# THE DICTIONARY OF SODIUM, FATS, AND CHOLESTEROL

# THE DICTIONARY OF SODIUM, FATS, AND CHOLESTEROL

## BY BARBARA KRAUS

A GD/PERIGEE BOOK

For Robert Alden and William E. Pecot, Jr.

Perigee Books
are published by
The Putnam Publishing Group
200 Madison Avenue
New York, New York 10016

Library of Congress catalog card number: 72-90848
ISBN 0-399-50945-3

First Perigee printing, 1983
Three previous Grosset & Dunlap printings
Printed in the United States of America
1 2 3 4 5 6 7 8 9

# CONTENTS

# INTRODUCTION

This dictionary lists the total fat, saturated and unsaturated fatty acids, cholesterol, and sodium content of several thousands of food items. These nutrients have been receiving increasing attention by nutritionists and the medical profession because of their possible relationship to atherosclerosis (coronary heart disease). Of course, diet is not the only factor to be considered in heart disease. Other considerations are heredity, obesity, high blood pressure, blood cholesterol, blood lipids, cigarette smoking, lack of exercise, stress, and certain ailments such as diabetes.

Patients with coronary disease and high blood pressure are often placed on diets in which one or more of these nutrients is controlled. Since physicians now believe that the conditions leading to early heart attacks are the result of a lifetime of habits that predispose individuals to such attacks, they recommend that certain changes in dietary patterns be made also in early childhood.

## Total Fat

The caloric intake from fat is often as much as 45% to 50% of the American diet. In the past 25 years, the consumption of fats and oils alone has increased, on the average, about 20%. In the same period, Americans have consumed over 18% more meat, which is also high in fat content. It is now frequently recommended that only about one-third of the calories be from fat, and of this amount, about two-thirds should be from polyunsaturated and monounsaturated fatty acids, amounting to approximately 10% to 15% of the diet.

Some fat in the diet is essential. It is used in the body to supply energy, yielding about nine calories per gram, more than twice as much as either protein or carbohydrate (the other energy-yielding nutrients in foods), which each supply about four calories per gram. Fat is also important in supplying essential fatty acids (those that cannot be synthesized by the body) and in the supply and utilization of fat soluble vitamins A, D, E, and K. Fat adds flavor and satiety value to otherwise bulky and bland diets.

## Fatty Acids

Fats are composed of "saturated" and "unsaturated" fatty acids. In scientific terms, they are saturated if the carbon atoms contain all the hydrogen they can hold. If there is one double bond where hydrogen can be added, the fat is monounsaturated; if there are two or more, the fat is polyunsaturated. In layman's terms: if the fat is solid at room temperature it is saturated, if liquid, it is unsaturated. This is a very rough rule of thumb and there are exceptions to it. Most foods contain both kinds of fat in varying proportions. Oils from plant foods and fish contain the most abundant amounts of polyunsaturated fats. Coconut oil is an exception. It is high in saturated fatty acids and is solid at room temperature.

Meats, cheeses, eggs, and most animal products are high in saturated fatty acids. The listings in this book showing the values for unsaturated fatty acids include both mono and polyunsaturated fats. At this time, the available information for many foods is not adequate to give a breakdown between these two forms. New federal requirements for labeling commercial products will result in more complete information in the future, and later editions of this book will incorporate such values.

the values for saturated and unsaturated fats are rounded to the nearest

Since the values for saturated and unsaturated fats are rounded to the nearest whole number they may add up to more or less than the figure given for total fat. In many cases, the values for unsaturated fat were derived by the subtraction of the saturated from the total fats. In a very few cases, manufactures reported analyzed saturated and unsaturated fats which did not add up to the total fat shown, because the undetermined fatty acids were, in their opinion, not present in significant amounts.

## Cholesterol

Cholesterol is one of the complex compounds known as sterols. It is an essential nutrient in normal metabolic processes and is synthesized in the body. It is also present in many foods of animal origin that we consume. Plant foods do not contain cholesterol in any significant amounts. Foods such as chocolate, cocoa, olive oil, coconut butter, and peanut butter are devoid of it since they are plant products.

Animal products are generally high in cholesterol. Organ and glandular meats such as brains, kidney, liver, sweetbreads, and heart are especially high in cholesterol. Egg yolk contains high concentrations of cholesterol, but it is absent in the white.

Cholesterol occurs in both the lean portions and the fatty portions of meat; the removal of fatty tissue if replaced by an equal amount of lean does not reduce the cholesterol intake. This is unlike the effect on the amount of fatty acids and must be taken into account in planning low cholesterol diets.

## Sodium

Sodium is an essential element in the growth of animals. It occurs naturally in many foods but the principle source in diets is sodium chloride or ordinary table salt. Salt is used in the processing of many foods in freezing, canning, and other manufacturing methods. It is also added in the home in cooking and at the table.

For some people, the use of salt is excessive and low-sodium diets are prescribed by physicians. Low-sodium diets are used in the treatment of diseases such as cardiac failure, edema formation, and high blood pressure.

## Summary

Always keep in mind that in making any drastic changes in dietary habits the advice and guidance of a competent physician should be sought. It is an essential of good health that the diet contain all the nutrients required by the individual and in adequate amounts. Reductions or increases in one or more of the essential nutrients may bring about adverse effects.

The tables given here are intended to provide basic information to help plan a varied and attractive diet within broad guidelines that are nutritionally adequate when one or more of the nutrients must be controlled.

## ARRANGEMENT OF THIS BOOK

Foods are listed alphabetically by brand name or by the name of the food. The singular form is used for the entries, that is, blackberry instead of blackberries. Most items are listed individually although a few are grouped (see p. xi). For example, all candies are listed together so that if you are looking for *Mars* bar, you look first under Candy, then under *M* in alphabetical order. But, if you are looking for a breakfast food such as Oatmeal, you will find it under *O* in the main alphabet. Many cross references are included to assist you in finding items known by different names.

Under the main headings, it was often not possible nor even desirable to follow an alphabetical arrangement. For basic foods, such as apricots, the first entries are for the fresh product weighed with seeds as it is purchased in the store, then the fruit in small portions as they may be eaten or measured. These entries are followed by the processed products, canned (although it may actually be a bottle or a jar), dehydrated, dried, and frozen items. This basic plan, with adaptations where necessary, was followed for fruits, vegetables, and meats.

In almost all entries, where data were available, the U.S. Department of Agriculture figures are shown first. The Department values represent averages from several manufacturers and are shown for comparison with the values from individual companies or for use where particular brands are not available.

All brand-name products have been italicized and company names appear in parentheses.

### Portions Used

The portion column is a most important one to read and note. Common household measures are used wherever possible. For some items, the amounts given are those commonly purchased in the store, such as one pound of meat, or a 15-ounce package of cake mix. These quantities can be divided into the number of servings used in the home and the nutritive values in each portion can then be readily determined. Any ingredients added in preparing such products must also be taken into account.

The smaller portions given are for foods as served or measured in moderate amounts, such as one-half cup of reconstituted juice, or four ounces of meat.Be sure to adjust the amount of the nutrients to the actual portions you use. For example, if you serve one cup of juice instead of one-half cup, multiply the amount of the nutrients shown for the smaller amount by two.

The size of portions you use is extremely important in controlling the intake of any nutrient. The amount of a nutrient is directly related to the weight of the food served. The weight of a volumetric measure, such as a cup or a pint may vary considerably depending on many factors; four ounces by weight may be very different from one-half cup or four fluid ounces. Ounces in the tables are always ounces by weight unless specified as fluid ounces, fractions of a cup, or other volumetric measure. Foods that are fluffy in texture such as flaked coconut and bean sprouts vary greatly in weight per cup, depending on how tightly they are packed. Such foods as canned green beans also vary when measured with and without liquid; for instance, canned beans with liquid weigh 4.2 ounces for one-half cup, but drained beans weigh 2.5 ounces for the same half cup. Check the weights of your serving portions regularly. Bear in mind that you can reduce or increase the intake of any nutrient by changing the serving size.

It was impossible to convert all the portions to a uniform basis. Some sources were able to report data only in terms of weights with no information on cup or other volumetric measures. We have shown small portions in quantities that might reasonably be expected to be served or measured in the home or institution.

You will find in the portion column the phrases "weighed with bone," and "weighed with skin and seeds." These descriptions apply to the products as you purchase them in the markets, but the nutritive values as shown are for the amount of edible food after you discard the bone, skin, seed, or other inedible part. The weight given in the "measure" or "quantity" column is to the nearest gram or fraction of an ounce.

Data on the composition of foods are constantly changing for many reasons. Better sampling and analytical methods, improvements in marketing procedures, and changes in formulas of mixed products may alter values for all of the nutrients. Weights of packaged foods are frequently changed. It is essential to read label information in order to be knowledgeable about these matters and to make intelligent use of food tables.


## Other Nutrients

These tables are not intended as a dietary guide. Any drastic change from a normal mixed diet should be undertaken only under the guidance of a qualified physician. Do not forget that other nutrients — protein, carbohydrate, minerals, and vitamins — are extremely important in diet planning. From a nutritional viewpoint, perhaps the best advice that can be given is to eat a varied diet with all classes of food represented. Meat, fish, chicken, fats and oils, milk, vegetables, fruits, and grain products are all important sources of essential nutrients and some foods from each of these classes should be included in the diet every day.

If your doctor has recommended the control of one or more of the nutrients shown in these tables, you can choose foods from this book under the doctor's guidance that will fit his specifications and will provide a varied selection of products that are acceptable. Control of certain nutrients such as cholesterol or sodium does not condemn you to a monotonous diet. There is a rich and varied assortment of foods in our markets that will meet any medical requirements. Choose wisely and eat well.

## Sources of Data

Values in this dictionary are based on publications issued by the U.S. Department of Agriculture and on data submitted by manufacturers and processors. The U.S. Department of Agriculture issues basic tables on food composition for use in the United States. The commercial products from U.S.D.A. publications represent average values obtained on products of more than one company. The figures designated as "home recipe" are based on recipes on file with the Department of Agriculture. Data on commercial products listed by brand name in this publication are based on values supplied by manufacturers and processors for their own individual products. Supermarket brand names, such as the A & P's *Ann Page*, or private labels could not be included in this book inasmuch as they are not usually analyzed under these trade names. Every care has been taken to interpret the data and the descriptions supplied by the companies as fully and as accurately as possible. Many values have been recalculated to different portions from those submitted, in order to bring about greater uniformity among similar items.

Analysis of foods to provide information on nutritive values are extremely expensive to conduct. Many small companies cannot afford to have their products analyzed and were unable to provide data or were able to provide only a portion of the data requested. Other companies have simply never gotten around to having the analyses done. New requirements for labeling nutritive values for products may provide information on additional items in the future. Wherever data were unavailable blank spaces were left which may be filled in by the reader at a later time.

## Foods Listed by Groups

Foods in the following classes are reported together rather than as individual items in the main alphabet: baby food, bread, cake icing, cake icing mix, candy, cheese, cookies, cookie mix, crackers, gravy, salad dressing, and sauce.

BARBARA KRAUS

# ABBREVIATIONS AND SYMBOLS

(USDA) = United States Department
     of Agriculture
    * = prepared as packaging directs[1]
    < = less than
    > = more than
    & = and
    " = inch
    + = values do not include amount
    of sodium found in the local
    water used in packaging
canned = bottles or jars as well as cans
  dia. = diameter
   fl. = fluid
  liq. = liquid

lb. = pound
med. = medium
oz. = ounce
pkg. = package
pt. = pint
qt. = quart
sq. = square
T. = tablespoon
Tr. = trace
tsp. = teaspoon
wt. = weight
mg. = milligram
gr. = gram

Italics or name in parentheses = registered trademark,®.
Where zero in parenthesis appears in the tabular column it means that (0) zero is imputed by author wherever there is a reasonable assumption that that nutrient is not present.

# EQUIVALENTS

| By Weight | By Volume |
|---|---|
| 1 pound = 16 ounces | 1 quart = 4 cups |
| 1 ounce = 28.35 grams | 1 cup = 8 fluid ounces |
| 3.52 ounces = 100 grams | 1 cup = ½ pint |
| 1 milligram = .001 gram | 1 cup = 16 tablespoons |
| | 2 tablespoons = 1 fluid ounce |
| | 1 tablespoon = 3 teaspoons |
| | 1 pound butter = 4 sticks or 2 cups |

[1]If the package directions call for whole or skim milk, the data given here are for whole milk, unless otherwise stated.

# THE DICTIONARY OF SODIUM, FATS, AND CHOLESTEROL

| Food and Description | Measure or Quantity | Sodium (mg.) | —Fats in grams— Total | Satu- rated | Unsatu- rated | Choles- terol (mg.) |
|---|---|---|---|---|---|---|

# A

**ABALONE** (USDA):
| | | | | | | |
|---|---|---|---|---|---|---|
| Raw, meat only | 4 oz. | | .6 | | | |
| Canned | 4 oz. | | .3 | | | |

***AC'CENT*** | ¼ tsp. (1 gram) | 129 | 0. | | | 0 |

**ACEROLA,** fresh (USDA):
| | | | | | | |
|---|---|---|---|---|---|---|
| Fruit | ½ lb. (weighed with seeds) | 15 | .6 | | | 0 |
| Juice | ½ cup (4.3 oz.) | 4 | .4 | | | 0 |

**ALBACORE,** raw, meat only (USDA) | 4 oz. | 45 | 8.6 | 3. | 5. | |

**ALCOHOLIC BEVERAGES** (See individual listings)

**ALEWIFE** (USDA):
| | | | | | | |
|---|---|---|---|---|---|---|
| Raw, meat only | 4 oz. | | 5.6 | | | |
| Canned, solids & liq. | 4 oz. | | 9.1 | | | |

**ALLSPICE** (Spice Islands):
| | | | | | | |
|---|---|---|---|---|---|---|
| Ground | 1 tsp. | 2 | | | | (0) |
| Whole | 1 tsp. | 1 | | | | (0) |

**ALMOND:**
In shell:
| | | | | | | |
|---|---|---|---|---|---|---|
| (USDA) | 4 oz. (weighed in shell) | 2 | 31.4 | 2. | 29. | 0 |
| (USDA) | 1 cup (2.8 oz.) | 2 | 21.7 | 2. | 20. | 0 |

Shelled:
Plain, unsalted:
| | | | | | | |
|---|---|---|---|---|---|---|
| Whole (USDA) | 1 oz. | 1 | 15.4 | 1. | 14. | 0 |
| Whole (USDA) | 1 cup (5 oz.) | 6 | 77.0 | 6. | 71. | 0 |
| Whole (USDA) | 13-15 almonds (.6 oz.) | <1 | 9.5 | <1. | 9. | 0 |
| Chopped (USDA) | 1 cup (4.5 oz.) | 5 | 68.8 | 5. | 64. | 0 |
| (Blue Diamond) | 1 cup (5.6 oz.) | 6 | 83.8 | 10. | 74. | (0) |

Blanched:
| | | | | | | |
|---|---|---|---|---|---|---|
| Salted (USDA) | 1 cup (5.5 oz.) | 311 | 90.6 | 8. | 83. | 0 |
| Slivered (Blue Diamond) | 1 cup (5.6 oz.) | 6 | 86.2 | 10. | 76. | (0) |

(USDA): United States Department of Agriculture
*Prepared as Package Directs

①

| Food and Description | Measure or Quantity | Sodium (mg.) | — Fats in grams — | | | Choles-terol (mg.) |
|---|---|---|---|---|---|---|
| | | | Total | Satu-rated | Unsatu-rated | |
| Chocolate-covered (See **CANDY**) | | | | | | |
| Flavored (Blue Diamond) barbecue, cheese, French-fried, onion-garlic or smokehouse-style | 1 oz. | 56 | | | | (0) |
| Roasted, salted: | | | | | | |
| (USDA) | 1 oz. | 56 | 16.4 | 1. | 15. | 0 |
| (USDA) | 1 cup (5.5 oz.) | 311 | 90.6 | 8. | 83. | 0 |
| Diced (Blue Diamond) | 1 oz. | 56 | | | | (0) |
| Dry (Flavor House) | 1 oz. | 56 | 16.4 | | | (0) |
| Dry (Planters) | 1 oz. | 340 | 16.4 | 1. | 15. | 0 |
| **ALMOND MEAL,** partially defatted (USDA) | 1 oz. | 2 | 5.2 | Tr. | 5. | 0 |
| *ALPHA-BITS,* oat cereal (Post) | 1 cup (1 oz.) | 150 | 1.1 | | | 0 |
| **AMARANTH,** raw (USDA): | | | | | | |
| Untrimmed | 1 lb. (weighed untrimmed) | | 1.4 | | | 0 |
| Trimmed | 4 oz. | | .6 | | | 0 |
| **AMBROSIA,** chilled, bottled (Kraft) | 4 oz. | 115 | 2.4 | | | (0) |
| *A.M.,* fruit juice drink (Mott's) | ½ cup | | .1 | | | (0) |
| **ANCHOVY PASTE,** canned (Crosse & Blackwell) | 1 T. (.5 oz.) | 1540 | .5 | | | |
| **ANCHOVY, PICKLED,** canned with or without added oil, not heavily salted (USDA) | 1 oz. | | 2.9 | | | |
| **ANGEL FOOD CAKE,** home recipe (USDA)[1] | $^1/_{12}$ of 8″ cake (1.4 oz.) | 113 | <.1 | | | 0 |
| **ANGEL FOOD CAKE MIX:** | | | | | | |
| Dry (USDA) | 4 oz. | 215 | .2 | | | 0 |
| *(USDA)[2] | $^1/_{12}$ of 10″ cake (1.9 oz.) | 77 | .1 | | | 0 |

(USDA): United States Department of Agriculture
*Prepared as Package Directs
[1]Made with sodium aluminum sulfate-type baking powder.
[2]Prepared with water, flavorings.

②

| Food and Description | Measure or Quantity | Sodium (mg.) | Fats in grams — Total | Satu- rated | Unsatu- rated | Choles- terol (mg.) |
|---|---|---|---|---|---|---|
| *(Betty Crocker): | | | | | | |
| 1 step | $^1/_{16}$ of cake | 172 | .1 | | | (0) |
| 2 step | $^1/_{16}$ of cake | 110 | .1 | | | (0) |
| Confetti | $^1/_{16}$ of cake | | .1 | | | (0) |
| Lemon custard | $^1/_{16}$ of cake | 133 | .1 | | | (0) |
| Strawberry | $^1/_{16}$ of cake | 148 | .1 | | | (0) |
| *(Duncan Hines) | $^1/_{12}$ of cake (2 oz.) | 89 | .1 | | | 0 |
| *(Swans Down) | $^1/_{12}$ of cake (1.8 oz.) | 95 | .1 | | | 0 |
| **ANISE SEED** (Spice Islands) | 1 tsp. | <1 | | | | (0) |
| **APPLE,** any variety: | | | | | | |
| Fresh (USDA): | | | | | | |
| Eaten with skin | 1 lb. (weighed with skin & core) | 4 | 2.5 | | | 0 |
| Eaten with skin | 1 med., 2½″ dia. (about 3 per lb.) | 1 | .8 | | | 0 |
| Eaten without skin | 1 lb. (weighed with skin & core) | 4 | 1.2 | | | 0 |
| Eaten without skin | 1 med., 2½″ dia. (about 3 per lb.) | 1 | .4 | | | 0 |
| Pared, diced | 1 cup (3.8 oz.) | 1 | .3 | | | 0 |
| Pared, quartered | 1 cup (4.3 oz.) | 1 | .4 | | | 0 |
| Canned (See **APPLESAUCE**) | | | | | | |
| Dehydrated: | | | | | | |
| Uncooked (USDA) | 1 oz. | 2 | .6 | | | 0 |
| Cooked, sweetened (USDA) | ½ cup (4.2 oz.) | 1 | .4 | | | 0 |
| Dried: | | | | | | |
| Uncooked (USDA) | 1 cup (3 oz.) | 4 | 1.4 | | | 0 |
| Uncooked (Del Monte) | 1 cup (3 oz.) | 75 | 1.6 | | | 0 |
| Cooked, unsweetened (USDA) | ½ cup (4.3 oz.) | 1 | .6 | | | 0 |
| Cooked, sweetened (USDA) | ½ cup (4.9 oz.) | 1 | .6 | | | 0 |
| Frozen, sweetened, slices, not thawed (USDA) | 4 oz. | 16 | .1 | | | 0 |
| **APPLE BROWN BETTY,** home recipe (USDA)[1] | 1 cup (8.1 oz.) | 352 | 8.0 | 2. | 6. | |
| **APPLE BUTTER:** | | | | | | |
| (USDA) | ½ cup (5 oz.) | 3 | 1.1 | | | 0 |

(USDA): United States Department of Agriculture
*Prepared as Package Directs
[1]Principal sources of fat: butter, bread crumbs.

| Food and Description | Measure or Quantity | Sodium (mg.) | Fats in grams — Total | Satu- rated | Unsatu- rated | Choles- terol (mg.) |
|---|---|---|---|---|---|---|
| (USDA) | 1 T. (.6 oz.) | <1 | .1 | | | 0 |
| (Bama) | 1 T. (.6 oz.) | 1 | <.1 | | | (0) |
| (Smucker's) spiced | 1 T. (.6 oz.) | 4. | .1 | | | (0) |
| **APPLE CAKE MIX,** cinnamon: | | | | | | |
| *(Betty Crocker) pudding cake | 1/6 of cake | 325 | 4.7 | | | |
| *(Betty Crocker) upside down | 1/9 of cake | 226 | 10.1 | | | |
| *(Duncan Hines) | 1/12 of cake (2.7 oz.) | 325 | 6.1 | | | 50 |
| **APPLE CIDER** (USDA) | ½ cup (4.4 oz.) | 1 | Tr. | | | 0 |
| **APPLE DRINK,** canned: | | | | | | |
| (Del Monte) | 6 fl. oz. (6.5 oz.) | 32 | Tr. | | | (0) |
| (Hi-C) | 6 fl. oz. (6.3 oz.) | <1 | Tr. | | | 0 |
| **APPLE DUMPLING,** frozen | | | | | | |
| (Pepperidge Farm) | 1 dumpling (3.3 oz.) | 206 | 16.4 | | | |
| **APPLE FRITTER,** frozen | | | | | | |
| (Mrs. Paul's) | 12 oz. pkg. | | 32.1 | | | |
| *APPLE JACKS*, cereal | | | | | | |
| (Kellogg's) | 1 cup (1 oz.) | 68 | .2 | | | (0) |
| **APPLE JELLY,** dietetic or low calorie: | | | | | | |
| (Diet Delight) | 1 T. (.6 oz.) | 5 | Tr. | | | (0) |
| (Kraft) | 1 oz. | 35 | <.1 | | | (0) |
| (S and W) *Nutradiet* | 1 T. (.5 oz.) | | <.1 | | | (0) |
| (Slenderella) | 1 T. (.6 oz.) | 22 | Tr. | | | (0) |
| (Tillie Lewis) | 1 T. (.5 oz.) | 3 | Tr. | | | (0) |
| **APPLE JUICE,** canned: | | | | | | |
| (USDA) | ½ cup (4.4 oz.) | 1 | Tr. | | | 0 |
| (Heinz) | 5½-fl.-oz. can | 5 | .2 | | | (0) |
| (Mott's) | ½ cup | | Tr. | | | (0) |
| (Mott's) McIntosh | ½ cup | | Tr. | | | (0) |
| **APPLE NECTAR** (Mott's) | ½ cup | | <.1 | | | (0) |
| **APPLE PIE:** | | | | | | |
| Home recipe, 2 crusts (USDA): | | | | | | |
| Made with lard & butter | 1/6 of 9" pie (5.6 oz.) | 476 | 17.5 | 6. | 11. | |

(USDA): United States Department of Agriculture
*Prepared as Package Directs

| Food and Description | Measure or Quantity | Sodium (mg.) | Fats in grams — Total | Satu- rated | Unsatu- rated | Choles- terol (mg.) |
|---|---|---|---|---|---|---|
| Made with vegetable shortening & butter | ¹/₆ of 9″ pie (5.6 oz.) | 476 | 17.5 | 5. | 13. | Tr. |
| (Hostess) | 4½ oz. pie | 589 | 11.0 | | | |
| (McDonald's) | 1 serving (3 oz.) | 395 | 15.4 | | | |
| (Tastykake) | 4-oz. pie | | 14.7 | | | |
| French apple (Tastykake) | 4½-oz. pie | | 18.4 | | | |
| Frozen: | | | | | | |
| Unbaked (USDA)[1] | 5 oz. | 251 | 11.8 | 3. | 9. | |
| Baked (USDA)[1] | 5 oz. | 302 | 14.3 | 3. | 11. | |
| (Banquet) | 5-oz. serving | | 15.4 | | | |
| (Morton) | ¹/₆ of 20-oz. pie | 229 | 10.8 | | | |
| (Morton) | ¹/₆ of 24-oz. pie | 242 | 11.5 | | | |
| (Morton) | ⅛ of 46-oz. pie | 287 | 16.5 | | | |
| (Mrs. Smith's) | ¹/₆ of 8″ pie (4.2 oz.) | 302 | 14.6 | | | |
| (Mrs. Smith's) old fashion | ¹/₆ of 9″ pie (5.8 oz.) | 547 | 22.7 | | | |
| (Mrs. Smith's) golden deluxe | ⅛ of 10″ pie (5.6 oz.) | 395 | 19.1 | | | |
| Dutch apple (Mrs. Smith's) | ¹/₆ of 8″ pie (4.2 oz.) | 284 | 14.2 | | | |
| Tart (Mrs. Smith's) | ¹/₆ of 8″ pie (4.2 oz.) | 207 | 9.9 | | | |
| **APPLE PIE FILLING,** canned: | | | | | | |
| Sweetened: | | | | | | |
| (Comstock) | ½ cup (5.4 oz.) | 9 | <.1 | | | |
| (Comstock) French | ½ cup (5.4 oz.) | 49 | .3 | | | |
| (Comstock-Greenwood) Pie, sliced | 1-lb. 1-oz. can | 9 | 1.4 | | | |
| (Lucky Leaf) | 8 oz. | 120 | .4 | | | |
| Unsweetened: | | | | | | |
| (Lucky Leaf) | 8 oz. | 5 | .5 | | | |
| (Wilderness) | 21-oz. can | 397 | | | | |
| **APPLESAUCE,** canned: | | | | | | |
| Sweetened: | | | | | | |
| (USDA) | ½ cup (4.5 oz.) | 3 | .1 | | | 0 |
| (Del Monte) | ½ cup (4.6 oz.) | 2 | .2 | | | 0 |
| (Hunt's) | 5-oz. can | 3 | .2 | | | (0) |
| (Mott's) | ½ cup (4.5 oz.) | | .1 | | | (0) |
| (Mott's) Golden Delicious | ½ cup (4.5 oz.) | | .2 | | | (0) |
| (Mott's) cinnamon, country style | ½ cup (4.5 oz.) | | .1 | | | (0) |
| (Stokely-Van Camp) | ½ cup (4.2 oz.) | | .1 | | | (0) |
| Unsweetened, dietetic or low calorie: | | | | | | |
| (USDA) | ½ cup (4.3 oz.) | 2 | .2 | | | 0 |

(USDA): United States Department of Agriculture
*Prepared as Package Directs
[1]Principal source of fat: vegetable shortening.

| Food and Description | Measure or Quantity | Sodium (mg.) | Total | Fats in grams — Satu-rated | Unsatu-rated | Choles-terol (mg.) |
|---|---|---|---|---|---|---|
| (Blue Boy) | 4 oz. | 1 | .1 | | | (0) |
| (Diet Delight) | ½ cup (4.4 oz.) | 4 | Tr. | | | (0) |
| (Mott's) | ½ cup (4.4 oz.) | | .2 | | | (0) |
| (S and W) *Nutradiet*, low calorie | 4 oz. | 1 | .1 | | | (0) |
| (S and W) *Nutradiet*, unsweetened | 4 oz. | 1 | <.1 | | | |
| (Tillie Lewis) | ½ cup (4.2 oz.) | <10 | .2 | | | (0) |
| **\*APPLESAUCE CAKE MIX,** raisin (Duncan Hines) | ¹/₉ of cake (2.7 oz.) | 331 | 5.3 | | | |
| **APPLE SOFT DRINK,** red, low calorie (Shasta) | 6 fl. oz. | 37 | 0. | | | 0 |
| **APPLE TURNOVER,** frozen (Pepperidge Farm) | 1 turnover (3.3 oz.) | 244 | 20.6 | | | |
| **APRICOT:** | | | | | | |
| Fresh (USDA): | | | | | | |
| Whole | 1 lb. (weighed with pits) | 4 | .9 | | | 0 |
| Whole | 3 apricots (about 12 per lb.) | 1 | .2 | | | 0 |
| Halves | 1 cup (5.5 oz.) | 2 | .3 | | | 0 |
| Canned, regular pack, solids & liq.: | | | | | | |
| Juice pack (USDA) | 4 oz. | 1 | .2 | | | 0 |
| Light syrup (USDA) | 4 oz. | 1 | .1 | | | 0 |
| Heavy syrup: | | | | | | |
| Halves & syrup (USDA) | ½ cup (4.4 oz.) | 1 | .1 | | | 0 |
| Halves & syrup (USDA) | 4 med. halves with 2 T. syrup (4.3 oz.) | 1 | .1 | | | 0 |
| (Del Monte) | ½ cup (4.4 oz.) | 15 | .4 | | | 0 |
| (Hunt's) | ½ cup (4.5 oz.) | 1 | .1 | | | (0) |
| (Stokely-Van Camp) | ½ cup (4.2 oz.) | | .1 | | | |
| Extra heavy syrup (USDA) | 4 oz. | 1 | .1 | | | 0 |
| Canned, unsweetened or low calorie: | | | | | | |
| Water pack, halves & liq. (USDA) | 4 oz. | 1 | .1 | | | 0 |
| Water pack, halves & liq. (USDA) | ½ cup (4.3 oz.) | 1 | .1 | | | 0 |
| (Diet Delight) | ½ cup (4.4 oz.) | 5 | <.1 | | | (0) |

(USDA): United States Department of Agriculture
\*Prepared as Package Directs

| Food and Description | Measure or Quantity | Sodium (mg.) | —Fats in grams— Total | Satu- rated | Unsatu- rated | Choles- terol (mg.) |
|---|---|---|---|---|---|---|
| (S and W) *Nutradiet,* low calorie, whole | 2 whole (3.5 oz.) | 2 | <.1 | | | (0) |
| (S and W) *Nutradiet,* low calorie, halves | 4 halves (3.5 oz.) | 2 | .1 | | | (0) |
| (S and W) *Nutradiet,* unsweetened, halves | 4 halves (3.5 oz.) | 3 | .1 | | | (0) |
| (Tillie Lewis) | ½ cup (4.3 oz.) | <10 | .1 | | | (0) |
| Dehydrated (USDA): | | | | | | |
| Uncooked | 4 oz. | 37 | 1.1 | | | 0 |
| Cooked, sugar added, solids & liq. | 4 oz. | 9 | .2 | | | 0 |
| Dried: | | | | | | |
| Uncooked: | | | | | | |
| (USDA) | 1 lb. | 118 | 2.3 | | | 0 |
| (USDA) | 14 large halves (½ cup or 2.8 oz.) | 21 | .4 | | | 0 |
| (USDA) | 10 small halves (¼ cup or 1.3 oz.) | 10 | .2 | | | 0 |
| (USDA) | ½ cup (2.3 oz.) | 17 | .3 | | | 0 |
| (Del Monte) | ½ cup (2.3 oz.) | 2 | .6 | | | 0 |
| Cooked (USDA): | | | | | | |
| Sweetened | ½ cup with liq. (12-13 halves, 5.7 oz.) | 11 | .2 | | | 0 |
| Unsweetened | ½ cup with liq. (4.3 oz.) | 10 | .2 | | | 0 |
| Frozen, sweetened, not thawed (USDA) | 4 oz. | 5 | .1 | | | 0 |
| **APRICOT-APPLE JUICE & PRUNE** (Sunsweet) | ½ cup | | <.1 | | | (0) |
| **APRICOT, CANDIED** (USDA) | 1 oz. | | <.1 | | | 0 |
| **APRICOT LIQUEUR** (Leroux) 60 proof | 1 fl. oz. | <1 | (0.) | | | (0) |
| **APRICOT NECTAR,** canned: | | | | | | |
| Sweetened: | | | | | | |
| (USDA) | ½ cup (4.2 oz.) | Tr. | .1 | | | 0 |
| (Del Monte) | ½ cup (4.3 oz.) | 8 | .2 | | | 0 |
| (Heinz) | 5½-fl.-oz. can | 5 | .2 | | | (0) |
| (Sunsweet) | ½ cup | | .1 | | | (0) |
| Low calorie (S and W) *Nutradiet* | 4 oz. (by wt.) | 2 | .1 | | | (0) |

(USDA): United States Department of Agriculture
*Prepared as Package Directs

(7)

| Food and Description | Measure or Quantity | Sodium (mg.) | —Fats in grams— | | | Choles-terol (mg.) |
|---|---|---|---|---|---|---|
| | | | Total | Satu-rated | Unsatu-rated | |
| **APRICOT-ORANGE PIE** | | | | | | |
| (Tastykake) | 4-oz. pie | | 15.6 | | | |
| **APRICOT PIE FILLING:** | | | | | | |
| (Comstock) | 1 cup (10¾ oz.) | 262 | .2 | | | |
| (Lucky Leaf) | 8 oz. | 182 | .2 | | | |
| **APRICOT & PINEAPPLE NECTAR,** | | | | | | |
| (S and W) *Nutradiet*, unsweetened | 4 oz. (by wt.) | 2 | .1 | | | (0) |
| **APRICOT & PINEAPPLE PRESERVE:** | | | | | | |
| Sweetened (Bama) | 1 T. (.7 oz.) | 2 | <.1 | | | (0) |
| Dietetic or low calorie: | | | | | | |
| (Diet Delight) | 1 T. (.6 oz.) | 3 | <.1 | | | (0) |
| (S and W) *Nutradiet* | 1 T. (.5 oz.) | | <.1 | | | (0) |
| (Tillie Lewis) | 1 T. (.5 oz.) | 3 | Tr. | | | 0 |
| **APRICOT PRESERVE,** sweetened | | | | | | |
| (Bama) | 1 T. (.7 oz.) | 2 | <.1 | | | (0) |
| **APRICOT SOUR COCKTAIL** | | | | | | |
| (National Distillers) *Duet*, 12½% | | | | | | |
| alcohol | 2 fl. oz. | Tr. | 0. | | | 0 |
| **ARROWROOT** (Spice Islands) | 1 tsp. | Tr. | | | | (0) |
| **ARTICHOKE,** Globe or French (See also **JERUSALEM ARTICHOKE**): | | | | | | |
| Raw, whole (USDA) | 1 lb. (weighed untrimmed) | 78 | .4 | | | 0 |
| Boiled without salt, drained (USDA) | 4 oz. | 34 | .2 | | | 0 |
| Frozen, hearts (Birds Eye) | 5-6 hearts (3 oz.) | | .2 | | | 0 |
| **ASPARAGUS:** | | | | | | |
| Raw, whole spears (USDA) | 1 lb. (weighed untrimmed) | 5 | .5 | | | 0 |
| Boiled without salt, whole spears (USDA) | 4 spears (½" dia. at base, 2.1 oz.) | <1 | .1 | | | 0 |
| Boiled without salt, 1½"-2" pieces, drained | 1 cup (5.1 oz.) | 1 | .3 | | | 0 |

(USDA): United States Department of Agriculture
*Prepared as Package Directs

(8)

| Food and Description | Measure or Quantity | Sodium (mg.) | —Fats in grams— | | | Choles- terol (mg.) |
|---|---|---|---|---|---|---|
| | | | Total | Satu- rated | Unsatu- rated | |
| **Canned, regular pack:** | | | | | | |
| Green: | | | | | | |
| Spears & liq. (USDA) | 4 oz. | 268 | .3 | | | 0 |
| Spears & liq. (USDA) | 1 cup (8.6 oz.) | 576 | .7 | | | 0 |
| Spears only (USDA) | 1 cup (7.6 oz.) | 507 | .9 | | | 0 |
| Spears only (USDA) | 6 med. spears (3.4 oz.) | 227 | .4 | | | 0 |
| Liq. only (USDA) | 2 T. (1.1 oz.) | 71 | Tr. | | | 0 |
| Cut spears & liq. (Green Giant) | ½ of 10½-oz. can | 492 | .1 | | | (0) |
| Spears & liq. (Green Giant) | ⅓ of 15-oz. can | 468 | .1 | | | (0) |
| Spears & liq. *LeSueur* | ¼ of 1-lb. 3-oz. can | 446 | .1 | | | (0) |
| Solids & liq. (Stokely- Van Camp) | ½ cup (3.9 oz.) | | .4 | | | (0) |
| Drained solids (Del Monte) | 1 cup (7.8 oz.) | 417 | .8 | | | 0 |
| White: | | | | | | |
| Spears & liq. (USDA) | 4 oz. | 268· | .3 | | | 0 |
| Spears & liq. (USDA) | 1 cup (8.4 oz.) | 564 | .7 | | | 0 |
| Spears & liq. (Del Monte) | 1 cup (8 oz.) | 865 | .2 | | | 0 |
| Spears only (USDA) | 1 cup (7.6 oz.) | 507 | 1.1 | | | 0 |
| Spears only (USDA) | 6 med. spears (3.4 oz.) | 227 | .5 | | | 0 |
| Spears only (Del Monte) | 1 cup (7.6 oz.) | 821 | .4 | | | 0 |
| Liq. only (USDA) | 2 T. (1.1 oz.) | 71 | Tr. | | | 0 |
| **Canned, dietetic pack:** | | | | | | |
| Green: | | | | | | |
| Spears & liq. (USDA) | 4 oz. | 3 | .2 | | | 0 |
| Spears & liq. (Blue Boy) | 4 oz. | 1 | .2 | | | (0) |
| Solids & liq. (Diet Delight) | 4 oz. | 7 | .1 | | | (0) |
| Solids & liq. (Tillie Lewis) | ½ cup (4.2 oz.) | <10 | .2 | | | (0) |
| Drained solids (USDA) | 4 oz. | 3 | .3 | | | 0 |
| Liq. only (USDA) | 4 oz. | 3 | Tr. | | | 0 |
| (S and W) *Nutradiet*. unseasoned | 5 spears (3.5 oz.) | 3 | .1 | | | (0) |
| White: | | | | | | |
| Spears & liq. (USDA) | 4 oz. | 5 | .2 | | | 0 |
| Drained solids (USDA) | 4 oz. | 5 | .2 | | | 0 |
| Drained liq. (USDA) | 4 oz. | 5 | Tr. | | | 0 |
| **Frozen:** | | | | | | |
| Cuts & tips. not thawed (USDA) | 4 oz. | 2 | .2 | | | 0 |
| Cuts & tips. boiled without salt. drained (USDA) | 4 oz. | 1 | .2 | | | 0 |
| Cuts & tips. boiled without salt. drained (USDA) | ½ cup (3.2 oz.) | <1 | .2 | | | 0 |

(USDA): United States Department of Agriculture
*Prepared as Package Directs

⑨

| Food and Description | Measure or Quantity | Sodium (mg.) | — Fats in grams — | | | Cholesterol (mg.) |
|---|---|---|---|---|---|---|
| | | | Total | Saturated | Unsaturated | |
| Cuts (Birds Eye) | ½ cup (3.3 oz.) | 2 | .2 | | | 0 |
| Cut spears in butter sauce (Green Giant) | ⅓ of 9-oz. pkg. | 353 | 2.6 | | | |
| Spears, not thawed (USDA) | 4 oz. | 2 | .2 | | | 0 |
| Spears, boiled without salt, drained (USDA) | 4 oz. | 1 | .2 | | | 0 |
| Spears (Birds Eye) | ⅓ of 10-oz. pkg. | 2 | .2 | | | 0 |
| Spears with Hollandaise sauce (Birds Eye) | ⅓ of 10-oz.pkg. | 88 | 8.5 | | | 57 |
| **ASPARAGUS SOUP,** Cream of, canned: | | | | | | |
| Condensed (USDA) | 8 oz. (by wt.) | 1861 | 3.2 | | | |
| *Prepared with equal volume water (USDA) | 1 cup (8.5 oz.) | 984 | 1.7 | | | |
| *Prepared with equal volume milk (USDA)[1] | 1 cup (8.5 oz.) | 1046 | 5.8 | 2. | 4. | |
| *(Campbell) | 1 cup (8 oz.) | 940 | 3.2 | 2. | 1. | |
| *AUNT JEMIMA SYRUP* | ¼ cup | 2 | 0. | | | (0) |
| **AVOCADO,** peeled, pitted (USDA): | | | | | | |
| All commercial varieties: | | | | | | |
| Whole | 1 lb. (weighed with seed & skin) | 14 | 55.8 | 11. | 45. | 0 |
| Diced | ½ cup (2.6 oz.) | 3 | 12.1 | 2 | 10. | 0 |
| Mashed | ½ cup (4.1 oz.) | 5 | 19.0 | 3. | 16. | 0 |
| California varieties, mainly Fuerte: | | | | | | |
| Whole | ½ avocado (3⅛" dia.) | 4 | 18.4 | 3. | 15. | 0 |
| ½" cubes | ½ cup (2.7 oz.) | 3 | 12.9 | 2. | 11. | 0 |
| Florida varieties: | | | | | | |
| Whole | ½ avocado (3⅝" dia.) | 6 | 16.7 | 3. | 14. | 0 |
| ½" cubes | ½ cup (2.7 oz.) | 3 | 8.4 | 2. | 7. | 0 |
| *AWAKE* (Birds Eye) | ½ cup (4.4 oz.) | 5 | .1 | | | 0 |
| *AYDS,* vanilla or chocolate | 1 piece (7 grams) | | .6 | | | 2 |

# B

| | | | | | | |
|---|---|---|---|---|---|---|
| **BABY FOOD:** | | | | | | |
| Apple: | | | | | | |
| & apricot, junior (Beech-Nut) | 7¾ oz. | 28 | .7 | | | |
| & apricot, strained (Beech-Nut) | 4¾ oz | 21 | .4 | | | |

(USDA): United States Department of Agriculture
*Prepared as Package Directs
[1]Principal source of fat: milk.

| Food and Description | Measure or Quantity | Sodium (mg.) | —Fats in grams— Total | Saturated | Unsaturated | Cholesterol (mg.) |
|---|---|---|---|---|---|---|
| & cranberry, junior (Heinz) | 7¾ oz. | 13 | .2 | | | |
| & cranberry, strained (Heinz) | 4¾ oz. | 9 | .1 | | | |
| & honey, junior (Heinz) | 7½ oz. | 15 | .2 | | | |
| & honey with tapioca, strained (Heinz) | 4½ oz. | 7 | Tr. | | | |
| & pear, junior (Heinz) | 7¾ oz. | 18 | .2 | | | |
| & pear, strained (Heinz) | 4½ oz. | 9 | .1 | | | |
| Dutch, dessert (Gerber): | | | | | | |
| Junior | 7⁸/₁₀ oz. | 61 | 1.6 | | | |
| Strained | 4⁷/₁₀ oz. | 36 | 1.3 | | | |
| Apple-apricot juice, strained (Heinz) | 4½ fl. oz. | 3 | .4 | | | |
| Apple Betty (Beech-Nut): | | | | | | |
| Junior | 7¾ oz. | 31 | 1.1 | | | |
| Strained | 4¾ oz. | 21 | .7 | | | |
| Apple-cherry juice: | | | | | | |
| Strained (Beech-Nut) | 4¹/₅ fl. oz. (4.4 oz.) | 1 | | | | |
| Strained (Gerber) | 4¹/₅ fl. oz. (4.6 oz.) | 2 | .1 | | | |
| Strained (Heinz) | 4½ fl. oz. | 3 | .1 | | | |
| Apple-grape juice: | | | | | | |
| Strained (Beech-Nut) | 4¹/₅ fl. oz. (4.4 oz.) | 1 | | | | |
| Strained (Heinz) | 4½ fl. oz. | 4 | Tr. | | | |
| Apple juice: | | | | | | |
| Strained (Beech-Nut) | 4¹/₅ fl. oz. (4.4 oz.) | 1 | | | | |
| Strained (Gerber) | 4¹/₅ fl. oz. (4.6 oz.) | 3 | .1 | | | |
| Strained (Heinz) | 4½ fl. oz. | 2 | .1 | | | |
| Apple pie (Heinz): | | | | | | |
| Junior | 7¾ oz. | 8 | 2.2 | | | |
| Strained | 4¾ oz. | 6 | 1.4 | | | |
| Apple-pineapple juice, strained (Heinz) | 4½ fl. oz. | 3 | .1 | | | |
| Apple-prune & honey (Heinz): | | | | | | |
| Junior | 7½ oz. | | .2 | | | |
| With tapioca, strained | 4½ oz. | | .1 | | | |
| Apple-prune juice, strained (Heinz) | 4½ fl. oz. | 6 | Tr. | | | |
| Applesauce: | | | | | | |
| Junior (Beech-Nut) | 7¾ oz. | 33 | .7 | | | |
| Junior (Gerber) | 7⁸/₁₀ oz. | 4 | .5 | | | |
| Junior (Heinz) | 7¾ oz. | 18 | .2 | | | |
| Strained (Beech-Nut) | 4¾ oz. | 17 | .3 | | | |
| Strained (Gerber) | 4⁷/₁₀ oz. | 2 | .2 | | | |
| Strained (Heinz) | 4½ oz. | 11 | .2 | | | |

(USDA): United States Department of Agriculture
*Prepared as Package Directs

⑪

| Food and Description | Measure or Quantity | Sodium (mg.) | —Fats in grams— Total | Satu- rated | Unsatu- rated | Choles- terol (mg.) |
|---|---|---|---|---|---|---|
| & apricots, junior (Gerber) | 7⁸/₁₀ oz. | 3 | .7 | | | |
| & apricots, junior (Heinz) | 7¾ oz. | 15 | .3 | | | |
| & apricots, strained (Gerber) | 4⁷/₁₀ oz. | 2 | .2 | | | |
| & apricots, strained (Heinz) | 4¾ oz. | 8 | .1 | | | |
| & cherries, junior (Beech-Nut) | 7¾ oz. | 18 | 1.1 | | | |
| & cherries, strained (Beech-Nut) | 4¾ oz. | 13 | .9 | | | |
| & pineapple, junior (Gerber) | 7⁸/₁₀ oz. | 4 | .3 | | | |
| & pineapple, strained (Gerber) | 4⁷/₁₀ oz. | 2 | .3 | | | |
| & raspberries, junior (Beech-Nut) | 7¾ oz. | 28 | 1.1 | | | |
| & raspberries, strained (Beech-Nut) | 4¾ oz. | 25 | .5 | | | |
| Apricot with tapioca: | | | | | | |
| Junior (Beech-Nut) | 7¾ oz. | 112 | .4 | | | |
| Junior (Gerber) | 7⁸/₁₀ oz. | 70 | .1 | | | |
| Junior (Heinz) | 7¾ oz. | 11 | .3 | | | |
| Strained (Beech-Nut) | 4¾ oz. | 52 | .1 | | | |
| Strained (Gerber) | 4⁷/₁₀ oz. | 42 | .1 | | | |
| Strained (Heinz) | 4¾ oz. | 15 | .5 | | | |
| Banana: | | | | | | |
| Strained (Heinz) | 4½ oz. | 7 | .3 | | | |
| Pie, junior (Heinz) | 7¾ oz. | 10 | 2.3 | | | |
| Pie, strained (Heinz) | 4¾ oz. | 6 | 1.4 | | | |
| & pineapple, junior (Heinz) | 7¾ oz. | 14 | .2 | | | |
| & pineapple, strained (Heinz) | 4¾ oz. | 12 | .1 | | | |
| & pineapple with tapioca: | | | | | | |
| Junior (Beech-Nut) | 7¾ oz. | 120 | .2 | | | |
| Junior (Gerber) | 7⁸/₁₀ oz. | 214 | .3 | | | |
| Strained (Beech-Nut) | 4¾ oz. | 95 | .5 | | | |
| Strained (Gerber) | 4⁷/₁₀ oz. | 40 | .3 | | | |
| Dessert, junior (Beech-Nut) | 7¾ oz. | 237 | .2 | | | |
| Pudding, junior (Gerber) | 7⁸/₁₀ oz. | 273 | 1.6 | | | |
| With tapioca: | | | | | | |
| Strained (Beech-Nut) | 4¾ oz. | 95 | .3 | | | |
| Strained (Gerber) | 4⁷/₁₀ oz. | 40 | .3 | | | |
| Bean, green: | | | | | | |
| Junior (Beech-Nut) | 7¼ oz. | 252 | .2 | | | |
| Strained (Beech-Nut) | 4½ oz. | 146 | .3 | | | |
| Strained (Gerber) | 4½ oz. | 146 | .1 | | | |
| Strained (Heinz) | 4½ oz. | 151 | .3 | | | |
| Creamed with bacon, junior (Gerber) | 7½ oz. | 652 | 5.4 | | | |
| In butter sauce, junior (Beech-Nut) | 7¼ oz. | 195 | 1.8 | | | |

(USDA): United States Department of Agriculture
*Prepared as Package Directs

| Food and Description | Measure or Quantity | Sodium (mg.) | —Fats in grams— Total | Satu- rated | Unsatu- rated | Choles- terol (mg.) |
|---|---|---|---|---|---|---|
| In butter sauce, strained (Beech-Nut) | 4½ oz. | 118 | 1.2 | | | |
| With potatoes & ham, casserole, toddler (Gerber) | 6¹/₅ oz. | 742 | 6.0 | | | |
| Beef: | | | | | | |
| Junior (Beech-Nut) | 3½ oz. | 162 | 3.9 | | | |
| Junior (Gerber) | 3½ oz. | 154 | 4.0 | | | |
| Strained (Beech-Nut) | 3½ oz. | 162 | 5.4 | | | |
| Strained (Gerber) | 3½ oz. | 180 | 4.1 | | | |
| Beef & beef broth (Heinz): | | | | | | |
| Junior | 3½ oz. | 157 | 4.4 | | | |
| Strained | 3½ oz. | 146 | 4.1 | | | |
| Beef & beef heart, strained (Gerber) | 3½ oz. | 149 | 3.7 | | | |
| Beef dinner: | | | | | | |
| Junior (Beech-Nut) | 4½ oz. | 125 | 7.2 | | | |
| Strained (Beech-Nut) | 4½ oz. | 165 | 8.4 | | | |
| & noodles, junior (Beech-Nut) | 7½ oz. | 273 | 6.4 | | | |
| & noodles, junior (Gerber) | 7½ oz. | 222 | 2.1 | | | |
| & noodles, strained (Beech-Nut) | 4½ oz. | 205 | 3.6 | | | |
| & noodles, strained (Gerber) | 4½ oz. | 163 | 1.1 | | | |
| & noodles, strained (Heinz) | 4½ oz. | 170 | 1.2 | | | |
| With vegetables: | | | | | | |
| Junior (Gerber) | 4½ oz. | 279 | 4.6 | | | |
| Strained (Gerber) | 4½ oz. | 194 | 4.7 | | | |
| Strained (Heinz) | 4¾ oz. | 126 | 5.4 | | | |
| With vegetables & cereal, junior (Heinz) | 4¾ oz. | 124 | 5.8 | | | |
| Beef lasagna, toddler (Gerber) | 6¹/₅ oz. | 768 | 4.1 | | | |
| Beef liver, strained (Gerber) | 3½ oz. | 160 | 3.2 | | | |
| Beef liver soup, strained (Heinz) | 4½ oz. | 115 | .6 | | | |
| Beef stew, toddler (Gerber) | 6¹/₅ oz. | 871 | 2.3 | | | |
| Beet: | | | | | | |
| Strained (Gerber) | 4½ oz. | 205 | .1 | | | |
| Strained (Heinz) | 4½ oz. | 98 | .2 | | | |
| Blueberry buckle (Gerber): | | | | | | |
| Junior | 7⁸/₁₀ oz. | 101 | .2 | | | |
| Strained | 4½ oz. | 57 | .1 | | | |
| Butterscotch pudding (Gerber): | | | | | | |
| Junior | 7½ oz. | 254 | 2.8 | | | |
| Strained | 4½ oz. | 157 | 3.1 | | | |
| Caramel pudding (Beech-Nut): | | | | | | |
| Junior | 7¾ oz. | 112 | .9 | | | |

(USDA): United States Department of Agriculture
*Prepared as Package Directs

⑬

| Food and Description | Measure or Quantity | Sodium (mg.) | Fats in grams — Total | Satu- rated | Unsatu- rated | Choles- terol (mg.) |
|---|---|---|---|---|---|---|
| Strained | 4¾ oz. | 84 | .7 | | | |
| Carrot: | | | | | | |
| Junior (Beech-Nut) | 7½ oz. | 269 | .2 | | | |
| Junior (Gerber) | 7½ oz. | 259 | .4 | | | |
| Junior (Heinz) | 7¾ oz. | 248 | .3 | | | |
| Strained (Beech-Nut) | 4½ oz. | 163 | .1 | | | |
| Strained (Gerber) | 4½ oz. | 156 | .2 | | | |
| Strained (Heinz) | 4½ oz. | 217 | .2 | | | |
| & pea, junior (Gerber) | 7½ oz. | 213 | .7 | | | |
| In butter sauce (Beech-Nut): | | | | | | |
| Junior | 7½ oz. | 301 | 1.5 | | | |
| Strained | 4½ oz. | 182 | .8 | | | |
| Cereal, dry: | | | | | | |
| Barley (Gerber) | 3 T. (7 grams) | 1 | .3 | | | |
| Barley, instant (Heinz) | 2 T. | 19 | .1 | | | |
| High protein (Gerber) | 3 T. (7 grams) | 1 | .4 | | | |
| High protein, instant (Heinz) | 2 T. | 15 | .2 | | | |
| Hi-protein (Beech-Nut) | 1 oz. | 24 | 1.4 | | | |
| Mixed (Beech-Nut) | 1 oz. | 26 | 1.3 | | | |
| Mixed (Gerber) | 3 T. (7 grams) | 1 | .3 | | | |
| Mixed (Heinz) | 2 T. | 7 | .2 | | | |
| Mixed, honey (Beech-Nut) | 1 oz. | 29 | 1.4 | | | |
| Mixed, with banana (Gerber) | 3 T. (7 grams) | 12 | .3 | | | |
| Oatmeal (Beech-Nut) | 1 oz. | 21 | 2.0 | | | |
| Oatmeal (Gerber) | 3 T. (7 grams) | 1 | .6 | | | |
| Oatmeal, honey (Beech-Nut) | 1 oz. | 34 | 1.8 | | | |
| Oatmeal, instant (Heinz) | 2 T. | 9 | .3 | | | |
| Oatmeal, with banana (Gerber) | 3 T. (7 grams) | 13 | .4 | | | |
| Rice (Beech-Nut) | 1 oz. | 26 | 1.6 | | | |
| Rice (Gerber) | 3 T. (7 grams) | 1 | .3 | | | |
| Rice, honey (Beech-Nut) | 1 oz. | 20 | 1.1 | | | |
| Rice, instant (Heinz) | 2 T. | 30 | .1 | | | |
| Rice, with strawberry (Gerber) | 3 T. (7 grams) | 5 | .4 | | | |
| Cereal, or mixed cereal: | | | | | | |
| With applesauce & banana: | | | | | | |
| Junior (Gerber) | 7⁸/₁₀ oz. | 196 | .6 | | | |
| Strained (Gerber) | 4⁷/₁₀ oz. | 134 | .9 | | | |
| Strained (Heinz) | 4¾ oz. | 8 | .5 | | | |
| With egg yolks & bacon: | | | | | | |
| Junior (Beech-Nut) | 7½ oz. | 229 | 12.3 | | | |
| Junior (Gerber) | 7½ oz. | 284 | 8.8 | | | |
| Junior (Heinz) | 7½ oz. | 872 | 8.7 | | | |
| Strained (Beech-Nut) | 4½ oz. | 198 | 7.3 | | | |

(USDA): United States Department of Agriculture
*Prepared as Package Directs

⑭

| Food and Description | Measure or Quantity | Sodium (mg.) | —Fats in grams— | | | Cholesterol (mg.) |
|---|---|---|---|---|---|---|
| | | | Total | Saturated | Unsaturated | |
| Strained (Gerber) | 4½ oz. | 172 | 5.0 | | | |
| Strained (Heinz) | 4½ oz. | 413 | 6.7 | | | |
| With fruit, strained (Beech-Nut) | 4¾ oz. | 142 | .3 | | | |
| High protein with apple & banana, strained (Heinz) | 4¾ oz. | 20 | .6 | | | |
| Oatmeal, with applesauce & banana, junior (Gerber) | 7⁸/₁₀ oz. | 306 | 1.5 | | | |
| Oatmeal with applesauce & banana, strained (Gerber) | 4⁷/₁₀ oz. | 196 | 1.2 | | | |
| Oatmeal, with fruit, strained (Beech-Nut) | 4¾ oz. | 204 | .9 | | | |
| Rice, with applesauce & banana, strained (Gerber) | 4⁷/₁₀ oz. | 163 | .8 | | | |
| Cheese: | | | | | | |
| Cottage, creamed with pineapple: | | | | | | |
| Junior (Beech-Nut) | 7¾ oz. | 322 | 2.2 | | | |
| Strained (Gerber) | 4⁷/₁₀ oz. | 195 | 6.0 | | | |
| Cottage, creamed with pineapple juice, strained (Beech-Nut) | 4¾ oz. | 154 | 1.3 | | | |
| Cottage, dessert, with pineapple (Gerber): | | | | | | |
| Junior | 7⁸/₁₀ oz. | 301 | 2.6 | | | |
| Strained | 4½ oz. | 175 | 1.5 | | | |
| Cottage, with banana (Heinz): | | | | | | |
| Junior | 7¾ oz. | 23 | .5 | | | |
| Strained | 4½ oz. | 14 | .3 | | | |
| Cherry vanilla pudding (Gerber): | | | | | | |
| Junior | 7⁸/₁₀ oz. | 110 | 1.6 | | | |
| Strained | 4⁷/₁₀ oz. | 69 | 1.3 | | | |
| Chicken: | | | | | | |
| Junior (Beech-Nut) | 3½ oz. | 162 | 4.9 | | | |
| Junior (Gerber) | 3½ oz. | 206 | 8.2 | | | |
| Strained (Beech-Nut) | 3½ oz. | 142 | 5.2 | | | |
| Strained (Gerber) | 3½ oz. | 168 | 8.5 | | | |
| Chicken & chicken broth (Heinz): | | | | | | |
| Junior | 3½ oz. | 134 | 5.7 | | | |
| Strained | 3½ oz. | 122 | 6.4 | | | |
| Chicken dinner: | | | | | | |
| Junior (Beech-Nut) | 4½ oz. | 221 | 4.6 | | | |
| Strained (Beech-Nut) | 4½ oz. | 191 | 5.0 | | | |
| Noodle: | | | | | | |
| Junior (Beech-Nut) | 7½ oz. | 199 | 2.1 | | | |

(USDA): United States Department of Agriculture
*Prepared as Package Directs

(15)

| Food and Description | Measure or Quantity | Sodium (mg.) | —Fats in grams— | | | Cholesterol (mg.) |
|---|---|---|---|---|---|---|
| | | | Total | Saturated | Unsaturated | |
| Junior (Gerber) | 7½ oz. | 320 | 1.0 | | | |
| Junior (Heinz) | 7½ oz. | 213 | 4.6 | | | |
| Strained (Beech-Nut) | 4½ oz. | 131 | 1.2 | | | |
| Strained (Gerber) | 4½ oz. | 147 | .9 | | | |
| Strained (Heinz) | 4½ oz. | 139 | 2.5 | | | |
| With vegetables: | | | | | | |
| Junior (Beech-Nut) | 7½ oz. | 191 | 1.3 | | | |
| Junior (Gerber) | 4½ oz. | 262 | 5.7 | | | |
| Junior (Heinz) | 4¾ oz. | 145 | 7.7 | | | |
| Strained (Beech-Nut) | 4½ oz. | 128 | 1.0 | | | |
| Strained (Gerber) | 4½ oz. | 172 | 5.3 | | | |
| Strained (Heinz) | 4¾ oz. | 138 | 7.3 | | | |
| Chicken soup: | | | | | | |
| Junior (Heinz) | 7½ oz. | 210 | 3.4 | | | |
| Strained (Heinz) | 4½ oz. | 116 | 2.1 | | | |
| Cream of, junior (Gerber) | 7½ oz. | 293 | 2.1 | | | |
| Cream of, strained (Gerber) | 4½ oz. | 177 | 1.3 | | | |
| Chicken stew, toddler (Gerber) | 6 oz. | 716 | 4.1 | | | |
| Chicken sticks: | | | | | | |
| Junior (Beech-Nut) | 2½ oz. | 203 | 11.1 | | | |
| Junior (Gerber) | 2½ oz. | 300 | 9.6 | | | |
| Cookie, animal-shaped (Gerber) | 1 cookie (6 grams) | 28 | 1.0 | | | |
| Cookie, assorted (Beech-Nut) | ½ oz. | 49 | 1.8 | | | |
| Corn, creamed: | | | | | | |
| Junior (Gerber) | 7½ oz. | 214 | .5 | | | |
| Junior (Heinz) | 7½ oz. | 232 | .8 | | | |
| Strained (Beech-Nut) | 4½ oz. | 118 | .9 | | | |
| Strained (Gerber) | 4½ oz. | 129 | .3 | | | |
| Strained (Heinz) | 4½ oz. | 103 | .5 | | | |
| Custard: | | | | | | |
| Junior (Beech-Nut) | 7¾ oz. | 272 | 3.9 | | | |
| Junior (Heinz) | 7¾ oz. | 270 | 5.9 | | | |
| Strained (Beech-Nut) | 4½ oz. | 150 | 2.2 | | | |
| Strained (Heinz) | 4½ oz. | 84 | 3.0 | | | |
| Chocolate, junior (Gerber) | 7⁸/₁₀ oz. | 221 | 3.3 | | | |
| Chocolate, strained (Beech-Nut) | 4½ oz. | 133 | 2.0 | | | |
| Chocolate, strained (Gerber) | 4½ oz. | 129 | 2.1 | | | |
| Vanilla, junior (Gerber) | 7½ oz. | 229 | 3.5 | | | |
| Vanilla, strained (Gerber) | 4½ oz. | 129 | 1.6 | | | |
| Egg yolk: | | | | | | |
| Strained (Beech-Nut) | 3⅓ oz. | 94 | 15.6 | | | |
| Strained (Gerber) | 3³/₁₀ oz. | 168 | 16.7 | | | |
| Strained (Heinz) | 3¼ oz. | 110 | 15.9 | | | |

(USDA): United States Department of Agriculture
*Prepared as Package Directs

| Food and Description | Measure or Quantity | Sodium (mg.) | —Fats in grams— Total | Satu- rated | Unsatu- rated | Choles- terol (mg.) |
|---|---|---|---|---|---|---|
| & bacon, strained (Beech-Nut) | 3⅓ oz. | 206 | 13.3 | | | |
| & ham, strained (Gerber) | 3³/₁₀ oz. | 312 | 16.1 | | | |
| Fruit (Heinz): | | | | | | |
| Mixed, & honey, junior | 7½ oz. | 10 | .2 | | | |
| Mixed, & honey, with tapioca, strained | 4½ oz. | 5 | .2 | | | |
| Fruit dessert: | | | | | | |
| Junior (Heinz) | 7¾ oz. | 14 | 0. | | | |
| Strained (Heinz) | 4½ oz. | 13 | .1 | | | |
| Tropical, junior (Beech-Nut) | 7¾ oz. | 191 | .4 | | | |
| With tapioca: | | | | | | |
| Junior (Beech-Nut) | 7¾ oz. | 116 | .7 | | | |
| Junior (Gerber) | 7⁸/₁₀ oz. | 91 | .3 | | | |
| Strained (Beech-Nut) | 4¾ oz. | 77 | .1 | | | |
| Strained (Gerber) | 4⁷/₁₀ oz. | 51 | .4 | | | |
| Fruit juice: | | | | | | |
| Mixed, strained (Beech-Nut) | 4¹/₅ fl. oz. (4.4 oz.) | 1 | .2 | | | |
| Mixed, strained (Gerber) | 4¹/₅ fl. oz. (4.6 oz.) | 3 | .3 | | | |
| Ham: | | | | | | |
| Junior (Gerber) | 3½ oz. | 204 | 6.0 | | | |
| Strained (Beech-Nut) | 3½ oz. | 183 | 6.6 | | | |
| Strained (Gerber) | 3½ oz. | 200 | 6.2 | | | |
| Ham dinner: | | | | | | |
| Junior (Beech-Nut) | 4½ oz. | 224 | 6.9 | | | |
| Strained (Beech-Nut) | 4½ oz. | 228 | 8.2 | | | |
| With vegetables: | | | | | | |
| Junior (Gerber) | 4½ oz. | 263 | 3.6 | | | |
| Junior (Heinz) | 4¾ oz. | 297 | 7.1 | | | |
| Strained (Gerber) | 4½ oz. | 224 | 3.8 | | | |
| Strained (Heinz) | 4¾ oz. | 263 | 7.0 | | | |
| Lamb: | | | | | | |
| Junior (Beech-Nut) | 3½ oz. | 173 | 4.8 | | | |
| Junior (Gerber) | 3½ oz. | 201 | 3.9 | | | |
| Strained (Beech-Nut) | 3½ oz. | 142 | 4.5 | | | |
| Strained (Gerber) | 3½ oz. | 164 | 4.0 | | | |
| & noodles, junior (Beech-Nut) | 7½ oz. | 231 | 6.4 | | | |
| Lamb & lamb broth (Heinz): | | | | | | |
| Junior | 3½ oz. | 158 | 4.6 | | | |
| Strained | 3½ oz. | 116 | 3.5 | | | |
| Liver with liver broth, strained (Heinz) | 3½ oz. | 170 | 2.7 | | | |
| Macaroni: | | | | | | |
| Alphabets & beef casserole, toddler (Gerber) | 6¹/₅ oz. | 881 | 3.1 | | | |

(USDA): United States Department of Agriculture
*Prepared as Package Directs

17

| Food and Description | Measure or Quantity | Sodium (mg.) | — Fats in grams — Total | Satu- rated | Unsatu- rated | Choles- terol (mg.) |
|---|---|---|---|---|---|---|
| & bacon, junior (Beech-Nut) | 7½ oz. | 299 | 10.6 | | | |
| & beef with vegetables, junior (Beech-Nut) | 7½ oz. | 131 | 5.9 | | | |
| With tomato, beef & bacon: | | | | | | |
| Junior (Gerber) | 7½ oz. | 265 | 3.0 | | | |
| Junior (Heinz) | 7½ oz. | 293 | 4.4 | | | |
| Strained (Gerber) | 4½ oz. | 137 | 2.4 | | | |
| Strained (Heinz) | 4½ oz. | 166 | 3.0 | | | |
| With tomato sauce, beef & bacon dinner, strained (Beech-Nut) | 4½ oz. | 166 | 5.6 | | | |
| Meat sticks, junior (Beech-Nut) | 2½ oz. | 279 | 9.9 | | | |
| Meat sticks, junior (Gerber) | 2½ oz. | 326 | 7.5 | | | |
| Noodles & beef, junior (Heinz) | 7½ oz. | 234 | 2.8 | | | |
| Orange-apple juice, strained: | | | | | | |
| (Beech-Nut) | 4⅕ fl. oz. (4.4 oz.) | 1 | .2 | | | |
| (Gerber) | 4⅕ fl. oz. (4.6 oz.) | 3 | .5 | | | |
| Orange-apple-banana juice, strained: | | | | | | |
| (Gerber) | 4⅕ fl. oz. (4.6 oz.) | 4 | .3 | | | |
| (Heinz) | 4½ fl. oz. | 4 | .2 | | | |
| Orange-apricot juice, strained: | | | | | | |
| (Beech-Nut) | 4⅕ fl. oz. (4.4 oz.) | 1 | .4 | | | |
| (Gerber) | 4⅕ fl. oz. (4.6 oz.) | 2 | .2 | | | |
| (Heinz) | 4½ fl. oz. | 2 | .1 | | | |
| Orange-banana juice, strained (Beech-Nut) | 4⅕ fl. oz. (4.4 oz.) | 1 | .5 | | | |
| Orange juice, strained: | | | | | | |
| (Beech-Nut) | 4⅕ fl. oz. (4.4 oz.) | 1 | .4 | | | |
| (Gerber) | 4⅕ fl. oz. (4.6 oz.) | 3 | .5 | | | |
| (Heinz) | 4½ fl. oz. | 1 | .2 | | | |
| Orange-pineapple dessert, strained (Beech-Nut) | 4¾ oz. | 130 | .7 | | | |
| Orange-pineapple juice, strained: | | | | | | |
| (Beech-Nut) | 4⅕ fl. oz. (4.4 oz.) | 1 | .4 | | | |
| (Gerber) | 4⅕ fl. oz. (4.6 oz.) | 2 | .2 | | | |
| (Heinz) | 4½ fl. oz. | 2 | Tr. | | | |
| Orange pudding, strained: | | | | | | |
| (Gerber) | 4⁷⁄₁₀ oz. | 129 | 1.2 | | | |
| (Heinz) | 4½ oz. | 79 | .4 | | | |
| Pea: | | | | | | |
| Strained (Beech-Nut) | 4½ oz. | 129 | .5 | | | |
| Strained (Gerber) | 4½ oz. | 129 | .4 | | | |

(USDA): United States Department of Agriculture
*Prepared as Package Directs

| Food and Description | Measure or Quantity | Sodium (mg.) | — Fats in grams — Total | Satu-rated | Unsatu-rated | Choles-terol (mg.) |
|---|---|---|---|---|---|---|
| Pea, creamed (Heinz): | | | | | | |
| Junior | 7¾ oz. | 205 | 3.8 | | | |
| Strained | 4½ oz. | 88 | 2.3 | | | |
| Pea, in butter sauce (Beech-Nut): | | | | | | |
| Junior | 7¼ oz. | 269 | 2.5 | | | |
| Strained | 4½ oz. | 164 | 1.7 | | | |
| Peach: | | | | | | |
| Junior (Beech-Nut) | 7¾ oz. | 31 | .4 | | | |
| Junior (Gerber) | 7⁸/₁₀ oz. | 12 | .7 | | | |
| Junior (Heinz) | 7½ oz. | 10 | .3 | | | |
| Strained (Beech-Nut) | 4¾ oz. | 15 | .3 | | | |
| Strained (Gerber) | 4⁷/₁₀ oz. | 3 | .1 | | | |
| Strained (Heinz) | 4½ oz. | 7 | .3 | | | |
| Peach cobbler (Gerber): | | | | | | |
| Junior | 7⁸/₁₀ oz. | 38 | .3 | | | |
| Strained | 4⁷/₁₀ oz. | 23 | .3 | | | |
| Peach & honey (Heinz): | | | | | | |
| Junior | 7½ oz. | 11 | .1 | | | |
| With tapioca, strained | 4½ oz. | 9 | .2 | | | |
| Peach Melba (Beech-Nut): | | | | | | |
| Junior | 7¾ oz. | 177 | .9 | | | |
| Strained | 4¾ oz. | 51 | .4 | | | |
| Peach pie (Heinz): | | | | | | |
| Junior | 7¾ oz. | 13 | 2.2 | | | |
| Strained | 4¾ oz. | 8 | 1.3 | | | |
| Pear: | | | | | | |
| Junior (Beech-Nut) | 7½ oz. | 19 | 0. | | | |
| Junior (Gerber) | 7⁸/₁₀ oz. | 4 | .4 | | | |
| Junior (Heinz) | 7¾ oz. | 2 | .3 | | | |
| Strained (Beech-Nut) | 4½ oz. | 19 | .3 | | | |
| Strained (Gerber) | 4⁷/₁₀ oz. | 3 | .1 | | | |
| Strained (Heinz) | 4½ oz. | 3 | .3 | | | |
| Pear & pineapple: | | | | | | |
| Junior (Beech-Nut) | 7½ oz. | 32 | .2 | | | |
| Junior (Gerber) | 7⁸/₁₀ oz. | 4 | .6 | | | |
| Junior (Heinz) | 7¾ oz. | 3 | .2 | | | |
| Strained (Beech-Nut) | 4½ oz. | 31 | .1 | | | |
| Strained (Gerber) | 4⁷/₁₀ oz. | 3 | .2 | | | |
| Strained (Heinz) | 4¾ oz. | 2 | .2 | | | |
| Pineapple dessert, strained (Beech-Nut) | 4¾ oz. | 163 | .1 | | | |
| Pineapple-grapefruit juice drink, strained (Gerber) | 4⅕ fl. oz. (4.6 oz.) | 3 | .1 | | | |

(USDA): United States Department of Agriculture
*Prepared as Package Directs

| Food and Description | Measure or Quantity | Sodium (mg.) | — Fats in grams — | | | Choles- terol (mg.) |
|---|---|---|---|---|---|---|
| | | | Total | Satu- rated | Unsatu- rated | |
| Pineapple juice, strained (Heinz) | 4½ fl. oz. | 2 | .2 | | | |
| Pineapple-orange dessert (Heinz): | | | | | | |
| Junior | 7¾ oz. | 46 | .4 | | | |
| Strained | 4½ oz. | 31 | .2 | | | |
| Pineapple pie (Heinz): | | | | | | |
| Junior | 7¾ oz. | 15 | 3.3 | | | |
| Strained | 4¾ oz. | 16 | 1.8 | | | |
| Plum with tapioca: | | | | | | |
| Junior (Beech-Nut) | 7¾ oz. | 90 | .4 | | | |
| Junior (Gerber) | 7⁸/₁₀ oz. | 12 | .4 | | | |
| Strained (Beech-Nut) | 4¾ oz. | 47 | .3 | | | |
| Strained (Gerber) | 4⁷/₁₀ oz. | 6 | .2 | | | |
| Strained (Heinz) | 4½ oz. | 8 | .1 | | | |
| Pork: | | | | | | |
| Junior (Beech-Nut) | 3½ oz. | 178 | 5.9 | | | |
| Junior (Gerber) | 3½ oz. | 241 | 6.1 | | | |
| Strained (Beech-Nut) | 3½ oz. | 170 | 6.4 | | | |
| Strained (Gerber) | 3½ oz. | 218 | 6.0 | | | |
| Pork with pork broth, strained (Heinz) | 3½ oz. | 98 | 4.0 | | | |
| Potatoes, creamed, with ham, toddler (Gerber) | 6 oz. | 750 | 9.3 | | | |
| Pretzel (Gerber) | 1 piece (5 grams) | 30 | .1 | | | |
| Prune-orange juice: | | | | | | |
| Strained (Beech-Nut) | 4¹/₅ fl. oz. (4.4 oz.) | 2 | .1 | | | |
| Strained (Gerber) | 4¹/₅ fl. oz. (4.6 oz.) | 5 | .2 | | | |
| Strained (Heinz) | 4½ fl. oz. | 3 | .1 | | | |
| Prune with tapioca: | | | | | | |
| Junior (Beech-Nut) | 7¾ oz. | 81 | .2 | | | |
| Junior (Gerber) | 7⁸/₁₀ oz. | 44 | .5 | | | |
| Strained (Beech-Nut) | 4¾ oz. | 59 | .1 | | | |
| Strained (Gerber) | 4⁷/₁₀ oz. | 26 | .2 | | | |
| Strained (Heinz) | 4¾ oz. | 6 | .2 | | | |
| Raspberry cobbler (Gerber): | | | | | | |
| Junior | 7⁸/₁₀ oz. | 101 | .2 | | | |
| Strained | 4½ oz. | 62 | .1 | | | |
| *Similac:* | | | | | | |
| Advance | 1 fl. oz. (1 oz.) | 12 | .5 | | | <1 |
| Isomil | 1 fl. oz. (1 oz.) | 9 | 1.0 | | | 0 |
| *Powder | 1 fl. oz. (1 oz.) | 11 | 1.0 | | | Tr. |
| Ready-to-feed | 1 fl. oz. (1 oz.) | 9 | 1.0 | | | Tr. |
| Spaghetti & meat balls, toddler (Gerber) | 6¹/₅ oz. | 813 | 1.2 | | | |

(USDA): United States Department of Agriculture
*Prepared as Package Directs

| Food and Description | Measure or Quantity | Sodium (mg.) | —Fats in grams— | | Choles- terol (mg.) |
|---|---|---|---|---|---|
| | | | Total | Satu- rated | Unsatu- rated |
| Spaghetti, tomato sauce & beef: | | | | | |
| Junior (Beech-Nut) | 7½ oz. | 352 | 6.8 | | |
| Junior (Gerber) | 7½ oz. | 483 | 1.6 | | |
| Junior (Heinz) | 7½ oz. | 272 | 4.4 | | |
| Spaghetti, tomato sauce & meat, strained (Heinz) | 4½ oz. | 48 | 2.9 | | |
| Spinach, creamed: | | | | | |
| Junior (Gerber) | 7½ oz. | 320 | 2.2 | | |
| Strained (Gerber) | 4½ oz. | 150 | 1.0 | | |
| Strained (Heinz) | 4½ oz. | 112 | 1.5 | | |
| Split pea with bacon, junior (Gerber) | 7½ oz. | 267 | 5.4 | | |
| Split pea, vegetables & bacon: | | | | | |
| Junior (Heinz) | 7½ oz. | 334 | 8.9 | | |
| Strained (Heinz) | 4½ oz. | 213 | 4.8 | | |
| Split pea, vegetables & ham, junior (Beech-Nut) | 7½ oz. | 390 | 2.8 | | |
| Squash: | | | | | |
| Junior (Beech-Nut) | 7½ oz. | 254 | .4 | | |
| Junior (Gerber) | 7½ oz. | 214 | .5 | | |
| Strained (Beech-Nut) | 4½ oz. | 148 | .4 | | |
| Strained (Gerber) | 4½ oz. | 129 | .2 | | |
| Strained (Heinz) | 4½ oz. | 108 | .3 | | |
| In butter sauce (Beech-Nut): | | | | | |
| Junior | 7½ oz. | 267 | 1.7 | | |
| Strained | 4½ oz. | 147 | 1.0 | | |
| Sweet potato: | | | | | |
| Junior (Beech-Nut) | 7¾ oz. | 241 | .2 | | |
| Junior (Gerber) | 7⁸/₁₀ oz. | 222 | .2 | | |
| Strained (Beech-Nut) | 4½ oz. | 223 | 1.3 | | |
| Strained (Gerber) | 4⁷/₁₀ oz. | 135 | .1 | | |
| Strained (Heinz) | 4½ oz. | 40 | .1 | | |
| In butter sauce (Beech-Nut): | | | | | |
| Junior | 7¾ oz. | 250 | 1.5 | | |
| Strained (Beech-Nut) | 4½ oz. | 202 | .9 | | |
| Teething biscuit (Gerber) | 1 piece (.4 oz.) | 60 | .6 | | |
| Teething ring, honey (Beech-Nut) | ½ oz. | 101 | .9 | | |
| Tuna with noodles, strained (Heinz) | 4½ oz. | 176 | .5 | | |
| Turkey: | | | | | |
| Junior (Beech-Nut) | 3½ oz. | 199 | 4.5 | | |
| Junior (Gerber) | 3½ oz. | 166 | 4.7 | | |
| Strained (Beech-Nut) | 3½ oz. | 169 | 5.1 | | |

(USDA): United States Department of Agriculture
*Prepared as Package Directs

| Food and Description | Measure or Quantity | Sodium (mg.) | Total | Fats in grams Satu-rated | Unsatu-rated | Choles-terol (mg.) |
|---|---|---|---|---|---|---|
| Strained (Gerber) | 3½ oz. | 180 | 8.1 | | | |
| Turkey dinner: | | | | | | |
| Junior (Beech-Nut) | 4½ oz. | 225 | 3.2 | | | |
| Strained (Beech-Nut) | 4½ oz. | 250 | 4.0 | | | |
| With rice: | | | | | | |
| Junior (Gerber) | 7½ oz. | 316 | 1.5 | | | |
| Strained (Beech-Nut) | 4½ oz. | 175 | .8 | | | |
| Strained (Gerber) | 4½ oz. | 129 | 1.2 | | | |
| With rice & vegetables, junior (Beech-Nut) | 7½ oz. | 199 | 1.1 | | | |
| With vegetables: | | | | | | |
| Junior (Gerber) | 4½ oz. | 322 | 4.5 | | | |
| Strained (Gerber) | 4½ oz. | 195 | 4.1 | | | |
| Strained (Heinz) | 4¾ oz. | 149 | 3.3 | | | |
| Tutti frutti dessert (Heinz): | | | | | | |
| Junior | 7¾ oz. | 79 | .5 | | | |
| Strained | 4½ oz. | 69 | .5 | | | |
| Veal: | | | | | | |
| Junior (Beech-Nut) | 3½ oz. | 158 | 3.7 | | | |
| Junior (Gerber) | 3½ oz. | 166 | 4.2 | | | |
| Strained (Beech-Nut) | 3½ oz. | 169 | 6.1 | | | |
| Strained (Gerber) | 3½ oz. | 177 | 4.0 | | | |
| Veal dinner: | | | | | | |
| Junior (Beech-Nut) | 4½ oz. | 145 | 8.2 | | | |
| Strained (Beech-Nut) | 4½ oz. | 177 | 6.9 | | | |
| With vegetables: | | | | | | |
| Junior (Gerber) | 4½ oz. | 289 | 1.6 | | | |
| Junior (Heinz) | 4¾ oz. | 150 | 4.7 | | | |
| Strained (Gerber) | 4½ oz. | 161 | 1.8 | | | |
| Strained (Heinz) | 4¾ oz. | 167 | 2.7 | | | |
| Veal & veal broth (Heinz): | | | | | | |
| Junior | 3½ oz. | 200 | 3.8 | | | |
| Strained | 3½ oz. | 143 | 3.6 | | | |
| Vegetables: | | | | | | |
| Garden, strained (Beech-Nut) | 4½ oz. | 134 | .3 | | | |
| Garden, strained (Gerber) | 4½ oz. | 142 | .3 | | | |
| Mixed, junior (Gerber) | 7½ oz. | 286 | .3 | | | |
| Mixed, junior (Heinz) | 7½ oz. | 208 | .1 | | | |
| Mixed, strained (Gerber) | 4½ oz. | 218 | .1 | | | |
| Vegetables & bacon: | | | | | | |
| Junior (Beech-Nut) | 7½ oz. | 337 | 8.3 | | | |
| Junior (Gerber) | 7½ oz. | 362 | 5.2 | | | |
| Junior (Heinz) | 7½ oz | 289 | 8.4 | | | |

(USDA): United States Department of Agriculture
*Prepared as Package Directs

| Food and Description | Measure or Quantity | Sodium (mg.) | —Fats in grams— | | | Choles- terol (mg.) |
|---|---|---|---|---|---|---|
| | | | Total | Satu- rated | Unsatu- rated | |
| Strained (Beech-Nut) | 4½ oz. | 137 | 5.1 | | | |
| Strained (Gerber) | 4½ oz. | 183 | 3.9 | | | |
| Strained (Heinz) | 4½ oz. | 170 | 2.4 | | | |
| Vegetables & beef: | | | | | | |
| Junior (Beech-Nut) | 7½ oz. | 337 | 6.4 | | | |
| Junior (Gerber) | 7½ oz. | 310 | 3.3 | | | |
| Junior (Heinz) | 7½ oz. | 270 | 2.0 | | | |
| Strained (Beech-Nut) | 4½ oz. | 157 | 4.1 | | | |
| Strained (Gerber) | 4½ oz. | 173 | 2.6 | | | |
| Strained (Heinz) | 4½ oz. | 226 | 2.0 | | | |
| Vegetables & chicken (Gerber): | | | | | | |
| Junior | 7½ oz. | 227 | .6 | | | |
| Strained | 4½ oz. | 137 | .8 | | | |
| Vegetables, dumplings, beef & bacon (Heinz): | | | | | | |
| Junior | 7½ oz. | 253 | 6.5 | | | |
| Strained | 4½ oz. | 182 | 4.3 | | | |
| Vegetables, egg noodles & chicken (Heinz): | | | | | | |
| Junior | 7½ oz. | 210 | 4.9 | | | |
| Strained | 4½ oz. | 134 | 2.5 | | | |
| Vegetables, egg noodles & turkey, junior (Heinz) | 7½ oz. | 206 | 3.2 | | | |
| Vegetables & ham: | | | | | | |
| Junior (Heinz) | 7½ oz. | 238 | 5.8 | | | |
| Strained (Beech-Nut) | 4½ oz. | 259 | 3.1 | | | |
| With bacon, junior (Gerber) | 7½ oz. | 445 | 4.0 | | | |
| With bacon, strained (Gerber) | 4½ oz. | 298 | 2.6 | | | |
| With bacon, strained (Heinz) | 4½ oz. | 198 | 4.1 | | | |
| Vegetables & lamb: | | | | | | |
| Junior (Beech-Nut) | 7½ oz. | 290 | 5.1 | | | |
| Junior (Gerber) | 7½ oz. | 273 | 2.9 | | | |
| Junior (Heinz) | 7½ oz. | 251 | 2.5 | | | |
| Strained (Gerber) | 4½ oz. | 184 | 1.7 | | | |
| Strained (Heinz) | 4½ oz. | 149 | 1.3 | | | |
| Vegetables & liver: | | | | | | |
| Junior (Beech-Nut) | 7½ oz. | 184 | 1.1 | | | |
| Strained (Beech-Nut) | 4½ oz. | 186 | .5 | | | |
| With bacon, junior (Gerber) | 7½ oz. | 498 | 2.0 | | | |
| With bacon, strained (Gerber) | 4½ oz. | 262 | 3.6 | | | |
| Vegetables & turkey: | | | | | | |
| Junior (Gerber) | 7½ oz. | 224 | .6 | | | |
| Strained (Gerber) | 4½ oz. | 157 | .5 | | | |

(USDA): United States Department of Agriculture
*Prepared as Package Directs

| Food and Description | Measure or Quantity | Sodium (mg.) | Fats in grams | | | Cholesterol (mg.) |
|---|---|---|---|---|---|---|
| | | | Total | Saturated | Unsaturated | |
| Toddler, casserole (Gerber) | 6¹/₅ oz. | 991 | 5.6 | | | |
| Vegetable soup: | | | | | | |
| Junior (Beech-Nut) | 7½ oz. | 189 | .2 | | | |
| Junior (Heinz) | 7½ oz. | 225 | 1.3 | | | |
| Strained (Beech-Nut) | 4½ oz. | 163 | .1 | | | |
| Strained (Heinz) | 4½ oz. | 292 | .8 | | | |
| **BAC ONION:** | | | | | | |
| (Lawry's) | 1 pkg. (3½ oz.) | | 8.2 | | | |
| (Lawry's) | 1 tsp. (4 grams) | | .3 | | | |
| **BACO NOIR BURGUNDY WINE** | | | | | | |
| (Great Western) 12.5% alcohol | 3 fl. oz. | 36 | 0. | | | 0 |
| **BAC*OS** (General Mills) | 1 T. | 341 | 1.3 | | | |
| **BACON, cured:** | | | | | | |
| Raw: | | | | | | |
| (USDA) sliced | 1 lb. | 3084 | 314.3 | 101. | 213. | |
| (USDA) sliced | 1 oz. | 193 | 19.6 | 6. | 13. | |
| (USDA) slab | 1 lb. (weighed with rind) | 2900 | 295.5 | 95. | 200. | |
| (Hormel) Black Label | 1 piece (.8 oz.) | 270 | 12.9 | | | |
| (Hormel) *Range Brand* | 1 piece (1.6 oz.) | 832 | 28.1 | 9. | 15. | 34 |
| (Wilson) | 1 oz. | 193 | 17.7 | 6. | 11. | 20 |
| Broiled or fried, crisp, drained: | | | | | | |
| (USDA) thin slice | 1 slice (5 grams) | 51 | 2.6 | <1. | 2. | |
| (USDA) medium slice | 1 slice (8 grams) | 77 | 3.9 | 1. | 3. | |
| (USDA) thick slice | 1 slice (.4 oz.) | 123 | 6.2 | 2. | 4. | |
| (Oscar Mayer) 11–14 slices per lb. raw | 1 slice (.4 oz.) | 209 | 6.3 | 2. | 4. | 6 |
| (Oscar Mayer) 18–26 slices per lb. raw | 1 slice (6 grams) | 114 | 3.4 | 1. | 2. | 3 |
| (Oscar Mayer) 25–30 slices per ¾ lb. raw | 1 slice (4 grams) | 76 | 2.3 | <1. | 1. | 2 |
| Canned (USDA) | 3 oz. | | 60.8 | 20. | 41. | |
| **BACON BITS:** | | | | | | |
| (Wilson) | 1 oz. | 778 | 10.2 | 4. | 6. | 27 |
| Imitation: | | | | | | |
| (Durkee) | 1 tsp. (2 grams) | 229 | .4 | | | |
| (French's) | 1 tsp. (2 grams) | 40 | .3 | | | |
| (McCormick) | 1 tsp. (2 grams) | 14 | .4 | | | |

(USDA): United States Department of Agriculture
*Prepared as Package Directs

| Food and Description | Measure or Quantity | Sodium (mg.) | —Fats in grams— | | | Choles- terol (mg.) |
|---|---|---|---|---|---|---|
| | | | Total | Satu- rated | Unsatu- rated | |
| **BACON, CANADIAN:** | | | | | | |
| Unheated: | | | | | | |
| (USDA) | 1 oz. | 538 | 4.1 | 1. | 3. | |
| (Oscar Mayer) | 1-oz. slice | 343 | 2.3 | | | |
| (Wilson) | 1 oz. | 293 | 2.3 | | | 18 |
| Broiled or fried, drained (USDA) | 1 oz. | 724 | 5.0 | 2. | 3. | |
| | | | | | | |
| **BAGEL** (USDA): | | | | | | |
| Egg | 3″ dia. (1.9 oz.) | | 2.0 | | | |
| Water | 3″ dia. (1.9 oz.) | | 2.0 | | | |
| | | | | | | |
| **BAKING POWDER:** | | | | | | |
| Regular: | | | | | | |
| Phosphate (USDA) | 1 tsp. (5 grams) | 386 | Tr. | | | 0 |
| SAS (USDA) | 1 tsp. (4 grams) | 405 | Tr. | | | 0 |
| Tartrate (USDA) | 1 tsp. (4 grams) | 270 | Tr. | | | 0 |
| (Calumet) SAS | 1 tsp. (4 grams) | 276 | | | | 0 |
| (Royal) tartrate | 1 tsp. (4 grams) | 250 | Tr. | | | 0 |
| Low sodium, commercial (USDA) | 1 tsp. (4 grams) | <1 | Tr. | | | 0 |
| | | | | | | |
| **BAKON DELITES** (Wise): | | | | | | |
| Regular | ½-oz. bag | 295 | 4.3 | | | |
| Barbecue flavor | ½-oz. bag | 352 | 4.1 | | | |
| | | | | | | |
| **BAMBOO SHOOT,** raw (USDA): | | | | | | |
| Untrimmed | ½ lb. (weighed untrimmed) | | .2 | | | 0 |
| Trimmed | 4 oz. | | .3 | | | 0 |
| | | | | | | |
| **BANANA:** | | | | | | |
| Common: | | | | | | |
| Fresh: | | | | | | |
| Whole (USDA) | 1 lb. (weighed with skin) | 3 | .6 | | | 0 |
| Small size (USDA) | 4.9-oz. banana (7¾″ x 1¹¹/₃₂″) | 1 | .2 | | | 0 |
| Small size (Del Monte) | 1 peeled banana (3.5 oz.) | 2 | .5 | | | 0 |
| Medium size (USDA) | 6.2-oz. banana (8¾″ x 1¹³/₃₂″) | 1 | .2 | | | 0 |
| Large size (USDA) | 7-oz. banana (9¾″ x 1⁷/₁₆″) | 1 | .3 | | | 0 |

(USDA): United States Department of Agriculture
*Prepared as Package Directs

| Food and Description | Measure or Quantity | Sodium (mg.) | —Fats in grams— Total | Satu- rated | Unsatu- rated | Choles- terol (mg.) |
|---|---|---|---|---|---|---|
| Chunks (USDA) | 1 cup (5 oz.) | 1 | .3 | | | 0 |
| Mashed (USDA) | 1 cup (2 med., 7.8 oz.) | 2 | .4 | | | 0 |
| Sliced (USDA) | 1 cup (1¼ med., 5.1 oz.) | 1 | .3 | | | 0 |
| Dehydrated (USDA): | | | | | | |
| Flakes | ½ cup (1.8 oz.) | 2 | .4 | | | 0 |
| Powder | 1 oz. | 1 | .2 | | | 0 |
| Red, fresh, whole (USDA) | 1 lb. (weighed with skin) | 3 | .6 | | | 0 |
| Red, fresh, peeled (USDA) | 4 oz. | 1 | .2 | | | 0 |

## BANANA, BAKING (See PLANTAIN)

## BANANA CAKE MIX:

| | | | | | | |
|---|---|---|---|---|---|---|
| *(Betty Crocker) layer | $^1/_{12}$ of cake | 244 | 5.7 | | | |
| *(Duncan Hines) | $^1/_{12}$ of cake (2.7 oz.) | 339 | 6.1 | | | 50 |

## BANANA PIE, cream or custard:

| | | | | | | |
|---|---|---|---|---|---|---|
| Home recipe (USDA) | $^1/_6$ of 9″ pie (5.4 oz.) | 295 | 14.1 | | | |
| (Tastykake) | 4-oz. pie | | 15.2 | | | |
| Frozen (Banquet) | 2½-oz. serving | | 8.7 | | | |
| Frozen (Morton) | $^1/_6$ of 14.4-oz. pie | 125 | 9.3 | | | |
| Frozen (Mrs. Smith's) | $^1/_6$ of 8″ pie (2.3 oz.) | 95 | 11.8 | | | |

## BANANA PUDDING, canned

| | | | | | | |
|---|---|---|---|---|---|---|
| (Del Monte) | 5-oz. can | 251 | 5.3 | | | |

## BANANA PUDDING & PIE MIX:

| | | | | | | |
|---|---|---|---|---|---|---|
| *Instant (Jell-O) | ½ cup (5.3 oz.) | 406 | 4.7 | | | 13 |
| *Instant (Royal) | ½ cup (5.1 oz.) | 350 | 4.2 | | | 14 |
| *Regular (Jell-O) | ½ cup (5.2 oz.) | 224 | 4.6 | | | 13 |
| *Regular (Royal) | ½ cup (5.1 oz.) | 170 | 4.4 | | | 14 |

## BARBADOS CHERRY
(See ACEROLA)

## BARBECUE DINNER MIX

| | | | | | | |
|---|---|---|---|---|---|---|
| (Hunt's) Skillet[1] | 2-lb. 1-oz. pkg. | 5813 | 30.7 | 8. | 22. | |

## BARBECUE SAUCE (See SAUCE, Barbecue)

(USDA): United States Department of Agriculture
*Prepared as Package Directs
[1]Principal source of fat: vegetable shortening.

| Food and Description | Measure or Quantity | Sodium (mg.) | —Fats in grams— | | | Choles-terol (mg.) |
|---|---|---|---|---|---|---|
| | | | Total | Satu-rated | Unsatu-rated | |
| **BARBECUE SEASONING** (French's) | 1 tsp. (2 grams) | 70 | .3 | | | |
| | | | | | | |
| **BARLEY,** pearled, dry: | | | | | | |
|   Light: | | | | | | |
|     (USDA) | ¼ cup (1.8 oz.) | 2 | .5 | | | 0 |
|     (Albers) | ¼ cup | | .5 | | | (0) |
|     (Quaker Scotch) | ¼ cup (1.7 oz.) | 4 | .6 | | | (0) |
|   Pot or Scotch (USDA) | 2 oz. | | .6 | | | 0 |
| | | | | | | |
| **BARRACUDA,** raw, meat only | | | | | | |
|   (USDA) | 4 oz. | | 2.9 | | | |
| | | | | | | |
| **BASS** (USDA): | | | | | | |
|   Black sea: | | | | | | |
|     Raw, whole | 1 lb. (weighed whole) | 120 | 2.1 | | | |
|     Baked, home recipe[1] | 4 oz. | | 17.9 | | | |
|   Smallmouth & largemouth, raw: | | | | | | |
|     Whole | 1 lb. (weighed whole) | | 3.7 | | | |
|     Meat only | 4 oz. | | 2.9 | | | |
|   Striped: | | | | | | |
|     Raw, whole | 1 lb. (weighed whole) | | 5.3 | | | |
|     Raw, meat only | 4 oz. | | 3.1 | | | |
|     Oven-fried[2] | 4 oz. | | 9.6 | | | |
|   White, raw, whole | 1 lb. (weighed whole) | | 4.1 | | | |
|   White, raw, meat only | 4 oz. | | 2.6 | | | |
| | | | | | | |
| **BASIL** (Spice Islands) | 1 tsp. | Tr. | | | | (0) |
| | | | | | | |
| **BAVARIAN PIE FILLING,** canned | | | | | | |
|   (Lucky Leaf) | 8 oz. | 268 | 10.8 | | | |
| | | | | | | |
| **BAVARIAN-STYLE BEANS & SPAETZLE,** frozen (Birds Eye) | ⅓ of 10-oz. pkg. | 411 | 8.4 | | | 0 |
| | | | | | | |
| **BAY LEAF** (Spice Islands) | 1 med. leaf | Tr. | | | | (0) |

(USDA): United States Department of Agriculture
*Prepared as Package Directs
[1]Prepared with bacon, butter, onion, celery & bread cubes.
[2]Prepared with milk, bread crumbs, butter & salt.

| Food and Description | Measure or Quantity | Sodium (mg.) | — Fats in grams — Total | Satu- rated | Unsatu- rated | Choles- terol (mg.) |
|---|---|---|---|---|---|---|
| **BEAN, BAKED:** | | | | | | |
| Canned with brown sugar sauce: | | | | | | |
| (B & M) red kidney bean | 1 cup (8 oz.) | 780 | 8.9 | | | |
| (B & M) yellow eye bean | 1 cup (8 oz.) | 965 | 10.6 | | | |
| (Homemaker's) red kidney bean | 1 cup (8 oz.) | 999 | 8.4 | | | |
| Canned in molasses sauce: | | | | | | |
| (Heinz) | 1 cup (9¼ oz.) | 1072 | 1.1 | | | |
| & brown sugar sauce (Campbell) | 1 cup | 651 | 7.7 | | | |
| Canned with pork: | | | | | | |
| (Campbell) Home Style | 1 cup | 848 | 4.0 | | | |
| (Hunt's) *Snack Pack*[1] | 5-oz. can | 561 | .7 | | | |
| (Van Camp) | 1 cup (7.7 oz.) | | 6.0 | | | |
| Canned with pork & molasses sauce: | | | | | | |
| (USDA)[2] | 1 cup (9 oz.) | 969 | 12.0 | 5. | 7. | |
| (B & M) Michigan Pea, New England-style | 1 cup (7.9 oz.) | 811 | 7.8 | | | |
| (Heinz) Boston-style | 1 cup (8¾ oz.) | 754 | 4.4 | | | |
| (Homemaker's) Michigan Pea, New England-style | 1 cup (8 oz.) | 840 | 7.3 | | | |
| Canned with pork & tomato sauce: | | | | | | |
| (USDA)[2] | 1 cup (9 oz.) | 1181 | 6.6 | 3. | 4. | |
| (Campbell) | 1 cup | 1134 | 3.0 | | | |
| (Heinz) | 1 cup (9¼ oz.) | 1148 | 4.5 | | | |
| Canned with tomato sauce: | | | | | | |
| (USDA) | 1 cup (9 oz.) | 862 | 1.3 | | | 0 |
| (Heinz) *Campside* | 1 cup (9½ oz.) | 1307 | 9.6 | | | |
| (Heinz) Vegetarian | 1 cup (9¼ oz.) | 1184 | 1.4 | | | (0) |
| (Van Camp) | 1 cup (8.1 oz.) | | 1.2 | | | |
| **BEAN, BARBECUE** (Campbell) | 1 cup | 1089 | 3.4 | | | |
| **BEAN, BAYO,** dry (USDA) | 4 oz. | 28 | 1.7 | | | 0 |
| *BEAN 'N BEEF* (Campbell) | 1 cup | 1211 | 6.1 | | | |
| **BEAN, BLACK,** dry (USDA) | 4 oz. | 28 | 1.7 | | | 0 |
| **BEAN, BROWN,** dry (USDA) | 4 oz. | 28 | 1.7 | | | 0 |
| **BEAN, CALICO,** dry (USDA) | 4 oz. | 11 | 1.4 | | | 0 |

(USDA): United States Department of Agriculture
*Prepared as Package Directs
[1]Principal source of fat: bacon.
[2]Principal source of fat: pork.

| Food and Description | Measure or Quantity | Sodium (mg.) | —Fats in grams— | | Choles-terol (mg.) |
|---|---|---|---|---|---|
| | | | Total | Satu- rated | Unsatu- rated |

**BEAN & FRANKFURTER, canned:**

| | | | | | | |
|---|---|---|---|---|---|---|
| (USDA) | 1 cup (9 oz.) | 1374 | 18.1 | | | |
| (Campbell) in tomato & molasses sauce | 1 cup | 1143 | 16.1 | | | |
| (Heinz) | 1 can (8¾ oz.) | 1121 | 19.8 | | | |
| (Van Camp) *Beanie-Weenee* | 1 cup (7.8 oz.) | | 15.6 | | | |

**BEAN & FRANKFURTER DINNER, frozen:**
(Banquet):

| | | | | | | |
|---|---|---|---|---|---|---|
| Meat compartment | 6¼ oz. | | 32.3 | | | |
| Apple compartment | 2½ oz. | | .3 | | | |
| Cornbread compartment | 2 oz. | | 3.0 | | | |
| Complete dinner | 10 ¾-oz. dinner | | 35.7 | | | |
| (Morton) | 12-oz. dinner | 881 | 17.9 | | | |
| (Swanson) | 11½-oz. dinner | 1085 | 28.7 | | | |

**BEAN, GREAT NORTHERN**
(See **BEAN, WHITE**)

**BEAN, GREEN or SNAP:**
Fresh (USDA):

| | | | | | | |
|---|---|---|---|---|---|---|
| Whole | 1 lb. (weighed untrimmed) | 28 | .8 | | | 0 |
| 1½" to 2" pieces | ½ cup (1.8 oz.) | 4 | .1 | | | 0 |
| French-style | ½ cup (1.4 oz.) | 3 | <.1 | | | 0 |
| Boiled without salt, drained, whole (USDA) | ½ cup (2.2 oz.) | 2 | .1 | | | 0 |
| Boiled without salt, drained, 1½" to 2" pieces (USDA) | ½ cup (2.4 oz.) | 3 | .1 | | | 0 |
| Canned, regular pack: | | | | | | |
| Solids & liq. (USDA) | ½ cup (4.2 oz.) | 283 | .1 | | | 0 |
| Drained solids, whole (USDA) | 4 oz. | 268 | .2 | | | 0 |
| Drained solids, cut (USDA) | ½ cup (2.5 oz.) | 165 | .1 | | | 0 |
| Drained liq. (USDA) | 4 oz. | 268 | .1 | | | 0 |
| Cut, solids & liq. (Comstock-Greenwood) | ½ cup (3 oz.) | 200 | .2 | | | (0) |
| Solids & liq. (Del Monte) | ½ cup (4 oz.) | 440 | .3 | | | 0 |
| Whole, solids & liq. (Green Giant) | ¼ of 16-oz. can | 415 | .1 | | | (0) |
| Cut, solids & liq. (Green Giant) | ¼ of 16-oz. can | 415 | .1 | | | (0) |
| Solids & liq. (Green Giant) French style | ½ of 8-oz. can | 415 | .1 | | | (0) |

(USDA): United States Department of Agriculture
*Prepared as Package Directs

29

| Food and Description | Measure or Quantity | Sodium (mg.) | — Fats in grams — | | | Choles- terol (mg.) |
|---|---|---|---|---|---|---|
| | | | Total | Satu- rated | Unsatu- rated | |
| Solids & liq. (Stokely- Van Camp) | ½ cup (3.9 oz.) | | .1 | | | (0) |
| Drained. whole or cut (Del Monte) | ½ cup (2.5 oz.) | 274 | .2 | | | 0 |
| Seasoned. solids & liq. (Del Monte) | ½ cup (4 oz.) | 526 | .2 | | | 0 |
| Seasoned. drained solids (Del Monte) | ½ cup (2.5 oz.) | 325 | .2 | | | 0 |
| Seasoned. drained liq. (Del Monte) | 4 oz. | 523 | .1 | | | 0 |
| With bacon (Comstock- Greenwood) | 4 oz. | 778 | .9 | | | |
| With mushroom. solids & liq. (Comstock-Greenwood) | 4 oz. | 473 | .2 | | | |
| Canned. dietetic pack: | | | | | | |
| Solids & liq. (USDA) | 4 oz. | 2 | .1 | | | 0 |
| Drained solids (USDA) | 4 oz. | 2 | .1 | | | 0 |
| Drained liq. (USDA) | 4 oz. | 2 | .1 | | | 0 |
| Cut. solids & liq. (Blue Boy) | 4 oz. | 9 | .1 | | | (0) |
| Cut (S and W) *Nutradiet,* unseasoned | 4 oz. | 1 | .1 | | | (0) |
| Solids & liq. (Diet Delight) | ½ cup (4.2 oz.) | 4 | .1 | | | (0) |
| Solids & liq. (Tillie Lewis) | ½ cup (4.2 oz.) | <10 | .1 | | | 0 |
| Frozen: | | | | | | |
| Whole (Birds Eye) | ⅓ of 9-oz. pkg. | 1 | .1 | | | 0 |
| Cut. not thawed (USDA) | 10-oz. pkg. | 3 | .3 | | | 0 |
| Cut. boiled without salt. drained (USDA) | 4 oz. | 1 | .1 | | | 0 |
| Cut. boiled without salt. drained (USDA) | ½ cup (2.8 oz.) | <1 | <.1 | | | 0 |
| Cut (Birds Eye) | ⅓ of 9-oz. pkg. | 1 | .1 | | | 0 |
| French-style. not thawed (USDA) | 10-oz. pkg. | 6 | .3 | | | 0 |
| French-style. boiled. drained (USDA) | ½ cup (2.8 oz.) | 2 | <.1 | | | 0 |
| French-style (Birds Eye) | ⅓ of 9-oz. pkg. | 2 | .1 | | | 0 |
| French-style with sliced mushrooms (Birds Eye) | ⅓ of 9-oz. pkg. | 153 | .1 | | | 0 |
| French-style. with toasted almonds (Birds Eye) | ½ cup (3 oz.) | 360 | 2.8 | | | 0 |
| In butter sauce. cut or French-style (Green Giant) | ⅓ of 9-oz. pkg. | 361 | 1.7 | | | |
| In mushroom sauce. casserole (Green Giant) | ⅓ of 12-oz. pkg. | 414 | 1.9 | | | |

(USDA): United States Department of Agriculture
*Prepared as Package Directs

| Food and Description | Measure or Quantity | Sodium (mg.) | — Fats in grams — | | | Choles- terol (mg.) |
|---|---|---|---|---|---|---|
| | | | Total | Satu- rated | Unsatu- rated | |
| With onions & bacon (Green Giant) | ⅓ of 9-oz. pkg. | 327 | 1.5 | | | |
| In mushroom sauce, cut (Green Giant) | ⅓ of 10-oz. pkg. | 321 | .6 | | | |

**BEAN, ITALIAN** (See **BROADBEAN**)

**BEAN, KIDNEY or RED:**
Dry:

| | | | | | | |
|---|---|---|---|---|---|---|
| (USDA) | 4 oz. | 11 | 1.7 | | | 0 |
| (USDA) | ½ cup (3.3 oz.) | 9 | 1.4 | | | 0 |
| Cooked without salt (USDA) | ½ cup (3.3 oz.) | 3 | .5 | | | 0 |
| Canned: | | | | | | |
| Solids & liq. (USDA) | ½ cup (4.5 oz.) | 4 | .5 | | | 0 |
| Red kidney & chili gravy (Nalley's) | 4 oz. | | 2.3 | | | |

**BEAN, LIMA,** young:

| | | | | | | |
|---|---|---|---|---|---|---|
| Raw, whole (USDA) | 1 lb. (weighed in pod) | 4 | .9 | | | 0 |
| Raw, without shell (USDA) | 1 lb. (weighed shelled) | 9 | 2.3 | | | 0 |
| Boiled without salt, drained (USDA) | ½ cup (3 oz.) | <1 | .4 | | | 0 |
| Canned, regular pack: | | | | | | |
| Solids & liq. (USDA) | ½ cup (4.4 oz.) | 293 | .4 | | | 0 |
| Drained solids (USDA) | ½ cup (3.1 oz.) | 205 | .3 | | | 0 |
| Drained liq. (USDA) | 4 oz. | 268 | Tr. | | | 0 |
| Drained solids (Del Monte) | ½ cup (3.1 oz.) | 292 | .2 | | | 0 |
| Seasoned, drained solids (Del Monte) | ½ cup (3.1 oz.) | 266 | .2 | | | 0 |
| Solids & liq. (Stokely- Van Camp) | ½ cup (4.1 oz.) | | .4 | | | (0) |
| With ham (Nalley's) | 4 oz. | | 4.8 | | | |
| Canned, dietetic pack: | | | | | | |
| Solids & liq., low sodium (USDA) | 4 oz. | 5 | .3 | | | 0 |
| Drained solids, low sodium (USDA) | 4 oz. | 5 | .3 | | | 0 |
| Solids & liq., unseasoned (Blue Boy) | 4 oz. | 5 | .3 | | | (0) |

(USDA): United States Department of Agriculture
*Prepared as Package Directs

㉛

| Food and Description | Measure or Quantity | Sodium (mg.) | —Fats in grams— | | | Cholesterol (mg.) |
|---|---|---|---|---|---|---|
| | | | Total | Saturated | Unsaturated | |
| **Frozen:** | | | | | | |
| Baby butter beans (Birds Eye) | ⅓ of 10-oz. pkg. | 367 | .2 | | | 0 |
| Baby limas: | | | | | | |
| Not thawed (USDA) | 4 oz. | 167 | .2 | | | 0 |
| Boiled, drained (USDA) | ½ cup (3 oz.) | 111 | .2 | | | 0 |
| (Birds Eye) | ½ cup (3.3 oz.) | 138 | .2 | | | 0 |
| In butter sauce (Green Giant) | ⅓ of 10-oz. pkg. | 439 | 2.8 | | | |
| Tiny (Birds Eye) | ½ cup (2.5 oz.) | 104 | .1 | | | 0 |
| Fordhooks: | | | | | | |
| Not thawed (USDA) | 4 oz. | 146 | .1 | | | 0 |
| Boiled, drained (USDA) | ½ cup (3 oz.) | 85 | <.1 | | | 0 |
| (Birds Eye) | ⅓ of 10-oz. pkg. | 121 | .1 | | | 0 |
| **BEAN, LIMA,** mature: | | | | | | |
| Dry: | | | | | | |
| Baby (USDA) | ½ cup (3.4 oz.) | 4 | 1.5 | | | 0 |
| Large (USDA) | ½ cup (3.1 oz.) | 4 | 1.4 | | | 0 |
| Boiled without salt, drained (USDA) | ½ cup (3.4 oz.) | 2 | .6 | | | 0 |
| **BEAN, MUNG,** dry (USDA) | ½ cup (3.7 oz.) | 6 | 1.4 | | | 0 |
| **BEAN, NAVY or PEA** (See **BEAN, WHITE**) | | | | | | |
| **BEAN, PINTO:** | | | | | | |
| Dry (USDA) | 4 oz. | 11 | 1.4 | | | 0 |
| Dry (USDA) | ½ cup (3.4 oz.) | 10 | 1.2 | | | 0 |
| *(Uncle Ben's) including broth | ¾ cup (6 oz.) | 16 | .6 | | | 0 |
| **BEAN, RED** (See **BEAN. KIDNEY** or **BEAN, RED MEXICAN**) | | | | | | |
| **BEAN, RED MEXICAN,** dry (USDA) | 4 oz. | 11 | 1.4 | | | 0 |
| **BEAN SALAD,** canned, solids & liq.: | | | | | | |
| (Comstock-Greenwood) | 4 oz. | 536 | 2.1 | | | |
| (Hunt's) *Snack Pack*[1] | 5-oz. can | 547 | 1.2 | Tr. | <1. | |
| (Le Sueur) | ¼ of 1-lb. 1-oz. can | 458 | .8 | | | |

(USDA): United States Department of Agriculture
*Prepared as Package Directs
[1]Principal source of fat: cottonseed oil.

| Food and Description | Measure or Quantity | Sodium (mg.) | Fats in grams | | | Cholesterol (mg.) |
|---|---|---|---|---|---|---|
| | | | Total | Saturated | Unsaturated | |
| **BEAN, SEMI-MATURE,** shelled, in brine, drained (B & M) | ½ of 8¾-oz. can | 320 | .7 | | | (0) |
| **BEAN SOUP,** canned: | | | | | | |
| *(Manischewitz) | 1 cup | | 1.9 | | | |
| *With bacon (Campbell) | 1 cup | 852 | 4.8 | 1. | 4. | |
| With pork, condensed (USDA) | 8 oz. (by wt.) | 1830 | 10.4 | | | |
| *With pork, prepared with equal volume water (USDA) | 1 cup (8.8 oz.) | 1008 | 5.8 | | | |
| With smoked ham (Heinz) *Great American* | 1 cup (8¾ oz.) | 1215 | 6.8 | | | |
| *With smoked pork (Heinz) | 1 cup (8½ oz.) | 1080 | 5.7 | | | |
| **BEAN SOUP, BLACK,** canned: | | | | | | |
| *(Campbell) | 1 cup | 816 | 1.6 | Tr. | 1. | |
| (Crosse & Blackwell) | 6½ oz. (½ can) | | .6 | | | |
| ***BEAN SOUP, LIMA,** canned (Manischewitz) | 1 cup | | 1.6 | | | |
| **BEAN SOUP, NAVY,** dehydrated (USDA) | 1 oz. | | .3 | | | |
| **BEAN SPROUT:** | | | | | | |
| Mung: | | | | | | |
| Raw (USDA) | ½ lb. | 12 | .4 | | | 0 |
| Raw (USDA) | ½ cup (1.6 oz.) | 2 | <.1 | | | 0 |
| Boiled without salt, drained (USDA) | ½ cup (2.2 oz.) | 2 | .1 | | | 0 |
| Soy: | | | | | | |
| Raw (USDA) | ½ lb. | | 3.2 | | | 0 |
| Raw (USDA) | ½ cup (1.9 oz.) | | .8 | | | 0 |
| Boiled without salt, drained (USDA) | 4 oz. | | 1.6 | | | 0 |
| Canned (Hung's) | 8 oz. | | 1.0 | | | (0) |
| **BEAN, WHITE,** dry: | | | | | | |
| Raw: | | | | | | |
| Great Northern (USDA) | ½ cup (3.1 oz.) | 17 | 1.4 | | | 0 |
| Navy or pea (USDA) | ½ cup (3.7 oz.) | 20 | 1.7 | | | 0 |
| All other white (USDA) | 1 oz. | 5 | .5 | | | 0 |

(USDA): United States Department of Agriculture
*Prepared as Package Directs

33

| Food and Description | Measure or Quantity | Sodium (mg.) | —Fats in grams— | | | Cholesterol (mg.) |
|---|---|---|---|---|---|---|
| | | | Total | Saturated | Unsaturated | |
| Cooked without salt: | | | | | | |
| Great Northern (USDA) | ½ cup (3 oz.) | 6 | .5 | | | 0 |
| Navy or pea (USDA) | ½ cup (3.4 oz.) | 7 | .6 | | | 0 |
| All other white (USDA) | 4 oz. | 8 | .7 | | | 0 |
| **BEAN, YELLOW or WAX:** | | | | | | |
| Raw. whole (USDA) | 1 lb. (weighed untrimmed) | 28 | .8 | | | 0 |
| Boiled without salt. drained (USDA) | 4 oz. | 3 | .2 | | | 0 |
| Boiled without salt. drained 1″ pieces (USDA) | ½ cup (2.9 oz.) | 2 | .2 | | | 0 |
| Canned. regular pack: | | | | | | |
| Solids & liq. (USDA) | ½ cup (4.2 oz.) | 283 | .2 | | | 0 |
| Drained solids (USDA) | ½ cup (2.2 oz.) | 146 | .2 | | | 0 |
| Drained liq. (USDA) | 4 oz. | 268 | .1 | | | 0 |
| Cut. solids & liq. (Comstock-Greenwood) | ½ cup (3 oz.) | 200 | .2 | | | (0) |
| Solids & liq. (Del Monte) | ½ cup (4 oz.) | 438 | .2 | | | 0 |
| Drained solids (Del Monte) | ½ cup (2.5 oz.) | 275 | .2 | | | 0 |
| Cut, solids & liq. (Green Giant) | ½ of 8.5-oz. can | 428 | .1 | | | (0) |
| Solids & liq. (Stokely-Van Camp) | ½ cup (4.1 oz.) | | .2 | | | (0) |
| Canned, dietetic pack: | | | | | | |
| Solids & liq. (USDA) | 4 oz. | 2 | .1 | | | 0 |
| Drained solids (USDA) | 4 oz. | 2 | .1 | | | 0 |
| Drained liq. (USDA) | 4 oz. | 2 | .1 | | | 0 |
| Solids & liq. (Blue Boy) | 4 oz. | 2 | .1 | | | (0) |
| Frozen: | | | | | | |
| Cut, not thawed (USDA) | 4 oz. | 1 | .1 | | | 0 |
| Boiled, drained (USDA) | 4 oz. | 1 | .1 | | | 0 |
| Cut (Birds Eye) | ⅓ of 9-oz. pkg. | 14 | .1 | | | 0 |
| **BEAVER,** roasted (USDA) | 4 oz. | | 15.5 | | | |
| **BEECHNUT:** | | | | | | |
| Whole (USDA) | 4 oz. (weighed in shell) | | 34.6 | 3. | 32. | 0 |
| Shelled (USDA) | 1 oz. (weighed shelled) | | 14.2 | 1. | 13. | 0 |

(USDA): United States Department of Agriculture
*Prepared as Package Directs

| Food and Description | Measure or Quantity | Sodium (mg.) | — Fats in grams — | | | Choles-terol (mg.) |
|---|---|---|---|---|---|---|
| | | | Total | Satu-rated | Unsatu-rated | |

**BEEF.** Values for beef cuts are given below for "lean and fat" and for "lean only." Beef purchased by the consumer at the retail store usually is trimmed to about one-half inch layer of fat. This is the meat described as "lean and fat." If all the fat that can be cut off with a knife is removed, the remainder is the "lean only." These cuts still contain flecks of fat known as "marbling" distributed through the meat. Cooked meats are medium done. Choice grade cuts (USDA):

| Food and Description | Measure or Quantity | Sodium (mg.) | Total | Satu-rated | Unsatu-rated | Choles-terol (mg.) |
|---|---|---|---|---|---|---|
| Brisket: | | | | | | |
| Raw, lean & fat | 1 lb. (weighed with bone) | 248 | 112.4 | 54. | 58. | 259 |
| Raw, lean & fat | 1 lb. (weighed without bone) | 295 | 133.8 | 64. | 69. | 308 |
| Raw, lean only | 1 lb. | 295 | 37.2 | 18. | 20. | 295 |
| Braised: | | | | | | |
| Lean & fat | 4 oz. | 68 | 39.5 | 19. | 21. | 107 |
| Lean only | 4 oz. | 68 | 11.9 | 6. | 6. | 103 |
| Chuck: | | | | | | |
| Raw, lean & fat | 1 lb. (weighed with bone) | 248 | 75.0 | 36. | 39. | 259 |
| Raw, lean & fat | 1 lb. (weighed without bone) | 295 | 88.9 | 43. | 46. | 308 |
| Raw, lean only | 1 lb. | 295 | 33.6 | 18. | 15. | 295 |
| Braised or pot-roasted: | | | | | | |
| Lean & fat | 4 oz. | 68 | 27.1 | 13. | 14. | 107 |
| Lean only | 4 oz. | 68 | 10.8 | 5. | 6. | 103 |
| Dried (See **BEEF, CHIPPED**) | | | | | | |
| Fat, separable, raw | 1 oz. | | 21.6 | 10. | 11. | 21 |
| Fat, separable, cooked | 1 oz. | | 22.1 | 10. | 12. | |

Filet Mignon. There are no data available on its composition. For dietary estimates, the data for sirloin steak, lean only, afford the closest approximation.

| Food and Description | Measure or Quantity | Sodium (mg.) | Total | Satu-rated | Unsatu-rated | Choles-terol (mg.) |
|---|---|---|---|---|---|---|
| Flank: | | | | | | |
| Raw, 100% lean | 1 lb. | 295 | 25.9 | 12. | 13. | 295 |
| Braised, 100% lean | 4 oz. | 68 | 8.3 | 4. | 4. | 103 |

(USDA): United States Department of Agriculture
*Prepared as Package Directs

| Food and Description | Measure or Quantity | Sodium (mg.) | — Fats in grams — | | | Cholesterol (mg.) |
|---|---|---|---|---|---|---|
| | | | Total | Saturated | Unsaturated | |
| Foreshank: | | | | | | |
| Raw. lean & fat | 1 lb. (weighed with bone) | 156 | 34.8 | 17. | 18. | 163 |
| Simmered: | | | | | | |
| Lean & fat | 4 oz. | 68 | 19.4 | 9. | 10. | 107 |
| Lean only | 4 oz. | 68 | 6.6 | 3. | 3. | 103 |
| Ground: | | | | | | |
| Regular: | | | | | | |
| Raw | 1 lb. | 118 | 96.2 | 48. | 48. | 308 |
| Raw | 1 cup (8 oz.) | 104 | 47.9 | 23. | 25. | 154 |
| Broiled | 4 oz. | 53 | 23.0 | 11. | 12. | 107 |
| Lean: | | | | | | |
| Raw | 1 lb. | 236 | 45.4 | 22. | 23. | 295 |
| Raw | 1 cup (8 oz.) | 118 | 22.6 | 11. | 11. | 147 |
| Broiled | 4 oz. | 54 | 12.8 | 6. | 7. | 103 |
| Heel of round: | | | | | | |
| Raw. lean & fat | 1 lb. | 295 | 64.4 | 31. | 34. | 308 |
| Raw. lean only | 1 lb. | 295 | 21.3 | 9. | 12. | 295 |
| Roasted: | | | | | | |
| Lean & fat | 4 oz. | 68 | 18.3 | 9. | 10. | 107 |
| Lean only | 4 oz. | 68 | 6.5 | 3. | 3. | 103 |
| Hindshank: | | | | | | |
| Raw. lean & fat | 1 lb. (weighed with bone) | 136 | 48.9 | 23. | 25. | 142 |
| Raw. lean & fat | 1 lb. (weighed without bone) | 295 | 106.1 | 51. | 55. | 308 |
| Raw. lean only | 1 lb. | 295 | 20.9 | 10. | 11. | 295 |
| Simmered: | | | | | | |
| Lean & fat | 4 oz. | 68 | 31.9 | 15. | 17. | 107 |
| Lean only | 4 oz. | 68 | 6.7 | 3. | 4. | 103 |
| Neck: | | | | | | |
| Raw, lean & fat | 1 lb. (weighed with bone) | 237 | 57.7 | 28. | 30. | 247 |
| Pot-roasted: | | | | | | |
| Lean & fat | 4 oz. | 68 | 22.3 | 11. | 12. | 107 |
| Lean only | 4 oz. | 68 | 8.3 | 4. | 4. | 103 |
| Oxtail, raw | 1 lb. (weighed with bone) | 73 | 7.9 | 4. | 4. | 73 |
| Oxtail, raw | 1 lb. (weighed without bone) | 295 | 31.8 | 15. | 17. | 295 |
| Plate: | | | | | | |
| Raw, lean & fat | 1 lb. (weighed with bone) | 263 | 150.6 | 72. | 78. | 275 |

(USDA): United States Department of Agriculture
*Prepared as Package Directs

| Food and Description | Measure or Quantity | Sodium (mg.) | — Fats in grams — | | | Choles- terol (mg.) |
|---|---|---|---|---|---|---|
| | | | Total | Satu- rated | Unsatu- rated | |
| Raw, lean & fat | 1 lb. (weighed without bone) | 295 | 169.2 | 81. | 88. | 308 |
| Raw, lean only | 1 lb. | 295 | 37.2 | 18. | 20. | 295 |
| Simmered: | | | | | | |
|    Lean & fat | 4 oz. | 68 | 48.5 | 23. | 25. | 107 |
|    Lean only | 4 oz. | 68 | 11.9 | 6. | 6. | 103 |
| Rib roast: | | | | | | |
| Raw, lean & fat | 1 lb. (weighed with bone) | 271 | 156.1 | 75. | 81. | 284 |
| Raw, lean & fat | 1 lb. (weighed without bone) | 295 | 169.6 | 81. | 88. | 308 |
| Raw, lean only | 1 lb. | 295 | 52.6 | 27. | 25. | 295 |
| Roasted: | | | | | | |
|    Lean & fat | 4 oz. | 68 | 44.7 | 21. | 23. | 107 |
|    Lean only | 4 oz. | 68 | 15.2 | 7. | 8. | 103 |
|    Lean only, chopped | 1 cup (4.5 oz.) | 77 | 17.2 | 8. | 9. | 116 |
|    Lean only, diced | 1 cup (5 oz.) | 86 | 19.2 | 9. | 10. | 130 |
| Round: | | | | | | |
| Raw, lean & fat | 1 lb. (weighed with bone) | 286 | 53.9 | 26. | 28. | 299 |
| Raw, lean & fat | 1 lb. (weighed without bone) | 295 | 55.8 | 27. | 29. | 308 |
| Raw, lean only | 1 lb. | 295 | 21.3 | 9. | 12. | 295 |
| Broiled: | | | | | | |
|    Lean & fat | 4 oz. | 68 | 17.5 | 8. | 9. | 107 |
|    Lean only | 4 oz. | 68 | 6.9 | 3. | 4. | 103 |
| Rump: | | | | | | |
| Raw, lean & fat | 1 lb. (weighed with bone) | 251 | 97.4 | 47. | 50. | 262 |
| Raw, lean & fat | 1 lb. (weighed without bone) | 295 | 114.8 | 55. | 60. | 308 |
| Raw, lean only | 1 lb. | 295 | 34.0 | 15. | 19. | 295 |
| Roasted: | | | | | | |
|    Lean & fat | 4 oz. | 68 | 31.0 | 15. | 16. | 107 |
|    Lean only | 4 oz. | 68 | 10.5 | 5. | 5. | 103 |
| Steak, club: | | | | | | |
| Raw, lean & fat | 1 lb. (weighed with bone) | 229 | 132.1 | 63. | 69. | 259 |
| Raw, lean & fat | 1 lb. (weighed without bone) | 295 | 157.9 | 76. | 82. | 308 |
| Raw, lean only | 1 lb. | 295 | 46.7 | 22. | 25. | 295 |
| Broiled: | | | | | | |
|    Lean & fat | 4 oz. | 68 | 46.0 | 22. | 24. | 107 |

(USDA): United States Department of Agriculture
*Prepared as Package Directs

| Food and Description | Measure or Quantity | Sodium (mg.) | —Fats in grams— | | | Choles-terol (mg.) |
|---|---|---|---|---|---|---|
| | | | Total | Satu-rated | Unsatu-rated | |
| Lean only | 4 oz. | 68 | 14.7 | 7. | 8. | 103 |
| One 8-oz. steak (weighed without bone before cooking) will give you: | | | | | | |
| Lean & fat | 5.9 oz. | 100 | 67.4 | 32. | 35. | 156 |
| Lean only | 3.4 oz. | 58 | 12.5 | 6. | 7. | 87 |
| Steak, porterhouse: | | | | | | |
| Raw, lean & fat | 1 lb. (weighed with bone) | 268 | 148.8 | 71. | 78. | 281 |
| Broiled: | | | | | | |
| Lean & fat | 4 oz. | 68 | 47.9 | 23. | 25. | 107 |
| Lean only | 4 oz. | 68 | 11.9 | 6. | 6. | 103 |
| One 16-oz. steak (weighed with bone before cooking) will give you: | | | | | | |
| Lean & fat | 10.2 oz. | 173 | 121.5 | 59. | 63. | 271 |
| Lean only | 5.9 oz. | 100 | 17.4 | 8. | 9. | 151 |
| Steak, ribeye, broiled: | | | | | | |
| One 10-oz. steak (weighed without bone before cooking) will give you: | | | | | | |
| Lean & fat | 7.3 oz. | 124 | 81.6 | 39. | 42. | 195 |
| Lean only | 3.8 oz. | 64 | 14.3 | 7. | 7. | 97 |
| Steak, sirloin, double-bone: | | | | | | |
| Raw, lean & fat | 1 lb. (weighed with bone) | 242 | 108.4 | 52. | 56. | 253 |
| Raw, lean & fat | 1 lb. (weighed without bone) | 295 | 132.0 | 63. | 69. | 308 |
| Raw, lean only | 1 lb. | 295 | 33.6 | 18. | 15. | 295 |
| Broiled: | | | | | | |
| Lean & fat | 4 oz. | 68 | 39.3 | 19. | 20. | 107 |
| Lean only | 4 oz. | 68 | 10.8 | 5. | 6. | 103 |
| One 16-oz. steak (weighed with bone before cooking) will give you: | | | | | | |
| Lean & fat | 8.9 oz. | 151 | 87.4 | 42. | 45. | 237 |
| Lean only | 5.9 oz. | 100 | 15.8 | 8. | 8. | 151 |
| One 12-oz. steak (weighed with bone before cooking) will give you: | | | | | | |
| Lean & fat | 6.6 oz. | 113 | 65.2 | 31. | 34. | 177 |
| Lean only | 4.4 oz. | 74 | 11.8 | 6. | 6. | 113 |

(USDA): United States Department of Agriculture
*Prepared as Package Directs

| Food and Description | Measure or Quantity | Sodium (mg.) | —Fats in grams— Total | Satu- rated | Unsatu- rated | Choles- terol (mg.) |
|---|---|---|---|---|---|---|
| Steak, sirloin, hipbone: | | | | | | |
| Raw, lean & fat | 1 lb. (weighed with bone) | 251 | 149.3 | 72. | 78. | 262 |
| Raw, lean & fat | 1 lb. (weighed without bone) | 295 | 176.0 | 84. | 92. | 308 |
| Raw, lean only | 1 lb. | 295 | 44.9 | 21. | 24. | 295 |
| Broiled: | | | | | | |
| Lean & fat | 4 oz. | 68 | 50.9 | 24. | 26. | 107 |
| Lean only | 4 oz. | 68 | 14.2 | 7. | 7. | 103 |
| Steak, sirloin, wedge & round-bone: | | | | | | |
| Raw, lean & fat | 1 lb. (weighed with bone) | 274 | 112.3 | 54. | 58. | 287 |
| Raw, lean & fat | 1 lb. (weighed without bone) | 295 | 121.1 | 58. | 63. | 308 |
| Raw, lean only | 1 lb. | 295 | 25.9 | 12. | 14. | 295 |
| Broiled: | | | | | | |
| Lean & fat | 4 oz. | 68 | 36.3 | 17. | 19. | 107 |
| Lean only | 4 oz. | 68 | 8.7 | 4. | 5. | 103 |
| Steak, T-bone: | | | | | | |
| Raw, lean & fat | 1 lb. (weighed with bone) | 263 | 149.1 | 72. | 78. | 275 |
| Broiled: | | | | | | |
| Lean & fat | 4 oz. | 68 | 49.0 | 24. | 26. | 107 |
| Lean only | 4 oz. | 68 | 11.7 | 6. | 6. | 103 |
| One 16-oz. steak (weighed with bone before cooking) will give you: | | | | | | |
| Lean & fat | 9.8 oz. | 167 | 120.1 | 58. | 63. | 261 |
| Lean only | 5.5 oz. | 94 | 16.1 | 8. | 8. | 142 |
| **BEEFAMATO COCKTAIL** | | | | | | |
| (Mott's) | ½ cup | | .3 | | | |
| **BEEFARONI,** canned (Chef Boy-Ar-Dee) | ⅓ of 40-oz. can | 1371 | 6.4 | | | |
| **BEEF BOUILLON/BROTH,** cubes or powder (See also **BEEF SOUP**): | | | | | | |
| (Croyden House) instant | 1 tsp. (5 grams) | 490 | .1 | Tr. | 0. | |
| (Herb-Ox) | 1 cube (4 grams) | 900 | .1 | | | |
| (Herb-Ox) instant | 1 packet (4 grams) | 1000 | .1 | | | |
| (Maggi) | 1 cube (4 grams) | 735 | .2 | | | |

(USDA): United States Department of Agriculture
*Prepared as Package Directs

| Food and Description | Measure or Quantity | Sodium (mg.) | Total | Fats in grams Satu-rated | Unsatu-rated | Choles-terol (mg.) |
|---|---|---|---|---|---|---|
| (Maggi) instant | 1 tsp. (4 grams) | 809 | .2 | | | |
| (Steero) | 1 cube (4 grams) | | .2 | | | |
| (Wyler's) | 1 cube (4 grams) | | .2 | | | |
| (Wyler's) instant | 1 tsp. | | .2 | | | |
| (Wyler's) no salt added | 1 cube (4 grams) | 10 | .3 | | | |
| **BEEF & CABBAGE,** casserole, frozen | | | | | | |
| (Mrs. Paul's) | 12-oz. pkg. | | 29.1 | | | |
| **BEEF, CHIPPED:** | | | | | | |
| Uncooked: | | | | | | |
| (USDA) | 2 oz. (about ⅓ cup) | 2451 | 3.6 | 2. | 2. | |
| (USDA) | ½ cup (2.9 oz.) | 3526 | 5.2 | 2. | 3. | |
| (Armour Star) | 1 oz. | | .7 | | | |
| Cooked, creamed, home recipe | | | | | | |
| (USDA)[1] | 1 cup (8.6 oz.) | 1754 | 25.2 | 15. | 11. | 66 |
| Cooked (Oscar Mayer) thin sliced | 1 slice (5 grams) | 74 | .2 | | | |
| Canned, creamed (Swanson) | 1 cup | 1908 | 10.0 | | | |
| Frozen, creamed (Banquet) | 5-oz. bag | | 4.1 | | | |
| **BEEF, CHOPPED or** | | | | | | |
| **DICED,** canned: | | | | | | |
| (Armour Star) | 12-oz. can | | 92.2 | | | |
| (Hormel) | 12-oz. can | | 71.1 | | | |
| Freeze dry (Wilson) *Campsite:* | | | | | | |
| Dry | 2 oz. | 437 | 8.3 | 4. | 4. | 113 |
| *Reconstituted | 4 oz. | 304 | 6.2 | 3. | 3. | 86 |
| **BEEF, CORNED** (See **CORNED BEEF**) | | | | | | |
| **BEEF DINNER,** frozen: | | | | | | |
| (Banquet): | | | | | | |
| Corn compartment | 1.9 oz. | | 1.2 | | | |
| Meat compartment | 6.3 oz. | | 6.2 | | | |
| Potato compartment | 2.8 oz. | | .9 | | | |
| Complete dinner | 11-oz. dinner | | 8.3 | | | |
| (Morton) | 11-oz. dinner | 938 | 9.4 | | | |
| (Swanson) | 11½-oz. dinner | 790 | 13.5 | | | |
| (Swanson) 3-course | 15-oz. dinner | 1403 | 21.5 | | | |
| Beef steak & carrots | | | | | | |
| (Weight Watchers) | 10-oz. luncheon | | 31.5 | | | |

(USDA): United States Department of Agriculture
*Prepared as Package Directs
[1]Principal sources of fat: milk, butter & beef.

| Food and Description | Measure or Quantity | Sodium (mg.) | —Fats in grams— Total | Satu- rated | Unsatu- rated | Choles- terol (mg.) |
|---|---|---|---|---|---|---|
| Beef steak & cauliflower | | | | | | |
| (Weight Watchers) | 11-oz. luncheon | | 31.2 | | | |
| Chopped (Banquet): | | | | | | |
| Meat compartment | 3.9 oz. | | 19.8 | | | |
| Potato compartment | 2.8 oz. | | .7 | | | |
| Corn compartment | 2.3 oz. | | 1.2 | | | |
| Complete dinner | 9-oz. dinner | | 21.7 | | | |
| Chopped sirloin (Swanson) | 10-oz. dinner | 978 | 19.9 | 7. | 13. | |
| Chopped (Weight Watchers) | 18-oz. dinner | | 54.4 | | | |
| Pot roast, includes whole oven- browned potatoes, peas & corn | | | | | | |
| (USDA) | 10 oz. | 736 | 9.1 | 6. | 3. | |
| Sliced (Morton) 3-course | 1-lb. 1-oz. dinner | 1476 | 20.7 | | | |
| | | | | | | |
| **BEEF & EGGPLANT,** casserole, | | | | | | |
| frozen (Mrs. Paul's) | 12-oz. pkg. | | 26.0 | | | |
| | | | | | | |
| **BEEF GOULASH:** | | | | | | |
| Canned (Heinz) | 8½-oz. can | 1070 | 12.3 | | | |
| Seasoning mix (Lawry's) | 1.7-oz. pkg. | | 1.3 | | | |
| | | | | | | |
| **BEEF & GREEN PEPPER,** casserole, | | | | | | |
| frozen (Mrs. Paul's) | 12-oz. pkg. | | 21.9 | | | |
| | | | | | | |
| **BEEF, GROUND,** seasoning mix: | | | | | | |
| (Durkee) | 1⅛-oz. pkg. | 8852 | .7 | | | |
| With onions (French's) | 1⅛-oz. pkg. | | .3 | | | |
| | | | | | | |
| **BEEF HASH, ROAST:** | | | | | | |
| Canned (Hormel) *Mary Kitchen* | 7½ oz. | 1327 | 27.1 | 10. | 13. | 62 |
| Frozen (Stouffer's) | 11½-oz. pkg. | | 26.1 | | | |
| | | | | | | |
| **BEEF JERKY** (General Mills) | 1 piece (¼ oz.) | 203 | .7 | | | |
| | | | | | | |
| **BEEF PATTIES:** | | | | | | |
| Canned, freeze dry (Wilson) | | | | | | |
| *Campsite:* | | | | | | |
| Dry | 2-oz. can | 1311 | 14.4 | 7. | 7. | 161 |
| *Reconstituted | 4 oz. | 1043 | 11.6 | 6. | 6. | 130 |
| Frozen (Morton House): | | | | | | |
| & Burgundy sauce | 4¹/₆-oz. serving | 637 | 8.9 | 4. | 4. | 30 |
| & Italian sauce | 4¹/₆-oz. serving | 832 | 8.9 | 4. | 4. | 30 |
| & Mexican sauce | 4¹/₆-oz. serving | 654 | 9.0 | 4. | 4. | 30 |

(USDA): United States Department of Agriculture
*Prepared as Package Directs

| Food and Description | Measure or Quantity | Sodium (mg.) | Total | —Fats in grams— Satu- rated | Unsatu- rated | Choles- terol (mg.) |
|---|---|---|---|---|---|---|
| **BEEF PIE:** | | | | | | |
| Baked, home recipe (USDA)[1] | 4¼" pie (8 oz. before baking) | 645 | 32.9 | 9. | 24. | 48 |
| Baked, home recipe (USDA)[1] | ⅓ of 9" pie (7.4 oz.) | 596 | 30.4 | 8. | 22. | 44 |
| Frozen: | | | | | | |
| Commercial, unheated (USDA)[1] | 1 pie (7.6 oz.) | 791 | 21.4 | 6. | 15. | 39 |
| (Banquet) | 8-oz. pie | | 19.9 | | | |
| (Banquet) | 2-lb 4-oz. pie | | 56.3 | | | |
| (Morton) | 8-oz. pie | 1051 | 18.2 | | | |
| (Stouffer's) | 10-oz. pkg. | 1807 | 35.0 | | | |
| (Swanson) | 8-oz. pie | 1060 | 24.1 | | | |
| (Swanson) deep dish | 16-oz. pie | 1922 | 37.9 | | | |
| **BEEF, POTTED** (USDA) | 1 oz. | | 5.4 | | | |
| **BEEF PUFFS,** frozen (Durkee) | 1 piece (.5 oz.) | | 4.5 | | | |
| **BEEF, ROAST,** canned: | | | | | | |
| (USDA) | 4 oz. | | 15.0 | 7. | 8. | |
| (Wilson) *Tender Made* | 4 oz. | 492 | 2.9 | 1. | 2. | 77 |
| **BEEF, SLICED,** with barbecue sauce | | | | | | |
| (Banquet) | 5-oz. bag | | 5.0 | | | |
| **BEEF SOUP,** canned: | | | | | | |
| *(Campbell) | 1 cup | 795 | 2.3 | <1. | 1. | |
| (Campbell) *Chunky* | 1 cup | 896 | 6.6 | | | |
| *Barley (Manischewitz) | 1 cup | | 2.7 | | | |
| Bouillon, condensed (USDA) | 8 oz. (by wt.) | 1480 | 0. | | | |
| *Bouillon, prepared with equal volume water (USDA) | 1 cup (8.5 oz.) | 782 | 0. | | | |
| Broth: | | | | | | |
| Condensed (USDA) | 8 oz. (by wt.) | 1480 | 0. | | | |
| *Prepared with equal volume water (USDA) | 1 cup (8.5 oz.) | 782 | 0. | | | |
| (Swanson) | 1 cup | 680 | .8 | | | |
| *Cabbage (Manischewitz) | 1 cup | | 1.3 | | | |
| Consommé: | | | | | | |
| Condensed (USDA) | 8 oz. (by wt.) | 1480 | 0. | | | |
| *Prepared with equal volume water (USDA) | 1 cup (8.5 oz.) | 782 | 0. | | | |
| *(Campbell) | 1 cup | 642 | 0. | | | |

(USDA): United States Department of Agriculture
*Prepared as Package Directs
[1]Principal sources of fat: vegetable shortening & beef.

| Food and Description | Measure or Quantity | Sodium (mg.) | —Fats in grams— | | | Choles- terol (mg.) |
|---|---|---|---|---|---|---|
| | | | Total | Satu- rated | Unsatu- rated | |
| Noodle: | | | | | | |
| Condensed (USDA) | 8 oz. (by wt.) | 1734 | 5.0 | | | |
| *Prepared with equal volume water (USDA) | 1 cup (8.5 oz.) | 917 | 2.6 | | | |
| *(Campbell) | 1 cup | 792 | 2.2 | <1. | 2. | 7 |
| *(Heinz) | 1 cup (8.5 oz.) | 972 | 2.9 | | | |
| *(Manischewitz) | 1 cup | | 1.6 | | | |
| *Curly, with chicken (Campbell) | 1 cup | 1099 | 2.5 | | | |
| With dumplings (Heinz) *Great American* | 1 cup (8¾ oz.) | 967 | 4.3 | | | |
| Sirloin burger (Campbell) *Chunky* | 1 cup | 930 | 7.0 | | | |
| *Vegetable (Manischewitz) | 1 cup | | 1.3 | | | |
| *With broth (Campbell) | 1 cup | 760 | 0. | | | |
| **BEEF SOUP MIX:** | | | | | | |
| *Barley (Wyler's) | 6 fl. oz. | | .8 | | | |
| Broth (Lipton) *Cup-a-Soup* | 1 pkg. (8 grams) | 899 | .1 | Tr. | 0. | |
| Noodle: | | | | | | |
| (USDA)[1] | 1 oz. | 672 | 2.1 | <1 | 2 | |
| *(USDA) | 1 cup (8.1 oz.) | 401 | 1.1 | | | |
| (Lipton) *Cup-a-Soup* | 1 pkg. (.4 oz.) | 892 | .3 | Tr. | Tr. | 5 |
| *With vegetable (Lipton) | 1 cup | 1258 | 1.3 | Tr. | <1. | 17 |
| *(Wyler's) | 6 fl. oz. | | .5 | | | |
| **BEEF STEAK,** freeze dry. canned (Wilson) *Campsite:* | | | | | | |
| Dry | 2-oz. can | 1267 | 4.7 | 2. | 3. | 169 |
| *Reconstituted | 4 oz. | 1043 | 3.9 | 2. | 2. | 137 |
| **BEEF STEW:** | | | | | | |
| Home recipe. made with lean beef chuck (USDA)[2] | 1 cup (8.6 oz.) | 91 | 10.5 | 5. | 6. | 64 |
| Canned: | | | | | | |
| (USDA) | 1 cup (8.6 oz.) | 1007 | 7.6 | | | 34 |
| (Armour Star) | 24-oz. can | | 32.6 | | | |
| (B & M) | 1 cup (7.9 oz.) | 1010 | 4.5 | | | |
| (Dinty Moore) | 8 oz. | 887 | 9.8 | 4. | 5. | 36 |
| (Heinz) | 8½-oz. can | 1272 | 10.7 | | | |
| (Nalley's) | 8 oz. | | 10.4 | | | |
| (Swanson) | 1 cup | 882 | 5.7 | | | |
| (Van Camp) | ½ cup (4.6 oz.) | | 4.2 | | | |

(USDA): United States Department of Agriculture
*Prepared as Package Directs
[1]Principal sources of fat: vegetable shortening & egg.
[2]Principal source of fat: beef.

| Food and Description | Measure or Quantity | Sodium (mg.) | Total | — Fats in grams — Saturated | Unsaturated | Cholesterol (mg.) |
|---|---|---|---|---|---|---|
| (Wilson) | 15½-oz. can | 1850 | 13.2 | 7. | 7. | 75 |
| Dietetic (Claybourne) | 8-oz. can | 66 | 23.8 | | | |
| Dietetic (Slim-ette) | 8-oz. can | 132 | 5.6 | | | |
| Freeze dry (Wilson) *Campsite:* | | | | | | |
| Dry | 4½-oz. can | 3424 | 25.3 | 12 | 14 | |
| *Reconstituted | 16 oz. | 2676 | 25.4 | 12 | 14 | |
| Meatball (Hormel) | 1-lb. 8-oz. can | | 41.5 | | | |
| Frozen: | | | | | | |
| Buffet (Banquet) | 2-lb. pkg. | | 25.0 | | | |
| **BEEF STEW SEASONING MIX:** | | | | | | |
| (Durkee) | 1¾-oz. pkg. | 6953 | .6 | | | |
| (French's) | 1 pkg. (1⅞ oz.) | 4400 | .5 | | | |
| *(Kraft) | 1 oz. | 52 | 4.0 | | | |
| (Lawry's) | 1 pkg. (1³/₃ oz.) | | 1.3 | | | |
| **BEEF STOCK BASE** (French's) | 1 tsp. (4 grams) | | Tr. | | | |
| **BEEF STROGANOFF:** | | | | | | |
| Canned (Hormel) | 1-lb. can | | 39.0 | | | |
| Mix (Chef Boy-Ar-Dee) | 6⅔-oz. pkg. | 1067 | 7.9 | | | |
| Mix (Hunt's) *Skillet*[1] | 1-lb. 2-oz. pkg. | 3984 | 40.7 | 21. | 19. | |
| Mix, dinner (Jeno's) | | | | | | |
| Add 'n Heat | 40-oz. pkg. | 95.3 | | | | |
| *Mix, *Noodle-Roni* | 4 oz. | 446 | 2.7 | | | |
| Seasoning mix (Lawry's) | 1½-oz. pkg. | | .5 | | | |
| **BEEF & ZUCCHINI,** casserole, frozen (Mrs. Paul's) | 12-oz. pkg. | | 21.0 | | | |
| **BEER,** canned: | | | | | | |
| Regular: | | | | | | |
| (USDA) 4.5% alcohol | 12 fl. oz. | 25 | 0. | | | 0 |
| *Budweiser,* 4.9% alcohol | 12 fl. oz. | 20–40 | 0. | | | 0 |
| *Budweiser,* 3.9% alcohol | 12 fl. oz. | 20–40 | 0. | | | 0 |
| *Busch Bavarian,* 4.9% alcohol | 12 fl. oz. | 20–40 | 0. | | | 0 |
| *Busch Bavarian,* 3.9% alcohol | 12 fl. oz. | 20–40 | 0. | | | 0 |
| *Michelob,* 4.9% alcohol | 12 fl. oz. | 20–40 | 0. | | | 0 |
| *Pabst Blue Ribbon* | 12 fl. oz. | 7 | (0.) | | | (0) |
| *Schlitz* | 12 fl. oz. | 24 | (0.) | | | (0) |
| Low carbohydrate: | | | | | | |
| *Gablinger's,* 4.5% alcohol | 12 fl. oz. | 21 | 0. | | | (0) |
| *Meister Brau Lite,* 4.6% alcohol | 12 fl. oz. | Tr. | 0. | | | (0) |

(USDA): United States Department of Agriculture
*Prepared as Package Directs
[1]Principal sources of fat: sour cream, cottonseed oil & egg.

| Food and Description | Measure or Quantity | Sodium (mg.) | Fats in grams — Total | Satu- rated | Unsatu- rated | Choles- terol (mg.) |
|---|---|---|---|---|---|---|
| **BEER, NEAR,** *Kingsbury* | | | | | | |
| (Heileman) 0.4% alcohol | 12 fl. oz. | 41 | | | | 0 |
| | | | | | | |
| **BEET:** | | | | | | |
| Raw (USDA) | 1 lb. (weighed with skins, part tops) | 133 | .2 | | | 0 |
| Raw (USDA) | 1 lb. (weighed with skins, without tops) | 190 | .3 | | | 0 |
| Raw, diced (USDA) | ½ cup (2.4 oz.) | 40 | <.1 | | | 0 |
| Boiled without salt: | | | | | | |
| Whole, drained (USDA) | 2 beets (2″ dia., 3.5 oz.) | 43 | .1 | | | 0 |
| Diced, drained (USDA) | ½ cup (3 oz.) | 37 | <.1 | | | 0 |
| Sliced, drained (USDA) | ½ cup (3.6 oz.) | 44 | .1 | | | 0 |
| Canned, regular pack: | | | | | | |
| Solids & liq. (USDA) | ½ cup (4.3 oz.) | 290 | .1 | | | 0 |
| Drained solids, whole (USDA) | ½ cup (2.8 oz.) | 188 | <.1 | | | 0 |
| Drained solids, diced (USDA) | ½ cup (2.9 oz.) | 194 | <.1 | | | 0 |
| Drained solids, sliced (USDA) | ½ cup (3.1 oz.) | 208 | <.1 | | | 0 |
| Drained liq. (USDA) | 4 oz. | 268 | Tr. | | | 0 |
| Solids & liq., sliced (Comstock-Greenwood) | ½ cup (2.6 oz.) | 177 | <.1 | | | (0) |
| Solids & liq. (Del Monte) | ½ cup (4 oz.) | 316 | .1 | | | 0 |
| Solids & liq., tiny, whole (Le Sueur) | ¼ of 1-lb. can | 437 | <.1 | | | (0) |
| Solids & liq. (Stokely-Van Camp) | ½ cup (4.1 oz.) | | .1 | | | (0) |
| Drained solids (Del Monte) | ½ cup (3.1 oz.) | 246 | .1 | | | 0 |
| Harvard, solids & liq. (Comstock-Greenwood) | 4 oz. | | <.1 | | | (0) |
| Pickled, solids & liq. (Comstock-Greenwood) | 4 oz. | | <.1 | | | (0) |
| Pickled, solids & liq. (Del Monte) | ½ cup (4 oz.) | 378 | .2 | | | 0 |
| Pickled, drained solids (Del Monte) | ½ cup (3.1 oz.) | 291 | .4 | | | 0 |
| Pickled, drained liq. (Del Monte) | 4 oz. | 378 | Tr. | | | 0 |
| Canned, dietetic pack: | | | | | | |
| Solids & liq. (USDA) | 4 oz. | 52 | Tr. | | | 0 |
| Drained solids (USDA) | 4 oz. | 52 | .1 | | | 0 |
| Drained liq. (USDA) | 4 oz. | 52 | Tr. | | | 0 |
| Whole (Blue Boy) | 10 small (3.5 oz.) | 44 | <.1 | | | (0) |
| Diced, solids & liq. (Blue Boy) | 4 oz. | 50 | <.1 | | | (0) |

(USDA): United States Department of Agriculture
*Prepared as Package Directs

| Food and Description | Measure or Quantity | Sodium (mg.) | Fats in grams Total | Satu- rated | Unsatu- rated | Choles- terol (mg.) |
|---|---|---|---|---|---|---|
| Diced, solids & liq. (Tillie Lewis) | ½ cup (4.3 oz.) | 55 | Tr. | | | (0) |
| Sliced (Blue Boy) | 10 slices (3.5 oz.) | 33 | <.1 | | | (0) |
| Sliced (S and W) *Nutradiet,* unseasoned | 4 oz. | 45 | .8 | | | (0) |
| Frozen, sliced, in orange flavor glaze (Birds Eye) | ⅓ of 10-oz. pkg. | 129 | .1 | | | 0 |
| **BEET GREENS** (USDA): | | | | | | |
| Raw, whole | 1 lb. (weighed untrimmed) | 330 | .8 | | | 0 |
| Boiled without salt, leaves & stems, drained | ½ cup (2.6 oz.) | 55 | .1 | | | 0 |
| **BELL PEPPER,** dried: | | | | | | |
| Green (Spice Islands) | 1 tsp. | 6 | | | | (0) |
| Red (Spice Islands) | 1 tsp. | 39 | | | | (0) |
| **BEVERAGE** (See individual listings) | | | | | | |
| *BIF* (Wilson) canned luncheon meat | 3 oz. | 935 | 23.8 | 12. | 12. | 56 |
| *BIG MAC* (McDonald's) | 1 hamburger (6.5 oz.) | 1064 | 31.9 | | | |
| *BIG WHEEL* (Hostess) | 1 cake (1.4 oz.) | 101 | 8.7 | | | |
| **BIRCH BEER,** soft drink (Yukon Club) | 6 fl. oz. | 14 | 0. | | | 0 |
| **BISCUIT:** | | | | | | |
| Baking powder, home recipe (USDA)[1]: | | | | | | |
| Made with regular flour & lard[2] | 1-oz. biscuit (2″ dia.) | 175 | 4.8 | 2. | 3. | |
| Made with regular flour & vegetable shortening[3] | 1-oz. biscuit (2″ dia.) | 175 | 4.8 | 1. | 4. | |
| Made with self-rising flour & lard[2] | 1-oz. biscuit (2″ dia.) | 185 | 4.9 | 2. | 3. | |
| Made with self-rising flour & vegetable shortening[3] | 1-oz. biscuit (2″ dia.) | 185 | 4.9 | 1. | 4. | |
| Egg (Stella D'oro): | | | | | | |
| Dietetic | 1 piece (.4 oz.) | 3 | 1.0 | | | |

(USDA): United States Department of Agriculture
*Prepared as Package Directs
[1]Made with sodium aluminum sulfate-type baking powder.
[2]Principal source of fat: lard.
[3]Principal source of fat: vegetable shortening.

| Food and Description | Measure or Quantity | Sodium (mg.) | —Fats in grams— | | | Choles- terol (mg.) |
|---|---|---|---|---|---|---|
| | | | Total | Satu- rated | Unsatu- rated | |
| Regular | 1 piece (.4 oz.) | | 1.0 | | | |
| Roman | 1 piece (1.1 oz.) | | 5.2 | | | |
| Sugared | 1 piece (.5 oz.) | | 1.1 | | | |
| **BISCUIT DOUGH:** | | | | | | |
| Frozen, commercial (DA)[1] | 1 oz. | 258 | 3.4 | <1. | 2. | |
| Refrigerated: | | | | | | |
| Commercial (USDA)[1] | 1 oz. | 246 | 1.8 | <1. | 2. | |
| *(Borden) | 1 biscuit (.8 oz.) | | 1.3 | | | |
| *Big 10's (Borden) | 1 biscuit (1 oz.) | | 4.0 | | | |
| *Buttered Up (Borden) | 1 biscuit (1 oz.) | | 4.6 | | | |
| *Gem (Borden) | 1 biscuit (1 oz.) | | 3.2 | | | |
| **BISCUIT MIX:** | | | | | | |
| Dry, with enriched flour (USDA)[1] | 1 oz. | 369 | 3.6 | <1. | 3 | |
| *Baked from mix, with added milk (USDA)[1] | 1-oz. biscuit | 276 | 2.6 | <1. | 2 | |
| Bisquick (Betty Crocker) | 1 cup | 1475 | 17.2 | | | |
| **BITTER LEMON,** soft drink: | | | | | | |
| (Canada Dry) bottle or can | 6 fl. oz. | 13+ | 0. | | | 0 |
| (Hoffman) | 6 fl. oz. | 25+ | 0. | | | 0 |
| (Schweppes) | 6 fl. oz. | 30 | 0. | 0 | | |
| **BITTER ORANGE,** soft drink | | | | | | |
| (Schweppes) | 6 fl. oz. | 5+ | 0. | | | 0 |
| *BITTERS* (Angostura) | | | | | | |
| 45% alcohol | 1 tsp. (5 grams) | Tr. | | | | (0) |
| **BLACKBERRY:** | | | | | | |
| Fresh (includes boysenberry. dewberry. youngberry): | | | | | | |
| With hulls (USDA) | 1 lb. (weighed untrimmed) | 4 | 3.9 | | | 0 |
| Hulled (USDA) | ½ cup (2.6 oz.) | <1 | .7 | | | 0 |
| Canned, regular, solids & liq. (USDA): | | | | | | |
| Juice pack | 4 oz. | 1 | .9 | | | 0 |
| Light syrup | 4 oz. | 1 | .7 | | | 0 |
| Heavy syrup | ½ cup (4.6 oz.) | 1 | .8 | | | 0 |
| Extra heavy syrup | 4 oz. | 1 | .7 | | | 0 |

(USDA): United States Department of Agriculture
*Prepared as Package Directs
[1]Principal source of fat: vegetable shortening.

| Food and Description | Measure or Quantity | Sodium (mg.) | —Fats in grams— | | | Choles- terol (mg.) |
|---|---|---|---|---|---|---|
| | | | Total | Satu- rated | Unsatu- rated | |
| Canned, water pack, solids & liq. (USDA) | ½ cup (4.3 oz.) | 1 | .7 | | | 0 |
| Canned, low calorie, solids & liq. (S and W) *Nutradiet* | 4 oz. | 2 | .1 | | | |
| Frozen (USDA): | | | | | | |
| Sweetened, not thawed | 4 oz. | 1 | .3 | | | 0 |
| Unsweetened, not thawed | 4 oz. | 1 | .3 | | | 0 |
| **BLACKBERRY JELLY,** low calorie: | | | | | | |
| (Slenderella) | 1 T. (.7 oz.) | 16 | Tr. | | | (0) |
| & apple (Kraft) | 1 oz. | 37 | <.1 | | | (0) |
| **BLACKBERRY JUICE,** canned, unsweetened (USDA) | ½ cup (4.3 oz.) | 1 | .7 | | | 0 |
| **BLACKBERRY PIE:** | | | | | | |
| Home recipe, 2-crust, made with lard (USDA)[1] | ¹/₆ of 9″ pie (5.6 oz.) | 423 | 17.4 | 6. | 11. | |
| Home recipe, 2-crust, made with vegetable shortening (USDA)[2] | ¹/₆ of 9″ pie (5.6 oz.) | 423 | 17.4 | 5. | 13. | |
| (Tastykake) | 4-oz. pie | | 14.6 | | | |
| Frozen (Banquet) | 5-oz. serving | | 15.3 | | | |
| **BLACKBERRY PIE FILLING,** canned: | | | | | | |
| (Comstock) | 1 cup (10¾ oz.) | 320 | <.1 | | | |
| (Lucky Leaf) | 8 oz. | 276 | .4 | | | |
| **BLACKBERRY PRESERVE or JAM:** | | | | | | |
| Sweetened (Bama) | 1 T. (.7 oz.) | 1 | <.1 | | | (0) |
| Low calorie: | | | | | | |
| (Diet Delight) | 1 T. (.6 oz.) | 4 | Tr. | | | (0) |
| (S and W) *Nutradiet* | 1 T. (.5 oz.) | | <.1 | | | (0) |
| **BLACK-EYED PEA,** frozen (See also **COWPEA**): | | | | | | |
| Not thawed (USDA) | 10-oz. pkg. | 142 | 1.1 | | | 0 |

(USDA): United States Department of Agriculture
*Prepared as Package Directs
[1]Principal sources of fat: lard, butter.
[2]Principal sources of fat: vegetable shortening, butter.

| Food and Description | Measure or Quantity | Sodium (mg.) | Fats in grams Total | Satu- rated | Unsatu- rated | Choles- terol (mg.) |
|---|---|---|---|---|---|---|
| Boiled, drained (USDA) | ½ cup (3 oz.) | 33 | .3 | | | 0 |
| (Birds Eye) | ½ cup (2.5 oz.) | 35 | .3 | | | 0 |

**BLANCMANGE** (See **VANILLA PUDDING**)

**BLOOD PUDDING or SAUSAGE**

| | | | | | | |
|---|---|---|---|---|---|---|
| (USDA) | 1 oz. | | 10.5 | 4. | 7. | |

**BLOODY MARY MIX** (Bar-

| | | | | | | |
|---|---|---|---|---|---|---|
| Tender's) | 1 serving (.3 oz.) | 510 | <.1 | | | (0) |

**BLUEBERRY:**

| | | | | | | |
|---|---|---|---|---|---|---|
| Fresh, whole (USDA) | 1 lb. (weighed untrimmed) | 4 | 2.1 | | | 0 |
| Fresh, trimmed (USDA) | ½ cup (2.6 oz.) | <1 | .4 | | | 0 |
| Canned, solids & liq. (USDA): | | | | | | |
| Syrup pack, extra heavy | ½ cup (4.4 oz.) | 1 | .2 | | | 0 |
| Water pack | ½ cup (4.3 oz.) | 1 | .2 | | | 0 |
| Frozen: | | | | | | |
| Sweetened, solids & liq. (USDA) | ½ cup (4 oz.) | 1 | .3 | | | 0 |
| Unsweetened, solids & liq. (USDA) | ½ cup (2.9 oz.) | <1 | .4 | | | 0 |
| Quick thaw (Birds Eye) | ½ cup (5 oz.) | 1 | .6 | | | 0 |

**BLUEBERRY PIE:**

| | | | | | | |
|---|---|---|---|---|---|---|
| Home recipe, 2 crust (USDA): | | | | | | |
| Made with lard[1] | ¹/₆ of 9″ pie (5.6 oz.) | 423 | 17.1 | 6. | 11. | |
| Made with vegetable shortening[2] | ¹/₆ of 9″ pie (5.6 oz.) | 423 | 17.1 | 5. | 12. | |
| (Tastykake) | 4-oz. pie | | 14.6 | | | |
| Frozen: | | | | | | |
| (Banquet) | 5-oz. serving | | 14.4 | | | |
| (Morton) | ¹/₆ of 20-oz. pie | 236 | 10.9 | | | |
| (Morton) | ⅛ of 46-oz. pie | 317 | 16.7 | | | |
| (Mrs. Smith's) | ¹/₆ of 8″ pie (4.2 oz.) | 302 | 14.2 | | | |
| (Mrs. Smith's) old fashion | ¹/₆ of 9″ pie (5.8 oz.) | 470 | 23.2 | | | |

(USDA): United States Department of Agriculture
*Prepared as Package Directs
[1]Principal sources of fat: lard, butter.
[2]Principal sources of fat: vegetable shortening, butter.

| Food and Description | Measure or Quantity | Sodium (mg.) | —Fats in grams— | | Choles- terol (mg.) |
|---|---|---|---|---|---|
| | | | Total | Satu- rated | Unsatu- rated | |

| Food and Description | Measure or Quantity | Sodium (mg.) | Total | Satu-rated | Unsatu-rated | Cholesterol (mg.) |
|---|---|---|---|---|---|---|
| (Mrs. Smith's) golden deluxe | ⅛ of 10″ pie (5.6 oz.) | 410 | 18.4 | | | |
| Tart (Pepperidge Farm) | 1 pie tart (3 oz.) | 188 | 14.9 | | | |
| **BLUEBERRY PIE FILLING,** canned: | | | | | | |
| (Comstock) | 1 cup (10¾ oz.) | 354 | .7 | | | |
| (Lucky Leaf) | 8 oz. | 298 | .6 | | | |
| (Wilderness) | 21-oz. can | 200 | | | | |
| **BLUEBERRY PRESERVE or JAM,** sweetened: | | | | | | |
| (Bama) | 1 T. (.7 oz.) | 2 | <.1 | | | (0) |
| (Smucker's) | 1 T. (.7 oz) | 6 | Tr. | | | (0) |
| **BLUEBERRY TURNOVER,** frozen (Pepperidge Farm) | 1 turnover (3.3 oz.) | 258 | 20.0 | | | |
| **BLUEFISH** (USDA): | | | | | | |
| Raw, whole | 1 lb. (weighed whole) | 171 | 7.6 | | | |
| Raw, meat only | 4 oz. | 84 | 3.7 | | | |
| Baked or broiled[1] | 4.4-oz. piece (3½″ x 3″ x ½″) | 130 | 6.5 | | | |
| Fried[2] | 5.3-oz. piece (3½″ x 3″ x ½″) | 219 | 14.7 | | | |
| **BOCKWURST** (USDA) | 1 oz. | | 6.7 | 3. | 4. | |
| **BOLOGNA:** | | | | | | |
| All meat (USDA) | 1 oz. | | 6.5 | | | |
| All meat, very thin slice (USDA) | ½-oz. slice (3″ x ⅛″) | | 3.0 | | | |
| With cereal (USDA) | 1 oz. | | 5.8 | | | |
| All meat (Armour Star) | 1 oz. | | 9.6 | | | |
| All meat (Hormel) | 1 oz. | 266 | 7.7 | 2. | 5. | 14 |
| All meat (Oscar Mayer): | | | | | | |
| 8–10 slices per ¾ lb. | 1 slice (1.3 oz.) | 342 | 11.0 | 5. | 6. | 14 |
| 8 slices per ½ lb. | 1 slice (1 oz.) | 252 | 8.1 | 3. | 5. | 11 |
| 10 slices per ½ lb. | 1 slice (.8 oz.) | 207 | 6.7 | 3. | 4. | 9 |
| Garlic | .8-oz. slice | 224 | 6.7 | | | |
| Wisconsin made, coarse | 1 oz. | 221 | 7.4 | | | |

(USDA): United States Department of Agriculture
*Prepared as Package Directs
[1]Prepared with butter or margarine.
[2]Prepared with egg, milk or water, & bread crumbs.

| Food and Description | Measure or Quantity | Sodium (mg.) | Total | Satu-rated | Unsatu-rated | Choles-terol (mg.) |
|---|---|---|---|---|---|---|
| | | | —Fats in grams— | | | |
| Wisconsin made, fine | 1 oz. | 221 | 7.9 | | | |
| Coarse ground (Hormel) | 1 oz. | 306 | 6.2 | 2. | 3. | 14 |
| Fine ground (Hormel) | 1 oz. | 306 | 7.3 | 3. | 4. | 16 |
| German brand (Oscar Mayer) | .8-oz. slice | 242 | 4.4 | | | |
| Lebanon, pure beef (Oscar Mayer) | .8-oz. slice | 269 | 2.5 | | | |
| Pure beef (Oscar Mayer): | | | | | | |
| 8 slices per ¾ lb. | 1 slice (1.3 oz.) | 332 | 11.0 | 5 | 6 | 16 |
| 10 slices per ½ lb. | 1 slice (.8 oz.) | 201 | 6.7 | 3 | 4 | 10 |
| (Vienna) | 1 oz. | | | | | |
| (Wilson) | 1 oz. | 312 | 7.9 | 3. | 5. | 17 |
| | | | | | | |
| **BONITO**, raw (USDA): | | | | | | |
| Whole | 1 lb. (weighed whole) | | 19.2 | | | |
| Meat only | 4 oz. | | 8.3 | | | |
| | | | | | | |
| **BORSCHT** (Manischewitz) | 1 cup | | <.1 | | | |
| | | | | | | |
| *BOSCO* (Best Foods)[1] | 1 T. (.7 oz.) | 33 | .3 | | | 0 |
| | | | | | | |
| **BOSTON BROWN BREAD** (See BREAD) | | | | | | |
| | | | | | | |
| **BOSTON CREAM PIE:** | | | | | | |
| Home recipe (USDA)[2] | 1/12 of 8" pie (2.4 oz.) | 128 | 6.5 | | | |
| *Mix (Betty Crocker) | ⅛ of pie | 451 | 7.6 | | | |
| | | | | | | |
| **BOUILON CUBE** (See also individual flavors) (USDA) | | | | | | |
| flavor not indicated | 1 cube (approx. ½", 4 grams) | 960 | .1 | | | |
| | | | | | | |
| **BOUQUET GARNI:** | | | | | | |
| For beef (Spice Islands) | 1 tsp. | <1 | | | | |
| For soup (Spice Islands) | 1 tsp. | 5 | | | | |
| | | | | | | |
| **BOURBON WHISKEY** (See DISTILLED LIQUOR) | | | | | | |

(USDA): United States Department of Agriculture
*Prepared as Package Directs
[1]Principal source of fat: cocoa.
[2]Made with sodium aluminum sulfate-type baking powder.

| Food and Description | Measure or Quantity | Sodium (mg.) | Total | — Fats in grams — Satu- rated | Unsatu- rated | Choles- terol (mg.) |
|---|---|---|---|---|---|---|
| **BOYSENBERRY:** | | | | | | |
| Fresh (See **BLACKBERRY,** fresh) | | | | | | |
| Canned, unsweetened or low calorie: | | | | | | |
| Water pack, solids & liq. | | | | | | |
| (USDA) | 4 oz. | 1 | .1 | | | 0 |
| Solids & liq. (S and W) | | | | | | |
| *Nutradiet* | 4 oz. | 2 | .1 | | | (0) |
| Frozen, not thawed (USDA): | | | | | | |
| Sweetened | 4 oz. | 1 | .3 | | | 0 |
| Unsweetened | 4 oz. | 1 | .3 | | | 0 |
| **BOYSENBERRY PIE,** frozen: | | | | | | |
| (Banquet) | 5-oz. serving | | 15.0 | | | |
| (Morton) | ¹/₆ of 20-oz. pie | 231 | 10.7 | | | |
| **BOYSENBERRY PIE FILLING** | | | | | | |
| (Comstock) | 1 cup (10¾ oz.) | 238 | .2 | | | |
| **BOYSENBERRY PRESERVE or JAM,** low calorie: | | | | | | |
| (S and W) *Nutradiet* | 1 T. (.5 oz.) | | <.1 | | | (0) |
| (Tillie Lewis) | 1 T. (.5 oz.) | 2 | Tr. | | | 0 |
| **BRAINS,** all animals, raw (USDA) | 4 oz. | 142 | 9.8 | | | 2268 |
| **BRAN** (USDA): | | | | | | |
| With added sugar & defatted wheat germ | 1 oz. | 139 | .5 | | | 0 |
| With added sugar & malt extract | 1 oz. | 301 | .9 | | | 0 |
| **BRAN BREAKFAST CEREAL:** | | | | | | |
| Plain: | | | | | | |
| *All-Bran* (Kellogg's) | ½ cup (1 oz.) | 287 | .7 | | | (0) |
| *Bran Buds* (Kellogg's) | ⅓ cup (1 oz.) | 63 | .7 | | | (0) |
| 40% bran flakes (USDA) | ½ cup (.6 oz.) | 162 | .3 | | | 0 |
| 40% bran flakes (Kellogg's) | ¾ cup (1 oz.) | 141 | .5 | | | (0) |
| 40% bran flakes (Post) | ⅔ cup (1 oz.) | 190 | .3 | | | 0 |
| 100% bran (Nabisco) | ½ cup (1 oz.) | 187 | 1.0 | | | (0) |
| Raisin bran flakes: | | | | | | |
| (USDA) | ½ cup (.9 oz.) | 200 | .4 | | | 0 |
| (Kellogg's) | ¾ cup (1 oz.) | 143 | .5 | | | (0) |
| (Post) | ½ cup (1 oz.) | 136 | .3 | | | 0 |
| Cinnamon (Post) | ½ cup (1 oz.) | 136 | .3 | | | 0 |

(USDA): United States Department of Agriculture
*Prepared as Package Directs

| Food and Description | Measure or Quantity | Sodium (mg.) | —Fats in grams— | | | Choles-terol (mg.) |
|---|---|---|---|---|---|---|
| | | | Total | Satu-rated | Unsatu-rated | |

**BRANDY** (See **DISTILLED LIQUOR**)

**BRANDY, BLACKBERRY**

| | | | | | | |
|---|---|---|---|---|---|---|
| (Leroux) 70 proof | 1 fl. oz. | 2 | (0.) | | | (0) |

**BRATWURST** (Oscar Mayer)

| | | | | | | |
|---|---|---|---|---|---|---|
| | 1 oz. | 221 | 8.5 | | | |

**BRAUNSCHWEIGER:**

| | | | | | | |
|---|---|---|---|---|---|---|
| (USDA) | 2 slices (2″ x ¼″, .7 oz.) | | 5.5 | 2. | 4. | |
| (Oscar Mayer) | 1 oz. | 310 | 10.2 | | | |
| (Wilson) | 1 oz. | 293 | 7.8 | 3. | 5. | 55 |
| Liver cheese (Oscar Mayer) | 1 slice (6 per ½ lb.) | 459 | 8.4 | | | |

**BRAZIL NUT** (USDA):

| | | | | | | |
|---|---|---|---|---|---|---|
| Whole | 1 lb. (weighed in shell) | 2 | 145.6 | 29. | 117. | 0 |
| Whole | 1 cup (14 nuts, 4.3 oz. with shell) | 1 | 39.2 | 8. | 31. | 0 |
| Shelled | ½ cup (2.5 oz.) | <1 | 46.8 | 9. | 38. | 0 |
| Shelled | 4 nuts (.6 oz.) | <1 | 11.7 | 2. | 9. | 0 |

**BREAD** (listed by type or brand name; toasting does not affect these nutritive values, only weight):

| | | | | | | |
|---|---|---|---|---|---|---|
| Boston brown (USDA) | 1.7-oz. slice (3″ x ¾″) | 120 | .6 | | | |
| Cheese, party (Pepperidge Farm) | 1 slice (6 grams) | 39 | .4 | | | |
| Cornbread (See **CORNBREAD**) | | | | | | |
| Corn & Molasses (Pepperidge Farm) | .9-oz. slice | 116 | .6 | | | |
| Cracked-wheat: | | | | | | |
| (USDA) | .8-oz. slice | 122 | .5 | | | |
| (USDA) 20 slices to 1 lb. | .9-oz. slice | 132 | .6 | | | |
| (Pepperidge Farm) | .9-oz. slice | 151 | 1.0 | | | |
| Honey (Wonder) | .8-oz. slice | 137 | .7 | | | |
| *Daffodil Farm* (Wonder) | .8-oz. slice | 140 | .6 | | | |
| Date-nut loaf (Thomas') | 1.1-oz. slice | 150 | 1.5 | | | |
| *Finn Crisp* | 1 piece (6 grams) | | <.1 | | | |
| French: | | | | | | |
| (USDA) 20 slices to 1 lb.[1] | .8-oz. slice | 133 | .7 | Tr. | <1. | |

(USDA): United States Department of Agriculture
*Prepared as Package Directs
[1]Principal source of fat: vegetable shortening.

| Food and Description | Measure or Quantity | Sodium (mg.) | —Fats in grams— Total | Satu- rated | Unsatu- rated | Choles- terol (mg.) |
|---|---|---|---|---|---|---|
| (Pepperidge Farm) | 1″ slice (1.1 oz.) | 173 | 1.2 | | | |
| *Glutogen Gluten* (Thomas') | .5-oz. slice | 80 | .1 | | | 0 |
| *Honey Wheatberry* (Pepperidge Farm) | 1.1-oz. slice | 172 | 1.1 | | | |
| Italian: | | | | | | |
| (USDA) 20 slices to 1 lb. | .8-oz. slice | 135 | .2 | | | |
| (Pepperidge Farm) | 1″ slice (1.2 oz.) | 179 | 1.3 | | | |
| *King's Bread* (Wasa) | 3.5-oz. piece | 400 | 2.0 | | | |
| Low sodium, 1-lb. loaf (Van de Kamp's) | .8-oz. slice | 7 | | | | |
| Natural Health (Arnold) | .9-oz. slice | | 1.9 | | | |
| Oatmeal: | | | | | | |
| (Arnold) | .8-oz. slice | | 1.2 | | | |
| (Pepperidge Farm) | .9-oz. slice | 166 | 1.0 | | | |
| *Profile*, dark (Wonder) | .8-oz. slice | 129 | .7 | | | |
| *Profile*, light (Wonder) | .8-oz. slice | 143 | .7 | | | |
| *Protogen Protein* (Thomas') | .7-oz. slice | 120 | .1 | | | 0 |
| Pumpernickel: | | | | | | |
| (USDA) 20 slices to 1 lb. | .8-oz. slice | 131 | .3 | | | |
| (Arnold) Jewish | 1.4-oz. slice | | 1.2 | | | |
| (Pepperidge Farm) family | 1.2-oz. slice | 239 | .8 | | | |
| (Pepperidge Farm) party | 1 slice (8 grams) | 58 | .2 | | | |
| (Wonder) | .8-oz. slice | 148 | .2 | | | |
| Raisin: | | | | | | |
| (USDA) 18 slices to 1 lb.[1] | .9-oz. slice | 91 | .7 | Tr. | Tr. | |
| Cinnamon (Pepperidge Farm) | .9-oz. slice | 66 | 1.6 | | | |
| Cinnamon (Thomas') | .8-oz. slice | 105 | .5 | | | 0 |
| Cinnamon (Wonder) | .8-oz slice | 83 | .5 | | | |
| Orange (Arnold) | .9-oz. slice | | 1.8 | | | |
| Tea (Arnold) | .9-oz. slice | | 1.9 | | | |
| *Rite Diet* (Thomas') | .7-oz. slice | 110 | .3 | | | |
| *Roman Meal* | .8-oz. slice | 126 | .7 | | | |
| Rye: | | | | | | |
| Light, 18 slices to 1 lb. (USDA) | .9-oz. slice | 139 | .3 | | | |
| (Arnold) Melba thin, Jewish | .6-oz. slice | | .6 | | | |
| (Arnold) Jewish, seeded or unseeded | 1.2-oz. slice | | 1.4 | | | |
| (Pepperidge Farm) family | 1.2-oz. slice | 232 | .8 | | | |
| (Pepperidge Farm) party | 1 slice (6 grams) | 86 | .2 | | | |
| (Pepperidge Farm) seedless | 1.2-oz. slice | 235 | .8 | | | |

(USDA): United States Department of Agriculture
*Prepared as Package Directs
[1]Prepared with vegetable shortening & nonfat dry milk.

| Food and Description | Measure or Quantity | Sodium (mg.) | — Fats in grams — | | | Choles- terol (mg.) |
|---|---|---|---|---|---|---|
| | | | Total | Satu- rated | Unsatu- rated | |
| *Ry-King* (Wasa): | | | | | | |
| Brown | 1 piece (.4 oz.) | 47 | .2 | Tr. | Tr. | |
| Golden | 1 piece (10 grams) | 35 | .2 | Tr. | Tr. | |
| Lite | 1 piece (8 grams) | 34 | .1 | Tr. | Tr. | |
| Seasoned | 1 piece (9 grams) | 49 | .2 | | | |
| (Wonder) | .8-oz. slice | 134 | .5 | | | |
| (Wonder) *Beefsteak* | 1.1-oz. slice | 213 | .7 | | | |
| (Wonder) *Beefsteak*, family | .8-oz. slice | 147 | .6 | | | |
| Salt-rising (USDA) | .9-oz. slice | 66 | .6 | Tr. | Tr. | |
| Toaster cake (See **TOASTER CAKE**) | | | | | | |
| Vienna, 20 slices to 1 lb. | | | | | | |
| (USDA) | .8-oz. slice | 133 | .7 | Tr. | Tr. | |
| Wheat (Wonder): | | | | | | |
| Golden | .9-oz. slice | 140 | .7 | | | |
| Home Pride | .9-oz. slice | 131 | .9 | | | |
| Wheat germ (Pepperidge Farm) | .9-oz. slice | 144 | .6 | | | |
| White, enriched or unenriched: | | | | | | |
| Prepared with 1-2% nonfat dry milk (USDA)[1] | .8-oz. slice | 117 | .7 | Tr. | <1. | |
| Prepared with 3-4% nonfat dry milk (USDA)[1] | .8-oz. slice | 117 | .7 | Tr. | <1. | |
| Prepared with 5-6% nonfat dry milk (USDA)[1] | .8-oz. slice | 114 | .9 | Tr. | <1. | |
| (Arnold) Melba thin, diet-slice | .5-oz. slice | | 1.0 | | | |
| (Arnold) sandwich, soft, 1½-lb. loaf | .9-oz. slice | | 1.6 | | | |
| (Arnold) small family | .8-oz. slice | | 1.5 | | | |
| (Arnold) toasting | 1.1-oz. slice | | 1.8 | | | |
| (Pepperidge Farm) large loaf | 1-oz. slice | 151 | 1.4 | | | |
| (Pepperidge Farm) large loaf, Calif. only | .8-oz. slice | 131 | 1.2 | | | |
| (Pepperidge Farm) sandwich | .8-oz. slice | 126 | 1.2 | | | |
| (Pepperidge Farm) toasting | 1.2-oz. slice | 230 | .9 | | | |
| (Pepperidge Farm) very thin slice, East | .5-oz. slice | 74 | .3 | | | |
| (Pepperidge Farm) very thin slice, Midwest | .6-oz. slice | 79 | .4 | | | |
| (Thomas') | .9-oz. slice | 190 | .6 | | | |
| (Wonder) | .9-oz. slice | 148 | .7 | | | |
| *Brick Oven* (Arnold) 1-lb. loaf | .8-oz. slice | | 1.5 | | | |
| *Brick Oven* (Arnold) 30-oz. loaf | 1.1-oz. slice | | 1.8 | | | |

(USDA): United States Department of Agriculture
*Prepared as Package Directs
[1]Principal source of fat: vegetable shortening.

| Food and Description | Measure or Quantity | Sodium (mg.) | Total | Fats in grams — Satu- rated | Unsatu- rated | Choles- terol (mg.) |
|---|---|---|---|---|---|---|
| *Brick Oven,* golden (Arnold) | | | | | | |
| 2-lb. loaf | 1-oz. slice | | 1.9 | | | |
| *English Tea Loaf* | | | | | | |
| (Pepperidge Farm) | .9-oz. slice | 146 | 1.5 | | | |
| *Hearthstone* (Arnold) 1-lb. loaf | .9-oz. slice | | 1.5 | | | |
| *Hearthstone* (Arnold) 2-lb. loaf | 1.1-oz. slice | | 1.8 | | | |
| *Home Pride* (Wonder) | .9-oz. slice | 145 | 1.0 | | | |
| Whole-wheat: | | | | | | |
| Made with 2% nonfat dry milk (USDA)[1] | .9-oz. slice | 132 | .8 | Tr. | <1. | |
| Made with water (USDA)[1] | .8-oz. slice | 122 | .6 | <1 | Tr. | |
| Made with water (USDA)[1] | .9-oz. slice | 132 | .6 | Tr. | Tr. | |
| (Arnold) Melba thin, diet slice | .6-oz. slice | | 1.1 | | | |
| (Arnold) small family | .8-oz. slice | | 1.7 | | | |
| (Pepperidge Farm) | .9-oz. slice | 107 | 1.2 | | | |
| (Thomas') 100% | .9-oz. slice | 140 | .6 | | | 0 |
| (Wonder) | .8-oz. slice | 136 | .9 | | | |
| *Brick Oven* (Arnold) 1-lb. loaf | .8-oz. slice | | 1.7 | | | |
| *Brick Oven* (Arnold) 2-lb. loaf | 1.1-oz. slice | | 2.1 | | | |
| **BREAD, CANNED:** | | | | | | |
| Banana nut (Dromedary) | ½" slice (1 oz.) | 212 | 2.0 | | | |
| Brown, plain (B & M) | ½" slice (1.5 oz.) | 209 | Tr. | | | |
| Brown with raisins (B & M) | ½" slice (1.6 oz.) | 201 | .3 | | | |
| Chocolate nut (Dromedary) | ½" slice (1 oz.) | 151 | 2.4 | | | |
| Date & nut (Crosse & Blackwell) | ½" slice (1 oz.) | | .5 | | | |
| Date & nut (Dromedary) | ½" slice (1 oz.) | 155 | 2.1 | | | |
| Orange nut (Dromedary) | ½" slice (1 oz.) | 133 | 2.0 | | | |
| **BREAD CRUMBS:** | | | | | | |
| Dry, grated (USDA) | 1 cup (3.5 oz.) | 736 | 4.6 | 1. | 4. | |
| Dry, grated (USDA)[1] | 1 T. (6 grams) | 47 | .3 | Tr. | Tr. | |
| (Buitoni) | 4 oz. | | 5.0 | | | |
| (Old London) | 1 cup (4.5 oz.) | | 3.6 | | | |
| Seasoned (Contadina) | 1 cup (4.1 oz.) | 3695 | 2.2 | | | |
| **BREAD DOUGH,** frozen (Morton) | 1 oz. | 141 | 1.3 | | | |
| **BREAD PUDDING** with raisins, home recipe (USDA)[2] | 1 cup (9.3 oz.) | 557 | 16.2 | 8. | 8. | 170 |

(USDA): United States Department of Agriculture
*Prepared as Package Directs
[1]Principal source of fat: vegetable shortening.
[2]Principal sources of fat: milk, butter, eggs & bread crumbs.

| Food and Description | Measure or Quantity | Sodium (mg.) | Fats in grams — Total | Satu- rated | Unsatu- rated | Choles- terol (mg.) |
|---|---|---|---|---|---|---|
| **BREAD STICK:** | | | | | | |
| Cheese (Keebler) | 1 piece (3 grams) | 25 | .1 | | | |
| Dietetic (Stella D'oro) | 1 piece (9 grams) | 3 | 1.0 | | | |
| Garlic (Keebler) | 1 piece (3 grams) | 28 | .1 | | | |
| Onion (Stella D'oro) | 1 piece (.4 oz.) | | 1.1 | | | |
| Regular (Stella D'oro) | 1 piece (10 grams) | | 1.0 | | | |
| Salt: | | | | | | |
| (USDA)[1] | 1 piece (3 grams) | 50 | <.1 | Tr. | Tr. | |
| Vienna type (USDA)[1] | 1 piece (3 grams) | 47 | <.1 | Tr. | Tr. | |
| (Keebler) | 1 piece (3 grams) | 30 | .1 | | | |
| Sesame (Keebler) | 1 piece (3 grams) | 41 | .1 | | | |
| Sesame (Stella D'oro) | 1 piece (9 grams) | | 1.6 | | | |
| **BREAD STUFFING MIX:** | | | | | | |
| Dry (USDA)[1] | 1 cup (2.5 oz.) | 945 | 2.7 | <1. | 2. | |
| *Crumb type, prepared with water & fat (USDA)[2] | 1 cup (5 oz.) | 1263 | 30.7 | 16. | 15. | |
| *Moist type, prepared with water, egg & fat (USDA)[3] | 1 cup (7.2 oz.) | 1023 | 26.0 | 14. | 12. | |
| Corn bread (Pepperidge Farm) | 8-oz. pkg. | 4142 | 9.2 | | | |
| Cube (Pepperidge Farm) | 7-oz. pkg. | 3389 | 4.0 | | | |
| Herb seasoned (Pepperidge Farm) | 8-oz. bag | 3931 | 3.0 | | | |
| Seasoned (Uncle Ben's) *Stuff 'n Such* | 6-oz. pkg. | 3381 | 2.9 | | | 0 |
| *Seasoned (Uncle Ben's) *Stuff 'n Such*, no added butter | ½ cup (2.9 oz.) | 647 | .6 | | | 0 |
| *(Uncle Ben's) *Stuff 'n Such*, with added butter | ½ cup (3.3 oz.) | 747 | 8.6 | | | |
| **BREADFRUIT,** fresh (USDA): | | | | | | |
| Whole | 1 lb. (weighed untrimmed) | 52 | 1.0 | | | 0 |
| Peeled & trimmed | 4 oz. | 17 | .3 | | | 0 |
| **BROADBEAN:** | | | | | | |
| Immature seed (USDA) | 1 lb. (weighed in pod) | 6 | .6 | | | 0 |
| Immature seed (USDA) | 1 oz. (without pod) | 1 | .1 | | | 0 |
| Mature seed, dry (USDA) | 1 oz. | | .5 | | | 0 |

(USDA): United States Department of Agriculture
*Prepared as Package Directs
[1]Principal source of fat: vegetable shortening.
[2]Principal sources of fat: vegetable shortening & butter.
[3]Principal sources of fat: butter, vegetable shortening & egg.

| Food and Description | Measure or Quantity | Sodium (mg.) | Total | Fats in grams — Satu- rated | Unsatu- rated | Choles- terol (mg.) |
|---|---|---|---|---|---|---|
| Canned, regular pack, drained solids (Del Monte) | ½ cup (2.5 oz.) | 368 | <.1 | | | (0) |
| Frozen, Italian bean (Birds Eye) | ⅓ of 9-oz. pkg. | 36 | .1 | | | 0 |
| Frozen, Italian bean, tomato sauce (Green Giant) | ⅓ of 10-oz. pkg. | 340 | .9 | | | |
| **BROCCOLI:** | | | | | | |
| Raw, whole (USDA) | 1 lb. (weighed untrimmed) | 42 | .8 | | | 0 |
| Raw, large leaves removed (USDA) | 1 lb. (weighed partially trimmed) | 53 | 1.1 | | | 0 |
| Boiled without salt, drained (USDA): | | | | | | |
| Whole stalk | 1 stalk (6.3 oz.) | 18 | .5 | | | 0 |
| ½" pieces | ½ cup (2.8 oz.) | 18 | .2 | | | 0 |
| Frozen: | | | | | | |
| Chopped or cut: | | | | | | |
| Not thawed (USDA) | 10-oz. pkg. | 48 | .8 | | | 0 |
| Boiled without salt, drained (USDA) | 1⅜ cups (10-oz. pkg.) | 25 | .8 | | | 0 |
| (Birds Eye) | ⅓ of 10-oz. pkg. | 56 | .3 | | | 0 |
| & noodle with sour cream sauce (Green Giant) | ⅓ of 10-oz. pkg. | 425 | 4.7 | | | |
| In cheese sauce (Green Giant) | ⅓ of 10-oz. pkg. | 331 | 2.1 | | | |
| Spears: | | | | | | |
| Not thawed (USDA) | 10-oz. pkg. | 37 | .6 | | | 0 |
| Boiled without salt, drained (USDA) | ½ cup (3.3 oz.) | 11 | .2 | | | 0 |
| (Birds Eye) | ⅓ of 10-oz. pkg. | 51 | .2 | | | 0 |
| Baby spears (Birds Eye) | ⅓ of 10-oz. pkg. | 12 | .2 | | | 0 |
| In butter sauce (Green Giant) | ⅓ of 10-oz. pkg. | 444 | 2.2 | | | |
| In Hollandaise sauce (Birds Eye) | ⅓ of 10-oz. pkg. | 96 | 8.5 | | | 57 |
| **BROTH & SEASONING** (See also individual kinds): | | | | | | |
| *Maggi* | 1 T. (.6 oz.) | 923 | 0. | | | |
| Golden (George Washington) | 1 packet (4 grams) | 1093 | <.1 | | | |
| Rich Brown (George Washington) | 1 packet (4 grams) | 1212 | <.1 | | | |
| **BROTWURST** (Oscar Mayer) | 3-oz. link | 663 | 23.8 | | | |

(USDA): United States Department of Agriculture
*Prepared as Package Directs

| Food and Description | Measure or Quantity | Sodium (mg.) | — Fats in grams — | | Choles-terol (mg.) |
|---|---|---|---|---|---|
| | | | Total | Satu-rated  Unsatu-rated | |

**BROWNIE** (See **COOKIE**)

*BROWN 'n SEASON* (Adolph's) — 1 tsp. (4 grams) — 21 — <.1 — Tr.   Tr. — 0

**BRUSSELS SPROUT:**

| Food and Description | Measure or Quantity | Sodium (mg.) | Total | Cholesterol (mg.) |
|---|---|---|---|---|
| Raw (USDA) | 1 lb. | 58 | 1.7 | 0 |
| Boiled without salt, 1¼"–1½" dia., drained (USDA) | 1 cup (7–8 sprouts, 5.5 oz.) | 16 | .6 | 0 |
| Frozen: | | | | |
| Not thawed (USDA) | 10-oz. pkg. | 45 | .6 | 0 |
| Boiled without salt, drained (USDA) | 4 oz. | 16 | .2 | 0 |
| Au gratin, casserole (Green Giant) | ⅓ of 10-oz. pkg. | 439 | 2.4 | |
| Baby sprouts (Birds Eye) | ½ cup (3.3 oz.) | 15 | .2 | 0 |
| In butter sauce (Green Giant) | ⅓ of 10-oz. pkg. | 421 | 2.6 | |

**BUCKWHEAT:**

Flour (See **FLOUR**)

Groats:

| Food and Description | Measure or Quantity | Sodium (mg.) | Total | Cholesterol (mg.) |
|---|---|---|---|---|
| (Pocono) | 1 oz. | | .7 | (0) |
| *Wolff's Kasha* (Birkett) | 1 oz. | | .5 | 0 |
| Whole-grain (USDA) | 1 oz. | | .7 | 0 |

*BUC WHEATS*, cereal

| Food and Description | Measure or Quantity | Sodium (mg.) | Total | Cholesterol (mg.) |
|---|---|---|---|---|
| (General Mills) | 1 cup | 264 | .5 | (0) |

**BUFFALOFISH,** raw (USDA):

| Food and Description | Measure or Quantity | Sodium (mg.) | Total |
|---|---|---|---|
| Whole | 1 lb. (weighed whole) | 76 | 6.1 |
| Meat only | 4 oz. | 59 | 4.8 |

**BULGUR** (from hard red winter wheat) (USDA):

| Food and Description | Measure or Quantity | Sodium (mg.) | Total | Cholesterol (mg.) |
|---|---|---|---|---|
| Dry | 1 lb. | | 6.8 | 0 |
| Canned, seasoned | 1 cup (4.8 oz.) | 621 | 4.5 | |
| Canned, unseasoned | 4 oz. | 679 | .8 | 0 |

**BULLHEAD,** raw (USDA):

| Food and Description | Measure or Quantity | Total |
|---|---|---|
| Whole | 1 lb. (weighed whole) | 1.4 |
| Meat only | 4 oz. | 1.8 |

(USDA): United States Department of Agriculture
*Prepared as Package Directs

| Food and Description | Measure or Quantity | Sodium (mg.) | Total | Satu- rated | Unsatu- rated | Choles- terol (mg.) |
|---|---|---|---|---|---|---|
| | | | — Fats in grams — | | | |

**BULLOCK'S-HEART** (See **CUSTARD APPLE**)

**BUN** (See **ROLL**)

**BURBOT,** raw (USDA):

| Food and Description | Measure or Quantity | Sodium (mg.) | Total | Satu-rated | Unsatu-rated | Cholesterol (mg.) |
|---|---|---|---|---|---|---|
| Whole | 1 lb. (weighed whole) | | .6 | | | |
| Meat only | 4 oz. | | 1.0 | | | |
| | | | | | | |
| **BURGUNDY WINE:** | | | | | | |
| (Gold Seal) 12% alcohol | 3 fl. oz. | 3 | 0. | | | (0) |
| (Great Western) 12.5% alcohol | 3 fl. oz. | 36 | 0. | | | 0 |
| | | | | | | |
| **BURGUNDY WINE, SPARKLING** | | | | | | |
| (Gold Seal) 12% alcohol | 3 fl. oz. | 3 | 0. | | | (0) |
| | | | | | | |
| **BUTTER:** | | | | | | |
| Salted: | | | | | | |
| (USDA) | ¼ lb. (1 stick, ½ cup) | 1119 | 92.0 | 52. | 40. | 284 |
| (USDA) | 1 T. (⅛ stick, .5 oz.) | 138 | 11.3 | 6. | 5. | 35 |
| (USDA) | 1 pat (1″ x 1″ x ⅓″, 5 grams) | 49 | 4.0 | 2. | 2. | 12 |
| (Breakstone) | 1 T. (.5 oz.) | 95 | 11.0 | | | 29 |
| (Sealtest) | 1 T. (.5 oz.) | 117 | 12.1 | | | |
| Whipped (USDA) | 2.7 oz. (1 stick, ½ cup) | 750 | 61.6 | 35. | 27. | 190 |
| Whipped (USDA) | 1 T. (⅛ stick, 9 grams) | 89 | 7.3 | 4. | 3. | 22 |
| Whipped (USDA) | 1 pat (1¼″ x 1¼″ x ⅓″. 4 grams) | 39 | 3.2 | 2. | 1. | 10 |
| Whipped (Breakstone) | 1 T. (9 grams) | 64 | 7.4 | | | 19 |
| Whipped (Sealtest) | 1 T. (9 grams) | 74 | 7.6 | | | |
| Unsalted: | | | | | | |
| (USDA) | ¼ lb. (1 stick, ½ cup) | 11 | 92.0 | 52. | 40. | 284 |
| (USDA) | 1 T. (⅛ stick, .5 oz.) | 1 | 11.3 | 6. | 5. | 35 |
| (USDA) | 1 pat (1″ x 1″ x ⅓″, 5 grams) | <1 | 4.0 | 2. | 2. | 12 |
| (Breakstone) | 1 T. (.5 oz.) | <1 | 11.0 | | | 29 |
| (Sealtest) | 1 T. (.5 oz.) | 1 | 12.1 | | | |
| Whipped (USDA) | ½ cup (1 stick, 2.7 oz.) | 8 | 61.6 | 35. | 27. | 190 |
| Whipped (USDA) | 1 T. (⅛ stick, 9 grams) | <1 | 7.3 | 4. | 3. | 22 |

(USDA): United States Department of Agriculture
*Prepared as Package Directs

| Food and Description | Measure or Quantity | Sodium (mg.) | — Fats in grams — | | | Choles- terol (mg.) |
|---|---|---|---|---|---|---|
| | | | Total | Satu- rated | Unsatu- rated | |
| Whipped (USDA) | 1 pat (1¼" x 1¼" x ⅓", 4 grams) | <1 | 3.2 | 2. | 1. | 10 |
| Whipped (Breakstone) | 1 T. (9 grams) | <1 | 7.4 | | | 19 |

**BUTTER BEAN** (See **BEAN, LIMA**)

***BUTTER BRICKLE LAYER CAKE MIX** (Betty Crocker) | ¹/₁₂ of cake | | 5.7 | | | |

**BUTTERFISH,** raw (USDA):
Gulf:
  Whole | 1 lb. (weighed whole) | | 6.7 | | | |
  Meat only | 4 oz. | | 3.3 | | | |
Northern:
  Whole | 1 lb. (weighed whole) | | 23.6 | | | |
  Meat only | 4 oz. | | 11.6 | | | |

**BUTTERMILK** (See **MILK**)

**BUTTERNUT** (USDA):
  Whole | 1 lb. (weighed in shell) | | 38.9 | | | 0 |
  Shelled | 4 oz. | | 69.4 | | | 0 |

**BUTTER OIL** or dehydrated butter (USDA) | 1 cup (7.2 oz.) | | 203.0 | 112. | 91. | |

**BUTTERSCOTCH MORSELS** (Nestlé's) | 6-oz. pkg. | | 52.7 | | | |

**BUTTERSCOTCH PIE:**
Home recipe, made with lard (USDA)[1] | ¹/₆ of 9" pie (5.4 oz.) | 325 | 16.7 | 6. | 11. | |
Home recipe, made with vegetable shortening (USDA)[2] | ¹/₆ of 9" pie (5.4 oz.) | 325 | 16.7 | 5. | 12. | |
Frozen, cream (Banquet) | 2½-oz. serving | | 7.9 | | | |

**BUTTERSCOTCH PIE FILLING MIX** (See **BUTTERSCOTCH PUDDING MIX**)

(USDA): United States Department of Agriculture
*Prepared as Package Directs
[1]Principal sources of fat: lard, butter.
[2]Principal sources of fat: vegetable shortening, butter.

| Food and Description | Measure or Quantity | Sodium (mg.) | Total | Fats in grams — Satu-rated | Unsatu-rated | Choles-terol (mg.) |
|---|---|---|---|---|---|---|
| **BUTTERSCOTCH PUDDING:** | | | | | | |
| Chilled (Breakstone) | 5-oz. container | 250 | 13.3 | | | 0 |
| Chilled (Sealtest) | 4 oz. | 298 | 3.3 | | | |
| Canned: | | | | | | |
| (Betty Crocker) | ½ cup | 204 | 4.9 | | | |
| (Del Monte) | 5-oz. can | 264 | 5.3 | | | |
| (Hunt's) | 5-oz. can | 242 | 12.4 | 2. | 10. | |
| (Thank You) | ½ cup (4.5 oz.) | | 4.7 | | | |
| **BUTTERSCOTCH PUDDING or PIE MIX:** | | | | | | |
| Sweetened: | | | | | | |
| *Instant (Jell-O) | ½ cup (5.3 oz.) | 406 | 4.7 | | | 13 |
| *Instant (Royal) | ½ cup (5.1 oz.) | 380 | 5.1 | | | 14 |
| *Regular (Jell-O) | ½ cup (5.2 oz.) | 224 | 4.6 | | | 13 |
| *Regular (Royal) | ½ cup (5.1 oz.) | 260 | 5.2 | | | 14 |
| *Low calorie (D-Zerta) | ½ cup (4.6 oz.) | 142 | 4.5 | | | 13 |
| ***B-V** (Wilson) | 1 tsp. (7 grams) | 978 | 0. | | | |

# C

| Food and Description | Measure or Quantity | Sodium (mg.) | Total | Satu-rated | Unsatu-rated | Choles-terol (mg.) |
|---|---|---|---|---|---|---|
| **CABBAGE:** | | | | | | |
| White (USDA): | | | | | | |
| Raw: | | | | | | |
| Whole | 1 lb. (weighed untrimmed) | 72 | .7 | | | 0 |
| Coarsely shredded or sliced | 1 cup (2.5 oz.) | 14 | .1 | | | 0 |
| Finely shredded or chopped | 1 cup (3.2 oz.) | 18 | .2 | | | 0 |
| Wedge | 3½" x 4½" wedge (3.5 oz.) | 20 | .2 | | | 0 |
| Boiled without salt, until tender: | | | | | | |
| Shredded, small amount of water, drained | ½ cup (2.6 oz.) | 10 | .1 | | | 0 |
| Wedges, in large amount of water, drained | ½ cup (3.2 oz.) | 12 | .2 | | | 0 |
| Dehydrated | 1 oz. | 54 | .5 | | | 0 |
| Red, raw (USDA): | | | | | | |
| Whole | 1 lb. (weighed untrimmed) | 93 | .7 | | | 0 |
| Coarsely shredded | 1 cup (2.5 oz.) | 18 | .1 | | | 0 |
| Red, canned (Comstock-Greenwood) | 4 oz. | | Tr. | | | (0) |

(USDA): United States Department of Agriculture
*Prepared as Package Directs

| Food and Description | Measure or Quantity | Sodium (mg.) | Fats in grams | | | Choles- terol (mg.) |
|---|---|---|---|---|---|---|
| | | | Total | Satu- rated | Unsatu- rated | |
| Savoy, raw (USDA): | | | | | | |
| Whole | 1 lb. (weighed untrimmed) | 79 | .7 | | | 0 |
| Coarsely shredded | 1 cup (2.5 oz.) | 15 | .1 | | | 0 |
| **CABBAGE, CHINESE or CELERY,** raw (USDA): | | | | | | |
| Whole | 1 lb. (weighed untrimmed) | 101 | .4 | | | 0 |
| 1″ pieces, leaves with stalk | ½ cup (1.3 oz.) | 9 | Tr. | | | 0 |
| **CABBAGE, SPOON or WHITE MUSTARD or PAKCHOY** (USDA): | | | | | | |
| Raw | 1 lb. (weighed untrimmed) | 112 | .9 | | | 0 |
| Boiled without salt, drained | ½ cup (3 oz.) | 15 | .2 | | | 0 |
| *CACTUS COOLER,* soft drink (Canada Dry) bottle or can | 6 fl. oz. | 13+ | 0. | | | (0) |

**CAKE.** Most cakes are listed elsewhere by kind of cake such as **ANGEL FOOD** or **CHOCOLATE** or brand name such as **YANKEE DOODLES.** Those listed below are made with sodium aluminum sulfate-type baking powder. (USDA):

Plain. home recipe:

| Food and Description | Measure or Quantity | Sodium | Total | Satu- rated | Unsatu- rated | Choles- terol |
|---|---|---|---|---|---|---|
| Without icing: | | | | | | |
| Made with butter[1] | ⅑ of 9″ sq. cake (3″ x 3″ x 1″, 3 oz.) | 258 | 10.9 | 6. | 5. | |
| Made with vegetable shortening[2] | ⅑ of 9″ sq. cake 3″ x 3″ x 1″, 3 oz.) | 258 | 12.0 | 3. | 8. | |
| With boiled white icing: | | | | | | |
| Made with butter[1] | ⅑ of 9″ sq. cake (4 oz.) | 299 | 12.0 | 7. | 5. | |
| Made with vegetable shortening[2] | ⅑ of 9″ sq. cake (4 oz.) | 299 | 12.0 | 3. | 9. | |
| With chocolate icing: | | | | | | |
| Made with butter[3] | ¹/₁₆ of 10″ layer cake (3.5 oz.) | 229 | 12.7 | 8. | 6. | |

(USDA): United States Department of Agriculture
*Prepared as Package Directs
[1]Principal sources of fat: butter, egg & milk.
[2]Principal sources of fat: vegetable shortening. egg & milk.
[3]Principal sources of fat: butter, egg. milk & chocolate.

| Food and Description | Measure or Quantity | Sodium (mg.) | Total | Satu-rated | Unsatu-rated | Choles-terol (mg.) |
|---|---|---|---|---|---|---|
| | | | | —Fats in grams— | | |
| Made with vegetable shortening[1] | 1/16 of 10″ layer cake (3.5 oz.) | 229 | 13.9 | 4. | 9. | |
| With uncooked white icing: | | | | | | |
| Made with butter[2] | 1/16 of 10″ layer cake (3.5 oz.) | 227 | 12.7 | 7. | 6. | |
| Made with vegetable shortening[3] | 1/16 of 10″ layer cake (3.5 oz.) | 227 | 11.8 | 3. | 9. | |
| White, home recipe: | | | | | | |
| Without icing: | | | | | | |
| Made with butter[2] | 1/9 of 9″ sq. cake (3″ x 3″ x 1″, 3 oz.) | 278 | 13.8 | 8. | 6. | |
| Made with vegetable shortening[3] | 1/9 of 9″ sq. cake (3″ x 3″ x 1″, 3 oz.) | 278 | 13.8 | 4. | 10. | |
| With coconut icing: | | | | | | |
| Made with butter[2] | 1/16 of 10″ layer cake (3.5 oz.) | 257 | 13.3 | 7. | 6. | |
| Made with vegetable shortening[3] | 1/16 of 10″ layer cake (3.5 oz.) | 257 | 13.3 | 4. | 9. | |
| With uncooked white icing: | | | | | | |
| Made with butter[2] | 1/16 of 10″ layer cake (3.5 oz.) | 234 | 12.9 | 7. | 6. | |
| Made with vegetable shortening[3] | 1/16 of 10″ layer cake (3.5 oz.) | 234 | 12.9 | 4. | 9. | |
| Yellow, home recipe: | | | | | | |
| Without icing: | | | | | | |
| Made with butter[2] | 1/9 of 9″ sq. cake (3″ x 3″ x 1″, 3 oz.) | 222 | 10.9 | 6. | 5. | |
| Made with vegetable shortening[3] | 1/9 of 9″ sq. cake (3″ x 3″ x 1″, 3 oz.) | 222 | 10.9 | 3. | 8. | |
| With caramel icing: | | | | | | |
| Made with butter[2] | 1/16 of 10″ layer cake (3.5 oz.) | 226 | 11.7 | 6. | 6. | |
| Made with vegetable shortening[3] | 1/16 of 10″ layer cake (3.5 oz.) | 226 | 11.7 | 3. | 9. | |
| With chocolate icing, 2-layer: | | | | | | |
| Made with butter[4] | 1/16 of 9″ cake (2.6 oz.) | 156 | 9.8 | 5. | 4. | |
| Made with vegetable shortening[5] | 1/16 of 9″ cake (2.6 oz.) | 156 | 9.8 | 3. | 7. | 33 |

(USDA): United States Department of Agriculture
*Prepared as Package Directs
[1]Principal sources of fat: vegetable shortening, egg, milk & chocolate.
[2]Principal sources of fat: butter, egg & milk.
[3]Principal sources of fat: vegetable shortening, egg & milk.
[4]Principal sources of fat: butter, egg, milk & chocolate.
[5]Principal sources of fat: vegetable shortening, egg, milk & chocolate.

| Food and Description | Measure or Quantity | Sodium (mg.) | —Fats in grams— | | | Choles-terol (mg.) |
|---|---|---|---|---|---|---|
| | | | Total | Satu-rated | Unsatu-rated | |

**CAKE FROSTING (See CAKE ICING & CAKE ICING MIX)**

**CAKE ICING:**

| Food and Description | Measure or Quantity | Sodium (mg.) | Total | Satu-rated | Unsatu-rated | Choles-terol (mg.) |
|---|---|---|---|---|---|---|
| Butterscotch (Betty Crocker) | $^1/_{12}$ of 16.5-oz. can | 157 | 6.7 | | | |
| Caramel, home recipe (USDA)[1] | 4 oz. | 94 | 7.6 | 4. | 3. | |
| Cherry (Betty Crocker) | $^1/_{12}$ of 16.5-oz. can | 97 | 6.6 | | | |
| Chocolate, home recipe (USDA)[2] | 1 cup (9.7 oz.) | 168 | 38.2 | 22. | 16. | |
| Chocolate (Betty Crocker) | $^1/_{12}$ of 16.5-oz. can | 113 | 7.7 | | | |
| Coconut, home recipe (USDA)[3] | 1 cup (5.8 oz.) | 196 | 12.8 | 12. | Tr. | |
| Dark Dutch fudge (Betty Crocker) | $^1/_{12}$ of 16.5-oz. can | 108 | 7.0 | | | |
| Lemon (Betty Crocker) | $^1/_{12}$ of 16.5-oz. can | 101 | 6.6 | | | |
| Milk chocolate (Betty Crocker) | $^1/_{12}$ of 16.5-oz. can | 107 | 7.0 | | | |
| Vanilla (Betty Crocker) | $^1/_{12}$ of 16.5-oz. can | 96 | 6.6 | | | |
| White, boiled, home recipe (USDA) | 1 cup (3.3 oz.) | 134 | 0. | | | |
| White, uncooked, home recipe (USDA)[1] | 4 oz. | 56 | 7.5 | 4. | 3. | |

**CAKE ICING MIX:**

| Food and Description | Measure or Quantity | Sodium (mg.) | Total | Satu-rated | Unsatu-rated | Choles-terol (mg.) |
|---|---|---|---|---|---|---|
| *Banana (Betty Crocker) | $^1/_{12}$ of cake's icing | 46 | 2.8 | | | |
| *Butter Brickle (Betty Crocker) | $^1/_{12}$ of cake's icing | 66 | 2.8 | | | |
| *Caramel (Betty Crocker) | $^1/_{12}$ of cake's icing | 75 | 2.7 | | | |
| *Caramel apple (Betty Crocker) | $^1/_{12}$ of cake's icing | 42 | 1.9 | | | |
| *Cherry, creamy (Betty Crocker) | $^1/_{12}$ of cake's icing | 69 | 2.8 | | | |
| *Cherry fluff (Betty Crocker) | $^1/_{12}$ of cake's icing | 29 | Tr. | | | |
| *Cherry fudge (Betty Crocker) | $^1/_{12}$ of cake's icing | 40 | 3.1 | | | |
| *Chocolate, fluffy (Betty Crocker) | $^1/_{12}$ of cake's icing | 32 | 2.6 | | | |
| Chocolate fudge (USDA)[4] | 1 oz. | 27 | 2.8 | <1. | 2. | |
| *Chocolate fudge, prepared with water & fat (USDA)[5] | 8 oz. | 354 | 32.7 | 14. | 19. | |
| *Chocolate fudge (Betty Crocker) | $^1/_{12}$ of cake's icing | 41 | 3.1 | | | |
| *Chocolate malt (Betty Crocker) | $^1/_{12}$ of cake's icing | 48 | 3.0 | | | |
| *Chocolate walnut (Betty Crocker) | $^1/_{12}$ of cake's icing | 37 | 3.6 | | | |
| *Coconut-pecan (Betty Crocker) | $^1/_{12}$ of cake's icing | 42 | 4.4 | | | |
| *Coconut, toasted (Betty Crocker) | $^1/_{12}$ of cake's icing | 72 | 3.3 | | | |
| *Dark chocolate fudge (Betty Crocker) | $^1/_{12}$ of cake's icing | 40 | 3.1 | | | |
| Fudge, creamy, contains nonfat | | | | | | |

(USDA): United States Department of Agriculture
*Prepared as Package Directs
[1]Principal sources of fat: butter & milk.
[2]Principal sources of fat: chocolate, butter & milk.
[3]Principal source of fat: coconut.
[4]Principal sources of fat: vegetable shortening & cocoa.
[5]Principal sources of fat: vegetable shortening, butter & cocoa.

| Food and Description | Measure or Quantity | Sodium (mg.) | Fats in grams Total | Satu- rated | Unsatu- rated | Choles- terol (mg.) |
|---|---|---|---|---|---|---|
| dry milk (USDA): | | | | | | |
| Dry[1] | 1 oz. | 75 | 2.1 | <1. | 2. | |
| *Prepared with water (USDA)[2] | 1 cup (8.6 oz) | 568 | 15.9 | | | |
| *Prepared with water & fat (USDA)[3] | 8 oz. | 728 | 34.5 | 16. | 19. | |
| *Fudge nugget (Betty Crocker) | $^1/_{12}$ of cake's icing | 33 | 3.0 | | | |
| *Lemon, creamy (Betty Crocker) | $^1/_{12}$ of cake's icing | 63 | 2.7 | | | |
| *Lemon fluff (Betty Crocker) | $^1/_{12}$ of cake's icing | 32 | Tr. | | | |
| *Milk chocolate (Betty Crocker) | $^1/_{12}$ of cake's icing | 47 | 2.2 | | | |
| *Orange (Betty Crocker) | $^1/_{12}$ of cake's icing | 66 | 2.7 | | | |
| *Pineapple (Betty Crocker) | $^1/_{12}$ of cake's icing | 63 | 2.7 | | | |
| *Sour cream, chocolate fudge (Betty Crocker) | $^1/_{12}$ of cake's icing | 40 | 3.1 | | | |
| *Sour cream, white (Betty Crocker) | $^1/_{12}$ of cake's icing | 65 | 2.0 | | | |
| *Spice, creamy (Betty Crocker) | $^1/_{12}$ of cake's icing | 77 | 2.8 | | | |
| *White, creamy (Betty Crocker) | $^1/_{12}$ of cake's icing | 66 | 2.7 | | | |
| *White, fluffy (Betty Crocker) | $^1/_{12}$ of cake's icing | 29 | Tr. | | | |

**CAKE MIX.** Most cake mixes are listed by kind of cake, such as **ANGEL FOOD CAKE MIX, CHOCOLATE CAKE MIX,** etc.

| Food and Description | Measure or Quantity | Sodium (mg.) | Total | Satu- rated | Unsatu- rated | Choles- terol (mg.) |
|---|---|---|---|---|---|---|
| White: | | | | | | |
| (USDA)[4] | 1 oz. | 106 | 3.4 | <1. | 2. | |
| *Made with egg whites & water, with chocolate icing, 2 layers (USDA)[5] | $^1/_{16}$ of 9″ cake (2.5 oz.) | 161 | 7.6 | 3. | 5. | 1 |
| *(Betty Crocker) layer | $^1/_{12}$ of cake | 273 | 4.8 | | | |
| *(Duncan Hines) | $^1/_{12}$ of cake (2.6 oz.) | 314 | 4.4 | | | |
| *(Swans Down) | $^1/_{12}$ of cake (2.5 oz.) | 350 | 2.5 | | | |
| *Sour cream (Betty Crocker) layer | $^1/_{12}$ of cake | 274 | 5.3 | | | |
| Yellow: | | | | | | |
| (USDA) | 1 oz. | 115 | 3.7 | | | |
| *Made with eggs & water, with chocolate icing (USDA) | $^1/_{16}$ of 9″ cake (2.6 oz.) | 170 | 8.5 | | | 36 |

(USDA): United States Department of Agriculture
*Prepared as Package Directs
[1]Contains nonfat dry milk.
[2]Principal sources of fat: vegetable shortening & cocoa.
[3]Principal sources of fat: vegetable shortening, butter & cocoa.
[4]Principal source of fat: vegetable shortening.
[5]Principal sources of fat: vegetable shortening, chocolate, egg & milk.

| Food and Description | Measure or Quantity | Sodium (mg.) | —Fats in grams— | | | Choles- terol (mg.) |
|---|---|---|---|---|---|---|
| | | | Total | Satu- rated | Unsatu- rated | |
| *(Betty Crocker) layer | ¹/₁₂ of cake | 273 | 5.6 | | | |
| *Butter recipe (Betty Crocker) | ¹/₁₂ of cake | 266 | 13.7 | | | |
| *(Duncan Hines) | ¹/₁₂ of cake (2.7 oz.) | 347 | 6.1 | | | 50 |
| *Golden butter (Duncan Hines) | ¹/₁₂ of cake (3.3 oz.) | 345 | 13.9 | | | |
| *(Swans Down) | ¹/₁₂ of cake (2.5 oz.) | 294 | 3.2 | | | 48 |

**CANADIAN WHISKY** (See
**DISTILLED LIQUOR**)

**CANDIED FRUIT** (See
individual kinds)

**CANDY.** The following values of candies from the U. S. Department of Agriculture are representative of the types sold commercially. These values may be useful when individual brands or sizes are not known:

| Food and Description | Measure or Quantity | Sodium (mg.) | Total | Satu- rated | Unsatu- rated | Choles- terol |
|---|---|---|---|---|---|---|
| Almond: | | | | | | |
| Chocolate-coated[1] | 1 oz. | 17 | 12.4 | 2. | 10. | |
| Chocolate-coated[1] | 1 cup (6.3 oz.) | 106 | 78.7 | 13. | 66. | |
| Sugar-coated or Jordan[2] | 1 oz. | 6 | 5.3 | Tr. | 5. | |
| Butterscotch[3] | 1 oz. | 19 | 1.0 | <1. | Tr. | |
| Candy Corn | 1 oz. | 60 | .6 | | | |
| Caramel: | | | | | | |
| Plain[4] | 1 oz. | 64 | 2.9 | 1. | 2. | |
| Plain with nuts[5] | 1 oz. | 58 | 4.6 | 2. | 3. | |
| Chocolate[6] | 1 oz. | 64 | 2.9 | 1. | 2. | |
| Chocolate with nuts[7] | 1 oz. | 58 | 4.6 | 2. | 3. | |
| Chocolate-flavored roll[4] | 1 oz. | 56 | 2.3 | 1. | 1. | |
| Chocolate: | | | | | | |
| Bittersweet[8] | 1 oz. | <1 | 11.3 | 6. | 5. | |
| Milk: | | | | | | |
| Plain[8] | 1 oz. | 27 | 9.2 | 5. | 4. | |
| With almonds | 1 oz. | 23 | 10.1 | | | |
| With peanuts | 1 oz. | 19 | 10.8 | | | |
| Semisweet[8] | 1 oz. | <1 | 10.1 | 6. | 4. | |

(USDA): United States Department of Agriculture
*Prepared as Package Directs
[1]Principal sources of fat: almonds, chocolate & vegetable shortening.
[2]Principal source of fat: almonds.
[3]Principal source of fat: butter.
[4]Principal sources of fat: animal & vegetable shortening.
[5]Principal sources of fat: vegetable shortening & nuts.
[6]Principal sources of fat: animal & vegetable shortening & chocolate.
[7]Principal sources of fat: chocolate, vegetable shortening & nuts.
[8]Principal sources of fat: chocolate & cacao butter.

| Food and Description | Measure or Quantity | Sodium (mg.) | —Fats in grams— | | | Cholesterol (mg.) |
|---|---|---|---|---|---|---|
| | | | Total | Saturated | Unsaturated | |
| Sweet[1] | 1 oz. | 9 | 10.0 | 6. | 4. | |
| Chocolate discs, sugar-coated[2] | 1 oz. | 20 | 5.6 | 3. | 2. | |
| Coconut center, chocolate-coated[2] | 1 oz. | 56 | 5.0 | 3. | 2. | |
| Fondant, plain[3] | 1 oz. | 60 | .6 | Tr. | Tr. | |
| Fondant, chocolate-covered[4] | 1 oz. | 52 | 3.0 | 1. | 2. | |
| Fudge: | | | | | | |
| Chocolate fudge[4] | 1 oz. | 54 | 3.5 | 1. | 2. | |
| Chocolate fudge, chocolate-coated[5] | 1 oz. | 65 | 4.5 | 2. | 3. | |
| Chocolate fudge with nuts[6] | 1 oz. | 48 | 4.9 | 2. | 3. | |
| Chocolate fudge with nuts, chocolate-coated[7] | 1 oz. | 58 | 5.9 | 2. | 4. | |
| Vanilla fudge[8] | 1 oz. | 59 | 3.1 | 1. | 2. | |
| Vanilla fudge with nuts[7] | 1 oz. | 53 | 4.6 | 2. | 3. | |
| With peanuts & caramel, chocolate-coated[9] | 1 oz. | 36 | 6.5 | 2. | 5. | |
| Gum drops | 1 oz. | 10 | .2 | | | |
| Hard | 1 oz. | 9 | .3 | | | |
| Honeycombed hard candy, with peanut butter, chocolate-covered[10] | 1 oz. | 46 | 5.5 | 2. | 4. | |
| Jelly beans | 1 oz. | 3 | .1 | | | |
| Marshmallows | 1 oz. | 11 | Tr. | | | |
| Mints, uncoated | 1 oz. | 60 | .6 | | | |
| Nougat & caramel, chocolate-covered[4] | 1 oz. | 49 | 3.9 | 2. | 2. | |
| Peanut bar[11] | 1 oz. | 3 | 9.1 | 2. | 7. | |
| Peanut brittle, no added salt or soda[11] | 1 oz. | 9 | 2.9 | <1. | 2. | |
| Peanuts, chocolate-covered[12] | 1 oz. | 17 | 11.7 | 3. | 9. | |
| Raisins, chocolate-covered[2] | 1 oz. | 18 | 4.8 | 3. | 2. | |
| Vanilla creams, chocolate-covered[5] | 1 oz. | 52 | 4.8 | 2. | 3. | |

(USDA): United States Department of Agriculture
*Prepared as Package Directs
[1]Principal sources of fat: chocolate & cacao butter.
[2]Principal sources of fat: chocolate, milk & cacao butter.
[3]Principal source of fat: butter.
[4]Principal sources of fat: animal & vegetable shortening & chocolate.
[5]Principal sources of fat: chocolate & vegetable shortening.
[6]Principal sources of fat: chocolate, animal & vegetable shortening & English walnuts.
[7]Principal sources of fat: animal & vegetable shortening & nuts.
[8]Principal sources of fat: animal & vegetable shortening.
[9]Principal sources of fat: vegetable shortening, chocolate & peanuts.
[10]Principal sources of fat: vegetable shortening, chocolate & peanut butter.
[11]Principal source of fat: peanuts.
[12]Principal sources of fat: peanuts, chocolate & vegetable shortening.

| Food and Description | Measure or Quantity | Sodium (mg.) | Total | Fats in grams — Satu- rated | Unsatu- rated | Choles- terol (mg.) |
|---|---|---|---|---|---|---|
| **CANDY, COMMERCIAL** (See also | | | | | | |
| **CANDY, DIETETIC):** | | | | | | |
| Almonds, chocolate-covered: | | | | | | |
| Candy-coated (Hershey's) | 1 oz. | 11 | 7.9 | | | |
| (Kraft) | 1 piece (3 grams) | 1 | 1.1 | | | |
| Almond Cluster (Kraft) | 1 piece (.4 oz.) | 7 | 4.7 | | | |
| Almond Toffee Bar (Kraft) | 1 oz. | 65 | 8.4 | | | |
| Brazil nuts, chocolate-covered | | | | | | |
| (Kraft) | 1 piece (6 grams) | 3 | 2.8 | | | |
| Bridge Mix: | | | | | | |
| Almond (Kraft) | 1 piece (4 grams) | 2 | 1.7 | | | |
| Caramelette (Kraft) | 1 piece (3 grams) | 6 | .5 | | | |
| Jelly (Kraft) | 1 piece (3 grams) | 7 | .5 | | | |
| Malted milk ball (Kraft) | 1 piece (3 grams) | 2 | 1.0 | | | |
| Mintette (Kraft) | 1 piece (3 grams) | 2 | .5 | | | |
| Peanut (Kraft) | 1 piece (1 gram) | <1 | .6 | | | |
| Peanut crunch (Kraft) | 1 piece (5 grams) | 26 | 1.2 | | | |
| Raisin (Kraft) | 1 piece (1 gram) | <1 | .2 | | | |
| (Nabisco) | 1 piece (2 grams) | | .3 | | | |
| *Butternut* (Hollywood) | 1¼-oz. bar | | 7.7 | | | |
| Butterscotch Skimmers (Nabisco) | 1 piece (6 grams) | | .2 | | | |
| Caramel: | | | | | | |
| Caramelette (Kraft) | 1 piece (3 grams) | 6 | .5 | | | |
| Chocolate (Kraft) | 1 piece (8 grams) | 21 | .7 | | | |
| Chocolate, bar (Kraft) | 1 piece (6 grams) | 17 | .6 | | | |
| Coconut (Kraft) | 1 piece (8 grams) | 18 | .9 | | | |
| Vanilla (Kraft) | 1 piece (8 grams) | 22 | .7 | | | |
| Vanilla, bar (Kraft) | 1 piece (6 grams) | 18 | .6 | | | |
| Vanilla, chocolate-covered | | | | | | |
| (Kraft) | 1 piece (9 grams) | 20 | 1.5 | | | |
| Vanilla, *Twisteroo* (Kraft) | 1 piece (6 grams) | 17 | .5 | | | |
| Cashew cluster (Kraft) | 1 piece (.4 oz.) | 7 | 4.2 | | | |
| Cashew crunch, canned (Planters) | 1 oz. | 55 | 7.3 | | | 0 |
| *Charleston Chew:* | | | | | | |
| 10¢ size | 1 bar (1⅛ oz.) | | 4.1 | | | |
| 5¢ size | 1 bar (¾ oz.) | | 2.5 | | | |
| Bite-size | 1 piece (7 grams) | | .8 | | | |
| Cherry, chocolate-covered: | | | | | | |
| Dark (Nabisco) | 1 piece (.6 oz.) | | 1.5 | | | |
| Dark (Nabisco) *Welch's* | 1 piece (.6 oz.) | | 1.5 | | | |
| Milk (Nabisco) | 1 piece (.6 oz.) | | 1.4 | | | |
| Milk (Nabisco) *Welch's* | 1 piece (.6 oz.) | | 1.4 | | | |

(USDA): United States Department of Agriculture
*Prepared as Package Directs

69

| Food and Description | Measure or Quantity | Sodium (mg.) | Fats in grams — Total | Satu-rated | Unsatu-rated | Choles-terol (mg.) |
|---|---|---|---|---|---|---|
| Chocolate bar: | | | | | | |
| Milk chocolate: | | | | | | |
| (Ghirardelli) | 1.1-oz. bar | 26 | 9.5 | | | |
| (Hershey's) | 1 oz. | 28 | 9.5 | 6. | 4. | |
| (Hershey's) | ¼-oz. miniature | 7 | 2.4 | 1. | 1. | |
| Mint chocolate (Ghirardelli) | 1.1-oz. bar | 26 | 9.8 | | | |
| Semisweet (Ghirardelli) *Eagle* | 1 sq. (1 oz.) | | 8.9 | | | |
| Semisweet (Nestlé's) | 1 oz. | | 8.0 | | | |
| Special Dark (Hershey's) | 1 oz. | 4 | 9.5 | | | |
| Special Dark (Hershey's) | ¼-oz. miniature | 1 | 2.4 | | | |
| (Nestlé's) | 1 oz. | | 9.5 | | | |
| Chocolate bar with almonds: | | | | | | |
| (Ghirardelli) | 1.1-oz. bar | 25 | 10.4 | | | |
| (Hershey's) | 1 oz. | 23 | 10.4 | | | |
| (Nestlé's) | 1 oz. | | 10.8 | | | |
| Chocolate block, milk: | | | | | | |
| (Ghirardelli) | 1 sq. (1 oz.) | 23 | 8.4 | | | |
| (Hershey's) | 1 oz. | 16 | 8.8 | | | |
| Chocolate Crisp Bar (Ghirardelli) | 1-oz. bar | 25 | 9.2 | | | |
| Chocolate Crisp Bar (Kraft) | 1 oz. | 73 | 6.4 | | | |
| Chocolate Crunch Bar (Nestlé's) | 1 oz. | | 7.9 | | | |
| Cluster: | | | | | | |
| Crispy (Nabisco) | 1 piece (.6 oz.) | | .8 | | | |
| Peanut, chocolate-covered (Kraft) | 1 piece (.4 oz.) | 5 | 4.3 | | | |
| *Royal Clusters* (Nabisco) | 1 piece (.6 oz.) | | 4.7 | | | |
| *Coco-Mello* (Nabisco) | 1 piece (.7 oz.) | | 3.7 | | | |
| Coconut: | | | | | | |
| Bar (Nabisco) *Welch's* | 1 piece (1.1 oz.) | | 4.5 | | | |
| Cream egg (Hershey's) | 1 oz. | 2 | 4.5 | | | |
| Squares (Nabisco) | 1 piece (.5 oz.) | | 1.4 | | | |
| Eggs (Nabisco) *Chuckles* | 1 piece (2 grams) | | Tr. | | | |
| *Fiddle Faddle* | 1½-oz. packet | | 3.4 | | | |
| Frappe (Nabisco) *Welch's* | 1 piece (1.1 oz.) | | 3.9 | | | |
| *Fruit'n Nut* chocolate bar | | | | | | |
| (Nestlé's) | 1 oz. | | 8.3 | | | |
| Fudge: | | | | | | |
| Bar (Nabisco) *Welch's* | 1 piece (1.1 oz.) | | 6.5 | | | |
| Bar (Tom Houston) | 1 bar (1.5 oz.) | 72 | 7.3 | | | |
| Fudgies, bar (Kraft) | 1 piece (7 grams) | 15 | .9 | | | |
| Fudgies, regular (Kraft) | 1 piece (8 grams) | 19 | 1.0 | | | |
| Fudgies, *Twisteroo* (Kraft) | 1 piece (6 grams) | 15 | .8 | | | |
| *Home Style* (Nabisco) | 1 piece (.7 oz.) | | 3.5 | | | |
| Nut, bars or squares (Nabisco) | 1 piece (.5 oz.) | | 3.2 | | | |

(USDA): United States Department of Agriculture
*Prepared as Package Directs

| Food and Description | Measure or Quantity | Sodium (mg.) | —Fats in grams— | | | Choles- terol (mg.) |
|---|---|---|---|---|---|---|
| | | | Total | Satu- rated | Unsatu- rated | |
| *Good & Fruity* | 1 oz. | | <.1 | | | |
| *Good & Plenty* | 1 oz. | | <.1 | | | |
| Hard candy (F & F) *Sherbit* | 1 piece | | 0. | | | (0) |
| *Hershey-Ets,* candy-coated | 1 oz. | 10 | 5.8 | | | |
| *Hollywood* | 1½-oz. bar | | 6.1 | | | |
| Jelly (See also individual flavors and brand names in this section): | | | | | | |
| Beans, rings (Nabisco) *Chuckles* | 1 piece (.4 oz.) | | <.1 | | | |
| Jujubes (Nabisco) *Chuckles* | 1 piece (4 grams) | | Tr. | | | |
| *Kisses,* milk chocolate (Hershey's) | 1 piece (5 grams) | 5 | 1.5 | <1. | <1. | |
| *Krackel Bar* (Hershey's) | 1 oz. | 33 | 8.3 | | | |
| *Krackel Bar* (Hershey's) | ¼-oz. miniature | 8 | 2.1 | | | |
| Licorice (Nabisco) *Chuckles* | 1 piece (.4 oz.) | | Tr. | | | |
| Twist (American Licorice Co): | | | | | | |
| Black | 1 piece (10 grams) | 10 | .1 | | | |
| Red | 1 piece (9 grams) | 8 | .2 | | | |
| *Life Savers* (Beech-Nut): | | | | | | |
| All but butter rum & butterscotch | 1 drop (3 grams) | <1 | 0. | | | |
| Butter rum & butterscotch | 1 drop (3 grams) | 12 | 0. | | | |
| Mint | 1 piece (2 grams) | <1 | 0. | | | |
| Malted Milk Crunch (Nabisco) | 1 piece (2 grams) | | .5 | | | |
| Marshmallow: | | | | | | |
| Chocolate (Kraft) | 1 piece (7 grams) | 4 | .2 | | | |
| Coconut (Kraft) | 1 piece (.4 oz.) | 12 | 1.1 | | | |
| Eggs (Nabisco) *Chuckles* | 1 piece (10 grams) | | <.1 | | | |
| Flavored, miniature (Kraft) | 1 piece (<1 gram) | <1 | 0. | | | |
| Flavored, regular (Kraft) | 1 piece (7 grams) | <1 | 0. | | | |
| White, miniature (Kraft) | 1 piece (<1 gram) | <1 | 0. | | | |
| White, regular (Kraft) | 1 piece (7 grams) | <1 | 0. | | | |
| *Mary Jane* (Miller): | | | | | | |
| 1¢ size | 1 piece (9 grams) | | <.1 | Tr. | Tr. | |
| 5¢ size | 1 piece (1¼ oz.) | | .4 | Tr. | Tr. | |
| *Milk Shake* (Hollywood) | 1¼-oz. bar | | 4.0 | | | |
| Mint or peppermint: | | | | | | |
| Buttermint (Kraft) | 1 piece (2 grams) | 4 | <.1 | | | |
| Encore (Kraft) | 1 piece (2 grams) | 3 | 0. | | | |
| *Jamaica Mints* (Nabisco) | 1 piece (6 grams) | | <.1 | | | |
| *Liberty Mints* (Nabisco) | 1 piece (6 grams) | | <.1 | | | |
| *Mini-mint* (Kraft) | 1 piece (3 grams) | 2 | .5 | | | |
| Party (Kraft) | 1 piece (2 grams) | 4 | <.1 | | | |

(USDA): United States Department of Agriculture
*Prepared as Package Directs

| Food and Description | Measure or Quantity | Sodium (mg.) | Fats in grams — Total | Satu-rated | Unsatu-rated | Choles-terol (mg.) |
|---|---|---|---|---|---|---|
| Pattie, chocolate-covered: | | | | | | |
| *Junior* Mint Pattie (Nabisco) | 1 piece (2 grams) | | .2 | | | |
| Peppermint pattie (Nabisco) | 1 piece (.5 oz.) | | 1.4 | | | |
| *Sherbit*, pressed mints (F & F) | 1 piece | | 0. | | | |
| Thin (Nabisco) | 1 piece (.4 oz.) | | 1.0 | | | |
| Wafers (Nabisco) | 1 piece (2 grams) | | .6 | | | |
| *Mr. Goodbar* (Hershey's) | 1 oz. | 16 | 10.4 | | | |
| *Mr. Goodbar* (Hershey's) | ¼-oz. miniature | 4 | 2.6 | | | |
| *Nibs* (Y & S) cherry | 1¾ oz. | 100 | 1.3 | | | 0 |
| *Nibs* (Y & S) licorice | 1¾ oz. | 208 | 1.1 | | | 0 |
| *North Pole* (F & F) | 1⅜-oz. bar | | 2.3 | | | |
| Nougat centers (Nabisco) | | | | | | |
| *Chuckles* | 1 piece (4 grams) | | Tr. | | | |
| *Nutty Crunch* (Nabisco) | 1 piece (½ oz.) | | 3.2 | | | |
| *$100,000 Bar* (Nestlé's) | 1 oz. | | 5.4 | | | |
| Orange slices (Nabisco) *Chuckles* | 1 piece (8 grams) | | Tr. | | | |
| *Payday* (Hollywood) | 1¼-oz. bar | | 5.6 | | | |
| Peanut, chocolate-covered: | | | | | | |
| (Hershey's) candy-coated | 1 oz. | 7 | 7.1 | | | |
| (Kraft) | 1 piece (2 grams) | 1 | .9 | | | |
| (Nabisco) | 1 piece (4 grams) | | 1.7 | | | |
| (Tom Houston) | 1 oz. | 17 | 11.6 | | | |
| Peanut Brittle: | | | | | | |
| (Kraft) | 1 oz. | 145 | 5.0 | | | |
| Coconut (Kraft) | 1 oz. | 189 | 4.5 | | | |
| *Jumbo Peanut Block Bar* | | | | | | |
| (Planters) | 1 oz. | 55 | 7.3 | | | 0 |
| Peanut Butter Cup (Reese's) | 1 oz. | 99 | 8.6 | | | |
| Peanut Butter Egg (Reese's) | 1 oz. | 119 | 8.6 | | | |
| Peanut Plank (Tom Houston) | 1 bar (1.5 oz.) | 4 | 13.5 | | | |
| *Pom Poms* (Nabisco) | 1 piece (3 grams) | | .5 | | | |
| Raisin, chocolate-covered: | | | | | | |
| (Ghirardelli) | 1 bar (1.1 oz.) | 23 | 8.4 | | | |
| (Nabisco) | 1 piece (<1 gram) | | .2 | | | |
| *Screaming Yellow Zonkers* | 1 oz. | | 2.7 | | | |
| Spearmint leaves: | | | | | | |
| (Nabisco) *Chuckles* | 1 piece (8 grams) | | Tr. | | | |
| (Quaker City) | 1 oz. | | .2 | | | |
| Spice-flavored sticks & drops | | | | | | |
| (Nabisco) *Chuckles* | 1 piece (4 grams) | | Tr. | | | |
| Spice-flavored strings (Nabisco) | | | | | | |
| *Chuckles* | 1 piece (5 grams) | | Tr. | | | |
| Sprigs, sweet chocolate (Hershey's) | 1 oz. | 6 | 7.7 | | | |

(USDA): United States Department of Agriculture
*Prepared as Package Directs

| Food and Description | Measure or Quantity | Sodium (mg.) | —Fats in grams— | | Choles-terol (mg.) |
| | | | Total | Satu-rated | Unsatu-rated | |
|---|---|---|---|---|---|---|
| Stars, chocolate: | | | | | | |
| (Kraft) | 1 piece (3 grams) | | .7 | | | |
| (Nabisco) | 1 piece (3 grams) | | .9 | | | |
| *Sugar Babies* (Nabisco) | 1 piece (2 grams) | | <.1 | | | |
| *Sugar Daddy* (Nabisco): | | | | | | |
| Caramel sucker | 1 piece (1.1 oz.) | | 1.5 | | | |
| Giant sucker, caramel | 1 piece (1 lb.) | | 19.5 | | | |
| Junior | 1 piece (.4 oz.) | | .5 | | | |
| Junior sucker, choco-flavored | 1 piece (.4 oz.) | | .6 | | | |
| Nugget | 1 piece (.4 oz.) | | .5 | | | |
| Nugget | 1 piece (7 grams) | | .3 | | | |
| *Sugar Mama* (Nabisco) | 1 piece (.8 oz.) | | 2.6 | | | |
| Sugar Wafer (F & F) | 1¼-oz. pkg. | | 8.0 | | | |
| Taffy: | | | | | | |
| Chocolate (Kraft) | 1 piece (7 grams) | 22 | .7 | | | |
| Coffee (Kraft) | 1 piece (7 grams) | 22 | .7 | | | |
| Rum butter (Kraft) | 1 piece (7 grams) | 22 | .7 | | | |
| Vanilla (Kraft) | 1 piece (7 grams) | 22 | .7 | | | |
| *Tootsie Roll:* | | | | | | |
| Regular: | | | | | | |
| 1¢ size or midgee | 1 piece (7 grams) | 15 | .5 | Tr. | Tr. | 0 |
| 2¢ size | 1 piece (.4 oz.) | 25 | .8 | Tr. | Tr. | 0 |
| 5¢ size | 1 piece (¾ oz.) | 50 | 1.6 | Tr. | 1. | 0 |
| 10¢ size | 1 piece (1½ oz.) | 98 | 3.3 | Tr. | 3. | 0 |
| Twin pak | 10¢ size (1¼ oz.) | 84 | 2.7 | Tr. | 2. | 0 |
| Twin pak | 15¢ size (2 oz.) | 135 | 4.4 | <1. | 4. | 0 |
| Vending-machine size | 1 piece (5 grams) | 11 | .4 | Tr. | Tr. | 0 |
| Pop, 2 for 5¢ | 1 piece (.5 oz.) | 8 | .3 | Tr. | Tr. | 0 |
| Pop, 5¢ size | 1 piece (1 oz.) | 17 | .6 | Tr. | Tr. | 0 |
| Pop-drop | 1 piece (5 grams) | 3 | <.1 | Tr. | Tr. | 0 |
| *Triple Decker* bar (Nestlé's) | 1 oz. | | 9.4 | | | |
| *Twizzlers* (Y & S): | | | | | | |
| Chocolate | 1 oz. | 64 | .9 | | | 0 |
| Grape | 1 oz. | 52 | .2 | | | 0 |
| Licorice | 1¾ oz. | 220 | .8 | | | 0 |
| Strawberry | 1¾ oz. | 91 | .4 | | | 0 |
| Strawberry | 1-oz. bar | 52 | .2 | | | 0 |
| Variety pack (Nabisco) *Chuckles* | 1 piece (.4 oz.) | | .1 | | | |
| Variety pack (Nabisco) *Chuckles* | 2-oz. pack | | .5 | | | |
| *Walnut Hill* (F & F) | 1⅜-oz. bar | | 6.0 | | | |
| *Whirligigs* (Nabisco) | 1 piece (6 grams) | | .5 | | | |

(USDA): United States Department of Agriculture
*Prepared as Package Directs

| Food and Description | Measure or Quantity | Sodium (mg.) | Fats in grams — Total | Satu- rated | Unsatu- rated | Choles- terol (mg.) |
|---|---|---|---|---|---|---|
| **CANDY DIETETIC:** | | | | | | |
| Almonds, chocolate-covered | | | | | | |
| (Estee) | 1 piece (4 grams) | 4 | 1.5 | <1. | <1. | <1 |
| Chocolate, assorted: | | | | | | |
| Milk (Estee) | 1 piece (8 grams) | 9 | 3.7 | 2. | 2. | <1 |
| *Slimtreats* | 1 piece (2 grams) | | .7 | | | |
| Chocolate bar, almonds: | | | | | | |
| (Estee) | 1 bar (¾ oz.) | 28 | 9.1 | 5. | 4. | 1 |
| (Estee) | 1 section of 2-oz. bar | 3 | 1.0 | <1. | Tr. | Tr. |
| (Estee) | 1 section of 4-oz. bar | 19 | 6.1 | 3. | 3. | <1 |
| Chocolate bar, bittersweet: | | | | | | |
| (Estee) | 1 bar (¾ oz.) | 22 | 8.5 | 5. | 4. | <1 |
| (Estee) | 1 section of 2-oz. bar | 2 | .9 | <1. | Tr. | <1 |
| (Estee) | 1 section of 4-oz. bar | 15 | 5.7 | 3. | 2. | <1 |
| Chocolate bar, coconut (Estee) | 1 bar (¾ oz.) | 30 | 8.9 | 6. | 3. | 1 |
| Chocolate bar, crunch (Estee) | 1 bar (⅝ oz.) | | 6.7 | 4. | 3. | 1 |
| Chocolate bar, crunch (Estee) | 1 section of 3-oz. bar | | 4.0 | 2. | 2. | <1 |
| Chocolate bar, fruit-nut (Estee) | 1 section of 4-oz. bar | 16 | 5.4 | 3. | 3. | <1 |
| Chocolate bar, milk: | | | | | | |
| (Estee) | 1 bar (¾ oz.) | 31 | 8.9 | 5. | 4. | 1 |
| (Estee) | 1 section of 2-oz. bar | 3 | 1.0 | <1. | Tr. | <1 |
| (Estee) | 1 section of 4-oz. bar | 21 | 6.0 | 3. | 3. | <1 |
| Chocolate bar, peppermint (Estee) | 1 bar (¾ oz.) | 31 | 8.9 | 5. | 4. | 1 |
| Chocolate bar, white (Estee) | 1 section of 4-oz. bar | 23 | 5.1 | 4. | 1. | 2 |
| Chocolettes, milk or peppermint | | | | | | |
| (Estee) | 1 piece (3 grams) | 5 | 1.2 | 1. | Tr. | <1 |
| Creams, assorted or peppermint | | | | | | |
| (Estee) | 1 piece (8 grams) | 12 | 3.6 | 2. | 1. | <1 |
| Gum Drops (Estee) | 1 piece | <1 | Tr. | | | 0 |
| Hard candy: | | | | | | |
| Assorted (Estee) | 1 piece | <1 | Tr. | | | 0 |
| Coffee (Estee) | 1 piece | <1 | .1 | | | 0 |
| *Slimtreats* | 1 piece (3 grams) | | 0. | | | |
| Mint, any flavor (Estee) | 1 piece | Tr. | Tr. | | | 0 |
| Nut, chocolate-covered (Estee) | 1 piece (8 grams) | 9 | 3.4 | 2. | 2. | <1 |
| Peanut butter cup (Estee) | 1 piece (7 grams) | 6 | 3.1 | 2. | 1. | <1 |
| Peanut, chocolate-covered (Estee) | 1 piece (1 gram) | 1 | .5 | Tr. | Tr. | Tr. |
| Petit fours (Estee) | 1 piece (8 grams) | 8 | 2.9 | 1. | 2. | <1 |
| Raisin, chocolate-covered (Estee) | 1 piece (1 gram) | 1 | .3 | Tr. | Tr. | Tr. |
| TV mix (Estee) | 1 piece (2 grams) | 1 | .8 | Tr. | Tr. | Tr. |
| **CANE SYRUP** (USDA) | Any quantity | | 0. | | | 0 |

(USDA): United States Department of Agriculture
*Prepared as Package Directs

74

| Food and Description | Measure or Quantity | Sodium (mg.) | —Fats in grams— Total | Satu- rated | Unsatu- rated | Choles- terol (mg.) |
|---|---|---|---|---|---|---|
| **CANTALOUPE,** fresh: | | | | | | |
| Whole | 1 lb. (weighed whole) | 27 | .2 | | | 0 |
| Whole, medium (USDA) | 5″ dia. melon (1⅔ lbs., weighed with skin & cavity contents) | 46 | .4 | | | 0 |
| Cubed (USDA) | ½ cup (2.9 oz.) | 10 | <.1 | | | 0 |
| **CAPE GOOSEBERRY** (See **GROUND-CHERRY**) | | | | | | |
| **CAPERS** (Crosse & Blackwell) | 1 T. (.6 oz.) | 306 | | | | |
| **CAPICOLA or CAPACOLA SAUSAGE** (USDA) | 1 oz. | | 13.0 | 5. | 8. | |
| *CAP'N CRUNCH:* | | | | | | |
| (Quaker) | ¾ cup (1 oz.) | 280 | 3.0 | | | |
| Crunchberries (Quaker) | ¾ cup (1 oz.) | 147 | 2.1 | | | |
| Peanut butter (Quaker) | ¾ cup (1 oz.) | 250 | 3.8 | | | |
| Vanilly (Quaker) | ¾ cup (1 oz.) | 141 | 1.7 | | | |
| **CARAMBOLA,** raw (USDA): | | | | | | |
| Whole | 1 lb. (weighed whole) | 9 | 2.1 | | | 0 |
| Flesh only | 4 oz. | 2 | .6 | | | 0 |
| **CARAMEL CAKE,** home recipe (USDA)[1] : | | | | | | |
| Without icing[2] | 1/9 of 9″ sq. cake (3 oz.) | 262 | 14.9 | 8. | 7. | |
| With caramel icing | 3 oz. | 214 | 12.6 | | | |
| **CARAMEL CAKE MIX:** | | | | | | |
| *(Duncan Hines) | 1/12 of cake (2.7 oz.) | 397 | 6.1 | | | 50 |
| *Apple (Betty Crocker) layer | 1/12 of cake | 275 | 6.0 | | | |
| *Pudding (Betty Crocker) | 1/6 of cake | 328 | 4.7 | | | |
| **\*CARAMEL PUDDING MIX,** nut (Royal) | ½ cup (5.1 oz.) | 380 | 5.7 | | | 14 |

(USDA): United States Department of Agriculture
*Prepared as Package Directs
[1]Made with sodium aluminum sulfate-type baking powder.
[2]Principal sources of fat: butter, egg & milk.

| Food and Description | Measure or Quantity | Sodium (mg.) | Total | —Fats in grams— Satu- rated | Unsatu- rated | Choles- terol (mg.) |
|---|---|---|---|---|---|---|
| **CARAWAY SEED** (Information supplied by General Mills Laboratory) | 1 oz. | 13 | <.1 | | | (0) |
| (Spice Islands) | 1 tsp. | <1 | | | | (0) |
| **CARDAMOM:** | | | | | | |
| Ground (Spice Islands) | 1 tsp. | <1 | | | | (0) |
| Whole (Spice Islands) | 1 seed | Tr. | | | | (0) |
| **CARISSA or NATAL PLUM,** raw: | | | | | | |
| Whole (USDA) | 1 lb. (weighed whole) | | 5.1 | | | 0 |
| Flesh only (USDA) | 4 oz. | | 1.5 | | | 0 |
| *CARNATION INSTANT BREAKFAST:* | | | | | | |
| Butterscotch[1] | 1 pkg. (1.2 oz.) | 171 | .2 | Tr. | Tr. | <1 |
| Chocolate[2] | 1 pkg. (1.3 oz.) | 163 | .9 | Tr. | Tr. | Tr. |
| Chocolate fudge[2] | 1 pkg. (1.3 oz.) | 206 | 1.1 | <1. | <1. | Tr. |
| Chocolate malt[3] | 1 pkg. (1.2 oz.) | 196 | 1.4 | <1. | <1. | 2 |
| Chocolat marshmallow[2] | 1 pkg. (1.3 oz.) | 198 | .9 | Tr. | Tr. | Tr. |
| Coffee[4] | 1 pkg. (1.3 oz.) | 132 | .3 | Tr. | Tr. | <1 |
| Eggnog[1] | 1 pkg. (1.2 oz.) | 185 | .5 | Tr. | Tr. | 21 |
| Special Morning, chocolate[2] | 1 pkg. (1 oz.) | 280 | 1.3 | <1. | <1. | <1 |
| Special Morning, chocolate malt[3] | 1 pkg. (1 oz.) | 264 | 1.4 | <1. | <1. | 2 |
| Special Morning, strawberry[4] | 1 pkg. (1 oz.) | 312 | .4 | Tr. | Tr. | <1 |
| Special Morning, vanilla[4] | 1 pkg. (1 oz.) | 241 | .4 | Tr. | Tr. | <1 |
| Strawberry[1] | 1 pkg. (1.2 oz.) | 201 | .2 | Tr. | Tr. | <1 |
| Vanilla[1] | 1 pkg. (1.2 oz.) | 131 | .2 | Tr. | Tr. | <1 |
| Vanilla ice creme[1] | 1 pkg. (1.2 oz.) | 130 | .2 | Tr. | Tr. | <1 |
| **CAROB FLOUR** (See **FLOUR**) | | | | | | |
| *CAROUSEL WINE* (Gold Seal) | 3 fl. oz. (3.3 oz.) | 3 | 0. | | | (0) |
| **CARP,** raw (USDA): | | | | | | |
| Whole | 1 lb. (weighed whole) | 68 | 5.7 | | | |
| Meat only | 4 oz. | 57 | 4.8 | | | |

(USDA): United States Department of Agriculture
*Prepared as Package Directs
[1]Principal source of fat: milk.
[2]Principal sources of fat: milk, cocoa & lecithin.
[3]Principal sources of fat: wort solids, milk, cocoa & lecithin.
[4]Principal sources of fat: milk & lecithin.

| Food and Description | Measure or Quantity | Sodium (mg.) | —Fats in grams— | | | Choles-terol (mg.) |
|---|---|---|---|---|---|---|
| | | | Total | Satu-rated | Unsatu-rated | |
| **CARROT:** | | | | | | |
| Raw (USDA): | | | | | | |
| Whole | 1 lb. (weighed with full tops) | 126 | .5 | | | 0 |
| Partially trimmed | 1 lb. (weighed without tops, with skins) | 175 | .7 | | | 0 |
| Trimmed | 5½″ x 1″ carrot (1.8 oz.) | 24 | .1 | | | 0 |
| Trimmed | 25 thin strips (1.8 oz.) | 24 | .1 | | | 0 |
| Chunks | ½ cup (2.4 oz.) | 32 | .1 | | | 0 |
| Diced | ½ cup (2.5 oz.) | 34 | .1 | | | 0 |
| Grated or shredded | ½ cup (1.9 oz.) | 26 | .1 | | | 0 |
| Slices | ½ cup (2.3 oz.) | 30 | .1 | | | 0 |
| Strips | ½ cup (2 oz.) | 27 | .1 | | | 0 |
| Boiled, without salt (USDA): | | | | | | |
| Chunks, drained | ½ cup (2.9 oz.) | 27 | .2 | | | 0 |
| Diced, drained | ½ cup (2.5 oz.) | 23 | .1 | | | 0 |
| Slices, drained | ½ cup (2.7 oz.) | 25 | .2 | | | 0 |
| Canned, regular pack: | | | | | | |
| Diced, solids & liq. (USDA) | ½ cup (4.3 oz.) | 290 | .2 | | | 0 |
| Diced, drained solids (USDA) | ½ cup (2.8 oz.) | 189 | .2 | | | 0 |
| Drained liq. (USDA) | 4 oz. | 268 | 0. | | | 0 |
| Drained solids (Butter Kernel) | ½ cup (4.1 oz.) | | | | | |
| Drained solids (Del Monte) | ½ cup (2.8 oz.) | 1852 | | | 0 | |
| Sliced, solids & liq. (Comstock-Greenwood) | ½ cup (2.6 oz.) | 177 | .2 | | | (0) |
| Solids & liq. (Del Monte) | ½ cup (4 oz.) | 266 | .2 | | | 0 |
| Solids & liq. (Stokely-Van Camp) | ½ cup (4 oz.) | | .2 | | | (0) |
| Canned, dietetic pack: | | | | | | |
| Low sodium, solids & liq. (USDA) | 4 oz. (by wt.) | 44 | .1 | | | 0 |
| Low sodium, drained solids (USDA) | ½ cup (2.8 oz.) | 31 | <.1 | | | 0 |
| Diced, solids & liq. (Blue Boy) | 4 oz. | 36 | .7 | | | (0) |
| Diced, solids & liq. (Tillie Lewis) | ½ cup (4.3 oz.) | 40 | .1 | | | 0 |
| Sliced, solids & liq. (Blue Boy) | 4 oz. | 43 | <.1 | | | (0) |
| Sliced (S and W), *Nutradiet,* unseasoned | 4 oz. | 45 | .1 | | | (0) |
| Dehydrated (USDA) | 1 oz. | 76 | .4 | | | 0 |

(USDA): United States Department of Agriculture
*Prepared as Package Directs

⑦⑦

| Food and Description | Measure or Quantity | Sodium (mg.) | —Fats in grams— | | | Choles-terol (mg.) |
|---|---|---|---|---|---|---|
| | | | Total | Satu-rated | Unsatu-rated | |
| Frozen: | | | | | | |
| Nuggets in butter sauce (Green Giant) | ⅓ of 10-oz. pkg. | 350 | 2.4 | | | |
| Sliced, honey glazed (Green Giant) | ⅓ of 10-oz. pkg. | 217 | 1.7 | | | |
| With brown sugar glaze (Birds Eye) | ½ cup (3.3 oz.) | 500 | 2.4 | | | 0 |
| **CASABA MELON,** fresh (USDA): | | | | | | |
| Whole | 1 lb. (weighed whole) | 27 | Tr. | | | 0 |
| Flesh only | 4 oz. | 14 | Tr. | | | 0 |
| **CASHEW NUT:** | | | | | | |
| Salted: | | | | | | |
| (USDA) | 1 oz. | 57 | 13.0 | 2. | 11. | 0 |
| (USDA) | ½ cup (2.5 oz.) | 140 | 32.0 | 6. | 26. | 0 |
| (USDA) | 5 large or 8 med. (.4 oz.) | 21 | 4.9 | <1. | 4. | 0 |
| (Tom Houston) | 15 nuts (1.1 oz.) | 60 | 13.7 | | | (0) |
| Dry roasted (Flavor House) | 1 oz. | 36 | 13.4 | | | (0) |
| Dry roasted (Planters) | 1 oz. | 340 | 13.0 | 2. | 11. | 0 |
| Dry roasted (Skippy) | 1 oz. | 142 | 13.2 | 3. | 11. | 0 |
| Oil roasted, *Freshnut* | 1 oz. | 140 | 14.5 | 3. | 11. | 0 |
| Oil roasted (Planters) | 1 oz. | 220 | 14.1 | | | 0 |
| Unsalted: | | | | | | |
| (USDA) | 1 oz. | 4 | 13.0 | 2. | 11. | 0 |
| (USDA) | ½ cup (2.5 oz.) | 10 | 32.0 | 6. | 26. | 0 |
| (USDA) | 5 large or 8 med. (.4 oz.) | 2 | 4.9 | <1. | 4. | 0 |
| **CATAWBA WINE:** | | | | | | |
| (Gold Seal) 13-14% alcohol | 3 fl. oz. (3.3 oz.) | 3 | 0. | | | (0) |
| (Great Western) pink, 13% alcohol | 3 fl. oz. | 36 | 0. | | | 0 |
| **CATFISH,** freshwater, raw, fillet | | | | | | |
| (USDA) | 4 oz. | 68 | 3.5 | | | |
| **CATSUP:** | | | | | | |
| Regular pack: | | | | | | |
| (USDA) | ½ cup (5 oz.) | 1469 | .6 | | | 0 |
| (USDA) | 1 T. (.6 oz.) | 188 | <.1 | | | 0 |
| (Bama) | 1 T. (.6 oz.) | 180 | .3 | | | (0) |

(USDA): United States Department of Agriculture
*Prepared as Package Directs

| Food and Description | Measure or Quantity | Sodium (mg.) | —Fats in grams— | | | Choles-terol (mg.) |
|---|---|---|---|---|---|---|
| | | | Total | Satu-rated | Unsatu-rated | |
| (Del Monte) | 1 T. (.7 oz.) | 263 | <.1 | | | 0 |
| (Heinz) | 1 T. | 180 | Tr. | | | (0) |
| (Hunt's) | ½ cup (4.8 oz.) | 1620 | .3 | | | (0) |
| (Hunt's) | 1 T. (.6 oz.) | 202 | <.1 | | | (0) |
| (Nalley's) | 1 oz. | | .1 | | | (0) |
| (Stokely-Van Camp) | 1 T. (.6 oz.) | | <.1 | | | (0) |
| Dietetic pack: | | | | | | |
| Low sodium (USDA) | ½ cup (5 oz.) | 7-49 | .6 | | | 0 |
| Low sodium (USDA) | 1 T. (.6 oz.) | <1-6 | <.1 | | | 0 |
| (Tillie Lewis) | 1 T. (.5 oz.) | 4 | Tr. | | | (0) |
| **CAULIFLOWER:** | | | | | | |
| Raw (USDA): | | | | | | |
| Whole | 1 lb. (weighed untrimmed) | 23 | .4 | | | 0 |
| Flowerbuds | 1 lb. (weighed trimmed) | 59 | .9 | | | 0 |
| Buds | ½ cup (1.8 oz.) | 6 | .1 | | | 0 |
| Slices | ½ cup (1.5 oz.) | 5 | <.1 | | | 0 |
| Boiled, without salt, drained (USDA) | ½ cup (2.2 oz.) | 6 | .1 | | | 0 |
| Frozen: | | | | | | |
| Not thawed (USDA) | 10-oz. pkg. | 31 | .6 | | | 0 |
| Boiled, drained (USDA) | ½ cup (3.2 oz.) | 9 | .2 | | | 0 |
| (Birds Eye) | ⅓ of 10-oz. pkg. | 38 | .2 | | | 0 |
| Au gratin (Stouffer's) | ⅓ of 10-oz. pkg. | 279 | 8.0 | | | |
| Cut, in butter sauce (Green Giant) | ⅓ of 10-oz. pkg. | 321 | 2.4 | | | |
| Hungarian, with sour cream sauce, casserole (Green Giant) | ⅓ of 10-oz. pkg. | 529 | 3.3 | | | |
| In cheese sauce (Green Giant) | ⅓ of 10-oz. pkg. | 298 | 2.6 | | | |
| **CAULIFLOWER, SWEET, PICKLED** (Smucker's) | 1 bud (.5 oz.) | 150 | Tr. | | | (0) |
| **CAVIAR, STURGEON** (USDA): | | | | | | |
| Pressed | 1 oz. | | 4.7 | | | |
| Whole eggs | 1 oz. | 624 | 4.3 | | | >85 |
| Whole eggs | 1 T. (.6 oz.) | 352 | 2.4 | | | >48 |
| **CELERIAC ROOT,** raw (USDA): | | | | | | |
| Whole | 1 lb. (weighed unpared) | 390 | 1.2 | | | 0 |
| Pared | 4 oz. | 113 | .3 | | | 0 |

(USDA): United States Department of Agriculture
*Prepared as Package Directs

| Food and Description | Measure or Quantity | Sodium (mg.) | —Fats in grams— | | | Choles- terol (mg.) |
|---|---|---|---|---|---|---|
| | | | Total | Satu- rated | Unsatu- rated | |
| **CELERY,** all varieties: | | | | | | |
| Raw (USDA): | | | | | | |
| Whole | 1 lb. (weighed untrimmed) | 429 | .3 | | | 0 |
| 1 large outer stalk | 8″ x 1½″ at root end (1.4 oz.) | 50 | <.1 | | | 0 |
| 3 small inner stalks | 5″ x ¾″ (1.8 oz.) | 63 | <.1 | | | 0 |
| Diced, chopped or cut in chunks | ½ cup (2.1 oz.) | 76 | <.1 | | | 0 |
| Slices | ½ cup (1.9 oz.) | 67 | <.1 | | | 0 |
| Boiled without salt, drained: | | | | | | |
| Diced or cut in chunks | ½ cup (2.7 oz.) | 67 | <.1 | | | 0 |
| Slices | ½ cup (3 oz.) | 74 | <.1 | | | 0 |
| **CELERY CABBAGE** (See **CABBAGE, CHINESE**) | | | | | | |
| **CELERY SEASONING** (French's) | 1 tsp. (5 grams) | 1430 | .1 | | | (0) |
| **CELERY SEED:** | | | | | | |
| Ground (Spice Islands) | 1 tsp. | 2 | | | | (0) |
| Whole (Spice Islands) | 1 tsp. | 4 | | | | (0) |
| **CELERY SOUP,** Cream of: | | | | | | |
| Condensed (USDA)[1] | 8 oz. (by wt.) | 1805 | 9.5 | 2. | 7. | |
| *Prepared with equal volume water (USDA)[1] | 1 cup (8.5 oz.) | 955 | 5.0 | 1. | 4. | |
| *Prepared with equal volume milk (USDA)[1] | 1 cup (8.6 oz.) | 1039 | 9.3 | 2. | 7. | |
| *(Campbell) | 1 cup | 930 | 4.4 | 1. | 3. | |
| *(Heinz) | 1 cup (8½ oz.) | 1010 | 6.3 | | | |
| **CEREAL BREAKFAST FOODS** (See kind of cereal such as **CORN FLAKES** or brand name such as *KIX*) | | | | | | |
| **CERVELAT** (USDA): | | | | | | |
| Dry | 1 oz. | | 10.7 | | | |
| Soft | 1 oz. | | 6.9 | | | |
| **CHABLIS WINE:** | | | | | | |
| (Gold Seal) 12% alcohol | 3 fl. oz. | 3 | 0. | | | |
| (Great Western) 12.5% alcohol | 3 fl. oz. | 31 | 0. | | | 0 |

(USDA): United States Department of Agriculture
*Prepared as Package Directs
[1]Principal sources of fat: corn oil & milk.

| Food and Description | Measure or Quantity | Sodium (mg.) | — Fats in grams — | | | Cholesterol (mg.) |
|---|---|---|---|---|---|---|
| | | | Total | Saturated | Unsaturated | |
| (Great Western) Diamond, 12.5% alcohol | 3 fl. oz. | <1 | 0. | | | 0 |
| **CHAMPAGNE:** | | | | | | |
| (Gold Seal) brut, or pink, extra dry, 12% alcohol | 3 fl. oz. (3.2 oz.) | 3 | 0. | | | (0) |
| (Great Western) regular, brut, extra dry, pink or special reserve, 12.5% alcohol | 3 fl. oz. | 31 | 0. | | | 0 |
| **CHARD,** Swiss (USDA): | | | | | | |
| Raw, whole | 1 lb. (weighed untrimmed) | 613 | 1.3 | | | 0 |
| Raw, trimmed | 4 oz. | 167 | .3 | | | 0 |
| Boiled without salt, drained | ½ cup (3.4 oz.) | 83 | .2 | | | 0 |
| **CHARLOTTE RUSSE,** with ladyfingers, whipped cream filling, home recipe (USDA)[1] | 4 oz. | 49 | 16.6 | 8. | 9. | |
| **CHAYOTE,** raw (USDA): | | | | | | |
| Whole | 1 lb. (weighed unpared) | 19 | .4 | | | 0 |
| Pared | 4 oz. | 6 | .1 | | | 0 |
| ***CHEDDAR CHEESE SOUP,** canned (Campbell) | 1 cup | 886 | 9.4 | 4. | 6. | |
| *CHEERIOS,* cereal (General Mills) | 1¼ cups (1 oz.) | 320 | 2.0 | | | (0) |
| **CHEESE:** | | | | | | |
| American or cheddar: | | | | | | |
| Natural: | | | | | | |
| (USDA) | 1 oz. | 198 | 9.1 | 5. | 4. | 28 |
| (USDA) | 1" cube (.6 oz.) | 119 | 5.5 | 3. | 2. | 17 |
| Diced (USDA) | 1 cup (4.6 oz.) | 917 | 42.2 | 24. | 19. | 130 |
| Grated or shredded (USDA) | 1 cup (3.9 oz.) | 777 | 35.7 | 20. | 16. | 110 |
| Grated or shredded (USDA) | 1 T. (7 grams) | 48 | 2.2 | 1. | 1. | 7 |
| (Kraft) | 1 oz. | 193 | 9.1 | | | |
| Cheddar (Sealtest) | 1 oz. | 193 | 9.4 | | | |
| Grated (Kraft) | 1 oz. | 836 | 6.7 | | | |

(USDA): United States Department of Agriculture
*Prepared as Package Directs
[1]Principal sources of fat: cream & egg.

| Food and Description | Measure or Quantity | Sodium (mg.) | Total | —Fats in grams— Satu- rated | Unsatu- rated | Choles- terol (mg.) |
|---|---|---|---|---|---|---|
| Shredded (Kraft) | 1 oz. | 193 | 9.1 | | | |
| Sharp cheddar, *Wispride* | 1 T. (.5 oz.) | | 4.4 | | | |
| Process: | | | | | | |
| (USDA) regular | 1 oz. | 322 | 8.5 | 5. | 4. | 25 |
| (USDA) regular | 1″ cube (.6 oz.) | 204 | 5.4 | 3. | 3. | 16 |
| (USDA) regular | 3½″ x 3⅜″ x ⅛″ slice (1 oz.) | 322 | 8.5 | 5. | 4. | 25 |
| (USDA) reduced sodium | 1 oz. | 184 | 8.5 | 5. | 4. | 25 |
| (USDA) reduced sodium | 1″ cube (.6 oz.) | 117 | 5.4 | 3. | 3. | 16 |
| (Borden) | ¾-oz. slice | 247 | 6.7 | 5. | 2. | 31 |
| (Kraft) loaf or slice | 1 oz. | 554 | 8.6 | | | |
| (Sealtest) | 1 oz. | 369 | 8.6 | | | |
| Dried, sharp cheddar (Data from General Mills Laboratory) | 1 oz. | 521 | 14.2 | | | |
| Armenian String (Sierra) | 1 oz. | | 6.2 | | | |
| Asiago (Frigo) | 1 oz. | 193 | 9.1 | | | |
| Bleu or Blue: | | | | | | |
| Natural (USDA) | 1 oz. | | 8.6 | 5. | 4. | 24 |
| Natural (USDA) | 1″ cube (.6 oz.) | | 5.2 | 3. | 2. | 15 |
| Natural, crumbled (USDA) | 1 cup (4.8 oz.) | | 41.2 | 23. | 18. | 117 |
| (Frigo) | 1 oz. | 511 | 8.2 | | | |
| (Kraft) natural | 1 oz. | 510 | 8.2 | | | |
| (Stella) | 1 oz. | | 9.1 | | | |
| *Wispride* | 2 T. (1 oz.) | | 8.8 | | | |
| Bondost (Kraft) natural | 1 oz. | 147 | 8.4 | | | |
| Brick: | | | | | | |
| (USDA) natural | 1 oz. | | 8.6 | 5. | 4. | 26 |
| (Kraft) natural | 1 oz. | 204 | 8.4 | | | |
| (Kraft) process, slices | 1 oz. | 445 | 8.3 | | | |
| Camembert, domestic: | | | | | | |
| Natural (USDA) | 1 oz. | | 7.0 | 4. | 3. | 26 |
| Natural (USDA) | 2¼″ x 2⅛″ x 1⅛″ wedge (3 to a 4-oz. pkg.) | | 9.4 | 5. | 4. | 35 |
| (Borden) | 1 oz. | 290 | 7.1 | | | |
| (Kraft) natural | 1 oz. | 295 | 7.0 | | | |
| Caraway (Kraft) natural | 1 oz. | 193 | 8.9 | | | |
| Casino Swiss (Kraft) natural | 1 oz. | 85 | 7.9 | | | |
| Chantelle, natural (Kraft) | 1 oz. | 272 | 7.4 | | | |
| Cheddar (See American) | | | | | | |
| *Cheez-ola*, process (Fisher) | 1 oz. | 454 | 6.5 | <1. | 5. | 1 |
| Colby, natural: | | | | | | |
| (USDA) | 1 oz. | | 9.1 | | | 27 |

(USDA): United States Department of Agriculture
*Prepared as Package Directs

| Food and Description | Measure or Quantity | Sodium (mg.) | — Fats in grams — | | | Cholesterol (mg.) |
|---|---|---|---|---|---|---|
| | | | Total | Saturated | Unsaturated | |
| (Kraft) | 1 oz. | 193 | 9.0 | | | |
| Cottage cheese: | | | | | | |
| Creamed, unflavored: | | | | | | |
| (USDA) | 1 oz. | 65 | 1.2 | <1. | <1. | 5 |
| (USDA) | 8-oz. pkg. | 520 | 9.5 | 5. | 5. | 43 |
| (USDA) | 1 packed cup (8.6 oz.) | 561 | 10.3 | 5. | 5. | 47 |
| (USDA) | 1 T. (.5 oz.) | 34 | .6 | Tr. | Tr. | 3 |
| (Borden) | 8-oz. container | 519 | 9.5 | 4. | 5. | 34 |
| (Kraft) | 1 oz. | 141 | 1.2 | | | |
| (Sealtest) | 1 cup (7.9 oz.) | 907 | 9.2 | | | |
| *California* (Breakstone) | 8-oz. container | 920 | 9.3 | | | 24 |
| *California* (Breakstone) | 1 T. (.6 oz.) | 64 | .6 | | | 2 |
| *Light n' Lively* (Sealtest) | 1 cup (7.9 oz.) | 916 | 2.2 | | | |
| *Lite Line* (Borden) | 1 cup | 970 | 4.5 | | | |
| Low fat (Breakstone) | 8-oz. container | 1168 | 4.1 | | | 11 |
| Low fat (Breakstone) | 1 T. (.6 oz.) | 82 | .3 | | | <1 |
| Low fat, 2% fat (Sealtest) | 1 cup (7.9 oz.) | 934 | 4.5 | | | |
| Tangy small curd (Breakstone) | 8-oz. container | 920 | 9.3 | | | 24 |
| Tangy small curd (Breakstone) | 1 T. (.6 oz.) | 64 | .6 | | | 2 |
| Tiny soft curd (Breakstone) | 8-oz. container | 920 | 9.3 | | | 24 |
| Tiny soft curd (Breakstone) | 1 T. (.6 oz.) | 64 | .6 | | | 2 |
| Creamed, flavored: | | | | | | |
| Chive (Breakstone) | 8-oz. container | 920 | 9.3 | | | 24 |
| Chive (Breakstone) | 1 T. (.6 oz.) | 64 | .6 | | | 2 |
| Chive (Sealtest) | 1 cup (7.9 oz.) | 907 | 9.2 | | | |
| Chive-pepper (Sealtest) | 1 cup (7.9 oz.) | 853 | 9.0 | | | |
| Peach, low fat (Breakstone) | 8-oz. container | 784 | 4.3 | | | 11 |
| Peach, low fat (Breakstone) | 1 T. (.6 oz.) | 57 | .3 | | | <1 |
| Peach-pineapple (Sealtest) | 1 cup (7.9 oz.) | 728 | 7.6 | | | |
| Pineapple, low fat (Breakstone) | 8-oz. container | 784 | 4.3 | | | 11 |
| Pineapple, low fat (Breakstone) | 1 T. (.6 oz.) | 56 | .3 | | | 6 |
| Pineapple (Sealtest) | 1 cup (7.9 oz.) | 726 | 7.6 | | | |
| *Spring Garden Salad* (Sealtest) | 1 cup (7.9 oz.) | 903 | 9.4 | | | |
| Uncreamed: | | | | | | |
| (USDA) | 8-oz. pkg. | 658 | .7 | | | 16 |
| (USDA) | 1 oz. | 82 | <.1 | | | 2 |
| (USDA) | 1 packed cup (7 oz.) | 580 | .6 | | | 14 |
| (Sealtest) | 1 cup (7.9 oz.) | 13 | .7 | | | |
| Pot, unsalted (Borden) | 8-oz. pkg. | 45 | .7 | Tr. | Tr. | 3 |

(USDA): United States Department of Agriculture
*Prepared as Package Directs

| Food and Description | Measure or Quantity | Sodium (mg.) | Total | Fats in grams Satu- rated | Unsatu- rated | Choles- terol (mg.) |
|---|---|---|---|---|---|---|
| Pot style (Breakstone) | 8-oz. container | 920 | .7 | | | 0 |
| Pot style (Breakstone) | 1 T. (.6 oz.) | 64 | Tr. | | | 0 |
| Skim milk (Breakstone) | 8-oz. container | 16 | .7 | | | 0 |
| Skim milk (Breakstone) | 1 T. (.6 oz.) | 1 | Tr. | | | 0 |
| *Country Charm*, natural (Fisher) | 1 oz. | | 7.4 | | | 22 |
| Cream cheese: | | | | | | |
| Plain, unwhipped: | | | | | | |
| (USDA) | 1 oz. | 71 | 10.7 | 6. | 5. | 31 |
| (USDA) | 3-oz. pkg. (2⅞" x ⅞") | 212 | 32.0 | 18. | 14. | 94 |
| (USDA) | 8-oz. pkg. | 568 | 85.6 | 48. | 38. | 252 |
| (USDA) | ½ cup (4.1 oz.) | 288 | 43.4 | 24. | 19. | 128 |
| (USDA) | 1" cube (.6 oz.) | 40 | 6.0 | 3. | 3. | 18 |
| (USDA) | 1 T. (.5 oz.) | 35 | 5.3 | 3. | 2. | 16 |
| (Breakstone) | 1 oz. | 25 | 9.5 | | | 113 |
| (Breakstone) | 1 T. (.5 oz.) | 12 | 4.8 | | | 56 |
| (Kraft) | 1 oz. | 113 | 9.7 | | | |
| (Sealtest) | 1 oz. | 114 | 9.5 | | | |
| *Hostess* (Kraft) | 1 oz. | 113 | 9.5 | | | |
| *Philadelphia* (Kraft) | 1 oz. | 113 | 9.7 | | | |
| *Philadelphia*, imitation (Kraft) | 1 oz. | 204 | 3.4 | | | |
| Plain, whipped (Breakstone): | | | | | | |
| *Temp-Tee* | 1 oz. | 25 | 9.5 | | | 113 |
| *Temp-Tee* | 1 T. (9 grams) | 8 | 3.1 | | | 37 |
| Flavored, unwhipped: | | | | | | |
| Chive (Kraft) *Hostess* | 1 oz. | 170 | 8.0 | | | |
| Chive (Kraft) *Philadelphia* | 1 oz. | 170 | 8.0 | | | |
| Olive-pimento (Kraft) *Hostess* | 1 oz. | 193 | 8.3 | | | |
| Pimento (Kraft) *Hostess* | 1 oz. | 170 | 8.2 | | | |
| Pimento (Kraft) *Philadelphia* | 1 oz. | 170 | 8.2 | | | |
| Pineapple (Kraft) *Hostess* | 1 oz. | 125 | 7.8 | | | |
| Roquefort (Kraft) *Hostess* | 1 oz. | 261 | 7.5 | | | |
| Flavored, whipped (Kraft): | | | | | | |
| Bacon & horseradish | 1 oz. | 159 | 9.4 | | | |
| Blue | 1 oz. | 169 | 9.3 | | | |
| *Catalina* | 1 oz. | 261 | 9.1 | | | |
| Chive | 1 oz. | 170 | 8.8 | | | |
| Onion | 1 oz. | 180 | 8.8 | | | |
| Pimento | 1 oz. | 181 | 8.6 | | | |
| Salami | 1 oz. | 126 | 8.3 | | | |
| Smoked salmon | 1 oz. | 170 | 8.2 | | | |
| Edam: | | | | | | |
| Natural (USDA) | 1 oz. | | 7.9 | | | 29 |

(USDA): United States Department of Agriculture
*Prepared as Package Directs

| Food and Description | Measure or Quantity | Sodium (mg.) | —Fats in grams— | | | Choles- terol (mg.) |
|---|---|---|---|---|---|---|
| | | | Total | Satu- rated | Unsatu- rated | |
| (House of Gold) | 1 oz. | 204 | 7.9 | | | |
| Natural (Kraft) | 1 oz. | 204 | 7.9 | | | |
| Farmer, midget (Breakstone) | 1 oz. | 111 | 2.3 | | | 6 |
| Farmer, midget (Breakstone) | 1 T. (.5 oz.) | 53 | 1.1 | | | 3 |
| Fontina, natural (Kraft) | 1 oz. | 204 | 9.2 | | | |
| Fontina (Stella) | 1 oz. | | 9.1 | | | |
| Frankenmuth, natural (Kraft) | 1 oz. | 193 | 9.1 | | | |
| Gjetost, natural (Kraft) | 1 oz. | 170 | 8.2 | | | |
| Gorgonzola, natural (Kraft) | 1 oz. | 397 | 9.1 | | | |
| Gouda, natural (Kraft) | 1 oz. | 204 | 8.5 | | | |
| Gruyère: | | | | | | |
| Natural (Kraft) | 1 oz. | 91 | 8.4 | | | |
| *Swiss Knight* | 1 oz. | | 8.5 | | | |
| Jack-dry, natural (Kraft) | 1 oz. | 204 | 8.2 | | | |
| Jack-fresh, natural (Kraft) | 1 oz. | 181 | 7.7 | | | |
| Lager-Kase, natural (Kraft) | 1 oz. | 215 | 8.8 | | | |
| Leyden, natural (Kraft) | 1 oz. | 204 | 3.8 | | | |
| *Liederkranz* (Borden) | 1 oz. | 271 | 7.3 | | | |
| Limburger: | | | | | | |
| Natural (USDA) | 1 oz. | | 7.9 | 4. | 4. | 28 |
| Natural (Kraft) | 1 oz. | 227 | 7.9 | | | |
| Monterey Jack (Frigo) | 1 oz. | 204 | 8.3 | | | |
| Monterey Jack, natural (Kraft) | 1 oz. | 204 | 8.3 | | | |
| Mozzarella: | | | | | | |
| Low moisture, natural (USDA) | 1 oz. | | 7.5 | | | 27 |
| Low moisture, part-skim, natural (USDA) | 1 oz. | | 5.9 | | | 18 |
| (Frigo) | 1 oz. | 227 | 4.7 | | | |
| (Sierra) | 1 oz. | | 6.2 | | | |
| Low moisture, part-skim, natural (Kraft) | 1 oz. | 227 | 5.6 | | | |
| Low moisture part-skim, pizza, natural (Kraft) | 1 oz. | 227 | 4.7 | | | |
| Shredded (Kraft) | 1 oz. | 227 | 4.7 | | | |
| Muenster: | | | | | | |
| Natural (USDA) | 1 oz. | | 8.6 | | | 25 |
| Natural (Borden) | 1 oz. | | | | | |
| Natural (Kraft) | 1 oz. | 204 | 8.1 | | | |
| Process, slices (Kraft) | 1 oz. | 366 | 8.3 | | | |
| Neufchâtel: | | | | | | |
| Natural (USDA) | 2⅞" x 2" x ⅞" pkg. (3 oz.) | | 20.4 | | | 64 |
| Natural (Kraft) *Calorie-Wise* | 1 oz. | 113 | 6.1 | | | |

(USDA): United States Department of Agriculture
*Prepared as Package Directs

| Food and Description | Measure or Quantity | Sodium (mg.) | —Fats in grams— Total | Satu- rated | Unsatu- rated | Choles- terol (mg.) |
|---|---|---|---|---|---|---|
| Process (Borden) | 1 oz. | 149 | 6.5 | | | |
| *Nuworld*, natural (Kraft) | 1 oz. | 397 | 8.4 | | | |
| Old English, process, loaf or slices (Kraft) | 1 oz. | 445 | 8.6 | | | |
| Parmesan: | | | | | | |
| Natural: | | | | | | |
| (USDA) | 1 oz. | 208 | 7.4 | 4. | 3. | 27 |
| (Frigo) | 1 oz. | 341 | 6.7 | | | |
| (Kraft) | 1 oz. | 340 | 6.7 | | | |
| (Stella) | 1 oz. | | 7.5 | | | |
| Grated: | | | | | | |
| Natural (USDA) | 1 oz. | 247 | 9.4 | | | 32 |
| Natural (USDA) | 1 cup loosely packed (3.7 oz.) | 923 | 35.2 | | | 120 |
| Natural (USDA) | 1 cup pressed down (4.9 oz.) | 1219 | 46.5 | | | 158 |
| Natural (USDA) | 1 T. loosely packed (7 grams) | 58 | 2.2 | | | 8 |
| Natural (USDA) | 1 T. pressed down (9 grams) | 78 | 3.0 | | | 10 |
| (Borden) | 1 oz. | 323 | 7.1 | | | |
| (Buitoni) | 1 oz. | | 7.4 | | | |
| (Frigo) | 1 T. (6 grams) | 88 | 1.7 | | | |
| (Kraft) | 1 oz. | 408 | 7.9 | | | |
| Shredded (Kraft) | 1 oz. | 363 | 7.1 | | | |
| Parmesan & Romano, grated: | | | | | | |
| (Borden) natural | 1 oz. | | 8.6 | | | |
| (Kraft) | 1 oz. | 411 | 8.2 | | | |
| Pepato (Frigo) | 1 oz. | 341 | 7.7 | | | |
| Pimento American, process: | | | | | | |
| (USDA) | 1 oz. | | 8.6 | 4. | 4. | |
| Loaf or slices (Kraft) | 1 oz. | 445 | 8.5 | | | |
| Pinconning, natural (Kraft) | 1 oz. | 193 | 9.1 | | | |
| Pizza: | | | | | | |
| (Frigo) | 1 oz. | 227 | 3.8 | | | |
| Low fat, part skim, shredded (Kraft) | 1 oz. | 284 | 5.5 | | | |
| Port du Salut, natural (Kraft) | 1 oz. | 227 | 8.0 | | | |
| Primost, natural (Kraft) | 1 oz. | 170 | 8.2 | | | |
| Provolone: | | | | | | |
| Natural (USDA) | 1 oz. | | 7.8 | | | 28 |
| (Frigo) | 1 oz. | 284 | 7.6 | | | |
| Natural (Kraft) | 1 oz. | 284 | 7.6 | | | |

(USDA): United States Department of Agriculture
*Prepared as Package Directs

| Food and Description | Measure or Quantity | Sodium (mg.) | —Fats in grams— Total | Satu- rated | Unsatu- rated | Choles- terol (mg.) |
|---|---|---|---|---|---|---|
| Ricotta: | | | | | | |
| Natural (USDA) | 1 oz. | | 3.7 | | | 14 |
| Part skim, natural (USDA) | 1 oz. | | 2.3 | | | 9 |
| (Breakstone) | 1 oz. | 42 | 3.1 | | | 8 |
| (Breakstone) | 1 T. (.6 oz.) | 24 | 1.7 | | | 5 |
| Natural (Kraft) | 1 oz. | 23 | 3.3 | | | |
| (Sierra) | 1 oz. | | 3.6 | | | |
| Romano: | | | | | | |
| (Frigo) | 1 oz. | 341 | 7.7 | | | |
| Natural (Stella) | 1 oz. | | 7.8 | | | |
| Grated: | | | | | | |
| (Borden) | 1 oz. | 488 | 6.2 | | | |
| (Buitoni) | 1 oz. | | 8.1 | | | |
| (Frigo) | 1 T. (6 grams) | 90 | 2.0 | | | |
| (Kraft) | 1 oz. | 420 | 9.4 | | | |
| Shredded (Kraft) | 1 oz. | 374 | 8.5 | | | |
| Romano & Parmesan: | | | | | | |
| Plain (Kraft) | 1 oz. | 417 | 9.0 | | | |
| Flavored (Kraft): | | | | | | |
| Bacon smoke | 1 oz. | 562 | 8.6 | | | |
| Garlic | 1 oz. | 401 | 9.0 | | | |
| Onion | 1 oz. | 401 | 9.0 | | | |
| Roquefort, natural: | | | | | | |
| (USDA) | 1 oz. | | 8.6 | 4. | 4. | |
| (USDA) | 1″ cube (.6 oz.) | | 5.2 | 3. | 2 | |
| (Kraft) | 1 oz. | 465 | 8.8 | | | |
| Sage, natural (Kraft) | 1 oz. | 193 | 9.1 | | | |
| Sap Sago, natural (Kraft) | 1 oz. | 510 | 2.6 | | | |
| Sardo Romano, natural (Kraft) | 1 oz. | 397 | 7.7 | | | |
| Scamorze: | | | | | | |
| (Frigo) | 1 oz. | 227 | 4.7 | | | |
| Natural (Kraft) | 1 oz. | 215 | 7.7 | | | |
| Special cure, process, slices | | | | | | |
| (Kraft) | 1 oz. | 403 | 8.6 | | | |
| Supercure, process, slices | | | | | | |
| (Kraft) | 1 oz. | 403 | 8.6 | | | |
| Swiss, domestic: | | | | | | |
| Natural: | | | | | | |
| (USDA) | 1 oz. | 201 | 7.9 | 4. | 4. | 28 |
| (USDA) | 1″ cube (.5 oz.) | 106 | 4.2 | 2. | 2. | 15 |
| (USDA) | 1¼-oz. slice (7½″ x 4″ x ¹/₁₆″) | 248 | 9.8 | 5. | 5. | 35 |
| (Kraft) | 1 oz. | 85 | 7.9 | | | |

(USDA): United States Department of Agriculture
*Prepared as Package Directs

| Food and Description | Measure or Quantity | Sodium (mg.) | —Fats in grams— Total | Satu- rated | Unsatu- rated | Choles- terol (mg.) |
|---|---|---|---|---|---|---|
| (Sealtest) | 1 oz. | 85 | 8.0 | | | |
| Process: | | | | | | |
| (USDA) regular | 1-oz. slice (3½″ x 3⅜″ x ⅛″) | 331 | 7.6 | 4. | 3. | 26 |
| (USDA) regular | 1″ cube (.6 oz.) | 210 | 4.8 | 3. | 2. | 17 |
| (USDA) reduced sodium | 1-oz. slice (3½″ x 3⅜″ x ⅛″) | 193 | 7.6 | 4. | 3. | 26 |
| (USDA) reduced sodium | 1″ cube (.6 oz.) | 126 | 4.8 | 3. | 2. | 17 |
| (Borden) | 1-oz. slice | 308 | 7.0 | 5. | 2. | 37 |
| (Borden) | ¾-oz. slice | 231 | 5.2 | 4. | 2. | 28 |
| (Kraft) slices | 1 oz. | 445 | 7.1 | | | |
| With Muenster (Kraft) loaf | 1 oz. | 456 | 7.8 | | | |
| Washed curd, natural (Kraft) | 1 oz. | 193 | 8.6 | | | |
| **CHEESE CAKE,** frozen (Mrs. Smith's) | ¹/₆ of 8″ cake (4 oz.) | 320 | 11.3 | | | |
| **CHEESE CAKE MIX:** | | | | | | |
| *(Jell-O) | ⅛ of cake including crust (3.3 oz.) | 359 | 11.6 | | | 23 |
| *(Royal) *No-Bake* | ⅛ of 9″ cake including crust (3.2 oz.) | 400 | 10.8 | | | 8 |
| **CHEESE DIP** (See **DIP**) | | | | | | |
| **CHEESE FONDUE,** home recipe (USDA) | 4 oz. | 615 | 20.8 | 10. | 10. | |
| **CHEESE FOOD,** process: | | | | | | |
| American: | | | | | | |
| (USDA) | 1-oz. slice (3½″ x 3⅜″ x ⅛″) | | 6.8 | 4. | 3. | 20 |
| (USDA) | 1″ cube (.6 oz.) | | 4.3 | 2. | 2. | 13 |
| (USDA) | 1 T. (.5 oz.) | | 3 | 2. | 2. | 10 |
| (Borden) | 1″ x 1″ x 1 piece (.8 oz.) | 356 | 5.0 | | | 34 |
| Grated (Borden) | 1 oz. | 717 | 6.7 | | | |
| Grated, used in *Kraft Dinner* | 1 oz. | 769 | 6.7 | | | |
| Slices (Kraft) | 1 oz. | 396 | 6.9 | | | |
| Cheez'n bacon, slices (Kraft) | ¾-oz. slice | 343 | 6.2 | | | |
| Links (Kraft) *Handi-Snack:* | | | | | | |
| Bacon | 1 oz. | 393 | 6.9 | | | |
| Garlic | 1 oz. | 393 | 6.8 | | | |

(USDA): United States Department of Agriculture
*Prepared as Package Directs

| Food and Description | Measure or Quantity | Sodium (mg.) | — Fats in grams — | | | Choles- terol (mg.) |
|---|---|---|---|---|---|---|
| | | | Total | Satu- rated | Unsatu- rated | |
| Jalapeño | 1 oz. | 404 | 6.8 | | | |
| *Nippy* | 1 oz. | 393 | 6.8 | | | |
| *Smokelle* | 1 oz. | 393 | 7.0 | | | |
| Swiss | 1 oz. | 414 | 6.7 | | | |
| Loaf: | | | | | | |
| Munst-ett (Kraft) | 1 oz. | 553 | 8.0 | | | |
| *Pizzalone*, loaf (Kraft) | 1 oz. | 442 | 6.6 | | | |
| Super blend (Kraft) | 1 oz. | 376 | 6.9 | | | |
| Pimento, slices (Kraft) | 1 oz. | 405 | 6.8 | | | |
| Salami, slices (Kraft) | 1 oz. | 390 | 6.8 | | | |
| Swiss (Borden) | .7-oz. slice | 265 | 5.0 | 4. | 1. | 20 |
| Swiss (Borden) | .8-oz. slice | 290 | 5.5 | 4. | 1. | 22 |
| Swiss, slices (Kraft) | 1 oz. | 396 | 6.6 | | | |
| **CHEESE PIE:** | | | | | | |
| (Tastykake) | 4-oz. pie | | 15.0 | | | |
| Frozen, pineapple (Mrs. Smith's) | ¹/₆ of 8″ pie (4 oz.) | 415 | 11.8 | | | |
| Frozen, pineapple (Mrs. Smith's) | ¹/₈ of 10″ pie (5.4 oz.) | 523 | 14.5 | | | |
| **CHEESE PUFF,** frozen (Durkee) | 1 piece (.5 oz.) | | 5.8 | | | |
| **CHEESE SOUFFLE:** | | | | | | |
| Home recipe (USDA)[1] | 4 oz. | 413 | 19.4 | 10. | 9. | 189 |
| Home recipe (USDA)[1] | ¼ of 7″ soufflé (3.9 oz.) | 400 | 18.8 | 10. | 9. | 184 |
| Frozen (Stouffer's) | ⅓ of 12-oz. pkg. | 606 | 16.7 | | | |
| **CHEESE SPREAD:** | | | | | | |
| American, process: | | | | | | |
| (USDA) regular | 1 oz. (2¾″ x 2¼″ x ¼″) | 461 | 6.1 | | | 18 |
| (USDA) regular | 1 T. (.5 oz.) | 228 | 3.0 | | | 9 |
| (USDA) regular shredded | 1 packed cup (4 oz.) | 1836 | 24.2 | | | 72 |
| (USDA) reduced sodium | 1 oz. (2¾″ x 2¼″ x ¼″) | 323 | 6.1 | | | 18 |
| (USDA) reduced sodium | 1 T. (.5 oz.) | 159 | 3.0 | | | 9 |
| (USDA) reduced sodium | 1 packed cup (4 oz.) | 1287 | 24.2 | | | 72 |
| (Borden) | 1 oz. | 403 | 6.1 | 4. | 2. | 44 |
| (Borden) Vera Sharp | 1 oz. | | 5.7 | | | |
| (Kraft) *Swankyswig* | 1 oz. | 490 | 5.8 | | | |
| (Nabisco) *Snack Mate* | 1 tsp. (5 grams) | 65 | 1.1 | | | |
| Bacon, process (Kraft): | | | | | | |
| *Squeez-A-Snak* | 1 oz. | 516 | 6.9 | | | |

(USDA): United States Department of Agriculture
*Prepared as Package Directs
[1]Principal sources of fat: butter, cheese, egg & milk.

| Food and Description | Measure or Quantity | Sodium (mg.) | Total | — Fats in grams — Satu- rated | Unsatu- rated | Choles- terol (mg.) |
|---|---|---|---|---|---|---|
| *Swankyswig* | 1 oz. | 366 | 7.6 | | | |
| Cheddar, process (Nabisco) | | | | | | |
| *Snack Mate* | 1 tsp. (5 grams) | 62 | 1.1 | | | |
| Cheddar, seasoned, process | | | | | | |
| (Nabisco) *Snack Mate* | 1 tsp. (5 grams) | 58 | 1.1 | | | |
| *Cheez Whiz*, process (Kraft) | 1 oz. | 465 | 5.8 | | | |
| *Count Down* (Fisher) | 1 oz. | 439 | .3 | Tr. | Tr. | 1 |
| Garlic, process: | | | | | | |
| (Kraft) *Squeez-A-Snak* | 1 oz. | 530 | 7.0 | | | |
| (Kraft) *Swankyswig* | 1 oz. | 366 | 6.5 | | | |
| Hickory smoke, process | | | | | | |
| (Nabisco) *Snack Mate* | 1 tsp. (5 grams) | 64 | 1.1 | | | |
| Imitation (Fisher) *Chef's* | | | | | | |
| *Delight* | 1 oz. | 380 | 1.1 | | | 3 |
| Imitation (Fisher) | | | | | | |
| *Mellow Age* | 1 oz. | 380 | 1.1 | | | 3 |
| Imitation, process (Kraft) | | | | | | |
| *Calorie-Wise or Tasty-loaf* | 1 oz. | 488 | 1.7 | | | |
| Jalapeño, process (Kraft) | | | | | | |
| *Cheez Whiz* | 1 oz. | 445 | 5.7 | | | |
| Limburger natural (Kraft) | 1 oz. | 431 | 5.8 | | | |
| Neufchâtel: | | | | | | |
| Bacon & horseradish (Kraft) | | | | | | |
| *Party Snacks* | 1 oz. | 170 | 6.8 | | | |
| Chipped beef (Kraft) *Party* | | | | | | |
| *Snacks* | 1 oz. | 227 | 6.0 | | | |
| Chive (Kraft) *Party Snacks* | 1 oz. | 170 | 6.2 | | | |
| Clam (Kraft) *Party Snacks* | 1 oz. | 170 | 5.8 | | | |
| Olive-pimento (Kraft) | | | | | | |
| *Swankyswig* | 1 oz. | 204 | 6.5 | | | |
| Onion (Kraft) *Party Snacks* | 1 oz. | 242 | 6.1 | | | |
| Pimento (Kraft) *Party Snacks* | 1 oz. | 159 | 5.8 | | | |
| Pimento (Kraft) *Swankyswig* | 1 oz. | 125 | 5.8 | | | |
| Pineapple (Kraft) *Swankyswig* | 1 oz. | 102 | 5.8 | | | |
| Relish (Kraft) *Swankyswig* | 1 oz. | 136 | 5.8 | | | |
| Roka (Kraft) *Swankyswig* | 1 oz. | 295 | 7.5 | | | |
| Old English, process (Kraft) | | | | | | |
| *Swankyswig* | 1 oz. | 366 | 8.1 | | | |
| Onion, French, process (Nabisco) | | | | | | |
| *Snack Mate* | 1 tsp. (5 grams) | 65 | 1.1 | | | |
| Pimento: | | | | | | |
| (Kraft) *Cheez Whiz* | 1 oz. | 465 | 5.8 | | | |
| Process (Kraft) *Squeez-A-Snak* | 1 oz. | 556 | 7.3 | | | |

(USDA): United States Department of Agriculture
*Prepared as Package Directs

| Food and Description | Measure or Quantity | Sodium (mg.) | —Fats in grams — | | | Choles-terol (mg.) |
|---|---|---|---|---|---|---|
| | | | Total | Satu-rated | Unsatu-rated | |
| Process (Nabisco) *Snack Mate* | 1 tsp. (5 grams) | 60 | 1.1 | | | |
| (Sealtest) | 1 oz. | 239 | 5.8 | | | |
| *Velveeta*, process (Kraft) | 1 oz. | 462 | 5.8 | | | |
| Sharp, process (Kraft) *Squeez-A-Snak* | 1 oz. | 496 | 7.2 | | | |
| *Sharpie*, process (Kraft) | 1 oz. | 420 | 7.3 | | | |
| Smoke, process (Kraft) *Squeez-A-Snak* | 1 oz. | 519 | 6.9 | | | |
| *Smokelle*, process (Kraft) *Swankyswig* | 1 oz. | 366 | 7.2 | | | |
| *Velva Kreme*, process (Borden) | 1 oz. | 106 | 9.2 | 3. | 6. | |
| *Velveeta*, process (Kraft) | 1 oz. | 462 | 5.8 | | | |
| **CHEESE STRAW:** | | | | | | |
| Made with lard (USDA)[1] | 1 oz. | 204 | 8.5 | 4. | 5. | 9 |
| Made with lard (USDA)[1] | 5″ x ⅜″ x ⅜″ piece (6 grams) | 43 | 1.8 | <1. | 1. | 2 |
| Made with vegetable shortening (USDA)[2] | 1 oz. | 204 | 8.5 | 3. | 6. | |
| Frozen (Durkee) | 1 piece (8 grams) | | 2.2 | | | |
| **CHELOIS WINE** (Great Western) 12.5% alcohol | 3 fl. oz. | 37 | 0. | | | 0 |
| **CHERIMOYA,** raw (USDA): | | | | | | |
| Whole | 1 lb. (weighed with skin &seeds) | | 1.1 | | | 0 |
| Flesh only | 4 oz. | | .5 | | | 0 |
| ***CHERRI-BERRI,*** soft drink (Hoffman) | 6 fl. oz. | 15 | 0. | | | (0) |
| **CHERRY:** | | | | | | |
| Sour: | | | | | | |
| Fresh (USDA): | | | | | | |
| Whole | 1 lb. (weighed with stems) | 7 | 1.1 | | | 0 |
| Whole | 1 lb. (weighed without stems) | 8 | 1.3 | | | 0 |
| Pitted | ½ cup (2.7 oz.) | 2 | .2 | | | 0 |
| Canned. syrup pack. pitted (USDA): | | | | | | |
| Light syrup | 4 oz. (with liq.) | 1 | .2 | | | 0 |

(USDA): United States Department of Agriculture
*Prepared as Package Directs
[1]Principal sources of fat: lard & milk.
[2]Principal sources of fat: vegetable shortening. milk & lard.

| Food and Description | Measure or Quantity | Sodium (mg.) | —Fats in grams— | | | Cholesterol (mg.) |
|---|---|---|---|---|---|---|
| | | | Total | Saturated | Unsaturated | |
| Heavy syrup | 4 oz. (with liq.) | 1 | .2 | | | 0 |
| Heavy syrup | ½ cup (4.6 oz.) | 1 | .3 | | | 0 |
| Extra heavy syrup | 4 oz. (with liq.) | 1 | .2 | | | 0 |
| Canned, water pack, pitted, solids & liq.: | | | | | | |
| (USDA) | ½ cup (4.3 oz.) | 2 | .2 | | | 0 |
| (Stokely-Van Camp) | ½ cup (4 oz.) | | .2 | | | |
| Frozen, pitted (USDA): | | | | | | |
| Sweetened | ½ cup (4.6 oz.) | 3 | .5 | | | 0 |
| Unsweetened | 4 oz. | 2 | .5 | | | 0 |
| Sweet: | | | | | | |
| Fresh (USDA): | | | | | | |
| Whole, with stems | 1 lb. (weighed with stems) | 8 | 1.2 | | | 0 |
| Whole, with stems | ½ cup (2.3 oz.) | 1 | .2 | | | 0 |
| Pitted | ½ cup (2.9 oz.) | 2 | .2 | | | 0 |
| Canned, syrup pack, with pits, solids & liq.: | | | | | | |
| Light syrup (USDA) | 4 oz. | 1 | .2 | | | 0 |
| Heavy syrup (USDA) | 4 oz. | 1 | .2 | | | 0 |
| Heavy syrup, dark (Del Monte) | ½ cup (4.3 oz.) | 2 | .6 | | | 0 |
| Heavy syrup, Royal Anne (Del Monte) | ½ cup (4.6 oz.) | 2 | .5 | | | 0 |
| Heavy syrup, light or dark (Stokely-Van Camp) | ½ cup (4.2 oz.) | | .2 | | | (0) |
| Extra heavy syrup (USDA) | 4 oz. | 1 | .2 | | | 0 |
| Canned, syrup pack, pitted, solids & liq.: | | | | | | |
| Light syrup (USDA) | 4 oz. | 1 | .2 | | | 0 |
| Heavy syrup (USDA) | 4 oz. | 1 | .2 | | | 0 |
| Heavy syrup (USDA) | ½ cup (4.2 oz.) | 1 | .2 | | | 0 |
| Heavy syrup (Del Monte) | ½ cup (4.3 oz.) | 6 | 1.5 | | | (0) |
| Extra heavy syrup (USDA) | 4 oz. | 1 | .2 | | | 0 |
| Canned, water pack, with pits, solids & liq. (USDA) | 4 oz. | 1 | .2 | | | 0 |
| Canned, water or dietetic pack, pitted, solids & liq.: | | | | | | |
| (USDA) | 4 oz. | 1 | .2 | | | 0 |
| (Blue Boy) | 4 oz. | 1 | Tr. | | | (0) |
| Royal Anne: | | | | | | |
| (Diet Delight) | ½ cup (4.4 oz.) | 6 | Tr. | | | (0) |

(USDA): United States Department of Agriculture
*Prepared as Package Directs

| Food and Description | Measure or Quantity | Sodium (mg.) | —Fats in grams— | | Choles- terol (mg.) |
|---|---|---|---|---|---|
| | | | Total | Satu- rated | Unsatu- rated | |

| Food and Description | Measure or Quantity | Sodium (mg.) | Total | Satu- rated | Unsatu- rated | Choles- terol (mg.) |
|---|---|---|---|---|---|---|
| (S and W) *Nutradiet*, low calorie | 14 whole cherries (3.5 oz.) | 3 | Tr. | | | (0) |
| (S and W) *Nutradiet*, unsweetened | 14 whole cherries (3.5 oz.) | 2 | Tr. | | | (0) |
| (Tillie Lewis) | ½ cup (4.5 oz.) | <10 | .2 | | | 0 |
| Dark (S and W) *Nutradiet*, low calorie | 4 oz. | 1 | .1 | | | (0) |
| Frozen, quick-thaw (Birds Eye) | ½ cup (5 oz.) | 3 | .3 | | | 0 |

**CHERRY, BLACK, SOFT DRINK (See CHERRY SOFT DRINK)**

**CHERRY CAKE:**

| | | | | | | |
|---|---|---|---|---|---|---|
| *Mix (Duncan Hines) | 1/12 of cake (2.6 oz.) | 299 | 5.2 | | | |
| *Mix, chip, layer (Betty Crocker) | 1/12 of cake | 278 | 4.8 | | | |
| *Mix, upside down (Betty Crocker) | 1/9 of cake | 226 | 10.2 | | | |

**CHERRY, CANDIED (USDA)** 1 oz. .6 0

**CHERRY COLA (See COLA SOFT DRINK)**

**CHERRY DRINK (Hi-C)** 6 fl. oz. (6.3 oz.) Tr. Tr. 0

**CHERRY, MARASCHINO (USDA)** 1 oz. (with liq.) <.1 0

**CHERRY PIE:**

| | | | | | | |
|---|---|---|---|---|---|---|
| Home recipe, made with lard, 2 crust (USDA)[1] | 1/6 of 9″ pie (5.6 oz.) | 480 | 17.9 | 6. | 12. | |
| Home recipe, made with vegetable shortening, 2 crust (USDA)[2] | 1/6 of 9″ pie (5.6 oz.) | 480 | 17.9 | 5. | 13. | |
| (Hostess) | 4½-oz. pie | 637 | 10.8 | | | |
| Cherry-apple (Tastykake) | 4-oz. pie | | 14.7 | | | |
| Frozen: | | | | | | |
| Unbaked (USDA) | 5 oz. | 287 | 15.1 | 4. | 11. | |
| Baked (USDA) | 5 oz. | 325 | 17.0 | 4. | 13. | |
| (Banquet) | 5-oz. serving | | 15.0 | | | |
| (Morton) | 1/6 of 20-oz. pie | 239 | 10.9 | | | |
| (Morton) | 1/6 of 24-oz. pie | 407 | 18.4 | | | |
| (Morton) | 1/8 of 46-oz. pie | 299 | 16.7 | | | |

(USDA): United States Department of Agriculture
*Prepared as Package Directs
[1]Principal sources of fat: lard & butter.
[2]Principal sources of fat: vegetable shortening & butter.

| Food and Description | Measure or Quantity | Sodium (mg.) | Fats in grams Total | Satu- rated | Unsatu- rated | Choles- terol (mg.) |
|---|---|---|---|---|---|---|
| (Mrs. Smith's) | ¹/₆ of 8″ pie (4.3 oz.) | 302 | 14.2 | | | |
| (Mrs. Smith's) old fashion | ¹/₆ of 9″ pie (4.3 oz.) | 470 | 23.2 | | | |
| (Mrs. Smith's) golden deluxe | ⅛ of 10″ pie (5.6 oz.) | 410 | 18.4 | | | |
| Tart (Pepperidge Farm) | 3-oz. pie tart | 196 | 14.9 | | | |
| **CHERRY PIE FILLING:** | | | | | | |
| (Comstock) | 1 cup (10¾ oz.) | 240 | .5 | | | |
| (Lucky Leaf) | 8 oz. | 104 | .4 | | | |
| **CHERRY PRESERVE or JAM:** | | | | | | |
| Sweetened (Bama) | 1 T. (.7 oz.) | 2 | <.1 | | | |
| Dietetic or low calorie (S and W) | | | | | | |
| *Nutradiet* | 1 T. (.5 oz.) | | Tr. | | | (0) |
| **CHERRY SOFT DRINK:** | | | | | | |
| Sweetened: | | | | | | |
| (Canada Dry) bottle or can | 6 fl. oz. | 13+ | 0. | | | 0 |
| (Clicquot Club) | 6 fl. oz. | 12 | 0. | | | 0 |
| (Cott) | 6 fl. oz. | 12 | 0. | | | 0 |
| (Dr. Brown's) black | 6 fl. oz. | 14 | 0. | | | 0 |
| (Fanta) | 6 fl. oz. | 7 | 0. | | | 0 |
| (Hoffman) black | 6 fl. oz. | 14 | 0. | | | 0 |
| (Key Food) black | 6 fl. oz. | 14 | 0. | | | 0 |
| (Kirsch) black | 6 fl. oz. | <1 | 0. | | | 0 |
| (Mission) | 6 fl. oz. | 12 | 0. | | | 0 |
| (Nedick's) black | 6 fl. oz. | 14 | 0. | | | 0 |
| (Shasta) black | 6 fl. oz. | 22 | 0. | | | 0 |
| (Waldbaum) black | 6 fl. oz. | 14 | 0. | | | 0 |
| (Yukon Club) black | 6 fl. oz. | 14 | 0. | | | 0 |
| Unsweetened or low calorie: | | | | | | |
| (Clicquot Club) | 6 fl. oz. | 46 | 0. | | | 0 |
| (Cott) | 6 fl. oz. | 46 | 0. | | | 0 |
| (Dr. Brown's) black | 6 fl. oz. | 57 | 0. | | | 0 |
| (Hoffman) black | 6 fl. oz. | 57 | 0. | | | 0 |
| (Key Food) black | 6 fl. oz. | 57 | 0. | | | 0 |
| (Mission) | 6 fl. oz. | 46 | 0. | | | 0 |
| (No-Cal) black | 6 fl. oz. | 12 | 0. | | | 0 |
| (Shasta) black | 6 fl. oz. | 37 | 0. | | | 0 |
| (Waldbaum) black | 6 fl. oz. | 57 | 0. | | | 0 |
| (Yukon Club) black | 6 fl. oz. | 71 | 0. | | | 0 |
| **CHERRY SYRUP,** dietetic | | | | | | |
| (No-Cal) black | 1 tsp. | <1 | 0. | | | 0 |

(USDA): United States Department of Agriculture
*Prepared as Package Directs

| Food and Description | Measure or Quantity | Sodium (mg.) | —Fats in grams— | | | Cholesterol (mg.) |
|---|---|---|---|---|---|---|
| | | | Total | Saturated | Unsaturated | |

**CHERRY TURNOVER,** frozen

| | | | | | | |
|---|---|---|---|---|---|---|
| (Pepperidge Farm) | 3.3-oz. turnover | 259 | 20.0 | | | |

**CHERVIL:**

| | | | | | | |
|---|---|---|---|---|---|---|
| Raw (USDA) | 1 oz. | | .3 | | | 0 |
| Dry (Spice Islands) | 1 tsp. | <1 | | | | (0) |

**CHESTNUT** (USDA):

| | | | | | | |
|---|---|---|---|---|---|---|
| Fresh, in shell | 1 lb. (weighed in shell) | 22 | 5.5 | | | 0 |
| Fresh, shelled | 4 oz. | 7 | 1.7 | | | 0 |
| Dried, in shell | 1 lb. (weighed in shell) | 45 | 15.3 | | | 0 |
| Dried, shelled | 4 oz. | 14 | 4.6 | | | 0 |

**CHESTNUT FLOUR** (See **FLOUR, CHESTNUT**)

**CHEWING GUM:**

| | | | | | | |
|---|---|---|---|---|---|---|
| Sweetened: | | | | | | |
| *Beechies* | 1 tablet (2 grams) | <1 | 0. | | | (0) |
| *Beech-Nut* | 1 stick (3 grams) | <1 | 0. | | | (0) |
| *Doublemint* | 1 stick (3 grams) | <1 | Tr. | | | 0 |
| *Juicy Fruit* | 1 stick (3 grams) | <1 | Tr. | | | 0 |
| Spearmint (Wrigley's) | 1 stick (3 grams) | <1 | Tr. | | | 0 |
| Unsweetened or dietetic: | | | | | | |
| All flavors (Estee) | 1 stick | | <.1 | | | (0) |
| *Care*Free* (Beech-Nut) | 1 stick (3 grams) | <1 | 0. | | | (0) |
| (Harvey's) | 1 stick | Tr. | 0. | | | 0 |
| Peppermint (Amurol) | 1 stick | | | | | |

**CHICKEN** (See also **CHICKEN, CANNED**) (USDA):

| | | | | | | |
|---|---|---|---|---|---|---|
| Broiler, cooked, meat only | 4 oz. | 75 | 4.3 | 1. | 3. | 99 |
| Capon, raw, ready-to-cook | 1 lb. (weighed with bones) | | 70.2 | 22. | 48. | 324 |
| Capon, raw, meat with skin | 4 oz. | | 24.9 | | | 92 |
| Fryer: | | | | | | |
| Raw: | | | | | | |
| Ready-to-cook | 1 lb. (weighed with bone) | | 15.1 | 5. | 10. | 310 |
| Meat & skin | 1 lb. | | 23.1 | 7. | 16. | 367 |
| Meat only | 1 lb. | 263 | 12.2 | 4. | 8. | 358 |

(USDA): United States Department of Agriculture
*Prepared as Package Directs

95

| Food and Description | Measure or Quantity | Sodium (mg.) | — Fats in grams — | | | Cholesterol (mg.) |
|---|---|---|---|---|---|---|
| | | | Total | Saturated | Unsaturated | |
| Dark meat with skin | 1 lb. | 304 | 28.6 | 9. | 20. | 399 |
| Light meat with skin | 1 lb. | 227 | 17.7 | 5. | 12. | 304 |
| Dark meat without skin | 1 lb. | 304 | 17.2 | 5. | 12. | 399 |
| Light meat without skin | 1 lb. | 227 | 6.8 | 2. | 5. | 358 |
| Skin only | 4 oz. | | 19.4 | 6. | 14. | |
| Back | 1 lb. (weighed with bone) | | 23.5 | 8. | 16. | 198 |
| Breast | 1 lb. (weighed with bone) | | 8.6 | 3. | 6. | 239 |
| Leg or drumstick | 1 lb. (weighed with bone) | | 10.6 | 3. | 8. | 239 |
| Neck | 1 lb. (weighed with bone) | | 20.5 | 7. | 14. | 177 |
| Rib | 1 lb. (weighed with bone) | | 12.5 | 4. | 8. | 187 |
| Thigh | 1 lb. (weighed with bone) | | 19.1 | 6. | 13. | 275 |
| Wing | 1 lb. (weighed with bone) | | 16.5 | 5. | 12. | 180 |
| Fried. A 2½-pound chicken (weighed with bone before cooking) will give you: | | | | | | |
| Back[1] | 1 back (2.2 oz.) | | 8.5 | 3. | 6. | 35 |
| Breast[1] | ½ breast (3.3 oz.) | | 4.9 | 2. | 3. | 61 |
| Leg or drumstick[1] | 1 leg (2 oz.) | | 3.8 | 1. | 3. | 34 |
| Neck[1] | 1 neck (2.1 oz.) | | 7.3 | 3. | 5. | 37 |
| Rib[1] | 1 rib (.7 oz.) | | 2.2 | <1 | 2. | 12 |
| Thigh[1] | 1 thigh (2.3 oz.) | | 5.7 | 2. | 4. | 44 |
| Wing[1] | 1 wing (1¾ oz.) | | 4.3 | 1. | 3. | 25 |
| Fryer: | | | | | | |
| Fried: | | | | | | |
| Meat, skin & giblets[1] | 4 oz. | 88 | 13.4 | 3. | 10. | 91 |
| Meat & skin[1] | 4 oz. | 88 | 13.5 | 3. | 10. | 91 |
| Meat only[1] | 4 oz. | 88 | 8.8 | 3. | 6. | 88 |
| Dark meat with skin[1] | 4 oz. | 100 | 15.4 | 5. | 10. | 103 |
| Light meat with skin[1] | 4 oz. | 77 | 11.2 | 4. | 8. | 90 |
| Dark meat without skin[1] | 4 oz. | 100 | 10.5 | 3. | 7. | 103 |
| Light meat without skin[1] | 4 oz. | 77 | 6.9 | 2. | 5. | 103 |
| Skin only[1] | 1 oz. | | 8.2 | 3. | 6. | |
| Hen & cock: | | | | | | |
| Raw: | | | | | | |
| Ready-to-cook | 1 lb. (weighed with bones) | | 82.1 | 26. | 56. | 324 |

(USDA): United States Department of Agriculture
*Prepared as Package Directs
[1]Principal source of fat: vegetable shortening.

| Food and Description | Measure or Quantity | Sodium (mg.) | Fats in grams Total | Satu-rated | Unsatu-rated | Choles-terol (mg.) |
|---|---|---|---|---|---|---|
| Meat & skin | 1 lb. | | 85.3 | 27. | 58. | 367 |
| Meat only | 1 lb. | 263 | 31.8 | 10. | 21. | 445 |
| Dark meat without skin | 1 lb. | 304 | 34.0 | 11. | 23. | 399 |
| Light meat without skin | 1 lb. | 227 | 16.8 | 5. | 11. | 304 |
| Stewed: | | | | | | |
| Meat, skin & giblets | 4 oz. | | 25.2 | 8. | 17. | 91 |
| Meat & skin | 4 oz. | | 25.9 | 8. | 18. | 99 |
| Meat only | 4 oz. | 62 | 10.1 | 3. | 7. | 99 |
| Chopped | ½ cup (2.5 oz.) | 40 | 6.4 | 2. | 4. | 63 |
| Diced | ½ cup (2.4 oz.) | 37 | 6.0 | 2. | 4. | 58 |
| Ground | ½ cup (2 oz.) | 31 | 5.0 | 2. | 3. | 49 |
| Roaster: | | | | | | |
| Raw: | | | | | | |
| Ready-to-cook | 1 lb. (weighed with bones) | | 59.3 | 19. | 40. | 324 |
| Meat, skin & giblets | 1 lb. | | 54.0 | 18. | 36. | 445 |
| Meat & skin | 1 lb. | | 57.2 | 19. | 38. | 445 |
| Meat only | 1 lb. | 263 | 20.4 | 7. | 14. | 367 |
| Dark meat without skin | 1 lb. | 304 | 21.3 | 7. | 14. | 399 |
| White meat without skin | 1 lb. | 227 | 14.5 | 5. | 10. | 304 |
| Roasted: | | | | | | |
| Total edible | 4 oz. | | 22.9 | 7. | 16. | 99 |
| Meat, skin & giblets | 4 oz. | | 15.9 | 5. | 11. | 92 |
| Meat & skin | 4 oz. | | 16.7 | 5. | 11. | 99 |
| Meat only | 4 oz. | 87 | 7.1 | 2. | 5. | 99 |
| Dark meat without skin | 4 oz. | 100 | 7.4 | 2. | 5. | 99 |
| Light meat without skin | 4 oz. | 75 | 5.6 | 2. | 3. | 99 |
| **CHICKEN A LA KING:** | | | | | | |
| Home recipe (USDA) | 1 cup (8.6 oz.) | 760 | 34.3 | 12. | 22. | 186 |
| Canned (College Inn) | 5-oz. serving | | 10.0 | | | |
| Canned (Richardson & Robbins) | 1 cup (7.9 oz.) | 1055 | 14.8 | | | |
| Canned (Swanson) | 1 cup | 1000 | 16.0 | | | |
| Frozen (Banquet) | 5-oz. bag | | 5.0 | | | |
| **CHICKEN BOUILLON/BROTH,** cube or powder (See also **CHICKEN SOUP**): | | | | | | |
| (Croyden House) | 1 tsp. (5 grams) | 680 | Tr. | Tr. | 0. | |
| (Herb-Ox) | 1 cube (4 grams) | 910 | .1 | | | |
| (Herb-Ox) instant | 1 packet (5 grams) | 940 | .1 | | | |
| (Maggi) | 1 cube (4 grams) | 747 | .2 | | | |
| (Maggi) instant | 1 tsp. (4 grams) | 699 | .2 | | | |

(USDA): United States Department of Agriculture
*Prepared as Package Directs

| Food and Description | Measure or Quantity | Sodium (mg.) | Total | Fats in grams Satu-rated | Unsatu-rated | Choles-terol (mg.) |
|---|---|---|---|---|---|---|
| (Steero) | 1 cube (4 grams) | | .2 | | | |
| (Wyler's) regular | 1 cube (4 grams) | | .3 | | | |
| (Wyler's) no salt added | 1 cube (4 grams) | 2 | .4 | | | |
| (Wyler's) instant | 1 tsp. | | .3 | | | |
| **CHICKEN CACCIATORE,** canned | | | | | | |
| (Hormel) | 1-lb can | | 17.7 | | | |
| **CHICKEN, CANNED:** | | | | | | |
| Boned: | | | | | | |
| (USDA) | 4 oz. | | 13.3 | 5. | 9. | |
| (USDA) | ½ cup (3 oz.) | | 9.9 | 3. | 7. | |
| (Lynden Farms) solids & liq. | 5-oz. jar | 446 | 13.3 | 4. | 9. | |
| (Lynden Farms) with broth | 11-oz. jar | 980 | 29.5 | 10. | 20. | |
| (Lynden Farms) with broth | 29-oz. can | 2137 | 174.6 | 59. | 115. | |
| (Swanson) with broth | 5-oz. can | 705 | 11.0 | | | |
| Fat, rendered, with onion | | | | | | |
| (Lynden Farms) | ¼ of 12.5-oz. jar | 4 | 85.1 | 28. | 57. | |
| Whole (Lynden Farms) solids & liq. | ¼ of 52-oz. can | 1100 | 95.9 | 33. | 63. | |
| **CHICKEN, CREAMED,** frozen | | | | | | |
| (Stouffer's) | 11½-oz. pkg. | 1015 | 44.4 | | | |
| **CHICKEN DINNER:** | | | | | | |
| Canned: | | | | | | |
| Dumpling (College Inn) | 5-oz. serving (½ can) | | 11.0 | | | |
| Noodle (Heinz) | 8½-oz. can | 1123 | 7.6 | | | |
| Noodle (Lynden Farms) | 14-oz. jar | 993 | 23.8 | 10. | 14. | |
| Noodle with vegetables (Lynden Farms) | 15-oz. can | 2121 | 22.5 | 8. | 15. | |
| Frozen: | | | | | | |
| (Weight Watchers) | 10-oz. luncheon | | 2.8 | | | |
| Boneless chicken (Swanson) | | | | | | |
| *Hungry Man* | 19-oz. dinner | 1995 | 33.6 | | | |
| Chicken & dumplings: | | | | | | |
| Buffet (Banquet) | 2-lb. pkg. | | 57.1 | | | |
| (Morton) | 12-oz. dinner | 1506 | 17.4 | | | |
| (Morton) 3-course | 1-lb 5-oz. dinner | 1220 | 32.9 | | | |
| Chicken livers & onion (Weight Watchers) | 11½-oz. luncheon | | 2.0 | | | |
| Creole (Weight Watchers) | 12-oz. luncheon | 748 | 6.8 | | | |

(USDA): United States Department of Agriculture
*Prepared as Package Directs

98

| Food and Description | Measure or Quantity | Sodium (mg.) | —Fats in grams— | | | Choles- terol (mg.) |
|---|---|---|---|---|---|---|
| | | | Total | Satu- rated | Unsatu- rated | |
| Fried: | | | | | | |
| With mashed potato, carrots peas, corn & beans (USDA)[1] | 12 oz. | 1170 | 28.9 | 10. | 19. | |
| (Banquet): | | | | | | |
| Meat compartment | 5 oz. | | 21.4 | | | |
| Corn compartment | 2.5 oz. | | 1.9 | | | |
| Potato compartment | 3.5 oz. | | 1.7 | | | |
| Complete dinner | 11-oz. dinner | | 25.0 | | | |
| (Morton) | 11-oz. dinner | 1153 | 25.0 | | | |
| (Morton) 3-course | 1-lb. 1-oz. dinner | 1531 | 49.7 | | | |
| (Swanson) | 11½-oz. dinner | 1174 | 29.3 | 9. | 21. | |
| (Swanson) 3-course | 15-oz. dinner | 1431 | 27.3 | | | |
| With shoestring potato (Swanson) | 25-oz. pkg. | 1190 | 107.9 | | | |

**CHICKEN & DUMPLINGS** (See **CHICKEN DINNER**)

**CHICKEN, FREEZE DRY**

| | | | | | | |
|---|---|---|---|---|---|---|
| (Wilson) *Campsite:* | | | | | | |
| Dry | 2 oz. | 284 | 5.8 | 2. | 4. | 142 |
| *Reconstituted | 4 oz. | 217 | 4.6 | 1. | 3. | 114 |

**CHICKEN FRICASSEE:**

| | | | | | | |
|---|---|---|---|---|---|---|
| Home recipe (USDA)[2] | 1 cup (8.5 oz.) | 370 | 22.3 | 7. | 15. | 96 |
| Canned (Lynden Farms) | 14.5-oz. can | 1607 | 29.5 | 10. | 19. | |
| Canned (Richardson & Robbins) | 1 cup (7.9 oz.) | 1028 | 12.8 | | | |

**CHICKEN, FRIED,** frozen:

| | | | | | | |
|---|---|---|---|---|---|---|
| (Banquet) whole chicken | 2 lbs. | | 127.8 | | | |
| (Banquet) ½ chicken | 14 oz. | | 55.9 | | | |
| (Swanson) halves | 2 pieces (17¼ oz.) | 1086 | 69.6 | | | |
| (Swanson) quarters | 4 pieces (17¼ oz.) | 1087 | 68.4 | | | |
| (Swanson) | 16-oz. pkg. | 1176 | 73.5 | | | |
| (Swanson) | 32-oz. pkg. | 2322 | 145.2 | | | |
| With whipped potato (Swanson) | 7-oz. pkg. | 895 | 23.1 | | | |

**CHICKEN GIBLETS:**

| | | | | | | |
|---|---|---|---|---|---|---|
| Capon, raw | 2 oz. | | 8.3 | | | |
| Fryer, raw | 2 oz. | | 1.8 | | | |

(USDA): United States Department of Agriculture
*Prepared as Package Directs
[1]Principal sources of fat: vegetable shortening, chicken & butter.
[2]Principal source of fat: chicken.

| Food and Description | Measure or Quantity | Sodium (mg.) | —Fats in grams— | | | Choles- terol (mg.) |
|---|---|---|---|---|---|---|
| | | | Total | Satu- rated | Unsatu- rated | |
| Fryer, fried, from a 2½-lb. chicken | 1 heart, gizzard & liver (2.1 oz.) | | 6.7 | | | |
| Hen & cock, raw | 2 oz. | | 6.6 | | | |
| Roaster, raw | 2 oz. | | 2.7 | | | |
| **CHICKEN GIZZARD** (USDA): | | | | | | |
| Raw | 2 oz. | 37 | 1.5 | | | 82 |
| Simmered | 2 oz. | 32 | 1.9 | | | 111 |
| **CHICKEN LIVER PUFF,** frozen (Durkee) | 1 piece (.5 oz.) | | 4.7 | | | |
| **CHICKEN & NOODLES:** | | | | | | |
| Home recipe (USDA)[1] | 1 cup (8.5 oz.) | 600 | 18.5 | 5. | 14. | 96 |
| Canned (College Inn) | 5-oz. serving | | 7.0 | | | |
| Frozen (Banquet) buffet | 2-lb. pkg. | | 21.2 | | | |
| Frozen, escalloped (Stouffer's) | 11½-oz. pkg. | 1199 | 37.9 | | | |
| **CHICKEN PIE:** | | | | | | |
| Baked, home recipe (USDA)[2] | 4¼″ pie (8 oz.) | 581 | 30.6 | 11. | 19. | 70 |
| Baked, home recipe (USDA)[2] | ⅓ of 9″ pie (8.2 oz.) | 594 | 31.3 | 12. | 20. | 72 |
| Frozen: | | | | | | |
| Commercial, unheated (USDA)[3] | 8-oz. pie | 933 | 26.1 | 7. | 19. | 29 |
| (Banquet) | 8-oz. pie | | 21.1 | | | |
| (Banquet) | 2-lb. 4-oz. pie | | 62.3 | | | |
| (Morton) | 8-oz. pie | 1048 | 25.4 | | | |
| (Stouffer's) | 10-oz. pkg. | 1507 | 50.6 | | | |
| (Swanson) | 8-oz. pie | 981 | 24.4 | | | |
| (Swanson) deep dish | 16-oz. pie | 2090 | 38.8 | | | |
| **CHICKEN, POTTED** (USDA) | 1 oz. | | 5.4 | | | |
| **CHICKEN PUFF,** frozen (Durkee) | 1 piece (.5 oz.) | | 4.8 | | | |
| **CHICKEN RAVIOLI,** in sauce (Lynden Farms) | 14.5-oz. can | 2318 | 10.5 | 3. | 8. | |
| **CHICKEN SOUP,** canned: | | | | | | |
| (Campbell) *Chunky* | 1 cup | 960 | 5.4 | | | |
| *Barley (Manischewitz) | 1 cup | | 2.1 | | | |

(USDA): United States Department of Agriculture
*Prepared as Package Directs
[1]Principal sources of fat: chicken & egg.
[2]Principal sources of fat: vegetable shortening, cream, chicken & butter.
[3]Principal sources of fat: vegetable shortening, chicken, cream & corn oil.

| Food and Description | Measure or Quantity | Sodium (mg.) | Total | Fats in grams Satu-rated | Unsatu-rated | Choles-terol (mg.) |
|---|---|---|---|---|---|---|
| **Broth:** | | | | | | |
| *(Campbell) | 1 cup | 750 | 1.8 | Tr. | 2. | |
| (Lynden Farms) | 1 cup (8 oz.) | 848 | 0. | | | |
| (Richardson & Robbins) | 1 cup (8.1 oz.) | 1152 | 1.1 | | | |
| (Swanson) | 1 cup | 1056 | 1.6 | | | |
| *Dietetic (Claybourne) | 8 oz. (by wt.) | 27 | .9 | | | |
| *Diet (Slim-ette) | 8 oz. (by wt.) | 36 | .3 | | | |
| With rice (Richardson & Robbins) | 1 cup (8.1 oz.) | 1136 | 1.4 | | | |
| **Consommé:** | | | | | | |
| Condensed (USDA) | 8 oz. (by wt.) | 1367 | .2 | | | |
| *Prepared with equal volume water (USDA) | 1 cup (8.5 oz.) | 722 | Tr. | | | |
| **Cream of:** | | | | | | |
| Condensed (USDA) | 8 oz. (by wt.) | 1836 | 10.9 | 2. | 9. | |
| *Prepared with equal volume milk (USDA) | 1 cup (8.6 oz.) | 1054 | 10.3 | 2. | 8. | |
| *Prepared with equal volume water (USDA) | 1 cup (8 oz.) | 970 | 5.8 | Tr. | 6. | |
| *(Campbell) | 1 cup | 885 | 5.0 | 1. | 4. | |
| *(Heinz) | 1 cup (8.5 oz.) | 962 | 5.3 | | | |
| (Heinz) *Great American* | 1 cup (8.5 oz.) | 1080 | 5.4 | | | |
| *& Dumplings (Campbell) | 1 cup | 972 | 5.5 | 1. | 4. | |
| **Gumbo:** | | | | | | |
| Condensed (USDA) | 8 oz. (by wt.) | 1798 | 3.0 | | | |
| *Prepared with equal volume water (USDA) | 1 cup (8.5 oz.) | 950 | 1.4 | | | |
| *(Campbell) | 1 cup | 919 | 1.3 | Tr. | 1. | |
| Creole (Heinz) *Great American* | 1 cup (8¾ oz.) | 1031 | 2.0 | | | |
| *& Kasha (Manischewitz) | 1 cup | | 1.4 | | | |
| **& Noodle:** | | | | | | |
| Condensed (USDA) | 8 oz. (by wt.) | 1852 | 3.6 | | | |
| *Prepared with equal volume water (USDA) | 1 cup (8.8 oz.) | 1020 | 2.0 | | | |
| *(Campbell) | 1 cup | 930 | 1.7 | Tr. | 1. | 6 |
| *Noodle-O's* (Campbell) | 1 cup | 855 | 1.9 | 1. | 1. | |
| *(Heinz) | 1 cup (8.5 oz.) | 1091 | 2.5 | | | |
| *(Manischewitz) | 1 cup | | 1.2 | | | |
| Dietetic (Tillie Lewis) | 1 cup (8 oz.) | 40 | 1.4 | | | |
| With dumplings (Heinz) *Great American* | 1 cup (8.5 oz.) | 1123 | 3.4 | | | |
| *With stars (Campbell) | 1 cup | 1050 | 1.5 | Tr. | 1. | |
| *With stars (Heinz) | 1 cup (8.5 oz.) | 1058 | 2.3 | | | |

(USDA): United States Department of Agriculture
*Prepared as Package Directs

| Food and Description | Measure or Quantity | Sodium (mg.) | — Fats in grams — | | | Cholesterol (mg.) |
| --- | --- | --- | --- | --- | --- | --- |
| | | | Total | Saturated | Unsaturated | |
| **& Rice:** | | | | | | |
| Condensed (USDA) | 8 oz. (by wt.) | 1734 | 2.3 | | | |
| *Prepared with equal volume water (USDA) | 1 cup (8.5 oz.) | 917 | 1.2 | | | |
| *(Campbell) | 1 cup | 748 | 1.5 | Tr. | 1. | |
| *(Heinz) | 1 cup (8.5 oz.) | 996 | 2.7 | | | |
| *(Manischewitz) | 1 cup | | 1.1 | | | |
| With mushrooms (Heinz) *Great American* | 1 cup (8.5 oz.) | 1123 | 3.7 | | | |
| **Vegetable:** | | | | | | |
| Condensed (USDA) | 8 oz. (by wt.) | 1916 | 4.5 | | | |
| *Prepared with equal volume water (USDA) | 1 cup (8.6 oz.) | 1034 | 2.4 | | | |
| *(Campbell) | 1 cup | 912 | 2.0 | Tr. | 2. | |
| *(Heinz) | 1 cup (8.5 oz.) | 1070 | 3.6 | | | |
| *(Manischewitz) | 1 cup | | 1.5 | | | |
| **CHICKEN SOUP MIX:** | | | | | | |
| Cream of (Lipton) *Cup-a-Soup* | 1 pkg. (.8 oz.) | 859 | 5.1 | 4. | <1. | 4 |
| **& Noodle:** | | | | | | |
| (USDA)[1] | 2-oz. pkg. | 2438 | 5.7 | 2. | 4. | |
| *(USDA) | 1 cup (8.1 oz.) | 554 | 1.4 | | | |
| *(Lipton) | 1 cup | 888 | 1.8 | <1. | 1. | 16 |
| (Lipton) *Cup-a-Soup* | 1 pkg. (.4 oz.) | 931 | .8 | Tr. | <1. | 16 |
| *(Wyler's) | 1 cup | | 1.3 | | | |
| *Ring-O-Noodle* (Lipton) | 1 cup | 827 | 1.2 | Tr. | <1. | 24 |
| *With diced chicken (Lipton) | 1 cup | 971 | 2.2 | <1. | 2. | 21 |
| With meat (Lipton) *Cup-a-Soup* | 1 pkg. (.4 oz.) | 989 | .9 | Tr. | <1. | 12 |
| **& Rice:** | | | | | | |
| (USDA) | 1 oz. | 1237 | 1.9 | 1. | 1. | |
| *(USDA) | 1 cup (8 oz.) | 591 | .9 | | | |
| *(Lipton) | 1 cup (8 oz.) | 948 | 2.1 | | | |
| *(Wyler's) | 1 cup | | 1.2 | | | |
| *Vegetable (Lipton) | 1 cup | 1160 | 2.2 | <1. | 2. | 7 |
| **CHICKEN SPREAD:** | | | | | | |
| (Swanson) | 5-oz. can | 830 | 21.0 | | | |
| (Underwood) | 4¾-oz. can | 1014 | 21.9 | | | |
| (Underwood) | 1 T. (.5 oz.) | 104 | 2.3 | | | |
| **CHICKEN STEW:** | | | | | | |
| Canned: | | | | | | |
| (B & M) | 1 cup (7.9 oz.) | 936 | 2.7 | | | |

(USDA): United States Department of Agriculture
*Prepared as Package Directs
[1]Principal sources of fat: vegetable shortening & egg.

| Food and Description | Measure or Quantity | Sodium (mg.) | —Fats in grams— | | | Choles- terol (mg.) |
|---|---|---|---|---|---|---|
| | | | Total | Satu- rated | Unsatu- rated | |
| (Swanson) | l cup | 1018 | 5.9 | | | |
| With dumplings (Heinz) | 8.5-oz. can | 1174 | 8.2 | | | |
| Freeze dry, canned (Wilson) *Campsite:;* | | | | | | |
| Dry | 4½-oz. can | 3375 | 19.8 | 7. | 13. | |
| *Reconstituted | 1 lb. | 2608 | 15.4 | 5. | 10. | |
| **CHICKEN STOCK BASE** | | | | | | |
| (French's) | 1 tsp. (3 grams) | 480 | .2 | | | |
| **CHICKEN TAMALE PIE,** | | | | | | |
| canned (Lynden Farms) | ½ tamale pie with sauce (3.8 oz.) | 554 | 8.3 | 2. | 6. | |
| **CHICK PEA or GARBANZO** (USDA): | | | | | | |
| Dry | 1 lb. | 118 | 21.8 | 2. | 20. | 0 |
| Dry | 1 cup (7.1 oz.) | 52 | 9.6 | Tr. | 10. | 0 |
| **CHICORY GREENS,** raw (USDA): | | | | | | |
| Untrimmed | ½ lb. (weighed untrimmed) | | .6 | | | 0 |
| Trimmed | 4 oz. | | .3 | | | 0 |
| **CHICORY, WITLOOF,** Belgian or French endive, raw, bleached head (USDA): | | | | | | |
| Untrimmed | ½ lb. (weighed untrimmed) | 14 | .2 | | | 0 |
| Trimmed, cut | ½ cup (.9 oz.) | 2 | <.1 | | | 0 |
| **CHILI or CHILI CON CARNE:** | | | | | | |
| Canned, with beans: | | | | | | |
| (USDA) | 1 cup (8.8 oz.) | 1328 | 15.2 | 8. | 8. | |
| (Armour Star) | 15½-oz. can | | 33.8 | | | |
| (Chef Boy-Ar-Dee) | ¼ of 30-oz. can | 912 | 15.5 | | | |
| (Heinz) | 8¾-oz. can | 1332 | 18.4 | | | |
| (Hormel) | 7½ oz. | 933 | 17.9 | 6. | 9. | 32 |
| (Nalley's) mild or hot | 8 oz. | | 17.9 | | | |
| (Swanson) | l cup | 1041 | 13.2 | | | |
| (Van Camp) | 1 cup (8 oz.) | | 14.0 | | | |
| (Wilson) | ½ of 15½-oz. can | 1167 | 16.5 | 8. | 9. | 34 |
| Canned without beans: | | | | | | |
| (USDA) not less than 60% meat nor more than 8% cereal & seasonings[1] | 1 cup (9 oz.) | | 37.7 | 18. | 20. | |

(USDA): United States Department of Agriculture
*Prepared as Package Directs
[1]Principal source of fat: beef.

| Food and Description | Measure or Quantity | Sodium (mg.) | —Fats in grams— | | | Choles-terol (mg.) |
| --- | --- | --- | --- | --- | --- | --- |
| | | | Total | Satu-rated | Unsatu-rated | |
| (Armour Star) | 15½-oz. can | | 66.3 | | | |
| (Chef Boy-Ar-Dee) | ½ of 15¼-oz. can | 927 | 22.5 | | | |
| (Hormel) | 7½ oz. | 878 | 25.6 | | | |
| (Nalley's) | 8 oz. | | 20.4 | | | |
| (Van Camp) | 1 cup (8.1 oz.) | | 34.0 | | | |
| (Wilson) | ½ of 15½-oz. can | 1204 | 35.4 | 18. | 18. | 60 |
| Frozen, with beans (Banquet) | 8-oz. bag | | 18.4 | | | |
| **CHILI BEEF SOUP:** | | | | | | |
| *(Campbell) | 1 cup | 975 | 4.2 | 2. | 2. | |
| *(Heinz) | 1 cup (8¾ oz.) | 1130 | 5.5 | | | |
| (Heinz) *Great American* | 1 cup (8¾ oz.) | 1146 | 5.9 | | | |
| **CHILI CON CARNE MIX** (Durkee): | | | | | | |
| *With meat & beans | 2½ cups (2¼-oz. pkg.) | 2347 | 38.0 | | | |
| *Without meat & beans | 1¼ cups (2¼-oz. pkg.) | 2116 | 2.2 | | | |
| **CHILI CON CARNE SPREAD** (Oscar Mayer): | | | | | | |
| With beans | 1 oz. | 243 | 4.0 | | | |
| Without beans | 1 oz. | 453 | 5.7 | | | |
| ***CHILI DOG SAUCE MIX** (McCormick) | 1 serving (.9 oz.) | 97 | .2 | | | |
| **CHILI PEQUIN** (Spice Islands) | 1 pod | Tr. | | | | (0) |
| **CHILI POWDER:** | | | | | | |
| With added seasoning (USDA) | 1 T. (.5 oz.) | 236 | 1.9 | | | |
| (Chili Products) | ½ oz. | | 1.6 | | | |
| **CHILI SAUCE:** | | | | | | |
| (USDA) | ½ cup (4.4 oz.) | 1659 | .4 | | | |
| (USDA) | 1 T. (.5 oz.) | 201 | <.1 | | | |
| (USDA) low sodium | ½ cup (4.4 oz.) | 6–43 | .4 | | | |
| (USDA) low sodium | 1 T. (.5 oz.) | <1–5 | <.1 | | | |
| (Del Monte) | 1 T. (.5 oz.) | 280 | <.1 | | | |
| (Heinz) | 1 T. | 191 | Tr. | | | |
| (Hunt's) | ½ cup (4.8 oz.) | 1549 | .3 | | | |
| (Hunt's) | 1 T. (.6 oz.) | 194 | <.1 | | | |
| (Ortega) | ¼ cup (2.1 oz.) | 364 | Tr. | | | |
| (Stokely-Van Camp) | 1 T. (.5 oz.) | | Tr. | | | |

(USDA): United States Department of Agriculture
*Prepared as Package Directs

| Food and Description | Measure or Quantity | Sodium (mg.) | Fats in grams | | | Cholesterol (mg.) |
|---|---|---|---|---|---|---|
| | | | Total | Saturated | Unsaturated | |

**CHILI SEASONING MIX:**
| | | | | | | |
|---|---|---|---|---|---|---|
| *Chili-O* (French's) | 1¾-oz. pkg. | 3800 | 1.2 | | | |
| *(Kraft) | 1 oz. | 49 | 2.3 | | | |
| (Lawry's) | 1.6-oz. pkg. | | 2.5 | | | |
| *(Wyler's) | 6 fl. oz. | | .8 | | | |
| Powder (Spice Islands) | 1 tsp. | 1 | | | | |

**CHINESE DATE** (See **JUJUBE**)

**CHINESE DINNER,** frozen:
| | | | | | | |
|---|---|---|---|---|---|---|
| Beef chop suey (Chun King) | 11-oz. dinner | | 10.0 | | | |
| (Banquet) dinner: | | | | | | |
| Meat compartment | 7 oz. | | 5.0 | | | |
| Rice compartment | 4 oz. | | 2.6 | | | |
| Complete dinner | 11-oz. dinner | | 7.6 | | | |
| Chicken chow mein (Chun King) | 11-oz. dinner | | 12.0 | | | |
| Egg foo young (Chun King) | 11-oz. dinner | | 10.0 | | | |
| Shrimp chow mein (Chun King) | 11-oz. dinner | | 10.0 | | | |
| (Swanson) | 11-oz. dinner | 1606 | 12.6 | | | |

**CHINESE VEGETABLES**
(See **VEGETABLE, MIXED**)

**CHIPS** (See **CRACKERS** for corn chips and **POTATO CHIPS**)

**CHITTERLINGS,** canned (Hormel) | 1-lb. 2-oz. can | | 76.5 | | | |

**CHIVES,** raw (USDA) | 1 oz. | | <.1 | | | 0 |

**CHOCOLATE, BAKING:**
| | | | | | | |
|---|---|---|---|---|---|---|
| Bitter or unsweetened: | | | | | | |
| (USDA) | 1 oz. | 1 | 15.0 | 9. | 6. | 0 |
| Grated (USDA) | ½ cup (2.3 oz.) | 3 | 35.0 | 20. | 15. | 0 |
| (Baker's) | 1-oz. sq. | 4 | 14.3 | | | 0 |
| Pre-melted, *Choco-Bake* | 1-oz. packet | Tr. | 13.5 | | | |
| (Hershey's) | 1 oz. | 11 | 15.7 | | | |
| Sweetened: | | | | | | |
| Bittersweet (USDA) | 1 oz. | <1 | 11.3 | 7. | 5. | 0 |
| Chips, milk (Hershey's) | 1 oz. | 28 | 9.5 | | | |
| Chips, semisweet (Baker's) | ¼ cup (1.5 oz.) | 9 | 10.5 | | | 0 |
| Chips, semisweet (Ghirardelli) | ⅓ cup (2 oz.) | | 16.3 | | | |
| Chips, semisweet (Hershey's) | 1 oz. | 4 | 9.2 | | | |

(USDA): United States Department of Agriculture
*Prepared as Package Directs

| Food and Description | Measure or Quantity | Sodium (mg.) | Total | — Fats in grams — Satu- rated | Unsatu- rated | Choles- terol (mg.) |
|---|---|---|---|---|---|---|
| *German's,* sweet (Baker's) | 4½ sq. (1 oz.) | 7 | 9.3 | | | 0 |
| Morsels, milk (Nestlé's) | 1 oz. | <1 | 8.3 | | | |
| Morsels, semisweet (Nestlé's) | 6-oz. pkg. | 4 | 47.6 | | | |
| Morsels, semisweet (Nestlé's) | 1 oz. | <1 | 8.0 | | | |
| Semisweet, small pieces (USDA) | ½ cup (3 oz.) | 2 | 30.3 | 17. | 13. | |
| Semisweet (Baker's) | 1-oz. sq. | 1 | 8.9 | | | 0 |

**CHOCOLATE CAKE:**
Home recipe (USDA):
  Without icing:

| Food and Description | Measure or Quantity | Sodium (mg.) | Total | Satu- rated | Unsatu- rated | Choles- terol (mg.) |
|---|---|---|---|---|---|---|
|     Made with butter[1] | 3 oz. | 250 | 14.6 | 8. | 7. | |
|     Made with vegetable shortening[2] | 3 oz. | 250 | 14.6 | 4. | 10. | |
|   With chocolate icing, 2-layer | ¹/₁₆ of 10″ cake (4.2 oz.) | 282 | 19.7 | | | 52 |
|   With chocolate icing, 2-layer | ¹/₁₆ of 9″ cake (2.6 oz.) | 176 | 12.3 | | | 32 |
|   With uncooked white icing | ¹/₁₆ of 10″ cake (4.2 oz.) | 281 | 17.5 | | | |
| Fudge, frozen (Pepperidge Farm) | ¹/₆ of cake (3 oz.) | 299 | 15.0 | | | |
| German chocolate, frozen (Morton) | 2.2-oz. serving | 243 | 12.6 | | | |
| Golden, frozen (Pepperidge Farm) | ¹/₆ of cake (3 oz.) | 252 | 15.6 | | | |

**CHOCOLATE CAKE MIX** (See also **FUDGE CAKE MIX**):

| Food and Description | Measure or Quantity | Sodium (mg.) | Total | Satu- rated | Unsatu- rated | Choles- terol (mg.) |
|---|---|---|---|---|---|---|
| Chocolate malt (USDA)[3] | 1 oz. | 156 | 3.0 | 1. | 2. | |
| *Chocolate malt,[2] uncooked white icing (USDA)[4] | 4 oz. | 361 | 9.9 | | | |
| *Chocolate malt layer (Betty Crocker) | ¹/₁₂ of cake | 264 | 5.8 | | | |
| *Chocolate pudding (Betty Crocker) | ¹/₆ of cake | 338 | 4.9 | | | |
| *Deep chocolate (Duncan Hines) | ¹/₁₂ of cake (2.7 oz.) | 483 | 6.1 | | | 50 |
| *German chocolate layer (Betty Crocker) | ¹/₁₂ of cake | 286 | 5.8 | | | |
| *German chocolate (Swans Down) | ¹/₁₂ of cake (2.5 oz.) | 376 | 3.6 | | | |
| *Milk chocolate layer (Betty Crocker) | ¹/₁₂ of cake | 281 | 6.0 | | | |
| *Swiss chocolate (Duncan Hines) | ¹/₁₂ of cake (2.7 oz.) | 405 | 6.1 | | | 50 |

(USDA): United States Department of Agriculture
*Prepared as Package Directs
[1]Principal sources of fat: butter, chocolate, egg & milk.
[2]Principal sources of fat: vegetable shortening, chocolate, egg & milk.
[3]Principal sources of fat: vegetable shortening, chocolate & milk.
[4]Prepared with eggs & water.

| Food and Description | Measure or Quantity | Sodium (mg.) | — Fats in grams — | | | Choles- terol (mg.) |
|---|---|---|---|---|---|---|
| | | | Total | Satu- rated | Unsatu- rated | |

**CHOCOLATE CANDY** (See **CANDY**)

**CHOCOLATE DRINK:**

| | | | | | | |
|---|---|---|---|---|---|---|
| Canned (Borden) | 9½-fl.-oz. can | 47 | 6.7 | | | |
| Mix: | | | | | | |
| Hot (USDA)[1] | 1 oz. | 108 | 3.0 | 2. | 1. | |
| Hot (USDA)[1] | 1 cup (4.9 oz.) | 531 | 14.7 | 8. | 6. | |
| Dutch, instant (Borden) | 2 heaping tsps. (¾ oz.) | 5 | .7 | | | |
| Instant (Ghirardelli) | 1 T. (.4 oz.) | 2 | .5 | | | |
| *Quik* (Nestlé's) | 2 heaping tsp. (.6 oz.) | 32 | .3 | | | |

**CHOCOLATE, GROUND**

| | | | | | | |
|---|---|---|---|---|---|---|
| (Ghirardelli) | ¼ cup (1.3 oz.) | 46 | 3.8 | | | |

**CHOCOLATE, HOT,** home

| | | | | | | |
|---|---|---|---|---|---|---|
| recipe (USDA) | 1 cup (8.8 oz.) | 120 | 12.5 | 8. | 5. | 31 |

**CHOCOLATE ICE CREAM** (See also individual brands):

| | | | | | | |
|---|---|---|---|---|---|---|
| (Borden) 9.5% fat | ¼ pt. (2.3 oz.) | 31 | 6.3 | | | |
| (Prestige) French | ¼ pt. (2.6 oz.) | 36 | 10.9 | | | |
| (Sealtest) | ¼ pt. (2.3 oz.) | 42 | 6.4 | | | |

**CHOCOLATE PIE:**

| | | | | | | |
|---|---|---|---|---|---|---|
| Chiffon, home recipe (USDA): | | | | | | |
| Made with lard[2] | 1/6 of 9″ pie (4.9 oz.) | 353 | 21.4 | 8. | 13. | |
| Made with vegetable shortening[3] | 1/6 of 9″ pie (4.9 oz.) | 353 | 21.4 | 6. | 16. | |
| Meringue, home recipe (USDA): | | | | | | |
| Made with lard[2] | 1/6 of 9″ pie (4.9 oz.) | 358 | 16.8 | 6. | 11. | |
| Made with vegetable shortening[3] | 1/6 of 9″ pie (4.9 oz.) | 358 | 16.8 | 4. | 13. | |
| Nut (Tastykake) | 4½-oz. pie | | 18.4 | | | |
| Frozen: | | | | | | |
| Cream: | | | | | | |
| (Banquet) | 2½-oz. serving | | 8.7 | | | |
| (Mrs. Smith's) | 1/6 of 8″ pie (2.3 oz.) | 150 | 13.2 | | | |
| Tart (Pepperidge Farm) | 1 pie tart (3 oz.) | 211 | 18.0 | | | |
| Velvet nut (Kraft) | 1/6 of 16¾-oz. pie | 77 | 18.6 | | | |

(USDA): United States Department of Agriculture
*Prepared as Package Directs
[1]Principal sources of fat: chocolate & milk.
[2]Principal sources of fat: lard & butter.
[3]Principal sources of fat: vegetable shortening & butter.

| Food and Description | Measure or Quantity | Sodium (mg.) | Total | Fats in grams — Satu- rated | Unsatu- rated | Choles- terol (mg.) |
|---|---|---|---|---|---|---|
| **CHOCOLATE PIE FILLING** (See **CHOCOLATE PUDDING MIX**) | | | | | | |
| **CHOCOLATE PUDDING,** | | | | | | |
| sweetened: | | | | | | |
| Home recipe with starch base (USDA)[1] | ½ cup (4.6 oz.) | 73 | 6.1 | 4. | 2. | |
| Chilled: | | | | | | |
| Dark chocolate (Breakstone) | 5-oz. container | 195 | 13.2 | | | 0 |
| Light chocolate (Breakstone) | 5-oz. container | 145 | 13.5 | | | 0 |
| (Sealtest) | 4 oz. | 128 | 3.5 | | | |
| Canned: | | | | | | |
| (Betty Crocker) | ½ cup | 239 | 5.2 | | | |
| (Hunt's)[2] | 5-oz. can | 146 | 12.9 | 2. | 10. | |
| (Thank You) | ½ cup (4.5 oz.) | | 5.1 | | | |
| Fudge (Betty Crocker) | ½ cup | 175 | 5.2 | | | |
| Fudge (Del Monte) | 5-oz. can | 233 | 5.8 | | | |
| Fudge (Hunt's)[2] | 5-oz. can | 150 | 12.9 | 3. | 10. | |
| Milk chocolate (Del Monte) | 5-oz. can | 251 | 5.7 | | | |
| **CHOCOLATE PUDDING or PIE FILLING MIX:** | | | | | | |
| Sweetened: | | | | | | |
| Regular: | | | | | | |
| Dry (USDA)[3] | 1 oz. | 127 | 6.0 | 3. | 3. | |
| *Prepared with milk (USDA)[1] | ½ cup (4.6 oz.) | 168 | 3.9 | 3. | 1. | 16 |
| *(Jell-O) | ½ cup (5.2 oz.) | 167 | 5.1 | | | 13 |
| *(Royal) | ½ cup (5.1 oz.) | 140 | 5.5 | | | 14 |
| *(Royal) *Dark 'N' Sweet* | ½ cup (5.1 oz.) | 140 | 5.9 | | | 14 |
| *Fudge (Jell-O) | ½ cup (5.2 oz.) | 167 | 5.1 | | | 13 |
| *Milk chocolate (Jell-O) | ½ cup (5.2 oz.) | 167 | 5.1 | | | 13 |
| Instant: | | | | | | |
| Dry (USDA) | 1 oz. | 115 | .5 | | | |
| *Prepared with milk, without cooking (USDA)[1] | 4 oz. | 141 | 2.8 | 1. | 2. | |
| *(Jell-O) | ½ cup (5.4 oz.) | 486 | 5.2 | | | 13 |
| *(Royal) | ½ cup (5.1 oz.) | 320 | 5.5 | | | 14 |
| *(Royal) *Dark 'N' Sweet* | ½ cup (5.1 oz.) | 320 | 5.5 | | | 14 |
| *Fudge (Jell-O) | ½ cup (5.4 oz.) | 486 | 5.2 | | | 13 |
| *Low calories or dietetic (D-Zerta) | ½ cup (4.6 oz.) | 72 | 4.8 | | | 13 |

(USDA): United States Department of Agriculture
*Prepared as Package Directs
[1]Principal sources of fat: milk & chocolate.
[2]Principal source of fat: soybean oil.
[3]Principal source of fat: chocolate.

| Food and Description | Measure or Quantity | Sodium (mg.) | Total | Satu-rated | Unsatu-rated | Choles-terol (mg.) |
|---|---|---|---|---|---|---|
| **CHOCOLATE RENNET MIX:** | | | | | | |
| Powder: | | | | | | |
| Dry (Junket) | 1 oz. | 26 | .7 | | | |
| *(Junket) | 4 oz. | 61 | 4.1 | | | |
| Tablet: | | | | | | |
| Dry (Junket) | 1 tablet (<1 gram) | 197 | Tr. | | | |
| *& sugar (Junket) | 4 oz. | 98 | 3.9 | | | |
| **CHOCOLATE SOFT DRINK:** | | | | | | |
| Sweetened: | | | | | | |
| (Clicquot Club) cream | 6 fl. oz. | 11 | 0. | | | 0 |
| (Cott) cream | 6 fl. oz. | 11 | .0. | | | 0 |
| (Hoffman) *Cocoa Cooler* | 6 fl. oz. | 14 | 0. | | | 0 |
| (Hoffman) cream | 6 fl. oz. | 14 | 0. | | | 0 |
| (Mission) cream | 6 fl. oz. | 11 | 0. | | | 0 |
| (Yukon Club) cream | 6 fl. oz. | 14 | 0. | | | 0 |
| Low calorie: | | | | | | |
| (Clicquot Club) | 6 fl. oz. | 45 | 0. | | | 0 |
| (Cott) | 6 fl. oz. | 45 | 0. | | | 0 |
| (Hoffman) | 6 fl. oz. | 39 | 0. | | | 0 |
| (Mission) | 6 fl. oz. | 45 | 0. | | | 0 |
| (No-Cal) | 6 fl. oz. | 12 | 0. | | | 0 |
| (Shasta) | 6 fl. oz. | 37 | 0. | | | 0 |
| **CHOCOLATE SYRUP:** | | | | | | |
| Sweetened: | | | | | | |
| Fudge (USDA)[1] | 1 fl. oz. (1.3 oz.) | 34 | 5.2 | 3. | 2. | |
| Fudge (USDA)[1] | 1 T. (.7 oz.) | 17 | 2.6 | 1. | 1. | |
| Thin type (USDA) | 1 fl. oz. (1.3 oz.) | 20 | .8 | Tr. | Tr. | |
| Thin type (USDA) | 1 T. (.7 oz.) | 10 | .4 | Tr. | Tr. | |
| (Hershey's) | 1 T. (1 oz.) | 14 | .3 | | | |
| (Smucker's) | 1 T. (.6 oz.) | 8 | .2 | Tr. | Tr. | |
| Low calorie: | | | | | | |
| (Slim-ette) *Chocotop* | 1 T. (.5 oz.) | | .2 | | | |
| (Tillie Lewis) | 1 T. (.5 oz.) | | .2 | | | |
| ***CHOCO-NUT SUNDAE CONE*** | | | | | | |
| (Sealtest) | 2½ fl. oz. (2.1 oz.) | 57 | 9.9 | | | |
| **CHOP SUEY:** | | | | | | |
| Home recipe, with meat (USDA)[2] | 1 cup (8.8 oz.) | 1052 | 17.0 | 7. | 10. | 64 |

(USDA): United States Department of Agriculture
*Prepared as Package Directs
[1]Principal sources of fat: chocolate, animal & vegetable shortening & milk.
[2]Principal sources of fat: butter, beef & pork.

| Food and Description | Measure or Quantity | Sodium (mg.) | Total | Fats in grams Satu- rated | Unsatu- rated | Choles- terol (mg.) |
|---|---|---|---|---|---|---|
| Canned: | | | | | | |
| With meat (USDA)[1] | 1 cup (8.8 oz.) | 1378 | 8.0 | 2. | 6. | 7 |
| Chicken (Hung's) | 8 oz. | | 5.6 | | | |
| Meatless (Hung's) | 8 oz. | | 6.0 | | | |
| Mix: | | | | | | |
| (Durkee) | 1½-oz. pkg. | 828 | 2.1 | | | |
| *With meat & vegetables | | | | | | |
| (Durkee) | 3½ cups (1½-oz. pkg.) | 1164 | 64.8 | | | |
| Frozen: | | | | | | |
| Beef (Banquet) cooking bag | 7-oz. bag | | 4.2 | | | |
| Beef (Banquet) buffet | 2-lb. pkg. | | 19.3 | | | |
| Beef dinner (Banquet): | | | | | | |
| Meat compartment | 7 oz. | | 5.1 | | | |
| Rice compartment | 4 oz. | | 2.8 | | | |
| Complete dinner | 11-oz. dinner | | 7.9 | | | |

**CHOP SUEY VEGETABLES** (See
**VEGETABLE, MIXED**)

**CHOW CHOW:**

| | | | | | | |
|---|---|---|---|---|---|---|
| Sour (USDA) | 1 oz. | 379 | .4 | | | 0 |
| Sweet (USDA) | 1 oz. | 149 | .3 | | | 0 |
| (Crosse & Blackwell) | 1 T. (.6 oz.) | 254 | 0. | | | (0) |

**CHOW MEIN** (See also
**CHINESE DINNER**):

| | | | | | | |
|---|---|---|---|---|---|---|
| Home recipe, chicken, without noodles (USDA)[2] | 4 oz. | 325 | 4.5 | 1. | 3. | |
| Canned: | | | | | | |
| Beef (Chun King) *Divider-Pak* | 7-oz. serving (¼ can) | | 5.0 | | | |
| Chicken: | | | | | | |
| (USDA) without noodles | 4 oz. | 329 | .1 | | | |
| (Chun King) *Divider-Pak* | 7-oz. serving (¼ can) | | 3.0 | | | |
| (Hung's) | 8 oz. | | 4.6 | | | |
| Meatless (Hung's) | 8 oz. | | 5.0 | | | |
| Pork (Chun King) *Divider-Pak* | 7-oz. serving (¼ can) | | 9.0 | | | |
| Shrimp (Chun King) *Divider-Pak* | 7-oz. serving (¼ can) | | 1.0 | | | |
| Frozen: | | | | | | |
| Beef (Chun King) | 7½-oz. serving (½ pkg.) | | 3.0 | | | |
| Chicken: | | | | | | |
| (Banquet) cooking bag | 7-oz. bag | | 3.4 | | | |

(USDA): United States Department of Agriculture
*Prepared as Package Directs
[1]Principal sources of fat: pork, beef & corn oil.
[2]Principal sources of fat: chicken, corn oil & soybeans.

| Food and Description | Measure or Quantity | Sodium (mg.) | —Fats in grams— | | | Choles- terol (mg.) |
|---|---|---|---|---|---|---|
| | | | Total | Satu- rated | Unsatu- rated | |
| (Banquet) buffet | 2-lb. pkg. | | 15.8 | | | |
| (Chun King) | 7½-oz serving (½ pkg.) | | 4.0 | | | |
| With rice (Swanson) | 8½-oz. pkg. | 1080 | 4.7 | | | |
| Shrimp (Chun King) | 7½-oz. serving (½ pkg.) | | 2.0 | | | |

**CHOW MEIN NOODLES** (See **NOODLES, CHOW MEIN**)

**CHOW MEIN VEGETABLES** (See **VEGETABLES, MIXED**)

**CHUB,** raw (USDA):

| | | | | | | |
|---|---|---|---|---|---|---|
| Whole | 1 lb. (weighed whole) | | 13.2 | | | |
| Meat only | 4 oz. | | 10.0 | | | |

**CHUTNEY,** *Major Grey's* (Crosse & Blackwell)

| | | | | | | |
|---|---|---|---|---|---|---|
| | 1 T. (.8 oz.) | 294 | 0. | | | |

**CIDER** (See **APPLE CIDER**)

**CINNAMON:**

| | | | | | | |
|---|---|---|---|---|---|---|
| Ground (Information supplied by General Mills Laboratory) | 1 oz. | | 1.0 | | | (0) |
| Stick (Spice Islands) | 1 stick | <1 | | | | (0) |
| With sugar (French's) | 1 tsp. (4 grams) | | Tr. | | | (0) |

**CINNAMON STICKS,** frozen (Aunt Jemima)

| | | | | | | |
|---|---|---|---|---|---|---|
| | 3 pieces (1¾ oz.) | 283 | 5.2 | | | |

**CISCO** (See **LAKE HERRING**)

| | | | | | | |
|---|---|---|---|---|---|---|
| **CITRON, CANDIED** (USDA) | 1 oz. | 82 | <.1 | | | 0 |
| **CITRUS COOLER** (Hi-C) | 6 fl. oz. (6.3 oz.) | Tr. | Tr. | | | 0 |

**CITRUS SOFT DRINK,** low calorie:

| | | | | | | |
|---|---|---|---|---|---|---|
| *Flair,* sugar-free | 6 fl. oz. | 52+ | 0. | | | 0 |
| (No-Cal) | 6 fl. oz. | 11 | 0. | | | 0 |
| *CLACKERS,* cereal (General Mills) | 1 cup (1 oz.) | 360 | 2.3 | | | (0) |

(USDA): United States Department of Agriculture
*Prepared as Package Directs

| Food and Description | Measure or Quantity | Sodium (mg.) | Fats in grams — Total | Satu- rated | Unsatu- rated | Choles- terol (mg.) |
|---|---|---|---|---|---|---|
| **CLAM:** | | | | | | |
| Raw, all kinds, meat & liq. (USDA) | 4 oz. | | 1.0 | | | |
| Raw, all kinds, meat only (USDA) | 4 med. clams (3 oz.) | 102 | 1.4 | | | 42 |
| Raw, hard or round (USDA): | | | | | | |
| Meat & liq. | 1 lb. (weighed in shell) | | .6 | | | |
| Meat only | 1 cup (7 round chowders, 8 oz.) | 465 | 2.0 | | | 114 |
| Raw, soft (USDA): | | | | | | |
| Meat & liq. | 1 lb. (weighed in shell) | | 2.6 | | | |
| Meat only | 1 cup (19 large, 8 oz.) | 82 | 4.3 | | | 114 |
| Canned, all kinds: | | | | | | |
| Solids & liq. (USDA) | 4 oz. | | .8 | | | |
| Meat only (USDA) | ½ cup (2.8 oz.) | | 2.0 | | | 50 |
| Chopped (Snow) | 4 oz. | | .2 | | | |
| Creamed, with mushrooms (Snow) | 4 oz. | | 6.6 | | | |
| Minced (Snow) | 4 oz. | | .3 | | | |
| Frozen, fried (Mrs. Paul's) | 4 oz. | | 23.6 | | | |
| **CLAM CAKE,** frozen, thins (Mrs. Paul's) | 10-oz. pkg. | | 23.5 | | | |
| **CLAM CHOWDER:** | | | | | | |
| Manhattan, canned: | | | | | | |
| Condensed (USDA) | 8 oz. (by wt.) | 1739 | 4.8 | | | |
| *Prepared with equal volume water (USDA) | 1 cup (8.6 oz.) | 938 | 2.4 | | | |
| *(Campbell) | 1 cup | 878 | 2.4 | Tr. | 2. | |
| (Campbell) *Chunky* | 1 cup | 1055 | 3.2 | | | |
| (Crosse & Blackwell) | ½ can (6½ oz.) | 935 | 1.5 | | | |
| *(Doxsee) | 1 cup (8.6 oz.) | 926 | 2.7 | | | 22 |
| (Heinz) *Great American* | 1 cup (8½ oz.) | 1293 | 4.5 | | | |
| (Snow) | 8 oz. | 631 | 4.0 | <1. | 3. | |
| New England: | | | | | | |
| Canned: | | | | | | |
| *(Campbell) | 1 cup | 930 | 6.7 | | | |
| (Crosse & Blackwell) | ½ can (6½ oz.) | 935 | 3.5 | | | |
| *(Doxsee) | 1 cup (8.6 oz.) | 982 | 7.3 | | | 52 |
| (Snow) | 8 oz. | 1368 | 4.1 | <1. | 3. | |
| Frozen: | | | | | | |
| Condensed (USDA) | 8 oz. (by wt.) | 1975 | 14.5 | | | |

(USDA): United States Department of Agriculture
*Prepared as Package Directs

| Food and Description | Measure or Quantity | Sodium (mg.) | Fats in grams — Total | Satu- rated | Unsatu- rated | Choles- terol (mg.) |
|---|---|---|---|---|---|---|
| *Prepared with equal volume water (USDA) | 1 cup (8.5 oz.) | 1044 | 7.7 | | | |
| *Prepared with equal volume milk (USDA) | 1 cup (8.6 oz.) | 1129 | 12.2 | | | |
| **CLAM FRITTERS,** home recipe,[1] (USDA) | 1 fritter (2″ x 1¾″, 1.4 oz.) | | 6.0 | | | 52 |
| **CLAM JUICE/LIQUOR,** canned: | | | | | | |
| (USDA) | 1 cup (8.3 oz.) | | .2 | | | |
| (Snow) | 8 oz. | | .2 | | | |
| **CLAM STEW,** New England (Snow) | 8 oz. | | 10.3 | | | |
| **CLAM STICKS,** frozen (Mrs. Paul's) | 4 oz. | | 7.7 | | | |
| *CLAMATO COCKTAIL* (Mott's) | 4 oz. | | .3 | | | |
| **CLARET WINE** (Gold Seal) 12% alcohol | 3 fl. oz. (3.1 oz.) | 3 | 0. | | | (0) |
| **CLOVE:** | | | | | | |
| Ground (Spice Islands) | 1 tsp. | <1 | | | | (0) |
| Whole (Spice Islands) | 1 clove | <1 | | | | (0) |
| **CLUB SODA SOFT DRINK:** | | | | | | |
| Regular: | | | | | | |
| (Dr. Brown's) | 6 fl. oz. | 29 | 0. | | | 0 |
| (Fanta) | 6 fl. oz. | 39 | 0. | | | 0 |
| (Hoffman) | 6 fl. oz. | 29 | 0. | | | 0 |
| (Key food) | 6 fl. oz. | 29 | 0. | | | 0 |
| (Nedick's) | 6 fl. oz. | 29 | 0. | | | 0 |
| (Schweppes) | 6 fl. oz. | 26 | 0. | | | 0 |
| (Shasta) | 6 fl. oz. | 98 | 0. | | | 0 |
| (Waldbaum) | 6 fl. oz. | 29 | 0. | | | 0 |
| (Yukon Club) | 6 fl. oz. | 29 | 0. | | | 0 |
| Dietetic: | | | | | | |
| (Dr. Brown's) | 6 fl. oz. | 2 | 0. | | | 0 |
| (Hoffman) | 6 fl. oz. | 2 | 0. | | | 0 |
| (Key Food) | 6 fl. oz. | 2 | 0. | | | 0 |
| (Waldbaum) | 6 fl. oz. | 2 | 0. | | | 0 |

(USDA): United States Department of Agriculture
*Prepared as Package Directs
[1]Prepared with flour, baking powder, butter & eggs.

| Food and Description | Measure or Quantity | Sodium (mg.) | —Fats in grams— | | | Choles-terol (mg.) |
|---|---|---|---|---|---|---|
| | | | Total | Satu-rated | Unsatu-rated | |
| **COCOA,** dry: | | | | | | |
| Plain (USDA): | | | | | | |
| Low fat | ½ cup (1.5 oz.) | 3 | 3.4 | 2. | 2. | 0 |
| Low fat | 1 T. (5 grams) | <1 | .4 | Tr. | Tr. | 0 |
| Medium-low fat | ½ cup (1.5 oz.) | 3 | 5.5 | 3. | 2. | 0 |
| Medium-low fat | 1 T. (5 grams) | <1 | .7 | Tr. | Tr. | 0 |
| Medium-high fat | ½ cup (1.5 oz.) | 3 | 8.2 | 5. | 3. | 0 |
| Medium-high fat | 1 T. (5 grams) | <1 | 1.0 | <1. | Tr. | 0 |
| High-fat· | ½ cup (1.5 oz.) | 3 | 10.2 | 6. | 5. | 0 |
| High-fat | 1 T. (5 grams) | <1 | 1.3 | <1. | <1. | 0 |
| Processed with alkali (USDA): | | | | | | |
| Medium-low fat | ½ cup (1.5 oz.) | 308 | 5.5 | 3. | 2. | 0 |
| Medium-low fat | 1 T. (5 grams) | 39 | .7 | Tr. | Tr. | 0 |
| Medium-high fat | ½ cup (1.5 oz.) | 308 | 8.2 | 5. | 3. | 0 |
| Medium-high fat | 1 T. (5 grams) | 39 | 1.0 | <1. | Tr. | 0 |
| High-fat | ½ cup (1.5 oz.) | 308 | 10.2 | 6. | 5. | 0 |
| High-fat | 1 T. (5 grams) | 39 | 1.3 | <1. | <1. | 0 |
| Unsweetened (Droste) | 1 T. (7 grams) | | 1.7 | | | (0) |
| (Hershey's) | ½ cup (1.5 oz.) | 32 | 7.1 | | | (0) |
| (Hershey's) | 1-oz. packet | 21 | 4.7 | | | (0) |
| (Hershey's) | 1 T. (5 grams) | 4 | .9 | | | (0) |
| **COCOA, HOME RECIPE** (USDA) | 1 cup (8.8 oz.) | 128 | 11.5 | 8. | 4. | 35 |
| *COCOA KRISPIES,* cereal (Kellogg's) | 1 cup (1 oz.) | 167 | .7 | | | (0) |
| **COCOA MIX:** | | | | | | |
| With nonfat dry milk (USDA)[1] | 1 oz. | 149 | .8 | <1. | Tr. | |
| Without nonfat dry milk (USDA)[2] | 1 oz. | 76 | .6 | Tr. | Tr. | 0 |
| (Kraft) | 1 oz. | 73 | .5 | | | |
| *(Kraft) | 1 cup | 91 | .7 | | | |
| (Nestlé's) *EverReady* | 3 heaping tsp. (.8 oz.) | 84 | 1. | | | |
| Hot (Hershey's) | 1 oz. | 105 | 2.4 | | | |
| Hot (Nestlé's) | 1-oz. pkg. | 139 | .3 | | | |
| Instant: | | | | | | |
| (Hershey's) | 1 oz. | 60 | .6 | | | |
| (Swiss Miss) | 1 oz. | | .4 | | | |
| Chocolate marshmallow (Carnation)[3] | 1 pkg. (1 oz.) | 122 | 1.6 | 1. | Tr. | <1 |
| Milk chocolate (Carnation) | 1 pkg. (1 oz.) | 163 | 2.6 | 2. | Tr. | <1 |
| Rich chocolate (Carnation)[3] | 1 pkg. (1 oz.) | 121 | 1.6 | 1. | Tr. | <1 |

(USDA): United States Department of Agriculture
*Prepared as Package Directs
[1]Principal sources of fat: cocoa & milk.
[2]Principal source of fat: cocoa.
[3]Principal sources of fat: milk, cocoa & modified coconut oil.

| Food and Description | Measure or Quantity | Sodium (mg.) | Fats in grams | | | Choles-terol (mg.) |
|---|---|---|---|---|---|---|
| | | | Total | Satu-rated | Unsatu-rated | |
| *COCOA PEBBLES,* cereal (Post) | ⅞ cup (1 oz.) | 125 | .1 | | | 0 |
| *COCOA PUFFS,* cereal (General Mills) | 1 cup (1 oz.) | 184 | .5 | | | (0) |
| **COCONUT:** | | | | | | |
| Fresh (USDA): | | | | | | |
| Whole | 1 lb. (weighed in shell) | 54 | 83.3 | 72. | 11. | 0 |
| Meat only | 4 oz. | 26 | 40.0 | 34. | 6. | 0 |
| Meat only | 2″ x 2″ x ½″ piece (1.6 oz.) | 10 | 15.9 | 14. | 2. | 0 |
| Grated or shredded | 1 firmly packed cup (4.6 oz.) | 30 | 45.9 | 39. | 7. | 0 |
| Grated | 1 lightly packed cup (2.9 oz.) | 18 | 28.2 | 24. | 4. | 0 |
| Cream, liq. expressed from grated coconut | 4 oz. | 5 | 36.5 | 32. | 5. | 0 |
| Milk, liq. expressed from mixture of grated coconut & water | 4 oz. | | 28.2 | 25. | 3. | 0 |
| Water, liq. from coconut | 1 cup (8.5 oz.) | 60 | .5 | | | 0 |
| Dried, canned or packaged: | | | | | | |
| Sweetened, shredded (USDA) | ½ lightly packed cup (1.6 oz.) | | 18.0 | 16. | 2. | 0 |
| Unsweetened (USDA) | ½ lightly packed cup (1.6 oz.) | | 30.0 | 26. | 4. | 0 |
| *Angel Flake* (Baker's) | ½ cup (1.3 oz.) | 86 | 11.8 | | | 0 |
| Cookie (Baker's) | ½ cup (2 oz.) | 136 | 18.6 | | | 0 |
| *Crunchies* (Baker's) | ½ cup (2.1 oz.) | 144 | 30.2 | | | 0 |
| Premium shred (Baker's) | ½ cup (1.5 oz.) | 100 | 13.8 | | | 0 |
| Southern-style (Baker's) | ½ cup (1.5 oz.) | | 13.4 | | | 0 |
| **COCONUT CAKE,** frozen (Pepperidge Farm) | ⅙ of cake (3 oz.) | 252 | 15.1 | | | |
| ***COCONUT CAKE MIX** (Duncan Hines) | ¹/₁₂ of cake (2.7 oz.) | 377 | 6.1 | | | 50 |
| **COCONUT PIE:** | | | | | | |
| Cream: | | | | | | |
| (Tastykake) | 4-oz. pie | | 27.5 | | | |
| Frozen: | | | | | | |
| (Banquet) | 2½-oz. serving | | 11.6 | | | |

(USDA): United States Department of Agriculture
*Prepared as Package Directs

| Food and Description | Measure or Quantity | Sodium (mg.) | —Fats in grams— | | | Choles-terol (mg.) |
|---|---|---|---|---|---|---|
| | | | Total | Satu-rated | Unsatu-rated | |
| (Morton) | ¼ of 14.4-oz. pie | 189 | 15.4 | | | |
| (Mrs. Smith's) | ⅙ of 8″ pie (2.3 oz.) | 132 | 12.3 | | | |
| Tart (Pepperidge Farm) | 3-oz. pie tart | 206 | 20.1 | | | |
| Custard: | | | | | | |
| Home recipe (USDA) | ⅙ of 9″ pie (5.4 oz.) | 375 | 19.0 | | | |
| Frozen: | | | | | | |
| Baked (USDA) | 5 oz. | 358 | 17.0 | | | |
| Unbaked (USDA) | 5 oz. | 338 | 12.1 | | | |
| (Banquet) | 5-oz. serving | | 12.0 | | | |
| (Morton) | ⅙ of 20-oz. pie | 219 | 9.1 | | | |
| (Morton) | ⅛ of 46-oz. pie | 394 | 30.0 | | | |
| (Mrs. Smith's) | ⅙ of 8″ pie (4 oz.) | 338 | 13.2 | | | |
| (Mrs. Smith's⟩ | ⅛ of 10″ pie | | | | | |
| | (5.4 oz.) | 438 | 17.0 | | | |

## COCONUT PIE FILLING MIX
### (See also COCONUT PUDDING MIX):

| | | | | | | |
|---|---|---|---|---|---|---|
| Custard & pie crust, dry (USDA)[1] | 1 oz. | 178 | 5.7 | 2. | 3. | |
| *Custard made with egg yolk & milk (USDA)[2] | 5 oz. (including crust) | 334 | 11.2 | 4. | 7. | |

## COCONUT PUDDING MIX:

| | | | | | | |
|---|---|---|---|---|---|---|
| *Cream, regular (Jell-O) | ½ cup (5.2 oz.) | 205 | 6.0 | | | 13 |
| *Cream, instant (Jell-O) | ½ cup (5.3 oz.) | 313 | 6.1 | | | 13 |
| *Toasted, instant (Royal) | ½ cup (5.1 oz.) | 385 | 6.1 | | | 14 |

## COCO WHEATS, cereal

| | | | | | | |
|---|---|---|---|---|---|---|
| COCO WHEATS, cereal | 2 T. (.6 oz.) | 1 | .3 | | | (0) |

## COD:

| | | | | | | |
|---|---|---|---|---|---|---|
| Raw, whole (USDA) | 1 lb. (weighed whole) | 98 | .4 | | | 70 |
| Raw, meat only (USDA) | 4 oz. | 79 | .3 | | | 57 |
| Raw, meat rinsed in brine (USDA) | 4 oz. | 289 | .3 | | | 57 |
| Broiled (USDA) | 4 oz. | 125 | 6.0 | | | |
| Canned (USDA) | 4 oz. | | .3 | | | |
| Dehydrated, lightly salted (USDA) | 4 oz. | 9185 | 3.2 | | | |
| Dried, salted (USDA) | 4 oz. | | .8 | | | 93 |

(USDA): United States Department of Agriculture
*Prepared as Package Directs
[1]Principal sources of fat: vegetable shortening & coconut.
[2]Principal sources of fat: vegetable shortening, coconut, milk & egg.

| Food and Description | Measure or Quantity | Sodium (mg.) | Total | Fats in grams Satu- rated | Unsatu- rated | Choles- terol (mg.) |
|---|---|---|---|---|---|---|
| Dried, salted (USDA) | 5½" x 1½" x ½" (2.8 oz.) | | .6 | | | 66 |
| Frozen (Gorton) | ⅓ of 1-lb. pkg. | 107 | .5 | | | |

**CODFISH CAKE** (See **FISH CAKE**)

**COFFEE:**
Regular:

| | | | | | | |
|---|---|---|---|---|---|---|
| *(Chase & Sanborn) | ¾ cup | 1 | Tr. | | | 0 |
| *Max Pax | ¾ cup | 1 | Tr. | | | 0 |
| *(Maxwell House) | ¾ cup | Tr. | Tr. | | | 0 |
| *(Yuban) | ¾ cup | Tr. | Tr. | | | 0 |

Instant:

| | | | | | | |
|---|---|---|---|---|---|---|
| Dry (USDA) | 1 oz. | 20 | Tr. | | | 0 |
| Dry (USDA) | 1 rounded tsp. (2 grams) | 2 | Tr. | | | 0 |
| *(USDA) | 1 cup (8.4 oz.) | 2 | Tr. | | | 0 |
| (Borden) | 1 rounded tsp. (2 grams) | | <.1 | | | (0) |
| *(Chase & Sanborn) | ¾ cup | 1 | Tr. | | | 0 |
| Kava (Borden) | 1 tsp. (1 gram) | <1 | <.1 | | | (0) |
| *(Maxwell House) | ¾ cup | Tr. | Tr. | | | 0 |
| *(Yuban) | ¾ cup | Tr. | Tr. | | | 0 |

Decaffeinated:

| | | | | | | |
|---|---|---|---|---|---|---|
| Decaf | 1 tsp. (2 grams) | Tr. | 0. | | | (0) |
| *Sanka regular | ¾ cup | Tr. | Tr. | | | 0 |
| *Sanka instant | ¾ cup | Tr. | Tr. | | | 0 |
| *Siesta | ¾ cup | 1 | Tr. | | | 0 |

Freeze-dried:

| | | | | | | |
|---|---|---|---|---|---|---|
| *Maxim | ¾ cup | Tr. | Tr. | | | 0 |
| *Sanka | ¾ cup | Tr. | Tr. | | | 0 |

**COFFEE CAKE:**

| | | | | | | |
|---|---|---|---|---|---|---|
| Butterfly (Mrs. Smith's) | 1 piece (2¾ oz.) | 175 | 14.2 | | | |
| Cherry (Mrs. Smith's) | 1 piece (2¾ oz.) | 180 | 14.2 | | | |
| Cinnamon-raisin (Mrs. Smith's) | 1 piece (2¾ oz.) | 145 | 11.3 | | | |
| Cinnamon twist (Pepperidge Farm) | ⅙ cake (1.8 oz.) | 208 | 6.6 | | | |
| Danish, apple, frozen (Morton) | 1 cake (13.5 oz.) | 1243 | 47.4 | | | |
| Danish pastry, without fruit or nuts: | | | | | | |
| Individual round (USDA)[1] | 1 piece (2.3 oz.) | 238 | 15.3 | 5. | 11. | |
| Packaged ring (USDA)[1] | 12-oz. cake | 1244 | 79.9 | 24. | 56. | |

(USDA): United States Department of Agriculture
*Prepared as Package Directs
[1]Principal sources of fat: vegetable shortening, butter & egg.

| Food and Description | Measure or Quantity | Sodium (mg.) | Fats in grams — Total | Satu- rated | Unsatu- rated | Choles- terol (mg.) |
|---|---|---|---|---|---|---|
| Danish pecan twist, frozen | | | | | | |
| (Morton) | 12-oz. cake | 1539 | 80.6 | | | |
| Melt-A-Way, frozen (Morton) | 13-oz. cake | 1625 | 79.8 | | | |
| Meltaway (Mrs. Smith's) | 1 piece (2¾ oz.) | 185 | 26.9 | | | |
| Pecan roll (Mrs. Smith's) | 1 piece (2¾ oz.) | 135 | 19.8 | | | |
| **COFFEE CAKE MIX:** | | | | | | |
| Dry (USDA)[1] | 1 oz. | 174 | 3.1 | <1 | 3. | |
| *Prepared with egg & milk (USDA)[2] | 2 oz. | 244 | 5.4 | 1. | 4. | |
| *(Aunt Jemima) | ⅛ of cake (1.8 oz.) | 211 | 5.8 | | | |
| **COFFEE SOFT DRINK:** | | | | | | |
| Sweetened (Hoffman) | 6 fl. oz. | 14 | 0. | | | 0 |
| Low calorie (Hoffman) | 6 fl. oz. | 32 | 0. | | | 0 |
| Low calorie (No-Cal) | 6 fl. oz. | 20 | 0. | | | 0 |
| *COFFEE SOUTHERN,* liqueur, | | | | | | |
| 55 proof | 1 fl. oz. | Tr. | 0. | | | 0 |
| **COLA SOFT DRINK:** | | | | | | |
| Sweetened: | | | | | | |
| (Canada Dry) Jamaica | 6 fl. oz. | 0+ | 0. | | | 0 |
| (Clicquot Club) | 6 fl. oz. | 11 | 0. | | | 0 |
| *Coca-Cola* | 6 fl. oz. | Tr.+ | 0. | | | 0 |
| (Cott) | 6 fl. oz. | 11 | 0. | | | 0 |
| (Dr. Brown's) | 6 fl. oz. | 3 | 0. | | | 0 |
| (Hoffman) | 6 fl. oz. | 3 | 0. | | | 0 |
| (Key Food) | 6 fl. oz. | 3 | 0. | | | 0 |
| (Kirsch) | 6 fl. oz. | <1 | 0. | | | 0 |
| (Mission) | 6 fl. oz. | 11 | 0. | | | 0 |
| (Nedick's) | 6 fl. oz. | 3 | 0. | | | 0 |
| *Pepsi-Cola* | 6 fl. oz. | Tr.+ | 0. | | | 0 |
| *RC* with a twist (Royal Crown) | 6 fl. oz. (6.5 oz.) | 3+ | 0. | | | 0 |
| (Royal Crown) | 6 fl. oz. (6.5 oz.) | 3+ | 0. | | | 0 |
| (Shasta) | 6 fl. oz. | 10 | 0. | | | 0 |
| (Waldbaum) | 6 fl. oz. | 3 | 0. | | | 0 |
| (Yukon Club) | 6 fl. oz. | 3 | 0. | | | 0 |
| Cherry (Key Food) | 6 fl. oz. | 14 | 0. | | | 0 |
| Cherry (Shasta) | 6 fl. oz. | 10 | 0. | | | 0 |
| Low calorie: | | | | | | |
| (Canada Dry)sugar-free | 6 fl. oz. | 8+ | 0. | | | 0 |

(USDA): United States Department of Agriculture
*Prepared as Package Directs
[1]Principal source of fat: vegetable shortening.
[2]Principal sources of fat: vegetable shortening, egg & milk.

| Food and Description | Measure or Quantity | Sodium (mg.) | — Fats in grams — | | | Cholesterol (mg.) |
|---|---|---|---|---|---|---|
| | | | Total | Saturated | Unsaturated | |
| (Clicquot Club) | 6 fl. oz. | 38 | 0. | | | 0 |
| (Cott) | 6 fl. oz. | 38 | 0. | | | 0 |
| *Diet Pepsi-Cola*, sugar-free | 6 fl. oz. | 31+ | 0. | | | 0 |
| *Diet Rite*, sugar-free | 6 fl. oz. (6.4 oz.) | 29+ | 0. | | | 0 |
| (Dr. Brown's) | 6 fl. oz. | 40 | 0. | | | 0 |
| (Hoffman) | 6 fl. oz. | 40 | 0. | | | 0 |
| (Key Food) | 6 fl. oz. | 40 | 0. | | | 0 |
| (Mission) | 6 fl. oz. | 38 | 0. | | | 0 |
| (No-Cal) | 6 fl. oz. | 12 | 0. | | | 0 |
| (Shasta) | 6 fl. oz. | 37 | 0. | | | 0 |
| *RC Cola*, sugar-free | 6 fl. oz. | 29+ | 0. | | | 0 |
| *Tab* | 6 fl. oz. | 13 | 0. | | | 0 |
| (Waldbaum) | 6 fl. oz. | 40 | 0. | | | 0 |
| (Yukon Club) | 6 fl. oz. | 57 | 0. | | | 0 |
| Cherry (Shasta) | 6 fl. oz. | 37 | 0. | | | 0 |
| **COLA SYRUP,** low calorie (No-Cal) | 1 tsp. (5 grams) | <1 | 0. | | | 0 |
| **COLESLAW,** not drained (USDA): | | | | | | |
| Prepared with commercial French dressing[1] | 4 oz. | 304 | 8.3 | 1. | 7. | |
| Prepared with homemade French dressing, using corn oil[2] | 4 oz. | 149 | 13.9 | 1. | 13. | |
| Prepared with homemade French dressing, using cottonseed oil[3] | 4 oz. | 149 | 13.9 | 3. | 10. | |
| Prepared with mayonnaise[2] | 4 oz. | 136 | 15.9 | 2. | 14. | |
| Prepared with mayonnaise-type salad dressing[2] | 4 oz. | 141 | 9.0 | 1. | 8. | |
| **COLLARDS:** | | | | | | |
| Raw (USDA): | | | | | | |
| Leaves, including stems | 1 lb. | 195 | 3.2 | | | 0 |
| Leaves only | ½ lb. | | 1.2 | | | 0 |
| Boiled without salt, drained (USDA): | | | | | | |
| Leaves, cooked in large amount of water | ½ cup (3.4 oz.) | | .7 | | | 0 |
| Leaves & stems, cooked in small amount of water | 4 oz. | 28 | .7 | | | 0 |
| Leaves, cooked in small amount water | ½ cup (3.4 oz.) | | .7 | | | 0 |

(USDA): United States Department of Agriculture
*Prepared as Package Directs
[1]Principal sources of fat: soybean oil, cottonseed oil & corn oil.
[2]Principal source of fat: corn oil.
[3]Principal source of fat: cottonseed oil.

| Food and Description | Measure or Quantity | Sodium (mg.) | Fats in grams — Total | Satu- rated | Unsatu- rated | Choles- terol (mg.) |
|---|---|---|---|---|---|---|
| Frozen: | | | | | | |
|   Not thawed (USDA) | 10-oz. pkg. | 51 | 1.1 | | | 0 |
|   Boiled, chopped, drained (USDA) | ½ cup (3 oz.) | 14 | .3 | | | 0 |
|   Chopped (Birds Eye) | ⅓ of pkg. (3.3 oz.) | 17 | .4 | | | 0 |
| **COLLINS MIX** (Bar-Tender's) | 1 serving (⅝ oz.) | 32 | .2 | | | (0) |
| *CONCENTRATE,* cereal (Kellogg's) | ⅓ cup (1 oz.) | 82 | .1 | | | |
| **CONCORD WINE:** | | | | | | |
|   (Gold Seal) 13–14% alcohol | 3 fl. oz. (3.3 oz.) | 3 | 0. | | | (0) |
|   (Pleasant Valley) red, 12.5% alcohol | 3 fl. oz. | 23 | 0. | | | 0 |
| **CONSOMME,** canned, dietetic pack (Slim-ette) | 8 oz. (by wt.) | 5 | Tr. | | | |
| **CONSOMME MADRILENE,** canned, clear or red (Crosse & Blackwell) | ½ can (6½ oz.) | | 2.4 | | | |
| **COOKIE, COMMERCIAL:** | | | | | | |
| The following are listed by type or brand name: | | | | | | |
| Almond crescent (Nabisco) | 1 piece (7 grams) | 23 | 1.4 | | | |
| Almond toast, Mandel (Stella D'oro) | 1 piece (.5 oz.) | | .7 | | | |
| Angelica Goodies (Stella D'oro) | 1 piece (.8 oz.) | | 3.9 | | | |
| Anginetti (Stella D'oro) | 1 piece (5 grams) | | 1.7 | | | |
| Animal Cracker: | | | | | | |
|   (USDA) | 1 oz. | 86 | 2.7 | | | |
|   (Nabisco) *Barnum's* | 1 piece (3 grams) | 12 | .3 | | | |
|   (Sunshine) regular | 1 piece (2 grams) | | .3 | | | |
|   (Sunshine) iced | 1 piece (5 grams) | | 1.2 | | | |
| Anisette sponge (Stella D'oro) | 1 piece (.5 oz.) | | .8 | | | |
| Anisette toast (Stella D'oro) | 1 piece (.4 oz.) | | .5 | | | |
| Applesauce (Sunshine) regular or iced | 1 piece (.6 oz.) | | 3.8 | | | |
| Arrowroot (Sunshine) | 1 piece (4 grams) | 12 | .4 | | | |
| Assortment: | | | | | | |
|   (USDA) | 1 oz. | 103 | 5.7 | | | |
|   (Stella D'oro) *Lady Stella* | 1 piece (8 grams) | | 1.6 | | | |
|   (Sunshine) *Lady Joan* | 1 piece (9 grams) | | 1.9 | | | |
|   (Sunshine) *Lady Joan,* iced | 1 piece (.4 oz.) | | 2.4 | | | |

(USDA): United States Department of Agriculture
*Prepared as Package Directs

| Food and Description | Measure or Quantity | Sodium (mg.) | —Fats in grams— Total | Satu- rated | Unsatu- rated | Choles- terol (mg.) |
|---|---|---|---|---|---|---|
| *Aunt Sally*, iced (Sunshine) | 1 piece (.8 oz.) | | 1.6 | | | |
| *Bana-Bee* (Nabisco) | 6 pieces | | | | | |
| | (1¾-oz. pkg.) | 210 | 12.4 | | | |
| *Big Treat* (Sunshine) | 1 piece (1.3 oz.) | | 5.0 | | | |
| *Bordeaux* (Pepperidge Farm) | 1 piece (8 grams) | 23 | 1.6 | | | |
| *Breakfast Treats* (Stella D'oro) | 1 piece (.8 oz.) | | 3.7 | | | |
| Brown edge wafers (Nabisco) | 1 piece (6 grams) | 20 | 1.2 | | | |
| Brownie: | | | | | | |
| (Hostess) 2 to pkg. | 1 piece (.9 oz.) | 41 | 4.0 | | | |
| (Tastykake) | 1 pkg. (2¼ oz.) | | 10.3 | | | |
| Chocolate nut (Pepperidge Farm) | 1 piece (.4 oz.) | 22 | 3.5 | | | |
| Peanut butter (Tastykake) | 1 pkg. (1¾ oz.) | | 10.2 | | | |
| Pecan fudge (Keebler) | 1 piece (.9 oz.) | 47 | 5.7 | | | |
| Frozen, with nuts & chocolate | | | | | | |
| icing (USDA)[1] | 1 oz. | 57 | 5.8 | 1. | 4. | |
| *Brussels* (Pepperidge Farm) | 1 piece (8 grams) | 21 | 2.4 | | | |
| Butter: | | | | | | |
| Thin, rich (USDA)[2] | 1 oz. | 119 | 4.8 | 3. | 2. | |
| (Nabisco) | 1 piece (5 grams) | 17 | .9 | | | |
| (Sunshine) | 1 piece (5 grams) | | .9 | | | |
| *Buttercup* (Keebler) | 1 piece (5 grams) | 30 | 1.0 | | | |
| *Butterscotch Fudgies* (Tastykake) | 1 pkg. (1¾ oz.) | | 10.4 | | | |
| *Capri* (Pepperidge Farm) | 1 piece (.6 oz.) | 38 | 4.6 | | | |
| *Cardiff* (Pepperidge Farm) | 1 piece (4 grams) | 8 | .8 | | | |
| Cherry Coolers (Sunshine) | 1 piece (6 grams) | | 1.1 | | | |
| Chinese almond (Stella D'oro) | 1 piece (1.2 oz.) | | 9.2 | | | |
| Chocolate & chocolate-covered: | | | | | | |
| (USDA)[3] | 1 oz. | 39 | 4.5 | 1. | 3. | |
| *Como* (Stella D'oro) | 1 piece (1.1 oz.) | | 8.9 | | | |
| Creme (Wise) | 1 piece (7 grams) | 28 | 1.3 | | | |
| Peanut bars (Nabisco) *Ideal* | 1 piece (.6 oz.) | 66 | 5.4 | | | |
| *Pinwheels* (Nabisco) | 1 piece (1.1 oz.) | 30 | 5.8 | | | |
| Snaps (Nabisco) | 1 piece (4 grams) | 14 | .7 | | | |
| Snaps (Sunshine) | 1 piece (3 grams) | | .5 | | | |
| Wafers (Nabisco) *Famous* | 1 piece (6 grams) | 29 | .7 | | | |
| Chocolate chip: | | | | | | |
| (USDA)[3] | 1 oz. | 114 | 6.0 | 1. | 5. | |
| (Keebler) old fashioned | 1 piece (.6 oz.) | 60 | 3.7 | | | |
| (Nabisco) | 1 piece (7 grams) | 19 | 1.6 | | | |
| (Nabisco) *Chips Ahoy* | 1 piece (.4 oz.) | 31 | 2.1 | | | |

(USDA): United States Department of Agriculture
*Prepared as Package Directs
[1]Principal sources of fat: vegetable shortening. egg. milk. nuts & chocolate.
[2]Principal sources of fat: butter. egg & milk.
[3]Principal sources of fat: vegetable shortening. egg & milk.

| Food and Description | Measure or Quantity | Sodium (mg.) | Fats in grams — Total | Satu- rated | Unsatu- rated | Choles- terol (mg.) |
|---|---|---|---|---|---|---|
| (Nabisco) *Family Favorites* | 1 piece (7 grams) | 19 | .9 | | | |
| (Nabisco) Snaps | 1 piece (4 grams) | 16 | .7 | | | |
| (Pepperidge Farm) | 1 piece (.4 oz.) | 23 | 2.9 | | | |
| (Sunshine) *Chip-A-Roos* | 1 piece (.4 oz.) | | 2.9 | | | |
| (Tastykake) *Choc-O-Chip* | 4 pieces (1¾-oz. pkg.) | | 14.4 | | | |
| Cinnamon: | | | | | | |
| Crisp (Keebler) | 1 piece (4 grams) | 27 | .6 | | | |
| Spice, vanilla sandwich | | | | | | |
| (Nabisco) *Crinkles* | 6 pieces (1⅝-oz. pkg.) | 202 | 9.6 | | | |
| Sugar (Pepperidge Farm) | 1 piece (.4 oz.) | 31 | 2.4 | | | |
| Toast (Sunshine) | 1 piece (3 grams) | | .3 | | | |
| Coconut: | | | | | | |
| Bar (USDA)[1] | 1 oz. | 42 | 6.9 | 2. | 5. | |
| Bar (Nabisco) | 1 piece (9 grams) | 34 | .2 | | | |
| Bar (Sunshine) | 1 piece (.4 oz.) | | 2.3 | | | |
| (Nabisco) *Family Favorites* | 1 piece (3 grams) | 11 | .7 | | | |
| Chocolate chip (Nabisco) | 1 piece (.5 oz.) | 49 | 4.1 | | | |
| Chocolate chip (Sunshine) | 1 piece (.6 oz.) | | 4.3 | | | |
| Chocolate drop (Keebler) | 1 piece (.5 oz.) | 41 | 4.2 | | | |
| *Coconut Kiss* (Tastykake) | 4 pieces (1¾-oz. pkg.) | | 19.2 | | | |
| *Commodore* (Keebler) | 1 piece (.5 oz.) | 74 | 2.3 | | | |
| *Como Delight* (Stella D'oro) | 1 piece (1.1 oz.) | | 7.9 | | | |
| *Cowboys and Indians* (Nabisco) | 1 piece (2 grams) | 9 | .2 | | | |
| Cream Lunch (Sunshine) | 1 piece (.4 oz.) | | 1.4 | | | |
| Creme Wafer Stick (Nabisco) | 1 piece (9 grams) | 9 | 2.8 | | | |
| *Cup Custard* (Sunshine): | | | | | | |
| Chocolate | 1 piece (.5 oz.) | | 3.3 | | | |
| Vanilla | 1 piece (.5 oz.) | | 3.3 | | | |
| Devil's Food Cake (Nab) | 2 pieces (1¼-oz. pkg.) | 83 | 2.2 | | | |
| Devil's Food Cake (Nabisco) | 1 piece (.5 oz.) | 31 | .8 | | | |
| *Dixie Vanilla* (Sunshine) | 1 piece (.5 oz.) | | 1.8 | | | |
| *Dresden* (Pepperidge Farm) | 1 piece (.6 oz.) | 33 | 4.6 | | | |
| Egg Jumbo (Stella D'oro) | 1 piece (.4 oz.) | | .7 | | | |
| Fig bar: | | | | | | |
| (USDA) | 1 oz. | 71 | 1.6 | Tr. | 1. | |
| (Keebler) | 1 piece (.7 oz.) | 84 | 1.2 | | | |
| (Nab) *Fig Newtons* | 1 piece (1-oz. pkg.) | 97 | 2.2 | | | |
| (Nab) *Fig Newtons* | 2 pieces (2-oz. pkg.) | 193 | 4.3 | | | |

(USDA): United States Department of Agriculture
*Prepared as Package Directs
[1]Principal sources of fat: butter, egg & coconut.

| Food and Description | Measure or Quantity | Sodium (mg.) | Fats in grams | | | Choles-terol (mg.) |
|---|---|---|---|---|---|---|
| | | | Total | Satu-rated | Unsatu-rated | |
| (Nabisco) *Fig Newtons* | 1 piece (.6 oz.) | 53 | 1.2 | | | |
| (Sunshine) | 1 piece (.4 oz.) | | .8 | | | |
| Fruit, iced (Nabisco) | 1 piece (.6 oz.) | 77 | 1.5 | | | |
| Fudge: | | | | | | |
| (Sunshine) | 1 piece (.5 oz.) | | 3.7 | | | |
| Chip (Pepperidge Farm) | 1 piece (.4 oz.) | 33 | 2.5 | | | |
| *Fudge Stripes* (Keebler) | 1 piece (.4 oz.) | 36 | 2.7 | | | |
| Gingersnap: | | | | | | |
| (USDA)[1] | 1 oz. | 162 | 2.5 | Tr. | 2. | |
| (USDA) crumbs[1] | 1 cup (4.1 oz.) | 657 | 10.2 | 2. | 8. | |
| (Keebler) | 1 piece (6 grams) | 88 | .6 | | | |
| (Nabisco) old fashion | 1 piece (7 grams) | 41 | .7 | | | |
| (Sunshine) | 1 piece (6 grams) | | .6 | | | |
| *Zu Zu* (Nabisco) | 1 piece (4 grams) | 17 | .4 | | | |
| Golden Bars (Stella D'oro) | 1 piece (1 oz.) | | 5.9 | | | |
| Golden Fruit (Sunshine) | 1 piece (.7 oz.) | | .6 | | | |
| Graham Cracker (See **CRACKERS, GRAHAM)** | | | | | | |
| Hermit bar, frosted (Tastykake) | 1 pkg. (2 oz.) | | 7.2 | | | |
| *Home Plate* (Keebler) | 1 piece (.5 oz.) | 58 | 1.6 | | | |
| *Hostest With The Mostest* (Stella D'oro) | 1 piece (8 grams) | | 1.8 | | | |
| *Hydrox* (Sunshine): | | | | | | |
| Regular or mint | 1 piece (.4 oz.) | | 2.2 | | | |
| Vanilla | 1 piece (.4 oz.) | | 2.3 | | | |
| *Jan Hagel* (Keebler) | 1 piece (10 grams) | 51 | 1.6 | | | |
| *Keebies* (Keebler) | 1 piece (.4 oz.) | 44 | 2.3 | | | |
| Ladyfingers (USDA)[1] | .4-oz. ladyfinger (3¼" x 1⅜" x 1⅛") | 8 | .9 | Tr. | <1. | 40 |
| Lemon: | | | | | | |
| (Sunshine) | 1 piece (.5 oz.) | | 3.7 | | | |
| Jumble rings (Nabisco) | 1 piece (.5 oz.) | 46 | 2.3 | | | |
| *Lemon Coolers* (Sunshine) | 1 piece (6 grams) | | 1.1 | | | |
| Nut crunch (Pepperidge Farm) | 1 piece (.4 oz.) | 23 | 3.2 | | | |
| Snaps (Nabisco) | 1 piece (4 grams) | 12 | .4 | | | |
| *Lido* (Pepperidge Farm) | 1 piece (.6 oz.) | 32 | 5.3 | | | |
| *Lisbon* (Pepperidge Farm) | 1 piece (5 grams) | 13 | 1.5 | | | |
| Macaroon: | | | | | | |
| (USDA)[2] | 1 oz. | 10 | 6.6 | 5. | 2. | |
| Almond (Tastykake) | 2-oz. pkg. (2 pieces) | | 20.3 | | | |
| Coconut (Nabisco) *Bake Shop* | 1 piece (.7 oz.) | 17 | 4.0 | | | |

(USDA): United States Department of Agriculture
*Prepared as Package Directs
[1]Principal sources of fat: vegetable shortening. egg & milk.
[2]Principal sources of fat: coconut & almonds.

| Food and Description | Measure or Quantity | Sodium (mg.) | Fats in grams | | | Cholesterol (mg.) |
|---|---|---|---|---|---|---|
| | | | Total | Saturated | Unsaturated | |
| Sandwich (Nabisco) | 1 piece (.5 oz.) | 29 | 3.4 | | | |
| *Margherite*, chocolate (Stella D'oro) | 1 piece (.6 oz.) | | 3.0 | | | |
| *Margherite*, vanilla (Stella D'oro) | 1 piece (.6 oz.) | | 3.0 | | | |
| *Marquisette* (Pepperidge Farm) | 1 piece (8 grams) | 18 | 2.6 | | | |
| Marshmallow: | | | | | | |
| (USDA) | 1 oz. | 59 | 3.7 | | | |
| *Fancy Crests* (Nabisco) | 1 piece (.5 oz.) | 29 | 1.0 | | | |
| *Mallowmars* (Nabisco) | 1 piece (.5 oz.) | 19 | 2.5 | | | |
| *Mallo Puff* (Sunshine) | 1 piece (.6 oz.) | | 1.6 | | | |
| *Minarets* (Nabisco) | 1 piece (10 grams) | 14 | 2.4 | | | |
| Puffs (Nabisco) | 1 piece (.7 oz.) | 25 | 4.4 | | | |
| Sandwich (Nabisco) | 1 piece (8 grams) | 22 | .8 | | | |
| *Twirls* (Nabisco) | 1 piece (1.1 oz.) | 32 | 4.6 | | | |
| *Milano* (Pepperidge Farm) | 1 piece (.4 oz.) | 21 | 3.5 | | | |
| *Milano*, mint (Pepperidge Farm) | 1 piece (.5 oz.) | 21 | 4.4 | | | |
| Mint sandwich (Nabisco) *Mystic* | 1 piece (.6 oz.) | 46 | 4.6 | | | |
| Molasses (USDA)[1] | 1 oz. | 109 | 3.0 | <1. | 2. | |
| Molasses & Spice (Sunshine) | 1 piece (.6 oz.) | | 1.8 | | | |
| *Naples* (Pepperidge Farm) | 1 piece (6 grams) | 10 | 1.9 | | | |
| *Nassau* (Pepperidge Farm) | 1 piece (.6 oz.) | 51 | 4.9 | | | |
| Oatmeal: | | | | | | |
| (Keebler) old fashioned | 1 piece (.6 oz.) | 76 | 3.0 | | | |
| (Nabisco) | 1 piece (.6 oz.) | 65 | 3.1 | | | |
| (Nabisco) *Family Favorites* | 1 piece (5 grams) | 20 | .9 | | | |
| (Sunshine) | 1 piece (.4 oz.) | 150 | 2.3 | | | |
| Iced (Sunshine) | 1 piece (.5 oz.) | | 2.2 | | | |
| Irish (Pepperidge Farm) | 1 piece (.4 oz.) | 41 | 2.2 | | | |
| Peanut butter (Sunshine) | 1 piece (.6 oz.) | | 3.6 | | | |
| Raisin (USDA)[1] | 1 oz. | 46 | 4.4 | 1. | 3. | |
| Raisin (Nabisco) *Bake Shop* | 1 piece (.6 oz.) | 81 | 3.0 | | | |
| Raisin (Pepperidge Farm) | 1 piece (.4 oz.) | 54 | 2.6 | | | |
| Raisin bar (Tastykake) | 1 pkg. (2¼ oz.) | | 10.0 | | | |
| *Old Country Treats* (Stella D'oro) | 1 piece (.5 oz.) | | 2.9 | | | |
| *Orleans* (Pepperidge Farm) | 1 piece (6 grams) | 7 | 1.7 | | | |
| Peach-apricot pastry (Stella D'oro) | 1 piece (.8 oz.) | | 3.7 | | | |
| Peanut & peanut butter: | | | | | | |
| (USDA)[1] | 1 oz. | 49 | 5.4 | 1. | 4. | |
| Bars, cocoa-covered (Nabisco) | | | | | | |
| *Crowns* | 1 piece (.6 oz.) | 89 | 5.1 | | | |
| Caramel logs (Nabisco) *Heydays* | 1 piece (.8 oz.) | 35 | 6.6 | | | |
| Creme patties (Nab) | 3 pieces (½-oz. pkg.) | 38 | 3.8 | | | |
| Creme patties (Nab) | 6 pieces (1-oz. pkg.) | 77 | 7.6 | | | |

(USDA): United States Department of Agriculture
*Prepared as Package Directs
[1]Principal sources of fat: vegetable shortening, egg & milk.

| Food and Description | Measure or Quantity | Sodium (mg.) | —Fats in grams— | | | Choles- terol (mg.) |
| | | | Total | Satu- rated | Unsatu- rated | |
|---|---|---|---|---|---|---|
| Creme patties (Nabisco) | 1 piece (7 grams) | 18 | 1.8 | | | |
| Creme patties, cocoa-covered (Nabisco) *Fancy* | 1 piece (.4 oz.) | 25 | 3.3 | | | |
| Patties (Sunshine) | 1 piece (7 grams) | | 1.4 | | | |
| Sandwich (Nabisco) *Nutter Butter* | 1 piece (.5 oz.) | 57 | 3.1 | | | |
| *Pecan Sandies* (Keebler) | 1 piece (.6 oz.) | 52 | 5.1 | | | |
| *Penguins* (Keebler) | 1 piece (.8 oz.) | 66 | 5.7 | | | |
| *Pirouette* (Pepperidge Farm): | | | | | | |
| Chocolate laced | 1 piece (7 grams) | 11 | 2.1 | | | |
| Lemon or original | 1 piece (7 grams) | 12 | 2.0 | | | |
| *Pitter Patter* (Keebler) | 1 piece (.6 oz.) | 117 | 3.8 | | | |
| *Pizzelle*, Carolines (Stella D'oro) | 1 piece (.4 oz.) | | 2.0 | | | |
| Raisin: | | | | | | |
| (USDA)[1] | 1 oz. | 15 | 1.5 | Tr. | | 1. |
| Fruit biscuit (Nabisco) | 1 piece (.5 oz.) | 19 | .6 | | | |
| *Rich 'n Chips* (Keebler) | 1 piece (.5 oz.) | 44 | 3.8 | | | |
| *Rochelle* (Pepperidge Farm) | 1 piece (.6 oz.) | 38 | 4.5 | | | |
| Sandwich, creme: | | | | | | |
| (USDA)[1] | 1 oz. | 137 | 6.4 | 2. | | 5. |
| Cameo (Nabisco) | 1 piece (.5 oz.) | 49 | 2.6 | | | |
| Chocolate chip (Nabisco) | 1 piece (.5 oz.) | 36 | 3.8 | | | |
| Chocolate fudge: | | | | | | |
| (Keebler) | 1 piece (.7 oz.) | 97 | 4.7 | | | |
| Assorted (Nabisco) *Cookie Break* | 1 piece (.4 oz.) | 33 | 2.5 | | | |
| Chocolate (Nabisco) *Cookie Break* | 1 piece (.4 oz.) | 32 | 2.5 | | | |
| *Orbit* (Sunshine) | 1 piece (.4 oz.) | | 2.4 | | | |
| *Oreo* (Nab) | 4 pieces (1-oz. pkg.) | 136 | 6.0 | | | |
| *Oreo* (Nab) | 6 pieces (1⅝-oz. pkg.) | 222 | 9.7 | | | |
| *Oreo* (Nab) | 6 pieces (2⅛-oz. pkg.) | 290 | 12.7 | | | |
| *Oreo* (Nabisco) | 1 piece (.4 oz.) | 49 | 2.2 | | | |
| *Oreo & Swiss* (Nab) | 6 pieces (1⅝-oz. pkg.) | 159 | 10.5 | | | |
| *Oreo & Swiss* (Nab) | 6 pieces (2¼-oz. pkg.) | 220 | 14.5 | | | |
| *Oreo & Swiss*, assortment (Nabisco) | 1 piece (.4 oz.) | 35 | 2.3 | | | |
| *Pride* (Nabisco) | 1 piece (.4 oz.) | 31 | 2.6 | | | |

(USDA): United States Department of Agriculture
*Prepared as Package Directs
[1]Principal sources of fat: vegetable shortening, egg & milk.

| Food and Description | Measure or Quantity | Sodium (mg.) | Total | Fats in grams Satu- rated | Unsatu- rated | Choles- terol (mg.) |
|---|---|---|---|---|---|---|
| *Social Tea* (Nabisco) | 1 piece (.4 oz.) | 34 | 2.3 | | | |
| Swiss (Nab) | 4 pieces (1-oz. pkg.) | 59 | 7.2 | | | |
| Swiss (Nab) | 6 pieces (1¾-oz. pkg.) | 104 | 12.6 | | | |
| Swiss (Nabisco) | 1 piece (.4 oz.) | 22 | 2.6 | | | |
| (Tom Houston) | 1 piece (.5 oz.) | 149 | 3.6 | | | |
| Vanilla (Keebler) | 1 piece (.6 oz.) | 78 | 3.8 | | | |
| Vanilla (Nabisco) | 1 piece (.4 oz.) | 34 | 2.4 | | | |
| Vienna Finger (Sunshine) | 1 piece (.5 oz.) | | 2.9 | | | |
| Sesame, Regina (Stella D'oro) | 1 piece (.4 oz.) | | 2.3 | | | |
| Shortbread or shortcake: | | | | | | |
| (USDA) | 1 oz. | 17 | 6.5 | 2. | 5. | |
| (USDA) | 1¾"-square (8 grams) | 5 | 1.8 | Tr. | 1. | |
| (Nabisco) *Dandy* | 1 piece (.4 oz.) | 29 | 1.5 | | | |
| (Pepperidge Farm) | 1 piece (.5 oz.) | 39 | 3.9 | | | |
| *Lorna Doone* (Nab) | 4 pieces (1-oz. pkg.) | 146 | 6.1 | | | |
| *Lorna Doone* (Nab) | 6 pieces (1½-oz. pkg.) | 219 | 9.1 | | | |
| *Lorna Doone* (Nabisco) | 1 piece (8 grams) | 39 | 1.6 | | | |
| Pecan (Nabisco) | 1 piece (.5 oz.) | 44 | 4.6 | | | |
| *Scotties* (Sunshine) | 1 piece (8 grams) | | 1.8 | | | |
| Striped (Nabisco) | 1 piece (10 grams) | 13 | 2.3 | | | |
| Vanilla (Tastykake) | 6 pieces (2¼-oz. pkg.) | | 18.6 | | | |
| *Social Tea Biscuit* (Nabisco) | 1 piece (5 grams) | 18 | .6 | | | |
| Spiced wafers (Nabisco) | 1 piece (10 grams) | 58 | 1.1 | | | |
| *Sprinkles* (Sunshine) | 1 piece (.6 oz.) | 1.5 | | | | |
| Sugar cookie: | | | | | | |
| (Keebler) old fashioned | 1 piece (.6 oz.) | 55 | 2.8 | | | |
| (Pepperidge Farm) | 1 piece (.4 oz.) | 30 | 2.4 | | | |
| (Sunshine) | 1 piece (.6 oz.) | | 3.7 | | | |
| Brown (Nabisco) *Family Favorite* | 1 piece (5 grams) | 11 | 1.3 | | | |
| Brown (Pepperidge Farm) | 1 piece (.4 oz.) | 24 | 2.2 | | | |
| Rings (Nabisco) | 1 piece (.5 oz.) | 47 | 2.5 | | | |
| Sugar wafer: | | | | | | |
| (USDA)[1] | 1 oz. | 54 | 5.5 | 1. | 4. | |
| (Nab) *Biscos* | 3 pieces (⅞-oz. pkg.) | 32 | 6.1 | | | |
| (Nabisco) *Biscos* | 1 piece (4 grams) | 5 | .9 | | | |
| (Sunshine) | 1 piece (9 grams) | 36 | 1.8 | | | |
| *Krisp Kreem* (Kcebler) | 1 piece (6 grams) | 14 | 1.8 | | | |
| Lemon (Sunshine) | 1 piece (9 grams) | | 1.9 | | | |

(USDA): United States Department of Agriculture
*Prepared as Package Directs
[1]Principal sources of fat: vegetable shortening, egg & milk.

| Food and Description | Measure or Quantity | Sodium (mg.) | —Fats in grams— | | | Choles-terol (mg.) |
|---|---|---|---|---|---|---|
| | | | Total | Satu-rated | Unsatu-rated | |
| *Swedish Kreme* (Keebler) | 1 piece (5.7 oz.) | 81 | 5.2 | | | |
| *Tahiti* (Pepperidge Farm) | 1 piece (.5 oz.) | 17 | 5.4 | | | |
| Toy (Sunshine) | 1 piece (3 grams) | | .4 | | | |
| Vanilla creme (Wise) | 1 piece (7 grams) | 23 | 1.4 | | | |
| Vanilla snap (Nabisco) | 1 piece (3 grams) | 10 | .3 | | | |
| Vanilla wafer: | | | | | | |
| (USDA)[1] | 1 oz. | 71 | 4.6 | 1. | 3. | |
| (Keebler) | 1 piece (4 grams) | 18 | .9 | | | |
| (Nabisco) *Nilla* | 1 piece (4 grams) | 12 | .7 | | | |
| (Sunshine) small | 1 piece (3 grams) | | .6 | | | |
| *Venice* (Pepperidge Farm) | 1 piece (.4 oz.) | 13 | 3.3 | | | |
| Waffle creme (Nabisco) *Biscos* | 1 piece (8 grams) | 10 | 2.1 | | | |
| *Yum Yums* (Sunshine) | 1 piece (.5 oz.) | | 3.2 | | | |

**COOKIE, DIETETIC:**

| Food and Description | Measure or Quantity | Sodium (mg.) | Total | Satu-rated | Unsatu-rated | Choles-terol (mg.) |
|---|---|---|---|---|---|---|
| Almond chocolate wafer (Estee) | 1 piece | 2 | 1.7 | | | |
| Angel puffs (Stella D'oro) | 1 piece (3 grams) | 2 | 1.0 | | | |
| Apple pastry (Stella D'oro) | 1 piece (.8 oz.) | 42 | 3.9 | | | |
| Assorted (Estee) | 1 piece (6 grams) | 3 | 1.4 | Tr. | 1. | |
| Assorted filled wafers (Estee) | 1 piece (5 grams) | 3 | 1.3 | Tr. | 1. | |
| Banana wafers (Estee) | 1 piece | 12 | 8.5 | | | |
| *Beljuin Treats* (Estee) | 1 piece | 10 | 1.7 | | | |
| Chocolate chip (Estee) | 1 piece (6 grams) | 11 | 1.0 | Tr. | <1. | |
| Chocolate Holland filled wafer (Estee) | 1 piece (3 grams) | 1 | 1.2 | Tr. | <1. | 1 |
| Chocolate & vanilla wafer (Estee) | 1 piece (4 grams) | 3 | 1.3 | Tr. | 1. | |
| Fig pastry (Stella D'oro) | 1 piece (.9 oz.) | 20 | 3.7 | | | |
| Fruit flavored wafer (Estee) | 1 piece (4 grams) | 1 | 1.2 | Tr. | <1. | 1 |
| *Have-A-Heart* (Stella D'oro) | 1 piece (.7 oz.) | 22 | 5.1 | | | |
| Holland bittersweet wafer (Estee) | 1 piece | 3 | 8.3 | | | |
| Holland milk chocolate wafer (Estee) | 1 piece (.8 oz.) | 3 | 8.3 | 3. | 6. | 8 |
| Kichel (Stella D'oro) | 1 piece (1 gram) | 2 | .5 | | | |
| *Monties* (Estee) | 1 piece | 10' | 2.2 | | | |
| Oatmeal raisin (Estee) | 1 piece (7 grams) | 2 | 1.4 | Tr. | 1. | 2 |
| Pastry stick (Estee) | 1 piece (7 grams) | 3 | 2.1 | 2. | Tr. | |
| Peach-apricot pastry (Stella D'oro) | 1 piece (.8 oz.) | 14 | 4.2 | | | |
| Prune pastry (Stella D'oro) | 1 piece (.8 oz.) | 15 | 3.4 | | | |
| *Royal Nuggets* (Stella D'oro) | 1 piece (<1 gram) | 1 | .1 | | | |
| Sandwich, chocolate (Estee) | 1 piece (8 grams) | 3 | 2.1 | <1. | 2. | |
| Sandwich, Duplex (Estee) | 1 piece (9 grams) | 3 | 2.0 | <1. | 1. | |

(USDA): United States Department of Agriculture
*Prepared as Package Directs
[1]Principal sources of fat: vegetable shortening, egg & milk.

| Food and Description | Measure or Quantity | Sodium (mg.) | —Fats in grams— | | | Cholesterol (mg.) |
|---|---|---|---|---|---|---|
| | | | Total | Saturated | Unsaturated | |
| Sandwich, lemon (Estee) | 1 piece (.5 oz.) | 20 | 3.0 | 2. | 1. | <1 |
| Vanilla filled wafer (Estee) | 1 piece (4 grams) | 3 | 1.3 | Tr. | 1. | |
| Vanilla Holland filled wafer (Estee) | 1 piece (3 grams) | 1 | 1.2 | Tr. | <1. | 1 |
| Vanilla & strawberry wafer (Estee) | 1 piece | 3 | 1.3 | | | |
| Wafer cake (Estee) | 1 piece (9 grams) | 4 | 3.3 | 1. | 2. | 3 |
| **COOKIE DOUGH,** refrigerated: | | | | | | |
| Unbaked, plain (USDA)[1] | 1 oz. | 141 | 6.4 | 1. | 5. | |
| Baked, plain (USDA)[1] | 1 oz. | 155 | 7.1 | 2. | 6. | |
| **COOKIE, HOME RECIPE:** | | | | | | |
| Brownie with nuts (USDA): | | | | | | |
| Made with butter[2] | 1 oz. | 71 | 8.5 | 3. | 6. | 24 |
| Made with butter[2] | .7-oz. piece (1¾″ x 1¾″ x ⅞″) | 50 | 6.0 | 2. | 4. | 17 |
| Made with vegetable shortening[3] | 1 oz. | 71 | 8.9 | 2. | 7. | |
| Chocolate Chip (USDA): | | | | | | |
| Made with butter[4] | 1 oz. | 99 | 8.0 | 4. | 4. | |
| Made with vegetable shortening[5] | 1 oz. | 99 | 8.5 | 2. | 6. | |
| Sugar, soft, thick (USDA): | | | | | | |
| Made with butter[6] | 1 oz. | 90 | 4.3 | 2. | 2. | |
| Made with vegetable shortening[7] | 1 oz. | 90 | 4.8 | 1. | 4. | |
| **COOKIE MIX:** | | | | | | |
| Plain, dry (USDA)[8] | 1 oz. | 100 | 6.9 | 2. | 5. | |
| *Plain, prepared with egg & water (USDA)[1] | 1 oz. | 98 | 6.9 | 2. | 5. | |
| *Plain, prepared with milk (USDA)[9] | 1 oz. | 98 | 6.7 | 2. | 5. | |
| Brownie: | | | | | | |
| Dry, with egg (USDA)[10] | 1 oz. | 85 | 3.4 | <1. | 3. | |
| Dry, without egg (USDA)[11] | 1 oz. | 55 | 4.6 | 1. | 4. | |

(USDA): United States Department of Agriculture
*Prepared as Package Directs
[1]Principal sources of fat: vegetable shortening & egg.
[2]Principal sources of fat: pecans, butter, chocolate & egg.
[3]Principal sources of fat: pecans, vegetable shortening, chocolate & egg.
[4]Principal sources of fat: butter, chocolate, walnuts & egg.
[5]Principal sources of fat: vegetable shortening, chocolate, walnuts & egg.
[6]Principal sources of fat: butter, egg & milk.
[7]Principal sources of fat: vegetable shortening, egg & milk.
[8]Principal source of fat: vegetable shortening.
[9]Principal sources of fat: vegetable shortening & milk.
[10]Principal sources of fat: vegetable shortening, cocoa & egg.
[11]Principal sources of fat: vegetable shortening & cocoa.

| Food and Description | Measure or Quantity | Sodium (mg.) | —Fats in grams— | | | Choles-terol (mg.) |
|---|---|---|---|---|---|---|
| | | | Total | Satu-rated | Unsatu-rated | |
| *Dry, with egg, prepared with water & nuts (USDA)[1] | 1 oz. | 62 | 5.3 | <1. | 4. | |
| *Dry, without egg, prepared with egg, water & nuts (USDA)[1] | 1 oz. | 47 | 5.7 | 1. | 5. | |
| *Butterscotch (Betty Crocker) | 1½" sq. | 68 | 2.1 | | | |
| *"Cake like," family size (Duncan Hines) | 1/24 of pan (1.2 oz.) | 103 | 6.9 | | | |
| *"Cake like," regular size (Duncan Hines) | 1/16 of pan (1.2 oz.) | 106 | 7.1 | | | |
| *Fudge (Betty Crocker) | 1½" sq. | 36 | 2.2 | | | |
| *Fudge, supreme (Betty Crocker) | 1½" sq. | 28 | 2.2 | | | |
| *Fudge, chewy, family size (Duncan Hines) | 1/24 of pan (1.1 oz.) | 96 | 6.4 | 1. | 5. | |
| *Fudge, chewy, regular size (Duncan Hines) | 1/16 of pan (1.2 oz.) | 99 | 6.6 | 2. | 5. | |
| *German chocolate (Betty Crocker) | 1½" sq. | 38 | 2.4 | | | |
| *Walnut (Betty Crocker) | 1½" sq. | 35 | 2.9 | | | |
| Chocolate mint (Nestlé's) | 1 oz. | 111 | 5.3 | | | |
| *Date bar (Betty Crocker) | 2" x 1" bar | 35 | 2.5 | | | |
| *Macaroon, coconut (Betty Crocker) | 1 macaroon (1¾") | 11 | 3.6 | | | |
| Lemon (Nestlé's) | 1 oz. | 111 | 5.2 | | | |
| Sugar (Nestlé's) | 1 oz. | 111 | 5.2 | | | |
| *Toll House* (Nestlé's) | 1 oz. | 111 | 5.2 | | | |
| *Toll House, with morsels, prepared with egg (Nestlé's) | 1 piece (.4 oz.) | 34 | 2.4 | | | |
| *Toll House, without morsels, prepared without egg (Nestlé's) | 1 piece (8 grams) | 31 | 1.8 | | | |
| *Vienna Dream bar (Betty Crocker) | 1 bar (2" x 1⅓") | 65 | 4.9 | | | |

**COOKING FATS** (See **FATS**)

| | | | | | | |
|---|---|---|---|---|---|---|
| *COOL 'N CREAMY* (Birds Eye) | ½ cup (4.4 oz.) | 119 | 6.1 | | | 0 |
| **CORIANDER,** whole or ground (Spice Islands) | 1 tsp. | <1 | | | | (0) |

**CORN:**
| | | | | | | |
|---|---|---|---|---|---|---|
| Fresh, white or yellow (USDA): | | | | | | |
| Raw, untrimmed, on cob | 1 lb. (weighed in husk) | Tr. | 1.6 | | | 0 |

(USDA): United States Department of Agriculture
*Prepared as Package Directs
[1]Principal sources of fat: walnuts, vegetable shortening, cocoa & egg.

| Food and Description | Measure or Quantity | Sodium (mg.) | — Fats in grams — | | | Cholesterol (mg.) |
|---|---|---|---|---|---|---|
| | | | Total | Saturated | Unsaturated | |
| Raw, trimmed, on cob | 1 lb. (husk removed) | Tr. | 2.5 | | | 0 |
| Raw, kernels | 4 oz. | Tr. | 1.1 | | | 0 |
| Boiled without salt, kernels, cut from cob, drained | 1 cup (5.9 oz.) | Tr. | 1.7 | | | 0 |
| Boiled without salt, whole | 1 ear (5" x 1¾") (4.9 oz.) | Tr. | .8 | | | 0 |
| Canned, regular pack: | | | | | | |
| Golden or yellow, whole kernel: | | | | | | |
| Solids & liq., vacuum pack (USDA) | ½ cup (3.7 oz.) | 250 | .5 | | | 0 |
| Solids & liq., wet pack (USDA) | ½ cup (4.5 oz.) | 302 | .8 | | | 0 |
| Drained solids, wet pack (USDA) | ½ cup (3 oz.) | 203 | .7 | | | 0 |
| Drained liq., wet pack (USDA) | 4 oz. | 268 | Tr. | | | 0 |
| Solids & liq., vacuum pack (Del Monte) | ½ cup (3.7 oz.) | 220 | .5 | | | 0 |
| Drained solids, wet pack (Del Monte) Family Style | ½ cup (3 oz.) | 202 | .8 | | | 0 |
| Vacuum pack, *Niblets* | ⅓ of 12-oz. can | 318 | .6 | | | (0) |
| Solids & liq. (Green Giant) | ½ of 8.5-oz. can | 368 | .6 | | | (0) |
| Shoe peg (Le Sueur) | ¼ of 17-oz. can | 366 | .6 | | | (0) |
| Solids & liq., wet pack (Stokely-Van Camp) | ½ cup (4.5 oz.) | | .8 | | | (0) |
| With peppers, solids & liq. (Del Monte) | ½ cup (3.7 oz.) | 156 | .3 | | | 0 |
| With peppers, vacuum pack, *Mexicorn* | ⅓ of 12-oz. can | 352 | .6 | | | (0) |
| White, whole kernel: | | | | | | |
| Solids & liq., wet pack (USDA) | ½ cup (4.5 oz.) | 302 | .8 | | | 0 |
| Drained solids, wet pack (USDA) | ½ cup (2.8 oz.) | 189 | .6 | | | 0 |
| Drained liq., wet pack (USDA) | 4 oz. | 268 | Tr. | | | 0 |
| Vacuum pack (Green Giant) | ⅓ of 12-oz. can | 255 | .6 | | | (0) |
| Canned, white or yellow, dietetic pack: | | | | | | |
| Solids & liq., wet pack (USDA) | 4 oz. | 2 | .6 | | | 0 |
| Drained solids (USDA) | 4 oz. | 2 | .8 | | | 0 |
| Drained liq. (USDA) | 4 oz. (by wt.) | 2 | Tr. | | | 0 |
| Solids & liq. (Blue Boy) | 4 oz. | 3 | .6 | | | (0) |

(USDA): United States Department of Agriculture
*Prepared as Package Directs

| Food and Description | Measure or Quantity | Sodium (mg.) | — Fats in grams — | | | Choles- terol (mg.) |
|---|---|---|---|---|---|---|
| | | | Total | Satu- rated | Unsatu- rated | |
| Solids & liq. (Diet Delight) | ½ cup (4.4 oz.) | 5 | .5 | | | (0) |
| Solids & liq. (S and W) *Nutradiet*, unseasoned | 4 oz. | 7 | .4 | | | (0) |
| Solids & liq. (Tillie Lewis) | ½ cup | <10 | .6 | | | 0 |
| Canned, cream style, white or yellow, regular pack: | | | | | | |
| Solids & liq. (USDA) | ½ cup (4.4 oz.) | 295 | .8 | | | 0 |
| Golden, solids & liq. (Del Monte) | ½ cup (4.4 oz.) | 656 | .4 | | | (0) |
| Golden, solids & liq. (Green Giant) | ½ of 8.5-oz. can | 349 | .6 | | | (0) |
| Solids & liq. (Stokely-Van Camp) | ½ cup (4.1 oz.) | | .7 | | | (0) |
| Canned, cream style, dietetic pack: | | | | | | |
| Solids & liq. (USDA) | 4 oz. | 2 | 1.2 | | | 0 |
| Solids & liq. (Blue Boy) | 4 oz. | 3 | 1.2 | | | (0) |
| Solids & liq. (S and W) *Nutradiet* | 4 oz. | 2 | .5 | | | (0) |
| Frozen: | | | | | | |
| On the cob: | | | | | | |
| Not thawed (USDA) | 4 oz. | 1 | 1.1 | | | 0 |
| Boiled, drained (USDA) | 4 oz. | 1 | 1.1 | | | 0 |
| (Birds Eye) | 1 ear (3.5 oz.) | 1 | 1.0 | | | 0 |
| *Niblets Ears* | 1 ear (4.9 oz.) | 21 | .8 | | | (0) |
| Kernel, cut off cob: | | | | | | |
| Not thawed (USDA) | 4 oz. | 1 | .6 | | | 0 |
| Boiled, drained (USDA) | ½ cup (3.2 oz.) | <1 | .5 | | | 0 |
| (Birds Eye) | ½ cup (3.3 oz.) | 33 | .5 | | | 0 |
| Sweet white (Birds Eye) | ½ cup (3.3 oz.) | 1 | .5 | | | 0 |
| Cream style (Green Giant) | ⅓ of 10-oz. pkg. | 198 | .4 | | | (0) |
| In butter sauce: | | | | | | |
| & peppers (Green Giant) | ⅓ of 10-oz. pkg. | 312 | 2.8 | | | |
| Yellow, *Niblets* | ⅓ of 10-oz. pkg. | 383 | 2.4 | | | |
| White (Green Giant) | ⅓ of 10-oz. pkg. | 346 | 2.8 | | | |
| Scalloped casserole (Gr en Giant) | ⅓ of 10-oz. pkg. | 619 | 5.7 | | | |
| With peas & tomatoes (Birds Eye) | ⅓ of 10-oz. pkg. | 447 | .4 | | | 0 |

## CORNBREAD:

| Food and Description | Measure or Quantity | Sodium (mg.) | Total | Satu- rated | Unsatu- rated | Choles- terol (mg.) |
|---|---|---|---|---|---|---|
| Corn pone, home recipe, prepared with white, whole-ground corn-meal (USDA)[1] | 4 oz. | 449 | 6.0 | 2 | 4. | |

(USDA): United States Department of Agriculture
*Prepared as Package Directs
[1]Principal sources of fat: lard & egg.

| Food and Description | Measure or Quantity | Sodium (mg.) | —Fats in grams— | | | Choles-terol (mg.) |
|---|---|---|---|---|---|---|
| | | | Total | Satu-rated | Unsatu-rated | |
| Corn sticks, frozen (Aunt Jemima) | 3 pieces (1¾ oz.) | 360 | 5.1 | | | |
| Johnnycake, home recipe, prepared with yellow, degermed cornmeal (USDA)[1] | 4 oz. | 782 | 5.9 | 2. | 4. | |
| Southern-style, home recipe, prepared with degermed corn-meal (USDA)[1] | 2½" x 2½" x 1⅝" piece (2.9 oz.) | 491 | 5.0 | 1. | 4. | 58 |
| Southern-style, home recipe, prepared with whole-ground cornmeal (USDA)[1] | 4 oz. | 712 | 8.2 | 2. | 6. | |
| Spoonbread, home recipe, prepared with white, whole-ground cornmeal (USDA)[2] | 4 oz. | 547 | 12.9 | 5. | 8. | |
| **CORNBREAD MIX:** | | | | | | |
| Dry (USDA)[3] | 1 oz. | 328 | 3.6 | <1. | 3. | |
| *Prepared with egg & milk: | | | | | | |
| (USDA)[4] | 4 oz. | 844 | 9.5 | 3. | 6. | 78 |
| (USDA)[4] | 2⅜" muffin (1.4 oz.) | 298 | 3.4 | 1. | 2. | 28 |
| (USDA)[4] | 2½" x 2½" x 1⅜" piece (1.9 oz.) | 409 | 4.6 | 2. | 3. | 38 |
| *(Aunt Jemima) | ⅙ of cornbread (2.4 oz.) | 575 | 7.6 | | | |
| *(Dromedary) | 2" x 2" piece (1.4 oz.) | 294 | 4.6 | | | |
| *CORN CHEX*, cereal, dry | 1¼ cups (1 oz.) | 304 | .1 | | | (0) |
| **CORN CHIPS** (See **CRACKERS**) | | | | | | |
| **CORN CHOWDER,** New England (Snow) | 8 oz. | | 6.3 | | | |
| **CORNED BEEF:** | | | | | | |
| Uncooked, boneless, medium fat (USDA) | 1 lb. | 5897 | 113.4 | 54. | 59. | |
| Cooked, boneless, medium fat (USDA) | 4 oz. | 1973 | 34.5 | 17. | 17. | |

(USDA): United States Department of Agriculture
*Prepared as Package Directs
[1]Principal sources of fat: lard & egg.
[2]Principal sources of fat: lard, egg & milk.
[3]Principal sources of fat: vegetable shortening & egg.
[4]Principal sources of fat: vegetable shortening, milk & egg.

| Food and Description | Measure or Quantity | Sodium (mg.) | —Fats in grams— Total | Satu- rated | Unsatu- rated | Choles- terol (mg.) |
|---|---|---|---|---|---|---|
| Canned: | | | | | | |
| Lean (USDA) | 4 oz. | | 9.1 | 5. | 5. | |
| Medium fat (USDA) | 4 oz. | | 13.6 | 7. | 7. | |
| Fat (USDA) | 4 oz. | | 20.4 | 10. | 10. | |
| (Armour Star) | 4 oz. (from 12-oz. can) | | 22.0 | | | |
| (Hormel) *Dinty Moore* | 4 oz. | 1191 | 15.2 | 6. | 7. | 79 |
| Brisket (Wilson) *Tender Made* | 4 oz. | 1435 | 10.9 | 5. | 5. | 71 |
| Packaged (Oscar Mayer) | 5-gram slice (16 to 3 oz.) | 74 | .2 | | | |
| **CORNED BEEF HASH, canned:** | | | | | | |
| With potato (USDA)[1] | 4 oz. | 612 | 12.8 | 6. | 7. | |
| (Armour Star) | 15½-oz. can | | 60.1 | | | |
| (Hormel) | 7½ oz. | 1480 | 26.2 | | | |
| (Nalley's) | 4 oz. | | 11.3 | | | |
| (Van Camp) | ½ cup (4.1 oz.) | | 12.4 | | | |
| (Wilson) | 15½-oz. can | 3625 | 58.0 | 26. | 32. | 105 |
| **CORNED BEEF HASH DINNER,** | | | | | | |
| frozen (Banquet): | | | | | | |
| Meat compartment | 5.5 oz. | | 9.9 | | | |
| Apple compartment | 2.8 oz. | | .1 | | | |
| Peas compartment | 1.9 oz. | | .7 | | | |
| Complete dinner | 10.2-oz. dinner | | 10.7 | | | |
| **CORNED BEEF SPREAD:** | | | | | | |
| (Underwood) | 1 T. (.5 oz.) | 121 | 2.1 | | | |
| (Underwood) | 4½-oz. can | 1117 | 19.5 | | | |
| **CORN FLAKES, cereal:** | | | | | | |
| Whole (USDA) | 1 cup (1 oz.) | 291 | .1 | | | 0 |
| Crushed (USDA) | 1 cup (2.5 oz.) | 704 | .3 | | | 0 |
| Frosted (USDA) | 1 cup (1.4 oz.) | 310 | <.1 | | | 0 |
| *Country* (General Mills) | 1¼ cups (1 oz.) | 303 | .3 | | | (0) |
| (Kellogg's) | 1⅓ cups (1 oz.) | 268 | .1 | | | (0) |
| (Ralston) | 1 cup (1 oz.) | 290 | <.1 | | | (0) |
| (Van Brode) | 1 oz. | | <.1 | | | (0) |
| **CORN FRITTER:** | | | | | | |
| Home recipe (USDA)[2] | 4 oz. | 541 | 24.4 | 6. | 19. | |
| Frozen (Mrs. Paul's) | 12-oz. pkg. | | 31.8 | | | |

(USDA): United States Department of Agriculture
*Prepared as Package Directs
[1]Principal source of fat: beef.
[2]Principal sources of fat: vegetable shortening, egg, milk & butter.

| Food and Description | Measure or Quantity | Sodium (mg.) | —Fats in grams— Total | Satu- rated | Unsatu- rated | Choles- terol (mg.) |
|---|---|---|---|---|---|---|
| **CORN GRITS** (See **HOMINY**) | | | | | | |
| **CORNMEAL MIX:** | | | | | | |
| Bolted (Aunt Jemima/Quaker) | ¼ cup (1 oz.) | 370 | .8 | | | (0) |
| Degermed (Aunt Jemima/Quaker) | ¼ cup (1 oz.) | 370 | .3 | | | (0) |
| **CORNMEAL, WHITE or YELLOW:** | | | | | | |
| Dry (USDA): | | | | | | |
| Bolted | 1 cup (4.3 oz.) | 1 | 4.1 | Tr. | 4. | 0 |
| Degermed | 1 cup (4.3 oz.) | 1 | 1.7 | | | 0 |
| Self-rising, degermed | 1 cup (5 oz.) | 1946 | 1.6 | | | 0 |
| Self-rising, whole-ground | 1 cup (5 oz.) | 1946 | 4.1 | Tr. | 4. | 0 |
| Whole-ground, unbolted | 1 cup (4.3 oz.) | 1 | 4.8 | Tr. | 5. | 0 |
| Cooked: | | | | | | |
| *Bolted (Aunt Jemina/Quaker) | ⅔ cup | <1 | .7 | | | (0) |
| Degermed (USDA) | 1 cup (8.5 oz.) | 264 | .5 | | | 0 |
| *Degermed (Albers) | 1 cup | | .5 | | | (0) |
| *Degermed (Aunt Jemima/Quaker) | ⅔ cup | <1 | .3 | | | (0) |
| **CORN PUDDING,** home recipe (USDA)[1] | 1 cup (8.6 oz.) | 1068 | 11.5 | 5. | 7. | 103 |
| **CORN SALAD,** raw (USDA): | | | | | | |
| Untrimmed | 1 lb. (weighed untrimmed) | | 1.7 | | | 0 |
| Trimmed | 4 oz. | | .5 | | | 0 |
| **CORN SOUFFLE,** frozen (Stouffer's) | 12-oz. pkg. | 1674 | 22.0 | | | |
| **CORNSTARCH:** | | | | | | |
| (USDA) | 1 cup (4.5 oz.) | Tr. | Tr. | | | 0 |
| (USDA) | 1 T. (8 grams) | Tr. | Tr. | | | 0 |
| (Argo) | 1 T. (10 grams) | Tr. | <.1 | | | 0 |
| (Duryea's) | 1 T. (10 grams) | Tr. | <.1 | | | 0 |
| (Kingsford's) | 1 T. (10 grams) | Tr. | <.1 | | | 0 |

**CORNSTARCH PUDDING** (See **VANILLA PUDDING**)

**CORN STICK** (See **CORNBREAD**)

(USDA): United States Department of Agriculture
*Prepared as Package Directs
[1]Principal sources of fat: milk, vegetable shortening & egg.

| Food and Description | Measure or Quantity | Sodium (mg.) | Fats in grams | | | Choles-terol (mg.) |
|---|---|---|---|---|---|---|
| | | | Total | Satu-rated | Unsatu-rated | |
| **CORN SYRUP,** light & dark blend: | | | | | | |
| (USDA) | 1 cup (11.5 oz.) | 221 | 0. | | | 0 |
| (USDA) | 1 T. (.7 oz.) | 14 | 0. | | | 0 |
| *CORN TOTAL,* cereal (General Mills) | 1¼ cups (1 oz.) | 316 | .2 | | | (0) |
| **COTTAGE PUDDING,** home recipe (USDA)[1] : | | | | | | |
| Without sauce[2] | 2 oz. | 170 | 6.4 | 4. | 3. | |
| With chocolate sauce | 2 oz. | 132 | 5.0 | | | |
| With strawberry sauce | 2 oz. | 132 | 5.0 | | | |
| **COUGH DROP:** | | | | | | |
| (Beech-Nut) | 1 drop (2 grams) | <1 | 0. | | | (0) |
| (Estee) | 1 drop | <1 | Tr. | | | (0) |
| (Pine Bros.) | 1 drop (3 grams) | <1 | 0 | | | (0) |
| *COUNT CHOCULA,* cereal (General Mills) | 1 cup (1 oz.) | 152 | .8 | | | (0) |
| **COUNTRY-STYLE SAUSAGE,** smoked links (USDA)[3] | 1 oz. | | 8.8 | 3. | 6. | |
| **COWPEA,** including black-eyed peas (USDA): | | | | | | |
| Immature seeds: | | | | | | |
| Raw, whole | 1 lb. (weighed in pods) | 5 | 2.0 | | | 0 |
| Raw, shelled | ½ cup (2.5 oz.) | 1 | .6 | | | 0 |
| Boiled without salt, drained | ½ cup (2.9 oz.) | <1 | 1.7 | | | 0 |
| Canned, solids & liq. | 4 oz. | 268 | .3 | | | 0 |
| Frozen (See **BLACK-EYED PEA,** frozen) | | | | | | |
| Young pods with seeds: | | | | | | |
| Raw, whole | 1 lb. (weighed untrimmed) | 17 | 1.2 | | | 0 |
| Boiled without salt, drained | 4 oz. | 3 | .3 | | | 0 |
| Mature seeds, dry: | | | | | | |
| Raw | ½ cup (3 oz.) | 29 | 1.3 | | | 0 |
| Boiled without salt, drained | ½ cup (4.4 oz.) | 10 | .4 | | | 0 |

(USDA): United States Department of Agriculture
*Prepared as Package Directs
[1]Made with sodium aluminum sulfate-type baking powder.
[2]Principal sources of fat: butter, egg & milk.
[3]Principal source of fat: pork.

| Food and Description | Measure or Quantity | Sodium (mg.) | —Fats in grams— Total | Satu-rated | Unsatu-rated | Choles-terol (mg.) |
|---|---|---|---|---|---|---|
| **CRAB,** all species: | | | | | | |
| Fresh (USDA): | | | | | | |
| Steamed, whole | 1 lb. (weighed in shell) | | 4.1 | | | 218 |
| Steamed, meat only | 1 cup (4.4 oz.) | | 2.4 | | | 125 |
| Canned: | | | | | | |
| Drained solids (USDA) | 1 packed cup (5.6 oz.) | 1600 | 4.0 | | | 162 |
| (Del Monte) Alaska King | 7½-oz. can | 1178 | .6 | | | |
| Frozen (Wakefield's) Alaska King, thawed & drained | 4 oz. | 1 | 1.1 | | | 113 |
| **CRAB APPLE,** fresh (USDA): | | | | | | |
| Whole | 1 lb. (weighed whole) | 4 | 1.3 | | | 0 |
| Flesh only | 4 oz. | 1 | .3 | | | 0 |
| **CRAB CAKE,** frozen, thins (Mrs. Paul's) | 10-oz. pkg. | | 30.9 | | | |
| **CRAB, DEVILED:** | | | | | | |
| Home recipe (USDA)[1] | 1 cup (8.5 oz.) | 2081 | 22.6 | | | 245 |
| Frozen (Mrs. Paul's) | 4 oz. | | 10.8 | | | |
| Frozen, miniature (Mrs. Paul's) | 4 oz. | | 12.1 | | | |
| **CRAB IMPERIAL,** home recipe (USDA)[2] | 1 cup (7.8 oz.) | 1602 | 16.7 | | | 308 |
| **CRAB NEWBURG,** frozen (Stouffer's) | 12-oz. pkg. | 1158 | 45.5 | | | |
| **CRAB SOUP** (Crosse & Blackwell) | ½ can (6½ oz.) | | .9 | | | |
| **CRACKER, PUFFS and CHIPS:** | | | | | | |
| *American Harvest* (Nabisco) | 1 piece (3 grams) | 36 | .8 | | | |
| Arrowroot biscuit (Nabisco) | 1 piece (5 grams) | 11 | .8 | | | |
| Bacon-flavored thins (Nabisco) | 1 piece (2 grams) | 32 | .6 | | | |
| *Bacon Nips* | 1 oz. | 700 | 9.4 | 3. | 6. | 0 |
| Bacon rinds (Wonder) | 1 oz. | 220 | 7.8 | | | |
| Bacon toast (Keebler) | 1 piece (3 grams) | 28 | .7 | | | |
| *Bakon Tasters* (Old London) | ½-oz. bag | 237 | 2.1 | | | |

(USDA): United States Department of Agriculture
*Prepared as Package Directs
[1]Prepared with bread cubes, butter, parsley, eggs, lemon juice & catsup.
[2]Prepared with butter, flour, milk, onion, green pepper, eggs & lemon juice.

| Food and Description | Measure or Quantity | Sodium (mg.) | — Fats in grams — | | | Choles- terol (mg.) |
|---|---|---|---|---|---|---|
| | | | Total | Satu- rated | Unsatu- rated | |
| *Bugles* (General Mills) | 15 pieces (½ oz.) | 138 | 5.3 | | | |
| Butter (USDA)[1] | 1 oz. | 310 | 5.0 | 2. | 3. | |
| Butter thins (Nabisco) | 1 piece (3 grams) | 16 | .5 | | | |
| Cheese flavored (See also individual brand names in this grouping): | | | | | | |
| (USDA) | 1 oz. | 295 | 6.0 | 2. | 4. | |
| Cheese'n Bacon, sandwich (Nab) | 6 pieces (1¼-oz. pkg.) | 307 | 9.6 | | | |
| Cheese'n Cracker (Kraft) | 4 crackers & ¾-oz. cheese | 68 | 1.2 | | | |
| Cheese *Nips* (Nab) | 24 pieces (⅞-oz. pkg.) | 422 | 4.2 | | | |
| Cheese *Nips* (Nabisco) | 1 piece (1 gram) | 19 | .2 | | | |
| Cheese'n Rye, sandwich (Nab) | 6 pieces (1¼-oz. pkg.) | 490 | 11.8 | | | |
| *Cheese Pixies* (Wise) | 1-oz. bag | 334 | 11.7 | | | |
| *Chee.Tos*, baked | 1 oz. | 470 | 9.9 | 3. | 7. | 0 |
| *Chee.Tos*, fried | 1 oz. | 290 | 9.8 | 3. | 6. | 0 |
| *Cheez Doodles* (Old London) | 1⅛-oz. bag | 244 | 9.6 | | | |
| *Cheez-Its* (Sunshine) | 1 piece (1 gram) | | .3 | | | |
| Cheez Waffles (Old London) | 1 piece (2 grams) | 50 | .6 | | | |
| *Che-zo* (Keebler) | 1 piece (<1 gram) | 9 | .2 | | | |
| *Ritz* (Nabisco) | 1 piece (3 grams) | 35 | .9 | | | |
| Sandwich (Nab) | 6 pieces (1¼-oz. pkg.) | 426 | 10.6 | | | |
| *Shapies*. dip delights (Nabisco) | 1 piece (2 grams) | 24 | .6 | | | |
| *Shapies*. shells (Nabisco) | 1 piece (2 grams) | 26 | .6 | | | |
| Thins (Pepperidge Farm) | 2 pieces (5 grams) | 50 | .5 | | | |
| Thins. dietetic (Estee) | 1 piece | | .2 | | | |
| *Tid-Bit* (Nab) | 32 pieces (1⅛-oz. pkg.) | 524 | 6.8 | | | |
| *Tid-Bit* (Nabisco) | 1 piece (<1 gram) | 15 | .2 | | | |
| Toast (Keebler) | 1 piece (3 grams) | 31 | .8 | | | |
| Twists (Nalley) | 1 oz. | | 10.2 | | | |
| Twists (Wonder) | 1 oz. | 333 | 9.6 | | | |
| Cheese & peanut butter sandwich: | | | | | | |
| (USDA)[2] | 1 oz. | 281 | 6.8 | 2. | 5. | |
| (Nab) *O-So-Gud* | 4 pieces (1-oz. pkg.) | 358 | 6.8 | | | |
| (Nab) squares | 4 pieces (1-oz. pkg.) | 332 | 7.1 | | | |
| (Nab) squares | 6 pieces (1½-oz. pkg.) | 498 | 10.7 | | | |

(USDA): United States Department of Agriculture
*Prepared as Package Directs
[1]Principal sources of fat: vegetable shortening & butter.
[2]Principal sources of fat: vegetable shortening, cheese & peanut butter.

| Food and Description | Measure or Quantity | Sodium (mg.) | —Fats in grams— | | Choles- terol (mg.) |
|---|---|---|---|---|---|
| | | | Total | Satu- rated | Unsatu- rated | |

| Food and Description | Measure or Quantity | Sodium (mg.) | Total | Satu- rated | Unsatu- rated | Choles- terol (mg.) |
|---|---|---|---|---|---|---|
| (Nab) squares | 6 pieces (1¾-oz. pkg.) | 581 | 12.5 | | | |
| (Nab) variety pack | 6 pieces (1½-oz. pkg.) | 520 | 10.5 | | | |
| (Nab) variety pack | 6 pieces (1¾-oz. pkg.) | 606 | 12.3 | | | |
| *Chicken in a Biskit* (Nabisco) | 1 piece (2 grams) | 19 | .5 | | | |
| *Chippers* (Nabisco) | 1 piece (3 grams) | 48 | .7 | | | |
| *Chipsters* (Nabisco) | 1 piece (<1 gram) | 8 | .1 | | | |
| Clam-flavored crisps (Snow) | 1 oz. | | 8.6 | | | |
| Club (Keebler) | 1 piece (3 grams) | 44 | .7 | | | |
| *Corn Capers* (Wonder) | 1 oz. | 220 | 10.0 | | | |
| Corn cheeze (Tom Houston) | 10 pieces (5 grams) | 3 | 2.2 | | | |
| Corn chips: | | | | | | |
|   *Cornetts* | 1 oz. | | 8.5 | | | 0 |
|   *Fritos*, regular | 1 oz. | 160 | 10.5 | 3. | 8. | 0 |
|   *Fritos*, barbecued | 1 oz. | 190 | 10.1 | 2. | 8. | 0 |
|   *Korkers* (Nabisco) | 1 piece (2 grams) | 11 | .5 | | | |
|   (Old London) | 1¾-oz. bag | 921 | 16.3 | | | |
|   (Wise) | 1¾-oz. bag | 229 | 17.7 | | | |
|   (Wonder) | 1 oz. | 220 | 10.7 | | | |
|   Barbecue (Wise) | 1¾-oz. bag | 278 | 17.6 | | | |
| *Corn Diggers* (Nabisco) | 1 piece (<1 gram) | 10 | .2 | | | |
| *Crown Pilot* (Nabisco) | 1 piece (.6 oz.) | 64 | 1.9 | | | |
| *Dipsy Doodles* (Old London) | 1¾-oz. bag | 366 | 18.3 | | | |
| *Doo Dads* (Nabisco) | 1 piece (<1 gram) | 7 | .1 | | | |
| *Escort* (Nabisco) | 1 piece (4 grams) | 37 | .9 | | | |
| *Flings*, cheese-flavored curls (Nabisco) | 1 piece (2 grams) | 28 | .8 | | | |
| *Flings*, Swiss'n ham (Nabisco) | 1 piece (2 grams) | 16 | .7 | | | |
| *Goldfish* (Pepperidge Farm): | | | | | | |
|   Cheddar cheese | 10 pieces (6 grams) | 87 | 1.3 | | | |
|   Lightly salted | 10 pieces (6 grams) | 84 | 1.2 | | | |
|   Parmesan cheese | 10 pieces (6 grams) | 87 | 1.2 | | | |
|   Pizza | 10 pieces (6 grams) | 77 | 1.4 | | | |
|   Pretzel | 10 pieces (7 grams) | 195 | .6 | | | |
|   Onion | 10 pieces (6 grams) | 81 | 1.2 | | | |
|   Sesame garlic | 10 pieces (6 grams) | 84 | 1.3 | | | |
| Graham: | | | | | | |
|   (USDA)[1] | 2½" sq. (7 grams) | 47 | .7 | Tr. | <1. | |
|   (Nabisco) | 1 piece (7 grams) | 44 | .7 | | | |

(USDA): United States Department of Agriculture
*Prepared as Package Directs
[1]Principal source of fat: vegetable shortening.

| Food and Description | Measure or Quantity | Sodium (mg.) | — Fats in grams — | | | Choles- terol (mg.) |
|---|---|---|---|---|---|---|
| | | | Total | Satu- rated | Unsatu- rated | |
| Chocolate or cocoa-covered: | | | | | | |
| (USDA)[1] | 1 oz. | 115 | 6.7 | 2. | 5. | |
| (Keebler) Deluxe | 1 piece (9 grams) | 27 | 2.0 | | | |
| (Nabisco) | 1 piece (.4 oz.) | 34 | 2.7 | | | |
| (Nabisco) *Fancy* | 1 piece (.5 oz.) | 41 | 3.3 | | | |
| (Nabisco) *Pantry* | 1 piece (.4 oz.) | 41 | 2.8 | | | |
| *Sweet-Tooth* (Sunshine) | 1 piece (.4 oz.) | | 2.2 | | | |
| Sugar-honey coated (USDA)[2] | 1 oz. | 143 | 3.2 | <1. | 2. | |
| Sugar-honey coated (Nabisco) | | | | | | |
| *Honey Maid* | 1 piece (7 grams) | 52 | .7 | | | |
| *Hi-Ho* (Sunshine) | 1 piece (4 grams) | | 1.0 | | | |
| *Hot Potatas* (Old London) | ⅝-oz. bag | 276 | 3.4 | | | |
| Matzo (See **MATZO**) | | | | | | |
| Melba toast (See **MELBA**) | | | | | | |
| Milk lunch (Nabisco) *Royal Lunch* | 1 piece (.4 oz.) | 66 | 2.2 | | | |
| *Munchos* | 1 oz. | 230 | 10.6 | 4. | 7. | 0 |
| Onion flavored: | | | | | | |
| Crisps (Snow) | 1 oz. | | 9.2 | | | |
| French (Nabisco) | 1 piece (2 grams) | 31 | .5 | | | |
| *Funyuns* (Frito-Lay) | 1 oz. | 230 | 5.7 | <1. | 5. | 0 |
| *Meal Mates* (Nabisco) | 1 piece (4 grams) | 51 | .5 | | | |
| *Onyums* (General Mills) | 30 pieces (.5 oz.) | 111 | 5.4 | | | |
| Rings (Old London) | ½-oz. bag | 170 | 2.8 | | | |
| Rings (Wise) | ½-oz. bag | 133 | 2.2 | | | |
| Rings (Wonder) | 1 oz. | 440 | 6.0 | | | |
| Thins (Pepperidge Farm) | 1 piece (3 grams) | 20 | .2 | | | |
| Toast (Keebler) | 1 piece (3 grams) | 29 | .7 | | | |
| Oyster: | | | | | | |
| (USDA)[2] | 10 pieces (.4 oz.) | 110 | 1.3 | Tr. | 1. | |
| (USDA)[2] | 1 cup (1 oz.) | 312 | 3.7 | <1. | 3. | |
| (Keebler) | 1 piece (<1 gram) | 4 | <.1 | | | |
| *Dandy* (Nabisco) | 1 piece (<1 gram) | 11 | <.1 | | | |
| Mini (Sunshine) | 1 piece (<1 gram) | | .1 | | | |
| *Oysterettes* (Nabisco) | 1 piece (<1 gram) | 12 | <.1 | | | |
| Peanut butter 'n cheez crackers | | | | | | |
| (Kraft) | 4 crackers & ¾ oz. peanut butter | 264 | 13.4 | | | |
| Peanut butter sandwich: | | | | | | |
| *Adora* (Nab) | 6 pieces (1½-oz. pkg.) | 498 | 8.6 | | | |
| Cheese crackers (Wise) | 1 piece (6 grams) | 68 | 1.7 | | | |

(USDA): United States Department of Agriculture
*Prepared as Package Directs
[1]Principal sources of fat: vegetable shortening, chocolate or cocoa.
[2]Principal source of fat: vegetable shortening.

| Food and Description | Measure or Quantity | Sodium (mg.) | Fats in grams — Total | Satu- rated | Unsatu- rated | Choles- terol (mg.) |
|---|---|---|---|---|---|---|
| Malted milk (Nab) | 4 pieces (1-oz. pkg.) | 188 | 6.7 | | | |
| Malted milk (Nab) | 6 pieces (1⅜-oz. pkg.) | 259 | 9.2 | | | |
| Toasted crackers (Wise) | 1 piece (6 grams) | 52 | 1.5 | | | |
| *Pizza Spins* (General Mills) | 32 pieces (½ oz.) | 218 | 3.8 | | | |
| *Pizza Wheels* (Wise) | ¾-oz. bag | 272 | 2.4 | | | |
| Potato crisps (General Mills) | 16 pieces (½ oz.) | 171 | 5.1 | | | |
| *Ritz*, plain (Nabisco) | 1 piece (3 grams) | 32 | .8 | | | |
| Rye thins (Pepperidge Farm) | 1 piece (3 grams) | 13 | .2 | | | |
| Rye toast (Keebler) | 1 piece (4 grams) | 39 | .8 | | | |
| Rye wafers, whole grain (USDA) | 1 piece (1⅞" x 3½," 6 grams) | 11 | .2 | | | |
| Rye wafers (Nabisco) *Meal Mates* | 1 piece (4 grams) | 59 | .4 | | | |
| *Ry-Krisp:* | | | | | | |
| Seasoned | 1 whole cracker (7 grams) | 96 | .6 | | | |
| Traditional | 1 whole cracker (6 grams) | 75 | <.1 | | | |
| Saltine: | | | | | | |
| (USDA)[1] | 4 crackers (.4 oz.) | 121 | 1.3 | Tr. | 1. | |
| *Krispy* (Sunshine) salted tops | 1 piece (3 grams) | 50 | .2 | | | |
| *Krispy* (Sunshine) unsalted tops | 1 piece (3 grams) | 21 | .3 | | | |
| *Premium* (Nab) | 8 pieces (¾-oz. pkg.) | 263 | 2.4 | | | |
| *Premium* (Nabisco) | 1 piece (3 grams) | 35 | .3 | | | |
| *Zesta* (Keebler) | 1 section (3 grams) | 34 | .3 | | | |
| Sea toast (Keebler) | 1 piece (.5 oz.) | 112 | 1.4 | | | |
| Sesame: | | | | | | |
| (Sunshine) *La Lanne* | 1 piece (3 grams) | | .7 | | | |
| Buttery flavored (Nabisco) | 1 piece (3 grams) | 35 | .8 | | | |
| Wafer (Keebler) | 1 piece (3 grams) | 32 | .8 | | | |
| Wafer (Nabisco), *Meal Mates* | 1 piece (5 grams) | 65 | .7 | | | |
| *Sip 'n Chips* (Nabisco) | 1 piece (2 grams) | 29 | .5 | | | |
| *Sociables* (Nabisco) | 1 piece (2 grams) | 30 | .4 | | | |
| Soda: | | | | | | |
| (USDA)[1] | 1 oz. | 312 | 3.7 | <1. | 3. | |
| (USDA)[1] | 2½" sq. (6 grams) | 60 | .7 | Tr. | <1. | |
| (Nabisco) *Premium*, unsalted tops | 1 piece (3 grams) | 23 | .3 | | | |
| (Sunshine) | 1 piece (4 grams) | | .5 | | | |
| Soya (Sunshine) *La Lanne* | 1 piece (3 grams) | | .9 | | | |
| *Star Lites* (Wise) | 1 cup (.5 oz.) | 197 | 2.4 | | | |
| Swedish rye wafer (Keebler) | 1 piece (5 grams) | 54 | .3 | | | |
| Taco corn chips (Old London) | 1¼-oz. bag | 205 | 7.0 | | | |

(USDA): United States Department of Agriculture
*Prepared as Package Directs
[1]Principal source of fat: vegetable shortening.

| Food and Description | Measure or Quantity | Sodium (mg.) | Fats in grams Total | Satu- rated | Unsatu- rated | Choles- terol (mg.) |
|---|---|---|---|---|---|---|
| Taco tortilla chips (Wonder) | 1 oz. | 241 | 8.1 | | | |
| Tortilla Chips, *Doritos*, regular | 1 oz. | 130 | 6.2 | 1. | 5. | 0 |
| Tortilla chips, *Doritos*, taco flavor | 1 oz. | 240 | 6.1 | 1. | 5. | 0 |
| Tortilla chips (Old London) | 1½-oz. bag | 300 | 9.8 | | | |
| Tortilla chips (Wonder) | 1 oz. | 165 | 7.9 | | | |
| *Town House* | 1 piece (3 grams) | 42 | 1.0 | | | |
| *Triangle Thins* (Nabisco) | 1 piece (2 grams) | 24 | .3 | | | |
| *Triscuit* (Nabisco) | 1 piece (4 grams) | 30 | .8 | | | |
| *Twigs*, sesame & cheese (Nabisco) | 1 piece (3 grams) | 32 | .7 | | | |
| *Uneeda Biscuit* (Nabisco) unsalted tops | 1 piece (5 grams) | 35 | .6 | | | |
| *Wafer-ets* (Hol-Grain): | | | | | | |
|   Rice, salted | 1 piece (3 grams) | 2 | <.1 | | | |
|   Rice, unsalted | 1 piece (3 grams) | <1 | <.1 | | | |
|   Wheat, salted | 1 piece (2 grams) | 5 | <.1 | | | |
|   Wheat, unsalted | 1 piece (2 grams) | <1 | <.1 | | | |
| *Waldorf*, low salt (Keebler) | 1 piece (3 grams) | <1 | .4 | | | |
| *Waverly* wafer (Nabisco) | 1 piece (4 grams) | 46 | .8 | | | |
| Wheat chips (General Mills) | 12 pieces (.5 oz.) | 139 | 4.5 | | | |
| Wheat thins (Nabisco) | 1 piece (2 grams) | 23 | .4 | | | |
| Wheat toast (Keebler) | 1 piece (3 grams) | 25 | .7 | | | |
| *Whistles* (General Mills) | 17 pieces (.5 oz.) | 265 | 3.8 | | | |
| White thins (Pepperidge Farm) | 1 piece (3 grams) | 22 | .2 | | | |
| Whole-wheat (USDA)[1] | 1 oz. | 155 | 3.9 | 1. | 3. | |
| Whole-wheat, natural (Froumine) | 1 piece (.4 oz.) | 1 | 1.2 | | | |
| **CRACKER CRUMBS:** | | | | | | |
|   Graham (USDA)[1] | 1 cup (3 oz.) | 576 | 8.1 | 2. | 6. | |
|   Graham (Keebler) | 3 oz. | 460 | 9.9 | | | |
|   Graham (Nabisco) | 1½ cups (4.6 oz. or 9" pie shell) | 823 | 14.0 | | | |
|   Graham (Sunshine) | 3 oz. | | 7.5 | | | |
| ***CRACKER JACK*** (See **POPCORN**) | | | | | | |
| **CRACKER MEAL:** | | | | | | |
|   (USDA)[1] | 3 oz. | 935 | 11.1 | 3. | 8. | |
|   (USDA) | 1 T. (.4 oz.) | 110 | 1.3 | Tr. | 1. | |
|   (Keebler): | | | | | | |
|     Fine, medium or coarse | 3 oz. | 5 | .9 | | | |
|     Zesty | 3 oz. | 1047 | 9.5 | | | |

(USDA): United States Department of Agriculture
*Prepared as Package Directs
[1]Principal source of fat: vegetable shortening.

141

| Food and Description | Measure or Quantity | Sodium (mg.) | Total | Fats in grams Satu- rated | Fats in grams Unsatu- rated | Choles- terol (mg.) |
|---|---|---|---|---|---|---|
| (Sunshine) | 3 oz. | | .9 | | | |
| Salted (Nabisco) | 1 cup (3 oz.) | 1022 | 1.4 | | | |
| Unsalted (Nabisco) | 1 cup (3 oz.) | 51 | 1.4 | | | |
| **CRACKER PIE CRUST MIX** (See **PIECRUST MIX**) | | | | | | |
| *CRANAPPLE DRINK* (Ocean Spray): | | | | | | |
| Regular | ½ cup (4.5 oz.) | 3 | .3 | | | 0 |
| Low calorie | ½ cup (4.2 oz.) | 4 | .1 | | | 0 |
| *Frozen | ½ cup (4.4 oz.) | 2 | Tr. | | | 0 |
| **CRANBERRY:** | | | | | | |
| Fresh: | | | | | | |
| Untrimmed (USDA) | 1 lb. (weighed with stems) | 9 | 3.0 | | | 0 |
| Stems removed (USDA) | 1 cup (4 oz.) | 2 | .8 | | | 0 |
| (Ocean Spray) | 1 oz. | <1 | .4 | | | 0 |
| Dehydrated (USDA) | 1 oz. | 5 | 1.9 | | | |
| **CRANBERRY JUICE COCKTAIL:** | | | | | | |
| (USDA) approx. 33% cranberry juice | ½ cup (4.4 oz.) | 1 | .1 | | | 0 |
| Regular (Ocean Spray) | ½ cup (4.4 oz.) | 2 | <.1 | | | 0 |
| Low calorie (Ocean Spray) | ½ cup (4.4 oz.) | 5 | <.1 | | | 0 |
| Frozen (Ocean Spray) | ½ cup (4.4 oz.) | 1 | Tr. | | | |
| *CRANORANGE JUICE DRINK,* frozen (Ocean Spray) | ½ cup (4.4 oz.) | 1 | .2 | | | |
| **CRANBERRY-ORANGE RELISH:** | | | | | | |
| Uncooked (USDA) | 4 oz. | 1 | .5 | | | 0 |
| (Ocean Spray) | 4 oz. | 12 | .4 | | | 0 |
| **CRANBERRY PIE** (Tastykake) | 4-oz. pie | | 14.6 | | | |
| **CRANBERRY SAUCE:** | | | | | | |
| Home recipe, sweetened, unstrained (USDA) | 4 oz. | 1 | .3 | | | 0 |
| Canned: | | | | | | |
| Sweetened, strained (USDA) | ½ cup (4.8 oz.) | 1 | .3 | | | 0 |
| Jellied (Ocean Spray) | 4 oz. | | 1.5 | | | 0 |
| Whole berry (Ocean Spray) | 4 oz. | | .4 | | | 0 |

(USDA): United States Department of Agriculture
*Prepared as Package Directs

| Food and Description | Measure or Quantity | Sodium (mg.) | —Fats in grams— | | | Choles- terol (mg.) |
|---|---|---|---|---|---|---|
| | | | Total | Satu- rated | Unsatu- rated | |
| **CRANBREAKER MIX** | | | | | | |
| (Bar-Tender's) | 1 serving (⅝ oz.) | Tr. | .2 | | | (0) |
| *CRANPRUNE* (Ocean Spray) | ½ cup (4.4 oz.) | 3 | .1 | | | 0 |
| **CRAPPIE,** white, raw, meat only | | | | | | |
| (USDA) | 4 oz. | | .9 | | | |
| **CRAYFISH,** freshwater (USDA): | | | | | | |
| Raw, in shell | 1 lb. (weighed in shell) | | .3 | | | |
| Raw, meat only | 4 oz. | | .6 | | | |
| **CREAM:** | | | | | | |
| Half & half: | | | | | | |
| (USDA) | 1 cup (8.5 oz.) | 111 | 28.3 | 15. | 14. | 104 |
| (USDA) | 1 T. (.5 oz.) | 7 | 1.8 | <1. | <1. | 6 |
| 10.5% fat (Sealtest) | 1 cup (8.5 oz.) | 104 | 25.2 | | | |
| 12% fat (Sealtest) | 1 cup (8.5 oz.) | 102 | 28.8 | | | |
| Light, table, or coffee: | | | | | | |
| (USDA) | 1 cup (8.5 oz.) | 103 | 49.4 | 26. | 23. | 158 |
| (USDA) | 1 T. (.5 oz.) | 6 | 3.1 | 2. | 1. | 10 |
| 16% fat (Sealtest) | 1 T. (.5 oz.) | 6 | 2.4 | | | |
| 18% fat (Sealtest) | 1 T. (.5 oz.) | 6 | 2.7 | | | |
| 25% fat (Sealtest) | 1 T. (.5 oz.) | 6 | 3.8 | | | |
| Light whipping: | | | | | | |
| (USDA) | 1 cup (8.4 oz.) | 86 | 74.8 | 41. | 34. | |
| (USDA) | 1 T. (.5 oz.) | 5 | 4.7 | 3. | 2. | |
| 30% fat (Sealtest) | 1 T. (.5 oz.) | 5 | 4.5 | | | |
| Whipped topping, pressurized: | | | | | | |
| (USDA) | 1 cup (2.1 oz.) | | 14. | 8. | 6. | 51 |
| (USDA) | 1 T. (3 grams) | | <1. | Tr. | Tr. | 3 |
| Heavy whipping: | | | | | | |
| Unwhipped (USDA) | 1 cup (8.4 oz. or 2 cups whipped) | 76 | 89.5 | 50. | 40. | 317 |
| Unwhipped (USDA) | 1 T. (.5 oz.) | 5 | 5.6 | 3. | 2. | 20 |
| 36% fat (Sealtest) | 1 T. (.5 oz.) | 5 | 5.4 | | | |
| Sour: | | | | | | |
| (USDA) | 1 cup (8.1 oz.) | 99 | 47.4 | 25. | 22. | 152 |
| (USDA) | 1 T. (.4 oz.) | 5 | 2.5 | 1. | 1. | 8 |
| (Borden) | 1 cup (8.6 oz.) | 96 | 43.2 | | | |
| (Borden) | 1 T. (.5 oz.) | 6 | 2.7 | | | |
| (Breakstone) | 8-oz. container | 112 | 41.5 | | | 112 |

(USDA): United States Department of Agriculture
*Prepared as Package Directs

| Food and Description | Measure or Quantity | Sodium (mg.) | —Fats in grams— | | | Choles-terol (mg.) |
|---|---|---|---|---|---|---|
| | | | Total | Satu-rated | Unsatu-rated | |
| (Breakstone) | 1 T. (.5 oz.) | 8 | 2.8 | | | 8 |
| (Sealtest) | 1 T. (.5 oz.) | 6 | 2.7 | | | |
| Half & half (Sealtest) | 1 T. (.5 oz.) | 6 | 1.8 | | | |
| Imitation: | | | | | | |
| (Sealtest) non-dairy | 1 T. (.5 oz.) | 16 | 2.7 | | | |
| *Sour Treat* (Delite) | 1 T. (.5 oz.) | 6 | 2.2 | | | |
| *Zest* (Borden) 13.5% vegetable fat | 1 T. | 16 | 2.0 | | | |
| Sour cream, dried (Data from General Mills) | 1 oz. | 87 | 16.2 | | | |
| Sour dairy dressing (Sealtest) | 1 T. (.5 oz.) | 7 | 1.8 | | | |
| Sour dressing or sour cream, made with nonfat dry milk: | | | | | | |
| (USDA) | 1 cup (8.3 oz.) | | 38. | 35. | 3. | |
| (USDA) | 1 T. (.4 oz.) | | 2. | 2. | Tr. | |
| Sour dressing, cultured (Breakstone) | 1 T. (.5 oz.) | 9 | 2.4 | | | 0 |
| *CREAMIES* (Tastykake): | | | | | | |
| Banana cake | 1⅞-oz. pkg. | | 10.1 | | | |
| Chocolate | 1⅞-oz. pkg. | | 17.7 | | | |
| Koffee Kake | 1⅞-oz. pkg. | | 10.3 | | | |
| Vanilla | 1⅞-oz. pkg. | | 16.5 | | | |
| **CREAM PUFF,** home recipe, with custard filling (USDA)[1] | 3½″ x 2″ (4.6 oz.) | 108 | 18.1 | 5. | 13. | 187 |
| ***CREAM OF RICE,** cereal, no salt added | 4 oz. | <1 | <.1 | | | |
| **CREAMSICLE** (Popsicle Industries) | 2½-fl. oz. bar (1.9 oz.) | 14 | 2.6 | | | |
| **CREAM or CREME SOFT DRINK:** | | | | | | |
| Sweetened: | | | | | | |
| (Canada Dry) vanilla | 6 fl. oz. | 13+ | 0. | | | 0 |
| (Clicquot Club) | 6 fl. oz. | 16 | 0. | | | 0 |
| (Cott) | 6 fl. oz. | 16 | 0. | | | 0 |
| (Dr. Brown's) | 6 fl. oz. | 14 | 0. | | | 0 |
| (Fanta) | 6 fl. oz. | 6 | 0. | | | 0 |
| (Hoffman) | 6 fl. oz. | 14 | 0. | | | 0 |
| (Key Food) | 6 fl. oz. | 14 | 0. | | | 0 |

(USDA): United States Department of Agriculture
*Prepared as Package Directs
[1]Principal sources of fat: vegetable shortening, egg & milk.

| Food and Description | Measure or Quantity | Sodium (mg.) | —Fats in grams— | | | Choles- terol (mg.) |
| --- | --- | --- | --- | --- | --- | --- |
| | | | Total | Satu- rated | Unsatu- rated | |
| (Kirsch) | 6 fl. oz. | <1 | 0. | | | 0 |
| (Mission) | 6 fl. oz. | 16 | 0. | | | 0 |
| (Nedick's) | 6 fl. oz. | 14 | 0. | | | 0 |
| (Shasta) | 6 fl. oz. | 20 | 0. | | | 0 |
| (Waldbaum) | 6 fl. oz. | 14 | 0. | | | 0 |
| (Yukon Club) | 6 fl. oz. | 14 | 0. | | | 0 |
| Low calorie: | | | | | | |
| (Clicquot Club) | 6 fl. oz. | 45 | 0. | | | 0 |
| (Cott) | 6 fl. oz. | 45 | 0. | | | 0 |
| (Dr. Brown's) | 6 fl. oz. | 35 | 0. | | | 0 |
| (Hoffman) | 6 fl. oz. | 35 | 0. | | | 0 |
| (Key Food) | 6 fl. oz. | 35 | 0. | | | 0 |
| (Mission) | 6 fl. oz. | 45 | 0. | | | 0 |
| (No-Cal) | 6 fl. oz. | 12 | 0. | | | 0 |
| (Shasta) | 6 fl. oz. | 39 | 0. | | | 0 |
| (Waldbaum) | 6 fl. oz. | 35 | 0. | | | 0 |
| (Yukon Club) | 6 fl. oz. | 69 | 0. | | | 0 |

**CREAM SUBSTITUTE:**

| Food and Description | Measure or Quantity | Sodium (mg.) | Total | Satu- rated | Unsatu- rated | Choles- terol (mg.) |
| --- | --- | --- | --- | --- | --- | --- |
| Liquid, frozen (USDA) | 1 cup (8.6 oz.) | | 27.0 | 25. | 2. | |
| Liquid, frozen (USDA) | 1 tsp. (5 grams) | | .6 | <1. | Tr. | |
| Powdered (USDA) | 1 cup (3.3 oz.) | | 33.0 | 31. | 2. | |
| Powdered (USDA) | 1 tsp. (2 grams) | | 1.0 | <1. | Tr. | |
| *Coffee-mate* (Carnation)[1] | 1 tsp. (2 grams) | 3 | .7 | <1. | Tr. | Tr. |
| *Coffee-mate* (Carnation)[1] | 1 packet (3 grams) | 4 | 1.1 | 1. | Tr. | Tr. |
| *Coffee Rich* | 1 tsp. (5 grams) | 2 | .6 | | | 0 |
| *Coffee Twin* (Sealtest) | ½ fl. oz. (.5 oz.) | 6 | 1.2 | | | |
| *Cremora* (Borden) | 1 tsp. (2 grams) | 2 | .7 | | | |
| *Perx* | 1 tsp. (5 grams) | <1 | .6 | <1. | 0. | 0 |
| *Poly Perx* | 1 oz. | 4 | 2.8 | Tr. | 2. | 0 |

**CREAM OF TARTAR**

| Food and Description | Measure or Quantity | Sodium (mg.) | Total | Satu- rated | Unsatu- rated | Choles- terol (mg.) |
| --- | --- | --- | --- | --- | --- | --- |
| (Spice Islands) | 1 tsp. | 8 | | | | (0) |

***CREAM OF WHEAT*, cereal:**

| Food and Description | Measure or Quantity | Sodium (mg.) | Total | Satu- rated | Unsatu- rated | Choles- terol (mg.) |
| --- | --- | --- | --- | --- | --- | --- |
| Instant, dry | 1 oz. (¾ cup cooked) | 2 | .3 | | | |
| Mix 'n Eat: | | | | | | |
| Regular, dry | 3½ T. (1 oz.) | 220 | .4 | | | |
| Baked apple & cinnamon, dry | 3¾ T. (1¼ oz.) | 228 | .7 | | | |
| Maple & brown sugar, dry | 3¾ T. (1¼ oz.) | 206 | .5 | | | |
| Quick, dry | 1 oz. (¾ cup cooked) | 78 | .3 | | | |
| Regular, dry | 1 oz. (¾ cup cooked) | <1 | .3 | | | |

(USDA): United States Department of Agriculture
*Prepared as Package Directs
[1]Principal source of fat: modified coconut oil.

| Food and Description | Measure or Quantity | Sodium (mg.) | Fats in grams Total | Satu- rated | Unsatu- rated | Choles- terol (mg.) |
|---|---|---|---|---|---|---|
| **CRESS, GARDEN** (USDA): | | | | | | |
| Raw, whole | 1 lb. (weighed untrimmed) | 45 | 2.3 | | | 0 |
| Boiled without salt, in small amount of water, short time, drained (USDA) | 1 cup (6.3 oz.) | 14 | 1.1 | | | 0 |
| Boiled without salt, large amount of water, long time, drained (USDA) | 1 cup (6.3 oz.) | 14 | 1.1 | | | 0 |
| *CRISP RICE,* cereal (Van Brode) | 1 oz. | | <.1 | | | (0) |
| *CRISPY CRITTERS,* cereal (Post) | 1 cup (1 oz.) | 170 | 1.1 | | | 0 |
| **CROAKER** (USDA): | | | | | | |
| Atlantic: | | | | | | |
| Raw, whole | 1 lb. (weighed whole) | 134 | 3.4 | | | |
| Raw, meat only | 4 oz. | 99 | 2.5 | | | |
| Baked | 4 oz. | 136 | 3.6 | | | |
| White, raw, meat only | 4 oz. | | .9 | | | |
| Yellowfin, raw, meat only | 4 oz. | | .9 | | | |
| **CRULLER** (See **DOUGHNUT**) | | | | | | |
| **CUCUMBER,** fresh (USDA): | | | | | | |
| Eaten with skin | ½ lb. (weighed with skin) | 13 | .2 | | | 0 |
| Eaten without skin | ½ lb. (weighed with skin) | 10 | .2 | | | 0 |
| Not pared, 10-oz. cucumber | 7½" x 2" pared cucumber (7.3 oz.) | 12 | .2 | | | 0 |
| Pared | 6 slices (2" x ⅛", 1.8 oz.) | 3 | <.1 | | | 0 |
| Pared & diced | ½ cup (2.5 oz.) | 4 | <.1 | | | 0 |
| **CUMIN SEED,** whole or ground (Spice Islands) | 1 tsp. | <1 | | | | (0) |
| **CUPCAKE:** | | | | | | |
| Home recipe (USDA)[1]: | | | | | | |
| Made with butter, without icing[2] | 2¾" cupcake (1.4 oz.) | 120 | 5.1 | 3. | 2. | |

(USDA): United States Department of Agriculture
*Prepared as Package Directs
[1]Made with sodium aluminum sulfate-type baking powder.
[2]Principal sources of fat: butter, egg & milk.

| Food and Description | Measure or Quantity | Sodium (mg.) | —Fats in grams— | | | Choles- terol (mg.) |
|---|---|---|---|---|---|---|
| | | | Total | Satu- rated | Unsatu- rated | |
| Made with vegetable shortening, without icing[1] | 2¾" cupcake (1.4 oz.) | 120 | 5.6 | 2. | 4. | |
| With chocolate icing | 2¾" cupcake (1.8 oz.) | 114 | 7.0 | | | |
| With boiled white icing | 2¾" cupcake (1.8 oz.) | 131 | 5.2 | | | |
| With uncooked white icing | 2¾" cupcake (1.8 oz.) | 114 | 5.9 | | | |
| Commercial: | | | | | | |
| Chocolate (Tastykake) | 1 cupcake (1 oz.) | | 5.7 | | | |
| Chocolate, chocolate-creme filled (Tastykake) | 1 cupcake (1¼ oz.) | | 3.0 | | | |
| Coconut (Tastykake) | 1 cupcake (¾ oz.) | | 2.3 | | | |
| Creme-filled, chocolate butter cream (Tastykake) | 1 cupcake (1⅛ oz.) | | 6.7 | | | |
| Devil's food cake (Hostess): | | | | | | |
| 2 to pkg. | 1 cupcake (1¾ oz.) | 194 | 4.6 | | | |
| 12 to pkg. | 1 cupcake (1.3 oz.) | 148 | 3.5 | | | |
| Lemon, creme-filled (Tastykake) | 1 cupcake (⅞ oz.) | | 5.7 | | | |
| Orange (Hostess): | | | | | | |
| 2 to pkg. | 1 cupcake (1.5 oz.) | 124 | 4.3 | | | |
| 12 to pkg. | 1 cupcake (1.3 oz.) | 110 | 3.8 | | | |
| Orange, creme-filled (Tastykake) | 1 cupcake (⅞ oz.) | | 6.7 | | | |
| Vanilla, creme-filled (Tastykake) | 1 cupcake (⅞ oz.) | | 5.9 | | | |
| Vanilla *Triplets* (Tastykake) | 1 cupcake (.8 oz.) | | 3.6 | | | |

**CUPCAKE MIX:**

| | | | | | | |
|---|---|---|---|---|---|---|
| (USDA)[2] | 4 oz. | 676 | 15.4 | 3. | 12. | |
| *Prepared with eggs, milk, without icing (USDA)[1] | 2½" cupcake (.9 oz.) | 113 | 3.0 | <1. | 2. | |
| *Prepared with eggs, milk, with chocolate icing (USDA)[3] | 2½" cupcake (1.2 oz.) | 121 | 4.5 | 2. | 3. | |
| *(Flako) | 1 large cupcake (1.3 oz., ¹/₁₂ of pkg.) | 178 | 5.0 | | | |

**CURRANT:**

| | | | | | | |
|---|---|---|---|---|---|---|
| Fresh (USDA): | | | | | | |
| Black European: | | | | | | |
| Whole | 1 lb. (weighed with stems) | 13 | .4 | | | 0 |
| Stems removed | 4 oz. | 3 | .1 | | | 0 |
| Red & white: | | | | | | |
| Whole | 1 lb. (weighed with stems) | 9 | .9 | | | 0 |

(USDA): United States Department of Agriculture
*Prepared as Package Directs
[1]Principal sources of fat: vegetable shortening, egg & milk.
[2]Principal source of fat: vegetable shortening.
[3]Principal sources of fat: vegetable shortening, chocolate, egg & milk.

| Food and Description | Measure or Quantity | Sodium (mg.) | Fats in grams — Total | Satu- rated | Unsatu- rated | Choles- terol (mg.) |
|---|---|---|---|---|---|---|
| Stems removed | 1 cup (3.9 oz.) | 2 | .2 | | | 0 |
| Dried, Zante (Del Monte) | ½ cup (2.5 oz.) | 20 | .2 | | | 0 |
| **CURRY POWDER:** | | | | | | |
| (Crosse & Blackwell) | 1 T. (6 grams) | | .2 | | | (0) |
| (Spice Islands) | 1 tsp. | 1 | | | | (0) |
| **CUSK** (USDA): | | | | | | |
| Raw, drawn | 1 lb. (weighed drawn, head & tail on) | | .5 | | | |
| Raw, meat only | 4 oz. | | .2 | | | |
| Steamed | 4 oz. | 84 | .8 | | | |
| **CUSTARD:** | | | | | | |
| Home recipe, baked (USDA) | ½ cup (4.7 oz.) | 104 | 7.3 | 4. | 3. | 139 |
| Chilled (Sealtest) | 4 oz. | 53 | 3.8 | | | |
| **CUSTARD APPLE,** bullock's heart, fresh (USDA): | | | | | | |
| Whole | 1 lb. (weighed with skin & seeds) | | 1.6 | | | 0 |
| Flesh only | 4 oz. | | .7 | | | 0 |
| **CUSTARD, FROZEN** (See **ICE CREAM**) | | | | | | |
| **CUSTARD PIE:** | | | | | | |
| Home recipe (USDA)[1] | ¹/₆ of 9″ pie (5.4 oz.) | 436 | 16.9 | | | 160 |
| Frozen (Banquet) | 5-oz. serving | | 9.1 | | | |
| **CUSTARD PUDDING MIX:** | | | | | | |
| Dry, with vegetable gum base (USDA) | 1 oz. | 84 | <.1 | | | |
| *Prepared with whole milk (USDA) | 4 oz. | 112 | 4.0 | 2. | 2. | |
| *No egg yolk (Jell-O) | ½ cup (5 oz.) | 180 | 5.8 | | | 29 |
| Real egg (Lynden Farms) | 4-oz. pkg. | 338 | 5.7 | 2. | 3. | |
| *Regular (Royal) | ½ cup (5.1 oz.) | 125 | 4.9 | | | 14 |

(USDA): United States Department of Agriculture
*Prepared as Package Directs
[1]Principal source of fat: lard.

| Food and Description | Measure or Quantity | Sodium (mg.) | —Fats in grams— | | | Choles- terol (mg.) |
|---|---|---|---|---|---|---|
| | | | Total | Satu- rated | Unsatu- rated | |

# D

**DAIQUIRI COCKTAIL:**
  (National Distillers)

| | | | | | | |
|---|---|---|---|---|---|---|
| *Duet*, 12½% alcohol | 8 fl.-oz. can | Tr. | 0. | | | (0) |
| Mix (Bar-tender's) | 1 serving (⅝ oz.) | 48 | .2 | | | (0) |

**DAMSON PLUM (See PLUM)**

**DANDELION GREENS,** raw
  (USDA):

| | | | | | | |
|---|---|---|---|---|---|---|
| Trimmed | 1 lb. | 345 | 3.2 | | | 0 |
| Boiled without salt, drained | ½ cup (3.2 oz.) | 40 | .5 | | | 0 |

**DANISH PASTRY (See COFFEE CAKE)**

**DANISH-STYLE VEGETABLES,**
  frozen (Birds Eye)

| | | | | | | |
|---|---|---|---|---|---|---|
| | ⅓ of 10-oz. pkg. | 402 | 7.0 | | | 0 |

*DANNY* (See **YOGURT**)

**DATE,** dry:
  Domestic:

| | | | | | | |
|---|---|---|---|---|---|---|
| With pits (USDA) | 1 lb. (weighed with pits) | 4 | 2.0 | | | 0 |
| Without pits (USDA) | 4 oz. | 1 | .6 | | | 0 |
| Without pits, chopped (USDA) | 1 cup (6.1 oz.) | 2 | .9 | | | 0 |
| Whole (Cal-Date) | 1 date (.8 oz.) | <1 | .1 | | | |
| Diced (Cal-Date) | 4 oz. | 1 | .7 | | | |
| Chopped (Dromedary) | 1 cup (5 oz.) | 17 | 2.5 | | | |
| Pitted (Dromedary) | 1 cup (5 oz.) | 17 | 1.3 | | | |
| Imported, Iraq (Bordo): | | | | | | |
| Whole | 4 average dates (.9 oz.) | 52 | .6 | | | |
| Diced | ¼ cup (2 oz.) | 114 | 1.4 | | | |

**DELAWARE WINE:**

| | | | | | | |
|---|---|---|---|---|---|---|
| (Gold Seal) 12% alcohol | 3 fl. oz. (3.2 oz.) | 3 | 0. | | | (0) |
| (Great Western) 12.5% alcohol | 3 fl. oz. | 2 | 0. | | | |

*DESSERT CUP* (Del Monte):

| | | | | | | |
|---|---|---|---|---|---|---|
| Pudding 'n apricot | 5-oz. container | 241 | 3.3 | | | |

(USDA): United States Department of Agriculture
*Prepared as Package Directs

| Food and Description | Measure or Quantity | Sodium (mg.) | —Fats in grams— | | | Choles- terol (mg.) |
|---|---|---|---|---|---|---|
| | | | Total | Satu- rated | Unsatu- rated | |
| Pudding 'n peach | 5-oz. container | 266 | 3.0 | | | |
| Pudding 'n pineapple | 5-oz. container | 244 | 3.4 | | | |
| *DEVIL DOGS* (Drakes) | 1 piece (1.6 oz.) | | 7.6 | | | |
| **DEVIL'S FOOD CAKE:** | | | | | | |
| Home recipe (USDA)[1]: | | | | | | |
| Without icing | 3″ x 2″ x 1½″ (1.9 oz.) | 162 | 9.5 | | | |
| With chocolate icing, 2-layer | 1/16 of 9″ cake (2.6 oz.) | 176 | 12.3 | | | 32 |
| With chocolate icing, 2-layer | 1/16 of 10″ cake (4.2 oz.) | 282 | 19.7 | | | 52 |
| With uncooked white icing | 1/16 of 10″ cake (4.2 oz.) | 281 | 17.5 | | | |
| Commercial, frozen: | | | | | | |
| With chocolate icing (USDA)[2] | 2 oz. | 238 | 10.0 | 5. | 5. | |
| With whipped-cream filling & chocolate icing (USDA)[3] | 2 oz. | 108 | 12.4 | 4. | 8. | |
| (Pepperidge Farm) | 1/6 of cake (3.1 oz.) | 305 | 14.0 | | | |
| Layer (Mrs. Smith's) | 1/6 of 14-oz. cake | 227 | 6.6 | | | |
| **DEVIL'S FOOD CAKE MIX:** | | | | | | |
| Dry (USDA)[4] | 1 oz. | 130 | 3.3 | <1. | 3. | |
| *With chocolate icing (USDA)[5] | 1/16 of 9″ cake (2.4 oz.) | 181 | 8.5 | 3. | 5. | 33 |
| *(Duncan Hines) | 1/12 of cake (2.7 oz.) | 491 | 6.8 | | | 50 |
| *(Swans Down) | 1/12 of cake (2.4 oz.) | 441 | 3.2 | | | 48 |
| *Butter (Betty Crocker) | 1/12 of cake | 358 | 13.1 | | | |
| *Layer (Betty Crocker) | 1/12 of cake | 320 | 5.9 | | | |
| **DEWBERRY,** fresh (See **BLACKBERRY,** fresh) | | | | | | |
| **DEWBERRY PRESERVE** (Bama) | 1 T. (.7 oz.) | 1 | <.1 | | | |
| **DILL:** | | | | | | |
| Seed (Data from General Mills) | 1 oz. | 28 | | | | (0) |
| Seed (Spice Islands) | 1 tsp. | <1 | | | | (0) |
| Weed (Spice Islands) | 1 tsp. | <1 | | | | (0) |

(USDA): United States Department of Agriculture
*Prepared as Package Directs
[1]Made with sodium aluminum sulfate-type baking powder.
[2]Principal sources of fat: butter, vegetable shortening, chocolate, egg & milk.
[3]Principal sources of fat: vegetable shortening, cream, chocolate, egg & milk.
[4]Principal source of fat: vegetable shortening.
[5]Principal sources of fat: vegetable shortening, chocolate, egg & milk.

| Food and Description | Measure or Quantity | Sodium (mg.) | Total | —Fats in grams— Satu- rated | Unsatu- rated | Choles- terol (mg.) |
|---|---|---|---|---|---|---|
| ***DING DONG*** (Hostess): | | | | | | |
| Dark chocolate, 2 to pkg. | 1 piece (1.4 oz.) | 96 | 9.1 | | | |
| Dark chocolate, 12 to pkg. | 1 piece (1.3 oz.) | 93 | 8.8 | | | |
| Milk chocolate, 2 to pkg. | 1 piece (1.4 oz.) | 101 | 8.7 | | | |
| Milk chocolate, 12 to pkg. | 1 piece (1.3 oz.) | 98 | 8.4 | | | |
| | | | | | | |
| **DINNER,** frozen (See individual listings such as **BEEF DINNER, CHICKEN DINNER, CHINESE DINNER, ENCHILADA DINNER,** etc.) | | | | | | |
| | | | | | | |
| **DIP:** | | | | | | |
| Bacon & horseradish: | | | | | | |
| (Breakstone) | 2 T. (1.1 oz.) | 224 | 5.5 | | | 12 |
| (Kraft) *Teez* | 1 oz. | 201 | 5.0 | | | |
| (Kraft) *Ready Dip,* Neufchâtel cheese | 1 oz. | 227 | 6.7 | | | |
| Bacon & smoke (Sealtest) *Dip'n Dressing* | 1 oz. | 157 | 3.9 | | | |
| Blue cheese: | | | | | | |
| (Breakstone) | 2 T. (1.1 oz.) | 228 | 5.8 | | | 15 |
| (Kraft) *Ready Dip,* Neufchâtel cheese | 1 oz. | 272 | 6.0 | | | |
| (Kraft) *Teez* | 1 oz. | 156 | 4.6 | | | |
| (Sealtest) *Dip 'n Dressing* | 1 oz. | 205 | 4.2 | | | |
| *Casino* (Sealtest) *Dip 'n Dressing* | 1 oz. | 164 | 3.5 | | | |
| Chipped beef (Sealtest) *Dip 'n Dressing* | 1 oz. | 192 | 3.6 | | | |
| Clam: | | | | | | |
| (Kraft) *Ready Dip,* Neufchâtel cheese | 1 oz. | 170 | 5.8 | | | |
| (Kraft) *Teez* | 1 oz. | 143 | 3.9 | | | |
| Cucumber & onion (Breakstone) | 2 T. (1.1 oz.) | 184 | 4.7 | | | 12 |
| Dill pickle (Kraft) *Ready Dip,* Neufchâtel cheese | 1 oz. | 215 | 5.8 | | | |
| Garlic (Kraft) *Teez* | 1 oz. | 120 | 4.3 | | | |
| Green goddess (Kraft) *Teez* | 1 oz. | 200 | 4.2 | | | |
| Jalapeño bean (Fritos) | 1 oz. | 170 | 1.4 | <1. | <1. | |
| Onion: | | | | | | |
| (Borden) French | 1 oz. | | 5.3 | | | |
| (Breakstone) | 2 T. (1.1 oz.) | 174 | 5.1 | | | 13 |
| (Kraft) French onion, *Teez* | 1 oz. | 145 | 3.9 | | | |

(USDA): United States Department of Agriculture
*Prepared as Package Directs

| Food and Description | Measure or Quantity | Sodium (mg.) | Total | — Fats in grams — Satu- rated | Unsatu- rated | Choles- terol (mg.) |
|---|---|---|---|---|---|---|
| (Kraft) *Ready Dip*, Neufchâtel cheese | 1 oz. | 242 | 6.1 | | | |
| (Sealtest) French onion, *Dip'n Dressing* | 1 oz. | 159 | 3.7 | | | |
| & garlic (Sealtest) *Dip'n Dressing* | 1 oz. | 166 | 3.7 | | | |
| Tasty Tartar (Borden) | 1 oz. | | 4.1 | | | |
| Western Bar B-Q (Borden) | 1 oz. | | 4.1 | | | |
| **DIP MIX:** | | | | | | |
| Any flavor (Fritos) | 1 pkg. (.6 oz.) | | | | | 0 |
| Green onion (Lawry's) | 1 pkg. (.6 oz.) | | .1 | | | |
| Guacomole (Lawry's) | 1 pkg. (.6 oz.) | | 3.5 | | | |
| Toasted onion (Lawry's) | 1 pkg. (.6 oz.) | | .2 | | | |
| **DISTILLED LIQUOR,** 80 proof to 100 proof (USDA) | 1 fl. oz. (1 oz.) | <1 | | | | 0 |
| **DOCK,** including **SHEEP SORREL** (USDA): | | | | | | |
| Raw, whole | 1 lb. (weighed un- trimmed) | 16 | 1.0 | | | 0 |
| Raw, trimmed | 4 oz. | 6 | .3 | | | 0 |
| Boiled, without salt, drained | 4 oz. | 3 | .2 | | | 0 |
| **DOGFISH,** Spiny, raw, meat only (USDA) | 4 oz. | | 10.2 | | | |
| **DOLLY VARDEN,** raw, meat & skin (USDA) | 4 oz. | | 7.4 | | | |
| **DOUGHNUT:** | | | | | | |
| Cake type: | | | | | | |
| (USDA)[1] | 1 piece (1.1 oz.) | 160 | 6.0 | 1. | 5. | |
| (Hostess) 10 to pkg. | 1 piece (1¼ oz.) | 178 | 6.7 | | | |
| Powdered, frozen (Morton) | 1 piece (.6 oz.) | 38 | 4.8 | | | |
| Sugar & spice, frozen (Morton) | 1 piece (.6 oz.) | 34 | 5.0 | | | |
| Yeast-leavened (USDA)[1] | 2 oz. | 133 | 15.1 | 3. | 12. | |
| *DR. BROWN'S CEL-RAY TONIC,* soft drink: | | | | | | |
| Regular | 6 fl. oz. | 7 | 0. | | | 0 |
| Low calorie | 6 fl. oz. | 30 | 0. | | | 0 |

(USDA): United States Department of Agriculture
*Prepared as Package Directs
[1]Principal sources of fat: vegetable shortening & egg.

| Food and Description | Measure or Quantity | Sodium (mg.) | —Fats in grams— | | | Cholesterol (mg.) |
|---|---|---|---|---|---|---|
| | | | Total | Satu-rated | Unsatu-rated | |
| **DR. PEPPER,** soft drink: | | | | | | |
| Regular, canned or bottled | 6 fl. oz. | 10+ | 0. | | | (0) |
| Sugar free | 6 fl. oz. | 18+ | 0. | | | (0) |
| **DRUM,** raw (USDA): | | | | | | |
| Freshwater: | | | | | | |
| Whole | 1 lb. (weighed whole) | 83 | 6.1 | | | |
| Meat only | 4 oz. | 79 | 5.9 | | | |
| Red: | | | | | | |
| Whole | 1 lb. (weighed whole) | 102 | .7 | | | |
| Meat only | 4 oz. | 62 | .5 | | | |
| **DUCK,** raw (USDA): | | | | | | |
| Domesticated: | | | | | | |
| Ready-to-cook | 1 lb. (weighed with bones) | | 106.4 | | | |
| Meat & skin | 4 oz. | | 32.4 | | | |
| Meat only | 4 oz. | 84 | 9.3 | | | |
| Wild: | | | | | | |
| Dressed | 1 lb. (weighed dressed) | | 41.6 | | | |
| Meat, skin and giblets | 4 oz. | | 17.9 | | | |
| Meat only | 4 oz. | | 5.9 | | | |

# E

| Food and Description | Measure or Quantity | Sodium (mg.) | Total | Satu-rated | Unsatu-rated | Cholesterol (mg.) |
|---|---|---|---|---|---|---|
| **ECLAIR,** home recipe, with custard filling & chocolate icing (USDA)[1] | 4 oz. | 93 | 15.4 | 5. | 11. | |
| **EEL** (USDA): | | | | | | |
| Raw, meat only | 4 oz. | | 20.8 | 5. | 16. | |
| Smoked, meat only | 4 oz. | | 31.5 | 7. | 25. | |
| **EGG BEATERS** (Fleischmann's) | ¼ cup (2.1 oz.) | | 7.5 | | | <1 |
| **EGG, BREAKFAST:** | | | | | | |
| Frozen, scrambled (Swanson): | | | | | | |
| With coffee cake | 6½-oz. breakfast | 706 | 35.9 | | | |
| With link sausage & coffee cake | 5½-oz. breakfast | 703 | 31.4 | | | |
| Mix (Durkee): | | | | | | |
| Scrambled, plain | 1 pkg. (.8 oz.) | 320 | 9.5 | 3. | 7. | 226 |

(USDA): United States Department of Agriculture
*Prepared as Package Directs
[1]Principal sources of fat: vegetable shortening, egg, milk, chocolate & butter.

| Food and Description | Measure or Quantity | Sodium (mg.) | Total | —Fats in grams— Satu- rated | Unsatu- rated | Choles- terol (mg.) |
|---|---|---|---|---|---|---|
| Scrambled, with bacon | 1 pkg. (1¼ oz.) | 476 | 13.4 | 4. | 10. | 357 |
| Western omelet | 1 pkg. (1¼ oz.) | 489 | 10.5 | 3. | 7. | 259 |
| **EGG, CHICKEN** (USDA): | | | | | | |
| Raw: | | | | | | |
| White only | 1 large egg (1.2 oz.) | 48 | Tr. | | | 0 |
| White only | 1 cup (9 oz.) | 372 | Tr. | | | 0 |
| Yolk only | 1 large egg (.6 oz.) | 9 | 5.2 | 2. | 4. | 250 |
| Yolk only | 1 cup (8.5 oz.) | 125 | 73.4 | 24. | 49. | 3552 |
| Whole, small | 1 egg (1.3 oz.) | 45 | 4.3 | 1. | 3. | 186 |
| Whole, medium | 1 egg (1.5 oz.) | 53 | 5.0 | 2. | 3. | 220 |
| Whole | 1 cup (8.8 oz.) | 306 | 28.9 | 10. | 19. | 1265 |
| Whole, large | 1 egg (1.8 oz.) | 61 | 5.7 | 2. | 4. | 251 |
| Whole, extra large | 1 egg (2 oz.) | 70 | 6.6 | 2. | 4. | 289 |
| Whole, jumbo | 1 egg (2.3 oz.) | 79 | 7.4 | 3. | 5. | 325 |
| Cooked: | | | | | | |
| Boiled without salt | 1 large egg (1.8 oz.) | 61 | 5.7 | 2. | 4. | 251 |
| Fried in butter[1] | 1 large egg (1.6 oz.) | 155 | 7.9 | 3. | 5. | |
| Omelet, mixed with milk & cooked in fat[2] | 1 large egg (2.2 oz.) | 159 | 8.0 | 3. | 5. | |
| Poached | 1 large egg (1.7 oz.) | 130 | 5.6 | 2. | 4. | 242 |
| Scrambled, mixed with milk & cooked in fat[2] | 1 cup (7.8 oz.) | 565 | 28.4 | 11. | 17. | 904 |
| Scrambled, mixed with milk & cooked in fat[2] | 1 large egg (2.3 oz.) | 164 | 8.3 | 3. | 5. | 263 |
| Dried: | | | | | | |
| White, flakes | 1 oz. | 293 | <.1 | | | |
| White, powder | 1 oz. | 313 | <.1 | | | |
| Yolk | 1 cup (3.4 oz.) | 96 | 54.3 | 17. | 37. | 2525 |
| Whole | 1 cup (3.8 oz.) | 461 | 44.5 | 14. | 30. | 2052 |
| Whole, glucose reduced | 1 oz. | 126 | 12.2 | 4. | 8. | |
| Frozen, whole, raw | 1 oz. | 35 | 3.3 | 1. | 2. | |
| **EGG, DUCK,** raw (USDA) | 1 egg (2.8 oz.) | 98 | 11.6 | | | |
| **EGG, GOOSE,** raw (USDA) | 1 egg (5.8 oz.) | | 21.8 | | | |
| **EGG, TURKEY,** raw (USDA) | 1 egg (3.1 oz.) | | 10.4 | | | |
| *EGG McMUFFIN,* (McDonald's) | 1 piece (4.5 oz.) | 1130 | 11.3 | | | |

(USDA): United States Department of Agriculture
*Prepared as Package Directs
[1]Principal sources of fat: egg & butter.
[2]Principal sources of fat: egg, milk & vegetable fat.

| Food and Description | Measure or Quantity | Sodium (mg.) | —Fats in grams— | | | Cholesterol (mg.) |
|---|---|---|---|---|---|---|
| | | | Total | Saturated | Unsaturated | |

**EGG NOG** Dairy:
| | | | | | | |
|---|---|---|---|---|---|---|
| (Borden) 4.69% fat[1] | ½ cup (4.2 oz.) | | 5.9 | | | |
| (Borden) 6% fat[1] | ½ cup (4.3 oz.) | | 8.1 | | | |
| (Borden) 8% fat[1] | ½ cup (4.3 oz.) | | 10.5 | | | |
| (Sealtest) 6% butterfat | ½ cup (4.6 oz.) | 80 | 8.7 | | | |
| (Sealtest) 8% butterfat | ½ cup (4.6 oz.) | 73 | 11.3 | | | |

**EGGPLANT:**
| | | | | | | |
|---|---|---|---|---|---|---|
| Raw, whole (USDA) | 1 lb. (weighed untrimmed) | 7 | .7 | | | 0 |
| Boiled without salt, drained (USDA) | 4 oz. | 1 | .2 | | | 0 |
| Boiled without salt, drained, diced (USDA) | 1 cup (7.1 oz.) | 2 | .4 | | | 0 |
| Frozen, fried sticks (Mrs. Paul's) | 7-oz. pkg. | | 27.6 | | | |
| Frozen, parmesan (Mrs. Paul's) | 11-oz. pkg. | | 35.3 | | | |
| Frozen, parmigiana (Buitoni) | 4 oz. | | 10.7 | | | |
| Frozen, slices (Mrs. Paul's) | 9-oz. pkg. | | 48.2 | | | |

**EGG ROLL,** shrimp, frozen (Hung's)
| | | | | | | |
|---|---|---|---|---|---|---|
| | 1 roll | | 5.1 | | | |

***EGGSTRA** (Tillie Lewis)
| | | | | | | |
|---|---|---|---|---|---|---|
| | 1 large egg (1.8 oz.) | 80 | 1.2 | | | 57 |

**ELDERBERRY,** fresh (USDA):
| | | | | | | |
|---|---|---|---|---|---|---|
| Whole | 1 lb. (weighed with stems) | | 2.1 | | | 0 |
| Stems removed | 4 oz. | | .6 | | | 0 |

**ENCHILADA,** beef, frozen:
| | | | | | | |
|---|---|---|---|---|---|---|
| With cheese & chili gravy (Banquet) | 8 enchiladas (2 lbs.) | | 60.4 | | | |
| With rice (Swanson) | 9⅝-oz. pkg. | 1018 | 16.1 | | | |
| With sauce (Banquet) | 6-oz. bag | | 12.2 | | | |

**ENCHILADA DINNER,** frozen:
| | | | | | | |
|---|---|---|---|---|---|---|
| (Banquet): | | | | | | |
| Meat compartment | 6¼ oz. | | 12.4 | | | |
| Rice compartment | 3 oz. | | .1 | | | |
| Beans compartment | 3¼ oz. | | 4.0 | | | |
| Complete dinner | 12-oz. dinner | | 16.6 | | | |
| (Patio) 5-compartment | 13-oz. dinner | | 17.0 | | | |
| (Patio) 3-compartment | 13-oz. dinner | | 16.0 | | | |
| (Swanson) | 15-oz. dinner | 2420 | 27.2 | | | |

(USDA): United States Department of Agriculture
*Prepared as Package Directs
[1]Principal sources of fat: milk and egg yolk.

| Food and Description | Measure or Quantity | Sodium (mg.) | Fats in grams Total | Satu- rated | Unsatu- rated | Choles- terol (mg.) |
|---|---|---|---|---|---|---|
| Cheese: | | | | | | |
| (Banquet): | | | | | | |
| Meat compartment | 6¼ oz. | | 14.0 | | | |
| Rice compartment | 3 oz. | | .1 | | | |
| Beans compartment | 3¼ oz. | | 2.4 | | | |
| Complete dinner | 12½-oz. dinner | | 16.6 | | | |
| (Patio) 5-compartment | 12-oz. dinner | | 15.0 | | | |
| (Patio) 3-compartment | 12-oz. dinner | | 13.0 | | | |
| **ENCHILADA MIX** (Lawry's) | 1.6-oz. pkg. | | 1.8 | | | |
| **ENDIVE, BELGIAN or FRENCH** (See **CHICORY, WITLOOF**) | | | | | | |
| **ENDIVE, CURLY, or ESCAROLE,** raw (USDA): | | | | | | |
| Untrimmed | 1 lb. (weighed un- trimmed) | 56 | .4 | | | 0 |
| Trimmed | ½ lb. | 32 | .2 | | | 0 |
| Cut up or shredded | 1 cup (2.5 oz.) | 10 | <.1 | | | 0 |
| **ESCAROLE** (See **ENDIVE**) | | | | | | |
| **EULACHON or SMELT,** raw, meat only (USDA) | 4 oz. | | 7.0 | | | |

## F

| Food and Description | Measure or Quantity | Sodium (mg.) | Fats in grams Total | Satu- rated | Unsatu- rated | Choles- terol (mg.) |
|---|---|---|---|---|---|---|
| **FARINA** (See also **CREAM OF WHEAT**): | | | | | | |
| Regular: | | | | | | |
| Dry: | | | | | | |
| (USDA) | 1 cup (6 oz.) | 3 | 1.5 | | | 0 |
| Cream, enriched (H-O) | 1 cup (6.1 oz.) | 3 | 1.4 | | | 0 |
| *Pearls of Wheat* (Albers) | 1 cup | | 1.4 | | | (0) |
| Cooked: | | | | | | |
| (USDA) | 1 cup (8.4 oz.) | 343 | .2 | | | 0 |
| (Quaker) | 1 cup (1 oz. dry) | <1 | .2 | | | (0) |
| Quick-cooking (USDA): | | | | | | |
| Dry | 1 oz. | 71 | .3 | | | 0 |
| Cooked | 1 cup (8.6 oz.) | 466 | .2 | | | 0 |
| Instant-cooking (USDA): | | | | | | |
| Dry | 1 oz. | 2 | .3 | | | 0 |
| Cooked | 4 oz. | 213 | .1 | | | 0 |

(USDA): United States Department of Agriculture
*Prepared as Package Directs

| Food and Description | Measure or Quantity | Sodium (mg.) | Fats in grams — Total | Satu- rated | Unsatu- rated | Choles- terol (mg.) |
|---|---|---|---|---|---|---|
| **FAT, COOKING:** | | | | | | |
| Lard (USDA) | 1 cup (7.2 oz.) | 0. | 205. | 78. | 127. | |
| Lard (USDA) | 1 T. (.5 oz.) | 0. | 13.0 | 5. | 8. | |
| Vegetable (USDA) | 1 cup (7.1 oz.) | 0. | 200.0 | 50. | 150. | 0 |
| Vegetable (USDA) | 1 T. (.4 oz.) | 0. | 12.0 | 3. | 9. | 0 |
| *Crisco* | 1 T. (.4 oz.) | 0. | 11.7 | 3. | 9. | 0 |
| *Fluffo* | 1 T. (.4 oz.) | 0. | 11.7 | 4. | 7. | Tr. |
| *Light Spry* | 1 T. (.4 oz.) | 0. | 10.6 | 3. | 8. | 0. |
| *Light Spry* | ¼ lb. | 0. | 113.4 | 32. | 82. | 0. |
| | | | | | | |
| **FENNEL LEAVES,** raw, (USDA): | | | | | | |
| Untrimmed | 1 lb. (weighed un- trimmed) | | 1.7 | | | 0 |
| Trimmed | 4 oz. | | .5 | | | 0 |
| | | | | | | |
| **FENNEL SEED** (Spice Islands) | 1 tsp. | 1 | | | | (0) |
| | | | | | | |
| **FIG:** | | | | | | |
| Fresh: | | | | | | |
| (USDA) | 1 lb. | 9 | 1.4 | | | 0 |
| Small (USDA) | 1.3-oz. fig (1½″) | <1 | .1 | | | 0 |
| Candied (USDA) | 1 oz. | | <.1 | | | 0 |
| Candied (Bama) | 1 T. (.7 oz.) | <1 | <.1 | | | |
| Canned, regular pack, solids & liq.: | | | | | | |
| Light syrup (USDA) | 4 oz. | 2 | .2 | | | 0 |
| Heavy syrup: | | | | | | |
| (USDA) | ½ cup (4.4 oz.) | 3 | .3 | | | 0 |
| (USDA) | 3 figs & 2 T. syrup | 2 | .2 | | | 0 |
| (Del Monte) | ½ cup (4.4 oz.) | 1 | .4 | | | 0 |
| (Stokely-Van Camp) | ½ cup (4.2 oz.) | | .2 | | | (0) |
| Extra heavy syrup (USDA) | 4 oz. | 2 | .2 | | | 0 |
| Canned, unsweetened or dietetic pack, solids & liq.: | | | | | | |
| Water pack (USDA) | 4 oz. | 2 | .2 | | | 0 |
| Kadota (Diet Delight) | ½ cup (4.4 oz.) | 4 | .1 | | | (0) |
| (Tillie Lewis) | ½ cup (4.5 oz.) | <10 | .2 | | | (0) |
| Whole: | | | | | | |
| (S and W) *Nutradiet,* low calorie | 6 whole figs (3.5 oz.) | 2 | .1 | | | (0) |
| (S and W) *Nutradiet,* un- sweetened | 6 whole figs (3.5 oz.) | 2 | 1 | | | (0) |
| Dried: | | | | | | |
| Chopped (USDA) | 1 cup (6 oz.) | 58. | 2.2 | | | 0 |

(USDA): United States Department of Agriculture
*Prepared as Package Directs

| Food and Description | Measure or Quantity | Sodium (mg.) | Fats in grams — Total | Satu- rated | Unsatu- rated | Choles- terol (mg.) |
|---|---|---|---|---|---|---|
| (USDA) | .7-oz. fig (2″ x 1″) | 7 | .3 | | | 0 |
| Calimyrna (Del Monte) | 1 cup (5.4 oz.) | 27 | 3.0 | | | (0) |
| Mission (Del Monte) | 1 cup (5.4 oz.) | 30 | 3.5 | | | (0) |
| **FIG PRESERVE,** sweetened (Bama) | 1 T. | 1 | <.1 | | | (0) |
| **FILBERT or HAZELNUT** (USDA): | | | | | | |
| Whole | 1 lb. (weighed in shell) | 4 | 130.2 | 7. | 123. | 0 |
| Shelled | 1 oz. | <1 | 17.7 | <1. | 17. | 0 |
| **FINE HERBES** (Spice Islands) | 1 tsp. | <1 | | | | (0) |
| **FINNAN HADDIE** (See **HADDOCK, SMOKED**) | | | | | | |
| **FISH** (See individual listings) | | | | | | |
| **FISH CAKE:** | | | | | | |
| Home recipe,[1] fried (USDA) | 2 oz. | | 4.5 | | | |
| Frozen: | | | | | | |
| Fried, reheated (USDA) | 2 oz. | | 10.1 | | | |
| (Mrs. Paul's) | 4 oz. | | 4.6 | | | |
| Thins (Mrs. Paul's) | 10-oz. pkg. | | 17.3 | | | |
| **FISH & CHIPS,** frozen: | | | | | | |
| (Gorton) | ½ of 1-lb. pkg. | 55 | 17.0 | | | |
| (Mrs. Paul's) | 14-oz. pkg. | | 21.4 | | | |
| (Swanson) | 5-oz. pkg. | 558 | 11.5 | | | |
| **FISH CHOWDER,** New England | | | | | | |
| (Snow) | 8 oz. | | 6.0 | | | |
| **FISH DINNER,** frozen: | | | | | | |
| (Morton) | 8¾-oz. dinner | 556 | 13.5 | | | |
| Filet of ocean fish (Swanson) | 11½-oz. dinner | 1111 | 14.9 | | | |
| With French fries (Swanson) | 9¾-oz. dinner | 1368 | 17.7 | | | |
| With green beans & peach (Weight Watchers) | 18-oz. dinner | | 2.0 | | | |
| With pineapple chunks (Weight Watchers) | 9½-oz. luncheon | | 2.2 | | | |
| **FISH FILLET** | | | | | | |
| Sandwich (McDonald's) | 1 sandwich (4.8 oz.) | 759 | 21.7 | | | |

(USDA): United States Department of Agriculture
*Prepared as Package Directs
[1]Prepared with canned flaked fish, potato & egg.

| Food and Description | Measure or Quantity | Sodium (mg.) | — Fats in grams — | | | Choles- terol (mg.) |
|---|---|---|---|---|---|---|
| | | | Total | Satu- rated | Unsatu- rated | |
| **Frozen:** | | | | | | |
| Breaded, fried (Mrs. Paul's) | 14-oz. pkg. | | 26.0 | | | |
| Buttered (Mrs. Paul's) | 10-oz. pkg. | | 19.0 | | | |
| Crisps (Gorton) | ½ of 8-oz. pkg. | 36 | 14.0 | | | |
| **FISH FLAKES,** canned (USDA) | 4 oz. | | .7 | | | |
| **FISH LOAF,** home recipe (USDA)[1] | 4 oz. | | 4.2 | | | |
| **FISH PUFFS,** frozen (Gorton) | ½ of 8-oz. pkg. | 4.1 | 17.0 | | | |
| **FISH STICK,** frozen: | | | | | | |
| Cooked, commercial, 3¾" x 1" x ½" sticks (USDA) | 10 sticks (8-oz. pkg.) | | 20.2 | | | |
| (Gorton) | ½ of 8-oz. pkg. | 80 | 10.0 | | | |
| Breaded, fried (Mrs. Paul's) | 14-oz. pkg. | | 28.7 | | | |
| **FLAN PUDDING,** chilled (Breakstone) | 5-oz. container | 175 | 3.7 | | | 10 |
| **FLOUNDER:** | | | | | | |
| Raw (USDA): | | | | | | |
| Whole | 1 lb. (weighed whole) | 117 | 1.2 | | | 75 |
| Meat only | 4 oz. | 88 | .9 | | | 57 |
| Baked (USDA) | 4 oz. | 269 | 9.3 | | | |
| Frozen: | | | | | | |
| (Gorton) | 1-lb. pkg. | 351 | 3.6 | | | |
| Dinner (Weight Watchers) | 18-oz. dinner | | 3.0 | | | |
| & broccoli (Weight Watchers) | 9½-oz. luncheon | | 4.8 | | | |
| **FLOUR:** | | | | | | |
| Buckwheat, dark, sifted (USDA) | 1 cup (3.5 oz.) | | 2.4 | | | 0 |
| Buckwheat, light, sifted (USDA) | 1 cup (3.5 oz.) | | 1.2 | | | 0 |
| Carob or St. John's-bread (USDA) | 1 oz. | | .4 | | | 0 |
| Chestnut (USDA) | 1 oz. | 3 | 1.0 | | | 0 |
| Corn, sifted (USDA) | 1 cup (3.9 oz.) | 1 | 2.9 | Tr. | 3. | 0 |
| Cottonseed (USDA) | 1 oz. | | 1.9 | <1. | 1. | 0 |
| Cottonseed (Data from General Mills) | 1 oz. | 8 | 1.2 | | | (0) |

(USDA): United States Department of Agriculture
*Prepared as Package Directs
[1]Prepared with canned flaked fish, bread crumbs, eggs, tomatoes, onion & fat.

| Food and Description | Measure or Quantity | Sodium (mg.) | Fats in grams — Total | Satu- rated | Unsatu- rated | Choles- terol (mg.) |
|---|---|---|---|---|---|---|
| Fish, from whole fish (USDA) | 1 oz. | 48 | <.1 | | | |
| Fish, from fillets (USDA) | 1 oz. | 11 | .1 | | | |
| Fish, from fillet waste (USDA) | 1 oz. | 62 | .6 | | | |
| Lima bean (USDA) | 1 oz. | | .4 | | | 0 |
| Peanut, defatted (USDA) | 1 oz. | 3 | 2.6 | <1. | 2. | 0 |
| Potato (USDA) | 1 oz. | 10 | .2 | | | 0 |
| Rice, stirred, spooned (USDA) | 1 cup (5.6 oz.) | 8 | .8 | | | 0 |
| Rye: | | | | | | |
| Light (USDA): | | | | | | |
| Unsifted, spooned | 1 cup (3.6 oz.) | 1 | 1.0 | | | 0 |
| Sifted, spooned | 1 cup (3.1 oz.) | <1 | .9 | | | 0 |
| Medium (USDA) | 1 oz. | <1 | .5 | | | 0 |
| Dark (USDA): | | | | | | |
| Unstirred | 1 cup (4.5 oz.) | 1 | 3.3 | | | 0 |
| Stirred | 1 cup (4.5 oz.) | 1 | 3.3 | | | 0 |
| Soybean (USDA): | | | | | | |
| Defatted, stirred | 1 cup (3.6 oz.) | 1 | .9 | | | 0 |
| Low fat, stirred | 1 cup (3.1 oz.) | <1 | 5.9 | <1. | 5. | 0 |
| Full fat, stirred | 1 cup (2.5 oz.) | <1 | 14.6 | 2. | 12. | 0 |
| High fat | 1 oz. | <1 | 3.4 | <1. | 3. | 0 |
| Sunflower seed, partially defat- ted (USDA) | 1 oz. | 16 | 1.0 | Tr. | 1. | 0 |
| Tapioca, unsifted, spooned (USDA) | 1 cup (3.8 oz.) | 3 | .2 | | | 0 |
| Wheat: | | | | | | |
| All-purpose: | | | | | | |
| (USDA) | 1 oz. | <1 | .3 | | | 0 |
| Unsifted, dipped (USDA) | 1 cup (5 oz.) | 3 | 1.4 | | | 0 |
| Unsifted, spooned (USDA) | 1 cup (4.4 oz.) | 3 | 1.3 | | | 0 |
| Sifted, spooned (USDA) | 1 cup (4.1 oz.) | 2 | 1.2 | | | 0 |
| Bread: | | | | | | |
| (USDA) | 1 oz. | <1 | .3 | | | 0 |
| Unsifted, dipped (USDA) | 1 cup (4.8 oz.) | 3 | 1.5 | | | 0 |
| Unsifted, spooned (USDA) | 1 cup (4.3 oz.) | 2 | 1.4 | | | 0 |
| Sifted, spooned (USDA) | 1 cup (4.1 oz.) | 2 | 1.3 | | | 0 |
| Cake or pastry: | | | | | | |
| (USDA) | 1 oz. | <1 | .2 | | | 0 |
| Unsifted, dipped (USDA) | 1 cup (4.2 oz.) | 2 | 1.0 | | | 0 |
| Unsifted, spooned (USDA) | 1 cup (3.9 oz.) | 2 | .9 | | | 0 |
| Sifted, spooned (USDA) | 1 cup (3.5 oz.) | 2 | .8 | | | 0 |
| Gluten: | | | | | | |
| (USDA) | 1 oz. | <1 | .5 | | | 0 |
| Unsifted, dipped (USDA) | 1 cup (5 oz.) | 3 | 2.7 | | | 0 |
| Unsifted, spooned (USDA) | 1 cup (4.8 oz.) | 3 | 2.6 | | | 0 |

(USDA): United States Department of Agriculture
*Prepared as Package Directs

| Food and Description | Measure or Quantity | Sodium (mg.) | —Fats in grams— | | | Choles- terol (mg.) |
|---|---|---|---|---|---|---|
| | | | Total | Satu- rated | Unsatu- rated | |
| Sifted, spooned (USDA) | 1 cup (4.8 oz.) | 3 | 2.6 | | | 0 |
| Self-rising: | | | | | | |
| (USDA) | 1 oz. | 306 | .3 | | | 0 |
| Unsifted, dipped (USDA) | 1 cup (4.6 oz.) | 1403 | 1.3 | | | 0 |
| Unsifted, spooned (USDA) | 1 cup (4.5 oz.) | 1370 | 1.3 | | | 0 |
| Sifted, spooned (USDA) | 1 cup (3.7 oz.) | 1144 | 1.1 | | | 0 |
| Whole wheat: | | | | | | |
| (USDA) | 1 oz. | <1 | .6 | | | 0 |
| Stirred, spooned (USDA) | 1 cup (4.8 oz.) | 4 | 2.7 | | | 0 |
| *Aunt Jemima*, self-rising (Quaker Oats) | 1 cup (4 oz.) | 1400 | 1.2 | | | (0) |
| *Gold Medal* (Betty Crocker): | | | | | | |
| Regular | 1 cup | 3 | 1.4 | | | (0) |
| Better-for-bread | 1 cup | 3 | 1.4 | | | (0) |
| Self-rising | 1 cup | 1743 | 1.3 | | | (0) |
| *Wondra* | 1 cup | 3 | 1.4 | | | (0) |
| *Presto*, self-rising | 1 cup (3.9 oz.) | 1320 | .9 | | | 0 |
| (Quaker) | 1 cup (4 oz.) | 4 | 1.2 | | | (0) |
| *Softasilk* for cakes (Betty Crocker) | 1 cup | 2 | .9 | | | (0) |
| **FOURNIER NATURE,** wine (Gold Seal) 12% alcohol | 3 fl. oz. | 3 | 0. | | | (0) |
| **FRANKENBERRY,** cereal (General Mills) | 1 cup (1 oz.) | 150 | .8 | | | (0) |
| **FRANKFURTER or WIENER:** | | | | | | |
| Raw: | | | | | | |
| All kinds (USDA) | 1.6-oz. frankfurter | 499 | 12.5 | | | |
| All meat (USDA) | 1.6-oz. frankfurter | | 11.6 | | | 29 |
| With cereal (USDA) | 1.6-oz. frankfurter | | 9.3 | | | |
| With nonfat dry milk (USDA) | 1.6-oz. frankfurter | | 11.6 | | | |
| With nonfat dry milk & cereal (USDA) | 1.6-oz. frankfurter | | 9.8 | | | |
| (Armour Star) all meat | 1.6-oz. frankfurter | | 15.1 | | | |
| (Hormel) all beef: | | | | | | |
| 10 per 12-oz. pkg. | 1.2-oz. frankfurter | 275 | 9.3 | 4. | 5. | 23 |
| 10 per 1-lb. pkg. | 1.6-oz. frankfurter | 364 | 12.3 | 5. | 6. | 31 |
| 12 per 12-oz. pkg. | 1-oz. frankfurter | 231 | 7.8 | 3. | 4. | 20 |
| (Hormel) all meat: | | | | | | |
| 10 per 12-oz. pkg. | 1.2-oz. frankfurter | 258 | 9.8 | 3. | 5. | 16 |
| 10 per 1-lb. pkg. | 1.6-oz. frankfurter | 342 | 13.0 | 4. | 7. | 21 |

(USDA): United States Department of Agriculture
*Prepared as Package Directs

| Food and Description | Measure or Quantity | Sodium (mg.) | —Fats in grams— | | | Choles-terol (mg.) |
|---|---|---|---|---|---|---|
| | | | Total | Satu-rated | Unsatu-rated | |
| 12 per 12-oz. pkg. | 1-oz. frankfurter | 217 | 8.2 | 2. | 4. | 13 |
| (Oscar Mayer) all meat, imperial size, 5 per lb. | 3.2-oz. frankfurter | 884 | 26.3 | | | |
| (Oscar Mayer) all meat, Little Wiener, 16 per 5½ oz. | .7-oz. frankfurter | 244 | 7.5 | | | |
| (Oscar Mayer) all meat, 1883, 6 per lb. | 2.7-oz. frankfurter | 678 | 18.9 | | | |
| (Oscar Mayer) all meat wieners: | | | | | | |
| 8 per lb. | 2-oz. frankfurter | 544 | 16.5 | 6. | 10. | 25 |
| 10 per lb. | 1.6-oz. frankfurter | 430 | 13.0 | 5. | 8. | 20 |
| (Oscar Mayer) pure beef: | | | | | | |
| 8 per lb. | 2-oz. frankfurter | 508 | 16.5 | 7. | 9. | 27 |
| 10 per lb. | 1.6-oz. frankfurter | 401 | 13.0 | 6. | 7. | 22 |
| (Oscar Mayer) pure beef, Machiaeh Brand | 2-oz. frankfurter | 531 | 15.9 | | | |
| (Wilson) all beef | 1.6-oz. frankfurter | 499 | 12.2 | 6. | 6. | 28 |
| (Wilson) skinless, all meat | 1.6-oz. frankfurter | 499 | 12.7 | 5. | 7. | 27 |
| Cooked, all kinds, 10 per lb. raw (USDA) | 1 frankfurter | | 12.2 | | | 28 |
| Canned (USDA) | 2 oz. | | 10.3 | | | |
| Canned (Hormel) | 12-oz. can | | 88.1 | | | |

**FRANKS & BEANS** (See **BEANS & FRANKS**)

*FRANKS-N-BLANKETS,* frozen
(Durkee) — 1 piece (.4 oz.) — 3.8

**FRENCH TOAST,** frozen:
| | | | | | | |
|---|---|---|---|---|---|---|
| (Aunt Jemima) | 1 slice (1.5 oz.) | 220 | 2.2 | | | |
| With link sausage (Swanson) | 4½-oz. breakfast | 664 | 15.0 | | | |

*FRESCA,* soft drink — 6 fl. oz. — 31 — Tr. — — — 0

**FROG LEGS,** raw (USDA):
| | | | | | | |
|---|---|---|---|---|---|---|
| Bone in | 1 lb. (weighed with bone) | | .9 | | | 147 |
| Meat only | 4 oz. | | .3 | | | 57 |

*FROOT LOOPS,* cereal (Kellogg's) — 1 cup (1 oz.) — 65 — .8 — — — (0)

*FROSTED RICE KRINKLES,* cereal
(Post) — ⅞ cup (1 oz.) — 204 — .1 — — — 0

(USDA): United States Department of Agriculture
*Prepared as Package Directs

| Food and Description | Measure or Quantity | Sodium (mg.) | —Fats in grams— | | | Choles- terol (mg.) |
|---|---|---|---|---|---|---|
| | | | Total | Satu- rated | Unsatu- rated | |
| **FROSTED SHAKE,** canned, any flavor | | | | | | |
| (Borden) | 9¼-fl.-oz. can | 300 | 12.5 | | | |
| **FROSTED TREAT** (Weight Watchers) 1 serving (4¾ oz.) | | | 1.4 | | | |
| **FROSTING** (See **CAKE ICING**) | | | | | | |
| **FROSTY O's,** cereal (General Mills) | 1 cup (1 oz.) | 155 | 1.2 | | | (0) |
| **FROZEN CUSTARD** (See **ICE CREAM**) | | | | | | |
| **FROZEN DESSERT:** | | | | | | |
| *Charlotte Freeze* (Borden): | | | | | | |
| Chocolate | ⅓ pt. (3 oz.) | | 5.2 | | | |
| Vanilla | ⅓ pt. (3 oz.) | | 5.0 | | | |
| Cherry (SugarLo): | | | | | | |
| 4% fat, ice milk | ⅓ pt. (3.5 oz.) | 69 | 4.0 | 2. | 2. | 13 |
| 10% fat, ice cream | ⅓ pt. (3.5 oz.) | 67 | 10.2 | 6. | 5. | 32 |
| Chocolate: | | | | | | |
| (Borden) | ⅓ pt. (3.4 oz.) | 68 | 8.0 | | | |
| Chocolate chip, mint (Borden) | ⅓ pt. (3.4 oz.) | 68 | 9.1 | | | |
| (SugarLo) 4.6% fat, ice milk | ⅓ pt. (3.5 oz.) | 69 | 4.6 | 2. | 2. | 13 |
| (SugarLo) 10.8% fat, ice cream | ⅓ pt. (3.5 oz.) | 67 | 10.8 | 6. | 5. | 32 |
| Coffee (SugarLo): | | | | | | |
| 4% fat, ice milk | ⅓ pt. (3.5 oz.) | 69 | 4.0 | 2. | 2. | 13 |
| 10% fat, ice cream | ⅓ pt. (3.5 oz.) | 67 | 10.2 | 6. | 5. | 32 |
| Lemon chiffon (SugarLo): | | | | | | |
| 4% fat, ice milk | ⅓ pt. (3.5 oz.) | 69 | 4.0 | 2. | 2. | 13 |
| 10% fat, ice cream | ⅓ pt. (3.5 oz.) | 67 | 10.2 | 6. | 5. | 32 |
| Maple (SugarLo): | | | | | | |
| 4% fat, ice milk | ⅓ pt. (3.5 oz.) | 69 | 4.0 | 2. | 2. | 13 |
| 10% fat, ice cream | ⅓ pt. (3.5 oz.) | 67 | 10.2 | 6. | 5. | 32 |
| Orange-Pineapple (SugarLo): | | | | | | |
| 3.6% fat, ice milk | ⅓ pt. (3.5 oz.) | 64 | 3.6 | 2. | 2. | 11 |
| 9% fat, ice cream | ⅓ pt. (3.5 oz.) | 61 | 9.0 | 5. | 4. | 28 |
| Raspberry, black (Borden) | ⅓ pt. (3.4 oz.) | 68 | 7.7 | | | |
| Shake (SugarLo) chocolate | ⅓ pt. (3.2 oz.) | 112 | .9 | Tr. | Tr. | 3 |
| Shake (SugarLo) vanilla & strawberry | ⅓ pt. (3.2 oz.) | 108 | .9 | Tr. | Tr. | 3 |
| Strawberry (SugarLo): | | | | | | |
| 3.6%, ice milk | ⅓ pt. (3.5 oz.) | 64 | 3.6 | 2. | 2. | 11 |
| 9%, ice cream | ⅓ pt. (3.5 oz.) | 61 | 9.0 | 5. | 4. | 28 |

(USDA): United States Department of Agriculture
*Prepared as Package Directs

| Food and Description | Measure or Quantity | Sodium (mg.) | — Fats in grams — | | | Cholesterol (mg.) |
| --- | --- | --- | --- | --- | --- | --- |
| | | | Total | Saturated | Unsaturated | |
| **Vanilla:** | | | | | | |
| (Borden) | ⅓ pt. (3.4 oz.) | 68 | 7.7 | | | |
| (SugarLo) 4% fat, ice milk | ⅓ pt. (3.5 oz.) | 69 | 4.0 | 2. | 2. | 13 |
| (SugarLo) 10% fat, ice cream | ⅓ pt. (3.5 oz.) | 67 | 10.2 | 6. | 5. | 32 |
| Chocolate spin (Borden) | ⅓ pt. (3.4 oz.) | 68 | 8.4 | | | |
| Fudge or raspberry swirl: | | | | | | |
| (SugarLo) 3.9% fat, ice milk | ⅓ pt. (3.5 oz.) | 56 | 3.9 | 2. | 2. | 12 |
| (SugarLo) 10% fat, ice cream | ⅓ pt. (3.5 oz.) | 59 | 10.0 | 6. | 4. | 31 |
| Vanilla-coated: | | | | | | |
| Ice cream bar (SugarLo) | 2½-oz. bar | 57 | 9.6 | 5. | 4. | 22 |
| Ice milk bar (SugarLo) | 2½-oz. bar | 46 | 7.0 | 4. | 3. | 9 |
| **FRUIT CAKE (USDA):** | | | | | | |
| Dark, home recipe[1] | 1-lb. loaf | 717 | 69.4 | | | 206 |
| Dark, home recipe[1] | 1/30 of 8" loaf (.5 oz.) | 24 | 2.3 | | | 7 |
| Dark, home recipe[1] | 2" x 2" x ½" slice (1.1 oz.) | 47 | 4.6 | | | 14 |
| Light, home recipe, made with butter[2] | 1-lb. loaf | 875 | 71.2 | 26. | 45. | |
| Light, home recipe, made with butter[2] | 2" x 2" x ½" slice (1.1 oz.) | 58 | 4.7 | 2. | 3. | |
| Light, home recipe, made with butter[2] | 1/30 of 8" loaf (.5 oz.) | 29 | 2.4 | <1. | 1. | |
| Light, home recipe, made with vegetable shortening[3] | 1-lb. loaf | 875 | 74.8 | 16. | 59. | |
| Light, home recipe, made with vegetable shortening[3] | 2" x 2" x ½" slice (1.1 oz.) | 58 | 5.0 | 1. | 4. | |
| Light, home recipe, made with vegetable shortening[3] | 1/30 of 8" loaf (.5 oz.) | 29 | 2.5 | <1. | 2. | |
| **FRUIT COCKTAIL:** | | | | | | |
| Canned, regular pack, solids & liq.: | | | | | | |
| Light syrup (USDA) | 4 oz. | 6 | .1 | | | 0 |
| Heavy syrup (USDA) | ½ cup (4.5 oz.) | 6 | .1 | | | 0 |
| Heavy syrup (Del Monte) | ½ cup (4.3 oz.) | 11 | .1 | | | 0 |
| Heavy syrup (Dole) | ½ cup (including 3 T. syrup) | 6 | .1 | | | 0 |
| Heavy syrup (Hunt's) | ½ cup (4.5 oz.) | 6 | .1 | | | (0) |

(USDA): United States Department of Agriculture
*Prepared as Package Directs
[1]Made with sodium aluminum sulfate-type baking powder.
[2]Principal sources of fat: butter, almonds & cream.
[3]Principal sources of fat: vegetable shortening, almonds & cream.

| Food and Description | Measure or Quantity | Sodium (mg.) | —Fats in grams— | | | Cholesterol (mg.) |
|---|---|---|---|---|---|---|
| | | | Total | Saturated | Unsaturated | |
| Heavy syrup (Stokely-Van Camp) | ½ cup (4 oz.) | | .1 | | | (0) |
| Extra heavy syrup (USDA) | 4 oz. | 6 | .1 | | | 0 |
| Canned, unsweetened or dietetic pack, solids & liq.: | | | | | | |
| Water pack (USDA) | 4 oz. | 6 | .1 | | | 0 |
| (S and W) *Nutradiet,* low calorie | 4 oz. | 3 | .1 | | | (0) |
| (Diet Delight) | ½ cup (4.4 oz.) | 5 | <.1 | | | (0) |
| (S and W) *Nutradiet,* unsweetened | 4 oz. | 3 | <.1 | | | (0) |
| (Tillie Lewis) | ½ cup (4.3 oz.) | <10 | .1 | | | 0 |
| *FRUIT CUP,* solids & liq. | | | | | | |
| (Del Monte): | | | | | | |
| Fruit cocktail | 5¼-oz. container | 13 | .1 | | | (0) |
| Mixed fruits | 5-oz. container | 18 | 0. | | | (0) |
| Peaches, diced | 5¼-oz. container | 15 | 0. | | | (0) |
| Pineapple, in its own juice | 4¼-oz. container | 23 | .2 | | | (0) |
| **FRUIT MIX,** soft drink: | | | | | | |
| (Hoffman) | 6 fl. oz. | 14 | 0. | | | 0 |
| (Nedick's) | 6 fl. oz. | 14 | 0. | | | 0 |
| **FRUIT, MIXED:** | | | | | | |
| Dried (Del Monte) | 1 cup (6.2 oz.) | 56 | .5 | | | (0) |
| Frozen, quick thaw (Birds Eye) | ½ cup (5 oz.) | Tr. | Tr. | | | 0 |
| **FRUIT PUNCH:** | | | | | | |
| (Del Monte) tropical | 6 fl. oz. | 2 | Tr. | | | (0) |
| Soft drink, sweetened (Nehi) | 6 fl. oz. | 8+ | 0. | | | 0 |
| **FRUIT SALAD:** | | | | | | |
| Bottled, chilled (Kraft) | 4 oz. | 115 | .1 | | | (0) |
| Canned, regular pack, solids & liq.: | | | | | | |
| Light syrup (USDA) | 4 oz. | 1 | .1 | | | 0 |
| Heavy syrup (USDA) | ½ cup (4.3 oz.) | 1 | .1 | | | 0 |
| Heavy syrup (Del Monte): | | | | | | |
| Fruits for salad | ½ cup (4.3 oz.) | 30 | .1 | | | 0 |
| Tropical | ½ cup (4.4 oz.) | 30 | .4 | | | 0 |
| Heavy syrup (Stokely-Van Camp) | ½ cup (4.2 oz.) | | .1 | | | (0) |
| Extra heavy syrup (USDA) | 4 oz. | 1 | .1 | | | 0 |
| Canned, unsweetened or dietetic pack: | | | | | | |
| Water pack (USDA) | 4 oz. | 1 | .1 | | | 0 |
| (Diet Delight) | ½ cup (4.4 oz.) | 6 | <.1 | | | (0) |
| (S and W) *Nutradiet,* low calorie | 4 oz. | 5 | .1 | | | (0) |
| (S and W) *Nutradiet,* unsweetened | 4 oz. | 3 | .1 | | | (.0) |

(USDA): United States Department of Agriculture
*Prepared as Package Directs

| Food and Description | Measure or Quantity | Sodium (mg.) | —Fats in grams— | | Choles-terol (mg.) |
|---|---|---|---|---|---|
| | | | Total | Satu-rated | Unsatu-rated | |

| Food and Description | Measure or Quantity | Sodium (mg.) | Total | Satu-rated | Unsatu-rated | Choles-terol (mg.) |
|---|---|---|---|---|---|---|
| **FRUIT TREATS**, apple (Mott's): | | | | | | |
| & apricots | ½ cup (4.4 oz.) | | .1 | | | (0) |
| & cherries | ½ cup (4.6 oz.) | | .1 | | | (0) |
| & pineapple | ½ cup (5.4 oz.) | | .2 | | | (0) |
| & raspberries | ½ cup (4.7 oz.) | | .1 | | | (0) |
| & strawberries | ½ cup (4.4 oz.) | | .1 | | | (0) |
| **FRUITY PEBBLES**, cereal (Post) | ⅞ cup (1 oz.) | 128 | .1 | | | 0 |
| **FUDGE CAKE MIX:** | | | | | | |
| *Butter recipe (Duncan Hines) | ¹/₁₂ of cake (3.3 oz.) | 439 | 14.8 | | | |
| *Cherry (Betty Crocker) | ¹/₁₂ of cake | 320 | 5.9 | | | |
| *Dark chocolate (Betty Crocker) | ¹/₁₂ of cake | 293 | 5.9 | | | |
| *Marble (Duncan Hines) | ¹/₁₂ of cake (2.7 oz.) | 381 | 6.1 | | | 50 |
| *Sour cream, chocolate flavor layer (Betty Crocker) | ¹/₁₂ of cake | 243 | 5.9 | | | |
| **FUDGE ICE BAR:** | | | | | | |
| *Fudgesicle* (Popsicle Industries) | 2½-fl. oz. bar (2.8 oz.) | 52 | .3 | | | |
| (Sealtest) | 2½-fl.-oz. bar (2.6 oz.) | 55 | .2 | | | |
| **FUDGE PUDDING**, canned (Thank You) | ½ cup (4.5 oz.) | | 5.5 | | | |

# G

| Food and Description | Measure or Quantity | Sodium (mg.) | Total | Satu-rated | Unsatu-rated | Choles-terol (mg.) |
|---|---|---|---|---|---|---|
| **GARBANZO**, dry (See **CHICK PEA**, dry) | | | | | | |
| **GARBANZO SOUP**, canned (Hormel) | 15-oz. can | | 23.8 | | | |
| **GARLIC**, raw (USDA): | | | | | | |
| Whole | 2 oz. (weighed with skin) | 10 | .1 | | | 0 |
| Peeled | 1 oz. | 5 | <.1 | | | 0 |
| **GARLIC:** | | | | | | |
| Dried, chips (Spice Islands) | 1 tsp. | 1 | | | | (0) |
| Powdered (Spice Islands) | 1 tsp. | 1 | | | | (0) |
| **GARLIC SPREAD** (Lawry's) | 1 T. (.5 oz.) | | 8.2 | | | |

(USDA): United States Department of Agriculture
*Prepared as Package Directs

| Food and Description | Measure or Quantity | Sodium (mg.) | —Fats in grams— | | | Choles-terol (mg.) |
|---|---|---|---|---|---|---|
| | | | Total | Satu-rated | Unsatu-rated | |
| **GAZPACHO SOUP,** canned | | | | | | |
| (Crosse & Blackwell) | ½ can (6½ oz.) | | 2.4 | | | |
| **GEFILTE FISH:** | | | | | | |
| (Manischewitz): | | | | | | |
| 2-lb. jar | 1 piece (2.4 oz.) | | 2.7 | | | |
| 24-oz. jar | 1 piece (2.6 oz.) | | 3.0 | | | |
| 1-lb. jar | 1 piece (2.2 oz.) | | 2.5 | | | |
| 4-piece can | 1 piece (3.7 oz.) | | 4.2 | | | |
| 2-piece can | 1 piece (3.5 oz.) | | 4.0 | | | |
| Fish balls | 1 piece (1.5 oz.) | | 1.7 | | | |
| Fishlets | 1 piece (7 grams) | | .3 | | | |
| Whitefish & pike: | | | | | | |
| 2-lb. jar | 1 piece (1.7 oz.) | | 1.2 | | | |
| 1-lb. jar | 1 piece (1.5 oz.) | | 1.1 | | | |
| 4-piece can | 1 piece (3.8 oz.) | | 2.7 | | | |
| 2-piece can | 1 piece (3.5 oz.) | | 2.5 | | | |
| Fishlets | 1 piece (7 grams) | | .2 | | | |
| **GELATIN,** unflavored, dry: | | | | | | |
| (USDA) | 1 envelope (7 grams) | | Tr. | | | 0 |
| (Knox) | 1 envelope (7 grams) | 0 | 0. | | | (0) |
| **GELATIN DESSERT POWDER:** | | | | | | |
| Regular: | | | | | | |
| Dry (USDA) | 3-oz. pkg. | 270 | 0. | | | 0 |
| Dry (USDA) | ½ cup (3.3 oz.) | 297 | 0. | | | 0 |
| *Prepared with water (USDA) | ½ cup (4.2 oz.) | 61 | 0. | | | 0 |
| *Prepared with fruit added (USDA) | ½ cup (4.3 oz.) | 41 | .2 | | | 0 |
| *All flavors (Jells Best) | ½ cup | 23 | 0. | | | 0 |
| *All flavors (Royal) | ½ cup (4.2 oz.) | 90 | | | | 0 |
| *Regular flavors (Jell-O) | ½ cup (4.9 oz.) | 46 | Tr. | | | 0 |
| *Wild flavors (Jell-O) | ½ cup (4.9 oz.) | 64 | Tr. | | | 0 |
| *Dietetic, all flavors (D-Zerta) | ½ cup (4.3 oz.) | 6 | Tr. | | | 0 |
| **GELATIN DRINK,** plain or flavored | | | | | | |
| (Knox) | 1 envelope (.7 oz.) | 0 | 0. | | | (0) |
| ***GEL CUP*** (Del Monte): | | | | | | |
| Lemon-lime with pineapple | 5-oz. container | 120 | 0. | | | (0) |
| Orange with peaches | 5-oz. container | 122 | 0. | | | (0) |
| Strawberry with peaches | 5-oz. container | 126 | 0. | | | (0) |

(USDA): United States Department of Agriculture
*Prepared as Package Directs

| Food and Description | Measure or Quantity | Sodium (mg.) | —Fats in grams— | | | Cholesterol (mg.) |
|---|---|---|---|---|---|---|
| | | | Total | Saturated | Unsaturated | |
| **GERMAN DINNER,** frozen | | | | | | |
| (Swanson) | 11-oz. dinner | 1372 | 14.7 | | | |
| **GINGER** (Spice Islands): | | | | | | |
| Whole | 1 average piece | 1 | | | | (0) |
| Ground | 1 tsp. | 1 | | | | (0) |
| **GINGER ALE,** soft drink: | | | | | | |
| Sweetened: | | | | | | |
| (Canada Dry) bottled | 6 fl. oz. | 0+ | 0. | | | 0 |
| (Canada Dry) cannned | 6 fl. oz. | Tr.+ | 0. | | | 0 |
| (Clicquot Club) | 6 fl. oz. | <1 | 0. | | | 0 |
| (Cott) | 6 fl. oz. | <1 | 0. | | | 0 |
| (Dr. Brown's) | 6 fl. oz. | 8 | 0. | | | 0 |
| (Fanta) | 6 fl. oz. | 13 | 0. | | | 0 |
| (Hoffman) pale dry | 6 fl. oz. | 24 | 0. | | | 0 |
| (Key Food) | 6 fl. oz. | 8 | 0. | | | 0 |
| (Kirsch) pale dry | 6 fl. oz. | <1 | 0. | | | 0 |
| (Mission) | 6 fl. oz. | <1 | 0. | | | 0 |
| (Nedick's) pale dry | 6 fl. oz. | 8 | 0. | | | 0 |
| (Schweppes) | 6 fl. oz. | Tr. | 0. | | | 0 |
| (Shasta) | 6 fl. oz. | 10 | 0. | | | 0 |
| (Waldbaum) | 6 fl. oz. | 8 | 0. | | | 0 |
| (Yukon Club) golden | 6 fl. oz. | 3 | 0. | | | 0 |
| (Yukon Club) pale dry | 6 fl. oz. | 8 | 0. | | | 0 |
| Low calorie: | | | | | | |
| (Canada Dry) bottle or can | 6 fl. oz. | 11+ | 0. | | | 0 |
| (Clicquot Club) | 6 fl. oz. | 32 | 0. | | | 0 |
| (Cott) | 6 fl. oz. | 32 | 0. | | | 0 |
| (Dr. Brown's) pale dry | 6 fl. oz. | 8 | 0. | | | 0 |
| (Hoffman) pale dry | 6 fl. oz. | 8 | 0. | | | 0 |
| (Key Food) pale dry | 6 fl. oz. | 8 | 0. | | | 0 |
| (Mission) | 6 fl. oz. | 32 | 0. | | | 0 |
| (No-Cal) | 6 fl. oz. | 11 | 0 | | | 0 |
| (Shasta) | 6 fl. oz. | 37 | 0. | | | 0 |
| (Waldbaum) pale dry | 6 fl. oz. | 8 | 0. | | | 0 |
| (Yukon Club) pale dry | 6 fl. oz. | 25 | 0. | | | 0 |
| **GINGER BEER,** soft drink, | | | | | | |
| regular (Schweppes) | 6 fl. oz. | 31 | 0. | | | 0 |
| **GINGERBREAD,** home recipe | | | | | | |
| (USDA)[1]: | | | | | | |

(USDA): United States Department of Agriculture
*Prepared as Package Directs
[1]Made with sodium aluminum sulfate-type baking powder.

| Food and Description | Measure or Quantity | Sodium (mg.) | Total | Fats in grams — Satu- rated | Unsatu- rated | Choles- terol (mg.) |
|---|---|---|---|---|---|---|
| Made with butter[1] | 1.9-oz. piece (2″ x 2″ x 2″) | 130 | 5.3 | 3. | 3. | |
| Made with vegetable shortening[2] | 1.9-oz. piece (2″ x 2″ x 2″) | 130 | 5.9 | 2. | 4. | |
| **GINGERBREAD MIX:** | | | | | | |
| Dry (USDA)[3] | 1 oz. | 131 | 2.9 | <1. | 2. | |
| *Prepared with water (USDA)[4] | 1/9 of 8″ sq. (2.2 oz.) | 192 | 4.3 | <1. | 4. | <1 |
| *(Betty Crocker) | 1/9 of cake | 320 | 4.8 | | | |
| *(Dromedary) | 1.2-oz. piece (2″ x 2″) | 180 | 2.2 | | | |
| **GINGER ROOT,** fresh (USDA): | | | | | | |
| With skin | 1 oz. | 2 | .3 | | | 0 |
| Without skin | 1 oz. | 2 | .3 | | | 0 |
| *GOLD 'n CRUST* (Adolph's) | 1 tsp. (4 grams) | 18 | Tr. | Tr. | Tr. | 0 |
| **GOOD HUMOR:** | | | | | | |
| Toasted almond bar | 1 piece (2.1 oz.) | 73 | 13.6 | 6. | 8. | 16 |
| Vanilla ice cream bar | 1 piece (2.4 oz.) | 27 | 13.8 | 8. | 6. | 16 |
| **GOOSE,** domesticated (USDA): | | | | | | |
| Raw, ready-to-cook | 1 lb. (weighed with bones) | | 104.3 | | | |
| Raw, total edible | 1 lb. | | 142.9 | | | |
| Raw, meat & skin | 1 lb. | | 152.4 | | | |
| Raw, meat only | 1 lb. | | 32.2 | | | |
| Roasted, total edible | 4 oz. | | 40.8 | | | |
| Roasted, meat & skin | 4 oz. | | 43.2 | | | |
| Roasted, meat only | 4 oz. | 141 | 11.1 | | | |
| **GOOSEBERRY** (USDA): | | | | | | |
| Fresh | 1 lb. | 5 | .9 | | | 0 |
| Fresh | 1 cup (5.3 oz.) | 2 | .3 | | | 0 |
| Canned, solids & liq.: | | | | | | |
| Regular pack, heavy or extra heavy syrup | 4 oz. | 1 | .1 | | | 0 |
| Water pack | 4 oz. | 1 | .1 | | | 0 |

(USDA): United States Department of Agriculture
*Prepared as Package Directs
[1]Principal sources of fat: butter, egg & milk.
[2]Principal sources of fat: vegetable shortening, egg & milk.
[3]Principal source of fat: vegetable shortening.
[4]Principal sources of fat: vegetable shortening & egg.

| Food and Description | Measure or Quantity | Sodium (mg.) | —Fats in grams— | | | Choles-terol (mg.) |
|---|---|---|---|---|---|---|
| | | | Total | Satu-rated | Unsatu-rated | |
| **GOOSE, GIBLET,** raw (USDA) | 4 oz. | | 7.9 | | | |
| **GOOSE GIZZARD,** raw (USDA) | 4 oz. | | 6.0 | | | |
| **GOULASH DINNER** (Chef Boy-Ar-Dee) | 7⅓-oz. pkg. | 1216 | 10.2 | | | |
| **GRANOLA:** | | | | | | |
| *Sun Country*, regular or honey almond | ½ cup (2 oz.) | | 9.0 | | | (0) |
| *Vita-Crunch:* | | | | | | |
| Regular | ½ cup (2.4 oz.) | 328 | 9.4 | | | (0) |
| Date | ½ cup | 308 | 9.4 | | | (0) |
| Raisin | ½ cup | 308 | 8.0 | | | (0) |
| Toasted almonds | ½ cup | 295 | 9.3 | | | (0) |
| **GRAPE:** | | | | | | |
| Fresh: | | | | | | |
| American type (slip skin), Con-cord, Delaware, Niagara, Cataw-ba & Scuppernong, pulp only: | | | | | | |
| (USDA) | ½ lb. (weighed with stem, skin & seeds) | 4 | 1.4 | | | 0 |
| (USDA) | ½ cup (2.7 oz.) | 2 | .8 | | | 0 |
| (USDA) | 3½″ x 3″ bunch (3.5 oz.) | 2 | .6 | | | 0 |
| European type (adherent skin), Malaga, Muscat, Thompson seedless, Emperor & Flame Tokay, with skin: | | | | | | |
| (USDA) | ½ lb. (weighed with stems & seeds) | 6 | .6 | | | 0 |
| Whole (USDA) | 20 grapes (¾″ dia.) | 2 | .2 | | | 0 |
| Whole (USDA) | ½ cup (3.1 oz.) | 3 | .3 | | | 0 |
| Halves (USDA) | ½ cup (3 oz.) | 3 | .3 | | | 0 |
| Canned, solids & liq. (USDA): | | | | | | |
| Thompson seedless, heavy syrup | 4 oz. | 5 | .1 | | | 0 |
| Thompson seedless, water pack | 4 oz. | 5 | .1 | | | 0 |
| **GRAPEADE,** chilled (Sealtest) | 6 fl. oz. (6.5 oz.) | <1 | | | | (0) |
| **GRAPE BERRY,** juice drink (Ocean Spray) | ½ cup (5 oz.) | 4 | .4 | | | 0 |

(USDA): United States Department of Agriculture
*Prepared as Package Directs

| Food and Description | Measure or Quantity | Sodium (mg.) | —Fats in grams— | | | Choles-terol (mg.) |
|---|---|---|---|---|---|---|
| | | | Total | Satu-rated | Unsatu-rated | |
| **GRAPE DRINK:** | | | | | | |
| Canned: | | | | | | |
| (Del Monte) | 6 fl. oz. (6.5 oz.) | 16 | Tr. | | | (0) |
| (Hi-C) | 6 fl. oz. (4.2 oz.) | <1 | Tr. | | | 0 |
| **GRAPE JAM:** | | | | | | |
| (Bama) | 1 T. (.7 oz.) | 3 | <.1 | | | (0) |
| (Smucker's) | 1 T. (.7 oz.) | 5 | <.1 | | | (0) |
| **GRAPE JELLY,** low calorie: | | | | | | |
| (Kraft) | 1 oz. | 37 | <.1 | | | (0) |
| (Diet Delight) Concord | 1 T. (.6 oz.) | 21 | Tr. | | | (0) |
| (S and W) *Nutradiet*, Concord | 1 T. (.5 oz.) | | <.1 | | | (0) |
| (Slenderella) | 1 T. (.7 oz.) | 34 | <.1 | | | (0) |
| (Smucker's) | 1 T. (.7 oz.) | Tr. | Tr. | | | (0) |
| (Tillie Lewis) | 1 T. (.5 oz.) | 4 | Tr. | | | 0 |
| **GRAPE JUICE:** | | | | | | |
| Canned: | | | | | | |
| (USDA) | ½ cup (4.4 oz.) | | Tr. | | | 0 |
| (Heinz) | 5½-fl.-oz. can | 2 | .2 | | | (0) |
| (S and W) *Nutradiet* | 4 oz. (by wt.) | 2 | .1 | | | (0) |
| Frozen, concentrate, sweetened: | | | | | | |
| (USDA) | 6-fl.-oz. can (7.6 oz.) | 6 | Tr. | | | 0 |
| Diluted with 3 parts water | | | | | | |
| (USDA) | ½ cup (4.4 oz.) | 1 | Tr. | | | 0 |
| *(Minute Maid) | ½ cup (4.2 oz.) | 1 | Tr. | | | 0 |
| *(Snow Crop) | ½ cup (4.2 oz.) | 1 | Tr. | | | 0 |
| **GRAPE JUICE DRINK,** canned (USDA) approximately 30% grape juice | 1 cup (8.8 oz.) | 2 | Tr. | | | 0 |
| *GRAPE-NUTS,* cereal (Post) | ¼ cup (1 oz.) | 147 | .1 | | | 0 |
| *GRAPE-NUTS FLAKES,* cereal (Post) | ⅔ cup (1 oz.) | 150 | .3 | | | 0 |
| **GRAPE PIE** (Tastykake) | 4-oz. pie | | 16.2 | | | |
| **GRAPE SOFT DRINK:** | | | | | | |
| Sweetened: | | | | | | |
| (Canada Dry) bottle or can | 6 fl. oz. | 13+ | 0. | | | 0 |
| (Dr. Brown's) | 6 fl. oz. | 15 | 0. | | | 0 |

(USDA): United States Department of Agriculture
*Prepared as Package Directs

| Food and Description | Measure or Quantity | Sodium (mg.) | —Fats in grams— Total | Satu-rated | Unsatu-rated | Choles-terol (mg.) |
|---|---|---|---|---|---|---|
| (Fanta) | 6 fl. oz. | 6 | 0. | | | 0 |
| (Hoffman) | 6 fl. oz. | 15 | 0. | | | 0 |
| (Key Food) | 6 fl. oz. | 15 | 0. | | | 0 |
| (Kirsch) | 6 fl. oz. | <1 | 0. | | | 0 |
| (Nedick's) | 6 fl. oz. | 15 | 0. | | | 0 |
| (Nehi) | 6 fl. oz. (6.6 oz.) | 0+ | 0. | | | 0 |
| (Shasta) | 6 fl. oz. | 18 | 0. | | | 0 |
| (Waldbaum) | 6 fl. oz. | 15 | 0. | | | 0 |
| (Yukon Club) | 6 fl. oz. | 15 | 0. | | | 0 |
| Low calorie: | | | | | | |
| (Dr. Brown's) | 6 fl. oz. | 71 | 0. | | | 0 |
| (Hoffman) | 6 fl. oz. | 71 | 0 | | | 0 |
| (Key Food) | 6 fl. oz. | 71 | 0. | | | 0 |
| (No-Cal) | 6 fl. oz. | 12 | 0. | | | 0 |
| (Shasta) | 6 fl. oz. | 45 | 0. | | | 0 |
| (Waldbaum) | 6 fl. oz. | 71 | 0. | | | 0 |
| (Yukon Club) | 6 fl. oz. | 69 | 0 | | | 0 |

**GRAPE SYRUP,** low calorie

| Food and Description | Measure or Quantity | Sodium (mg.) | Total | Satu-rated | Unsatu-rated | Choles-terol (mg.) |
|---|---|---|---|---|---|---|
| (No-Cal) | 1 tsp. (5 grams) | <1 | 0. | | | 0 |

**GRAPEFRUIT:**

Fresh, pulp only:

Pink & red:

| Food and Description | Measure or Quantity | Sodium (mg.) | Total | Satu-rated | Unsatu-rated | Choles-terol (mg.) |
|---|---|---|---|---|---|---|
| Seeded type (USDA) | 1 lb. (weighed with seeds and skin) | 2 | .2 | | | 0 |
| Seeded type (USDA) | ½ med. grapefruit (3¾", 8.5 oz.) | 1 | .1 | | | 0 |
| Seedless type (USDA) | 1 lb. (weighed with skin) | 2 | .2 | | | 0 |
| Seedless type (USDA) | ½ med. grapefruit (8.5 oz.) | 1 | .1 | | | 0 |
| White: | | | | | | |
| Seeded type (USDA) | 1 lb. (weighed with seeds & skin) | 2 | .2 | | | 0 |
| Seeded type (USDA) | ½ med. grapefruit (3¾", 8.5 oz.) | 1 | .1 | | | 0 |
| Seedless type (USDA) | 1 lb. (weighed with skin) | 2 | .2 | | | 0 |
| Seedless type, sections (USDA) | 1 cup (7 oz.) | 2 | .2 | | | 0 |
| Seedless type (USDA) | ½ med. grapefruit (3¾", 8.5 oz.) | 1 | .1 | | | 0 |
| (Sunkist) | ½ grapefruit (8.5 oz.) | 1 | Tr. | | | 0 |

(USDA): United States Department of Agriculture
*Prepared as Package Directs

| Food and Description | Measure or Quantity | Sodium (mg.) | — Fats in grams — | | | Cholesterol (mg.) |
|---|---|---|---|---|---|---|
| | | | Total | Saturated | Unsaturated | |
| Bottled, chilled, sweetened sections (Kraft) | 4 oz. | 115 | .1 | | | (0) |
| Bottled, chilled, unsweetened sections (Kraft) | 4 oz. | 115 | .1 | | | (0) |
| Canned, sections, syrup pack, solids & liq.: | | | | | | |
| (USDA) | ½ cup (4.5 oz.) | 1 | .1 | | | 0 |
| (Del Monte) | ½ cup (4.5 oz.) | 2 | | | | 0 |
| Light syrup (Stokely-Van Camp) | ½ cup (4 oz.) | | .1 | | | (0) |
| Canned, sections, unsweetened or dietetic pack, solids & liq.: | | | | | | |
| Water pack (USDA) | ½ cup (4.2 oz.) | 5 | .1 | | | 0 |
| Juice pack (Del Monte) | ½ cup (4.5 oz.) | 1 | .5 | | | 0 |
| (Diet Delight) unsweetened | ½ cup (4.3 oz.) | 5 | <.1 | | | (0) |
| (S and W) *Nutradiet*, low calorie | 4 oz. | 2 | .1 | | | (0) |
| (S and W) *Nutradiet*, unsweetened | 4 oz. | 2 | .2 | | | (0) |
| (Tillie Lewis) | ½ cup (4.4 oz.) | <10 | .1 | | | (0) |
| **GRAPEFRUIT JUICE:** | | | | | | |
| Fresh, pink, red or white, all varieties (USDA) | ½ cup (4.3 oz.) | 1 | .1 | | | 0 |
| Bottled, chilled, sweetened (Kraft) | ½ cup (4.3 oz.) | 1 | .1 | | | (0) |
| Bottled, chilled, unsweetened (Kraft) | ½ cup (4.3 oz.) | 1 | .1 | | | (0) |
| Canned: | | | | | | |
| Sweetened: | | | | | | |
| (USDA) | ½ cup (4.4 oz.) | 1 | .1 | | | 0 |
| (Del Monte) | ½ cup (4.3 oz.) | 1 | Tr. | | | 0 |
| (Heinz) | 5½-fl.-oz. can | 2 | .5 | | | (0) |
| (Stokely-Van Camp) | ½ cup (4.4 oz.) | | .1 | | | (0) |
| Unsweetened: | | | | | | |
| (USDA) | ½ cup (4.4 oz.) | 1 | .1 | | | 0 |
| (Del Monte) | ½ cup (4.3 oz.) | 5 | .2 | | | 0 |
| (Diet Delight) | ½ cup (4 oz.) | 7 | Tr. | | | (0) |
| (Heinz) | 5½-fl.-oz. can | 2 | .5 | | | (0) |
| (Stokely-Van Camp) | ½ cup (4.5 oz.) | | .1 | | | (0) |
| Frozen, concentrate: | | | | | | |
| Sweetened: | | | | | | |
| (USDA) | 6-fl.-oz. can (7.4 oz.) | 6 | .6 | | | 0 |

(USDA): United States Department of Agriculture
*Prepared as Package Directs

173

| Food and Description | Measure or Quantity | Sodium (mg.) | Fats in grams — Total | Satu- rated | Unsatu- rated | Choles- terol (mg.) |
|---|---|---|---|---|---|---|
| *Diluted with 3 parts water | | | | | | |
| (USDA) | ½ cup (4.4 oz.) | 1 | .1 | | | 0 |
| *(Minute Maid) | ½ cup (4.2 oz.) | <1 | Tr. | | | 0 |
| *(Snow Crop) | ½ cup (4.2 oz.) | <1 | Tr. | | | 0 |
| Unsweetened: | | | | | | |
| (USDA) | 6-fl.-oz. can (7.3 oz.) | 8 | .8 | | | 0 |
| *Diluted with 3 parts water | | | | | | |
| (USDA) | ½ cup (4.4 oz.) | 1 | .1 | | | 0 |
| *(Florida Diet) | ½ cup (4.3 oz.) | | .6 | | | (0) |
| *(Minute Maid) | ½ cup (4.2 oz.) | <1 | Tr. | | | 0 |
| *(Snow Crop) | ½ cup (4.2 oz.) | <1 | Tr. | | | 0 |
| Dehydrated, crystals: | | | | | | |
| (USDA) | 4-oz. can | 11 | 1.1 | | | 0 |
| *Reconstituted (USDA) | ½ cup (4.4 oz.) | 1 | .1 | | | 0 |

## GRAPEFRUIT-ORANGE JUICE (See ORANGE-GRAPEFRUIT JUICE)

## GRAPEFRUIT PEEL, CANDIED

| Food and Description | Measure or Quantity | Sodium (mg.) | Total | Satu- rated | Unsatu- rated | Choles- terol (mg.) |
|---|---|---|---|---|---|---|
| (USDA) | 1 oz. | | <.1 | | | 0 |

## GRAPEFRUIT SOFT DRINK:

| Food and Description | Measure or Quantity | Sodium (mg.) | Total | Satu- rated | Unsatu- rated | Choles- terol (mg.) |
|---|---|---|---|---|---|---|
| Sweetened: | | | | | | |
| (Clicquot Club) | 6 fl. oz. | 11 | 0. | | | 0 |
| (Cott) | 6 fl. oz. | 11 | 0. | | | 0 |
| (Fanta) | 6 fl. oz. | 12 | Tr. | | | 0 |
| (Hoffman) | 6 fl. oz. | 14 | 0. | | | 0 |
| (Mission) | 6 fl. oz. | 11 | 0. | | | 0 |
| (Shasta) | 6 fl. oz. | 22 | 0. | | | 0 |
| Low calorie: | | | | | | |
| (Canada Dry) golden or pink, bottle or can | 6 fl. oz. | 13+ | 0. | | | 0 |
| (Clicquot Club) | 6 fl. oz. | 43 | 0. | | | 0 |
| (Cott) | 6 fl. oz. | 43 | 0. | | | 0 |
| (Hoffman) | 6 fl. oz. | 64 | 0. | | | 0 |
| (Mission) | 6 fl. oz. | 43 | 0. | | | 0 |
| (No-Cal) pink | 6 fl. oz. | 14 | 0. | | | 0 |
| (Shasta) | 6 fl. oz. | 37 | 0. | | | 0 |

## GRAVY, canned:

| Food and Description | Measure or Quantity | Sodium (mg.) | Total | Satu- rated | Unsatu- rated | Choles- terol (mg.) |
|---|---|---|---|---|---|---|
| Beef (Franco-American) | ¼ cup | 278 | 2.0 | | | |
| Brown with onion (Franco-American) | ¼ cup | 324 | 1.2 | | | |

(USDA): United States Department of Agriculture
*Prepared as Package Directs

| Food and Description | Measure or Quantity | Sodium (mg.) | —Fats in grams— | | | Choles- terol (mg.) |
|---|---|---|---|---|---|---|
| | | | Total | Satu- rated | Unsatu- rated | |
| Chicken (Franco-American) | ¼ cup | 284 | 3.6 | | | |
| Chicken giblet (Franco-American) | ¼ cup | 348 | 1.4 | | | |
| Mushroom: | | | | | | |
| (B in B) | ¼ cup | | .8 | | | |
| *Dawn Fresh*, brown | 5¾-oz. can | 668 | 1.6 | | | |
| (Franco-American) | ¼ cup | 306 | 1.4 | | | |
| *Ready Gravy* | ¼ cup (2.2 oz.) | 344 | .8 | | | |
| ***GRAVY MASTER*** | 1 fl. oz. (1.3 oz.) | 560 | 0. | | | 0 |
| **GRAVY with MEAT or TURKEY,** frozen: | | | | | | |
| Giblet & sliced turkey (Banquet): | | | | | | |
| Cooking bag | 5-oz. bag | | 6.9 | | | |
| Buffet | 2-lb. pkg. | | 20.1 | | | |
| Sliced beef, frozen (Banquet): | | | | | | |
| Cooking bag | 5-oz. bag | | 6.9 | | | |
| Buffet | 2-lb. pkg. | | 49.9 | | | |
| Sliced beef (Morton House) | 6¼ oz. | 995 | 12.3 | 6. | 6. | 42 |
| Sliced pork (Morton House) | 6¼ oz. | 975 | 11.9 | 5. | 7. | 43 |
| Sliced turkey (Morton House) | 6¼ oz. | 1076 | 6.5 | 2. | 4. | 47 |
| **GRAVY MIX:** | | | | | | |
| *Au jus (Durkee) | 1 cup (1-oz. pkg.) | 2256 | .2 | | | |
| Au jus (French's) | ¾-oz. pkg. | 2400 | .6 | | | |
| *Au jus (French's) | ¼ cup | 300 | .1 | | | |
| Beef: | | | | | | |
| (Swiss Products) | 1¼-oz. pkg. | | .8 | | | |
| (Swiss Products) | ⅞-oz. pkg. | | .5 | | | |
| *(Wyler's) | 2-oz. serving | | .4 | | | |
| Brown: | | | | | | |
| *(Durkee) | 1 cup (.8-oz. pkg.) | 1512 | .8 | | | |
| (French's) | ¾-oz. pkg. | 940 | 1.8 | | | |
| *(French's) | ¼ cup | 235 | .5 | | | |
| (Kraft) | 2-oz. serving | 242 | .5 | | | |
| (Lawry's) | 1¼-oz. pkg. | | 5.3 | | | |
| (McCormick) | ⅞-oz. pkg. | 680 | 1.2 | | | |
| *(McCormick) | 2-oz. serving | 168 | .4 | | | |
| Cheese: | | | | | | |
| (McCormick) | 1¼-oz. pkg. | 685 | 12.6 | | | |
| *(McCormick) | 2-oz. serving | 200 | 5.0 | | | |
| Chicken: | | | | | | |
| *(Durkee) | 1 cup (1-oz. pkg.) | 2168 | 3.2 | | | |

(USDA): United States Department of Agriculture
*Prepared as Package Directs

| Food and Description | Measure or Quantity | Sodium (mg.) | Fats in grams Total | Satu- rated | Unsatu- rated | Choles- terol (mg.) |
|---|---|---|---|---|---|---|
| (French's) | 1¼-oz. pkg. | 900 | 4.6 | | | |
| *(French's) | ¼ cup | 225 | 1.2 | | | |
| *(Kraft) | 2-oz. serving | 211 | 1.5 | | | |
| (Lawry's) | 1-oz. pkg. | | 4.2 | | | |
| *(McCormick) | 2-oz. serving | 325 | 3.0 | | | |
| (Swiss) | 1¼-oz. pkg. | | .6 | | | |
| (Swiss) | ⅞-oz. pkg. | | .4 | | | |
| *(Wyler's) | 2-oz. serving | | .7 | | | |
| *Herb (McCormick) | 2-oz. serving | 160 | .8 | | | |
| Homestyle (French's) | ⅞-oz. pkg. | 1540 | 3.0 | | | 6 |
| *Homestyle (French's) | ¼ cup | 380 | 1.0 | | | 2 |
| Mushroom: | | | | | | |
| *(Durkee) | 1 cup (.8-oz. pkg.) | 1696 | .8 | | | |
| (French's) | ¾-oz. pkg. | 1000 | 2.0 | | | |
| *(French's) | ¼ cup | 250 | .5 | | | |
| (Lawry's) | 1.3-oz. pkg. | | 6.6 | | | |
| *(McCormick) | 2-oz. serving | 170 | .3 | | | |
| *(Wyler's) | 2-oz. serving | | .6 | | | |
| Onion: | | | | | | |
| *(Durkee) | 1 cup (1-oz. pkg.) | 1408 | .8 | | | |
| (French's) | 1-oz. pkg. | 1100 | 1.6 | | | |
| *(French's) | ¼ cup | 275 | .4 | | | |
| *(Kraft) | 2-oz. serving | 175 | .5 | | | |
| *(McCormick) | 2-oz. serving | 364 | 1.6 | | | |
| *(Wyler's) | 2-oz. serving | | .5 | | | |
| Pork: | | | | | | |
| (French's) | ¾-oz. pkg. | 1180 | 2.2 | | | |
| *(French's) | ¼ cup | 295 | .6 | | | |
| Turkey: | | | | | | |
| (French's) | ⅞-oz. pkg. | 1250 | 3.2 | | | |
| *(French's) | ¼ cup | 313 | .8 | | | |
| **GREAT HONEY CRUNCHERS:** | | | | | | |
| Rice | 1 cup (1 oz.) | 50 | 1.0 | | | (0) |
| Wheat | 1 cup (1 oz.) | 50 | 1.4 | | | (0) |

**GREEN PEA** (See **PEA**)

**GRITS** (See **HOMINY GRITS**)

**GROUND-CHERRY,** Poha or Cape
Gooseberry, fresh (USDA):

| | | | | | | |
|---|---|---|---|---|---|---|
| Whole | 1 lb. (weighed with husks & stems) | | 2.9 | | | 0 |
| Flesh only | 4 oz. | | .8 | | | 0 |

(USDA): United States Department of Agriculture
*Prepared as Package Directs

| Food and Description | Measure or Quantity | Sodium (mg.) | —Fats in grams— | | Choles- terol (mg.) |
|---|---|---|---|---|---|
| | | | Total | Satu- rated | Unsatu- rated | |

| Food and Description | Measure or Quantity | Sodium (mg.) | Total | Satu-rated | Unsatu-rated | Choles-terol (mg.) |
|---|---|---|---|---|---|---|
| **GROUPER,** raw (USDA): | | | | | | |
| Whole | 1 lb. (weighed whole) | | 1.0 | | | |
| Meat only | 4 oz. | | .6 | | | |
| | | | | | | |
| **GUAVA, COMMON,** fresh (USDA): | | | | | | |
| Whole | 1 lb. (weighed untrimmed) | 18 | 2.6 | | | 0 |
| Whole | 1 guava (2.8 oz.) | 3 | .5 | | | 0 |
| Flesh only | 4 oz. | 5 | .7 | | | 0 |
| | | | | | | |
| **GUAVA, STRAWBERRY,** fresh (USDA): | | | | | | |
| Whole | 1 lb. (weighed untrimmed) | 18 | 2.7 | | | 0 |
| Flesh only | 4 oz. | 5 | .7 | | | 0 |
| | | | | | | |
| **GUINEA HEN,** raw (USDA): | | | | | | |
| Ready-to-cook | 1 lb.(weighed with bones) | | 24.4 | | | |
| Meat & skin | 4 oz. | | 7.3 | | | |
| Giblets | 2 oz. | | 4.0 | | | |

**GUM** (See **CHEWING GUM**)

# H

| Food and Description | Measure or Quantity | Sodium (mg.) | Total | Satu-rated | Unsatu-rated | Choles-terol (mg.) |
|---|---|---|---|---|---|---|
| **HADDOCK:** | | | | | | |
| Raw (USDA): | | | | | | |
| Whole | 1 lb. (weighed whole) | 133 | .2 | | | 131 |
| Meat only | 4 oz. | 69 | .1 | | | 68 |
| Fried, dipped in egg, milk & bread crumbs (USDA) | 4" x 3" x ½" fillet (3.5 oz.) | 177 | 6.4 | | | |
| Frozen (Gorton) | ⅓ of 1-lb. pkg. | 93 | .2 | | | |
| Smoked, canned or not (USDA) | 4 oz. | | .5 | | | |
| | | | | | | |
| **HADDOCK MEALS,** frozen: | | | | | | |
| (Banquet): | | | | | | |
| Fish compartment | 5 oz. | | 7.7 | | | |
| Potato compartment | 1.6 oz. | | 7.6 | | | |

(USDA): United States Department of Agriculture
*Prepared as Package Directs

| Food and Description | Measure or Quantity | Sodium (mg.) | — Fats in grams — | | | Choles- terol (mg.) |
|---|---|---|---|---|---|---|
| | | | Total | Satu- rated | Unsatu- rated | |
| Peas compartment | 2.2 oz. | | 1.4 | | | |
| Complete dinner | 8.8-oz. dinner | | 16.7 | | | |
| (Weight Watchers) | 18-oz. dinner | | 1.5 | | | |
| & spinach (Weight Watchers) | 9½-oz. luncheon | | 4.7 | | | |
| **HAKE,** raw (USDA): | | | | | | |
| Whole | 1 lb. (weighed whole) | 144 | .8 | | | |
| Meat only | 4 oz. | 84 | .5 | | | |
| **HALF & HALF,** milk & cream (See **CREAM**) | | | | | | |
| **HALF & HALF SOFT DRINK:** | | | | | | |
| Sweetened: | | | | | | |
| (Dr. Brown's) | 6 fl. oz. | 14 | 0. | | | 0 |
| (Hoffman) | 6 fl. oz. | 14 | 0. | | | 0 |
| (Key Food) | 6 fl. oz. | 14 | 0. | | | 0 |
| (Kirsch) | 6 fl. oz. | <1 | 0. | | | 0 |
| (Waldbaum) | 6 fl. oz. | 14 | 0. | | | 0 |
| (Yukon Club) | 6 fl. oz. | 14 | 0. | | | 0 |
| Low calorie (Hoffman) | 6 fl. oz. | 63 | 0. | | | 0 |
| **HALIBUT:** | | | | | | |
| Atlantic & Pacific: | | | | | | |
| Raw (USDA): | | | | | | |
| Whole | 1 lb. (weighed whole) | 145 | 3.2 | | | 134 |
| Meat only, not dipped in brine | 4 oz. | 61 | 1.4 | | | 57 |
| Meat only, dipped in brine (USDA) | 4 oz. | 408 | 1.4 | | | 57 |
| Broiled with vegetable shortening (USDA) | 6½" x 2½" x 8" or 4" x 3" x ½" steak (4.4 oz.) | 168 | 8.8 | | | 75 |
| Smoked (USDA) | 4 oz. | | 17.0 | | | |
| California, raw, meat only (USDA) | 4 oz. | | 1.6 | | | |
| **HAM** (See also **PORK**): | | | | | | |
| Boiled: | | | | | | |
| Luncheon meat (USDA)[1] | 1 oz. | | 4.8 | 2. | 3. | |

(USDA): United States Department of Agriculture
*Prepared as Package Directs
[1]Principal source of fat: pork.

| Food and Description | Measure or Quantity | Sodium (mg.) | —Fats in grams— | | | Choles- terol (mg.) |
|---|---|---|---|---|---|---|
| | | | Total | Satu- rated | Unsatu- rated | |
| Luncheon meat, chopped | | | | | | |
| (USDA)[1] | 1 cup (4.8 oz.) | | 23.1 | 8. | 15. | |
| Luncheon meat, diced (USDA)[1] | 1 cup (5 oz.) | | 24.0 | 8. | 16. | |
| (Hormel) | 1 oz. | 319 | 1.4 | Tr. | <1. | 15 |
| Chopped, sliced (Hormel) | 1 oz. | 289 | 5.8 | | | |
| Minced (Oscar Mayer) | 1 slice (10 per ½ lb.) | 251 | 4.4 | | | |
| Smoked (Oscar Mayer) | 1 slice (8 per 6 oz.) | 246 | 1.5 | | | |
| Smoked, thin sliced (Oscar Mayer) | 1 slice (10 per 3 oz.) | 87 | .6 | | | |
| Canned: | | | | | | |
| (USDA) | 1 oz. | 312 | 3.5 | 1. | 2. | |
| (Armour Golden Star) | 1 oz. | | 1.4 | | | |
| (Armour Star) | 1 oz. | | 3.5 | | | |
| (Hormel) | 1 oz. (8-lb. can) | | 4.2 | | | |
| (Hormel) | 1 oz. (6-lb. can) | | 2.6 | | | |
| (Hormel) | 1 oz. (4-lb. can) | | 3.1 | | | |
| (Hormel) | 1 oz. (1-lb. 8-oz. can) | | 3.1 | | | |
| (Oscar Mayer) *Jubilee*, bone in | 1 lb. | 5307 | 54.4 | | | |
| (Oscar Mayer) *Jubilee*, boneless | 1 lb. | 5307 | 54.4 | | | |
| (Oscar Mayer) *Jubilee*, boneless | ½-lb. slice | 2654 | 15.9 | | | |
| (Oscar Mayer) *Jubilee*, special trim, as purchased | 1 oz. | 276 | 2.3 | | | |
| (Oscar Mayer) *Jubilee*, special trim, cooked | 1 oz. | 298 | 1.4 | <1. | <1. | 8 |
| (Oscar Mayer) steak | 1 slice (8 to lb.) | 663 | 3.4 | | | |
| (Swift) | 1¾-oz. slice (5" x 2¼" x ¼") | 422 | 7.8 | | | |
| (Swift) *Hostess* | 1 oz. (4-lb. can) | 269 | 1.6 | | | |
| (Wilson) | 1 oz. | 272 | 2.8 | 1. | 2. | 16 |
| (Wilson) *Tender Made* | 1 oz. | 305 | 2.6 | <1. | 1. | 18 |
| Chopped or minced, canned: | | | | | | |
| (USDA)[1] | 1 oz. | | 4.8 | 2. | 3. | |
| (Armour Star) | 1 oz. | | 7.3 | | | |
| (Hormel) | 1 oz. (8-lb. can) | 369 | 7.9 | 3. | 5. | 13 |
| (Oscar Mayer) | 1-oz. slice | 310 | 4.8 | | | |
| Chopped, spiced or unspiced, canned: | | | | | | |
| (USDA)[1] | 1 oz. | 350 | 7.1 | 3. | 5. | |
| Chopped (USDA)[1] | 1 cup (4.8 oz.) | 1678 | 33.9 | 12. | 22. | |
| Diced (USDA)[1] | 1 cup (5 oz.) | 1740 | 35.1 | 13. | 22. | |
| (Hormel) | 1 oz. (5-lb. can) | | 6.6 | | | |

(USDA): United States Department of Agriculture
*Prepared as Package Directs
[1]Principal source of fat: pork.

| Food and Description | Measure or Quantity | Sodium (mg.) | — Fats in grams — | | | Choles- terol (mg.) |
|---|---|---|---|---|---|---|
| | | | Total | Satu- rated | Unsatu- rated | |
| Deviled, canned: | | | | | | |
| (USDA)[1] | 1 oz. | | 9.2 | 3. | 6. | |
| (USDA)[1] | 1 T. (.5 oz.) | | 4.2 | 2. | 3. | |
| (Armour Star) | 1 oz. | | 6.7 | | | |
| (Hormel) | 1 oz. (3-oz. can) | | 6.1 | | | |
| (Underwood) | 4½-oz. can | 1156 | 40.8 | | | |
| (Underwood) | 1 T. (.5 oz.) | 122 | 4.3 | | | |
| Freeze-dry, diced, canned (Wilson) *Campsite:* | | | | | | |
| Dry | ¾-oz. can | 490 | 6.2 | 2. | 4. | 41 |
| *Reconstituted | 1 oz. | 326 | 4.1 | 2. | 3. | 28 |
| **HAM & CHEESE:** | | | | | | |
| Loaf (Oscar Mayer) | 1-oz. slice | 287 | 5.4 | | | |
| Roll (Oscar Mayer) | 1 oz. | 287 | 4.8 | | | |
| Spread (Oscar Mayer) | 1 oz. | 287 | 6.0 | | | |
| **HAM CROQUETTE,** home recipe (USDA)[2] | 4 oz. | 388 | 17.1 | 7. | 10. | |
| **HAM DINNER:** | | | | | | |
| Frozen: | | | | | | |
| (Banquet) | | | | | | |
| Meat compartment | 5.2 oz. | | 7.4 | | | |
| Apple compartment | 2.8 oz. | | 1.1 | | | |
| Peas & carrots compartment | 2.1 oz. | | .2 | | | |
| Complete dinner | 10-oz. dinner | | 8.8 | | | |
| (Morton) | 10-oz. dinner | 278 | 18.1 | | | |
| (Swanson) | 10¼-oz. dinner | 1258 | 11.9 | 3. | 9. | |
| *Mix, au gratin (Jeno's) *Add 'n Heat* | 35-oz. pkg. | | 83.3 | | | |
| **HAM SPREAD,** salad (Oscar Mayer) | 1 oz. | 254 | 4.0 | | | |
| **HAMBURGER** (See also **BEEF,** Ground): | | | | | | |
| Regular (McDonald's) | 1 hamburger (3.4 oz.) | 542 | 9.6 | | | |
| Regular, cheese (McDonald's) | 1 hamburger (3.9 oz.) | 821 | 13.9 | | | |
| ¼ pound, (McDonald's) | 1 hamburger (5.5 oz.) | 690 | 19.3 | | | |
| ¼ pound, cheese (McDonald's) | 1 hamburger (6.6 oz.) | 1173 | 27.7 | | | |

(USDA): United States Department of Agriculture
*Prepared as Package Directs
[1]Principal source of fat: pork.
[2]Principal sources of fat: butter, ham & vegetable shortening.

| Food and Description | Measure or Quantity | Sodium (mg.) | — Fats in grams — Total | Satu- rated | Unsatu- rated | Choles- terol (mg.) |
|---|---|---|---|---|---|---|
| Freeze dry, canned (Wilson) | | | | | | |
| *Campsite:* | | | | | | |
| Dry | 3¼-oz. can | 1413 | 35.6 | 18. | 18. | 216 |
| *Reconstituted | 4 oz. | 261 | 17.9 | 9. | 9. | 109 |
| **HAWAIIAN DINNER MIX** | | | | | | |
| (Hunt's) *Skillet*[1] | 1-lb. pkg. | 3041 | 6.2 | 3. | 3. | |
| **HAWAIIAN-STYLE VEGETABLES,** | | | | | | |
| frozen (Birds Eye) | ⅓ of 10-oz. pkg. | 416 | 5.0 | | | 0 |
| **HAWS, SCARLET,** raw (USDA): | | | | | | |
| Whole | 1 lb. (weighed with core) | | 2.5 | | | 0 |
| Flesh & skin | 4 oz. | | .8 | | | 0 |
| **HAZELNUT** (See **FILBERT**) | | | | | | |
| **HEADCHEESE:** | | | | | | |
| (USDA)[2] | 1 oz. | | 6.2 | 2. | 4. | |
| (Oscar Mayer) | 1 slice (8 per ½ lb.) | 332 | 3.1 | | | |
| **HEART** (USDA): | | | | | | |
| Beef: | | | | | | |
| Lean, raw | 1 lb. | 390 | 16.3 | | | 680 |
| Lean, braised | 4 oz. | 118 | 6.5 | | | 311 |
| Lean, braised, chopped or diced | 1 cup (5.1 oz.) | 151 | 8.3 | | | 397 |
| Lean with visible fat, raw | 1 lb. | | 93.9 | | | |
| Lean with visible fat, braised | 4 oz. | | 32.9 | | | |
| Calf, raw | 1 lb. | 426 | 26.8 | | | |
| Calf, braised | 4 oz. | 128 | 10.3 | | | |
| Chicken, raw | 1 lb. | 358 | 27.2 | | | 771 |
| Chicken, simmered | 1 heart (5 grams) | 3 | .4 | | | 12 |
| Chicken, simmered, chopped or diced | 1 cup (5.1 oz.) | 100 | 10.4 | | | 335 |
| Hog, raw | 1 lb. | 245 | 20.0 | | | |
| Hog, braised | 4 oz. | 74 | 7.8 | | | |
| Lamb, raw | 1 lb. | | 43.5 | | | |
| Lamb, braised | 4 oz. | | 16.3 | | | |
| Turkey, raw | 1 lb. | 313 | 50.8 | | | 680 |
| Turkey, simmered | 4 oz. | 69 | 15.0 | | | 270 |
| Turkey, simmered, chopped or diced | 1 cup (5.1 oz.) | 88 | 19.1 | | | 345 |

(USDA): United States Department of Agriculture
*Prepared as Package Directs
[1]Principal source of fat: almonds.
[2]Principal source of fat: pork.

| Food and Description | Measure or Quantity | Sodium (mg.) | — Fats in grams — | | | Choles- terol (mg.) |
|---|---|---|---|---|---|---|
| | | | Total | Satu- rated | Unsatu- rated | |
| ***HEARTLAND,*** cereal (Pet) | 1 oz. | | 3.7 | | | (0) |
| **HERRING:** | | | | | | |
| Raw (USDA): | | | | | | |
| Atlantic, whole | 1 lb. (weighed whole) | | 26.1 | 5. | 21. | 197 |
| Atlantic, meat only | 4 oz. | | 12.8 | 2. | 11. | 96 |
| Pacific, meat only | 4 oz. | 84 | 2.9 | Tr. | 3. | |
| Canned: | | | | | | |
| Plain, solids & liq. (USDA) | 4 oz. | | 15.4 | | | 110 |
| Plain, solids & liq. (USDA) | 15-oz. can | | 57.8 | | | 412 |
| Bismark, drained (Vita) | 5-oz. jar | | 15.6 | | | |
| Cocktail, drained (Vita) | 8-oz. jar | | 13.7 | | | |
| In cream sauce (Vita) | 8-oz. jar | | 25.3 | | | |
| In tomato sauce, solids & liq. (USDA) | 4 oz. | | 11.9 | | | |
| In wine sauce, drained (Vita) | 8-oz. jar | | 22.0 | | | |
| Lunch, drained (Vita) | 8-oz. jar | | 30.9 | | | |
| Matjis, drained (Vita) | 8 oz. | | 8.7 | | | |
| Party snacks, drained (Vita) | 8-oz. jar | | 22.0 | | | |
| Tastee Bits, drained (Vita) | 8-oz. jar | | 17.8 | | | |
| Pickled, Bismarck type (USDA) | 4 oz. | | 17.1 | | | |
| Salted or brined (USDA) | 4 oz. | | 17.2 | | | |
| Smoked (USDA): | | | | | | |
| Bloaters | 4 oz. | | 14.1 | | | |
| Hard | 4 oz. | 7066 | 17.9 | | | |
| Kippered | 4 oz. | | 14.6 | | | |
| **HICKORY NUT** (USDA): | | | | | | |
| Whole | 1 lb. (weighed in shell) | | 109.1 | 9. | 100. | 0 |
| Shelled | 4 oz. | | 77.9 | 7. | 71. | 0 |
| ***HO-HO*** (Hostess): | | | | | | |
| 2 to pkg. | 1 piece (.9 oz.) | 59 | 5.0 | | | |
| 10 to pkg. | 1 piece (.9 oz.) | 61 | 5.1 | | | |
| **HOMINY GRITS:** | | | | | | |
| Dry: | | | | | | |
| Degermed (USDA) | ½ cup (2.8 oz.) | <1 | .6 | | | 0 |
| Instant (Quaker) | .8-oz. packet | 347 | .1 | | | |
| Cooked: | | | | | | |
| Degermed (USDA) | 1 cup (8.6 oz.) | 502 | .2 | | | 0 |

(USDA): United States Department of Agriculture
*Prepared as Package Directs

| Food and Description | Measure or Quantity | Sodium (mg.) | Total | —Fats in grams— Satu- rated | Unsatu- rated | Choles- terol (mg.) |
|---|---|---|---|---|---|---|
| (Albers) | 1 cup | | .2 | | | |
| (Aunt Jemima/Quaker) | ²/₃ cup | <1 | .2 | | | |
| **HONEY,** strained: | | | | | | |
| (USDA) | ½ cup (5.7 oz.) | 8 | 0. | | | 0 |
| (USDA) | 1 T. (.7 oz.) | 1 | 0. | | | 0 |
| *HONEYCOMB,* cereal (Post) | 1⅓ cups (1 oz.) | 150 | .1 | | | 0 |
| **HONEYDEW,** fresh (USDA): | | | | | | |
| Whole | 1 lb. (weighed whole) | 34 | .9 | | | 0 |
| Wedge | 2″ x 7″ wedge (5.3 oz.) | 11 | .3 | | | 0 |
| Flesh only | 4 oz. | 14 | .3 | | | 0 |
| Flesh only, diced | 1 cup (5.9 oz.) | 20 | .5 | | | 0 |
| **HORSERADISH:** | | | | | | |
| Raw (USDA): | | | | | | |
| Whole | 1 lb. (weighed un-pared) | 26 | 1.0 | | | 0 |
| Pared | 1 oz. | 2 | <.1 | | | 0 |
| Dehydrated (Heinz) | 1 T. | 95 | .2 | | | (0) |
| Dry (Spice Islands) | 1 tsp. | <1 | | | | (0) |
| Prepared: | | | | | | |
| (USDA) | 1 oz. | 27 | <.1 | | | 0 |
| (Kraft) | 1 oz. | 312 | <.1 | | | (0) |
| Cream style (Kraft) | 1 oz. | 312 | .5 | | | (0) |
| Oil style (Kraft) | 1 oz. | 312 | 1.9 | | | (0) |
| *HOTCHAS* (General Mills) | 15 pieces (.5 oz.) | 148 | 3.1 | | | (0) |
| ***HOT DOG BEAN SOUP,** canned | | | | | | |
| (Campbell) | 1 cup | 904 | 3.9 | 2. | 2. | |
| **HYACINTH BEAN** (USDA): | | | | | | |
| Young pod, raw: | | | | | | |
| Whole | 1 lb. (weighed un-trimmed) | 8 | 1.2 | | | 0 |
| Trimmed | 4 oz. | 2 | .3 | | | 0 |
| Dry seeds | 4 oz. | | 1.7 | | | 0 |

(USDA): United States Department of Agriculture
*Prepared as Package Directs

| Food and Description | Measure or Quantity | Sodium (mg.) | Total | —Fats in grams— Satu- rated | Unsatu- rated | Choles- terol (mg.) |
|---|---|---|---|---|---|---|
| **ICE CREAM and FROZEN CUS-TARD** (See also listing by flavor or brand name, e.g., **CHOCOLATE ICE CREAM** or *DREAMSICLE* and **FROZEN DESSERT**) with salt added (USDA): | | | | | | |
| 10% fat, regular ice cream | 3-fl.-oz. container (1.8 oz.) | 32 | 5.3 | 3. | 2. | 20 |
| 10% fat, regular ice cream | 1 cup (4.7 oz.) | 84 | 14.1 | 8. | 6. | 53 |
| 10% fat, frozen custard or French ice cream | 1 cup (4.7 oz.) | 84 | 14.1 | | | 97 |
| 10% fat, frozen custard or French ice cream | 3-fl.-oz. container (1.8 oz.) | 32 | 5.3 | | | 36 |
| 12% fat, ice cream | 2½-oz. slice (⅛ of qt. brick) | 28 | 8.9 | 5. | 4. | |
| 12% fat, ice cream | 3½-fl.-oz. container (2.2 oz.) | 25 | 7.8 | 4. | 3. | |
| 12% fat, ice cream | 1 cup (5 oz.) | 57 | 17.8 | 10. | 8. | |
| 16% fat, rich ice cream | 1 cup (5.2 oz.) | 49 | 23.8 | 13. | 11. | 84 |
| **ICE CREAM BAR,** chocolate-coated (Sealtest) | 2½-fl.-oz. bar (1.7 oz.) | 24 | 10.5 | | | |
| **ICE CREAM CONE,** cone only: | | | | | | |
| (USDA)[1] | 1 piece (5 grams) | 12 | .1 | Tr. | Tr. | |
| (Comet) | 1 piece (4 grams) | 4 | .2 | | | |
| Assorted colors (Comet) | 1 piece (4 grams) | 5 | .2 | | | |
| Rolled sugar (Comet) | 1 piece (.4 oz.) | 54 | .5 | | | |
| **ICE CREAM CUP,** cup only: | | | | | | |
| (Comet) | 1 piece (5 grams) | 5 | .2 | | | |
| Assorted colors (Comet) | 1 piece (5 grams) | 6 | .2 | | | |
| *Pilot* (Comet) | 1 piece (4 grams) | 4 | .2 | | | |
| **ICE CREAM SANDWICH** (Sealtest) | 3 fl. oz. (2.2 oz.) | 92 | 6.2 | | | |
| **ICE MILK:** | | | | | | |
| Hardened, with salt added (USDA) | 1 cup (4.6 oz.) | 89 | 6.7 | 4. | 3. | 26 |

(USDA): United States Department of Agriculture
*Prepared as Package Directs
[1]Principal source of fat: vegetable shortening.

| Food and Description | Measure or Quantity | Sodium (mg.) | —Fats in grams— | | | Choles-terol (mg.) |
|---|---|---|---|---|---|---|
| | | | Total | Satu-rated | Unsatu-rated | |
| Soft-serve, with salt added | | | | | | |
|   (USDA) | 1 cup (6.2 oz.) | 119 | 8.9 | 5. | 4. | 35 |
| Any flavor (Borden) 2.5% fat | ¼ pt. (2.3 oz.) | 39 | 1.6 | | | |
| Any flavor (Borden) 3.25% fat | ¼ pt. (2.4 oz.) | | 2.2 | | | |
| Any flavor (Borden) *Lite-line* | ¼ pt. | | 1.9 | | | |
| *Light n' Lively* (Sealtest): | | | | | | |
|   Banana | ¼ pt. (2.4 oz.) | 48 | 1.9 | | | |
|   Banana strawberry twirl | ¼ pt. (2.5 oz.) | 45 | 1.7 | | | |
|   Buttered almond | ¼ pt. (2.4 oz.) | 130 | 4.0 | | | |
|   Caramel nut | ¼ pt. (2.4 oz.) | 102 | 3.9 | | | |
|   Cherry pineapple | ¼ pt. (2.4 oz.) | 46 | 1.8 | | | |
|   Chocolate | ¼ pt. (2.4 oz.) | 47 | 2.2 | | | |
|   Coffee | ¼ pt. (2.4 oz.) | 56 | 2.1 | | | |
|   Lemon | ¼ pt. (2.4 oz.) | 56 | 2.2 | | | |
|   Lemon chiffon | ¼ pt. (2.4 oz.) | 46 | 1.8 | | | |
|   Orange pineapple | ¼ pt. (2.4 oz.) | 51 | 2.0 | | | |
|   Peach | ¼ pt. (2.4 oz.) | 47 | 1.8 | | | |
|   Raspberry | ¼ pt. (2.4 oz.) | 53 | 2.0 | | | |
|   Strawberry | ¼ pt. (2.4 oz.) | 47 | 1.8 | | | |
|   Strawberry royale | ¼ pt. (2.5 oz.) | 50 | 1.9 | | | |
|   Toffee | ¼ pt. (2.4 oz.) | 78 | 2.8 | | | |
|   Toffee crunch | ¼ pt. (2.4 oz.) | 85 | 3.3 | | | |
|   Vanilla | ¼ pt. (2.3 oz.) | 56 | 2.2 | | | |
|   Vanilla fudge royale | ¼ pt. (2.5 oz.) | 65 | 2.4 | | | |
| **ICE MILK BAR,** chocolate-coated | | | | | | |
|   (Sealtest) | 2½-fl.-oz. bar (1.8 oz.) | 31 | 7.7 | | | |
| **ICE STICK,** Twin Pops (Sealtest) | 3 fl. oz. (3.1 oz.) | | Tr. | | | |
| **ICES** (See **LIME ICE**) | | | | | | |
| **ICING** (See **CAKE ICING**) | | | | | | |
| **INCONNU or SHEEFISH,** raw: | | | | | | |
|   Whole (USDA) | 1 lb. (weighed whole) | | 19.4 | | | |
|   Meat only (USDA) | 4 oz. | | 7.7 | | | |
| **INDIAN PUDDING,** New England | | | | | | |
|   (B & M) | ½ cup (4 oz.) | 189 | .3 | | | |

(USDA): United States Department of Agriculture
*Prepared as Package Directs

| Food and Description | Measure or Quantity | Sodium (mg.) | Total | —Fats in grams— Satu- rated | Unsatu- rated | Choles- terol (mg.) |
|---|---|---|---|---|---|---|
| **INSTANT BREAKFAST** (See individual brand name or company listings) | | | | | | |
| **IRISH WHISKEY** (See **DISTILLED LIQUOR)** | | | | | | |
| **ITALIAN DINNER,** frozen: | | | | | | |
| (Banquet): | | | | | | |
| Meat compartment | 2¾ oz. | | 10.3 | | | |
| Mostaccioli compartment | 7¾ oz. | | 5.6 | | | |
| Bread compartment | 5 oz. | | 1.8 | | | |
| Complete dinner | 11-oz. dinner | | 17.7 | | | |
| (Swanson) | 13½-oz. dinner | 1244 | 18.1 | | | |
| **ITALIAN HERBS** (Spice Islands) | 1 tsp. | <1 | | | | (0) |
| **ITALIAN-STYLE VEGETABLES,** frozen (Birds Eye) | ⅓ of 10-oz. pkg. | 468 | 6.8 | | | 0 |

# J

| Food and Description | Measure or Quantity | Sodium (mg.) | Total | —Fats in grams— Satu- rated | Unsatu- rated | Choles- terol (mg.) |
|---|---|---|---|---|---|---|
| **JACKFRUIT,** fresh (USDA): | | | | | | |
| Whole | 1 lb. (weighed with seeds & skin) | 3 | .4 | | | 0 |
| Flesh only | 4 oz. | 2 | .3 | | | 0 |
| **JACK MACKEREL,** raw, meat only (USDA) | 4 oz. | | 6.4 | | | |
| **JACK ROSE MIX** (Bar-Tender's) | 1 serving (⅝ oz.) | 46 | .2 | | | (0) |
| **JAM,** sweetened (See also individual listings by flavor): | | | | | | |
| (USDA) | 1 oz. | 3 | <.1 | | | 0 |
| (USDA) | 1 T. (.7 oz.) | 2 | Tr. | | | 0 |
| **JAPANESE-STYLE VEGETABLES,** frozen (Birds Eye) | ⅓ of 10-oz. pkg. | 107 | 8.2 | | | 0 |
| **JELLY,** sweetened (See also individual listings by flavor): | | | | | | |
| (USDA) | 1 oz. | 5 | <.1 | | | 0 |
| (USDA) | 1 T. (.6 oz.) | 3 | Tr. | | | 0 |

(USDA): United States Department of Agriculture
*Prepared as Package Directs

| Food and Description | Measure or Quantity | Sodium (mg.) | —Fats in grams— | | | Choles-terol (mg.) |
|---|---|---|---|---|---|---|
| | | | Total | Satu-rated | Unsatu-rated | |
| All flavors (Bama) | 1 T. (.7 oz.) | 2 | <.1 | | | (0) |
| All flavors (Kraft) | 1 oz. | <1 | <.1 | | | |
| All flavors (Smucker's) | 1 T. (.7 oz.) | <1 | 0. | | | (0) |

**JERUSALEM ARTICHOKE**
(USDA):

| Unpared | 1 lb. (weighed with skin) | | .3 | | | 0 |
| Pared | 4 oz. | | .1 | | | 0 |

**JORDAN ALMOND** (See **CANDY**)

**JUICE** (See individual flavors)

**JUJUBE or CHINESE DATE**
(USDA):

| Fresh, whole | 1 lb. (weighed with seeds) | 13 | .8 | | | 0 |
| Fresh, flesh only | 4 oz. | 3 | .2 | | | 0 |
| Dried, whole | 1 lb. (weighed with seeds) | | 4.4 | | | 0 |
| Dried, flesh only | 1 oz. | | .3 | | | 0 |

**JUNIOR FOOD** (See **BABY FOOD**)

*JUNIORS* (Tastykake):

| Chocolate | 2¾-oz. pkg. | | 9.9 | | | |
| Chocolate devil food | 2¾-oz. pkg. | | 9.7 | | | |
| Coconut | 2¾-oz. pkg. | | 6.5 | | | |
| Coconut devil food | 2¾-oz. pkg. | | 6.8 | | | |
| Jelly square | 3¼-oz. pkg. | | 4.4 | | | |
| Koffee Kake | 2½-oz. pkg. | | 13.5 | | | |
| Lemon | 2¾-oz. pkg. | | 6.9 | | | |

| **JUNIPER BERRY** (Spice Islands) | 1 berry | Tr. | | | | (0) |

*JUNKET* **RENNET MIX** (See individual flavors)

# K

| *KABOOM*, cereal (General Mills) | 1 cup (1 oz.) | 196 | .7 | | | (0) |

(USDA): United States Department of Agriculture
*Prepared as Package Directs

| Food and<br>Description | Measure or<br>Quantity | Sodium<br>(mg.) | —Fats in grams—<br>Total | Satu-<br>rated | Unsatu-<br>rated | Choles-<br>terol<br>(mg.) |
|---|---|---|---|---|---|---|
| **KALE:** | | | | | | |
| Raw, leaves only (USDA) | 1 lb. (weighed un-<br>trimmed) | 218 | 2.3 | | | 0 |
| Raw, leaves including stems<br>(USDA) | 1 lb. (weighed<br>trimmed) | 252 | 2.7 | | | 0 |
| Boiled without salt,<br>leaves only (USDA) | 4 oz. | 49 | .8 | | | 0 |
| Boiled without salt,<br>including stems (USDA) | ½ cup (1.9 oz.) | 24 | .4 | | | 0 |
| Frozen: | | | | | | |
| Not thawed (USDA) | 4 oz. | 29 | .6 | | | 0 |
| Boiled, drained (USDA) | ½ cup (3.2 oz.) | 19 | .5 | | | 0 |
| Chopped (Birds Eye) | ½ cup (3.3 oz.) | 24 | .5 | | | 0 |
| ***KARO,* syrup:** | | | | | | |
| Dark corn | 1 cup (11.7 oz.) | 447 | 0. | | | 0 |
| Dark corn | 1 T. (.7 oz.) | 28 | 0. | | | 0 |
| Imitation maple | 1 cup (11.6 oz.) | 328 | 0. | | | 0 |
| Imitation maple | 1 T. (.7 oz.) | 20 | 0. | | | 0 |
| Light corn | 1 cup (11.7 oz.) | 381 | 0. | | | 0 |
| Light corn | 1 T. (.7 oz.) | 23 | 0. | | | 0 |
| Pancake & waffle | 1 cup (11.5 oz.) | 331 | 0. | | | 0 |
| Pancake & waffle | 1 T. (.7 oz.) | 20 | 0. | | | 0 |
| **KASHA** (See **BUCKWHEAT,**<br>Groats) | | | | | | |
| **KETCHUP** (See **CATSUP**) | | | | | | |
| **KIDNEY** (USDA): | | | | | | |
| Beef, raw | 4 oz. | 200 | 7.6 | | | 425 |
| Beef, braised | 4 oz. | 287 | 13.6 | | | 912 |
| Beef braised, ¼″ slices | 1 cup (4.9 oz.) | 354 | 16.8 | | | 1126 |
| Calf, raw | 4 oz. | | 5.2 | | | 425 |
| Hog, raw | 4 oz. | 130 | 4.1 | | | 425 |
| Lamb, raw | 4 oz. | 257 | 3.7 | | | 425 |
| **KIELBASA** (Oscar Mayer) | 6-oz. link | 1658 | 4.4 | | | |
| **KINGFISH,** raw (USDA): | | | | | | |
| Whole | 1 lb. (weighed<br>whole) | 166 | 6.0 | | | |
| Meat only | 4 oz. | 94 | 3.4 | | | |

(USDA): United States Department of Agriculture
*Prepared as Package Directs

| Food and Description | Measure or Quantity | Sodium (mg.) | —Fats in grams— | | | Choles- terol (mg.) |
|---|---|---|---|---|---|---|
| | | | Total | Satu- rated | Unsatu- rated | |
| **KING VITAMAN** (Quaker) | ¾ cup (1 oz.) | 210 | 2.0 | | | (0) |
| **KIPPERS** (See **HERRING**) | | | | | | |
| **KIX,** cereal (General Mills) | 1½ cups (1 oz.) | 330 | .6 | | | (0) |
| **KNOCKWURST:** | | | | | | |
| (USDA) | 1 oz. | | 6.6 | | | |
| *Chubbies*, all meat (Oscar Mayer) | 1 link (2.4 oz.) | 663 | 19.0 | | | |
| **KOHLRABI** (USDA): | | | | | | |
| Raw, whole | 1 lb. (weighed with skin, without leaves) | 26 | .3 | | | 0 |
| Raw, diced | 1 cup (4.9 oz.) | 11 | .1 | | | 0 |
| Boiled without salt, drained | 1 cup (5.5 oz.) | 9 | .2 | | | 0 |
| ***KOOL-AID** (General Foods): | | | | | | |
| Regular | 1 cup (9.3 oz.) | 13 | Tr. | | | 0 |
| Sugar sweetened | 1 cup (9.3 oz.) | 13 | Tr. | | | 0 |
| **KOOL-POPS** (General Foods) | 1 bar (1.5 oz.) | 14 | Tr. | | | 0 |
| **KOTTBULLAR,** canned (Hormel) | 1 oz. (1-lb. can) | | 3.5 | | | |
| **KRIMPETS** (Tastykake): | | | | | | |
| Apple spice | .9-oz. cake | | 2.9 | | | |
| Butterscotch | .9-oz. cake | | 2.7 | | | |
| Chocolate | .9-oz. cake | | 2.8 | | | |
| Jelly | .9-oz. cake | | 1.4 | | | |
| Lemon | .9-oz. cake | | 2.4 | | | |
| Orange | .9-oz. cake | | 2.4 | | | |
| **KRUMBLES,** cereal (Kellogg's) | ¾ cup (1 oz.) | 167 | .4 | | | (0) |
| **KUMQUAT,** fresh (USDA): | | | | | | |
| Whole | 1 lb. (weighed with seeds) | 30 | .4 | | | 0 |
| Flesh & skin | 4 oz. | 8 | .1 | | | 0 |

# L

| | | | | | | |
|---|---|---|---|---|---|---|
| **LAKE COUNTRY WINE** (Taylor): | | | | | | |
| Red dinner, 12½% alcohol | 3 fl. oz. | | | | | 0 |
| White dinner, 12½% alcohol | 3 fl. oz. | | | | | 0 |

(USDA): United States Department of Agriculture
*Prepared as Package Directs

| Food and Description | Measure or Quantity | Sodium (mg.) | Total | Fats in grams Satu- rated | Unsatu- rated | Choles- terol (mg.) |
|---|---|---|---|---|---|---|
| **LAKE HERRING,** raw (USDA): | | | | | | |
| Whole | 1 lb. (weighed whole) | 111 | 5.4 | | | |
| Meat only | 4 oz. | 53 | 2.6 | | | |
| | | | | | | |
| **LAKE TROUT,** raw (USDA): | | | | | | |
| Drawn | 1 lb. (weighed with head, fins & bone) | | 16.8 | | | |
| Meat only | 4 oz. | | 11.3 | | | |
| | | | | | | |
| **LAKE TROUT or SISCOWET,** raw (USDA): | | | | | | |
| Less than 6.5 lb. whole | 1 lb. (weighed whole) | | 33.4 | | | |
| Less than 6.5 lb. whole | 4 oz. (meat only) | | 22.6 | | | |
| More than 6.5 lb. whole | 1 lb. (weighed whole) | | 88.8 | | | |
| More than 6.5 lb. whole | 4 oz. (meat only) | | 61.7 | | | |
| | | | | | | |
| **LAMB,** choice grade (USDA): | | | | | | |
| Chop, broiled: | | | | | | |
| Loin. One 5-oz. chop (weighed with bone before cooking) will give you: | | | | | | |
| Lean & fat | 2.8 oz. | 55 | 22.9 | 13. | 10. | 76 |
| Lean only | 2.3 oz. | 46 | 4.9 | 3 | 2 | 65 |
| Rib. One 5-oz. chop (weighed with bone before cooking) will give you: | | | | | | |
| Lean & fat | 2.9 oz. | 57 | 29.2 | 16. | 13. | 80 |
| Lean only | 2 oz. | 39 | 5.9 | 3. | 3. | 56 |
| Fat, separable, cooked | 1 oz. | | 21.4 | 12. | 10. | |
| Leg: | | | | | | |
| Raw, lean & fat | 1 lb. (weighed with bone) | 280 | 61.7 | 35. | 27. | 271 |
| Roasted, lean & fat | 4 oz. | 79 | 21.4 | 12. | 9. | 111 |
| Roasted, lean only | 4 oz. | 79 | 7.9 | 4. | 4. | 113 |
| Shoulder: | | | | | | |
| Raw, lean & fat | 1 lb. (weighed with bone) | 280 | 92.0 | 52. | 40. | 274 |
| Roasted, lean & fat | 4 oz. | 79 | 30.8 | 17. | 14. | 111 |
| Roasted, lean only | 4 oz. | 79 | 11.3 | 6. | 5. | 113 |

(USDA): United States Department of Agriculture
*Prepared as Package Directs

| Food and Description | Measure or Quantity | Sodium (mg.) | Fats in grams | | Choles- terol (mg.) |
|---|---|---|---|---|---|
| | | | Total | Satu- rated | Unsatu- rated | |

| Food and Description | Measure or Quantity | Sodium (mg.) | Total | Satu-rated | Unsatu-rated | Choles-terol (mg.) |
|---|---|---|---|---|---|---|
| **LAMB'S QUARTERS** (USDA): | | | | | | |
| Raw, trimmed | 1 lb. | | 3.6 | | | 0 |
| Boiled, drained | 4 oz. | | .8 | | | 0 |
| | | | | | | |
| **LAMB STEW,** canned (B & M) | 1 cup (8.1 oz.) | 911 | 8.9 | | | |
| | | | | | | |
| **LARD:** | | | | | | |
| (USDA) | 1 lb. | 0 | 454.0 | 172. | 282. | 431 |
| (USDA) | 1 cup (7.2 oz.) | 0 | 205.0 | 78. | 127. | 195 |
| (USDA) | 1 T. (.5 oz.) | 0 | 13.0 | 5. | 8. | 12 |
| | | | | | | |
| **LASAGNE:** | | | | | | |
| Canned (Chef Boy-Ar-Dee) | 1/3 of 40-oz. can | 1459 | 12.9 | | | |
| Canned (Nalley's) | 8 oz. | | 7.3 | | | |
| Frozen (Buitoni) | 1/7 of 56-oz. pkg. | | 2.6 | | | |
| Frozen (Buitoni) | ½ of 15-oz. pkg. | | 10.8 | | | |
| Frozen (Celeste) | ¼ of 2-lb. pkg. | 1090 | 26.7 | | | |
| *Mix, dinner (Chef Boy-Ar-Dee) | 8¾-oz. pkg. | 1819 | 7.9 | | | |
| *Mix, dinner (Jeno's) | | | | | | |
|    *Add 'n Heat* | 30-oz. pkg. | | 89.3 | | | |
| Mix (Hunt's) *Skillet* | 1-lb. 2-oz. pkg. | 1933 | 21.7 | 7. | 15. | |
| Seasoning mix (Lawry's) | 1.1-oz. pkg. | | .2 | | | |
| | | | | | | |
| **LEEKS,** raw (USDA): | | | | | | |
| Whole | 1 lb. (weighed un-trimmed). | 12 | .7 | | | 0 |
| Trimmed | 4 oz. | 6 | .3 | | | 0 |
| | | | | | | |
| **LEMON,** fresh (USDA): | | | | | | |
| Fruit, including peel | 1 lb. (weighed whole) | 13 | 1.3 | | | 0 |
| Fruit, including peel | 2⅛" lemon (3.8 oz., seeds removed) | 3 | .3 | | | 0 |
| Peeled fruit | 1 med. lemon (2⅛") | 1 | .2 | | | 0 |
| | | | | | | |
| **LEMONADE:** | | | | | | |
| Chilled (Sealtest) | ½ cup (4.4 oz.) | <1 | .1 | | | (0) |
| Frozen, concentrate, sweetened: | | | | | | |
| (USDA) | 6-fl.-oz. can (7.7 oz.) | 4 | .2 | | | 0 |
|   *Diluted with 4⅓ parts water (USDA) | ½ cup (4.4 oz.) | Tr. | Tr. | | | 0 |
|   *(Minute Maid) | ½ cup (4.2 oz.) | <1 | Tr. | | | (0) |

(USDA): United States Department of Agriculture
*Prepared as Package Directs

(191)

| Food and Description | Measure or Quantity | Sodium (mg.) | —Fats in grams— | | | Choles- terol (mg.) |
|---|---|---|---|---|---|---|
| | | | Total | Satu- rated | Unsatu- rated | |
| (ReaLemon) | 6-oz. can | 4 | .2 | | | (0) |
| *(Snow Crop) | ½ cup (4.2 oz.) | <1 | Tr. | | | (0) |
| *Low calorie (Weight Watchers) | 6 fl. oz. (5.8 oz.) | | <.1 | | | (0) |
| **LEMON CAKE MIX:** | | | | | | |
| *(Duncan Hines) | ¹/₁₂ of cake (2.7 oz.) | 385 | 6.1 | | | 50 |
| *Chiffon (Betty Crocker) | ¹/₁₆ of cake | 148 | 3.5 | | | |
| *Layer (Betty Crocker) | ¹/₁₂ of cake | 271 | 5.6 | | | |
| *Pudding cake (Betty Crocker) | ¹/₆ of cake | 277 | 4.7 | | | |
| **LEMON DRINK,** chilled (Sealtest) | 6 fl. oz. (6.5 oz.) | Tr. | <.1 | | | |
| **LEMON JUICE:** | | | | | | |
| Fresh: | | | | | | |
| (USDA) | ½ cup (4.3 oz.) | 1 | .2 | | | 0 |
| (USDA) | 1 T. (.5 oz.) | <1 | <.1 | | | 0 |
| (Sunkist) | 1 lemon (3.9 oz.) | 1 | Tr. | | | 0 |
| (Sunkist) | 1 T. (.5 oz.) | Tr. | Tr. | | | 0 |
| Canned, unsweetened: | | | | | | |
| (USDA) | ½ cup (4.3 oz.) | 1 | .1 | | | 0 |
| (USDA) | 1 T. (.5 oz.) | <1 | <.1 | | | 0 |
| Plastic container: | | | | | | |
| (USDA) | ½ cup (4 oz.) | 1 | .1 | | | 0 |
| (ReaLemon) | 1 T. (.5 oz.) | 4 | Tr. | | | (0) |
| Frozen, unsweetened: | | | | | | |
| Concentrate (USDA) | ½ cup (5.1 oz.) | 7 | 1.3 | | | 0 |
| Single strength (USDA) | ½ cup (4.3 oz.) | 1 | .2 | | | 0 |
| Full strength, already reconstituted (Minute Maid) | ½ cup (4.2 oz.) | 1 | <.1 | | | 0 |
| Full strength, already reconstituted (Snow Crop) | ½ cup (4.2 oz.) | 1 | <.1 | | | 0 |
| **LEMON-LIMEADE,** sweetened, concentrate, frozen: | | | | | | |
| *(Minute Maid) | ½ cup | Tr. | Tr. | | | 0 |
| *(Snow Crop) | ½ cup | Tr. | Tr. | | | 0 |
| **LEMON-LIME SOFT DRINK:** | | | | | | |
| Sweetened: | | | | | | |
| (Dr. Brown's) | 6 fl. oz. | 32 | 0. | | | 0 |
| (Hoffman) | 6 fl. oz. | 32 | 0. | | | 0 |

(USDA): United States Department of Agriculture
*Prepared as Package Directs

| Food and Description | Measure or Quantity | Sodium (mg.) | Fats in grams Total | Satu- rated | Unsatu- rated | Choles- terol (mg.) |
|---|---|---|---|---|---|---|
| Key Food) | 6 fl. oz. | 32 | 0. | | | 0 |
| (Nedick's) | 6 fl. oz. | 32 | 0. | | | 0 |
| (Shasta) | 6 fl. oz. | 16 | 0. | | | 0 |
| (Waldbaum) | 6 fl. oz. | 32 | 0. | | | 0 |
| (Yukon Club) | 6 fl. oz. | 32 | 0. | | | 0 |
| Low calorie: | | | | | | |
| *Diet Rite* | 6 fl. oz. | 45+ | 0. | | | 0 |
| (Hoffman) | 6 fl. oz. | 72 | 0. | | | 0 |
| (Shasta) | 6 fl. oz. | 37 | 0. | | | 0 |
| (Yukon Club) | 6 fl. oz. | 72 | 0. | | | 0 |
| **LEMON PEEL:** | | | | | | |
| Raw (USDA) | 1 oz. | 2 | <.1 | | | 0 |
| Dried (Spice Islands) | 1 tsp. | <1 | | | | (0) |
| Candied (USDA) | 1 oz. | | <.1 | | | 0 |
| **LEMON PIE:** | | | | | | |
| (Hostess) | 4½-oz. pie | 605 | 13.7 | | | |
| (Tastykake) | 4-oz. pie | | 15.5 | | | |
| Chiffon, home recipe, made with lard (USDA)[1] | 1/6 of 9″ pie (3.8 oz.) | 282 | 13.6 | 5. | 9. | 183 |
| Chiffon, home recipe, made with vegetable shortening (USDA)[2] | 1/6 of 9″ pie (3.8 oz.) | 282 | 13.6 | 4. | 10. | |
| Cream, frozen: | | | | | | |
| (Banquet) | 2½-oz. serving | | 7.9 | | | |
| (Morton) | ¼ of 14.4-oz. pie | 190 | 13.9 | | | |
| (Mrs. Smith's) | 1/6 of 8″ pie (2.3 oz.) | 75 | 12.3 | | | |
| Meringue, home recipe, 1-crust made with lard (USDA)[1] | 1/6 of 9″ pie (4.9 oz.) | 395 | 14.3 | 5. | 9. | 130 |
| Meringue, home recipe, 1-crust made with vegetable shortening (USDA)[2] | 1/6 of 9″ pie (4.9 oz.) | 395 | 14.3 | 4. | 10. | |
| Meringue, frozen (Mrs. Smith's) | 1/6 of 8″ pie (3.7 oz.) | 263 | 12.8 | | | |
| Tart, frozen (Pepperidge Farm) | 1 pie tart (3 oz.) | 218 | 18.2 | | | |
| **LEMON PIE FILLING,** canned: | | | | | | |
| (Comstock) | ½ cup (5.4 oz.) | <1 | .3 | | | |
| (Lucky Leaf) | 8 oz. | 472 | 4.8 | | | |
| (Wilderness) | 22-oz. can | 395 | | | | |

**LEMON PIE FILLING MIX**
(See **LEMON PUDDING MIX**)

(USDA): United States Department of Agriculture
*Prepared as Package Directs
[1]Principal sources of fat: lard & butter.
[2]Principal sources of fat: vegetable shortening & butter.

| Food and Description | Measure or Quantity | Sodium (mg.) | —Fats in grams— | | | Choles-terol (mg.) |
| --- | --- | --- | --- | --- | --- | --- |
| | | | Total | Satu-rated | Unsatu-rated | |
| **LEMON PUDDING, canned:** | | | | | | |
| (Betty Crocker) | ½ cup | 129 | 3.8 | | | |
| (Hunt's)[1] | 5-oz. can | 90 | 4.2 | <.1 | 3. | |
| (Thank You) | ½ cup (4.5 oz.) | | 4.1 | | | |
| **LEMON PUDDING or PIE MIX:** | | | | | | |
| Regular: | | | | | | |
| *(Jell-O) | ½ cup (5.1 oz.) | 114 | 2.0 | | | 128 |
| *(Royal) | ⅛ of 9″ pie (includ-ing crust, 4.2 oz.) | 260 | 12.2 | | | 14 |
| Instant: | | | | | | |
| *(Jell-O) | ½ cup (5.3 oz.) | 406 | 4.7 | | | 65 |
| *(Royal) | ½ cup (5.1 oz.) | 280 | 4.5 | | | 14 |
| **LEMON RENNET MIX:** | | | | | | |
| Powder: | | | | | | |
| Dry (Junket) | 1 oz. | 9 | <.1 | | | |
| *(Junket) | 4 oz. | 54 | 3.9 | | | |
| Tablet: | | | | | | |
| Dry (Junket) | 1 tablet (9 grams) | 197 | Tr. | | | |
| *& sugar (Junket) | 4 oz. | 98 | 3.9 | | | |
| **LEMON SOFT DRINK:** | | | | | | |
| Sweetened: | | | | | | |
| (Canada Dry) bottle or can | 6 fl. oz. | 13+ | 0. | | | 0 |
| (Canada Dry) *Hi-Spot*, bottle or can | 6 fl. oz. | 19+ | 0. | | | 0 |
| (Clicquot Club) | 6 fl. oz. | 22 | 0. | | | 0 |
| (Cott) | 6 fl. oz. | 22 | 0. | | | 0 |
| (Mission) | 6 fl. oz. | 22 | 0. | | | 0 |
| (Royal Crown) | 6 fl. oz. | 10+ | 0. | | | 0 |
| Low calorie: | | | | | | |
| (Canada Dry) bottle or can | 6 fl. oz. | 7+ | 0. | | | |
| (Clicquot Club) | 6 fl. oz. | 34 | 0. | | | 0 |
| (Cott) | 6 fl. oz. | 34 | 0. | | | 0 |
| (Mission) | 6 fl. oz. | 34 | 0. | | | 0 |
| (No-Cal) | 6 fl. oz. | 11 | 0. | | | 0 |
| **LEMON TURNOVER,** frozen | | | | | | |
| (Pepperidge Farm) | 1 turnover (3.3 oz.) | 284 | 21.9 | | | |

(USDA): United States Department of Agriculture
*Prepared as Package Directs
[1]Principal source of fat: soybean oil.

| Food and Description | Measure or Quantity | Sodium (mg.) | —Fats in grams— | | | Choles-terol (mg.) |
|---|---|---|---|---|---|---|
| | | | Total | Satu-rated | Unsatu-rated | |
| **LENTIL:** | | | | | | |
| Whole: | | | | | | |
| Dry: | | | | | | |
| (USDA) | ½ lb. | 68 | 2.5 | | | 0 |
| (USDA) | 1 oz. | 9 | .3 | | | 0 |
| (USDA) | 1 cup (6.7 oz.) | 57 | 2.1 | | | 0 |
| Cooked, drained (USDA) | ½ cup (3.6 oz.) | | Tr. | | | 0 |
| Split, dry, without seed coat | | | | | | |
| (USDA) | ½ lb. | | 2.0 | | | 0 |
| | | | | | | |
| **LENTIL SOUP,** canned: | | | | | | |
| *(Manischewitz) | 1 cup | | 2.4 | | | |
| With ham (Crosse & Blackwell) | 6½ oz. (½ can) | 460 | 5.3 | | | |
| | | | | | | |
| **LETTUCE** (USDA): | | | | | | |
| Bibb, untrimmed | 1 lb. (weighed un-trimmed) | 30 | .7 | | | 0 |
| Bibb, untrimmed | 7.8-oz. head (4″ dia.) | 15 | .3 | | | 0 |
| Boston, untrimmed | 1 lb. (weighed un-trimmed) | 30 | .7 | | | 0 |
| Boston, untrimmed | 7.8-oz. head (4″ dia.) | 15 | .3 | | | 0 |
| Butterhead varieties (See Bibb) | | | | | | |
| Cos (See Romaine) | | | | | | |
| Dark green (See Romaine) | | | | | | |
| Grand Rapids | 1 lb. (weighed un-trimmed) | 26 | .9 | | | 0 |
| Grand Rapids | 2 large leaves (1.8 oz.) | 4 | .2 | | | 0 |
| Great Lakes, untrimmed | 1 lb. (weighed un-trimmed) | 39 | .4 | | | 0 |
| Great Lakes, trimmed | 1-lb. head (4¾″ dia., weighed trimmed) | 41 | .5 | | | 0 |
| Iceberg: | | | | | | |
| Untrimmed | 1 lb. (weighed un-trimmed) | 39 | .4 | | | 0 |
| Trimmed | 1-lb. head (4¾″ dia., weighed trimmed) | 41 | .5 | | | 0 |
| Leaves | 1 cup (2.3 oz.) | 6 | <.1 | | | 0 |
| Chopped | 1 cup (2 oz.) | 5 | <.1 | | | 0 |
| Chunks | 1 cup (2.6 oz.) | 7 | <.1 | | | |

(USDA): United States Department of Agriculture
*Prepared as Package Directs

| Food and Description | Measure or Quantity | Sodium (mg.) | Fats in grams Total | Satu- rated | Unsatu- rated | Choles- terol (mg.) |
|---|---|---|---|---|---|---|
| Loose leaf varieties (See Salad Bowl): | | | | | | |
| New York | 1 lb. (weighed un-trimmed) | 39 | .4 | | | 0 |
| New York | 1-lb. head (4¾″ dia., weighed trimmed) | 41 | .5 | | | 0 |
| Romaine: | | | | | | |
| Untrimmed | 1 lb. (weighed un-trimmed) | 26 | .9 | | | 0 |
| Shredded & broken into pieces | ½ cup (.8 oz.) | 2 | <.1 | | | 0 |
| Salad Bowl: | | | | | | |
| Untrimmed | 1 lb. (weighed un-trimmed) | 26 | .9 | | | 0 |
| Trimmed | 2 large leaves (1.8 oz.) | 4 | .2 | | | 0 |
| Simpson: | | | | | | |
| Untrimmed | 1 lb. (weighed un-trimmed) | 26 | .9 | | | 0 |
| Trimmed | 2 large leaves (1.8 oz.) | 4 | .2 | | | 0 |
| White Paris (See Romaine) | | | | | | |
| *LIFE,* cereal (Quaker) | ⅔ cup (1 oz.) | 176 | .6 | | | (0) |
| *LIKE,* soft drink | 6 fl. oz. | Tr.+ | 0. | | | 0 |
| **LIMA BEAN** (See **BEAN, LIMA**) | | | | | | |
| **LIME,** fresh, whole: | | | | | | |
| (USDA) | 1 lb. (weighed with skin & seeds) | 8 | .8 | | | 0 |
| (USDA) | 1 med. (2″ dia., 2.4 oz.) | 1 | .1 | | | 0 |
| **LIMEADE,** concentrate, sweetened, frozen: | | | | | | |
| (USDA) | 6-fl.-oz. can (7.7 oz.) | Tr. | .2 | | | 0 |
| *Diluted with 4⅓ parts water (USDA) | ½ cup (4.4 oz.) | Tr. | Tr. | | | 0 |
| (ReaLemon) | 6-oz. can | 4 | .2 | | | |
| *(Minute Maid) | ½ cup (4.2 oz.) | Tr. | Tr. | | | 0 |
| *(Snow Crop) | ½ cup (4.2 oz.) | Tr. | Tr. | | | 0 |

(USDA): United States Department of Agriculture
*Prepared as Package Directs

196

| Food and Description | Measure or Quantity | Sodium (mg.) | — Fats in grams — | | | Cholesterol (mg.) |
|---|---|---|---|---|---|---|
| | | | Total | Satu-rated | Unsatu-rated | |
| **LIME ICE,** home recipe (USDA) | 8 oz. (by wt.) | Tr. | Tr. | | | 0 |
| **LIME JUICE:** | | | | | | |
| Fresh (USDA) | 1 cup (8.7 oz.) | 2 | .2 | | | 0 |
| Canned or bottled, unsweetened: | | | | | | |
| (USDA) | 1 T. (.5 oz.) | Tr. | Tr. | | | 0 |
| (USDA) | 1 cup (8.7 oz.) | 2 | .2 | | | 0 |
| *ReaLime* | 1 T. | 5 | Tr. | | | (0) |
| **LIME PIE,** Key lime, cream, frozen (Banquet) | 2½-oz. serving | | 9.7 | | | |
| ***LIME PIE FILLING MIX,** Key lime (Royal) | ⅛ of 9″ pie (including crust, 4.2 oz.) | 250 | 12.2 | | | 65 |
| **LIME SOFT DRINK** (Yukon Club) | 6 fl. oz. | 14 | 0. | 0 | 0 | 0 |
| **LINGCOD,** raw (USDA): | | | | | | |
| Whole | 1 lb. (weighed whole) | 91 | 1.2 | | | |
| Meat only | 4 oz. | 67 | .9 | | | |
| **LITCHI NUT** (USDA): | | | | | | |
| Fresh: | | | | | | |
| Whole | 4 oz. (weighed in shell with seeds) | 2 | .2 | | | 0 |
| Flesh only | 4 oz. | 3 | .3 | | | 0 |
| Dried: | | | | | | |
| Whole | 4 oz. (weighed in shell with seeds) | 2 | .6 | | | 0 |
| Flesh only | 2 oz. | 2 | .7 | | | 0 |
| **LIVER:** | | | | | | |
| Beef, raw (USDA) | 1 lb. | 617 | 17.2 | | | 1361 |
| Beef, fried (USDA) | 4 oz. | 209 | 12.0 | | | 497 |
| Beef, fried (USDA) | 6½″ x 2⅜″ x ⅜″ slice (3 oz.) | 150 | 9.0 | | | 372 |
| Calf, raw (USDA) | 1 lb. | 331 | 21.3 | | | 1361 |
| Calf, fried (USDA) | 4 oz. | 134 | 15.0 | | | 497 |
| Calf, fried (USDA) | 6½″ x 2⅜″ x ⅜″ slice (3 oz.) | 100 | 11.2 | | | 372 |

(USDA): United States Department of Agriculture
*Prepared as Package Directs

| Food and Description | Measure or Quantity | Sodium (mg.) | Total | Fats in grams — Satu- rated | Fats in grams — Unsatu- rated | Choles- terol (mg.) |
|---|---|---|---|---|---|---|
| Chicken, raw (USDA) | 1 lb. | 318 | 16.8 | | | 2517 |
| Chicken, raw, frozen (Swanson) | 8-oz. pkg. | 138 | 6.1 | | | |
| Chicken, simmered (USDA) | 4 oz. | 69 | 5.0 | | | 846 |
| Chicken, simmered (USDA) | 2" x 2" x ⅝" liver (.9 oz.) | 15 | 1.1 | | | 186 |
| Goose, raw (USDA) | 1 lb. | 635 | 45.4 | | | |
| Hog, raw (USDA) | 1 lb. | 331 | 16.8 | 6. | 11. | 1301 |
| Hog, fried (USDA) | 4 oz. | 126 | 13.0 | 3. | 10. | 497 |
| Hog, fried (USDA) | 6½" x 2⅜" x ⅜" slice (3 oz.) | 94 | 9.8 | 3. | 7. | 372 |
| Lamb, raw (USDA) | 1 lb. | 236 | 17.7 | | | 1361 |
| Lamb, broiled (USDA) | 4 oz. | 96 | 14.1 | | | 497 |
| Lamb, broiled (USDA) | 6½" x 2⅜" x ⅜" slice (3 oz.) | 72 | 10.5 | | | 372 |
| Turkey, raw (USDA) | 1 lb. | 286 | 18.1 | | | 1973 |
| Turkey, simmered (USDA) | 4 oz. | 62 | 5.4 | | | 679 |
| Turkey, simmered, chopped (USDA) | 1 cup (4.9 oz.) | 77 | 6.7 | | | 839 |

**LIVER PATE** (See **PATE**)

**LIVER SAUSAGE or LIVER-WURST:**

| | | | | | | |
|---|---|---|---|---|---|---|
| Fresh (USDA) | 1 oz. | | 7.3 | | | |
| Sliced (Oscar Mayer) | .9-oz. slice (10 slices to 9 oz.) | 264 | 8.8 | | | |
| Ring (Oscar Mayer) | 1 oz. | 287 | 7.9 | | | |
| Smoked (USDA) | 1 oz. | | 7.8 | | | |

**LIVERWURST SPREAD**

| | | | | | | |
|---|---|---|---|---|---|---|
| (Underwood) | 1 T. (.5 oz.) | 105 | 3.8 | | | |

**LOBSTER** (USDA):

Raw:

| | | | | | | |
|---|---|---|---|---|---|---|
| Whole | 1 lb. (weighed whole) | | 2.2 | | | |
| Meat only | 4 oz. | 238 | 2.2 | | | 96 |
| Cooked, meat only | 4 oz. | | 1.7 | | | |
| Cooked, meat only | 1 cup (½" cubes, 5.1 oz.) | 304 | 2.2 | | | 123 |
| Canned, meat only | 4 oz. | 238 | 1.7 | | | |

(USDA): United States Department of Agriculture
*Prepared as Package Directs

| Food and Description | Measure or Quantity | Sodium (mg.) | —Fats in grams— | | | Choles- terol (mg.) |
|---|---|---|---|---|---|---|
| | | | Total | Satu- rated | Unsatu- rated | |
| **LOBSTER NEWBURG:** | | | | | | |
| Home recipe (USDA)[1] | 4 oz. | 260 | 12.0 | | | 206 |
| Home recipe (USDA)[1] | 1 cup (8.8 oz.) | 572 | 26.5 | | | 455 |
| Frozen (Stouffer's) | 11½-oz. pkg. | | 55.0 | | | |
| **LOBSTER PASTE,** canned (USDA) | 1 oz. | | 2.7 | | | |
| **LOBSTER SALAD,** home recipe (USDA) | 4 oz. | 141 | 7.3 | | | |
| **LOBSTER SOUP,** canned, cream of (Crosse & Blackwell) | ½ can (6½ oz.) | | 4.8 | | | |
| **LOGANBERRY** (USDA): | | | | | | |
| Fresh: | | | | | | |
| Untrimmed | 1 lb. (weighed with caps) | 4 | 2.6 | | | 0 |
| Trimmed | 1 cup (5.1 oz.) | 1 | .9 | | | 0 |
| Canned, solids & liq.: | | | | | | |
| Water pack | 4 oz. | 1 | .5 | | | 0 |
| Juice pack | 4 oz. | 1 | .6 | | | 0 |
| Light syrup | 4 oz. | 1 | .5 | | | 0 |
| Heavy syrup | 4 oz. | 1 | .5 | | | 0 |
| Extra heavy syrup | 4 oz. | 1 | .5 | | | 0 |
| ***LOG CABIN,*** syrup: | | | | | | |
| Regular | 1 T. (.7 oz.) | 2 | Tr. | | | 0 |
| Buttered | 1 T. (.7 oz.) | 10 | .3 | | | 0 |
| *Country Kitchen,* pancake & waffle | 1 T. | 2 | Tr. | | | 0 |
| Maple-honey | 1 T. | 2 | Tr. | | | 0 |
| **LONGAN** (USDA): | | | | | | |
| Fresh: | | | | | | |
| Whole | 1 lb. (weighed with shell & seeds) | | .2 | | | 0 |
| Flesh only | 4 oz. | | .1 | | | 0 |
| Dried: | | | | | | |
| Whole | 1 lb. (weighed with shell & seeds) | | .7 | | | 0 |
| Flesh | 4 oz. | | .5 | | | 0 |

(USDA): United States Department of Agriculture
*Prepared as Package Directs
[1]Prepared with butter, egg yolks, sherry & cream.

| Food and Description | Measure or Quantity | Sodium (mg.) | —Fats in grams— Total | Satu- rated | Unsatu- rated | Choles- terol (mg.) |
|---|---|---|---|---|---|---|
| **LOQUAT,** fresh (USDA): | | | | | | |
| Whole | 1 lb. (weighed with seeds) | | .7 | | | 0 |
| Flesh only | 4 oz. | | .2 | | | 0 |
| | | | | | | |
| *LUCKY CHARMS,* cereal (General Mills) | 1 cup (1 oz.) | 188 | 1.0 | | | (0) |
| | | | | | | |
| **LUNCHEON MEAT** (See also individual listings, e.g., **BOLOGNA**): | | | | | | |
| All meat (Oscar Mayer) | 1-oz. slice | 332 | 8.8 | | | |
| Bar-B-Q Loaf (Oscar Mayer) | 1-oz. slice | 321 | 2.3 | | | |
| Cocktail loaf (Oscar Mayer) | 1-oz. slice | 365 | 3.7 | | | |
| Ham & cheese (See **HAM & CHEESE**) | | | | | | |
| Honey loaf (Oscar Mayer) | 1-oz. slice | 365 | 1.7 | | | |
| Jellied: | | | | | | |
| Beef loaf (Oscar Mayer) | 1-oz. slice | 321 | 1.1 | | | |
| Corned beef loaf (Oscar Mayer) | 1-oz. slice | 299 | 1.1 | | | |
| Luncheon roll, sausage, all meat (Oscar Mayer) | .8-oz. slice | 260 | 1.2 | | | |
| *Luxury Loaf* (Oscar Mayer) | 1-oz. slice (8 per ½ lb.) | 299 | 1.7 | | | |
| Meat loaf (USDA) | 1 oz. | | 3.7 | | | |
| Minced roll sausage, all meat (Oscar Mayer) | .8-oz. slice | 242 | 4.1 | | | |
| Old fashioned loaf (Oscar Mayer) | 1-oz. slice | 321 | 4.0 | | | |
| Olive loaf (Oscar Mayer) | 1-oz. slice | 365 | 4.3 | | | |
| Peppered loaf (Oscar Mayer) | 1-oz. slice | 321 | 2.3 | | | |
| Pickle & pimento: | | | | | | |
| (Hormel) | 1 oz. (6-lb. can) | | 7.2 | | | |
| (Oscar Mayer) | 1-oz. slice | 365 | 3.7 | | | |
| (Sugardale) | 1-oz. slice | | | | | |
| Picnic loaf (Oscar Mayer) | 1-oz. slice | 310 | 4.8 | | | |
| Plain loaf (Oscar Mayer) | 1-oz. slice | 221 | 6.0 | | | |
| Pure beef (Oscar Mayer) | 1-oz. slice | 343 | 6.0 | | | |
| Spiced (Hormel) | 1 oz. | 312 | 6.3 | | | |
| | | | | | | |
| **LUNG,** raw (USDA): | | | | | | |
| Beef | 1 lb. | | 10.4 | | | |
| Calf | 1 lb. | | 17.2 | | | |
| Lamb | 1 lb. | | 10.4 | | | |

(USDA): United States Department of Agriculture
*Prepared as Package Directs

| Food and Description | Measure or Quantity | Sodium (mg.) | —Fats in grams— | | | Cholesterol (mg.) |
|---|---|---|---|---|---|---|
| | | | Total | Saturated | Unsaturated | |

# M

**MACADAMIA NUT** (USDA):

| | | | | | | |
|---|---|---|---|---|---|---|
| Whole | 1 lb. (weighed in shell) | | 100.7 | | | 0 |
| Shelled | 4 oz. | | 81.2 | | | 0 |

**MACARONI.** Plain macaroni products are essentially the same in caloric value and carbohydrate content on the same weight basis. The longer they are cooked, the more water is absorbed and this affects the nutritive values.[1]

| | | | | | | |
|---|---|---|---|---|---|---|
| Dry: | | | | | | |
| (USDA) | 1 oz. | <1 | .3 | | | 0 |
| Elbow type | 1 cup (4.8 oz.) | 3 | 1.6 | | | 0 |
| 1-inch pieces | 1 cup (3.8 oz.) | 2 | 1.3 | | | 0 |
| 2-inch pieces | 1 cup (3 oz.) | 2 | 1.0 | | | 0 |
| Cooked (USDA): | | | | | | |
| 8-10 minutes, firm | 4 oz. | 1 | .6 | | | 0 |
| 8-10 minutes, firm | 1 cup (4.6 oz.) | 1 | .6 | | | 0 |
| 14-20 minutes, tender | 1 cup (4.9 oz.) | 1 | .6 | | | 0 |
| 14-20 minutes, tender | (4 oz.) | 1 | .5 | | | 0 |
| 20% Protein, dry (Buitoni) | 1 oz. | | .6 | | | (0) |

**MACARONI & BEEF:**

| | | | | | | |
|---|---|---|---|---|---|---|
| Canned, tiny meatballs & sauce (Buitoni) | 4 oz. | | 4.5 | | | |
| Canned, in tomato sauce (Franco-American) | 1 cup | 1386 | 8.4 | | | |
| Frozen: | | | | | | |
| (Banquet) buffet | 2-lb. pkg. | | 52.9 | | | |
| In tomato sauce (Kraft) | 11½-oz. pkg. | 936 | 19.9 | | | |
| With tomatoes (Stouffer's) | 11½-oz. pkg. | 1133 | 19.0 | | | |
| (Swanson) | 11¼-oz. dinner | 1499 | 10.9 | | | |

**MACARONI & CHEESE:**

| | | | | | | |
|---|---|---|---|---|---|---|
| Home recipe, baked (USDA)[2] | 1 cup (7.1 oz.) | 1086 | 22.2 | 10. | 12. | 42 |
| Canned: | | | | | | |
| (USDA)[3] | 1 cup (8.5 oz.) | 730 | 9.6 | 5. | 5. | |

(USDA): United States Department of Agriculture
*Prepared as Package Directs
[1]Cholesterol applies to this plain macaroni which is made without milk.
[2]Principal sources of fat: cheese, margarine, milk & butter.
[3]Principal sources of fat: cheese, corn oil & milk.

| Food and Description | Measure or Quantity | Sodium (mg.) | —Fats in grams— Total | Satu- rated | Unsatu- rated | Choles- terol (mg.) |
|---|---|---|---|---|---|---|
| (Franco-American) | 1 cup | 1000 | 9.5 | | | |
| (Heinz) | 8¼-oz. can | 1253 | 9.7 | | | |
| Frozen: | | | | | | |
| (Banquet) cooking bag | 8-oz. bag | | 10.2 | | | |
| (Banquet) entrée | 8-oz. entrée | | 9.9 | | | |
| (Banquet) entrée | 20-oz. pkg. | | 31.9 | | | |
| (Kraft) | 12½-oz. pkg. | 1593 | 32.2 | | | |
| (Morton) casserole | 8-oz. pkg. | 934 | 13.7 | | | |
| (Stouffer's) | 12-oz. pkg. | | 20.3 | | | |

## *MACARONI & CHEESE MIX
| | | | | | | |
|---|---|---|---|---|---|---|
| cheddar sauce (Betty Crocker) | 1 cup | 1292 | 8.9 | | | |

## MACARONI DINNER:
| | | | | | | |
|---|---|---|---|---|---|---|
| & beef, frozen (Morton) | 11-oz. dinner | 989 | 12.1 | | | |
| & cheese: | | | | | | |
| *(Chef Boy-Ar-Dee) | 4½-oz. pkg. | 199 | 3.3 | | | |
| *(Kraft) | 4 oz. | 287 | 8.1 | | | |
| *(Kraft) deluxe | 4 oz. | 469 | 6.1 | | | |
| Frozen (Banquet): | | | | | | |
| Macaroni compartment | 8 oz. | | 7.9 | | | |
| Peas compartment | 1.9 oz. | | 1.1 | | | |
| Carrots compartment | 2.1 oz. | | 1.2 | | | |
| Complete dinner | 12-oz. dinner | | 10.2 | | | |
| Frozen (Morton) | 12¾-oz. dinner | 1182 | 13.9 | | | |
| Frozen (Swanson) | 12¾-oz. dinner | 1451 | 13.7 | | | |
| Creole, with mushrooms (Heinz) | 8¾-oz. can | 1577 | 3.9 | | | |
| *Italian-style (Kraft) | 4 oz. | 345 | 2 4 | | | |
| *Mexican-style (Kraft) | 4 oz. | 296 | 2.2 | | | |
| *Monte Bello (Betty Crocker) | 1 cup | 1205 | 12.9 | | | |

## MACARONI ENTREE, shells in
| | | | | | | |
|---|---|---|---|---|---|---|
| meat sauce (Buitoni) | 4 oz. | | 3.5 | | | |

## MACARONI SALAD,
| | | | | | | |
|---|---|---|---|---|---|---|
| canned (Nalley's) | 4 oz. | | 14.8 | | | |

| | | | | | | |
|---|---|---|---|---|---|---|
| **MACE,** ground (Spice Islands) | 1 tsp. | 2 | | | | (0) |

(USDA): United States Department of Agriculture
*Prepared as Package Directs

| Food and Description | Measure or Quantity | Sodium (mg.) | —Fats in grams— | | Choles-terol (mg.) |
| | | | Total | Satu-rated | Unsatu-rated | |
| --- | --- | --- | --- | --- | --- | --- |
| **MACKEREL** (USDA): | | | | | | |
| Atlantic: | | | | | | |
| Raw: | | | | | | |
| Whole | 1 lb. (weighed whole) | | 29.9 | | | 233 |
| Meat only | 4 oz. | | 13.8 | | | 108 |
| Broiled with butter or margarine | 8½″ x 2½″ x ½″ fillet (3.7 oz.) | | 16.6 | | | |
| Broiled with vegetable shortening | 8½″ x 2½″ x ½″ fillet (3.7 oz.) | | 16.6 | | | 106 |
| Canned, solids & liq. | 4 oz. | | 12.6 | | | 107 |
| Canned, solids & liq. | 15-oz. can | | 47.2 | | | 400 |
| Pacific: | | | | | | |
| Raw: | | | | | | |
| Dressed | 1 lb. (weighed with bones & skin) | | 23.8 | | | |
| Meat only | 4 oz. | | 8.3 | | | |
| Canned, solids & liq. | 4 oz. | | 11.3 | | | |
| Salted | 4 oz. | | 28.5 | | | |
| Smoked | 4 oz. | | 14.7 | | | |
| **MACKEREL, JACK** (See **JACK MACKEREL**) | | | | | | |
| **MAI TAI COCKTAIL:** | | | | | | |
| Canned (National Distillers) | | | | | | |
| *Duet*, 12½% alcohol | 8-fl.-oz. can | <1 | 0. | | | 0 |
| Dry mix (Bar-Tender's) | 1 serving (⅝ oz.) | 106 | .3 | | | |
| **MALT,** dry (USDA) | 1 oz. | | .5 | | | (0) |
| **MALTED MILK MIX:** | | | | | | |
| Dry powder, "unfortified" (USDA) | 1 oz. (3 heaping tsps.) | 125 | 2.4 | | | |
| *Prepared with whole milk (USDA) | 1 cup (8.3 oz.) | 214 | 10.3 | | | |
| Chocolate, instant (Borden) | 2 heaping tsps. (.7 oz.) | 64 | .9 | | | |
| Chocolate (Carnation)[1] | 3 heaping tsps. (.7 oz.) | 50 | .8 | Tr. | Tr. | |

(USDA): United States Department of Agriculture
*Prepared as Package Directs
[1]Principal sources of fat: wort solids, milk, cocoa & lecithin.

| Food and Description | Measure or Quantity | Sodium (mg.) | —Fats in grams— | | | Cholesterol (mg.) |
|---|---|---|---|---|---|---|
| | | | Total | Saturated | Unsaturated | |
| Chocolate, dry (Kraft) | 2 heaping tsps. (.4 oz.) | 55 | .7 | | | |
| *Chocolate (Kraft) | 1 cup (8.7 oz.) | 213 | 9.2 | | | |
| Natural, instant (Borden) | 2 heaping tsps. (.7 oz.) | 67 | 1.7 | | | |
| Natural (Carnation)[1] | 3 heaping tsps. (.7 oz.) | 98 | 1.7 | <1. | <1. | |
| Natural, dry (Kraft) | 2 heaping tsps. (.4 oz.) | 50 | 1.0 | | | |
| *Natural (Kraft) | 1 cup (8.6 oz.) | 201 | 9.6 | | | |
| *MALTEX*, cereal | 1 oz. | <1 | .4 | | | (0) |
| **MALT EXTRACT,** dried (USDA) | 1 oz. | 23 | Tr. | | | (0) |
| *MALT-O-MEAL*, cereal | ¾ cup (1 oz. dry) | <1 | .2 | | | 0 |
| **MAMEY or MAMMEE APPLE,** fresh (USDA): | | | | | | |
| Whole | 1 lb. (weighed with skin & seeds) | 42 | 1.4 | | | 0 |
| Flesh only | 4 oz. | 17 | .6 | | | 0 |
| **MANDARIN ORANGE, CANNED:** | | | | | | |
| Light syrup (Del Monte) | ½ cup (4.5 oz.) | 8 | Tr. | | | 0 |
| Low calorie, solids & liq. (Diet Delight) | ½ cup (4.3 oz.) | 5 | Tr. | | | (0) |
| Unsweetened, solids & liq. (S and W) *Nutradiet* | 4 oz. | 2 | Tr. | | | (0) |
| **MANDARIN ORANGE, FRESH** (See **TANGERINE**) | | | | | | |
| **MANGO,** fresh (USDA): | | | | | | |
| Whole | 1 lb. (weighed with seeds & skin) | 21 | 1.2 | | | 0 |
| Whole | 1 med. (7.1 oz.) | 9 | .5 | | | 0 |
| Flesh only, diced or sliced | ½ cup (2.9 oz.) | 6 | .3 | | | 0 |
| **MANHATTAN COCKTAIL:** Canned: (National Distillers) *Duet,* 20% alcohol | 8-fl.-oz. can | Tr. | 0. | | | 0 |

(USDA): United States Department of Agriculture
*Prepared as Package Directs
[1]Principal sources of fat: wort solids, milk & lecithin.

| Food and Description | Measure or Quantity | Sodium (mg.) | —Fats in grams— | | | Choles- terol (mg.) |
|---|---|---|---|---|---|---|
| | | | Total | Satu- rated | Unsatu- rated | |
| Brandy (National Distillers) | | | | | | |
| *Duet*, 20% alcohol | 8-fl.-oz. can | Tr. | 0. | | | 0 |
| Dry mix (Bar-Tender's) | 1 serving (¹/₃ oz.) | Tr. | <.1 | | | (0) |
| **MANICOTTI,** frozen: | | | | | | |
| Dinner (Celeste) | 2 manicotti (with sauce) | 1510 | 19.6 | | | |
| Without sauce (Buitoni) | 4 oz. | | 10.0 | | | |
| With sauce (Buitoni) | 4 oz. | | 5.8 | | | |
| **MAPLE RENNET MIX:** | | | | | | |
| Powder: | | | | | | |
| Dry (Junket) | 1 oz. | 14 | <.1 | | | |
| *(Junket) | 4 oz. | 57 | 3.9 | | | |
| Tablet: | | | | | | |
| Dry (Junket) | 1 tablet (<1 gram) | 197 | Tr. | | | |
| *& sugar (Junket) | 4 oz. | 98 | 3.9 | | | |
| **MAPLE SYRUP** (See also individual brand names): | | | | | | |
| (USDA) | 1 T. (.7 oz.) | 2 | | | | 0 |
| (Cary's) | 1 T. (.8 oz.) | 2 | 0. | | | 0 |
| Dietetic (Tillie Lewis) | 1 T. (.5 oz.) | 4 | Tr. | | | (0) |
| **MARBLE CAKE MIX:** | | | | | | |
| Dry (USDA)[1] | 1 oz. | 108 | 3.8 | <1. | 3. | |
| *Prepared with eggs, boiled white icing (USDA)[2] | 4 oz. | 294 | 9.9 | 3. | 6. | |
| *Layer (Betty Crocker) | ¹/₁₂ of cake | 279 | 5.7 | | | |
| **MARGARINE:** | | | | | | |
| Salted: | | | | | | |
| Made with hydrogenated fat, regular or soft: | | | | | | |
| (USDA) | 1 lb. | 4477 | 367.4 | 82. | 286. | 0 |
| (USDA) | 4 oz. (1 stick) | 1119 | 91.9 | 20. | 70. | 0 |
| (USDA) | 1 cup or 1 tub (8 oz.) | 2239 | 183.7 | 41. | 143. | 0 |
| (USDA) | 1 T. (⅛ of stick, .5 oz.) | 138 | 11.3 | 3. | 9. | 0 |
| (USDA) | 1 pat (1" x ⅓" x 1", 5 grams) | 49 | 4.0 | <1. | 3. | 0 |

(USDA): United States Department of Agriculture
*Prepared as Package Directs
[1]Principal source of fat: vegetable shortening.
[2]Principal sources of fat: vegetable shortening, chocolate, egg & milk.

| Food and Description | Measure or Quantity | Sodium (mg.) | Total | Fats in grams — Satu- rated | Unsatu- rated | Choles- terol (mg.) |
|---|---|---|---|---|---|---|
| Made with liquid oil, regular or soft: | | | | | | |
| (USDA) | 1 lb. | 4477 | 367.4 | 86. | 281. | 0 |
| (USDA) | 4 oz. (1 stick) | 1119 | 91.9 | 22. | 70. | 0 |
| (USDA) | 1 cup or 1 tub (8 oz.) | 2239 | 183.7 | 43. | 141. | 0 |
| (USDA) | 1 T. (.5 oz.) | 138 | 11.3 | 3. | 9. | 0 |
| (USDA) | 1 pat (1″ x ⅓″ x 1″, 5 grams) | 49 | 4.0 | <1. | 3. | 0 |
| Made with two-thirds animal fat & one-third vegetable fat: | | | | | | |
| (USDA) | 1 lb. | 4477 | 367.4 | | | 227 |
| (USDA) | 4 oz. (1 stick) | 1119 | 91.9 | | | 57 |
| (USDA) | 1 cup or 1 tub (8 oz.) | 2239 | 183.7 | | | 113 |
| (USDA) | 1 T. (⅛ of stick, .5 oz.) | 138 | 11.3 | | | 7 |
| (USDA) | 1 pat (1″ x ⅓″ x 1″, 5 grams) | 49 | 4.0 | | | 2 |
| (Blue Bonnet) regular | 1 T. (.5 oz.) | 110 | 11.2 | 2. | 9. | 0 |
| (Blue Bonnet) soft | 1 T. (.5 oz.) | 110 | 11.2 | 2. | 9. | 0 |
| (Borden) Danish flavor | 1 T. (.5 oz.) | 112 | 11.2 | 8. | 3. | |
| (Fleischmann's) regular | 1 T. (.5 oz.) | 110 | 11.2 | 2. | 9. | 0 |
| (Fleischmann's) soft | 1 T. (.5 oz.) | 110 | 10.2 | 2. | 8. | 0 |
| (Golden Glow) | 1 T. (.4 oz.) | 86 | 10.0 | | | |
| (Good Luck) soft | 1 T. (.4 oz.) | 86 | 10.0 | 2. | 8. | 0 |
| (Holiday) | 1 T. (.5 oz.) | 172 | 11.2 | | | 0 |
| (Imperial) stick | 1 T. (.5 oz.) | 112 | 11.2 | 2. | 9. | 0 |
| (Imperial) Sof-Spread | 1 T. (.5 oz.) | 96 | 11.2 | 2. | 9. | 0 |
| (Mazola)[1] | 1 T. (.5 oz.) | 119 | 11.2 | 2. | 9. | 0 |
| (Miracle) corn oil | 1 T. (9 grams) | 74 | 7.4 | | | |
| (Nucoa)[1] | 1 T. (.5 oz.) | 125 | 11.2 | 3. | 9. | 0 |
| (Nucoa) soft[1] | 1 T. (.4 oz.) | 109 | 10.0 | 2. | 8. | 0 |
| (Parkay) regular | 1 T. (.5 oz.) | 112 | 11.2 | | | |
| (Parkay) soft cup | 1 T. (.5 oz.) | 106 | 10.6 | | | |
| (Parkay) corn oil deluxe | 1 T. (.5 oz.) | 112 | 11.2 | | | |
| (Parkay) corn oil soft | 1 T. (.5 oz.) | 106 | 10.6 | | | |
| (Parkay) safflower oil, soft | 1 T. (.5 oz.) | 106 | 10.6 | | | |
| (Parkay) squeeze | 1 T. (.5 oz.) | 112 | 11.2 | | | |
| (Phenix) | 1 T. (.5 oz.) | 112 | 11.2 | | | |
| (Promise) soft | 1 T. (.5 oz.) | 96 | 11.2 | 2. | 10. | 0 |
| (Promise) stick | 1 T. (.5 oz.) | 112 | 11.2 | 2. | 10. | 0 |
| (Saffola) cube | 1 T. (.5 oz.) | 120 | 11.2 | 2. | 9. | 0 |
| (Saffola) soft | 1 T. (.5 oz.) | 114 | 11.2 | 2. | 10. | 0 |

(USDA): United States Department of Agriculture
*Prepared as Package Directs
[1]Principal source of fat: vegetable oil.

| Food and Description | Measure or Quantity | Sodium (mg.) | Total | —Fats in grams— Satu- rated | Unsatu- rated | Choles- terol (mg.) |
|---|---|---|---|---|---|---|
| Unsalted: | | | | | | |
| Made with hydrogenated fat, regular or soft: | | | | | | |
| (USDA) | 1 lb. | 45 | 367.4 | 82. | 286. | 0 |
| (USDA) | 4 oz. (1 stick) | 11 | 91.9 | 20. | 71. | 0 |
| (USDA) | 1 cup or 1 tub (8 oz.) | 23 | 183.7 | 41. | 143. | 0 |
| (USDA) | 1 T. (⅛ of stick, .5 oz.) | 1 | 11.3 | 3. | 9. | 0 |
| (USDA) | 1 pat (1″ x ⅓″ x 1″, 5 grams) | <1 | 4.0 | <1. | 3. | 0 |
| Made with liquid oil, regular or soft: | | | | | | |
| (USDA) | 1 lb. | 45 | 367.4 | 86. | 281 | 0 |
| (USDA) | 4 oz. (1 stick) | 11 | 91.9 | 22. | 70. | 0 |
| (USDA) | 1 cup or 1 tub (8 oz.) | 23 | 183.7 | 43. | 141. | 0 |
| (USDA) | 1 T. (⅛ stick, .5 oz.) | 1 | 11.3 | 3. | 9. | 0 |
| (USDA) | 1 pat (1″ x ⅓″ x 1″, 5 grams) | <1 | 4.0 | <1. | 3 | 0 |
| Made with two-thirds animal fat & one-third vegetable fat: | | | | | | |
| (USDA) | 1 lb. | 45 | 367.4 | | | 227 |
| (USDA) | 4 oz. (1 stick) | 11 | 91.9 | | | 57 |
| (USDA) | 1 cup or 1 tub (8 oz.) | 23 | 183.7 | | | 113 |
| (USDA) | 1 T. (⅛ stick, .5 oz.) | 1 | 11.3 | | | 7 |
| (USDA) | 1 pat (1″ x ⅓″ x 1″, 5 grams) | <1 | 4.0 | | | 2 |
| (Fleischmann's) regular | 1 T. (.5 oz.) | 1 | 11.2 | 2. | 9. | 0 |
| (Mazola)[1] | 1 T. (.5 oz.) | Tr. | 11.3 | 2. | 9. | 0 |
| **MARGARINE, IMITATION**, diet, salted: | | | | | | |
| (Fleischmann's) | 1 T. (.5 oz.) | 110 | 5.6 | 1. | 5. | 0 |
| (Imperial) | 1 T. (.5 oz.) | 136 | 5.5 | Tr. | 5. | (0) |
| (Mazola) | 1 cup (8.3 oz.) | 2338 | 92.6 | 17. | 76. | 0 |
| (Mazola) | 1 T. (.5 oz.) | 144 | 5.7 | 1. | 5. | 0 |
| (Parkay) | 1 T. (.5 oz.) | 120 | 5.9 | | | |
| **MARGARINE, WHIPPED:** | | | | | | |
| Salted: | | | | | | |
| (USDA) | 1 stick or ½ cup (2.7 oz.) | 750 | 61.6 | 14. | 48. | 0 |
| (Blue Bonnet) | 1 T. (9 grams) | 70 | 7.4 | 2. | 6. | 0 |

(USDA): United States Department of Agriculture
*Prepared as Package Directs
[1]Principal source of fat: vegetable oil.

| Food and Description | Measure or Quantity | Sodium (mg.) | —Fats in grams— | | | Cholesterol (mg.) |
|---|---|---|---|---|---|---|
| | | | Total | Satu-rated | Unsatu-rated | |
| (Imperial) | 1 T. (9 grams) | 62 | 7.2 | 1. | 6. | (0) |
| (Miracle) cottonseed-soybean | 1 T. (9 grams) | 74 | 7.4 | | | |
| (Parkay) cup | 1 T. (9 grams) | 74 | 7.4 | | | |
| Unsalted (USDA) | 1 stick or ½ cup (2.7 oz.) | 8 | 61.6 | 14. | 47. | 0 |
| **MARGARITA COCKTAIL,** dry mix (Bar-Tender's) | 1 serving (⅝ oz.) | 42 | .2 | | | (0) |
| **MARINADE MIX:** | | | | | | |
| (Adolph's) instant, meat | .8-oz. pkg. | 4068 | .5 | Tr. | Tr. | |
| *(Durkee) meat | 6 T. (.9-oz. pkg.) | 4022 | .3 | | | |
| (Lawry's) beef | 1.6-oz. pkg. | | .2 | | | |
| (Lawry's) lemon pepper | 2.7-oz. pkg. | | 3.3 | | | |
| **MARJORAM** (Spice Islands) | 1 tsp. | <1 | | | | (0) |
| **MARMALADE:** | | | | | | |
| Sweetened: | | | | | | |
| (USDA) | 1 T. (.7 oz.) | 3 | <.1 | | | 0 |
| (Bama) | 1 T. (.7 oz.) | 2 | <.1 | | | (0) |
| (Kraft) | 1 oz. | <1 | <.1 | | | (0) |
| (Smucker's) bitter | 1 T. (.7 oz.) | 8 | Tr. | | | (0) |
| (Smucker's) sweet | 1 T. (.7 oz.) | 4 | Tr. | | | (0) |
| Low calorie: | | | | | | |
| (Kraft) | 1 oz. | 15 | <.1 | | | (0) |
| (S and W) *Nutradiet* | 1 T. (.5 oz.) | | <.1 | | | (0) |
| (Slenderella) | 1 T. (.6 oz.) | <1 | 0. | | | (0) |
| **MARMALADE PLUM** (See **SAPOTE**) | | | | | | |
| **MARTINI COCKTAIL,** canned (National Distillers) *Duet,* 20% alcohol | 8-fl.-oz. can | Tr. | 0. | | | 0 |
| *MASA HARINA** (Quaker) | 2 tortillas (6″ dia.) | 5 | 1.5 | | | |
| *MASA TRIGO** (Quaker) | 2 tortillas (6″ dia.) | 300 | 4.0 | | | |
| **MATZO:** | | | | | | |
| Regular (Manischewitz) | 1 matzo (1.1 oz.) | <1 | .2 | | | |
| American (Manischewitz) | 1 matzo (1 oz.) | | 2.0 | | | |

(USDA): United States Department of Agriculture
*Prepared as Package Directs

| Food and Description | Measure or Quantity | Sodium (mg.) | —Fats in grams— | | | Choles-terol (mg.) |
|---|---|---|---|---|---|---|
| | | | Total | Satu-rated | Unsatu-rated | |
| Diet-10's (Goodman's) | 1 small square ($^1/_9$ of matzo, 3 grams) | Tr. | Tr. | | | |
| Diet-10's (Goodman's) | 1 matzo (1 oz.) | <1 | .6 | | | |
| Diet-thins (Manischewitz) | 1 matzo (1 oz.) | <1 | .3 | | | |
| Egg (Manischewitz) | 1 matzo (1.2 oz.) | 5 | 1.1 | | | |
| Egg 'n Onion (Manischewitz) | 1 matzo (1 oz.) | | .6 | | | |
| Onion Tams (Manischewitz) | 1 piece (2 grams) | | .5 | | | |
| Tam Tams (Manischewitz) | 1 piece (3 grams) | | .6 | | | |
| Tasteas (Manischewitz) | 1 matzo (1 oz.) | <1 | 1.3 | | | |
| Tea (Goodman's) | 1 matzo (.6 oz.) | <1 | .4 | | | |
| Tea (Goodman's) Midgetea | 1 matzo (.4 oz.) | <1 | .2 | | | |
| Thin tea (Manischewitz) | 1 matzo (1 oz.) | <1 | .3 | | | |
| Unsalted (Goodman's) | 1 matzo (1 oz.) | <1 | .6 | | | |
| Whole wheat (Manischewitz) | 1 matzo (1.2 oz.) | <1 | .7 | | | |
| **MATZO MEAL** (Manischewitz) | 1 cup (4.1 oz.) | 2 | .9 | | | |
| **MAYONNAISE:** | | | | | | |
| (USDA)[1] | 1 cup (7.8 oz.) | 1319 | 176.6 | 31. | 146. | 155 |
| (USDA)[1] | 1 T. (.5 oz.) | 84 | 11.2 | 2. | 9. | 10 |
| (Bama) | 1 T. (.5 oz.) | 16 | 13.2 | | | |
| (Bennett's) | 1 T. (.5 oz.) | 73 | 12.4 | | | 13 |
| (Best Foods) *Real*[2] | 1 T. (.5 oz.) | 74 | 11.2 | 2. | 10. | 5 |
| (Hellmann's) *Real*[2] | 1 T. (.5 oz.) | 74 | 11.2 | 2. | 10. | 5 |
| (Kraft) | 1 T. (.5 oz.) | 75 | 11.4 | | | |
| (Kraft) *Salad Bowl* | 1 T. (.5 oz.) | 73 | 11.4 | | | |
| (Nalley's) | 1 oz. | | 22.4 | | | |
| *Saffola* | 1 cup (7.2 oz.) | 1224 | 166.5 | 15. | 152. | 112 |
| *Saffola* | 1 T. (.5 oz.) | 78 | 10.6 | <1. | 10. | 7 |
| Salt free (Healthlife) | 1 oz. | 3 | 23.0 | 2. | 21. | 15 |
| *MAYPO,* cereal, dry, any flavor: | | | | | | |
| Instant | 1 oz. | <1 | 1.3 | | | |
| 1-minute | 1 oz. | <1 | 1.4 | | | |
| **MEAL** (See **CORNMEAL** or **CRACKER MEAL** or **MATZO MEAL**) | | | | | | |
| **MEATBALL:** | | | | | | |
| In sauce, canned (Prince) | 1 can (3.7 oz.) | | 11.4 | | | |

(USDA): United States Department of Agriculture
*Prepared as Package Directs
[1]Principal sources of fat: soybean oil, cottonseed oil, corn oil & egg.
[2]Principal sources of fat: vegetable oil & egg.

| Food and Description | Measure or Quantity | Sodium (mg.) | —Fats in grams— Total | Satu- rated | Unsatu- rated | Choles- terol (mg.) |
|---|---|---|---|---|---|---|
| Stew, canned (Chef Boy-Ar-Dee) | ¼ of 30-oz. can | 829 | 10.4 | | | |
| With gravy, canned (Chef Boy-Ar-Dee) | ¼ of 15¼-oz. can | 404 | 7.8 | | | |
| With gravy & whipped potato, frozen (Swanson) | 9¼-oz. pkg. | 524 | 16.5 | | | |
| **MEAT LOAF ENTREE,** frozen: | | | | | | |
| (Banquet) | 5-oz. serving | | 19.9 | | | |
| With tomato sauce (Swanson) | 9-oz. pkg. | 1175 | 17.2 | | | |
| **MEAT LOAF DINNER,** frozen: | | | | | | |
| With tomato sauce, mashed potato & peas (USDA) | 12 oz. | 1336 | 22.8 | | | |
| Banquet: | | | | | | |
| Meat compartment | 6½ oz. | | 22.0 | | | |
| Potato compartment | 2¾ oz. | | .4 | | | |
| Peas compartment | 2 oz. | | 1.1 | | | |
| Complete dinner | 11-oz. dinner | | 23.5 | | | |
| (Kraft) | 5 oz. | 771 | 21.3 | | | |
| (Morton) | 11-oz. dinner | 896 | 21.5 | | | |
| (Morton) 3-course | 1-lb. 1-oz. dinner | 1564 | 28.1 | | | |
| (Swanson) | 10¾-oz. dinner | 1006 | 19.3 | 7. | 13. | |
| (Swanson) 3-course | 16½-oz. dinner | 1915 | 24.2 | | | |
| In brown gravy (Morton House) | 4¹/₆-oz. serving | 663 | 12.1 | 6. | 6. | 41 |
| In tomato sauce (Morton House) | 4¹/₆-oz. serving | 779 | 12.2 | 6. | 6. | 41 |
| **MEAT LOAF SEASONING MIX:** | | | | | | |
| (Contadina) | 3¾-oz. pkg. | 4190 | 2.6 | | | |
| (Lawry's) | 3½-oz. pkg. | | 2.4 | | | |
| **MEAT, POTTED:** | | | | | | |
| (Armour Star) | 3-oz. can | | 14.6 | | | |
| (Hormel) | 3-oz. can | | 12.3 | | | |
| (Van Camp) | ½ cup (3.9 oz.) | | 21.1 | | | |
| **MEAT TENDERIZER:** | | | | | | |
| Unseasoned (Adolph's) | 1 tsp. (5 grams) | 1700 | Tr. | Tr. | Tr. | 0 |
| Unseasoned (French's) | 1 tsp. | 1760 | Tr. | | | |
| Seasoned (Adolph's) | 1 tsp. (5 grams) | 1600 | <.1 | Tr. | Tr. | 0 |
| Seasoned (French's) | 1 tsp. | 1520 | Tr. | | | |
| **MELBA TOAST:** | | | | | | |
| Garlic (Keebler) | 1 piece (2 grams) | 30 | .2 | | | |

(USDA): United States Department of Agriculture
*Prepared as Package Directs

| Food and Description | Measure or Quantity | Sodium (mg.) | Fats in grams Total | Satu- rated | Unsatu- rated | Choles- terol (mg.) |
|---|---|---|---|---|---|---|
| Garlic, round (Old London) | 1 piece (2 grams) | 42 | .2 | | | |
| Onion (Keebler) | 1 piece (2 grams) | 32 | .2 | | | |
| Onion, round (Old London) | 1 piece (2 grams) | 33 | .3 | | | |
| Plain (Keebler) | 1 piece (2 grams) | 32 | .2 | | | |
| Pumpernickel (Old London) | 1 piece (4 grams) | 72 | <.1 | | | |
| Rye (Old London) | 1 piece (4 grams) | 44 | <.1 | | | |
| Rye, unsalted (Old London) | 1 piece (4 grams) | <1 | <.1 | | | |
| Sesame (Keebler) | 1 piece (2 grams) | 24 | .5 | | | |
| Sesame, rounds (Old London) | 1 piece (2 grams) | 23 | .4 | | | |
| Wheat (Old London) | 1 piece (4 grams) | 35 | <.1 | | | |
| Wheat, unsalted (Old London) | 1 piece (4 grams) | <1 | <.1 | | | |
| White: | | | | | | |
|   (Keebler) | 1 piece (4 grams) | 39 | .1 | | | |
|   (Old London) | 1 piece (4 grams) | 37 | <.1 | | | |
|   Unsalted (Old London) | 1 piece (4 grams) | <1 | <.1 | | | |
| **MELLORINE** (Sealtest) | ¼ pt. (2.3 oz.) | 48 | 6.6 | | | |
| **MELON** (See individual listings, e.g., **CANTALOUPE, WATER-MELON,** etc.) | | | | | | |
| **MELON BALL,** in syrup, frozen (USDA) | ½ cup (4.1 oz.) | 10 | .1 | | | 0 |
| **MENHADEN,** Atlantic, canned, solids & liq. (USDA) | 4 oz. | | 11.6 | | | |
| **MEXICAN DINNER:** | | | | | | |
| Mix (Hunt's) *Skillet*[1] | 1-lb. 2-oz. pkg. | 3801 | 14.6 | 4. | 11. | |
| Combination dinner, frozen (Patio) | 11-oz. dinner | | 29.0 | | | |
| Mexican style, frozen: | | | | | | |
|   (Banquet): | | | | | | |
|     Meat compartment | 9 oz. | | 17.3 | | | |
|     Rice compartment | 3½ oz. | | .1 | | | |
|     Beans compartment | 3¾ oz. | | 3.6 | | | |
|     Complete dinner | 16¼-oz. dinner | | 21.0 | | | |
|   (Patio) 5-compartment | 12-oz. dinner | | 22.0 | | | |
|   (Patio) 3-compartment | 12-oz. dinner | | 18.0 | | | |
|   (Swanson) | 16¼-oz. dinner | 1866 | 31.3 | 11. | 20. | |
|   (Swanson) 3-course | 18-oz. dinner | 1935 | 26.7 | | | |

(USDA): United States Department of Agriculture
*Prepared as Package Directs
[1]Principal sources of fat: cottonseed oil, egg & cheese.

| Food and Description | Measure or Quantity | Sodium (mg.) | —Fats in grams— | | | Choles-terol (mg.) |
|---|---|---|---|---|---|---|
| | | | ·Total | Satu-rated | Unsatu-rated | |
| **MEXICAN-STYLE VEGETA-** | | | | | | |
| **BLES,** frozen (Birds Eye) | ⅓ of 10-oz. pkg. | 80 | 7.9 | | | 0 |
| **MILK, CONDENSED,** sweetened, | | | | | | |
| canned: | | | | | | |
| (USDA) | 1 cup (10.8 oz.) | 343 | 26.6 | 13. | 13. | 105 |
| *Dime Brand* | 1 T. (.7 oz.) | 21 | 1.7 | | | |
| *Eagle Brand* | 1 T. (.7 oz.) | 21 | 1.7 | | | |
| *Magnolia Brand* | 1 T. (.7 oz.) | 21 | 1.7 | | | |
| **MILK, DRY:** | | | | | | |
| Whole: | | | | | | |
| (USDA) packed | 1 cup (5.1 oz.) | 587 | 39.9 | 22. | 18. | 158 |
| (USDA) spooned | 1 cup (4.3 oz.) | 490 | 33.3 | 18. | 15. | 132 |
| Nonfat, instant: | | | | | | |
| ⅞ cup makes 1 qt. (USDA) | ⅞ cup (3.2 oz.) | 484 | .7 | | | 20 |
| 1⅓ cups make 1 qt. (USDA) | 1⅓ cups (3.2 oz.) | 479 | .7 | | | 20 |
| (Carnation) | 1 cup (2.4 oz.) | 347 | .5 | Tr. | Tr. | 2 |
| *(Carnation) | 1 cup (8.6 oz.) | 115 | .2 | Tr. | Tr. | <1 |
| Chocolate (Carnation) | 1 cup (2.4 oz.) | 371 | 5.2 | 3. | 2. | |
| *Chocolate (Carnation) | 1 cup (8.6 oz.) | 184 | 2.6 | 1. | 1. | |
| (Weight Watchers) | 1 packet (3 grams) | | <.1 | | | |
| **MILK, EVAPORATED,** canned: | | | | | | |
| Regular: | | | | | | |
| Unsweetened (USDA) | 1 cup (8.9 oz.) | 297 | 19.9 | 10. | 10. | 79 |
| (Borden) | 14.5-oz. can | 485 | 32.5 | | | |
| (Carnation) | 1 cup (8.9 oz.) | 297 | 19.9 | 12. | 8. | 62 |
| Skimmed: | | | | | | |
| (Carnation) | 1 cup (9 oz.) | 329 | .5 | Tr. | Tr. | 2 |
| *Sunshine* (Defiance Milk) | 1 cup (8.9 oz.) | | .5 | | | |
| **MILK, FRESH:** | | | | | | |
| Whole: | | | | | | |
| 3.5% fat (USDA) | 1 cup (8.6 oz.) | 122 | 8.5 | 5. | 4. | 34 |
| 3.7% fat (USDA) | 1 cup (8.5 oz.) | 121 | 8.9 | 5. | 4. | |
| 3.25% fat, homogenized (Borden) | 1 cup (8.6 oz.) | | 7.8 | | | |
| 3.25% fat (Sealtest) | 1 cup (8.6 oz.) | 110 | 7.9 | | | |
| 3.5% fat (Sealtest) | 1 cup (8.6 oz.) | 113 | 8.5 | | | |
| 3.7% fat (Sealtest) | 1 cup (8.6 oz.) | 115 | 9.0 | | | |
| Multivitamin (Sealtest) | 1 cup (8.6 oz.) | 113 | 8.5 | | | |
| Skim: | | | | | | |
| (USDA) | 1 cup (8.6 oz.) | 127 | .2 | | | 5 |

(USDA): United States Department of Agriculture
*Prepared as Package Directs

| Food and Description | Measure or Quantity | Sodium (mg.) | Total | Satu- rated | Unsatu- rated | Choles- terol (mg.) |
|---|---|---|---|---|---|---|
| | | | | —Fats in grams— | | |
| 1% fat with 1-2% nonfat milk solids added (USDA) | 1 cup (8.7 oz.) | | 2.5 | | | 15 |
| 2% fat with 1-2% nonfat milk solids added (USDA) | 1 cup (8.7 oz.) | 150 | 4.9 | 2. | 2. | 22 |
| (Borden) | 1 cup (8.6 oz.) | | .7 | | | |
| (Sealtest) | 1 cup (8.6 oz.) | 116 | .2 | | | |
| Diet (Sealtest) | 1 cup (8.6 oz.) | 143 | 1.0 | | | |
| *Light n' Lively*, low-fat (Sealtest) | 1 cup (8.6 oz.) | 140 | 2.4 | | | |
| *Lite-line*, fortified, low-fat (Borden) | 1 cup (8.6 oz.) | | 2.4 | | | |
| *Pro-Line*, 2% fat (Borden) | 1 cup (8.6 oz.) | | 4.8 | | | |
| *Skim-line*, fortified (Borden) | 1 cup (8.6 oz.) | | .7 | | | |
| *Vita Lure*, 2% fat (Sealtest) | 1 cup (8.6 oz.) | 140 | 4.9 | | | |
| Buttermilk, cultured, fresh: | | | | | | |
| (USDA) | 1 cup (8.6 oz.) | 318 | .2 | | | 5 |
| 0.1% fat (Borden) | 1 cup (8.6 oz.) | 317 | .2 | | | |
| 1.0% fat (Borden) | 1 cup (8.6 oz.) | 317 | 2.4 | | | |
| 3.5% fat (Borden) | 1 cup (8.6 oz.) | 122 | 8.5 | | | |
| *Golden Nugget* (Sealtest) | 1 cup (8.6 oz.) | 288 | 2.0 | | | |
| *Light n' Lively* (Sealtest) | 1 cup (8.6 oz.) | 244 | 2.0 | | | |
| Low-fat (Sealtest) | 1 cup (8.6 oz.) | 281 | 4.9 | | | |
| Skimmilk (Sealtest) | 1 cup (8.6 oz.) | 281 | .2 | | | |
| Buttermilk, cultured, dried (USDA) | 1 cup (4.2 oz.) | 608 | 6.4 | 4. | 3. | |
| Chocolate milk drink, fresh: | | | | | | |
| With whole milk: | | | | | | |
| (USDA) | 1 cup (8.8 oz.) | 118 | 8.5 | 4. | 5. | 32 |
| 3.4% fat (Sealtest) | 1 cup (8.6 oz.) | 172 | 8.2 | | | |
| With skim milk & 2% added butterfat (USDA) | 1 cup (8.8 oz.) | 115 | 5.8 | 2. | 3. | 20 |
| With skim milk: | | | | | | |
| 0.5% fat (Sealtest) | 1 cup (8.6 oz.) | 174 | 1.2 | | | |
| 1% fat (Sealtest) | 1 cup (8.6 oz.) | 174 | 2.5 | | | |
| 2% fat (Sealtest) | 1 cup (8.6 oz.) | 173 | 4.8 | | | |
| **MILK, GOAT,** whole (USDA) | 1 cup (8.6 oz.) | 83 | 9.8 | 5. | 5. | |
| **MILK, HUMAN** (USDA) | 1 oz. (by wt.) | 5 | 1.1 | <1. | <1. | |
| **MILK, REINDEER** (USDA) | 1 oz. (by wt.) | 45 | 5.6 | | | |
| **MILK SHAKE** (McDonald's): | | | | | | |
| Chocolate | 1 serving (9.5 oz.) | 296 | 7.3 | | | |

(USDA): United States Department of Agriculture
*Prepared as Package Directs

| Food and Description | Measure or Quantity | Sodium (mg.) | Total | Fats in grams — Saturated | Unsaturated | Cholesterol (mg.) |
|---|---|---|---|---|---|---|
| Strawberry | 1 serving (9.4 oz.) | 267 | 8.0 | | | |
| Vanilla | 1 serving (9.7 oz.) | 274 | 6.6 | | | |
| **MILLET,** whole-grain (USDA) | 1 lb. | | 13.2 | 4. | 9. | 0 |
| **MINCEMEAT:** | | | | | | |
| (Crosse & Blackwell) | ½ cup (5.2 oz.) | 328 | 1.6 | | | |
| Condensed (None Such) | 9-oz. pkg. | 1405 | 3.8 | | | |
| Ready-to-use (None Such) | ½ cup (5.1 oz.) | 473 | 2.0 | | | |
| With brandy & rum (None Such) | ½ cup (5.3 oz.) | 353 | 3.0 | | | |
| **MINCE PIE:** | | | | | | |
| Home recipe, 2-crust (USDA) | 1/6 of 9″ pie (5.6 oz.) | 708 | 18.2 | | | |
| (Tastykake) | 4-oz. pie | | 17.2 | | | |
| Frozen: | | | | | | |
| (Banquet) | 5-oz. serving | | 14.6 | | | |
| (Morton) | 1/6 of 20-oz. pie | 318 | 10.8 | | | |
| (Morton) | ⅛ of 46-oz. pie | 460 | 31.4 | | | |
| (Mrs. Smith's) | 1/6 of 8″ pie (4.2 oz.) | 395 | 16.1 | | | |
| (Mrs. Smith's) | ⅛ of 10″ pie (5.6 oz.) | 538 | 20.9 | | | |
| **MINESTRONE SOUP:** | | | | | | |
| Canned: | | | | | | |
| Condensed(USDA) | 8 oz. (by wt.) | 1844 | 6.4 | | | |
| *Prepared with equal volume water (USDA) | 1 cup (8.6 oz.) | 995 | 3.4 | | | |
| *(Campbell) | 1 cup | 905 | 2.7 | Tr. | 2. | |
| (Crosse & Blackwell) | 6½ oz. (½ can) | 380 | .8 | | | |
| **MINT MIST PIE,** frozen (Kraft) | ¼ of 13-oz. pie | 72 | 18.4 | | | |
| **MISO,** cereal & soybeans (USDA) | 4 oz. | 3345 | 5.2 | 1. | 4. | 0 |
| ***MOCHA NUT PUDDING MIX,** instant (Royal) | ½ cup (5.1 oz.) | 345 | 5.7 | | | 14 |
| **MOCHA PIE,** frozen (Kraft) | 3-oz. serving | 88 | 21.0 | | | |
| **MOLASSES:** | | | | | | |
| Blackstrap (USDA) | ½ cup (5.4 oz.) | 148 | | | | 0 |
| Blackstrap (USDA) | 1 T. (.7 oz.) | 18 | | | | 0 |

(USDA): United States Department of Agriculture
*Prepared as Package Directs

| Food and Description | Measure or Quantity | Sodium (mg.) | Total | Fats in grams —<br>Satu-<br>rated | Unsatu-<br>rated | Choles-<br>terol (mg.) |
|---|---|---|---|---|---|---|
| Light (USDA) | ½ cup (5.4 oz.) | 23 | | | | 0 |
| Light (USDA) | 1 T. (.7 oz.) | 3 | | | | 0 |
| Medium (USDA) | ½ cup (5.4 oz.) | 57 | | | | 0 |
| Medium (USDA) | 1 T. (.7 oz.) | 7 | | | | 0 |
| Unsulphured (Grandma's) | 1 T. (.7 oz.) | 21 | | | | (0) |
| *MOR* (Wilson) canned luncheon meat | 3 oz. | 1010 | 23.1 | 10. | 14. | 51 |
| **MORTADELLA,** sausage (USDA) | 1 oz. | | 7.1 | | | |
| *MR. PiBB,* soft drink | 6 fl. oz. | 8 | 0. | | | 0 |
| *MRS. BUTTERWORTH'S SYRUP* | 1 T. (.7 oz.) | 16 | .3 | Tr. | Tr. | Tr. |
| **MUFFIN:** | | | | | | |
| Blueberry, home recipe (USDA)[1] | 3" muffin (1.4 oz.) | 253 | 3.7 | 1. | 3. | |
| Blueberry, frozen (Morton) | 1.6-oz. muffin | 151 | 2.7 | | | |
| Bran: | | | | | | |
| Home recipe (USDA)[2] | 3" muffin (1.4 oz.) | 179 | 3.9 | 2. | 2. | |
| (Thomas') with raisins | 1.9-oz. muffin | 405 | 5.5 | | | |
| Corn: | | | | | | |
| Home recipe, prepared with whole ground cornmeal (USDA)[3] | 2⅜" muffin (1.4 oz.) | 198 | 4.1 | 2. | 3. | |
| Home recipe, prepared with degermed cornmeal (USDA)[3] | 2⅜" muffin (1.4 oz.) | 192 | 4.0 | 2. | 2. | |
| (Morton) frozen | 1 muffin (1.7 oz.) | 273 | 4.3 | | | |
| (Thomas') | 1 muffin (2 oz.) | 335 | 7.7 | | | |
| English: | | | | | | |
| (Arnold) | 1 muffin (2.2 oz.) | | 1.4 | | | |
| (Newly Weds) | 1 muffin (2.5 oz.) | 475 | .6 | | | |
| (Thomas') | 1 muffin (2.1 oz.) | 225 | .7 | | | 0 |
| (Wonder) | 1 muffin (2 oz.) | 265 | 1.0 | | | |
| *Golden Egg Toasting* (Arnold) | 2.2-oz. muffin | | 3.3 | | | |
| Plain, home recipe (USDA)[4] | 3" muffin (1.4 oz.) | 176 | 4.0 | <1. | 3. | 21 |
| Scone: | | | | | | |
| (Wonder) | 1 piece (2 oz.) | 197 | 1.3 | | | |
| *Raisin Round* (Wonder) | 1 piece (2.2 oz.) | 214 | 1.4 | | | |

(USDA): United States Department of Agriculture
*Prepared as Package Directs
[1]Principal sources of fat: vegetable shortening, egg & milk.
[2]Principal sources of fat: butter, egg & milk.
[3]Principal sources of fat: lard, milk & egg.
[4]Principal sources of fat: vegetable shortening & egg.

| Food and Description | Measure or Quantity | Sodium (mg.) | Total | — Fats in grams — | | Choles-terol (mg.) |
|---|---|---|---|---|---|---|
| | | | | Satu-rated | Unsatu-rated | |

**MUFFIN MIX:**

| Food and Description | Measure or Quantity | Sodium (mg.) | Total | Satu-rated | Unsatu-rated | Choles-terol (mg.) |
|---|---|---|---|---|---|---|
| *Apple cinnamon (Betty Crocker) | 2¾" muffin | 189 | 5.4 | | | |
| *Banana nut (Betty Crocker) | 2¾" muffin | 165 | 6.8 | | | |
| *Blueberry (Betty Crocker) | 2¾" muffin | 124 | 3.8 | | | |
| *Blueberry (Duncan Hines) | 1 muffin (1.2 oz.) | 183 | 2.7 | | | |
| *Butter pecan (Betty Crocker) | 2¾" muffin | 150 | 7.7 | | | |
| Corn: | | | | | | |
| With enriched flour (USDA)[1] | 1 oz. | 187 | 3.3 | <1. | 2. | |
| Prepared with egg & milk (USDA)[2] | 2⅜" muffin (1.4 oz.) | 136 | 3.1 | <1. | 2. | |
| With cake flour & nonfat dry milk (USDA)[1] | 1 oz. | 230 | 3.0 | <1. | 2. | |
| Prepared with egg & water (USDA)[3] | 2⅜" muffin (1.4 oz.) | 138 | 3.1 | <1. | 2. | |
| (Albers) | 1 oz. | 292 | 3.9 | | | |
| *(Betty Crocker) | 2¾" muffin | 322 | 4.8 | | | |
| *(Dromedary) | 2½" muffin (1.4 oz.) | 237 | 5.8 | | | |
| *(Flako) | 1.5-oz. muffin (¹/₁₂ of pkg.) | 295 | 4.3 | | | |
| *Date nut (Betty Crocker) | 2¾" muffin | 164 | 6.4 | | | |
| *Honey bran (Betty Crocker) | 2¾" muffin | 165 | 4.9 | | | |
| *Lemon (Betty Crocker) | 1 muffin | 150 | 5.4 | | | |
| *Oatmeal (Betty Crocker) | 2¾" muffin | 205 | 6.6 | | | |
| *Orange (Betty Crocker) | 1 muffin | 146 | 4.8 | | | |
| *Spice (Betty Crocker) | 1 muffin | 150 | 5.6 | | | |
| **MULLET,** raw (USDA): | | | | | | |
| Whole | 1 lb. (weighed whole) | 195 | 16.6 | | | |
| Meat only | 4 oz. | 92 | 7.8 | | | |
| **MUNG BEANSPROUT** (See **BEAN SPROUT**) | | | | | | |
| **MUSCATEL WINE** (Gold Seal) | | | | | | |
| 19% alcohol | 3 fl. oz. (3.3 oz.) | 3 | 0. | | | (0) |
| **MUSHROOM:** | | | | | | |
| Raw (USDA): | | | | | | |
| Whole | ½ lb. (weighed un-trimmed) | 33 | .6 | | | 0 |

(USDA): United States Department of Agriculture
*Prepared as Package Directs
[1]Principal source of fat: vegetable shortening.
[2]Principal sources of fat: vegetable shortening, milk & egg.
[3]Principal sources of fat: vegetable shortening & egg.

| Food and Description | Measure or Quantity | Sodium (mg.) | —Fats in grams— | | | Cholesterol (mg.) |
|---|---|---|---|---|---|---|
| | | | Total | Saturated | Unsaturated | |
| Trimmed, slices | ½ cup (1.2 oz.) | 5 | .1 | | | 0 |
| Powdered (Spice Islands) | 1 tsp. | <1 | | | | (0) |
| Canned, solids & liq.: | | | | | | |
| (USDA) | ½ cup (4.3 oz.) | 488 | .1 | | | 0 |
| Sliced, chopped or whole, broiled in butter (B in B) | 6-oz. can | 710 | 2.5 | | | |
| Whole or sliced (Green Giant) | 4-oz. can | 533 | .2 | | | (0) |
| Frozen, whole, in butter sauce (Green Giant) | ⅓ of 6-oz. pkg. | 120 | 2.0 | | | |
| **MUSHROOM SOUP, canned:** | | | | | | |
| *Barley (Manischewitz) | 8 fl. oz. | | 1.9 | | | |
| Bisque (Crosse & Blackwell) | 6½ oz. (½ can) | | 6.1 | | | |
| Cream of: | | | | | | |
| Condensed (USDA)[1] | 8 oz. (by wt.) | 1803 | 18.1 | 2. | 16. | |
| Prepared with equal volume water (USDA)[1] | 1 cup (8.5 oz.) | 955 | 9.6 | 2. | 7. | |
| Prepared with equal volume milk (USDA)[2] | 1 cup (8.6 oz.) | 1039 | 14.2 | 5. | 9. | |
| *(Campbell) | 1 cup | 1047 | 9.9 | 3. | 7. | 1 |
| *(Heinz) | 1 cup (8.5 oz.) | 1030 | 8.0 | | | |
| (Heinz) *Great American* | 1 cup (8¾ oz.) | 1170 | 7.1 | | | |
| *Dietetic (Claybourne) | 8 oz. | 57 | 3.2 | | | |
| *Dietetic (Slim-ette) | 8 oz. (by wt.) | 69 | 1.4 | | | |
| Low sodium (Campbell) | 7¼-oz. can | 20 | 9.2 | | | |
| *Golden (Campbell) | 1 cup | 966 | 4.0 | 1. | 3. | |
| **MUSHROOM SOUP MIX:** | | | | | | |
| (Wyler's) | 1 oz. | | 2.2 | | | |
| *Beef flavor (Lipton) | 1 cup | 929 | .8 | Tr. | <1. | |
| Cream of (Lipton) *Cup-a-Soup* | 1 pkg. (.7 oz.) | 527 | 4.5 | 4. | Tr. | |
| **MUSKELLUNGE, raw (USDA):** | | | | | | |
| Whole | 1 lb. (weighed whole) | | 5.6 | | | |
| Meat only | 4 oz. | | 2.8 | | | |
| **MUSKMELON (See CANTA-LOUPE, CASABA or HONEY-DEW)** | | | | | | |
| **MUSKRAT, roasted (USDA)** | 4 oz. | | 4.6 | | | |

(USDA): United States Department of Agriculture
*Prepared as Package Directs
[1]Principal sources of fat: corn oil & cream.
[2]Principal sources of fat: corn oil, milk & cream.

| Food and Description | Measure or Quantity | Sodium (mg.) | —Fats in grams— | | | Cholesterol (mg.) |
|---|---|---|---|---|---|---|
| | | | Total | Satu-rated | Unsatu-rated | |
| **MUSSEL** (USDA): | | | | | | |
| Raw, Atlantic & Pacific, with liq., in shell | 1 lb. (weighed in shell) | | 3.2 | | | |
| Raw, Atlantic & Pacific, meat only | 4 oz. | 328 | 2.5 | | | |
| Canned, Pacific, drained | 4 oz. | | 3.7 | | | |
| | | | | | | |
| **MUSTARD,** dry, hot or mayonnaise (Spice Islands) | 1 tsp. | <1 | | | | |
| | | | | | | |
| **MUSTARD,** prepared: | | | | | | |
| Brown: | | | | | | |
| (USDA) | 1 tsp. (9 grams) | 118 | .6 | | | 0 |
| (French's) spicy | 1 tsp. | 53 | .3 | | | (0) |
| (Heinz) | 1 tsp. | 58 | .4 | | | (0) |
| German style (Kraft) | 1 oz. | 408 | 1.8 | | | (0) |
| *Grey Poupon* | 1 tsp. (6 grams) | 70 | .2 | | | (0) |
| Horseradish (Best Foods)[1] | 1 tsp. (5 grams) | 91 | .2 | | | 0 |
| Horseradish (French's) | 1 tsp. | 93 | .3 | | | (0) |
| Horseradish (Kraft) | 1 oz. | 397 | 1.8 | | | (0) |
| Medford (French's) | 1 tsp. | 80 | .3 | | | (0) |
| Onion (French's) | 1 tsp. | 53 | .2 | | | (0) |
| *Ring Star* (French's) | 1 tsp. | 63 | .2 | | | (0) |
| Salad: | | | | | | |
| (French's) | 1 tsp. | 63 | .2 | | | (0) |
| Glass or squeeze pack (Kraft) | 1 oz. | 374 | 1.1 | | | (0) |
| Plastic squeeze bottle (Kraft) | 1 oz. | 373 | 1.1 | | | (0) |
| Yellow: | | | | | | |
| (USDA) | 1 tsp. (9 grams) | 113 | .4 | | | (0) |
| (Heinz) | 1 tsp. | 71 | .2 | | | (0) |
| | | | | | | |
| **MUSTARD GREENS:** | | | | | | |
| Raw, whole (USDA) | 1 lb. (weighed untrimmed) | 102 | 1.6 | | | 0 |
| Boiled without salt, drained (USDA) | 1 cup (7.8 oz.) | 40 | .9 | | | 0 |
| Frozen: | | | | | | |
| Not thawed (USDA) | 4 oz. | 14 | .5 | | | 0 |
| Boiled, drained (USDA) | ½ cup (3.8 oz.) | 11 | .4 | | | 0 |
| Chopped (Birds Eye) | ½ cup (3.3 oz.) | 24 | .4 | | | 0 |

(USDA): United States Department of Agriculture
*Prepared as Package Directs
[1]Principal source of fat: mustard seed.

| Food and Description | Measure or Quantity | Sodium (mg.) | Total | Satu- rated | Unsatu- rated | Choles- terol (mg.) |
|---|---|---|---|---|---|---|
| | | | | — Fats in grams — | | |

**MUSTARD SEED**
| | | | | | | |
|---|---|---|---|---|---|---|
| (Spice Islands) | 1 tsp. | <1 | | | | (0) |

**MUSTARD SPINACH** (USDA):
| | | | | | | |
|---|---|---|---|---|---|---|
| Raw | 1 lb. | | 1.4 | | | 0 |
| Boiled without salt, drained | 4 oz. | | .2 | | | 0 |

# N

**NATTO,** fermented soybean
| | | | | | | |
|---|---|---|---|---|---|---|
| (USDA) | 4 oz. | | 8.4 | 1. | 7. | |

**NATURAL CEREAL:**
| | | | | | | |
|---|---|---|---|---|---|---|
| 100% (Quaker) | ¼ cup (1 oz.) | 19 | 6.5 | | | |
| 100%, with fruit (Quaker) | ¼ cup (1 oz.) | 16 | 6.0 | | | |

**NEAR BEER** (See **BEER, NEAR**)

**NEAPOLITAN CREAM PIE,** frozen:
| | | | | | | |
|---|---|---|---|---|---|---|
| (Banquet) | 2½-oz. serving | | 7.9 | | | |
| (Morton) | ¼ of 14.4-oz. pie | 193 | 15.0 | | | |
| (Mrs. Smith's) | 1/6 of 8″ pie (2.3 oz.) | 95 | 12.8 | | | |

**NECTARINE,** fresh (USDA):
| | | | | | | |
|---|---|---|---|---|---|---|
| Whole | 1 lb. (weighed with pits) | 25 | Tr. | | | 0 |
| Flesh only | 4 oz. | 7 | Tr. | | | 0 |

**NEW ZEALAND SPINACH** (USDA):
| | | | | | | |
|---|---|---|---|---|---|---|
| Raw | 1 lb. | 721 | 1.4 | | | |
| Boiled without salt, drained | 4 oz. | 104 | .2 | | | |

**NIAGARA WINE,** white
| | | | | | | |
|---|---|---|---|---|---|---|
| (Pleasant Valley) | 12.5% alcohol | 24 | 0. | | | 0 |

**NOODLE** (USDA):
| | | | | | | |
|---|---|---|---|---|---|---|
| Dry, 1½″ strips[1] | 1 cup (2.6 oz.) | 4 | 3.4 | <1. | 3. | 67 |
| Dry, 1½″ strips[1] | 1 oz. | 1 | 1.3 | Tr. | 1. | 27 |
| Cooked[1] | 1 cup (5.6 oz.) | 3 | 2.4 | <1. | 2. | 50 |
| Cooked[1] | 1 oz. | <1 | .4 | Tr. | Tr. | 9 |

(USDA): United States Department of Agriculture
*Prepared as Package Directs
[1]Principal source of fat: egg.

| Food and Description | Measure or Quantity | Sodium (mg.) | —Fats in grams— | | | Choles- terol (mg.) |
|---|---|---|---|---|---|---|
| | | | Total | Satu- rated | Unsatu- rated | |
| **NOODLE & BEEF:** | | | | | | |
| Canned (Heinz) | 8½-oz. can | 1219 | 6.4 | | | |
| Canned (Nalley's) | 8 oz. | | 7.3 | | | |
| Frozen (Banquet) buffet | 2-lb. pkg. | | 14.1 | | | |
| **NOODLE, CHOW MEIN,** canned: | | | | | | |
| (USDA) | 1 cup (1.6 oz.) | | 10.6 | | | 5 |
| (Hung's) | 1 oz. | | 8.2 | | | |
| **NOODLE DINNER:** | | | | | | |
| *Cantong* dinner mix (Betty Crocker) | 1 cup | 224 | 21.2 | | | |
| *Romanoff, mix (Kraft) | 8 oz. | 499 | 25.6 | | | |
| *Stroganoff dinner mix (Betty Crocker) | 1 cup | 204 | 25.4 | | | |
| *With cheese, mix (Kraft) | 8 oz. | 524 | 20.4 | | | |
| *With chicken, mix (Kraft) | 8 oz. | 1021 | 5.9 | | | |
| With chicken, frozen (Swanson) | 11-oz. dinner | 1410 | 15.0 | | | |
| **NOODLE MIX:** | | | | | | |
| *Almondine (Betty Crocker) | ½ cup | 621 | 9.4 | | | |
| *Egg Noodles Plus* (Pennsylvania Dutch Brand): | | | | | | |
| Beef sauce | ½ cup | 757 | 2.4 | 1. | 1. | 45 |
| Butter sauce | ½ cup | 706 | 4.6 | 2. | 3. | 48 |
| Cheese sauce | ½ cup | 440 | 3.4 | 1. | 2. | 45 |
| Chicken sauce | ½ cup | 591 | 2.7 | <1. | 2. | 53 |
| Mushroom sauce | ½ cup | 802 | 2.2 | <1. | 2. | 43 |
| Onion sauce | ½ cup | 498 | 2.2 | <1. | 2. | 43 |
| *Italiano (Betty Crocker) | ½ cup | 833 | 8.0 | | | |
| *Romanoff (Betty Crocker) | ½ cup | 593 | 12.5 | | | |
| **NOODLE SOUP:** | | | | | | |
| Beef (See **BEEF SOUP**) | | | | | | |
| Chicken (See **CHICKEN SOUP**) | | | | | | |
| *Canned, with ground beef (Campbell) | 1 cup | 804 | 4.2 | 2. | 2. | |
| **NUT,** mixed (See also individual kinds): | | | | | | |
| Dry roasted, salted: | | | | | | |
| (Flavor House) | 1 oz. | 81 | 14.9 | | | (0) |
| (Planters) | 1 oz. | 340 | 14.2 | 2. | 12. | 0 |

(USDA): United States Department of Agriculture
*Prepared as Package Directs

| Food and Description | Measure or Quantity | Sodium (mg.) | Fats in grams Total | Satu-rated | Unsatu-rated | Choles-terol (mg.) |
|---|---|---|---|---|---|---|
| (Skippy) | 1 oz. | 147 | 15.1 | 2. | 13. | 0 |
| Oil roasted: | | | | | | |
| With peanuts (Planters) | 1 oz. | 220 | 14.3 | | | 0 |
| Without peanuts (Planters) | 1 oz. | 220 | 15.0 | | | 0 |

**NUT LOAF** (See **BREAD, CANNED**)

**NUTMEG:**

| | | | | | | |
|---|---|---|---|---|---|---|
| Whole (Spice Islands) | 1 nut | <1 | | | | (0) |
| Ground (Spice Islands) | 1 tsp. | <1 | | | | (0) |

| | | | | | | |
|---|---|---|---|---|---|---|
| *NUTRIMATO* (Mott's) | 4 oz. | | .3 | | | |

# O

| | | | | | | |
|---|---|---|---|---|---|---|
| **OAT FLAKES,** cereal (Post) | ⅔ cup (1 oz.) | 198 | 1.3 | | | 0 |

**OATMEAL:**
Instant:

| | | | | | | |
|---|---|---|---|---|---|---|
| (H-O) | 1 cup (2.4 oz.) | 1 | 3.9 | 1. | 3. | 0 |
| (H-O) | 1 T. (4 grams) | Tr. | .2 | Tr. | Tr. | 0 |
| *(Quaker) | 1-oz. packet (¾ cup cooked) | 255 | 1.7 | | | |
| (Ralston) | 4 T. (1 oz.) | 1 | .6 | | | |
| Sweet and Mellow (H-O) | 1 packet (1.4 oz.) | 272 | 1.7 | Tr. | 1. | 0 |
| With apple & cinnamon (Quaker) | 1⅛-oz. packet (¾ cup cooked) | 202 | 1.3 | | | |
| With chocolate flavor (Quaker) | 1¾-oz. packet (¾ cup cooked | 276 | 2.0 | | | |
| With dates & brown sugar (Quaker) | 1⅜-oz. packet (¾ cup cooked) | 228 | 1.2 | | | |
| With dates & caramel (H-O) | 1 packet (1.4 oz.) | 232 | 1.4 | Tr. | 1. | 0 |
| With maple & brown sugar (Quaker) | 1⅝-oz. packet (¾ cup cooked) | 275 | 1.8 | | | |
| With raisins & spice (H-O) | 1 packet (1.6 oz.) | 252 | 1.6 | Tr. | 1. | 0 |
| With raisins & spice (Quaker) | 1½-oz. packet (¾ cup cooked) | 253 | 1.3 | | | |

(USDA): United States Department of Agriculture
*Prepared as Package Directs

221

| Food and Description | Measure or Quantity | Sodium (mg.) | Total | Fats in grams — Satu- rated | Unsatu- rated | Choles- terol (mg.) |
|---|---|---|---|---|---|---|
| Quick: | | | | | | |
| Dry: | | | | | | |
| (H-O) | 1 cup (2.5 oz.) | 2 | 4.1 | 1. | 3. | 0 |
| (H-O) | 1 T. (4 grams) | Tr. | .3 | Tr. | Tr. | 0 |
| (Ralston Oats) | 5 T. (1 oz.) | 1 | 1.8 | | | |
| Cooked: | | | | | | |
| *(Albers) | 1 cup | | 2.8 | | | |
| *(Quaker) | ⅔ cup (1 oz. dry) | 1 | 1.7 | | | |
| Regular: | | | | | | |
| Dry: | | | | | | |
| (USDA) | 1 cup (2.5 oz.) | 1 | 5.3 | 1. | 4. | 0 |
| (USDA) | 1 T. (4 grams) | <1 | .3 | Tr. | Tr. | 0 |
| (H-O) old fashioned | 1 cup (2.6 oz.) | 1 | 4.1 | 1. | 3. | 0 |
| (H-O) old fashioned | 1 T. (5 grams) | Tr. | .3 | Tr. | Tr. | 0 |
| (Ralston) | 3⅓ T. (1 oz.) | 1 | .6 | | | |
| Cooked: | | | | | | |
| *(USDA) | 1 cup (8.5 oz.) | 523 | 2.4 | | | 0 |
| *(Albers) old fashioned | 1 cup | | 2.8 | | | (0) |
| *(Quaker) old fashioned | ⅔ cup (1 oz. dry) | 1 | 1.7 | | | (0) |
| | | | | | | |
| **OCEAN PERCH:** | | | | | | |
| Atlantic: | | | | | | |
| Raw, whole (USDA) | 1 lb. (weighed whole) | 111 | 1.7 | | | |
| Fried, dipped in egg, milk & bread crumbs (USDA) | 4 oz. | 174 | 15.1 | | | |
| Frozen, breaded, fried, reheated (USDA) | 4 oz. | | 21.4 | | | |
| Pacific, raw: | | | | | | |
| Whole (USDA) | 1 lb. (weighed whole) | 77 | 1.8 | | | |
| Meat only (USDA) | 4 oz. | 71 | 1.7 | | | |
| Frozen (Gorton) | ⅓ of 1-lb. pkg. | 120 | 1.8 | | | |
| | | | | | | |
| **OCEAN PERCH MEALS,** frozen: | | | | | | |
| (Banquet): | | | | | | |
| Fish compartment | 5 oz. | | 8.7 | | | |
| Potato compartment | 1.6 oz. | | 7.6 | | | |
| Corn compartment | 2.2 oz. | | .9 | | | |
| Complete dinner | 8.8-oz. dinner | | 17.1 | | | |
| (Weight Watchers) | 18-oz. dinner | | 6.1 | | | |
| & broccoli (Weight Watchers) | 9½-oz. luncheon | | 7.9 | | | |

(USDA): United States Department of Agriculture
*Prepared as Package Directs

| Food and Description | Measure or Quantity | Sodium (mg.) | — Fats in grams — | | | Choles- terol (mg.) |
|---|---|---|---|---|---|---|
| | | | Total | Satu- rated | Unsatu- rated | |
| **OCTOPUS,** raw, meat only | | | | | | |
| (USDA) | 4 oz. | | .9 | | | |
| **OIL,** salad or cooking: | | | | | | |
| Corn: | | | | | | |
| (USDA) | ½ cup (3.9 oz.) | 0 | 110.0 | 11. | 99. | 0 |
| (USDA) | 1 T. (.5 oz.) | 0 | 14.0 | 1. | 13. | 0 |
| (Kraft) | 1 oz. | 0 | 28.4 | 4. | 24. | 0 |
| (Mazola) | 1 cup (7.7 oz.) | 0 | 221.0 | 29. | 192. | 0 |
| (Mazola) | 1 T. (.5 oz.) | 0 | 14.0 | 2. | 12. | 0 |
| Cottonseed (USDA) | ½ cup (3.9 oz.) | 0 | 110.0 | 28. | 82. | 0 |
| Cottonseed (USDA) | 1 T. (.5 oz.) | 0 | 14.0 | 4. | 10. | 0 |
| *Crisco* | 1 T. | 0 | 14.0 | 2. | 12. | |
| Olive (USDA) | ½ cup (3.9 oz.) | 0 | 110.0 | 12. | 98. | 0 |
| Olive (USDA) | 1 T. (.5 oz.) | 0 | 14.0 | 2. | 12. | 0 |
| Peanut: | | | | | | |
| (USDA) | ½ cup (3.9 oz.) | 0 | 110.0 | 20. | 90. | 0 |
| (USDA) | 1 T. (.5 oz.) | 0 | 14.0 | 3. | 11. | 0 |
| (Planters) | 1 T. (.5 oz.) | Tr. | 14.0 | 3. | 11. | 0 |
| Safflower: | | | | | | |
| (USDA) | ½ cup (3.9 oz.) | 0 | 110.0 | 9. | 101. | 0 |
| (USDA) | 1 T. (.5 oz.) | 0 | 14.0 | 1. | 13. | 0 |
| (Kraft) | 1 oz. | | 28.4 | 3. | 26. | 0 |
| (Saff-o-life) | 1 T. | Tr. | 14.0 | | | (0) |
| *Saffola* | ½ cup (3.9 oz.) | 0 | 110.0 | 9. | 101. | 0 |
| *Saffola* | 1 T. (.5 oz.) | 0 | 14.0 | 1. | 13. | 0 |
| Sesame (USDA) | ½ cup (3.9 oz.) | 0 | 110.0 | 15. | 95. | 0 |
| Sesame (USDA) | 1 T. (.5 oz.) | 0 | 14.0 | 2. | 12. | 0 |
| Soybean (USDA) | ½ cup (3.9 oz.) | 0 | 110.0 | 16. | 94. | 0 |
| Soybean (USDA) | 1 T. (.5 oz.) | 0 | 14.0 | 2. | 12. | 0 |
| Vegetable (Kraft) | 1 oz. | 0 | 28.4 | 5. | 24. | 0 |
| *Wesson* | 1 T. (.5 oz.) | 0 | 14.0 | 3. | 11. | 0 |
| **OKRA:** | | | | | | |
| Raw, whole (USDA) | 1 lb. (weighed untrimmed) | 12 | 1.2 | | | 0 |
| Boiled without salt, drained (USDA): | | | | | | |
| Whole | ½ cup (3.1 oz.) | 2 | .3 | | | 0 |
| Pods | 8 pods (3" x ⅝", 3 oz.) | 2 | .3 | | | 0 |
| Slices | ½ cup (2.8 oz.) | 2 | .2 | | | 0 |
| Frozen: | | | | | | |
| Cut & pods, not thawed (USDA) | 4 oz. | 2 | .1 | | | 0 |

(USDA): United States Department of Agriculture
*Prepared as Package Directs

223

| Food and Description | Measure or Quantity | Sodium (mg.) | Fats in grams — Total | Satu- rated | Unsatu- rated | Choles- terol (mg.) |
|---|---|---|---|---|---|---|
| Cut, boiled, drained | | | | | | |
| (USDA) | ½ cup (3.2 oz.) | 2 | <.1 | | | 0 |
| Whole, boiled, drained | | | | | | |
| (USDA) | ½ cup (2.4 oz.) | 1 | <.1 | | | 0 |
| Cut (Birds Eye) | ½ cup (3.3 oz.) | 2 | Tr. | | | 0 |
| Whole (Birds Eye) | ½ cup (2.5 oz.) | 1 | Tr. | | | 0 |
| **OLD FASHIONED:** | | | | | | |
| Mix (Bar-Tender's) | 1 serving (⅙ oz.) | Tr. | <.1 | | | (0) |
| **OLEOMARGARINE (See MARGARINE)** | | | | | | |
| **OLIVE:** | | | | | | |
| Greek style, salt-cured, oil-coated: | | | | | | |
| Pitted (USDA) | 1 oz. | 932 | 10.1 | 1. | 9. | 0 |
| With pits, drained (USDA) | 4 oz. | 2992 | 32.6 | 4. | 29. | 0 |
| Green, pitted & drained: | | | | | | |
| (USDA) | 1 oz. | 680 | 3.6 | | | 0 |
| (USDA) | 4 med. or 3 extra large or 2 giant (.6 oz.) | 384 | 2.0 | | | 0 |
| (USDA) | 1 olive (¹³/₁₆″ x 1¹/₁₆″, 6 grams) | 132 | .7 | | | 0 |
| Ripe, by variety, pitted & drained: | | | | | | |
| Ascalano, any size (USDA) | 1 oz. | 230 | 3.9 | <1. | 3. | 0 |
| Manzanilla, any size (USDA) | 1 oz. | 230 | 3.9 | <1. | 3. | 0 |
| Mission, any size (USDA) | 1 oz. | 213 | 5.7 | <1. | 5. | 0 |
| Mission (USDA) | 3 small or 2 large (.4 oz.) | 75 | 2.0 | Tr. | 2. | 0 |
| Mission, slices (USDA) | ½ cup (2.2 oz.) | 465 | 12.5 | 1. | 11. | 0 |
| Sevillano, any size (USDA) | 1 oz. | 235 | 2.7 | Tr. | 2. | 0 |
| *1 ● 2 ● 3,* dessert (Jello-O) | ⅔ cup (5.3 oz.) | 44 | 3.3 | | | 0 |
| **ONION:** | | | | | | |
| Raw (USDA): | | | | | | |
| Whole | 1 lb. (weighed untrimmed) | 41 | .4 | | | 0 |
| Whole | 2½″ onion (3.9 oz.) | 10 | .1 | | | 0 |
| Chopped | ½ cup (3 oz.) | 9 | <.1 | | | 0 |

(USDA): United States Department of Agriculture
*Prepared as Package Directs

(224)

| Food and Description | Measure or Quantity | Sodium (mg.) | Fats in grams | | | Cholesterol (mg.) |
|---|---|---|---|---|---|---|
| | | | Total | Satu-rated | Unsatu-rated | |
| Chopped | 1 T. (.4 oz.) | 1 | <.1 | | | 0 |
| Grated | 1 T. (.5 oz.) | 1 | <.1 | | | 0 |
| Ground | 1 T. (.5 oz.) | 2 | <.1 | | | 0 |
| Slices | ½ cup (2 oz.) | 6 | <.1 | | | 0 |
| Boiled without salt (USDA): | | | | | | |
| Whole | ½ cup (3.7 oz.) | 7 | .1 | | | 0 |
| Halves or pieces | ½ cup (3.2 oz.) | 6 | <.1 | | | 0 |
| Pearl onions | ½ cup (3.2 oz.) | 6 | <.1 | | | 0 |
| Canned, boiled, solids & liq. (Comstock-Greenwood) | 4 oz. | 176 | .1 | | | (0) |
| Dehydrated: | | | | | | |
| Flakes (USDA) | 1 cup (2.3 oz.) | 56 | .8 | | | 0 |
| Flakes (USDA) | 1 tsp. (1 gram) | 1 | Tr. | | | 0 |
| Instant, minced or powder (Spice Islands) | 1 tsp. | 2 | | | | (0) |
| Frozen: | | | | | | |
| Chopped (Birds Eye) | ¼ cup (1 oz.) | 3 | Tr. | | | 0 |
| Whole, small (Birds Eye) | ½ cup (4 oz.) | 6 | .2 | | | 0 |
| Small with cream sauce (Birds Eye) | ⅓ of 9-oz. pkg. | 307 | .8 | | | Tr. |
| Small with cream sauce (Green Giant) | ⅓ of 10-oz. pkg. | 326 | .9 | | | |
| French-fried rings: | | | | | | |
| Canned (Durkee) *O&C* | 3½-oz. can | 451 | 48.6 | | | |
| Frozen (Birds Eye) | 2 oz. | 415 | 10.0 | | | Tr. |
| Frozen (Mrs. Paul's) | 9-oz. pkg. | | 34.8 | | | |
| Frozen (Mrs. Paul's) | 5-oz. pkg. | | 25.0 | | | |
| Pickled, cocktail (Crosse & Blackwell) | 1 T. (.5 oz.) | 227 | 0. | | | |

**ONION BOUILLON:**

| Food and Description | Measure or Quantity | Sodium (mg.) | Total | | | |
|---|---|---|---|---|---|---|
| (Herb-Ox) | 1 cube (4 grams) | 510 | .1 | | | |
| (Herb-Ox) instant | 1 packet (5 grams) | 750 | .2 | | | |
| (Steero) | 1 cube (4 grams) | | <.1 | | | |
| (Wyler's) | 1 cube (4 grams) | | .2 | | | |

**ONION, GREEN** (USDA):

| Food and Description | Measure or Quantity | Sodium (mg.) | Total | | | Cholesterol (mg.) |
|---|---|---|---|---|---|---|
| Raw: | | | | | | |
| Whole | 1 lb. (weighed untrimmed) | 22 | .9 | | | 0 |
| Bulb & entire top | 1 oz. | 1 | <.1 | | | 0 |
| Bulb & white portion of top | 3 small onions (.9 oz.) | 1 | <.1 | | | 0 |

(USDA): United States Department of Agriculture
*Prepared as Package Directs

225

| Food and Description | Measure or Quantity | Sodium (mg.) | Total | Fats in grams — Satu- rated | Unsatu- rated | Choles- terol (mg.) |
|---|---|---|---|---|---|---|
| Slices, bulb & white portion of top | ½ cup (1.8 oz.) | 2 | .1 | | | 0 |
| Tops only | 1 oz. | 1 | .1 | | | 0 |
| Dry, shredded (Spice Islands) | 1 tsp. | 11 | | | | (0) |
| **ONION SOUP:** | | | | | | |
| Condensed (USDA) | 8 oz. (by wt.) | 1984 | 4.8 | | | |
| *Prepared with equal volume water (USDA) | 1 cup (8.5 oz.) | 1051 | 2.4 | | | |
| *(Campbell) | 1 cup | 932 | 1.6 | <1. | 1. | |
| (Crosse & Blackwell) | 6½ oz. (½ can) | | 1.7 | | | |
| (Hormel) | 15-oz. can | | 7.2 | | | |
| **ONION SOUP MIX:** | | | | | | |
| Dry (USDA)[1] | 1½-oz. pkg. | 2871 | 4.6 | | | |
| *Prepared (USDA) | 1 cup (8.1 oz.) | 660 | 1.2 | | | |
| *(Lipton) | 1 cup | 872 | .8 | Tr. | <1. | |
| (Lipton) *Cup-a-Soup* | 1 pkg. (.4 oz.) | 920 | .5 | Tr. | Tr. | |
| (Wyler's) | 1 cup | | .7 | | | |
| **ONION, WELSH,** raw (USDA): | | | | | | |
| Whole | 1 lb. (weighed untrimmed) | | 1.2 | | | 0 |
| Trimmed | 4 oz. | | .5 | | | 0 |
| **OPOSSUM,** roasted, meat only (USDA) | 4 oz. | | 11.6 | | | |
| **ORANGE,** fresh: | | | | | | |
| All varieties: | | | | | | |
| Whole (USDA) | 1 lb. (weighed with rind & seeds) | 3 | .7 | | | 0 |
| Whole (USDA) | small orange (2½" dia., 5.3 oz.) | 1 | .2 | | | 0 |
| Whole (USDA) | med. orange (3" dia., 5.5 oz.) | 2 | .3 | | | 0 |
| Whole (USDA) | large orange (3⅜" dia., 8.4 oz.) | 2 | .5 | | | 0 |
| Diced or sliced, drained (USDA) | 1 cup (7.7 oz.) | 2 | .4 | | | 0 |
| Sections (USDA) | 1 cup (8.5 oz.) | 2 | .5 | | | 0 |
| Sections, sweetened, chilled, bottled (Kraft) | 4 oz. | 115 | .2 | | | (0) |

(USDA): United States Department of Agriculture
*Prepared as Package Directs
[1]Principal source of fat: vegetable shortening.

| Food and Description | Measure or Quantity | Sodium (mg.) | —Fats in grams— | | Choles-terol (mg.) |
| | | | Total | Satu-rated | Unsatu-rated | |
|---|---|---|---|---|---|
| Sections, unsweetened, chilled, bottled (Kraft) | 4 oz. | 115 | .1 | | (0) |
| California Navel: | | | | | |
| Whole (USDA) | 1 lb. (weighed with rind & seeds) | 3 | .3 | | 0 |
| Whole (USDA) | 2⁴/₅" orange (6.3 oz.) | 1 | .1 | | 0 |
| Sections (USDA) | 1 cup (8.5 oz.) | 2 | .2 | | 0 |
| California Navel or Valencia: Unpeeled, wedge or slice (Sunkist) | ¹/₆ orange (1.1 oz.) | 1 | Tr. | | 0 |
| Peeled, cut bite-size (Sunkist) | ½ cup (6.3-oz. orange) | 1 | Tr. | | 0 |
| California Valencia (USDA): | | | | | |
| Whole | 1 lb. (weighed with rind & seeds) | 3 | 1.0 | | 0 |
| Fruit, including peel | 2⅝" orange (6.3 oz.) | 4 | .5 | | 0 |
| Sections | 1 cup (8.5 oz.) | 2 | .7 | | 0 |
| Florida, all varieties (USDA): | | | | | |
| Whole | 1 lb. (weighed with rind & seeds) | 3 | .7 | | 0 |
| Whole | 3" orange (5.5 oz.) | 2 | .3 | | 0 |
| Sections | 1 cup (8.5 oz.) | 2 | .5 | | 0 |
| **ORANGEADE:** | | | | | |
| Chilled (Sealtest) | ½ cup (4.4 oz.) | <1 | .1 | | (0) |
| Frozen: | | | | | |
| *(Minute Maid) | ½ cup (4.2 oz.) | 47 | Tr. | | 0 |
| *(Snow Crop) | ½ cup (4.2 oz.) | 47 | Tr. | | 0 |
| **ORANGE-APRICOT JUICE DRINK,** canned: | | | | | |
| (USDA) 40% fruit juices | 1 cup (8.8 oz.) | Tr. | .2 | | 0 |
| (Del Monte) | 1 cup (8.6 oz.) | Tr. | Tr. | | (0) |
| **ORANGE CAKE MIX:** | | | | | |
| *Chiffon (Betty Crocker) | ¹/₁₆ of cake | 116 | 2.8 | | |
| *(Betty Crocker) layer | ¹/₁₂ of cake | 269 | 5.6 | | |
| *(Duncan Hines) | ¹/₁₂ of cake (2.7 oz.) | 374 | 6.1 | | 50 |
| **ORANGE CREAM BAR** (Sealtest) | 2½-fl.-oz. bar | 27 | 3.1 | | |

(USDA): United States Department of Agriculture
*Prepared as Package Directs

| Food and Description | Measure or Quantity | Sodium (mg.) | —Fats in grams— | | | Cholesterol (mg.) |
|---|---|---|---|---|---|---|
| | | | Total | Saturated | Unsaturated | |
| **ORANGE DRINK:** | | | | | | |
| Chilled (Sealtest) | 6 fl. oz. (6.5 oz.) | Tr. | <.1 | | | (0) |
| Canned (Del Monte) | 6 fl. oz. (6.5 oz.) | 15 | Tr. | | | (0) |
| Canned (Hi-C) | 6 fl. oz. (6.3 oz.) | <1 | Tr. | | | 0 |
| **ORANGE-GRAPEFRUIT JUICE:** | | | | | | |
| Bottled, chilled (Kraft) | ½ cup (4.5 oz.) | 1 | .1 | | | (0) |
| Canned: | | | | | | |
| Sweetened (USDA) | ½ cup (4.4 oz.) | 1 | .1 | | | 0 |
| Sweetened (Del Monte) | ½ cup (4.3 oz.) | 10 | .1 | | | 0 |
| Sweetened (Stokely-Van Camp) | ½ cup (4.4 oz.) | | .1 | | | (0) |
| Unsweetened (USDA) | ½ cup (4.3 oz.) | 1 | .2 | | | 0 |
| Unsweetened (Stokely-Van Camp) | ½ cup (4.4 oz.) | | .2 | | | (0) |
| Frozen, concentrate, unsweetened: | | | | | | |
| (USDA) | 6-fl.-oz. can (7.4 oz.) | 4 | .1 | | | 0 |
| *Diluted with 3 parts water | | | | | | |
| (USDA) | ½ cup (4.4 oz.) | Tr. | .1 | | | 0 |
| *(Minute Maid) | ½ cup (4.2 oz.) | <1 | <.1 | | | 0 |
| *(Snow Crop) | ½ cup (4.2 oz.) | <1 | <.1 | | | 0 |
| **ORANGE ICE** (Sealtest) | ¼ pt. (3.2 oz.) | Tr. | Tr. | | | |
| **ORANGE JUICE:** | | | | | | |
| Fresh: | | | | | | |
| All varieties (USDA) | ½ cup (4.4 oz.) | 1 | .2 | | | 0 |
| California Navel (USDA) | ½ cup (4.4 oz.) | 1 | .1 | | | 0 |
| California Valencia (USDA) | ½ cup (4.4 oz.) | 1 | .4 | | | 0 |
| California Navel or Valencia (Sunkist) | ½ cup (4.4 oz.) | <1 | Tr. | | | 0 |
| Florida, early or mid-season (USDA) | ½ cup (4.4 oz.) | 1 | .2 | | | 0 |
| Florida Temple (USDA) | ½ cup (4.4 oz.) | 1 | .2 | | | 0 |
| Florida Valencia (USDA) | ½ cup (4.4 oz.) | 1 | .2 | | | 0 |
| Chilled, fresh (Kraft) | ½ cup (4.4 oz.) | 1 | .2 | | | (0) |
| Chilled, fresh (Sealtest) | ½ cup (4.3 oz.) | 1 | .2 | | | (0) |
| Canned or bottled, sweetened: | | | | | | |
| (USDA) | ½ cup (4.4 oz.) | 1 | .3 | | | 0 |
| (Del Monte) | ½ cup (4.3 oz.) | 1 | .1 | | | 0 |
| (Heinz) | 5½-fl.-oz. can | 3 | .3 | | | (0) |
| (Stokely-Van Camp) | ½ cup (4.4 oz.) | | .2 | | | (0) |
| Canned or bottled, unsweetened: | | | | | | |
| (USDA) | ½ cup (4.4 oz.) | 1 | .2 | | | 0 |

(USDA): United States Department of Agriculture
*Prepared as Package Directs

| Food and Description | Measure or Quantity | Sodium (mg.) | —Fats in grams—<br>Total | Satu-<br>rated | Unsatu-<br>rated | Choles-<br>terol (mg.) |
|---|---|---|---|---|---|---|
| (Del Monte) | ½ cup (4.3 oz.) | 1 | .1 | | | 0 |
| (Heinz) | 5½-fl.-oz. can | 3 | .4 | | | (0) |
| *Reconstituted (Kraft) | ½ cup (4.4 oz.) | 1 | .1 | | | (0) |
| (Stokely-Van Camp) | ½ cup (4.4 oz.) | | .2 | | | (0) |
| Canned, concentrate, unsweetened: | | | | | | |
| (USDA) | 4 oz. | 1 | .3 | | | 0 |
| *Diluted with 5 parts water | | | | | | |
| (USDA) | ½ cup (4.4 oz.) | 1 | .4 | | | 0 |
| Dehydrated, crystals: | | | | | | |
| (USDA) | 4-oz. can | 9 | 1.9 | | | 0 |
| *Reconstituted (USDA) | ½ cup (4.4 oz.) | 1 | .2 | | | 0 |
| Frozen, concentrate: | | | | | | |
| (USDA) | 6-fl.-oz. can<br>(7.5 oz.) | 4 | .4 | | | 0 |
| *Diluted with 3 parts water | | | | | | |
| (USDA) | ½ cup (4.4 oz.) | 1 | .1 | | | 0 |
| *(Birds Eye) | ½ cup (4 oz.) | 1 | .1 | | | 0 |
| *(Lake Hamilton) | ½ cup (4.4 oz.) | | .2 | | | (0) |
| *(Minute Maid) | ½ cup (4.2 oz.) | <1 | <.1 | | | 0 |
| *(Nature's Best) | ½ cup (4.4 oz.) | | .2 | | | (0) |
| *(Snow Crop) | ½ cup (4.2 oz.) | <1 | <.1 | | | 0 |

**ORANGE, MANDARIN (See TANGERINE)**

**ORANGE PEEL:**

| | | | | | | |
|---|---|---|---|---|---|---|
| Raw (USDA) | 1 oz. | 1 | .1 | | | 0 |
| Dry (Spice Islands) | 1 tsp. | <1 | | | | (0) |
| Candied (USDA) | 1 oz. | | .1 | | | 0 |

**ORANGE-PINEAPPLE DRINK,**

| | | | | | | |
|---|---|---|---|---|---|---|
| canned (Hi-C) | 6 fl. oz. (6.3 oz.) | <1 | Tr. | | | 0 |

**ORANGE-PINEAPPLE JUICE,**

| | | | | | | |
|---|---|---|---|---|---|---|
| bottled, chilled (Kraft) | ½ cup (4.4 oz.) | 1 | .1 | | | (0) |

**ORANGE-PINEAPPLE PIE**

| | | | | | | |
|---|---|---|---|---|---|---|
| (Tastykake) | 4-oz. pie | | 14.8 | | | |

***ORANGE PLUS** (Birds Eye)*

| | | | | | | |
|---|---|---|---|---|---|---|
| *ORANGE PLUS* (Birds Eye) | ½ cup (4.4 oz.) | 10 | .1 | | | 0 |

**ORANGE RENNET MIX:**
Powder:

| | | | | | | |
|---|---|---|---|---|---|---|
| Dry (Junket) | 1 oz. | 14 | Tr. | | | |
| *(Junket) | 4 oz. | 57 | 3.8 | | | |

(USDA): United States Department of Agriculture
*Prepared as Package Directs

| Food and Description | Measure or Quantity | Sodium (mg.) | —Fats in grams— Total | Satu- rated | Unsatu- rated | Choles- terol (mg.) |
|---|---|---|---|---|---|---|
| Tablet: | | | | | | |
|   Dry (Junket) | 1 tablet (<1 gram) | 197 | Tr. | | | |
|   *& sugar (Junket) | 4 oz. | 98 | 3.9 | | | |

**ORANGE SHERBET** (See SHERBET)

**ORANGE SOFT DRINK:**

| | | | | | | |
|---|---|---|---|---|---|---|
| Sweetened: | | | | | | |
|   (Canada Dry) *Sunripe*, | | | | | | |
|     bottle or can | 6 fl. oz. | 15+ | 0. | | | 0 |
|   (Clicquot Club) | 6 fl. oz. | 12 | 0. | | | 0 |
|   (Cott) | 6 fl. oz. | 12 | 0. | | | 0 |
|   (Dr. Brown's) | 6 fl. oz. | 28 | 0. | | | 0 |
|   (Fanta) | 6 fl. oz. | 6 | Tr. | | | 0 |
|   (Hoffman) | 6 fl. oz. | 28 | 0. | | | 0 |
|   (Key Food) | 6 fl. oz. | 28 | 0. | | | 0 |
|   (Kirsch) | 6 fl. oz. | <1 | 0. | | | 0 |
|   (Mission) | 6 fl. oz. | 12 | 0. | | | 0 |
|   (Nedick's) | 6 fl. oz. | 28 | 0. | | | 0 |
|   (Nehi) | 6 fl. oz. (6.6 oz.) | 0+ | 0. | | | 0 |
|   (Shasta) draft | 6 fl. oz. | 22 | 0. | | | 0 |
|   (Waldbaum) | 6 fl. oz. | 28 | 0. | | | 0 |
|   (Yukon Club) | 6 fl. oz. | 28 | 0. | | | 0 |
| Low calorie: | | | | | | |
|   (Canada Dry) bottle | 6 fl. oz. | 14+ | 0. | | | 0 |
|   (Canada Dry) can | 6 fl. oz. | 15+ | 0. | | | 0 |
|   (Clicquot Club) | 6 fl. oz. | 45 | 0. | | | 0 |
|   (Cott) | 6 fl. oz. | 45 | 0. | | | 0 |
|   *Diet Rite* | 6 fl. oz. | 41+ | 0. | | | 0. |
|   (Dr. Brown's) | 6 fl. oz. | 46 | 0. | | | 0 |
|   (Hoffman) | 6 fl. oz. | 46 | 0. | | | 0 |
|   (Key Food) | 6 fl. oz. | 46 | 0. | | | 0 |
|   (Mission) | 6 fl. oz. | 45 | 0. | | | 0 |
|   (No-Cal) | 6 fl. oz. | 13 | 0. | | | 0 |
|   (Shasta) | 6 fl. oz. | 37 | 0 | | | 0 |
|   (Waldbaum) | 6 fl. oz. | 46 | 0. | | | 0 |
|   (Yukon Club) | 6 fl. oz. | 69 | 0. | | | 0 |
| **OREGANO** (Spice Islands) | 1 tsp. | <1 | | | | (0) |
| **ORIENTAL DINNER** (Hunt's) | | | | | | |
|   *Skillet* | 1-lb. 1-oz. pkg. | 3006 | .8 | | | |

(USDA): United States Department of Agriculture
*Prepared as Package Directs

| Food and Description | Measure or Quantity | Sodium (mg.) | —Fats in grams— | | | Cholesterol (mg.) |
|---|---|---|---|---|---|---|
| | | | Total | Saturated | Unsaturated | |
| *OVALTINE,* dry: | | | | | | |
| Chocolate | 1 oz. | 96 | 1.0 | | | |
| Malt | 1 oz. | 68 | 1.1 | | | |
| **OXTAIL SOUP** (Crosse & Blackwell) | 6½ oz. (½ can) | 530 | 1.1 | | | |
| **OYSTER:** | | | | | | |
| Raw: | | | | | | |
| Eastern, meat only: | | | | | | |
| (USDA) | 1 lb. (weighed with shell & liq.) | 33 | .8 | | | 23 |
| (USDA) | 12 oysters (weighed in shell, 4 lb.) | 132 | 3.2 | | | 92 |
| (USDA) | 4 oz. | 83 | 2.0 | | | 57 |
| (USDA) | 19-31 small or 13-19 med. oysters (1 cup, 8.5 oz.) | 175 | 4.3 | | | 120 |
| Pacific & Western, meat only: | | | | | | |
| (USDA) | 4 oz. | | 2.5 | | | 57 |
| (USDA) | 6-9 small or 4-6 med. oysters (1 cup, 8.5 oz.) | | 5.3 | | | 120 |
| Canned, solids & liq. (USDA) | 4 oz. | | 2.5 | | | 51 |
| Fried, dipped in egg, milk & bread crumbs (USDA) | 4 oz. | 234 | 15.8 | | | |
| Frozen, solids & liq. (USDA) | 4 oz. | 431 | 6.9 | | | |
| **OYSTER CRACKER** (See **CRACKER**) | | | | | | |
| **OYSTER STEW:** | | | | | | |
| Home recipe (USDA): | | | | | | |
| 1 part oysters to 1 part milk by volume | 1 cup (6-8 oysters, 8.5 oz.) | | 13.2 | | | |
| 1 part oysters to 2 parts milk by volume[1] | 1 cup (8.5 oz.) | 814 | 15.4 | | | 62 |
| 1 part oysters to 3 parts milk by volume[1] | 1 cup (8.5 oz.) | 487 | 12.7 | | | 58 |
| *Canned (Campbell) | 1 cup | 824 | 8.0 | 2. | 6. | |
| Frozen (USDA): | | | | | | |
| Condensed | 8 oz. (by wt.) | 1542 | 14.3 | | | |

(USDA): United States Department of Agriculture
*Prepared as Package Directs
[1]Prepared with added salt & butter.

| Food and Description | Measure or Quantity | Sodium (mg.) | Fats in grams Total | Satu- rated | Unsatu- rated | Choles- terol (mg.) |
|---|---|---|---|---|---|---|
| *Prepared with equal volume water | 1 cup (8.5 oz.) | 816 | 7.7 | | | |
| *Prepared with equal volume milk | 1 cup (8.5 oz.) | 878 | 11.8 | | | |

# P

**PANCAKE:**
| | | | | | | |
|---|---|---|---|---|---|---|
| Home recipe, wheat (USDA) | 4″ pancake (1 oz.) | 115 | 1.9 | <1. | 1. | |
| Frozen, breakfast, with link sausage (Swanson) | 6-oz. breakfast | 972 | 24.0 | | | |

**PANCAKE & WAFFLE MIX**
**(See also PANCAKE &**
**WAFFLE MIX, DIETETIC):**
Buckwheat:
| | | | | | | |
|---|---|---|---|---|---|---|
| (USDA) | 1 oz. | 378 | .5 | | | |
| (USDA) | 1 cup (4.8 oz.) | 1801 | 2.6 | | | |
| *Prepared with egg & milk (USDA) | 4″ pancake (1 oz.) | 125 | 2.5 | | | |
| *(Aunt Jemima) | 4″ pancake (1.2 oz.) | 148 | 2.4 | | | |
| Buttermilk: | | | | | | |
| (USDA) | 1 oz. | 406 | .5 | | | |
| (USDA) | 1 cup (4.8 oz.) | 1935 | 2.4 | | | |
| *Prepared with milk (USDA)[1] | 4″ pancake (1 oz.) | 122 | 1.5 | <1. | 1. | |
| *Prepared with milk & egg (USDA)[2] | 4″ pancake (1 oz.) | 182 | 2.0 | <1. | 1. | |
| *(Aunt Jemima) | 4″ pancake (1 oz.) | 245 | 3.0 | | | |
| *(Duncan Hines) | 4″ pancake (2 oz.) | 354 | 1.7 | | | |
| Flapjack (Albers) | 1 cup | | 1.4 | | | |
| Plain: | | | | | | |
| (USDA) | 1 oz. | 406 | .5 | | | |
| (USDA) | 1 cup (4.8 oz.) | 1935 | 2.4 | | | |
| *Prepared with milk (USDA)[1] | 4″ pancake (1 oz.) | 122 | 1.5 | <1. | 1. | |
| *Prepared with milk & egg (USDA)[2] | 4″ pancake (1 oz.) | 152 | 2.0 | <1. | 1. | 20 |
| *Prepared with milk & egg (USDA)[2] | 6″ x ½″ pancake (7 T. batter) | 412 | 5.3 | 2. | 3. | 54 |
| *(Aunt Jemima) Complete | 4″ pancake (1.2 oz.) | 193 | .8 | | | |

(USDA): United States Department of Agriculture
*Prepared as Package Directs
[1]Principal sources of fat: vegetable shortening & milk.
[2]Principal sources of fat: vegetable shortening, milk & egg.

| Food and Description | Measure or Quantity | Sodium (mg.) | — Fats in grams — | | | Choles-terol (mg.) |
|---|---|---|---|---|---|---|
| | | | Total | Satu-rated | Unsatu-rated | |
| *(Aunt Jemima) Easy Pour | 4" pancake (1.2 oz.) | 215 | 2.7 | | | |
| *(Aunt Jemima) Original | 4" pancake (1 oz.) | 150 | 2.3 | | | |
| Dry (Golden Mix) | 1 cup (4.3 oz.) | | 3.0 | | | |
| **\*PANCAKE & WAFFLE MIX, DIETETIC,** buttermilk or plain (Tillie Lewis) | 4" pancake (1.2 oz.) | | .2 | | | 2 |
| **PANCAKE & WAFFLE SYRUP** (See also individual brand names): Sweetened: | | | | | | |
| Cane & maple (USDA) | 1 T. (.7 oz.) | <1 | 0. | | | 0 |
| Chiefly corn, light & dark (USDA) | 1 T. (.7 oz.) | 14 | 0. | | | 0 |
| (Bama) | 1 T. (.7 oz.) | 6 | 0. | | | |
| (Golden Griddle) | 1 T. (.7 oz.) | 1 | 0. | | | 0 |
| Dietetic or low calorie: | | | | | | |
| (Diet Delight) | 1 T. (.6 oz.) | 10 | Tr. | | | |
| Boysenberry (Cary's) | 1 T. (.6 oz.) | 4 | 0. | | | 0 |
| Maple (Cary's) | 1 T. (.6 oz.) | 4 | 0. | | | 0 |
| Maple (Slim-ette) | 1 T. (.5 oz.) | | 0. | | | |
| **PANCREAS,** raw (USDA): | | | | | | |
| Beef, lean only | 4 oz. | 76 | 8.3 | | | |
| Beef, medium-fat | 4 oz. | | 28.4 | | | |
| Calf | 4 oz. | | 10.0 | | | |
| Hog or hog sweetbread | 4 oz. | 50 | 22.6 | | | |
| **PAPAW,** fresh (USDA): | | | | | | |
| Whole | 1 lb. (weighed with rind & seeds) | | 3.1 | | | 0 |
| Flesh only | 4 oz. | | 1.0 | | | 0 |
| **PAPAYA,** fresh (USDA): | | | | | | |
| Whole | 1 lb. (weighed with skin & seeds) | 9 | .3 | | | 0 |
| Flesh only | 4 oz. | 3 | .1 | | | 0 |
| Cubed | 1 cup (6.4 oz.) | 5 | .2 | | | 0 |
| **PAPRIKA** (Spice Islands) | 1 tsp. | <2 | | | | (0) |
| **PARISIAN-STYLE VEGETA-BLES,** frozen (Birds Eye) | ⅓ of 10-oz. pkg. | 137 | 6.5 | | | 0 |

(USDA): United States Department of Agriculture
*Prepared as Package Directs

| Food and Description | Measure or Quantity | Sodium (mg.) | Fats in grams Total | Satu- rated | Unsatu- rated | Choles- terol (mg.) |
|---|---|---|---|---|---|---|
| **PARSLEY:** | | | | | | |
| Fresh (USDA): | | | | | | |
| Whole | ½ lb. | 102 | 1.4 | | | 0 |
| Chopped | 1 T. (4 grams) | 2 | <.1 | | | 0 |
| Dry (Spice Islands) | 1 tsp. | 5 | | | | |
| | | | | | | |
| **PARSNIP** (USDA): | | | | | | |
| Raw, whole | 1 lb. (weighed unpared) | 46 | 1.9 | | | 0 |
| Boiled without salt, drained, cut in pieces | ½ cup (3.7 oz.) | 8 | .5 | | | 0 |
| | | | | | | |
| *PARV-A-ZERT* (SugarLo): | | | | | | |
| Chocolate | ⅓ pint (3.5 oz.) | 59 | 10.6 | 9. | 2. | 19 |
| Coffee, strawberry or vanilla | ⅓ pint (3.5 oz.) | 36 | 10.6 | 9. | 2. | 19 |
| | | | | | | |
| **PASSION FRUIT,** fresh (USDA): | | | | | | |
| Whole | 1 lb. (weighed with shell) | 66 | 1.7 | | | 0 |
| Pulp & seeds | 4 oz. | 32 | .8 | | | 0 |
| | | | | | | |
| **PASTINAS,** dry (USDA): | | | | | | |
| Carrot | 1 oz. | | .5 | | | |
| Egg[1] | 1 oz. | 1 | 1.2 | Tr. | <1. | |
| Spinach | 1 oz. | | .5 | | | |
| | | | | | | |
| **PASTRY SHELL** (See also **PIE CRUST**): | | | | | | |
| Home recipe, made with lard, baked (USDA)[2] | 1 shell (1.5 oz.) | 260 | 14.2 | 6. | 9. | |
| Home recipe, made with vegetable shortening, baked (USDA)[3] | 1 shell (1.5 oz.) | 260 | 14.2 | 3. | 11. | 0 |
| (Stella D'oro) | 1 shell (1 oz.) | | 7.8 | | | |
| Pot, bland (Stella D'oro) | 1 shell (1.6 oz.) | | 11.3 | | | |
| Pot pie, bland (Keebler) | 4″ shell (1.7 oz.) | 137 | 11.- | | | |
| Tart, sweet (Keebler) | 3″ shell (1 oz.) | 5 | 9.1 | | | |
| Frozen (Pepperidge Farm) | 1 shell (1.8 oz.) | 210 | 18.1 | | | |
| Frozen, tart (Pepperidge Farm) | 1 pie tart (3 oz.) | 176 | 15.5 | | | |

(USDA): United States Department of Agriculture
*Prepared as Package Directs
[1]Principal source of fat: egg.
[2]Principal source of fat: lard.
[3]Principal source of fat: vegetable shortening.

| Food and Description | Measure or Quantity | Sodium (mg.) | — Fats in grams — | | | Choles- terol (mg.) |
|---|---|---|---|---|---|---|
| | | | Total | Satu- rated | Unsatu- rated | |
| **PATE,** canned: | | | | | | |
| De foie gras (USDA) | 1 oz. | | 12.4 | | | |
| De foie gras (USDA) | 1 T. (.5 oz.) | | 6.6 | | | |
| Liver (Hormel) | 1 oz. | | 6.3 | | | |
| Liver (Sell's) | 1 T. (.5 oz.) | 105 | 3.8 | | | |
| | | | | | | |
| *PDQ:* | | | | | | |
| Chocolate | 1 T. (.6 oz.) | | .3 | | | |
| Egg Nog | 2 heaping tsps. (1 oz.) | | .4 | | | |
| Strawberry | 1T. (.5 oz.) | | Tr. | | | |
| | | | | | | |
| **PEA, GREEN:** | | | | | | |
| Raw (USDA): | | | | | | |
| In pod | 1 lb. (weighed in pod) | 3 | .7 | | | 0 |
| Shelled | 1 lb. | 9 | 1.8 | | | 0 |
| Shelled | ½ cup (2.4 oz.) | 1 | .3 | | | 0 |
| Boiled without salt, drained (USDA) | ½ cup (2.9 oz.) | <1 | .3 | | | 0 |
| Canned, regular pack: | | | | | | |
| Drained solids (Del Monte) | ½ cup (3 oz.) | 198 | .4 | | | 0 |
| Seasoned, drained solids (Del Monte) | ½ cup (3 oz.) | 204 | .4 | | | 0 |
| Alaska, Early or June, solids & liq. (USDA) | ½ cup (4.4 oz.) | 293 | .4 | | | 0 |
| Alaska, Early or June, drained solids (USDA) | ½ cup (3 oz.) | 203 | .3 | | | 0 |
| Alaska, Early or June, drained liq. (USDA) | 4 oz. | 268 | Tr. | | | 0 |
| Early, solids & liq., *April Showers* | ½ of 8½-oz. can | 374 | .4 | | | (0) |
| Early, solids & liq. (Le Sueur) | ½ of 8.5-oz. can | 374 | .2 | | | |
| Early, solids & liq. (Stokely- Van Camp) | ½ cup (4.1 oz.) | | .4 | | | (0) |
| Early June, with onions (Green Giant) | ¼ of 17-oz. can | 518 | .2 | | | (0) |
| Sweet, solids & liq. (USDA) | ½ cup (4.4 oz.) | 293 | .4 | | | 0 |
| Sweet, drained solids (USDA) | ½ cup (3 oz.) | 203 | .3 | | | 0 |
| Sweet, drained liq. (USDA) | 4 oz. | 268 | Tr. | | | 0 |
| Sweet, solids & liq. (Green Giant) | ½ of 8.5-oz. can | 337 | .4 | | | (0) |

(USDA): United States Department of Agriculture
*Prepared as Package Directs

| Food and Description | Measure or Quantity | Sodium (mg.) | —Fats in grams— | | | Choles- terol (mg.) |
|---|---|---|---|---|---|---|
| | | | Total | Satu- rated | Unsatu- rated | |
| Sweet, honey pod, solids & liq. (Stokely-Van Camp) | ½ cup (4 oz.) | | .4 | | | (0) |
| Canned, dietetic pack: | | | | | | |
| Alaska, Early or June, solids & liq. (USDA) | 4 oz. | 3 | .3 | | | 0 |
| Alaska, Early or June, drained solids (USDA) | 4 oz. | 3 | .5 | | | 0 |
| Alaska, Early or June, drained liq. (USDA) | 4 oz. | 3 | Tr. | | | 0 |
| Sweet, solids & liq. (USDA) | 4 oz. | 3 | .3 | | | 0 |
| Sweet, drained solids (USDA) | 4 oz. | 3 | .5 | | | 0 |
| Sweet, drained liq. (USDA) | 4 oz. | 3 | Tr. | | | 0 |
| Solids & liq. (Diet Delight) | ½ cup (4.4 oz.) | 10 | .2 | | | (0) |
| (S and W) *Nutradiet*, unseasoned | 4 oz. | 11 | .1 | | | (0) |
| Sweet, solids & liq. (Blue Boy) | 4 oz. | 8 | .2 | | | (0) |
| Sweet, solids & liq. (Tillie Lewis) | ½ cup (4.4 oz.) | <10 | .4 | | | 0 |
| Frozen: | | | | | | |
| Not thawed (USDA) | 1 cup (2.5 oz.) | 93 | .2 | | | 0 |
| Boiled, drained (USDA) | ½ cup (3 oz.) | 97 | .3 | | | 0 |
| Sweet (Birds Eye) | ½ cup (3.3 oz.) | 152 | .3 | | | 0 |
| Tender tiny (Birds Eye) | ½ cup (3.3 oz.) | 121 | .3 | | | 0 |
| In butter sauce, baby peas, (Le Sueur) | ⅓ of 10-oz. pkg. | 416 | 2.4 | | | |
| In butter sauce, sweet (Green Giant) | ⅓ of 10-oz. pkg. | 402 | 2.8 | | | |
| With cream sauce (Birds Eye) | ⅓ of pkg. (2.7 oz.) | 399 | 6.5 | | | Tr. |
| With cream sauce (Green Giant) | ⅓ of 10-oz. pkg. | 151 | .8 | | | |
| With sliced mushroom (Birds Eye) | ⅓ of 10-oz. pkg. | 258 | .3 | | | 0 |
| **PEA, MATURE SEED, dry:** | | | | | | |
| Raw: | | | | | | |
| Whole (USDA) | 1 lb. | 159 | 5.9 | | | 0 |
| Whole (USDA) | 1 cup (7.1 oz.) | 70 | 2.6 | | | 0 |
| Split, without seed coat (USDA) | 1 lb. | 181 | 4.5 | | | 0 |
| Split, without seed coat (USDA) | 1 cup (7.2 oz.) | 81 | 2.0 | | | 0 |
| Cooked without salt, split, without seed coat, drained (USDA) | ½ cup (3.4 oz.) | 13 | .3 | | | 0 |

(USDA): United States Department of Agriculture
*Prepared as Package Directs

| Food and Description | Measure or Quantity | Sodium (mg.) | — Fats in grams — | | | Choles- terol (mg.) |
|---|---|---|---|---|---|---|
| | | | Total | Satu- rated | Unsatu- rated | |
| **PEA POD,** edible-podded or | | | | | | |
| Chinese (USDA): | | | | | | |
| Raw | 1 lb. (weighed | | | | | |
| | untrimmed) | | .9 | | | 0 |
| Boiled, drained | 4 oz. | | .2 | | | 0 |
| **PEA & CARROT:** | | | | | | |
| Canned, regular pack, drained | | | | | | |
| (Del Monte) | ½ cup (3 oz.) | 308 | .4 | | | 0 |
| Canned, dietetic pack, solids & liq.: | | | | | | |
| (Blue Boy) | 4 oz. | 22 | .2 | | | (0) |
| (Diet Delight) | ½ cup (4.2 oz.) | 10 | .2 | | | (0) |
| (S and W) *Nutradiet* | 4 oz. | 24 | .2 | | | (0) |
| Frozen: | | | | | | |
| Not thawed (USDA) | 4 oz. | 104 | .3 | | | 0 |
| Boiled, drained (USDA) | ½ cup (3.1 oz.) | 73 | .3 | | | 0 |
| (Birds Eye) | ½ cup (3.3 oz.) | 86 | .3 | | | 0 |
| In cream sauce (Green Giant) | ⅓ of 10-oz. pkg. | 236 | .8 | | | |
| **PEA & CELERY,** frozen (Birds | | | | | | |
| Eye) | ½ cup (3.3 oz.) | 490 | .2 | | | 0 |
| **PEA & ONION,** frozen: | | | | | | |
| (Birds Eye) | ½ cup (3.3 oz.) | 428 | .3 | | | 0 |
| In butter sauce (Green Giant) | ⅓ of 10-oz. pkg. | 340 | 2.6 | | | |
| **PEA & POTATO,** with cream | | | | | | |
| sauce, frozen (Birds Eye) | ⅓ of pkg. (2.7 oz.) | 406 | 7.1 | | | Tr. |
| **PEA SOUP, GREEN:** | | | | | | |
| Canned, condensed: | | | | | | |
| (USDA) | 8 oz. (by wt.) | 1665 | 4.1 | | | |
| *Prepared with equal volume | | | | | | |
| water (USDA) | 1 cup (8.6 oz.) | 899 | 2.2 | | | |
| *Prepared with equal volume | | | | | | |
| milk (USDA) | 1 cup (8.6 oz.) | 963 | 6.4 | | | |
| *(Campbell) | 1 cup | 939 | 1.8 | 1. | <1. | |
| Canned, low sodium: | | | | | | |
| (Campbell) | 7½-oz. can | 40 | 2.3 | | | |
| *(Claybourne) | 8 oz. | 23 | .1 | | | |
| Dry mix: | | | | | | |
| (USDA) | 1 oz. | 669 | 1.2 | | | |

(USDA): United States Department of Agriculture
*Prepared as Package Directs

(237)

| Food and Description | Measure or Quantity | Sodium (mg.) | —Fats in grams— | | | Choles- terol (mg.) |
|---|---|---|---|---|---|---|
| | | | Total | Satu- rated | Unsatu- rated | |
| *(USDA) | 1 cup (8.5 oz.) | 787 | 1.5 | | | |
| *(Lipton) | 1 cup | 1078 | 1.7 | | | |
| (Lipton) *Cup-a-Soup* | 1.2-oz. pkg. | 694 | 1.4 | Tr. | 1. | |
| Frozen, condensed: | | | | | | |
| With ham (USDA) | 8 oz. (by wt.) | 1701 | 5.2 | | | |
| *With ham, prepared with | | | | | | |
| equal volume water (USDA) | 8 oz. (by wt.) | 850 | 2.7 | | | |
| **PEA SOUP, SPLIT:** | | | | | | |
| Canned, regular pack: | | | | | | |
| Condensed (USDA) | 8 oz. (by wt.) | 1790 | 5.9 | | | |
| *Prepared with equal volume | | | | | | |
| water (USDA) | 1 cup (8.6 oz.) | 941 | 3.2 | | | |
| *(Manischewitz) | 1 cup | | 3.1 | | | |
| *With ham (Campbell) | 1 cup | 864 | 3.0 | 1. | 2. | |
| *With ham (Heinz) | 1 cup (8¾ oz.) | 953 | 2.4 | | | |
| With smoked ham (Heinz) | | | | | | |
| *Great American* | 1 cup (9 oz.) | 1132 | 5.2 | | | |
| *Canned, dietetic (Slim-ette) | 8 oz. (by wt.) | 24 | .5 | | | |
| Canned, low sodium (Tillie | | | | | | |
| Lewis) | 1 cup (8 oz.) | 25 | .5 | | | |
| **PEACH:** | | | | | | |
| Fresh, without skin (USDA): | | | | | | |
| Whole | 1 lb. (weighed unpeeled) | 4 | .4 | | | 0 |
| Whole | 4-oz. peach (2½″ dia.) | 1 | .1 | | | 0 |
| Diced | ½ cup (4.7 oz.) | 1 | .1 | | | 0 |
| Slices | ½ cup (3 oz.) | 1 | .1 | | | 0 |
| Canned, regular pack, solids & liq.: | | | | | | |
| Juice pack (USDA) | 4 oz. | 2 | .1 | | | 0 |
| Light syrup (USDA) | 4 oz. | 2 | .1 | | | 0 |
| Heavy syrup (USDA) | 2 med. halves & 2 T. syrup (4.1 oz.) | 2 | .1 | | | 0 |
| Heavy syrup, halves (USDA) | ½ cup (4.5 oz.) | 3 | .1 | | | 0 |
| Heavy syrup, slices (USDA) | ½ cup (4.4 oz.) | 3 | .1 | | | 0 |
| Heavy syrup (Del Monte) cling | ½ cup (4.6 oz.) | 15 | .2 | | | 0 |
| Heavy syrup (Del Monte) freestone | ½ cup (4.6 oz.) | 16 | .2 | | | 0 |
| Heavy syrup (Hunt's) | ½ cup (4.5 oz.) | 3 | .1 | | | 0 |
| Extra heavy syrup (USDA) | 4 oz. | 2 | .1 | | | 0 |

(USDA): United States Department of Agriculture
*Prepared as Package Directs

| Food and Description | Measure or Quantity | Sodium (mg.) | — Fats in grams — | | Choles-terol (mg.) |
| | | | Total | Satu-rated | Unsatu-rated | |

| Food and Description | Measure or Quantity | Sodium (mg.) | Total | Satu-rated | Unsatu-rated | Choles-terol (mg.) |
|---|---|---|---|---|---|---|
| Spiced, heavy syrup | | | | | | |
| (Del Monte) | ½ cup (4.5 oz.) | 4 | Tr. | | | 0 |
| (Stokely-Van Camp) | ½ cup (4 oz.) | | .1 | | | (0) |
| Canned, dietetic or unsweetened pack: | | | | | | |
| Water pack, solids & liq. | | | | | | |
| (USDA) | ½ cup (4.3 oz.) | 2 | .1 | | | 0 |
| (Blue Boy) slices, solids & liq. | 4 oz. | 1 | Tr. | | | (0) |
| (Diet Delight) cling, halves or slices | ½ cup (4.4 oz.) | 5 | <.1 | | | (0) |
| (Diet Delight) freestone, halves or slices | ½ cup (4.4 oz.) | 5 | <.1 | | | (0) |
| (S and W) *Nutradiet*, cling, halves, low calorie, undrained | 2 halves (3.5 oz.) | 2 | .1 | | | (0) |
| (S and W) *Nutradiet*, cling, halves, unsweetened | 2 halves (3.5 oz.) | 2 | .1 | | | (0) |
| (S and W) *Nutradiet*, cling, slices, low calorie, undrained | 4 oz. | 2 | .1 | | | (0) |
| (S and W) *Nutradiet*, cling, slices, unsweetened | 4 oz. | 2 | <.1 | | | (0) |
| (S and W) *Nutradiet*, freestone, halves, low calorie, undrained | 4 halves (3.5 oz.) | 5 | .1 | | | (0) |
| (S and W) *Nutradiet*, freestone, slices, low calorie, solids & liq. | 4 oz. | 2 | .1 | | | (0) |
| (Tillie Lewis) cling, solids & liq. | ½ cup (4.3 oz.) | <10 | .1 | | | 0 |
| (Tillie Lewis) Elberta, solids & liq. | ½ cup (4.3 oz.) | 10 | .1 | | | 0 |
| Dehydrated, sulfured, nugget or pieces: | | | | | | |
| Uncooked (USDA) | 1 oz. | 6 | .3 | | | 0 |
| Cooked with added sugar, solids & liq. (USDA) | ½ cup (5-6 halves & 3 T. liq., 5.4 oz.) | 8 | .3 | | | 0 |
| Dried: | | | | | | |
| Uncooked (USDA) | 1 lb. | 73 | 3.2 | | | 0 |
| Uncooked (USDA) | ½ cup (3.1 oz.) | 14 | .6 | | | 0 |
| Cooked, unsweetened (USDA) | ½ cup (5-6 halves & 3 T. liq., 4.8 oz.) | 7 | .3 | | | 0 |
| Cooked, with added sugar (USDA) | ½ cup (5-6 halves & 3 T. liq., 5.4 oz.) | 6 | .3 | | | 0 |
| Uncooked (Del Monte) | ½ cup (3.1 oz.) | 4 | .7 | | | 0 |

(USDA): United States Department of Agriculture
*Prepared as Package Directs

| Food and Description | Measure or Quantity | Sodium (mg.) | Total | Fats in grams Satu- rated | Fats in grams Unsatu- rated | Choles- terol (mg.) |
|---|---|---|---|---|---|---|
| Frozen: | | | | | | |
| Not thawed, slices, sweetened: | | | | | | |
| (USDA) | 12-oz. pkg. | 7 | .3 | | | 0 |
| (USDA) | 16-oz. can | 9 | .5 | | | 0 |
| (USDA) | ½ cup (4.2 oz.) | 2 | .1 | | | 0 |
| Quick thaw (Birds Eye) | ½ cup (5 oz.) | 1 | .1 | | | 0 |
| **PEACH BUTTER** (Smucker's) | 1 T. (.6 oz.) | 2 | Tr. | | | (0) |
| **PEACH DUMPLING,** frozen | | | | | | |
| (Pepperidge Farm) | 1 dumpling (3.3 oz.) | 220 | 16.4 | | | |
| **PEACH NECTAR,** canned: | | | | | | |
| (USDA) | 1 cup (8.8 oz.) | 2 | Tr. | | | 0 |
| (Del Monte) | 1 cup (8.7 oz.) | 15 | Tr. | | | 0 |
| **PEACH PIE:** | | | | | | |
| Home recipe, 2-crust (USDA): | | | | | | |
| Made with lard[1] | ¹/₆ of 9″ pie (5.6 oz.) | 423 | 17.5 | 6. | 11. | |
| Made with vegetable shortening[2] | ¹/₆ of 9″ pie (5.6 oz.) | 423 | 16.9 | 6. | 11. | |
| (Tastykake) | 4-oz. pie | | 15.0 | | | |
| Frozen: | | | | | | |
| (Banquet) | 5-oz. serving | | 13.8 | | | |
| (Morton) | ¹/₆ of 20-oz. pie | 244 | 10.8 | | | |
| (Morton) | ¹/₆ of 24-oz. pie | 265 | 10.9 | | | |
| (Morton) | ⅛ of 46-oz. pie | 311 | 16.5 | | | |
| (Mrs. Smith's) | ¹/₆ of 8″ pie (4.2 oz.) | 283 | 14.2 | | | |
| (Mrs. Smith's) old fashion | ¹/₆ of 9″ pie (5.8 oz.) | 470 | 22.7 | | | |
| (Mrs. Smith's) | ⅛ of 10″ pie (5.6 oz.) | 381 | 18.4 | | | |
| **PEACH PIE FILLING:** | | | | | | |
| (Comstock) | ½ cup (5.1 oz.) | 183 | <.1 | | | |
| (Lucky Leaf) | 8 oz. | 132 | .2 | | | |
| **PEACH PRESERVE:** | | | | | | |
| Sweetened (Bama) | 1 T. (.7 oz.) | 20 | <.1 | | | (0) |
| Low calorie or dietetic: | | | | | | |
| (Kraft) | 1 oz. | 42 | <.1 | | | (0) |
| (Tillie Lewis) | 1 T. (.5 oz.) | 3 | Tr. | | | 0 |

(USDA): United States Department of Agriculture
*Prepared as Package Directs
[1]Principal sources of fat: lard & butter.
[2]Principal sources of fat: vegetable shortening & butter.

| Food and Description | Measure or Quantity | Sodium (mg.) | Fats in grams — Total | Satu- rated | Unsatu- rated | Choles- terol (mg.) |
|---|---|---|---|---|---|---|
| **PEACH TURNOVER,** frozen | | | | | | |
| (Pepperidge Farm) | 1 turnover (3.3 oz.) | 254 | 19.9 | | | |
| **PEANUT:** | | | | | | |
| Raw (USDA): | | | | | | |
| In shell | 1 lb. (weighed in shell) | 17 | 157.3 | 35. | 122. | 0 |
| With skins | 1 oz. | 1 | 13.5 | 3. | 11. | 0 |
| Without skins, whole, unsalted | 1 oz. | 1 | 13.7 | 3. | 11. | 0 |
| Boiled (USDA) | 1 oz. | 1 | 8.9 | 2. | 7. | 0 |
| Roasted: | | | | | | |
| Whole, unsalted (USDA) | 1 lb. (weighed in shell) | 15 | 148.0 | 33. | 115. | 0 |
| With skins, unsalted (USDA) | 1 oz. | 1 | 13.8 | 3. | 11. | 0 |
| Without skins, salted (USDA) | 1 oz. | 119 | 14.1 | 3. | 11. | 0 |
| Halves, salted (USDA) | ½ cup (2.5 oz.) | 301 | 35.9 | 8. | 28. | 0 |
| Chopped, salted (USDA) | ½ cup (2.4 oz.) | 288 | 34.4 | 8. | 27. | 0 |
| Chopped, salted (USDA) | 1 T. (9 grams) | 38 | 4.5 | 1. | 3. | 0 |
| Dry (Franklin) | 1 oz. | 283 | 12.0 | | | (0) |
| Dry (Frito-Lay) | 1 oz. | 340 | 14.5 | 3. | 12. | 0 |
| Dry, salted (Flavor House) | 1 oz. | 119 | 14.1 | | | (0) |
| Dry (Planters) | 1 oz. (jar) | 340 | 13.3 | 3. | 11. | 0 |
| Dry (Skippy) | 1 oz. | 194 | 14.5 | 3. | 12. | 0 |
| Oil (Planters) cocktail | ¾-oz. bag | 165 | 10.9 | | | 0 |
| Oil (Planters) cocktail | 1 oz. (can) | 220 | 14.6 | | | 0 |
| Salted (Nabisco) *Nab* | ¾-oz. pkg. | 155 | 10.6 | | | (0) |
| Salted (Nabisco) *Nab* | 1¼-oz. pkg. | 258 | 17.7 | | | (0) |
| Salted (Nabisco) *Nab* | 1⅞-oz. pkg. | 387 | 26.5 | | | (0) |
| Toasted (Tom Houston) | 2 T. (1.1 oz.) | 125 | 14.9 | | | (0) |
| Spanish, oil-roasted, *Freshnut* | 1 oz. | 160 | 14.7 | 3. | 12. | 0 |
| Spanish, dry-roasted (Planters) | 1 oz. (jar) | 340 | 14.4 | | | 0 |
| Spanish, oil-roasted (Planters) | 1 oz. (can) | 220 | 15.3 | | | 0 |
| **PEANUT BUTTER:** | | | | | | |
| (USDA): | | | | | | |
| Small amounts of fat & salt added | ½ cup (4.4 oz.) | 765 | 62.2 | 11. | 51. | 0 |
| Small amounts of fat & salt added | 1 T. (.6 oz.) | 97 | 7.9 | 1. | 6. | 0 |
| Small amounts of fat, sweetener & salt added | ½ cup (4.4 oz.) | 764 | 62.4 | 11. | 51. | 0 |
| Small amounts of fat, sweetener & salt added | 1 T. (.6 oz.) | 97 | 7.9 | 1. | 6. | 0 |
| Moderate amounts of fat, sweetener & salt added | ½ cup (4.4 oz.) | 762 | 63.8 | 11. | 52. | 0 |

(USDA): United States Department of Agriculture
*Prepared as Package Directs

| Food and Description | Measure or Quantity | Sodium (mg.) | —Fats in grams— | | | Cholesterol (mg.) |
|---|---|---|---|---|---|---|
| | | | Total | Satu-rated | Unsatu-rated | |
| Moderate amounts of fat, sweetener & salt added | 1 T. (.6 oz.) | 97 | 8.1 | 1. | 7. | 0 |
| (Bama) crunchy | 1 T. (.6 oz.) | 70 | 7.7 | 1. | 7. | (0) |
| (Bama) smooth | 1 T. (.6 oz.) | 87 | 8.4 | 1. | 7. | (0) |
| (Jif) | 1 T. (.6 oz.) | 89 | 8.6 | 2. | 7. | 0 |
| (Peter Pan) | 1 T. (.6 oz.) | 78 | 7.8 | | | 0 |
| (Planters) | 1 T. (.5 oz.) | 95 | 8.1 | 3. | 6. | 0 |
| (Skippy) creamy[1] | 1 T. (.6 oz.) | 77 | 8.2 | 2. | 6. | 0 |
| (Skippy) chunk[1] | 1 T. (.6 oz.) | 77 | 8.5 | 2. | 7. | 0 |
| (Smucker's) creamy or crunchy | 1 T. (.5 oz.) | 81 | 6.7 | 1. | 6. | (0) |
| (Smucker's) old fashioned | 1 T. (.5 oz.) | 81 | 6.9 | 1. | 6. | (0) |
| & jelly (Smucker's) *Goober* | 1 T. (.5 oz.) | 43 | 3.3 | <1. | 3. | (0) |
| With crackers (See **CRACKERS**) | | | | | | |
| **PEANUT SPREAD:** | | | | | | |
| (USDA)[2] | 1 oz. | 169 | 14.8 | 3. | 12. | 0 |
| Diet (Peter Pan) | 1 T. (.5 oz.) | 3 | 8.2 | | | 0 |
| **PEAR:** | | | | | | |
| Fresh: | | | | | | |
| Whole (USDA) | 1 lb. (weighed with stems & core) | 8 | 1.7 | | | 0 |
| Whole (USDA) | 6.4-oz. pear (3″ x 2½″) | 3 | .6 | | | 0 |
| Quartered (USDA) | ½ cup (3.4 oz.) | 2 | .4 | | | 0 |
| Slices, including skin (USDA) | ½ cup (2.9 oz.) | 2 | .3 | | | 0 |
| Canned, regular pack, solids & liq.: | | | | | | |
| Juice pack (USDA) | 4 oz. | 1 | .3 | | | 0 |
| Light syrup (USDA) | 4 oz. | 1 | .2 | | | 0 |
| Heavy syrup, halves (USDA) | ½ cup (4 oz.) | 1 | .2 | | | 0 |
| Heavy syrup, halves (USDA) | 2 med. halves & 2 T. syrup (4.1 oz.) | 1 | .2 | | | 0 |
| Heavy syrup (Del Monte) | ½ cup (4 oz.) | 7 | .6 | | | 0 |
| Heavy syrup (Hunt's) | ½ cup (4.5 oz.) | 1 | .3 | | | (0) |
| Extra heavy syrup (USDA) | 4 oz. | 1 | .2 | | | 0 |
| (Stokely-Van Camp) | ½ cup (4 oz.) | | .2 | | | (0) |
| Canned, unsweetened or low calorie: | | | | | | |
| Water pack, solids & liq. (USDA) | ½ cup (4.3 oz.) | 1 | .2 | | | 0 |
| Solids & liq. (Blue Boy) Bartlett | 4 oz. | 1 | .1 | | | (0) |

(USDA): United States Department of Agriculture
*Prepared as Package Directs
[1]Principal sources of fat: peanuts & vegetable oil.
[2]Principal sources of fat: peanuts & vegetable shortening.

| Food and Description | Measure or Quantity | Sodium (mg.) | Total | Satu- rated | Unsatu- rated | Choles- terol (mg.) |
|---|---|---|---|---|---|---|
| | | | | — Fats in grams — | | |
| Solids & liq. (Diet Delight) halves or quarters | ½ cup (4.4 oz.) | 4 | <.1 | | | (0) |
| (S and W) *Nutradiet*, halves, low calorie, undrained | 4 halves (3.5 oz.) | 3 | .1 | | | (0) |
| (S and W) *Nutradiet*, halves, unsweetened | 2 halves (3.5 oz.) | 4 | <.1 | | | (0) |
| (S and W) *Nutradiet*, quartered, low calorie, undrained | 4 oz. | 2 | .1 | | | (0) |
| (S and W) *Nutradiet*, quartered, unsweetened | 4 oz. | 2 | <.1 | | | (0) |
| Solids & liq. (Tillie Lewis) Bartlett | ½ cup (4.3 oz.) | <10 | .2 | | | 0 |
| Dried: | | | | | | |
| (USDA) | 1 lb. | 32 | 8.2 | | | 0 |
| Uncooked (Del Monte) | ½ cup (2.8 oz.) | 3 | .6 | | | 0 |
| Cooked without added sugar, solids & liq. (USDA) | 4 oz. | 3 | .9 | | | 0 |
| Cooked with added sugar, solids & liq. (USDA) | 4 oz. | 3 | .9 | | | 0 |
| **PEAR, CANDIED** (USDA) | 1 oz. | | .2 | | | (0) |
| **PEAR NECTAR:** | | | | | | |
| Sweetened (USDA) | 1 cup (8.5 oz.) | 2 | .5 | | | 0 |
| Sweetened (Del Monte) | 1 cup (8.7 oz.) | 17 | Tr. | | | 0 |
| (S and W) *Nutradiet* | 4 oz. (by wt.) | 2 | .1 | | | (0) |
| **PEAR PRESERVE** (Bama) | 1 T. (.7 oz.) | 1 | <.1 | | | (0) |
| **PECAN:** | | | | | | |
| In shell (USDA) | 1 lb. (weighed in shell) | Tr. | 171.2 | 12. | 159. | 0 |
| Shelled, unsalted (USDA): | | | | | | |
| Whole | 1 lb. | Tr. | 323.0 | 23. | 300. | 0 |
| Halves | ½ cup (1.9 oz.) | Tr. | 38.4 | 3. | 36. | 0 |
| Halves | 12-14 halves (.5 oz.) | Tr. | 10.0 | <1. | 9. | 0 |
| Chopped | ½ cup (1.8 oz.) | Tr. | 37.0 | 3. | 34. | 0 |
| Chopped | 1 T. (7 grams) | Tr. | 5.0 | Tr. | 5. | 0 |
| Dry, roasted, salted (Flavor House) | 1 oz. | 32 | 20.2 | | | (0) |
| Dry, roasted (Planters) | 1 oz. | 340 | 20.2 | 2. | 18. | 0 |

(USDA): United States Department of Agriculture
*Prepared as Package Directs

243

| Food and Description | Measure or Quantity | Sodium (mg.) | —Fats in grams— Total | Satu- rated | Unsatu- rated | Choles- terol (mg.) |
|---|---|---|---|---|---|---|
| **PECAN PIE:** | | | | | | |
| Home recipe, 1-crust (USDA): | | | | | | |
|   Made with lard[1] | ¹/₆ of 9″ pie (4.9 oz.) | 305 | 31.6 | 6. | 26. | |
|   Made with vegetable | | | | | | |
|     shortening[2] | ¹/₆ of 9″ pie (4.9 oz.) | 305 | 31.6 | 4. | 27. | |
| Frozen (Morton) | ¹/₆ of 20-oz. pie | 320 | 15.4 | | | |
| Frozen (Morton) | ⅛ of 46-oz. pie | 565 | 23.5 | | | |
| Frozen (Mrs. Smith's) | ¹/₆ of 8″ pie (4 oz.) | 338 | 21.3 | | | |
| Frozen (Mrs. Smith's) | ⅛ of 10″ pie (4.5 oz.) | 365 | 23.4 | | | |
| | | | | | | |
| ***PEP,*** cereal (Kellogg's) | 1 cup (1 oz.) | 184 | .4 | | | (0) |
| | | | | | | |
| **PEPPER:** | | | | | | |
| Black: | | | | | | |
|   (USDA) | 1 cup (3.9 oz.) | 13 | 7.5 | | | 0 |
|   (USDA) | 1 tsp. (2 grams) | <1 | .2 | | | 0 |
|   Seasoned (French's) | 1 tsp. (3 grams) | 4 | .2 | | | (0) |
|   Seasoned (Lawry's) | 1 pkg. (1.6 oz.) | | 2.4 | | | (0) |
|   Seasoned (Lawry's) | 1 tsp. (2 grams) | | .1 | | | (0) |
|   Whole or ground (Spice Islands) | 1 tsp. | <1 | | | | (0) |
| Cayenne (Spice Islands) | 1 tsp. | <1 | | | | (0) |
| Lemon (Durkee) | 1 tsp. (3 grams) | 698 | Tr. | | | (0) |
| & lemon seasoning (French's) | 1 tsp. (3 grams) | 800 | Tr. | | | (0) |
| White, whole or ground | | | | | | |
|   (Spice Islands) | 1 tsp. | <1 | | | | (0) |
| | | | | | | |
| **PEPPER, HOT CHILI:** | | | | | | |
| Green (USDA): | | | | | | |
|   Raw, whole | 4 oz. | | .2 | | | 0 |
|   Raw, without seeds | 4 oz. | | .2 | | | 0 |
|   Canned, chili sauce | 1 oz. | | <.1 | | | 0 |
|   Canned, pods, without seeds, | | | | | | |
|     solids & liq. | 4 oz. | | 1.1 | | | 0 |
| Red: | | | | | | |
|   Raw, whole (USDA) | 4 oz. (weighed with seeds) | | 2.6 | | | 0 |
|   Raw, trimmed, pods only (USDA) | 4 oz. | 21 | 3.2 | | | 0 |
|   Canned, chili sauce (USDA) | 1 oz. | | .2 | | | 0 |
|   Canned, solids & liq. (Del | | | | | | |
|     Monte) | ¼ cup | 554 | .3 | | | 0 |
|   Canned, drained (Ortega) | ¼ cup (1.8 oz.) | 42 | .1 | | | (0) |

(USDA): United States Department of Agriculture
*Prepared as Package Directs
[1]Principal sources of fat: pecans, lard & egg.
[2]Principal sources of fat: pecans, vegetable shortening & egg.

| Food and Description | Measure or Quantity | Sodium (mg.) | —Fats in grams— | | | Choles-terol (mg.) |
|---|---|---|---|---|---|---|
| | | | Total | Satu-rated | Unsatu-rated | |
| Dried: | | | | | | |
| Pods (USDA) | 1 oz. | 106 | 2.6 | | | 0 |
| Pods (Chili Products) | 1 oz. | | 2.5 | | | (0) |
| Powder with added seasoning (USDA) | 1 T. (.5 oz.) | 236 | 1.9 | | | 0 |
| *PEPPER POT SOUP, canned (Campbell) | 1 cup | 1093 | 3.6 | 1. | 2. | |
| PEPPER, STUFFED: | | | | | | |
| Home recipe, with beef & crumbs (USDA)[1] | 2¾" x 2½" pepper with 1⅛ cups stuffing (6.5 oz.) | 5881 | 10.2 | 6. | 5. | 56 |
| Frozen, with veal (Weight Watchers) | 12-oz. dinner | 1123 | 6.8 | | | |
| PEPPER, SWEET: | | | | | | |
| Green: | | | | | | |
| Raw, whole (USDA) | 1 lb. (weighed untrimmed) | 48 | .7 | | | 0 |
| Raw, without stem & seeds: | | | | | | |
| (USDA) | 1 med. pepper (2.6 oz.) | 8 | .1 | | | 0 |
| Chopped (USDA) | ½ cup (2.6 oz.) | 10 | .2 | | | 0 |
| Slices (USDA) | ½ cup (1.4 oz.) | 5 | .1 | | | 0 |
| Strips (USDA) | ½ cup (1.7 oz.) | 6 | .1 | | | 0 |
| Boiled without salt, drained, (USDA) | 1 med. pepper (2.6 oz.) | 7 | .1 | | | 0 |
| Boiled without salt, strips, drained (USDA) | ½ cup (2.4 oz.) | 6 | .1 | | | 0 |
| Red (USDA): | | | | | | |
| Raw, whole | 1 lb. (weighed with stems & seeds) | | 1.1 | | | 0 |
| Raw, without stem & seeds | 1 med. pepper (2.2 oz.) | | .2 | | | 0 |
| PEPPERMINT, dry (Spice Islands) | 1 tsp. | 3 | | | | (0) |
| PEPPERMINT PIE, pink, frozen (Kraft) | ¼ of 13-oz. pie (3.2 oz.) | 69 | 17.6 | | | |

(USDA): United States Department of Agriculture
*Prepared as Package Directs
[1]Principal sources of fat: beef, butter, bread & milk.

| Food and Description | Measure or Quantity | Sodium (mg.) | —Fats in grams— Total | Satu-rated | Unsatu-rated | Choles-terol (mg.) |
|---|---|---|---|---|---|---|
| **PEPPERONI** (Hormel) | 1 oz. | 425 | 13.0 | | | |
| | | | | | | |
| **PERCH:** | | | | | | |
| Raw (USDA): | | | | | | |
| White, whole | 1 lb. (weighed whole) | | 6.5 | | | |
| White, meat only | 4 oz. | | 4.5 | | | |
| Yellow, whole | 1 lb. (weighed whole) | 120 | 1.6 | | | |
| Yellow, meat only | 4 oz. | 77 | 1.0 | | | |
| Frozen, breaded (Gorton) | ⅓ of 11-oz. pkg. | 63 | 1.1 | | | |
| | | | | | | |
| **PERSIMMON** (USDA): | | | | | | |
| Japanese or Kaki, fresh: | | | | | | |
| With seeds | 1 lb. (weighed with skin, calyx & seeds) | 22 | 1.5 | | | 0 |
| With seeds | 4.4-oz. persimmon | 6 | .4 | | | 0 |
| Seedless | 1 lb. (weighed with skin & calyx) | 23 | 1.5 | | | 0 |
| Seedless | 4.4-oz. persimmon | 6 | .4 | | | 0 |
| Native, fresh, whole | 1 lb. (weighed with seeds & calyx) | 4 | 1.5 | | | 0 |
| Native, fresh, flesh only | 4 oz. | 1 | .5 | | | 0 |
| | | | | | | |
| **PETITE MARMITE SOUP,** | | | | | | |
| canned (Crosse & Blackwell) | 6½ oz. (½ can) | | .7 | | | |
| | | | | | | |
| ***PETTIJOHNS*** (Quaker) | | | | | | |
| rolled whole wheat | ⅔ cup (1 oz. dry) | <1 | .6 | | | (0) |
| | | | | | | |
| **PHEASANT,** raw (USDA): | | | | | | |
| Ready-to-cook | 1 lb. (weighed with bones) | | 20.5 | | | |
| Meat & skin | 4 oz. | | 5.9 | | | |
| Meat only | 4 oz. | | 7.7 | | | |
| Giblets | 2 oz. | | 2.8 | | | |
| | | | | | | |
| **PICKEREL,** chain, raw (USDA): | | | | | | |
| Whole | 1 lb. (weighed whole) | | 1.2 | | | |
| Meat only | 4 oz. | | .6 | | | |

(USDA): United States Department of Agriculture
*Prepared as Package Directs

| Food and Description | Measure or Quantity | Sodium (mg.) | — Fats in grams — | | | Choles- terol (mg.) |
|---|---|---|---|---|---|---|
| | | | Total | Satu- rated | Unsatu- rated | |

**PICKLE:**

Chow chow (See **CHOW CHOW**)

Cucumber, fresh or bread & butter:

| | | | | | | |
|---|---|---|---|---|---|---|
| (USDA) | ½ cup (3 oz.) | 572 | .2 | | | 0 |
| (USDA) | 3 slices (¼" x 1½", .7 oz.) | 141 | <.1 | | | 0 |
| (Aunt Jane's) | 4 slices or sticks (1 oz.) | 191 | <.1 | | | (0) |
| (Aunt Jane's) | 1 spear (1 oz.) | 280 | | | | (0) |
| (Del Monte) | 3 med. pieces (.9 oz.) | 345 | <.1 | | | 0 |
| (Fanning's) | 14-fl.-oz. bottle | 2231 | .4 | | | 0 |
| (Heinz) | 3 slices | 160 | Tr. | | | (0) |

Dill:

| | | | | | | |
|---|---|---|---|---|---|---|
| (USDA) | 4" x 1¾" pickle (4.8 oz.) | 1928 | .3 | | | 0 |
| (USDA) | 3¾" x 1¼" pickle (2.3 oz.) | 928 | .1 | | | 0 |
| (Aunt Jane's) | 1 pickle (2 oz.) | 811 | .1 | | | (0) |
| (Del Monte) | 1 large pickle (3.5 oz.) | 1940 | .i | | | 0 |
| (Heinz) | 4" pickle | 1207 | .1 | | | (0) |
| Processed (Heinz) | 3" pickle | 511 | .1 | | | (0) |
| (Smucker's) baby, fresh pack | 2¾" pickle (.8 oz.) | 283 | Tr. | | | (0) |
| Dill, candied sticks (Smucker's) | 4" pickle (.8 oz.) | 182 | Tr. | | | (0) |
| Dill, hamburger (Heinz) | 3 slices | 245 | Tr. | | | (0) |
| Dill, hamburger (Smucker's) | 3 slices (.4 oz.) | 141 | Tr. | | | (0) |
| Hot, mixed (Smucker's) | 4 pieces (.7 oz.) | 290 | Tr. | | | (0) |
| Hot peppers (Smucker's) | 4" pepper (1 oz.) | 401 | Tr. | | | (0) |
| Kosher dill (Smucker's) | 3½" pickle (.5 oz.) | 642 | Tr. | | | (0) |

Sour:

| | | | | | | |
|---|---|---|---|---|---|---|
| Cucumber (USDA) | 1¾" x 4" pickle (4.8 oz.) | 1827 | .3 | | | 0 |
| (Aunt Jane's) | 1 pickle (2 oz.) | 769 | .1 | | | (0) |
| Cucumber (Del Monte) | 1 large pickle (3.5 oz.) | 1490 | .2 | | | 0 |
| (Heinz) | 2" pickle | 166 | Tr. | | | (0) |

Sweet:

Cucumber (USDA):

| | | | | | | |
|---|---|---|---|---|---|---|
| Whole | 1 oz. | | .1 | | | 0 |
| Whole, gherkin | 2½" x ¾" pickle (.5 oz.) | | <.1 | | | 0 |
| Chopped | ½ cup (2.6 oz.) | | .3 | | | 0 |

(USDA): United States Department of Agriculture
*Prepared as Package Directs

| Food and Description | Measure or Quantity | Sodium (mg.) | Fats in grams Total | Satu-rated | Unsatu-rated | Choles-terol (mg.) |
|---|---|---|---|---|---|---|
| Chopped | 1 T. (9 grams) | | <.1 | | | 0 |
| (Aunt Jane's) | 1 pickle (1.5 oz.) | 420 | .2 | | | (0) |
| (Del Monte) | 1 med. pickle (.4 oz.) | 99 | <.1 | | | 0 |
| (Smucker's) | 2½" pickle (.4 oz.) | 119 | Tr. | | | (0) |
| Candied (Borden) | 1 pickle (1.5 oz.) | 420 | .2 | | | (0) |
| Candied, midgets (Smucker's) | 2" pickle (9 grams) | 89 | Tr. | | | (0) |
| Cherry (Del Monte) | ½ cup (1.9 oz.) | 1023 | .6 | | | 0 |
| Chips, fresh pack (Smucker's) | 1 piece (5 grams) | 42 | Tr. | | | (0) |
| Gherkin (Heinz) | 2" pickle | 76 | Tr. | | | (0) |
| Mixed (Heinz) | 3 pieces | 120 | Tr. | | | (0) |
| Mixed (Smucker's) | 1 piece (8 grams) | 82 | Tr. | | | (0) |
| Sticks, fresh pack (Smucker's) | 4" stick (1.1 oz.) | 246 | Tr. | | | (0) |
| Wax, mild (Del Monte) | ½ cup (2.1 oz.) | 1008 | .4 | | | 0 |
| **PICKLING SPICE** (Spice Islands) | 1 tsp. | 1 | | | | (0) |

**PIE** (See individual kinds)

**PIECRUST** (See also **PASTRY SHELL**):

| | | | | | | |
|---|---|---|---|---|---|---|
| Home recipe, baked, 9": | | | | | | |
| Made with lard[1] | 1 crust (6.3 oz.) | 1100 | 60.1 | 23. | 37. | |
| Made with vegetable shortening[2] | 1 crust (6.3 oz.) | 1100 | 60.1 | 14. | 46. | |
| Frozen: | | | | | | |
| (Mrs. Smith's) | 8" shell (5 oz.) | 1130 | 56.7 | | | |
| (Mrs. Smith's) old fashioned | 9" shell (7 oz.) | 1580 | 79.4 | | | |
| (Mrs. Smith's) | 10" shell (8 oz.) | 1810 | 87.9 | | | |

**PIECRUST MIX:**

| | | | | | | |
|---|---|---|---|---|---|---|
| Dry, pkg. or stick (USDA)[2] | 10-oz. pkg. (2 crusts) | 1968 | 92.9 | 20 | 73. | |
| *Prepared with water, baked (USDA)[2] | 4 oz. | 922 | 33.0 | 8. | 25. | |
| *Double crust (Betty Crocker) | 1/6 of 2 crusts | 389 | 21.5 | | | |
| *Graham cracker (Betty Crocker) | 1/6 of crust | 137 | 7.9 | | | |
| *(Flako) | 1/6 of 9" shell | 147 | 7.0 | | | |

**PIE FILLING** (See individual kinds)

**PIGEON** (See **SQUAB**)

(USDA): United States Department of Agriculture
*Prepared as Package Directs
[1]Principal source of fat: lard.
[2]Principal source of fat: vegetable shortening.

248

| Food and Description | Measure or Quantity | Sodium (mg.) | Fats in grams — Total | Satu- rated | Unsatu- rated | Choles- terol (mg.) |
|---|---|---|---|---|---|---|
| **PIGEONPEA** (USDA): | | | | | | |
| Raw, immature seeds in pods | 1 lb. | 9 | 1.1 | | | 0 |
| Dry seeds | 1 lb. | 118 | 6.4 | | | 0 |
| | | | | | | |
| **PIGNOLIA** (See **PINE NUT**) | | | | | | |
| | | | | | | |
| **PIGS FEET,** pickled: | | | | | | |
| (USDA) | 4 oz. | | 16.8 | 6. | 11. | |
| (Hormel) | 1-pt. can (8.6 oz.) | | 37.3 | | | |
| | | | | | | |
| **PIKE,** raw (USDA): | | | | | | |
| Blue, whole | 1 lb. (weighed whole) | | 1.8 | | | |
| Blue, meat only | 4 oz. | | 1.0 | | | |
| Northern, whole | 1 lb. (weighed whole) | | 1.3 | | | |
| Northern, meat only | 4 oz. | | 1.2 | | | |
| Walleye, whole | 1 lb. (weighed whole) | 132 | 3.1 | | | |
| Walleye, meat only | 4 oz. | 58 | 1.4 | | | |
| | | | | | | |
| **PILI NUT** (USDA): | | | | | | |
| In shell | 1 lb. (weighed in shell) | 2 | 58.0 | | | 0 |
| Shelled | 4 oz. | 3 | 80.6 | | | 0 |
| | | | | | | |
| **PIMIENTO,** canned: | | | | | | |
| Solids & liq. (USDA) | 1 med. pod (1.3 oz.) | | .2 | | | 0 |
| Whole pods, slices, pieces (Dromedary) | 1 oz. | 2 | .2 | | | (0) |
| Drained (Ortega) | ¼ cup (1.7 oz.) | 18 | .1 | | | (0) |
| Solids & liq. (Stokely-Van Camp) | ½ cup (4.1 oz.) | | .6 | | | (0) |
| | | | | | | |
| *PINA COLADA* (Party Tyme) | ½-oz. pkg. | 20 | 0. | | | (0) |
| | | | | | | |
| *PINCH of HERBS:* | | | | | | |
| (Lawry's) | 1 pkg. (2.2 oz.) | | 10.3 | | | (0) |
| (Lawry's) | 1 tsp. (3 grams) | | .4 | | | (0) |
| | | | | | | |
| **PINEAPPLE:** | | | | | | |
| Fresh: | | | | | | |
| Whole (USDA) | 1 lb. (weighed untrimmed) | 2 | .5 | | | 0 |

(USDA): United States Department of Agriculture
*Prepared as Package Directs

| Food and Description | Measure or Quantity | Sodium (mg.) | —Fats in grams— Total | Satu- rated | Unsatu- rated | Choles- terol (mg.) |
|---|---|---|---|---|---|---|
| Diced (USDA) | ½ cup (2.8 oz.) | <1 | .2 | | | 0 |
| Slices (USDA) | ¾" x 3½" slice | | | | | |
| | (3 oz.) | <1 | .2 | | | 0 |
| (Del Monte) | ½ cup (2.5 oz.) | <1 | .4 | | | (0) |
| Canned, regular pack, solids & liq.: | | | | | | |
| Juice pack: | | | | | | |
| (USDA) | 4 oz. | 1 | .1 | | | 0 |
| (Del Monte) | ½ cup (4.9 oz.) | 26 | .3 | | | 0 |
| Chunks or crushed (Dole) | ½ cup (includes 2½ | | | | | |
| | T. juice, 3.7 oz.) | 1 | .1 | | | 0 |
| Slices (Dole) | 2 med. slices & 2½ | | | | | |
| | T. juice (3.7 oz.) | 1 | .1 | | | 0 |
| Light syrup (USDA) | 4 oz. | 1 | .1 | | | 0 |
| Heavy syrup: | | | | | | |
| Crushed (USDA) | ½ cup (4.6 oz.) | 1 | .1 | | | 0 |
| Slices (USDA) | ½ cup (4.9 oz.) | 1 | .1 | | | 0 |
| Slices (USDA) | 2 small or 1 large slice & 2 T. syrup | | | | | |
| | (4.3 oz.) | 1 | .1 | | | 0 |
| Tidbits (USDA) | ½ cup (4.6 oz.) | 1 | .1 | | | 0 |
| (Del Monte) | ½ cup (5 oz.) | 14 | .2 | | | 0 |
| Chunks (Dole) | 10 pieces & 2½ | | | | | |
| | T. syrup (4 oz.) | 1 | .1 | | | 0 |
| Crushed or tidbits (Dole) | ½ cup (includes 2½ | | | | | |
| | T. syrup, 4 oz.) | 1 | .1 | | | 0 |
| Slices (Dole) | 2 med. slices & 2½ | | | | | |
| | T. syrup (4 oz.) | 1 | .1 | | | 0 |
| Slices, chunks or crushed (Stokely-Van Camp) | ½ cup (4 oz.) | | .1 | | | (0) |
| Extra heavy syrup (USDA) | 4 oz. | 1 | .1 | | | 0 |
| Canned, unsweetened, low calorie or dietetic, solids & liq.: | | | | | | |
| Water pack, except crushed (USDA) | 4 oz. | 1 | .1 | | | 0 |
| Chunks: | | | | | | |
| (Diet Delight) | ½ cup (4.4 oz.) | 5 | Tr. | | | (0) |
| (S and W) Nutradiet | 4 oz. | 3 | Tr. | | | (0) |
| Crushed (Diet Delight) | ½ cup (4.4 oz.) | 9 | Tr. | | | (0) |
| Slices: | | | | | | |
| (Diet Delight) | ½ cup (4.4 oz.) | 5 | Tr. | | | (0) |
| (S and W) Nutradiet, low calorie | 2½ slices (3.5 oz.) | 3 | Tr. | | | (0) |

(USDA): United States Department of Agriculture
*Prepared as Package Directs

| Food and Description | Measure or Quantity | Sodium (mg.) | —Fats in grams— | | Choles-terol (mg.) |
| | | | Total | Satu-rated | Unsatu-rated | |
|---|---|---|---|---|---|---|
| (S and W) *Nutradiet*, unsweetened | 2½ slices (3.5 oz.) | 2 | .1 | | | (0) |
| Tidbits: | | | | | | |
| (Diet Delight) | ½ cup (4.4 oz.) | 5 | Tr. | | | (0) |
| (S and W) *Nutradiet*, low calorie | 4 oz. | 3 | Tr. | | | (0) |
| (S and W) *Nutradiet*, unsweetened | 4 oz. | 1 | .1 | | | (0) |
| (Tillie Lewis) | ½ cup (4.4 oz.) | <10 | .1 | | | 0 |
| Frozen: | | | | | | |
| Chunks, sweetened, not thawed (USDA) | ½ cup (4.3 oz.) | 2 | .1 | | | 0 |
| Chunks in heavy syrup (Dole) | 11 chunks & 2½ T. syrup (4 oz.) | 2 | .1 | | | 0 |
| **PINEAPPLE-APRICOT JUICE DRINK** (Del Monte) | 1 cup (8.6 oz.) | 25 | .2 | | | (0) |
| **PINEAPPLE CAKE MIX:** | | | | | | |
| *(Betty Crocker) layer | $^1/_{12}$ of cake | 271 | 5.6 | | | |
| *(Duncan Hines) | $^1/_{12}$ of cake (2.7 oz.) | 366 | 6.1 | | | 50 |
| (Pillsbury) | 1 oz. | | | | | |
| **PINEAPPLE, CANDIED** (USDA) | 1 oz. | | .1 | | | 0 |
| **PINEAPPLE-CHERRY JUICE DRINK,** canned (Del Monte) *Merry* | ½ cup (4.3 oz.) | 2 | Tr. | | | |
| **PINEAPPLE & GRAPEFRUIT JUICE DRINK,** canned: | | | | | | |
| (USDA) 40% fruit juices | ½ cup (4.4 oz.) | Tr. | Tr. | | | 0 |
| (Del Monte) | ½ cup (4.3 oz.) | 42 | Tr. | | | 0 |
| (Del Monte) pink | ½ cup (4.3 oz.) | 42 | Tr. | | | 0 |
| (Dole) regular or pink | 6-fl.-oz. can | Tr. | Tr. | | | 0 |
| (Dole) regular or pink | ½ cup (4.3 oz.) | Tr. | Tr. | | | 0 |
| (Hi-C) | ½ cup (4.2 oz.) | 40 | Tr. | | | 0 |
| **PINEAPPLE JUICE:** | | | | | | |
| Canned, unsweetened: | | | | | | |
| (USDA) | ½ cup (4.4 oz.) | 1 | .1 | | | 0 |
| (Del Monte) | ½ cup (4.3 oz.) | 1 | | | | 0 |
| (Dole) | 6-fl.-oz. can | 2 | .2 | | | 0 |

(USDA): United States Department of Agriculture
*Prepared as Package Directs

| Food and Description | Measure or Quantity | Sodium (mg.) | Fats in grams Total | Satu-rated | Unsatu-rated | Choles-terol (mg.) |
|---|---|---|---|---|---|---|
| (Dole) | ½ cup (4.6 oz.) | 1 | .1 | | | 0 |
| (Heinz) | 5½-fl.-oz. can | 3 | .3 | | | (0) |
| (S and W) *Nutradiet* | 4 oz. (by wt.) | 1 | .1 | | | (0) |
| (Stokely-Van Camp) | ½ cup (3.7 oz.) | | .1 | | | (0) |
| Frozen, concentrate: | | | | | | |
| Unsweetened, undiluted (USDA) | 6-fl.-oz. can (7.6 oz.) | 6 | .2 | | | 0 |
| *Unsweetened, diluted with | | | | | | |
| 3 parts water (USDA) | ½ cup (4.4 oz.) | 1 | Tr. | | | 0 |
| Unsweetened, undiluted | | | | | | |
| (Dole) | 6-fl.-oz. can | 7 | .2 | | | 0 |

**PINEAPPLE & ORANGE JUICE**
**DRINK,** canned:

| | | | | | | |
|---|---|---|---|---|---|---|
| (USDA) 40% fruit juices | ½ cup (4.4 oz.) | Tr. | .1 | | | 0 |
| (Del Monte) | ½ cup (4.3 oz.) | 22 | Tr. | | | 0 |

**PINEAPPLE-PEAR JUICE**
**DRINK,** canned (Del Monte)

| | | | | | | |
|---|---|---|---|---|---|---|
| | ½ cup (4.3 oz.) | 26 | Tr. | | | (0) |

**PINEAPPLE PIE:**
Home recipe, 2-crust (USDA):

| | | | | | | |
|---|---|---|---|---|---|---|
| Made with lard[1] | 1/6 of 9″ pie (5.6 oz.) | 271 | 16.9 | 5. | 12. | |
| Made with vegetable shortening[2] | 1/6 of 9″ pie (5.6 oz.) | 428 | 16.9 | 5. | 12. | |
| Chiffon, 1-crust: | | | | | | |
| Made with lard[3] | 1/6 of 9″ pie (3.8 oz.) | 276 | 13.1 | 4. | 9. | |
| Made with vegetable shortening[4] | 1/6 of 9″ pie (3.8 oz.) | 276 | 13.1 | 3. | 10. | |
| Custard, 1-crust: | | | | | | |
| Made with lard[5] | 1/6 of 9″ pie (5.4 oz.) | 283 | 13.2 | 5. | 9. | |
| Made with vegetable shortening[6] | 1/6 of 9″ pie (5.4 oz.) | 283 | 13.2 | 3. | 10. | |
| (Tastykake) | 4-oz. pie | | 15.6 | | | |
| With cheese (Tastykake) | 4-oz. pie | | 20.3 | | | |
| Frozen (Morton) | 1/8 of 46-oz. pie | 315 | 16.4 | | | |

**PINEAPPLE PIE FILLING,** canned:

| | | | | | | |
|---|---|---|---|---|---|---|
| (Comstock) | ½ cup (5.4 oz.) | 1 | <.1 | | | |
| (Lucky Leaf) | 8 oz. | 134 | .2 | | | |

(USDA): United States Department of Agriculture
*Prepared as Package Directs
[1]Principal sources of fat: lard & butter.
[2]Principal sources of fat: vegetable shortening & butter.
[3]Principal sources of fat: lard & cream.
[4]Principal sources of fat: vegetable shortening & cream.
[5]Principal sources of fat: lard, egg & milk.
[6]Principal sources of fat: vegetable shortening, egg & milk.

| Food and Description | Measure or Quantity | Sodium (mg.) | Fats in grams — Total | Satu- rated | Unsatu- rated | Choles- terol (mg.) |
|---|---|---|---|---|---|---|
| **\*PINEAPPLE PUDDING MIX, CREAM,** instant (Jell-O) | ½ cup (5.3 oz.) | 406 | 4.7 | | | 13 |
| **PINEAPPLE PRESERVE:** | | | | | | |
| Sweetened (Bama) | 1 T. (.7 oz.) | 1 | <.1 | | | (0) |
| Low calorie (Tillie Lewis) | 1 T. (.5 oz.) | 3 | Tr. | | | 0 |
| **PINEAPPLE SOFT DRINK,** sweetened: | | | | | | |
| (Hoffman) | 6 fl. oz. | 14 | 0. | | | 0 |
| (Kirsch) | 6 fl. oz. | <1 | 0. | | | 0 |
| (Nedick's) | 6 fl. oz. | 14 | 0. | | | 0 |
| **PINE NUT** (USDA): | | | | | | |
| Pignolias, shelled | 4 oz. | | 53.8 | | | 0 |
| Piñon, whole | 4 oz. (weighed in shell) | | 39.8 | | | 0 |
| Piñon, shelled | 4 oz. | | 68.6 | | | 0 |
| *PINK PANTHER FLAKES,* cereal (Post) | ⅔ cup (1 oz.) | 209 | .1 | | | 0 |
| **PISTACHIO NUT:** | | | | | | |
| In shell (USDA) | 4 oz. (weighed in shell) | | 30.4 | 3. | 27. | 0 |
| In shell (USDA) | ½ cup (2.3 oz.) | | 17.8 | 2. | 16. | 0 |
| Shelled (USDA) | ½ cup (2.2 oz.) | | 33.3 | 3. | 30. | 0 |
| Shelled (USDA) | 1 T. (8 grams) | | 4.2 | Tr. | 4. | 0 |
| Dry, roasted, salted (Flavor House) | 1 oz. | 32 | 15.2 | | | (0) |
| **\*PISTACHIO NUT PUDDING MIX,** instant (Royal) | ½ cup (5.1 oz.) | 350 | 4.8 | | | 14 |
| **PITANGA,** fresh (USDA): | | | | | | |
| Whole | 1 lb. (weighed whole) | | 1.5 | | | 0 |
| Flesh only | 4 oz. | | .5 | | | 0 |
| **PIZZA PIE:** | | | | | | |
| Home recipe, with cheese topping: | | | | | | |
| (USDA)[1] | 4 oz. | 796 | 9.4 | 3. | 6. | |
| (USDA)[1] | 5½" sector (⅛ of 14" pie, 2.6 oz.) | 527 | 6.2 | 2. | 4. | |

(USDA): United States Department of Agriculture
\*Prepared as Package Directs
[1]Principal sources of fat: cheese, vegetable shortening & olive oil.

| Food and Description | Measure or Quantity | Sodium (mg.) | Fats in grams — Total | Satu- rated | Unsatu- rated | Choles- terol (mg.) |
|---|---|---|---|---|---|---|
| Home recipe, with sausage topping: | | | | | | |
| (USDA)[1] | 4 oz. | 827 | 10.5 | 3. | 7. | |
| (USDA)[1] | 5½" sector (⅛ of 14" pie, 2.6 oz.) | 547 | 7.0 | 2. | 5. | |
| Chilled, partially baked (USDA)[2] | 4 oz. | 610 | 6.6 | 2. | 4. | |
| Chilled, baked (USDA)[2] | 4 oz. | 718 | 7.7 | 2. | 5. | |
| Frozen: | | | | | | |
| Partially baked (USDA)[2] | 4 oz. | 686 | 7.5 | 2. | 5. | |
| Baked (USDA)[2] | 4 oz. | 734 | 8.1 | 2. | 6. | |
| Baked (USDA)[2] | ⅛ of 14" pie (2.6 oz.) | 485 | 5.3 | 2. | 4. | |
| (Celeste) Bambino | 10-oz. pie | 1560 | 28.8 | | | |
| With cheese (Buitoni) | 4 oz. | | 8.9 | | | |
| With cheese (Celeste) | 20-oz. pie | 3280 | 50.4 | | | |
| With cheese (Chef Boy-Ar-Dee) | ⅙ of 12½" pie (2.1 oz.) | 161 | 4.2 | | | |
| With cheese, little (Chef Boy-Ar-Dee) | 1 pie (2½ oz.) | 373 | 5.1 | | | |
| With cheese (Jeno's) | 13-oz. pie | | 28.4 | | | |
| With cheese (Jeno's) Serv-A-Slice | 1 slice (1.7 oz.) | | 4.6 | | | |
| With cheese (Jeno's) snack tray | ½-oz. pizza | | .5 | | | |
| With cheese (Kraft) | 14-oz. pie | 2596 | 29.4 | | | |
| With cheese, Pee Wee (Kraft) | 2½-oz. pie | 484 | 6.5 | | | |
| With hamburger (Jeno's) | 13½-oz. pie | | 28.3 | | | |
| With pepperoni (Buitoni) | 4 oz. | | 10.5 | | | |
| With pepperoni (Chef Boy-Ar-Dee) | ⅙ of 14-oz. pie | 271 | 6.0 | | | |
| With pepperoni (Jeno's) | 13¼-oz. pie | | 45.8 | | | |
| With pepperoni (Jeno's) Serv-A-Slice | 1 slice (1.8 oz.) | | 6.6 | | | |
| With pepperoni (Jeno's) snack tray | ½-oz. pizza | | 1.3 | | | |
| With sausage (Buitoni) | 4 oz. | | 10.1 | | | |
| With sausage (Celeste) | 23-oz. pie | 3880 | 78.4 | | | |
| With sausage (Celeste) Bambino | 9-oz. pie | 1340 | 27.6 | | | |
| With sausage (Chef Boy-Ar-Dee) | ⅙ of 13¼-oz. pie | 159 | 5.1 | | | |
| With sausage, little (Chef Boy-Ar-Dee) | 2½-oz. pie | 387 | 5.4 | | | |

(USDA): United States Department of Agriculture
*Prepared as Package Directs
[1]Principal sources of fat: sausage, vegetable shortening & olive oil.
[2]Principal sources of fat: cheese, vegetable shortening & olive oil.

| Food and Description | Measure or Quantity | Sodium (mg.) | Fats in grams — Total | Satu- rated | Unsatu- rated | Choles- terol (mg.) |
|---|---|---|---|---|---|---|
| With sausage (Jeno's) | 13½-oz. pie | | 28.3 | | | |
| With sausage (Jeno's) Serv-A-Slice | 1 slice (2 oz.) | | 5.2 | | | |
| With sausage (Jeno's) snack tray | ½-oz. pizza | | 1.1 | | | |
| With sausage (Kraft) | 14½-oz. pie | 2852 | 47.7 | | | |
| With sausage, *Pee Wee* (Kraft) | 2½-oz. pie | 365 | 9.2 | | | |
| **PIZZA PIE MIX:** | | | | | | |
| *With cheese (Chef Boy-Ar-Dee) | ⅕ of 15½-oz. pie | 548 | 5.4 | | | |
| *With cheese (Kraft) | 4 oz. | 1293 | 10.8 | | | |
| *With sausage (Chef Boy-Ar-Dee) | ⅕ of 17-oz. pie | 695 | 7.8 | | | |
| *With sausage (Kraft) | 4 oz. | 1182 | 12.2 | | | |
| **PIZZA ROLL,** frozen (Jeno's): | | | | | | |
| Cheeseburger, 12 to pkg. | ½-oz. roll | | 2.1 | | | |
| Pepperoni, 12 to pkg. | ½-oz. roll | | 1.8 | | | |
| Sausage, 12 to pkg. | ½-oz. roll | | 2.0 | | | |
| Shrimp, 12 to pkg. | ½-oz. roll | | 1.5 | | | |
| Snack tray: | | | | | | |
| Hamburger | ½-oz. roll | | 2.0 | | | |
| Pepperoni | ½-oz. roll | | 1.8 | | | |
| Sausage | ½-oz. roll | | 2.0 | | | |
| **PIZZA SAUCE:** | | | | | | |
| Canned (Buitoni) | 4 oz. | | 2.9 | | | |
| Canned (Chef Boy-Ar-Dee) | ½ of 10½-oz. can | 987 | 8.5 | | | |
| Canned (Contadina) | 1 cup | 1064 | 4.0 | | | |
| Mix (French's) | 1-oz. pkg. | 1790 | .1 | | | |
| *Mix (French's) | 2 T. | 155 | .1 | | | |
| **PIZZA SEASONING** (French's) | 1 tsp. (4 grams) | 390 | .1 | | | (0) |
| **PIZZARIA MIX** (Hunt's) *Skillet*[1] | 14.1-oz. pkg. | 2844 | 11.1 | 7. | 4. | |
| **PLANTAIN,** raw (USDA): | | | | | | |
| Whole | 1 lb. (weighed with skin) | 16 | 1.3 | | | 0 |
| Flesh only | 4 oz. | 6 | .5 | | | 0 |
| **PLUM:** | | | | | | |
| Damson, fresh (USDA): | | | | | | |
| Whole | 1 lb. (weighed with pits) | 8 | Tr. | | | 0 |

(USDA): United States Department of Agriculture
*Prepared as Package Directs
[1]Principal sources of fat: cheese & egg.

| Food and Description | Measure or Quantity | Sodium (mg.) | Fats in grams — Total | Satu-rated | Unsatu-rated | Choles-terol (mg.) |
|---|---|---|---|---|---|---|
| Flesh only | 4 oz. | 2 | Tr. | | | 0 |
| Japanese & hybrid, fresh (USDA): | | | | | | |
| Whole | 1 lb. (weighed with pits) | 4 | .9 | | | 0 |
| Whole | 2″ plum (2.1 oz.) | <1 | .1 | | | 0 |
| Diced | ½ cup (2.3 oz.) | <1 | .2 | | | 0 |
| Halves | ½ cup (3.1 oz.) | <1 | .2 | | | 0 |
| Slices | ½ cup (3 oz.) | <1 | .2 | | | 0 |
| Prune-type, fresh (USDA): | | | | | | |
| Whole | 1 lb. (weighed with pits) | 4 | .9 | | | 0 |
| Halves | ½ cup (2.8 oz.) | <1 | .2 | | | 0 |
| Canned, purple, regular pack, solids & liq.: | | | | | | |
| Light syrup (USDA) | 4 oz. | 1 | .1 | | | 0 |
| Heavy syrup (USDA) | ½ cup (with pits, 4.5 oz.) | 1 | .1 | | | 0 |
| Heavy syrup (USDA) | ½ cup (without pits, 4.2 oz.) | 1 | .1 | | | 0 |
| Heavy syrup (USDA) | 3 plums without pits & 2 T. syrup (4.3 oz.) | 1 | .1 | | | 0 |
| Heavy syrup (Del Monte) | ½ cup (4.1 oz.) | 6 | .1 | | | 0 |
| Extra heavy syrup (USDA) | 4 oz. | 1 | .1 | | | 0 |
| (Stokely-Van Camp) | ½ cup (4.2 oz.) | | .1 | | | (0) |
| Canned, unsweetened or low calorie, solids & liq.: | | | | | | |
| Greengage, water pack (USDA) | 4 oz. | 1 | .1 | | | 0 |
| Purple: | | | | | | |
| Water pack (USDA) | 4 oz. | 2 | .2 | | | 0 |
| (Diet Delight) | ½ cup (4.4 oz.) | 4 | <.1 | | | (0) |
| (S and W) *Nutradiet* | 4 oz. | 2 | .1 | | | (0) |
| (Tillie Lewis) | ½ cup (4.5 oz.) | <10 | .2 | | | (0) |
| **PLUM PIE** (Tastykake) | 4-oz. pie | | 15.0 | | | |
| **PLUM PRESERVE or JAM,** sweetened, Damson or red (Bama) | 1 T. (.7 oz.) | 2 | <.1 | | | (0) |
| **PLUM PUDDING:** | | | | | | |
| (Crosse & Blackwell) | 4 oz. | | 1.0 | | | |
| (Richardson & Robbins) | ½ cup (4 oz.) | 173 | 1.4 | | | |
| *P.M.,* fruit juice drink | | | | | | |
| (Mott's) | ½ cup | | .1 | | | (0) |

(USDA): United States Department of Agriculture
*Prepared as Package Directs

| Food and Description | Measure or Quantity | Sodium (mg.) | —Fats in grams— | | | Choles-terol (mg.) |
|---|---|---|---|---|---|---|
| | | | Total | Satu-rated | Unsatu-rated | |

**POHA** (See **GROUND-CHERRY**)

**POKE SHOOTS** (USDA):
| | | | | | | |
|---|---|---|---|---|---|---|
| Raw | 1 lb. | | 1.8 | | | 0 |
| Boiled, drained | 4 oz. | | .5 | | | 0 |

**POLISH-STYLE SAUSAGE:**
| | | | | | | |
|---|---|---|---|---|---|---|
| (USDA) | 1 oz. | | 7.3 | | | |
| (Oscar Mayer) all meat | 1 oz. (from 8-oz. link) | 221 | 6.8 | | | |
| Kolbase (Hormel) | 1 oz. | 315 | 6.9 | 3. | 4. | 17 |

**POLLOCK** (USDA):
| | | | | | | |
|---|---|---|---|---|---|---|
| Raw, drawn | 1 lb. (weighed with head, tail, fins & bones) | 98 | 1.8 | | | |
| Raw, meat only | 4 oz. | 5.4 | 1.0 | | | |
| Creamed[1] | 4 oz. | 126 | 6.7 | | | |

**POLYNESIAN-STYLE DINNER,**
| | | | | | | |
|---|---|---|---|---|---|---|
| frozen (Swanson) | 11¾-oz. dinner | 1490 | 20.0 | | | |

**POMEGRANATE,** raw (USDA):
| | | | | | | |
|---|---|---|---|---|---|---|
| Whole | 1 lb. (weighed whole) | 8 | .8 | | | 0 |
| Pulp only | 4 oz. | 3 | .3 | | | 0 |

**POMPANO,** raw (USDA):
| | | | | | | |
|---|---|---|---|---|---|---|
| Whole | 1 lb. (weighed whole) | 119 | 24.1 | | | |
| Meat only | 4 oz. | 53 | 10.8 | | | |

**POPCORN:**
| | | | | | | |
|---|---|---|---|---|---|---|
| Unpopped (USDA) | 1 oz. | <1 | 1.3 | Tr. | 1. | 0 |
| Popped (USDA): | | | | | | |
| Plain, large kernel | 1 oz. | <1 | 1.4 | Tr. | 1. | 0 |
| Plain, large kernel | 1 cup (6 grams) | <1 | .3 | Tr. | Tr. | 0 |
| Butter & salt added[2] | 1 oz. | 550 | 6.2 | 3. | 3. | |
| Butter & salt added[2] | 1 cup (9 grams) | 175 | 2.0 | <1. | 1. | |
| Coconut oil & salt added[3] | 1 oz. | 550 | 6.2 | 4. | 2. | |
| Coconut oil & salt added[3] | 1 cup (9 grams) | 175 | 2.0 | 1. | <1. | |

(USDA): United States Department of Agriculture
*Prepared as Package Directs
[1]Prepared with flour, butter & milk.
[2]Principal source of fat: butter.
[3]Principal source of fat: coconut oil.

| Food and Description | Measure or Quantity | Sodium (mg.) | —Fats in grams— | | | Cholesterol (mg.) |
|---|---|---|---|---|---|---|
| | | | Total | Saturated | Unsaturated | |
| Sugar-coated, without salt[1] | 1 oz. | <1 | 1.0 | Tr. | <1. | |
| Sugar-coated, without salt[1] | 1 cup (1.2 oz.) | <1 | 1.2 | Tr. | <1. | |
| (Jiffy Pop) | ½ pkg. (2½ oz.) | 936 | 11.6 | | | |
| (Tom Houston) | 1 cup (.5 oz.) | 291 | 3.3 | | | |
| Buttered (Jiffy Pop) | ½ pkg. (2½ oz.) | 936 | 12.2 | | | |
| Buttered (Wise) | 1-oz. bag | 235 | 7.1 | | | |
| Caramel-coated: | | | | | | |
| Without peanuts (Old London) | 1¾-oz. bag | 372 | 1.6 | | | |
| With peanuts (Old London) | 1 cup (1.3 oz.) | 258 | 1.6 | | | |
| *Cracker Jack*[2] | ¾-oz. bag | | 2.0 | | | |
| *Cracker Jack*[2] | 1⅜-oz. box | | 3.6 | | | |
| Cheese (Old London) | ¾-oz. bag | 102 | 6.3 | | | |
| Cheese (Wise) | ⅝-oz. bag | 167 | 5.2 | | | |
| Seasoned (Old London) | 1¼-oz. bag | 69 | 8.6 | | | |

**POPOVER:**

| Food and Description | Measure or Quantity | Sodium (mg.) | Total | Saturated | Unsaturated | Cholesterol (mg.) |
|---|---|---|---|---|---|---|
| Home recipe (USDA)[3] | 1.4-oz. popover (2¾" dia. at top, ¼ cup batter) | 88 | 3.7 | 1. | 2. | 59 |
| *Mix (Flako) | 2.3-oz. popover (¹/₆ of pkg.) | 300 | 4.8 | | | |

**POPPY SEED** (Spice Islands)

| Food and Description | Measure or Quantity | Sodium (mg.) | Total | Saturated | Unsaturated | Cholesterol (mg.) |
|---|---|---|---|---|---|---|
| POPPY SEED (Spice Islands) | 1 tsp. | <1 | | | | (0) |

***POPSICLE***, fruit flavors

| Food and Description | Measure or Quantity | Sodium (mg.) | Total | Saturated | Unsaturated | Cholesterol (mg.) |
|---|---|---|---|---|---|---|
| (Popsicle Industries) | 3-fl.-oz. bar (3.4 oz.) | 7 | 0. | | | (0) |

**POP-UP** (See **TOASTER CAKE**)

**PORGY,** raw (USDA):

| Food and Description | Measure or Quantity | Sodium (mg.) | Total | Saturated | Unsaturated | Cholesterol (mg.) |
|---|---|---|---|---|---|---|
| Whole | 1 lb. (weighed whole) | 117 | 6.3 | | | |
| Meat only | 4 oz. | 71 | 3.9 | | | |

**PORK,** medium-fat:
Fresh (USDA):
All lean cuts:
Lean only:

| Food and Description | Measure or Quantity | Sodium (mg.) | Total | Saturated | Unsaturated | Cholesterol (mg.) |
|---|---|---|---|---|---|---|
| Raw, diced | 1 cup (8.2 oz.) | 667 | 26.4 | 10. | 17. | 140 |
| Raw, strips | 1 cup (8.2 oz.) | 664 | 26.3 | 10. | 17. | 140 |
| Roasted, chopped | 1 cup (5 oz.) | 554 | 20.0 | 7. | 13. | 125 |

(USDA): United States Department of Agriculture
*Prepared as Package Directs
[1]Principal source of fat: coconut oil.
[2]Principal sources of fat: corn & peanut oil.
[3]Principal sources of fat: vegetable shortening, egg & milk.

| Food and Description | Measure or Quantity | Sodium (mg.) | Total | —Fats in grams— Satu- rated | Unsatu- rated | Choles- terol (mg.) |
|---|---|---|---|---|---|---|
| Boston butt: | | | | | | |
| Raw | 1 lb. (weighed with bone & skin) | 260 | 104.1 | 37. | 67. | 264 |
| Roasted, lean & fat | 4 oz. | 74 | 32.3 | 11. | 21. | 101 |
| Roasted, lean only | 4 oz. | 74 | 16.2 | 6. | 10. | 100 |
| Chop: | | | | | | |
| Broiled, lean & fat | 4-oz. chop (weighed with bone) | 49 | 23.9 | 8. | 16. | 67 |
| Broiled, lean & fat | 3-oz. chop (weighed without bone) | 55 | 26.9 | 9. | 18. | 76 |
| Broiled, lean only | 3-oz. chop (weighed without bone) | 55 | 13.1 | 5. | 8. | 75 |
| Fat, separable, cooked | 1 oz. | | 23.6 | 9. | 15. | |
| Ham (See also **HAM**): | | | | | | |
| Raw | 1 lb. (weighed with bone & skin) | 320 | 102.6 | 37. | 66. | 239 |
| Roasted, lean & fat | 4 oz. | 74 | 34.7 | 12. | 22. | 101 |
| Roasted, lean only | 4 oz. | 74 | 11.3 | 5. | 7. | 100 |
| Loin: | | | | | | |
| Raw | 1 lb. (weighed with bone) | 260 | 89.0 | 32. | 57. | 221 |
| Broiled, lean & fat | 4 oz. | 74 | 35.9 | 12. | 24. | 101 |
| Broiled, lean only | 4 oz. | 74 | 17.5 | 7. | 11. | 100 |
| Roasted, lean & fat | 4 oz. | 74 | 32.3 | 11. | 21. | 101 |
| Roasted, lean only | 4 oz. | 74 | 16.1 | 6. | 10. | 100 |
| Picnic: | | | | | | |
| Raw | 1 lb. (weighed with bone & skin) | 260 | 92.2 | 33. | 59. | 231 |
| Simmered, lean & fat | 4 oz. | 74 | 34.6 | 12. | 22. | 101 |
| Simmered, lean only | 4 oz. | 74 | 11.1 | 5. | 7. | 100 |
| Spareribs: | | | | | | |
| Raw, with bone | 1 lb. (weighed with bone) | 775 | 89.7 | 32. | 58. | 169 |
| Raw, without bone | 1 lb. (weighed without bone) | 1295 | 150.6 | 54. | 97. | 281 |
| Braised, lean & fat | 4 oz. | 74 | 44.1 | 16. | 28. | 101 |
| Cured, light commercial cure: | | | | | | |
| Bacon (see **BACON**) | | | | | | |
| Boston butt (USDA): | | | | | | |
| Raw | 1 lb. (weighed with bone & skin) | | 101.7 | 37. | 65. | |
| Roasted, lean & fat | 4 oz. | | 29.1 | 10. | 19. | |
| Roasted, lean only | 4 oz. | 1055 | 15.6 | 7. | 9. | |

(USDA): United States Department of Agriculture
*Prepared as Package Directs

| Food and Description | Measure or Quantity | Sodium (mg.) | Total | Fats in grams — Satu-rated | Fats in grams — Unsatu-rated | Choles-terol (mg.) |
|---|---|---|---|---|---|---|
| Smoked, Tasty Meat | | | | | | |
| (Wilson) | 4 oz. | 1174 | 25.4 | 11. | 15. | 70 |
| Ham (See also **HAM**): | | | | | | |
| Raw (USDA) | 1 lb. (weighed with bone & skin) | | 89.7 | 32. | 58. | |
| Raw, lean only, ground | | | | | | |
| (USDA) | 1 cup (6 oz.) | 1870 | 14.4 | 5. | 9. | |
| Roasted, lean & fat (USDA) | 4 oz. | | 25.1 | 9. | 16. | |
| Roasted, lean only: | | | | | | |
| (USDA) | 4 oz. | 1055 | 10.0 | 3. | 7. | |
| Chopped (USDA) | 1 cup (4.9 oz.) | 1283 | 12.1 | 4. | 8. | |
| Diced (USDA) | 1 cup (5.2 oz.) | 1367 | 12.9 | 4. | 9. | |
| Ground (USDA) | 1 cup (3.8 oz.) | 1014 | 9.6 | 3. | 6. | |
| Fully cooked, bone-in (Hormel) | 4 oz. | 1361 | 15.3 | | | |
| Fully cooked, boneless: | | | | | | |
| Parti-Style (Armour Star) | 4 oz. | | 8.3 | | | |
| *Cure 81* (Hormel) | 4 oz. | 953 | 11.9 | | | |
| *Curemaster* (Hormel) | 4 oz. | 1361 | 5.0 | | | |
| (Wilson) Certified, rolled | 4 oz. | 1145 | 15.8 | 7. | 9. | 70 |
| (Wilson) Festival, smoked | 4 oz. | 1281 | 11.1 | 4. | 7. | 70 |
| Picnic: | | | | | | |
| Raw (USDA) | 1 lb. (weighed with bone & skin) | | 87.8 | 32. | 56. | |
| Raw (Wilson) smoked | 4 oz. | 1247 | 24.4 | 10. | 15. | 70 |
| Roasted, lean & fat (USDA) | 4 oz. | | 28.6 | 10. | 18. | |
| Roasted, lean only (USDA) | 4 oz. | 1055 | 11.2 | 5. | 7. | |
| Canned (Hormel) | 4 oz. (3-lb. can) | | 14.5 | | | |
| | | | | | | |
| **PORK, CANNED,** chopped | | | | | | |
| luncheon meat: | | | | | | |
| (USDA)[1] | 1 oz. | 350 | 7.1 | 3. | 5. | |
| Chopped (USDA)[1] | 1 cup (4.8 oz.) | 1678 | 33.9 | 12. | 22. | |
| Diced (USDA)[1] | 1 cup (5 oz.) | 1740 | 35.1 | 13. | 22. | |
| (Hormel) | 1 oz. (8-lb. can) | | 5.8 | | | |
| | | | | | | |
| **PORK DINNER,** loin of pork, | | | | | | |
| frozen (Swanson) | 10-oz. dinner | 820 | 21.9 | 6. | 15. | |
| | | | | | | |
| **PORK, FREEZE DRY,** | | | | | | |
| canned (Wilson) *Campsite:* | | | | | | |
| Chop, dry | 2-oz. can | 874 | 17.1 | 6. | 11. | 146 |

(USDA): United States Department of Agriculture
*Prepared as Package Directs
[1]Principal source of fat: pork.

| Food and Description | Measure or Quantity | Sodium (mg.) | —Fats in grams— | | | Choles- terol (mg.) |
|---|---|---|---|---|---|---|
| | | | Total | Satu- rated | Unsatu- rated | |
| *Chop, reconstituted | 4 oz. | 695 | 13.8 | 5. | 9. | 119 |
| Patties, dry | 2-oz. can | 1413 | 18.7 | 7. | 12. | 146 |
| *Patties, reconstituted | 4 oz. | 1174 | 15.2 | 6. | 10. | 119 |
| **PORK & GRAVY,** 90% pork, canned(USDA) | 4 oz. | | 20.2 | 7. | 13. | |
| **PORK LOIN** (Oscar Mayer) thin sliced | 1 slice (16 to 3 oz.) | 58 | .7 | | | |
| **PORK RINDS,** fried, *Baken · ets* (See also other brand names) | 1 oz. | 490 | 7.4 | 3. | 5. | 6 |
| **PORK ROAST,** canned (Wilson) *Tender Made* | 1 oz. | 127 | 2.2 | <1. | 1. | 18 |
| **PORK SAUSAGE:** | | | | | | |
| Uncooked: | | | | | | |
| Links or bulk (USDA)[1] | 1 oz. | 210 | 14.4 | 5. | 9. | |
| (Armour Star) | 1-oz. sausage | | 13.5 | | | |
| Country style (Hormel) | 1 oz. | 270 | 9.7 | 4. | 6. | 31 |
| *Little Sizzlers* (Hormel) | 1 piece (.8 oz.) | 292 | 10.5 | | | |
| Midget (Hormel) | 1 piece (.8 oz.) | 286 | 7.4 | 3. | 4. | 23 |
| Smoked (Hormel) | 1 oz. | 318 | 8.9 | 3. | 5. | 14 |
| Bulk style (Oscar Mayer) | 1 oz. | 210 | 12.8 | | | |
| Italian Brand (Oscar Mayer) | 1 oz. | 299 | 13.3 | | | |
| *Little Friers* (Oscar Mayer): | | | | | | |
| 6-8 per lb. | 1 link (2.3 oz.) | 482 | 29.9 | | | |
| 14-18 per lb. | 1 link (1 oz.) | 210 | 13.0 | | | |
| (Wilson) | 1 oz. | 207 | 13.6 | 5. | 8. | 18 |
| Cooked: | | | | | | |
| Links or bulk (USDA)[1] | 1 oz. | 272 | 12.5 | 5. | 8. | |
| Links, 16 per lb. raw (USDA)[1] | 1 link | 125 | 5.7 | 2. | 4. | |
| Bulk style (Oscar Mayer) | 1 oz. | 409 | 7.9 | | | |
| Italian Brand (Oscar Mayer) | 1 oz. | 299 | 6.8 | | | |
| *Little Friers* (Oscar Mayer): | | | | | | |
| 6-8 per lb. raw | 1 link (1 oz. cooked) | 396 | 8.7 | 3. | 5. | 17 |
| 14-18 per lb. raw | 1 link (.4 oz. cooked) | 164 | 3.6 | 1. | 2. | 7 |
| Canned, solids & liq. (USDA)[1] | 1 oz. | | 10.9 | 4. | 7. | |
| Canned, drained (USDA)[1] | 1 oz. | | 9.3 | 3. | 6. | |

(USDA): United States Department of Agriculture
*Prepared as Package Directs
[1]Principal source of fat: pork.

| Food and Description | Measure or Quantity | Sodium (mg.) | Fats in grams | | | Choles- terol (mg.) |
|---|---|---|---|---|---|---|
| | | | Total | Satu- rated | Unsatu- rated | |
| **PORK, SWEET & SOUR,** frozen | | | | | | |
| (Chun King) | 7½-oz. serving (½ pkg.) | | 10.0 | | | |
| **PORT WINE:** | | | | | | |
| (Gold Seal) 19% alcohol | 3 fl. oz. (3.3 oz.) | 3 | 0. | | | (0) |
| (Great Western) Solera, 18% alcohol | 3 fl. oz. | 34 | 0. | | | 0 |
| (Great Western) Solera, tawny, 18% alcohol | 3 fl. oz. | 34 | 0. | | | 0 |
| *POST TOASTIES,* cereal (Post) | 1 cup (1 oz.) | 238 | .1 | | | 0 |
| *\*POSTUM,* instant | 1 cup (6 oz.) | 3 | Tr. | | | 0 |
| **POTATO:** | | | | | | |
| Raw, whole (USDA) | 1 lb. (weighed unpared) | 11 | .4 | | | 0 |
| Raw, pared (USDA): | | | | | | |
| Chopped | 1 cup (5.2 oz.) | 4 | .1 | | | 0 |
| Diced | 1 cup (5.5 oz.) | 5 | .2 | | | 0 |
| Slices | 1 cup (5.2 oz.) | 4 | .1 | | | 0 |
| Cooked: | | | | | | |
| Au gratin or scalloped, without cheese (USDA)[1] | ½ cup (4.3 oz.) | 433 | 4.8 | 2. | 2. | 7 |
| Au gratin, with cheese (USDA)[2] | ½ cup (4.3 oz.) | 545 | 9.6 | 5. | 5. | 18 |
| Baked, peeled after baking, no salt added (USDA) | 2½" dia. potato (3.5 oz., 3 raw per lb.) | 4 | .1 | | | 0 |
| Baked, peeled after baking, salt added (USDA) | 2½" dia. potato (3.5 oz., 3 raw per lb.) | 234 | .1 | | | 0 |
| Boiled, peeled after boiling, no salt added (USDA) | 4.8-oz. potato (3 raw per lb.) | 4 | .1 | | | 0 |
| Boiled, peeled after boiling, salt added (USDA) | 4.8-oz. potato (3 raw per lb.) | 321 | .1 | | | 0 |

(USDA): United States Department of Agriculture
*Prepared as Package Directs
[1]Principal sources of fat: butter & milk.
[2]Principal sources of fat: cheese, butter & milk.

| Food and Description | Measure or Quantity | Sodium (mg.) | Total | Satu- rated | Unsatu- rated | Choles- terol (mg.) |
|---|---|---|---|---|---|---|
| **Boiled, peeled before boiling, no salt added (USDA):** | | | | | | |
| Whole | 4.3-oz. potato (3 raw per lb.) | 2 | .1 | | | 0 |
| Diced | ½ cup (2.8 oz.) | 2 | <.1 | | | 0 |
| Mashed | ½ cup (3.7 oz.) | 2 | .1 | | | 0 |
| Riced | ½ cup (4 oz.) | 2 | .1 | | | 0 |
| Slices | ½ cup (2.8 oz.) | 2 | <.1 | | | 0 |
| **Boiled, peeled before boiling, salt added (USDA):** | | | | | | |
| Whole | 4.3-oz. potato (3 raw per lb.) | 288 | .1 | | | 0 |
| Diced | ½ cup (2.8 oz.) | 184 | <.1 | | | 0 |
| Mashed | ½ cup (3.7 oz.) | 245 | .1 | | | 0 |
| Riced | ½ cup (4 oz.) | 269 | .1 | | | 0 |
| Slices | ½ cup (2.8 oz.) | 189 | <.1 | | | 0 |
| **French-fried in deep fat, no salt added (USDA)[1]** | 10 pieces (2" x ½" x ½", 2 oz.) | 3 | 7.5 | 2. | 6. | |
| **French-fried in deep fat, salt added (USDA)[1]** | 10 pieces (2" x ½" x ½", 2 oz.) | 135 | 7.5 | 2. | 6. | |
| French-fried (McDonald's) | 1 serving (2.4 oz.) | 117 | 10.4 | | | |
| Hash-browned (USDA)[2] | ½ cup (3.4 oz.) | 281 | 11.4 | 3. | 8. | |
| Mashed, milk added (USDA) | ½ cup (3.5 oz.) | 295 | .7 | | | |
| Mashed, milk & butter added (USDA)[3] | ½ cup (3.5 oz.) | 324 | 4.2 | 2. | 2. | |
| Pan-fried from raw (USDA) | ½ cup (3 oz.) | 190 | 12.1 | 3. | 10. | |
| Scalloped (See Au gratin) | | | | | | |
| **Canned:** | | | | | | |
| Solids & liq., no added salt (USDA) | 1 cup (8.8 oz.) | 2 | .5 | | | 0 |
| Solids & liq., added salt (USDA) | 1 cup (8.8 oz.) | 590 | .5 | | | 0 |
| White (Butter Kernel) | 3-4 small potatoes (4.1 oz.) | | 2.3 | | | (0) |
| Solids & liq. (Stokely-Van Camp) | ½ cup (4.1 oz.) | | .2 | | | (0) |
| Whole, new, solids & liq. (Del Monte) | ½ cup (2.6 oz.) | 382 | Tr. | | | 0 |

(USDA): United States Department of Agriculture
*Prepared as Package Directs
[1]Principal source of fat: cottonseed oil.
[2]Principal source of fat: vegetable shortening.
[3]Principal sources of fat: butter & milk.

| Food and Description | Measure or Quantity | Sodium (mg.) | —Fats in grams— | | | Choles-terol (mg.) |
|---|---|---|---|---|---|---|
| | | | Total | Satu-rated | Unsatu-rated | |
| Whole. new. drained solids (Del Monte) | ½ cup (2.5 oz.) | 261 | <.1 | | | 0 |
| Dehydrated. mashed: | | | | | | |
| Flakes. without milk (USDA): | | | | | | |
| Dry | ½ cup (.8 oz.) | 20 | .1 | | | 0 |
| *Prepared with water. milk & fat[1] | ½ cup (3.8 oz.) | 247 | 3.4 | 2. | 1. | |
| Granules. without milk (USDA): | | | | | | |
| Dry | ½ cup (3.5 oz.) | 84 | .6 | | | 0 |
| *Prepared with water. milk & butter[1] | ½ cup (3.7 oz.) | 256 | 3.8 | 2. | 2. | |
| Granules with milk (USDA): | | | | | | |
| Dry | ½ cup (3.5 oz.) | 82 | 1.1 | | | |
| *Prepared with water & fat[2] | ½ cup (3.7 oz.) | 246 | 2.3 | 1. | 1. | |
| Frozen: | | | | | | |
| Au gratin (Stouffer's) | 11½-oz. pkg. | | 11.5 | | | |
| Diced for hash-browning. not thawed (USDA) | 4 oz. | 9 | Tr. | | | |
| Diced. hash-browned (USDA)[3] | 4 oz. | 339 | 13.0 | 3. | 10. | |
| French-fried: | | | | | | |
| Not thawed. no salt added (USDA)[3] | 9-oz. pkg. | 8 | 16.6 | 5. | 12. | |
| Not thawed. salt added (USDA)[3] | 9-oz. pkg. | 602 | 16.6 | 5. | 12. | |
| Heated. no added salt (USDA)[3] | 10 pieces (2" x ½" x ½". 2 oz.) | 2 | 4.8 | 2. | 3. | |
| Heated. salt added (USDA)[3] | 10 pieces (2" x ½" x ½". 2 oz.) | 135 | 4.8 | 2. | 3. | |
| Mashed. not thawed (USDA) | 4 oz. | 90 | .1 | | | |
| Mashed. heated (USDA)[1] | 4 oz. | 407 | 3.2 | 2. | <1. | |
| Stuffed. baked (Holloway House): | | | | | | |
| With cheese | 1 potato (6 oz.) | 842 | 13.6 | | | |
| With some cream & chives | 1 potato (6 oz.) | 646 | 13.6 | | | |
| **POTATO CHIP:** | | | | | | |
| (USDA)[3,4] | 1 oz. | 284 | 11.3 | 3. | 8. | 0 |
| (USDA)[3,4] | 10 2" chips or 7 3" chips (.7 oz.) | 200 | 8.0 | 2. | 6. | 0 |

(USDA): United States Department of Agriculture
*Prepared as Package Directs
[1]Principal source of fat: butter & milk.
[2]Principal source of fat: butter.
[3]Principal source of fat: cottonseed oil.
[4]Sodium content is variable & may be as high as 284 mg. per oz.

| Food and Description | Measure or Quantity | Sodium (mg.) | — Fats in grams — | | | Choles- terol (mg.) |
|---|---|---|---|---|---|---|
| | | | Total | Satu- rated | Unsatu- rated | |
| *Lay's* | 1 oz. | 230 | 11.1 | 3. | 8. | 0 |
| (Nalley's) | 1 oz. | | 10.5 | | | |
| (Pringle's) | 10 chips (.5 oz.) | 126 | 4.8 | 1. | 3. | 0 |
| (Pringle's) | 1 oz. | 255 | 9.6 | 3. | 7. | 0 |
| *Ruffles* | 1 oz. | 200 | 9.4 | 2. | 7. | 0 |
| (Tom Houston) | 10 chips (.7 oz.) | 200 | 8.0 | | | |
| (Wise) | 1-oz. bag | 104 | 10.3 | | | |
| (Wonder) | 1 oz. | 220 | 11.1 | | | |
| Barbecue, *Lay's* | 1 oz. | 380 | 10.8 | 3. | 8. | 0 |
| Barbecue (Wise) | 1-oz. bag | 149 | 9.7 | | | |
| Barbecue (Wonder) | 1 oz. | 199 | 10.6 | | | |
| Onion-garlic (Wise) | 1-oz. bag | 149 | 10.2 | | | |
| Ridgies (Wise) | 1-oz. bag | 119 | 10.1 | | | |

**POTATO MIX:**

| Food and Description | Measure or Quantity | Sodium (mg.) | Total | Satu- rated | Unsatu- rated | Choles- terol (mg.) |
|---|---|---|---|---|---|---|
| *Au gratin (Betty Crocker) | ½ cup | 468 | 7.0 | | | |
| Au gratin (French's) | 5½-oz. pkg. | 2880 | 13.0 | | | |
| *Au gratin (French's) | ½ cup | 480 | 2.2 | | | |
| *_Buds_ (Betty Crocker) | ½ cup | 401 | 6.4 | | | |
| Mashed, country style (French's) | 2⅔-oz. pkg. | 60 | .5 | | | |
| *Mashed, country style (French's) | ½ cup | 390 | 7.0 | | | |
| Mashed, granules (French's) | 3¼-oz. pkg. | 77 | .6 | | | |
| *Mashed, granules, salt added (French's) | ½ cup | 306 | 4.8 | | | |
| *Scalloped (Betty Crocker) | ½ cup | 668 | 5.8 | | | |
| Scalloped (French's) | 5⅝-oz. pkg. | 2160 | 1.1 | | | |
| *Scalloped (French's) | ½ cup | 383 | 2.1 | | | |
| Whipped (Borden) | ¼ cup (.5 oz.) | <.1 | | | | |

**POTATO PANCAKE MIX:**

| Food and Description | Measure or Quantity | Sodium (mg.) | Total | Satu- rated | Unsatu- rated | Choles- terol (mg.) |
|---|---|---|---|---|---|---|
| (French's) | 3-oz. pkg. | 1440 | .5 | | | |
| *(French's) | 3 small pancakes (¼ pkg.) | 375 | 1.4 | | | |

**POTATO SALAD:**

| Food and Description | Measure or Quantity | Sodium (mg.) | Total | Satu- rated | Unsatu- rated | Choles- terol (mg.) |
|---|---|---|---|---|---|---|
| Home recipe, with cooked salad dressing & seasonings (USDA)[1] | 4 oz. | 599 | 3.2 | 1. | 2. | |
| Home recipe, with mayonnaise & French dressing, hard-cooked eggs & seasonings (USDA)[2] | ½ cup (4.4 oz.) | 600 | 11.5 | 2. | 9. | 81 |
| Canned (Nalley's) | 4 oz. | | 9.9 | | | |

(USDA): United States Department of Agriculture
*Prepared as Package Directs
[1]Principal sources of fat: butter, milk & egg.
[2]Principal sources of fat: soybean oil, cottonseed oil, corn oil & eggs.

| Food and Description | Measure or Quantity | Sodium (mg.) | —Fats in grams— | | | Choles-terol (mg.) |
|---|---|---|---|---|---|---|
| | | | Total | Satu-rated | Unsatu-rated | |
| **POTATO SOUP,** Cream of: | | | | | | |
| *Canned (Campbell) | 1 cup | 1049 | 4.4 | <1. | 4. | |
| Frozen (USDA): | | | | | | |
| Condensed[1] | 8 oz. (by wt.) | 2223 | 9.8 | 5. | 5. | |
| *Prepared with equal volume water[1] | 1 cup (8.5 oz.) | 1176 | 5.3 | 2. | 3. | |
| *Prepared with equal volume milk[2] | 1 cup (8.6 oz.) | 1264 | 9.6 | 5. | 5. | |
| **POTATO SOUP MIX:** | | | | | | |
| *(Lipton) | 1 cup | 1272 | 1.2 | Tr. | <1. | |
| (Wyler's) | 1 oz. | | 1.0 | | | |
| **POTATO STICK:** | | | | | | |
| (USDA)[3,4] | 1 oz. | 284 | 10.3 | 3. | 8. | |
| (Durkee) *O & C* | 1¾-oz. can | 496 | 18.7 | | | |
| Julienne (Wise) | 1-oz. bag | 128 | 9.3 | | | |
| **POUND CAKE:** | | | | | | |
| Home recipe, old fashioned, equal weights flour, sugar, eggs & butter (USDA)[5] | 1.1-oz. slice (3½" x 3" x ½") | 33 | 7.9 | 4. | 4. | |
| Home recipe, old fashioned, equal weights flour, sugar, eggs & vegetable shortening (USDA)[6] | 1.1-oz. slice (3½" x 3" x ½") | 33 | 8.8 | 2. | 7. | |
| Home recipe, traditional, made with butter (USDA)[7] | 1.1-oz. slice (3½" x 3" x ½") | 53 | 4.8 | 2. | 2. | |
| Home recipe, traditional, made with vegetable shortening (USDA)[8] | 1.1-oz. slice (3½" x 3" x ½" | 53 | 5.6 | 2. | 4. | |
| Frozen (Morton) | 1 oz. | 136 | 5.9 | | | |

(USDA): United States Department of Agriculture
*Prepared as Package Directs
[1]Principal source of fat: cream.
[2]Principal sources of fat: cream & milk.
[3]Principal source of fat: cottonseed oil.
[4]Sodium content is variable & may be as high as 284 mg. per oz.
[5]Principal sources of fat: egg & butter.
[6]Principal sources of fat: egg & vegetable shortening.
[7]Principal sources of fat: butter, egg & milk.
[8]Principal sources of fat: vegetable shortening, egg & milk.

| Food and Description | Measure or Quantity | Sodium (mg.) | Total | Fats in grams — Satu- rated | Unsatu- rated | Choles- terol (mg.) |
|---|---|---|---|---|---|---|
| **POUND CAKE MIX:** | | | | | | |
| *(Betty Crocker) | $^1/_{12}$ of cake | 171 | 9.2 | | | |
| *(Dromedary) | 1" slice (2.9 oz.) | 388 | 14.9 | | | |
| | | | | | | |
| **PRESERVE,** sweetened (See also individual listings by flavor): | | | | | | |
| (USDA) | 1 oz. | 3 | <.1 | | | 0 |
| (USDA) | 1 T. (.7 oz.) | 2 | Tr. | | | 0 |
| (Kraft) | 1 oz. | <1 | <.1 | | | (0) |
| (Smucker's) | 1 T. (.7 oz.) | <1 | 0. | | | (0) |
| | | | | | | |
| **PRETZEL:** | | | | | | |
| (USDA)[1] | 1 oz. | 476 | 1.3 | | | |
| Dutch, twist (USDA)[1] | 1 pretzel (.6 oz.) | 269 | .7 | | | |
| Stick, small (USDA)[1] | 10 small sticks (2¼", 3 grams) | 50 | .1 | | | |
| Stick, regular (USDA)[1] | 5 regular sticks (3⅛", 3 grams) | 50 | .1 | | | |
| Thin, twist (USDA)[1] | 1 pretzel (6 grams) | 101 | .3 | | | |
| (Nab) *Mister Salty Veri-Thin* | 75 pieces (¾-oz. pkg.) | 671 | .5 | | | |
| (Nab) *Mister Salty Veri-Thin* | 150 pieces (1½- oz. pkg.) | 1342 | 1.0 | | | |
| (Nab) Pretzelette | 16 pieces (1¼-oz. pkg.) | 639 | 1.5 | | | |
| (Nabisco) *Mister Salty,* Dutch | 1 piece (.5 oz.) | 239 | .2 | | | |
| (Nabisco) *Mister Salty,* pretzelette | 1 piece (2 grams) | 31 | <.1 | | | |
| (Nabisco) *Mister Salty*, 3-ring | 1 piece (3 grams) | 56 | .1 | | | |
| (Nabisco) *Mister Salty Veri-Thin* | 1 piece (5 grams) | 88 | .2 | | | |
| (Nabisco) *Mister Salty Veri- Thin*, stick | 1 piece (<1 gram) | 9 | Tr. | | | |
| (Old London) nugget | 2-oz. bag | 1108 | 2.6 | | | |
| (Old London) ring | 1½-oz. bag | 1059 | 1.9 | | | |
| (Rold Gold) rod | 1 oz. | 390 | 1.1 | Tr. | <1. | 0 |
| (Rold Gold) twist | 1 oz. | 300 | .9 | Tr. | <1. | 0 |
| | | | | | | |
| **PRICKLY PEAR,** fresh (USDA): | | | | | | |
| Whole | 1 lb. (weighed with rind & seeds) | 4 | .2 | | | 0 |
| Flesh only | 4 oz. | 2 | .1 | | | 0 |

(USDA): United States Department of Agriculture
*Prepared as Package Directs
[1]Sodium content is variable. For example, very thin pretzel sticks contain about twice the average amount listed.

| Food and Description | Measure or Quantity | Sodium (mg.) | —Fats in grams— Total | Satu-rated | Unsatu-rated | Choles-terol (mg.) |
|---|---|---|---|---|---|---|
| **PRODUCT 19,** cereal (Kellogg's) | 1 cup (1 oz.) | 271 | .4 | | | (0) |
| **PRUNE:** | | | | | | |
| Dried, "softenized," uncooked: | | | | | | |
|   Small (USDA) | 1 prune (5 grams) | <1 | Tr. | | | 0 |
|   Medium, whole with pits (USDA) | 1 cup (6.6 oz.) | 13 | 1.0 | | | 0 |
|   Medium (USDA) | 1 prune (7 grams) | <1 | Tr. | | | 0 |
|   Large (USDA) | 1 prune (9 grams) | <1 | Tr. | | | 0 |
|   Pitted, chopped (USDA) | 1 cup (5.3 oz.) | 12 | .9 | | | 0 |
|   Pitted, ground (USDA) | 1 cup (9.7 oz.) | 22 | 1.6 | | | 0 |
| Dried, moist-pak (Del Monte) | 1 cup (8 oz.) | 5 | .9 | | | 0 |
| Dried, ready-to-eat (Del Monte) | 1 cup (6.6 oz.) | 2 | 4.7 | | | 0 |
| Dried, "softenized," cooked, unsweetened (USDA) | 1 cup (17-18 med. with ⅓ cup liq., 9.5 oz.) | 10 | .7 | | | 0 |
| Dried, "softenized," cooked with sugar (USDA) | 1 cup (16-18 prunes & ⅓ cup liq., 11.1 oz.) | 9 | .6 | | | 0 |
| Dehydrated (USDA): | | | | | | |
|   Nugget-type & pieces | 8 oz. | 25 | 1.1 | | | 0 |
|   Nugget-type & pieces, cooked with sugar, solids & liq. | 1 cup (8.9 oz.) | 10 | .5 | | | 0 |
| Canned: | | | | | | |
|   Cooked (Sunsweet) | 1 cup | | .4 | | | (0) |
|   Stewed (Del Monte) | 1 cup (9.4 oz.) | 3 | 1.1 | | | 0 |
|   Stewed, pitted (Del Monte) | 1 cup (9.2 oz.) | 14 | 1.3 | | | 0 |
| **PRUNE JUICE:** | | | | | | |
| (USDA) | ½ cup (4.5 oz.) | 2 | .1 | | | 0 |
| (Bennett's) | ½ cup (4.5 oz.) | 3 | .1 | | | 0 |
| (Del Monte) | ½ cup (4.3 oz.) | 10 | Tr. | | | 0 |
| (Heinz) | 5½-fl.-oz. can | 13 | .2 | | | (0) |
| (Mott's) Super | 4 oz. (by wt.) | | .1 | | | (0) |
| *RealPrune* | ½ cup (4.5 oz.) | 33 | .3 | | | (0) |
| (Sunsweet) | ½ cup | | <.1 | | | (0) |
| & apple (Sunsweet) | 4 oz. (by wt.) | | .1 | | | (0) |
| With lemon (Sunsweet) | ½ cup | | <.1 | | | (0) |

(USDA): United States Department of Agriculture
*Prepared as Package Directs

| Food and Description | Measure or Quantity | Sodium (mg.) | Fats in grams — Total | Satu- rated | Unsatu- rated | Choles- terol (mg.) |
|---|---|---|---|---|---|---|
| **PRUNE WHIP,** home recipe (USDA) | 1 cup (4.8 oz.) | 221 | .3 | | | |
| **PUDDING or PUDDING MIX** (See individual kinds) | | | | | | |
| **PUFF** (See **CRACKER** or individual kinds of hors d'oeuvres, such as **CHICKEN PUFF**) | | | | | | |
| *PUFFA PUFFA RICE,* cereal | 1 cup (1 oz.) | 25 | 3.0 | | | (0) |
| **PUFFED OAT CEREAL** (USDA): | | | | | | |
| Added nutrients | 1 oz. | 359 | 1.6 | | | 0 |
| Sugar-coated, added nutrients | 1 oz. | 167 | 1.0 | | | 0 |
| **PUFFED RICE CEREAL:** | | | | | | |
| (USDA) added nutrients, unsalted | 1 cup (.5 oz.) | <1 | <.1 | | | 0 |
| (USDA) honey & added nutrients | 1 oz. | 200 | .2 | | | 0 |
| (USDA) honey or cocoa fat, added nutrients | 1 oz. | 101 | 1.1 | | | 0 |
| (Checker) | ½ oz. | 2 | <.1 | | | (0) |
| (Quaker) | 1¼ cups (½ oz.) | <1 | .1 | | | (0) |
| (Sunland) | ½ oz. | 2 | <.1 | | | (0) |
| (Whiffs) | ½ oz. | 2 | <.1 | | | (0) |
| **PUMPKIN:** | | | | | | |
| Fresh, whole (USDA) | 1 lb. (weighed with rind & seeds) | 3 | .3 | | | 0 |
| Flesh only (USDA) | 4 oz. | 1 | .1 | | | 0 |
| Canned: | | | | | | |
| Salted (USDA) | ½ cup (4.3 oz.) | 288 | .4 | | | 0 |
| Unsalted (USDA) | ½ cup (4.3 oz.) | 2 | .4 | | | 0 |
| (Del Monte) | ½ cup (4.3 oz.) | 1 | .1 | | | 0 |
| (Stokely-Van Camp) | ½ cup (4.1 oz.) | | .4 | | | (0) |
| **PUMPKIN PIE:** | | | | | | |
| Home recipe, 1-crust (USDA): | | | | | | |
| Made with lard[1] | ⅙ of 9″ pie (5.4 oz.) | 325 | 17.0 | 6. | 11. | 93 |

(USDA): United States Department of Agriculture
*Prepared as Package Directs
[1]Principal sources of fat: lard & butter.

| Food and Description | Measure or Quantity | Sodium (mg.) | Fats in grams — Total | Satu- rated | Unsatu- rated | Choles- terol (mg.) |
|---|---|---|---|---|---|---|
| Made with vegetable shortening[1] | 1/6 of 9″ pie (5.4 oz.) | 325 | 17.0 | 5. | 12. | |
| (Tastykake) | 4-oz. pie | | 16.0 | | | |
| Frozen: | | | | | | |
| (Banquet) | 5-oz. serving | | 10.7 | | | |
| (Morton) | 1/6 of 20-oz. pie | 218 | 5.9 | | | |
| (Morton) | 1/8 of 46-oz. pie | 393 | 27.3 | | | |
| (Mrs. Smith's) | 1/6 of 8″ pie (4 oz.) | 245 | 9.4 | | | |
| (Mrs. Smith's) | 1/8 of 10″ pie (5.6 oz.) | 310 | 12.0 | | | |
| **PUMPKIN PIE FILLING:** | | | | | | |
| (Comstock) | ½ cup (5.4 oz.) | 298 | .3 | | | |
| (Del Monte) | 1 cup (9 oz.) | 512 | .5 | | | |
| **PUMPKIN PIE SPICE** | | | | | | |
| (Spice Islands) | 1 tsp | <1 | | | | (0) |
| **PUMPKIN SEED,** dry (USDA): | | | | | | |
| Whole | 4 oz. (weighed in hull) | | 39.2 | 7. | 32. | 0 |
| Hulled | 4 oz. | | 53.0 | 9. | 44. | 0 |
| **PUNCH DRINK** canned (Hi-C) | 6 fl. oz. (6.3 oz.) | <1 | | | | 0 |
| *PURPLE PASSION,* soft drink (Canada Dry) bottle or can | 6 fl. oz. | 13+ | 0. | | | (0) |
| **PURSLANE,** including stems (USDA): | | | | | | |
| Raw | 1 lb. | | 1.8 | | | 0 |
| Boiled, drained | 4 oz. | | .3 | | | 0 |
| **PUSSYCAT MIX** (Bar-Tender's) | 1 serving (⅔ oz.) | 21 | .2 | | | (0) |

# Q

| | | | | | | |
|---|---|---|---|---|---|---|
| **QUAIL,** raw (USDA): | | | | | | |
| Ready-to-cook | 1 lb. (weighed with bones) | | 27.8 | | | |
| Meat & skin only | 4 oz. | 45 | 7.9 | | | |
| Giblets | 2 oz. | | 3.5 | | | |

(USDA): United States Department of Agriculture
*Prepared as Package Directs
[1]Principal sources of fat: vegetable shortening & butter.

| Food and Description | Measure or Quantity | Sodium (mg.) | Total | Satu-rated | Unsatu-rated | Choles-terol (mg.) |
|---|---|---|---|---|---|---|
| | | | —Fats in grams— | | | |
| *QUAKE,* cereal (Quaker) | 1 cup (1 oz.) | 116 | 2.3 | | | 0 |
| *QUANGAROOS,* cereal (Quaker) | 1 cup (1 oz.) | 146 | 1.1 | | | 0 |
| *QUIK* (See individual kinds) | | | | | | |
| **QUINCE,** fresh (USDA): | | | | | | |
| Untrimmed | 1 lb. (weighed with skin & seeds) | 11 | .3 | | | 0 |
| Flesh only | 4 oz. | 5 | .1 | | | 0 |
| **QUININE SOFT DRINK or TONIC WATER:** | | | | | | |
| Sweetened: | | | | | | |
| (Canada Dry) bottle | 6 fl. oz. | 0+ | 0. | | | 0 |
| (Canada Dry) can | 6 fi. oz. | <1+ | 0. | | | 0 |
| (Dr. Brown's) | 6 fl. oz. | 3 | 0. | | | 0 |
| (Fanta) | 6 fl. oz. | 5 | 0. | | | 0 |
| (Hoffman) | 6 fl. oz. | 3 | 0. | | | 0 |
| (Kirsch) | 6 fl. oz. | <1 | 0. | | | 0 |
| (Schweppes) | 6 fl. oz. | 10 | 0. | | | 0 |
| (Shasta) | 6 fl. oz. | 10 | 0. | | | 0 |
| (Yukon Club) | 6 fl. oz. | 3 | 0. | | | 0 |
| Low calorie (No-Cal) | 6 fl. oz. | 12 | 0. | | | 0 |
| *QUISP,* cereal (Quaker) | 1¹/₆ cups (1 oz.) | 215 | 2.7 | | | 0 |

# R

| Food and Description | Measure or Quantity | Sodium (mg.) | Total | Satu-rated | Unsatu-rated | Choles-terol (mg.) |
|---|---|---|---|---|---|---|
| **RABBIT** (USDA): | | | | | | |
| Domesticated: | | | | | | |
| Ready-to-cook | 1 lb. (weighed with bones) | 154 | 29. | 11. | 18. | |
| Raw meat only | 4 oz. | 49 | 9.1 | | | 74 |
| Stewed, flesh only | 4 oz. | 46 | 11.5 | | | 103 |
| Stewed, flesh only, chopped or diced | 1 cup (4.9 oz.) | 57 | 14.1 | | | 127 |
| Wild, ready-to-cook | 1 lb. (weighed with bones) | | 18.1 | | | |
| Wild, raw, meat only | 4 oz. | | 5.7 | | | |
| **RACOON,** roasted, meat only (USDA) | 4 oz. | | 16.4 | | | |

(USDA): United States Department of Agriculture
*Prepared as Package Directs

(271)

| Food and Description | Measure or Quantity | Sodium (mg.) | — Fats in grams — Total | Satu- rated | Unsatu- rated | Choles- terol (mg.) |
|---|---|---|---|---|---|---|
| **RADISH** (USDA): | | | | | | |
| Common, raw: | | | | | | |
| Untrimmed, without tops | ½ lb. (weighed untrimmed) | 36 | .2 | | | 0 |
| Trimmed, whole | 4 small radishes (1.4 oz.) | 7 | <.1 | | | 0 |
| Trimmed, whole | 1 cup (4.7 oz.) | 24 | .1 | | | 0 |
| Trimmed, sliced | ½ cup (2 oz.) | 10 | <.1 | | | 0 |
| Oriental, raw, without tops | ½ lb. (weighed unpared) | | .2 | | | 0 |
| Oriental, raw, trimmed & pared | 4 oz. | | .1 | | | 0 |
| **RAISIN:** | | | | | | |
| Dried: | | | | | | |
| Whole (USDA) | 4 oz. | 31 | .2 | | | 0 |
| Whole (USDA) | 1 pkg. (.5 oz.) | 4 | <.1 | | | 0 |
| Whole, pressed down (USDA) | ½ cup (2.9 oz.) | 22 | .2 | | | 0 |
| Whole, pressed down (USDA) | 1 T. (.4 oz.) | 3 | <.1 | | | 0 |
| Chopped (USDA) | ½ cup (2.9 oz.) | 22 | .2 | | | 0 |
| Ground (USDA) | ½ cup (4.7 oz.) | 36 | .3 | | | 0 |
| Cinnamon-coated (Del Monte) | ½ cup (2.5 oz.) | 16 | .4 | | | (0) |
| Seeded, Muscat (Del Monte) | ½ cup (2.5 oz.) | 42 | .6 | | | (0) |
| Seeded, Muscat (Sun-Maid) | 15-oz. pkg. | | <.1 | | | 0 |
| Seeded, Muscat (Sun-Maid) | 1 oz. | | .1 | | | 0 |
| Seedless, California Thompson (Del Monte) | ½ cup (2.5 oz.) | 17 | .6 | | | (0) |
| Seedless, California Thompson (Sun-Maid) | ½ cup (2.8 oz.) | 14 | .2 | | | 0 |
| Seedless, California Thompson (Sun-Maid) | 1 T. (.4 oz.) | 2 | <.1 | | | 0 |
| Seedless, golden (Del Monte) | ½ cup (2.5 oz.) | 23 | .2 | | | 0 |
| Seedless, golden (Sun-Maid) | 15-oz. pkg. | 85 | .8 | | | 0 |
| Cooked, added sugar, solids & liq. (USDA) | ½ cup (4.3 oz.) | 16 | .1 | | | 0 |
| **RAISIN PIE:** | | | | | | |
| Home recipe, 2-crust (USDA): | | | | | | |
| Made with lard[1] | 1/6 of 9″ pie (5.6 oz.) | 450 | 16.9 | 6. | 11. | |
| Made with vegetable shortening[2] | 1/6 of 9″ pie (5.6 oz.) | 450 | 16.9 | 5. | 12. | |
| (Tastykake) | 4-oz. pie | | 14.6 | | | |
| **RAISIN PIE FILLING:** | | | | | | |
| (Comstock) | ½ cup (5.4 oz.) | 84 | <.1 | | | |
| (Lucky Leaf) | 8 oz. | 242 | 1.6 | | | |

(USDA): United States Department of Agriculture
*Prepared as Package Directs
[1]Principal sources of fat: lard & butter.
[2]Principal sources of fat: vegetable shortening & butter.

| Food and Description | Measure or Quantity | Sodium (mg.) | —Fats in grams— | | | Choles- terol (mg.) |
|---|---|---|---|---|---|---|
| | | | Total | Satu- rated | Unsatu- rated | |

**RAJA FISH** (See **SKATE**)

**RASPBERRY:**
  Black:
  Fresh:

| | | | | | | |
|---|---|---|---|---|---|---|
| (USDA) | ½ lb. (weighed with caps & stems) | 2 | 3.1 | | | 0 |
| (USDA) without caps & stems | ½ cup (2.4 oz.) | <1 | .9 | | | 0 |
| Canned, water pack, unsweet- ened, solids & liq. (USDA) | 4 oz. | 1 | 1.2 | | | 0 |

  Red:
  Fresh:

| | | | | | | |
|---|---|---|---|---|---|---|
| (USDA) | ½ lb. (weighed with caps & stems) | 2 | 1.1 | | | 0 |
| (USDA) without caps & stems | ½ cup (2.5 oz.) | <1 | .4 | | | 0 |

  Canned, water pack, un- sweetened, or low calorie:

| | | | | | | |
|---|---|---|---|---|---|---|
| Solids & liq. (USDA) | 4 oz. | 1 | .1 | | | 0 |
| Solids & liq. (Blue Boy) | 4 oz. | 1 | 1.0 | | | (0) |

  Frozen, sweetened:

| | | | | | | |
|---|---|---|---|---|---|---|
| Not thawed (USDA) | 10-oz. pkg. | 3 | .6 | | | 0 |
| Not thawed (USDA) | ½ cup (4.4 oz.) | 1 | .2 | | | 0 |
| Quick-thaw (Birds Eye) | ½ cup (5 oz.) | 1 | .4 | | | 0 |

**RASPBERRY PIE FILLING:**

| | | | | | | |
|---|---|---|---|---|---|---|
| Red (Comstock) | ½ cup (5.3 oz.) | 166 | .2 | | | |
| Red (Lucky Leaf) | 8 oz. | 260 | .4 | | | |

**RASPBERRY PRESERVE or JAM:**
  Sweetened, black or red

| | | | | | | |
|---|---|---|---|---|---|---|
| (Bama) | 1 T. (.7 oz.) | 2 | <.1 | | | (0) |

  Low calorie or dietetic:

| | | | | | | |
|---|---|---|---|---|---|---|
| (Diet Delight) | 1 T. (.6 oz.) | 9 | Tr. | | | (0) |
| Black (Kraft) | 1 oz. | 5 | <.1 | | | (0) |
| (S and W) *Nutradiet* | 1 T. (.5 oz.) | | <.1 | | | (0) |
| Low sugar, black (Slenderella) | 1 T. (.7 oz.) | 16 | <.1 | | | (0) |

**RASPBERRY RENNET MIX:**
  Powder:

| | | | | | | |
|---|---|---|---|---|---|---|
| Dry (Junket) | 1 oz. | 11 | Tr. | | | |

(USDA): United States Department of Agriculture
*Prepared as Package Directs

| Food and Description | Measure or Quantity | Sodium (mg.) | — Fats in grams — | | | Choles-terol (mg.) |
|---|---|---|---|---|---|---|
| | | | Total | Satu-rated | Unsatu-rated | |
| *(Junket) | 4 oz. | 56 | 3.8 | | | |
| Tablet: | | | | | | |
| Dry (Junket) | 1 tablet (<1 gram) | 197 | Tr. | | | |
| *& sugar (Junket) | 4 oz. | 98 | 3.9 | | | |
| **RASPBERRY SOFT DRINK:** | | | | | | |
| Sweetened: | | | | | | |
| (Clicquot Club) | 6 fl. oz. | 11 | 0. | | | 0 |
| (Cott) | 6 fl. oz. | 11 | 0. | | | 0 |
| (Dr. Brown's) black | 6 fl. oz. | 14 | 0. | | | 0 |
| (Hoffman) black | 6 fl. oz. | 14 | 0. | | | 0 |
| (Kirsch) black | 6 fl. oz. | <1 | 0. | | | 0 |
| (Mission) | 6 fl. oz. | 11 | 0. | | | 0 |
| (Shasta) Wild | 6 fl. oz. | 22 | 0. | | | 0 |
| (Yukon Club) black | 6 fl. oz. | 14 | 0. | | | 0 |
| Low calorie: | | | | | | |
| (Clicquot Club) | 6 fl. oz. | 45 | 0. | | | 0 |
| (Cott) | 6 fl. oz. | 45 | 0. | | | 0 |
| (Dr. Brown's) black | 6 fl. oz. | 20 | 0. | | | 0 |
| (Hoffman) black | 6 fl. oz. | 20 | 0. | | | 0 |
| (Key Food) black | 6 fl. oz. | 20 | 0. | | | 0 |
| (Mission) | 6 fl. oz. | 45 | 0. | | | 0 |
| (No-Cal) black | 6 fl. oz. | 12 | 0. | | | 0 |
| (Shasta) Wild | 6 fl. oz. | 37 | 0. | | | 0 |
| (Waldbaum) black | 6 fl. oz. | 20 | 0. | | | 0 |
| **RASPBERRY SYRUP,** low calorie: | | | | | | |
| (No-Cal) | 1 tsp. (5 grams) | <1 | 0. | | | (0) |
| **RASPBERRY TURNOVER,** | | | | | | |
| frozen (Pepperidge Farm) | 1 turnover (3.3 oz.) | 258 | 20.0 | | | |
| **RAVIOLI:** | | | | | | |
| Canned: | | | | | | |
| Beef or meat: | | | | | | |
| (Buitoni) | 8 oz. | | 4.5 | | | |
| In brine (Buitoni) | 8 oz. | | 3.8 | | | |
| (Chef Boy-Ar-Dee) | 1/5 of 40-oz. can | 1349 | 6.4 | | | |
| (Nalley's) | 8 oz. | | 10.2 | | | |
| (Prince) | 3.7-oz. can | | 4.8 | | | |
| Cheese: | | | | | | |
| (Buitoni) | 8 oz. | | 7.4 | | | |
| In brine (Buitoni) | 8 oz. | | 3.3 | | | |

(USDA): United States Department of Agriculture
*Prepared as Package Directs

| Food and Description | Measure or Quantity | Sodium (mg.) | —Fats in grams— | | | Choles- terol (mg.) |
|---|---|---|---|---|---|---|
| | | | Total | Satu- rated | Unsatu- rated | |
| (Chef Boy-Ar-Dee) | ½ of 15-oz. can | 1347 | 10.9 | | | |
| (Prince) | 3.7-oz. can | | 3.7 | | | |
| Chicken (Nalley's) | 8 oz. | | 10.0 | | | |
| Frozen: | | | | | | |
| Beef (Celeste) | 7 ravioli (4 oz.) | 300 | 5.7 | | | |
| Beef, dinner (Celeste) | ½ of 15-oz. pkg. | 660 | 6.4 | | | |
| Beef (Kraft) | 12½-oz. pkg. | 1628 | 14.9 | | | |
| Cheese (Buitoni) | 4 oz. | | 7.1 | | | |
| Cheese (Celeste) | 7 ravioli (4 oz.) | 250 | 6.3 | | | |
| Cheese, dinner (Celeste) | ½ of 15-oz. pkg. | 665 | 6.2 | | | |
| Cheese (Kraft) | 12½-oz. pkg. | 1848 | 16.6 | | | |
| Meat, without sauce (Buitoni) | 4 oz. | | 5.9 | | | |
| Meat, with sauce (Buitoni) | 4 oz. | | 4.4 | | | |
| *Raviolettes* (Buitoni) | 4 oz. | | 4.0 | | | |

**REDFISH** (See **DRUM, RED & OCEAN PERCH,** Atlantic)

**RED & GRAY SNAPPER,** raw:

| | | | | | | |
|---|---|---|---|---|---|---|
| Whole (USDA) | 1 lb. (weighed whole) | 158 | 2.1 | | | |
| Meat only (USDA) | 4 oz. | 76 | 1.0 | | | |

**REDHORSE, SILVER,** raw (USDA):

| | | | | | | |
|---|---|---|---|---|---|---|
| Drawn | 1 lb. (weighed eviscerated) | | 4.8 | | | |
| Meat only | 4 oz. | | 2.6 | | | |

| | | | | | | |
|---|---|---|---|---|---|---|
| ***RED POP,*** soft drink (No-Cal) | 6 fl. oz. | 12 | 0. | | | (0) |

**REINDEER,** raw, lean only (USDA)

| | | | | | | |
|---|---|---|---|---|---|---|
| | 4 oz. | | 4.3 | | | |

**RELISH:**

| | | | | | | |
|---|---|---|---|---|---|---|
| Barbecue (Crosse & Blackwell) | 1 T. (.7 oz.) | 220 | 0. | | | |
| Barbecue (Heinz) | 1 T. | 139 | .1 | | | |
| Corn (Crosse & Blackwell) | 1 T. (.6 oz.) | 340 | 0. | | | |
| Hamburger (Crosse & Blackwell) | 1 T. (.6 oz.) | 220 | 0. | | | |
| Hamburger (Del Monte) | 1 T. (.9 oz.) | 402 | <.1 | | | 0 |
| Hamburger (Heinz) | 1 T. | 146 | Tr. | | | |
| Hot dog (Crosse & Blackwell) | 1 T. (.7 oz.) | | 0. | | | |
| Hot dog (Del Monte) | 1 T. (.9 oz.) | 422 | .2 | | | 0 |

(USDA): United States Department of Agriculture
*Prepared as Package Directs

| Food and Description | Measure or Quantity | Sodium (mg.) | —Fats in grams— Total | Satu- rated | Unsatu- rated | Choles- terol (mg.) |
|---|---|---|---|---|---|---|
| Hot dog (Heinz) | 1 T. | 111 | .1 | | | |
| Hot pepper (Crosse & Blackwell) | 1 T. (.7 oz.) | | 0. | | | |
| India (Crosse & Blackwell) | 1 T. (.7 oz.) | 220 | 0. | | | |
| India (Heinz) | 1 T. | 115 | .1 | | | |
| Piccalilli (Crosse & Blackwell) | 1 T. (.7 oz.) | | 0. | | | |
| Piccalilli (Heinz) | 1 T. | 123 | .1 | | | |
| Sour (USDA) | ½ cup (4.3 oz.) | | 1.1 | | | 0 |
| Sour (USDA) | 1 T. (.5 oz.) | | .1 | | | 0 |
| Sweet: | | | | | | |
| (USDA) finely chopped | ½ cup (4.3 oz.) | 869 | .7 | | | 0 |
| (USDA) finely chopped | 1 T. (.5 oz.) | 107 | <.1 | | | 0 |
| (Aunt Jane's) | 1 rounded tsp. (.4 oz.) | 71 | <.1 | | | (0) |
| (Crosse & Blackwell) | 1 T. (.7 oz.) | | 0. | | | |
| (Del Monte) | 1 T. (.9 oz.) | 355 | .2 | | | 0 |
| (Heinz) | 1 T. | 181 | .1 | | | |
| (Smucker's) | 1 T. (.6 oz.) | 158 | Tr. | | | |

## RENNIN CUSTARD PRODUCTS
(See individual flavors)

## RHINE WINE:
| | | | | | | |
|---|---|---|---|---|---|---|
| (Gold Seal) 12% alcohol, | 3 fl. oz. (3.1 oz.) | 3 | 0. | | | (0) |
| (Great Western) 12.5% alcohol, regular | 3 fl. oz. | 25 | 0. | | | 0 |
| (Great Western) 12.5% alcohol, Dutchess | 3 fl. oz. | 27 | 0. | | | 0 |

## RHUBARB:
Fresh (USDA):
| | | | | | | |
|---|---|---|---|---|---|---|
| Partly trimmed | 1 lb. (weighed with part leaves, ends & trimmings) | 7 | .3 | | | 0 |
| Trimmed | 4 oz. | 2 | .1 | | | 0 |
| Diced | ½ cup (2.2 oz.) | 1 | <.1 | | | 0 |
| Cooked, sweetened, solids & liq. (USDA) | ½ cup (4.2 oz.) | 2 | .1 | | | 0 |
| Frozen, sweetened: | | | | | | |
| Not thawed (USDA) | ½ cup (3.9 oz.) | 4 | .2 | | | 0 |
| Cooked, added sugar, solids & liq. (USDA) | ½ cup (4.4 oz.) | 4 | .2 | | | 0 |
| (Birds Eye) | ½ cup (4 oz.) | 2 | .1 | | | 0 |

(USDA): United States Department of Agriculture
*Prepared as Package Directs

| Food and Description | Measure or Quantity | Sodium (mg.) | — Fats in grams — Total | Satu- rated | Unsatu- rated | Choles- terol (mg.) |
|---|---|---|---|---|---|---|
| **RHUBARB PIE,** home recipe, 2-crust (USDA) | ¹/₆ of 9″ pie (5.6 oz.) | 427 | 16.9 | 5. | 12. | |
| **RICE:** | | | | | | |
| Brown: | | | | | | |
| Raw (USDA) | ½ cup (3.7 oz.) | 9 | 2.0 | | | 0 |
| Raw (USDA) | 1 oz. | 3 | .5 | | | 0 |
| Cooked: | | | | | | |
| With salt added: | | | | | | |
| (USDA) | 4 oz. | 320 | .7 | | | 0 |
| (Carolina) | 4 oz. | 320 | .7 | | | (0) |
| (River Brand) | 4 oz. | 320 | .7 | | | (0) |
| (Water Maid) | 4 oz. | 320 | .7 | | | (0) |
| Parboiled (Uncle Ben's) with no added butter or salt | ⅔ cup (4.2 oz.) | 6 | 1.1 | | | 0 |
| Parboiled (Uncle Ben's) with added butter | ⅔ cup (4.3 oz.) | 32 | 3.2 | | | |
| Frozen, in beef stock (Green Giant) | ⅓ of 12-oz. pkg. | 782 | 2.8 | | | |
| White: | | | | | | |
| Instant or precooked: | | | | | | |
| Dry, long-grain (USDA) | ½ cup (1.9 oz.) | <1 | .1 | | | 0 |
| Dry, long-grain (USDA) | 1 oz. | <1 | <.1 | | | 0 |
| Cooked: | | | | | | |
| With salt added: | | | | | | |
| Long-grain (USDA) | ⅔ cup (3.3 oz.) | 254 | Tr. | | | 0 |
| (Carolina) | ⅔ cup (3.3 oz.) | 254 | Tr. | | | (0) |
| Without salt: | | | | | | |
| (Minute Rice) no added butter | ⅔ cup (4 oz.) | 1 | Tr. | | | 0 |
| Long-grain (Uncle Ben's Quick) no added butter | ⅔ cup (4 oz.) | 9 | <.1 | | | 0 |
| Long-grain (Uncle Ben's Quick) with added butter | ⅔ cup (4.1 oz.) | 37 | 2.5 | | | |
| Parboiled: | | | | | | |
| Dry, long-grain (USDA) | 1 oz. | 3 | <.1 | | | 0 |
| Cooked: | | | | | | |
| With added salt: | | | | | | |
| Long-grain (USDA) | ⅔ cup (4.1 oz.) | 419 | .1 | | | 0 |
| (Aunt Caroline) | ⅔ cup (4.1 oz.) | 419 | .1 | | | (0) |

(USDA): United States Department of Agriculture
*Prepared as Package Directs

| Food and Description | Measure or Quantity | Sodium (mg.) | — Fats in grams — | | | Choles- terol (mg.) |
|---|---|---|---|---|---|---|
| | | | Total | Satu- rated | Unsatu- rated | |
| No added salt, long-grain (Uncle Ben's Converted), no added butter | ⅔ cup (4.3 oz.) | 3 | .2 | | | 0 |
| Regular: | | | | | | |
| Raw (USDA) | ½ cup (3.5 oz.) | 5 | .4 | | | 0 |
| Cooked with salt: | | | | | | |
| (USDA) | ⅔ cup (4.8 oz.) | 512 | .1 | | | 0 |
| Extra long-grain (Carolina) | ⅔ cup (4.8 oz.) | 512 | .1 | | | (0) |
| Long-grain (Mahatma) | ⅔ cup (4.8 oz.) | 512 | .1 | | | (0) |
| (River Brand) fluffy | ⅔ cup (4.8 oz.) | 512 | .1 | | | (0) |
| (Water Maid) | ⅔ cup (4.8 oz.) | 512 | .1 | | | (0) |
| White & wild, frozen (Green Giant) | ⅓ of 12-oz. pkg. | 522 | 1.1 | | | |
| Wild (See **WILD RICE**) | | | | | | |
| **RICE BRAN** (USDA) | 1 oz. | Tr. | 4.5 | | | 0 |
| **RICE CEREAL** (USDA): | | | | | | |
| With casein & other added nutrients | 1 oz. | 170 | <.1 | | | 0 |
| Wheat gluten & other added nutrients | 1 oz. | 227 | <.1 | | | 0 |
| *RICE CHEX,* cereal (Ralston) | 1⅛ cups (1 oz.) | 261 | .1 | | | (0) |
| **RICE FLAKES,** cereal, added nutrients (USDA) | 1 cup (1.1 oz.) | 296 | <.1 | | | 0 |
| **RICE, FRIED:** | | | | | | |
| Frozen, with almonds (Green Giant) | ⅓ of 12-oz. pkg. | 743 | 6.8 | | | |
| Seasoning Mix (Durkee) | 1-oz. pkg. | 1931 | 1.1 | | | |
| *Seasoning Mix (Durkee) | 2 cups (1-oz. pkg.) | 3195 | 1.4 | | | |
| *RICE KRISPIES,* cereal (Kellogg's) | 1 cup (1 oz.) | 261 | .1 | | | (0) |
| **RICE MIX:** | | | | | | |
| Beef: | | | | | | |
| (Uncle Ben's) | 6-oz. pkg. | 3995 | 3.4 | | | 0 |
| *(Uncle Ben's) no added butter or salt | ½ cup (4.2 oz.) | 692 | .6 | | | Tr. |
| *(Uncle Ben's) with added butter, no added salt | ½ cup (4.3 oz.) | 715 | 2.5 | | | |

(USDA): United States Department of Agriculture
*Prepared as Package Directs

| Food and Description | Measure or Quantity | Sodium (mg.) | — Fats in grams — | | | Choles- terol (mg.) |
|---|---|---|---|---|---|---|
| | | | Total | Satu- rated | Unsatu- rated | |
| *(Village Inn) | ½ cup | | 1.7 | | | |
| Brown & wild: | | | | | | |
| (Uncle Ben's) | 6-oz. pkg. | 1980 | 5.1 | | | 0 |
| *(Uncle Ben's) no added butter or salt | ½ cup (4.3 oz.) | 319 | .8 | | | 0 |
| *(Uncle Ben's) with added butter, no added salt | ½ cup (4.3 oz.) | 344 | 2.9 | | | |
| Chicken: | | | | | | |
| (Uncle Ben's) | 6-oz. pkg. | 2542 | 5.4 | | | 0 |
| *(Uncle Ben's) no added butter or salt | ½ cup (3.6 oz.) | 416 | .9 | | | |
| *(Uncle Ben's) with added butter, no added salt | ½ cup (3.8 oz.) | 460 | 4.5 | | | |
| *(Village Inn) | ½ cup | | 1.7 | | | |
| Curried or curry: | | | | | | |
| (Uncle Ben's) | 6-oz. pkg. | 3179 | 1.2 | | | 0 |
| *(Uncle Ben's) no added butter or salt | ½ cup (4.2 oz.) | 541 | .2 | | | 0 |
| *(Uncle Ben's) with added butter, no added salt | ½ cup (4.2 oz.) | 564 | 2.1 | | | |
| *(Village Inn) | ½ cup | | 1.7 | | | |
| *Drumstick (Minute Rice) | ½ cup (4.1 oz.) | 634 | 5.7 | | | 23 |
| *Herb (Village Inn) | ½ cup | | 1.7 | | | |
| *Keriyaki dinner (Betty Crocker) | 1 cup | 223 | 20.3 | | | |
| Long-grain & wild: | | | | | | |
| (Uncle Ben's) | 6-oz. pkg. | 2926 | 1.5 | | | 0 |
| *(Uncle Ben's) no added butter or salt | ½ cup (4 oz.) | 482 | .2 | | | |
| *(Uncle Ben's) with added butter, no added salt | ½ cup (4.1 oz.) | 505 | 2.1 | | | |
| *(Village Inn) | ½ cup | | 1.7 | | | |
| *Milanese (Betty Crocker) | ½ cup | 797 | 6.4 | | | |
| *Oriental, dinner (Jeno's) Add 'n Heat | 40-oz. pkg. | | 81.6 | | | |
| Pilaf: | | | | | | |
| (Uncle Ben's) | 6-oz. pkg. | 2703 | 2.2 | | | 0 |
| *(Uncle Ben's) no added butter or salt | ½ cup (3.3 oz.) | 435 | .4 | | | |
| *(Uncle Ben's) with added butter, no added salt | ½ cup (3.5 oz.) | 479 | 3.9 | | | |
| *Provence (Betty Crocker) | ½ cup | 895 | 5.7 | | | |
| *Rib Roast (Minute Rice) | ½ cup (4.1 oz.) | 508 | 4.0 | | | 12 |

(USDA): United States Department of Agriculture
*Prepared as Package Directs

| Food and Description | Measure or Quantity | Sodium (mg.) | Total | Satu-rated | Unsatu-rated | Choles-terol (mg.) |
|---|---|---|---|---|---|---|
| | | | | — Fats in grams — | | |
| Spanish (See also **RICE, SPANISH**): | | | | | | |
| *(Minute Rice) | ½ cup (5.6 oz.) | 866 | 3.7 | | | 12 |
| (Uncle Ben's) | 5½-oz. pkg. | 4365 | .9 | | | 0 |
| *(Uncle Ben's) no added butter or salt | ½ cup (4.6 oz.) | 888 | .2 | | | 0 |
| *(Uncle Ben's) with added butter, no added salt | ½ cup (4.6 oz.) | 916 | 2.5 | | | |
| *(Village Inn) | ½ cup | | 1.7 | | | |
| *Yellow (Village Inn) | ½ cup | | 1.7 | | | |
| **RICE & PEAS with MUSH-ROOMS:** | | | | | | |
| Frozen (Birds Eye) | ⅓ of pkg. (2.3 oz.) | 536 | .1 | | | 0 |
| Frozen (Green Giant) | ⅓ of 12-oz. pkg. | 437 | 2.3 | | | |
| **RICE PILAF,** frozen (Green Giant) | ⅓ of 12-oz. pkg. | 607 | 1.1 | | | |
| **RICE POLISH** (USDA) | 1 oz. | Tr. | 3.6 | | | 0 |
| **RICE PUDDING:** | | | | | | |
| Home recipe, with raisins (USDA)[1] | ½ cup (4.7 oz.) | 94 | 4.1 | 3. | 2. | 15 |
| Canned: | | | | | | |
| (Betty Crocker) | ½ cup | 166 | 4.2 | | | |
| (Hunt's)[2] | 5-oz. can | 192 | 11.5 | 2. | 9. | |
| **RICE, SPANISH:** | | | | | | |
| Home recipe (USDA) | 4 oz. | 358 | 1.9 | | | |
| Canned: | | | | | | |
| (Heinz) | 8¾-oz. can | 1545 | 4.5 | | | |
| (Nalley's) | 4 oz. | | 1.6 | | | |
| (Van Camp) | ½ cup (.9 oz.) | | 1.8 | | | |
| Frozen (Green Giant) | ⅓ of 12-oz. pkg. | 476 | .6 | | | |
| **RICE, SPANISH, SEASONING MIX** (Lawry's) | 1½-oz. pkg. | | 1.3 | | | |
| **RICE VERDI,** frozen (Green Giant) | ⅓ of 12-oz. pkg. | 544 | 2.3 | | | |
| *ROAST 'n BOAST* (General Foods): | | | | | | |
| For beef | 1½-oz. pkg. | 2678 | .7 | | | 0 |
| For chicken | 1⅜-oz. pkg. | 3440 | .3 | | | 0 |

(USDA): United States Department of Agriculture
*Prepared as Package Directs
[1]Principal source of fat: milk.
[2]Principal source of fat: soybean oil.

| Food and Description | Measure or Quantity | Sodium (mg.) | — Fats in grams — | | | Choles-terol (mg.) |
|---|---|---|---|---|---|---|
| | | | Total | Satu-rated | Unsatu-rated | |
| For pork | 1¾-oz. pkg. | 5399 | .4 | | | 0 |
| For stew | 1½-oz. pkg. | 4106 | .7 | | | 0 |
| **ROCKFISH** (USDA): | | | | | | |
| Raw, meat only | 1 lb. | 272 | 8.2 | | | |
| Oven-steamed, with onion | 4 oz. | 77 | 2.8 | | | |
| **ROE** (USDA): | | | | | | |
| Raw, carp, cod, haddock, herring, pike or shad | 4 oz. | | 2.6 | | | |
| Raw, salmon, sturgeon, turbot | 4 oz. | | 11.8 | | | 401 |
| Baked or broiled,[1] cod & shad | 4 oz. | 83 | 3.2 | | | |
| Canned, cod, haddock or herring, solids & liq. | 4 oz. | | 3.2 | | | |
| **ROLL & BUN:** | | | | | | |
| Barbeque (Arnold) | 1 bun (1.6 oz.) | | 2.7 | | | |
| Brown & serve: | | | | | | |
|   Unbrowned (USDA)[2] | 1 oz. | 145 | 1.9 | Tr. | 2. | |
|   Browned (USDA)[2] | 1 oz. | 159 | 2.2 | Tr. | 2. | |
|   (Wonder) | 1 roll (1 oz.) | 134 | 1.5 | | | |
| Butter crescent (Pepperidge Farm) | 1 roll (1.2 oz.) | 203 | 8.0 | | | |
| Butterfly (Pepperidge Farm) | 1 roll (.6 oz.) | 87 | 2.1 | | | |
| Cinnamon nut (Pepperidge Farm) | 1 bun (1 oz.) | 76 | 4.8 | | | |
| Cloverleaf, home recipe (USDA)[3] | 1 roll (1.2 oz.) | 98 | 3.0 | <1. | 2. | |
| Club (Pepperidge Farm) | 1 roll (1.6 oz.) | 267 | .7 | | | |
| Deli Twist (Arnold) | 1 roll (1.2 oz.) | | 3.3 | | | |
| Diet size (Arnold) | 1 roll (.5 oz.) | | 1.1 | | | |
| Dinner (Arnold) 12 or 24 to pkg. | 1 roll (¾ oz.) | | 2.2 | | | |
| Dinner (Pepperidge Farm) | 1 roll (.7 oz.) | 90 | 1.6 | | | |
| *Dutch Egg*, sandwich (Arnold) | 1 bun (1.7 oz.) | | 3.9 | | | |
| Finger: | | | | | | |
|   (Arnold) handipan | 1 roll (.7 oz.) | | 1.7 | | | |
|   Egg (Arnold) family | 1 roll (.7 oz.) | | 1.7 | | | |
| Frankfurter: | | | | | | |
|   (USDA)[2] | 1 roll (1.4 oz.) | 202 | 2.2 | Tr. | 2. | |
|   (Arnold) | 1 roll (1.4 oz.) | | 2.6 | | | |
|   New England (Arnold) | 1 roll (1.6 oz.) | | 2.8 | | | |
|   (Pepperidge Farm) | 1 roll (1.4 oz.) | 205 | 2.3 | | | |
|   (Wonder) | 1 bun (1.5 oz.) | 232 | 2.2 | | | |

(USDA): United States Department of Agriculture
*Prepared as Package Directs
[1]Prepared with butter or margarine & lemon juice or vinegar.
[2]Principal source of fat: vegetable shortening.
[3]Principal sources of fat: vegetable shortening, milk & egg.

| Food and Description | Measure or Quantity | Sodium (mg.) | —Fats in grams— | | | Cholesterol (mg.) |
|---|---|---|---|---|---|---|
| | | | Total | Saturated | Unsaturated | |
| French: | | | | | | |
|   Triple (Pepperidge Farm) | 1 roll (3.5 oz.) | 589 | 1.5 | | | |
|   Twin (Pepperidge Farm) | 1 roll (5.2 oz.) | 867 | 2.1 | | | |
| Golden Twist (Pepperidge Farm) | 1 roll (1.2 oz.) | 178 | 6.7 | | | |
| Hamburger: | | | | | | |
|   (USDA)[1] | 1 roll (1.4 oz.) | 202 | 2.2 | Tr. | 2. | |
|   (Pepperidge Farm) | 1 roll (1.4 oz.) | 201 | 2.2 | | | |
|   (Wonder) | 1 bun (1.5 oz.) | 232 | 2.2 | | | |
| Hard, round or rectangular (USDA) | 1 roll (1.8 oz.) | 312 | 1.6 | <1. | 1. | |
| Hearth (Pepperidge Farm) | 1 roll (.8 oz.) | 118 | .9 | | | |
| Honey, frozen (Morton) | 1 serving (2.2 oz.) | 56 | 6.5 | | | |
| Kaiser, brown & serve (Arnold) | 1 roll (1.7 oz.) | | 1.8 | | | |
| Old Fashioned (Pepperidge Farm) | 1 roll (.6 oz.) | 90 | 2.2 | | | |
| Parker (Arnold) handipan | 1 roll (.7 oz.) | | 1.7 | | | |
| Party Pan (Pepperidge Farm): | | | | | | |
|   Finger | 1 roll (.7 oz.) | 84 | 1.5 | | | |
|   Round | 1 roll (.4 oz.) | 51 | .9 | | | |
| Pecan, coffee (Pepperidge Farm) | 1 bun (1.7 oz.) | 186 | 11.6 | | | |
| Plain (USDA)[1] | 1 roll (1 oz.) | 143 | 1.6 | Tr. | 1. | |
| Raisin (USDA)[1] | 1 oz. | 109 | .8 | Tr. | <1. | |
| Sandwich, soft (Arnold) | 1 roll (1.5 oz.) | | 4.0 | | | |
| Sesame crisp (Pepperidge Farm): | | | | | | |
|   Midwest | 1 roll (.8 oz.) | 112 | 1.4 | | | |
|   East | 1 roll (.9 oz.) | 119 | 1.5 | | | |
| Soft (Arnold) handipan | 1 roll (.7 oz.) | | 1.6 | | | |
| Sweet (USDA)[2] | 1 bun (1.5 oz.) | 167 | 3.9 | <1. | 3. | |
| Whole-wheat (USDA)[1] | 1 roll (1.3 oz.) | 214 | 1.1 | Tr. | <1. | |
| **ROLL DOUGH:** | | | | | | |
| Frozen, unraised (USDA)[1] | 1 oz. | 137 | 1.4 | Tr. | 1. | |
| Frozen, baked (USDA)[1] | 1 oz. | 159 | 1.5 | Tr. | 1. | |
| **ROLL MIX:** | | | | | | |
| Dry (USDA)[1] | 1 oz. | 117 | 1.7 | Tr. | 1. | |
| *Prepared with water (USDA)[1] | 1 oz. | 89 | 1.3 | Tr. | 1. | |
| (Pillsbury) hot | 1 oz. | | | | | |
| ***ROMAN MEAL CEREAL,** dry* | ¾ cup (1.3 oz.) | 2 | .7 | Tr. | <1. | 0 |
| **ROOT BEER SOFT DRINK:** | | | | | | |
| Sweetened: | | | | | | |
|   (Canada Dry) *Rooti* | 6 fl. oz. | 13+ | 0. | | | 0 |

(USDA): United States Department of Agriculture
*Prepared as Package Directs
[1]Principal source of fat: vegetable shortening.
[2]Principal sources of fat: vegetable shortening, milk & egg.

| Food and Description | Measure or Quantity | Sodium (mg.) | Fats in grams — | | | Choles- terol (mg.) |
| --- | --- | --- | --- | --- | --- | --- |
| | | | Total | Satu- rated | Unsatu- rated | |
| (Clicquot Club) | 6 fl. oz. | 12 | 0. | | | 0 |
| (Cott) | 6 fl. oz. | 12 | 0. | | | 0 |
| (Fanta) | 6 fl. oz. | 7 | 0. | | | 0 |
| (Dr. Brown's) | 6 fl. oz. | 3 | 0. | | | 0 |
| (Hires) | 6 fl. oz. | 2 | 0. | | | 0 |
| (Hoffman) | 6 fl. oz. | 3 | 0. | | | 0 |
| (Key Food) | 6 fl. oz. | 3 | 0. | | | 0 |
| (Kirsch) | 6 fl. oz. | <1 | 0. | | | 0 |
| (Mission) | 6 fl. oz. | 12 | 0. | | | 0 |
| (Nedick's) | 6 fl. oz. | 3 | 0. | | | 0 |
| (Nehi) | 6 fl. oz. (6.6 oz.) | 0+ | 0. | | | 0 |
| (Shasta) draft | 6 fl. oz. | 22 | 0. | | | 0 |
| (Waldbaum) | 6 fl. oz. | 3 | 0. | | | 0 |
| (Yukon Club) | 6 fl. oz. | 3 | 0. | | | 0 |
| Low calorie: | | | | | | |
| (Canada Dry) | 6 fl. oz. | 12+ | 0. | | | 0 |
| (Clicquot Club) | 6 fl. oz. | 45 | 0. | | | 0 |
| (Cott) | 6 fl. oz. | 45 | 0. | | | 0 |
| (Hoffman) | 6 fl. oz. | 35 | 0. | | | 0 |
| (Mission) | 6 fl. oz. | 45 | 0. | | | 0 |
| (No-Cal) | 6 fl. oz. | 11 | 0. | | | 0 |
| (Shasta) draft | 6 fl. oz. | 37 | 0. | | | 0 |
| (Yukon Club) | 6 fl. oz. | 64 | 0. | | | 0 |
| **ROSE APPLE,** raw (USDA): | | | | | | |
| Whole | 1 lb. (weighed with caps & seeds) | | .9 | | | 0 |
| Flesh only | 4 oz. | | .3 | | | 0 |
| **ROSEMARY** (Spice Islands) | 1 tsp. | <1 | | | | (0) |
| **ROSE WINE:** | | | | | | |
| (Great Western) 12.5% alcohol | 3 fl. oz. | 38 | 0. | | | 0 |
| (Great Western) Isabella, 12.5% alcohol | 3 fl. oz. | <1 | 0. | | | 0 |
| **RUSK:** | | | | | | |
| (USDA)[1] | 1 piece (.5 oz.) | 35 | 1.2 | Tr. | 1. | |
| Holland (Nabisco) | 1 piece (.4 oz.) | 34 | .6 | | | |
| **RUTABAGA:** | | | | | | |
| Raw, without tops (USDA) | 1 lb. (weighed with skin) | 19 | .4 | | | 0 |

(USDA): United States Department of Agriculture
*Prepared as Package Directs
[1]Principal sources of fat: vegetable shortening, egg & milk.

| Food and Description | Measure or Quantity | Sodium (mg.) | Total | Fats in grams — Satu- rated | Unsatu- rated | Choles- terol (mg.) |
|---|---|---|---|---|---|---|
| Raw, diced (USDA) | ½ cup (2.5 oz.) | 4 | <.1 | | | 0 |
| Boiled without salt, diced, drained (USDA) | ½ cup (3 oz.) | 3 | <.1 | | | 0 |
| Boiled without salt, mashed (USDA) | ½ cup (4.3 oz.) | 5 | .1 | | | 0 |
| Canned (King Pharr) | ½ cup | | | | | |
| **RYE,** whole grain (USDA) | 1 oz. | <1 | .5 | | | 0 |

**RYE FLOUR** (See **FLOUR**)

**RYE WHISKEY** (See **DISTILLED LIQUOR**)

*RYE-KRISP* (See **CRACKER**)

*RY-KING* (See **BREAD**)

# S

| | | | | | | |
|---|---|---|---|---|---|---|
| **SABLEFISH,** raw (USDA): | | | | | | |
| Whole | 1 lb. (weighed whole) | 107 | 28.4 | | | |
| Meat only | 4 oz. | 64 | 16.9 | | | |
| **SAFFLOWER SEED** (USDA): | | | | | | |
| Kernels, dry, in hull | ½ lb. (weighed in hull) | | 68.8 | 6. | 63. | |
| Kernels, dry, hulled | 1 oz. | | 16.9 | 1. | 15. | |
| Meal, partially defatted | 1 oz. | | 2.3 | Tr. | 2. | |
| **SAFFRON** (Spice Islands) | 1 tsp. | <1 | | | | (0) |
| **SAGE** (Spice Islands) | 1 tsp. | <1 | | | | (0) |

**SAINT JOHN'S-BREAD FLOUR** (See **FLOUR**, Carob)

| | | | | | | |
|---|---|---|---|---|---|---|
| **SALAD DRESSING** (See also **SALAD DRESSING, LOW CALORIE**): | | | | | | |
| Avocado, refrigerated (Marzetti) | 1 T. (.5 oz.) | | 8.2 | | | 10 |
| (Bama) | 1 T. (.5 oz.) | 315 | 5.1 | | | |

(USDA): United States Department of Agriculture
*Prepared as Package Directs

| Food and Description | Measure or Quantity | Sodium (mg.) | —Fats in grams— | | | Choles- terol (mg.) |
|---|---|---|---|---|---|---|
| | | | Total | Satu- rated | Unsatu- rated | |
| *Bennett's* | 1 T. (.5 oz.) | 127 | 4.7 | | | |
| Blendaise (Marzetti) | 1 T. (.5 oz.) | | 5.5 | | | 7 |
| Bleu or blue cheese: | | | | | | |
| (USDA)[1] | 1 oz. | 310 | 14.8 | 3. | 12. | |
| (USDA)[1] | 1 T. (.5 oz.) | 164 | 7.8 | 2. | 6. | |
| (Bernstein's) Danish | 1 T. (.5 oz.) | 115 | 4.4 | <1. | 4. | |
| (Kraft) Imperial | 1 T. (.5 oz.) | 138 | 7.1 | | | |
| (Kraft) refrigerated | 1 T. (.5 oz.) | 171 | 7.6 | | | |
| (Kraft) Roka | 1 T. (.5 oz.) | 177 | 5.4 | | | |
| (Lawry's) | 1 T. (.5 oz.) | | 5.8 | | | |
| (Marzetti) | 1 T. (.5 oz.) | | 7.0 | | | 7 |
| (Marzetti) refrigerated  . | 1 T. (.5 oz.) | | 8.6 | | | 9 |
| (Wish-Bone) chunky | 1 T. (.5 oz.) | 149 | 7.7 | 1. | 6. | 1 |
| Boiled, home recipe (USDA)[2] | 1 T. (.6 oz.) | 116 | 1.6 | <1. | <1. | 12 |
| Caesar (Kraft) Golden | 1 T. (.5 oz.) | 170 | 6.7 | | | |
| Caesar (Kraft) Imperial | 1 T. (.5 oz.) | 164 | 8.2 | | | |
| Caesar (Lawry's) | 1 T. (.5 oz.) | | 7.4 | | | |
| Canadian (Lawry's) | 1 T. (.5 oz.) | | 7.5 | | | |
| Coleslaw (Bernstein's) | 1 T. (.5 oz.) | 188 | 4.4 | <1. | 4. | |
| Coleslaw (Kraft) | 1 T. (.5 oz.) | 187 | 5.5 | | | |
| French: | | | | | | |
| Home recipe with corn oil (USDA)[3] | 1 T. (.6 oz.) | 105 | 11.2 | 1. | 10. | |
| Home recipe with cottonseed oil (USDA)[4] | 1 T. (.6 oz.) | 105 | 11.2 | 3. | 8. | |
| Commercial (USDA)[5] | 1 T. (.6 oz.) | 219 | 6.2 | 1. | 5. | |
| (Bennett's) | 1 T. (.5 oz.) | 217 | 7.2 | | | 0 |
| (Bernstein's) | 1 T. (.5 oz.) | 224 | 5.4 | <1. | 5. | |
| (Bernstein's) New Orleans | 1 T. (.5 oz.) | 292 | 5.4 | <1. | 5. | |
| (Hellmann's) Family[6] | 1 T. (.6 oz.) | 272 | 6.0 | <1. | 5. | 2 |
| (Kraft) | 1 T. (.5 oz.) | 231 | 6.5 | | | |
| (Kraft) Casino | 1 T. (.5 oz.) | 180 | 5.5 | | | |
| (Kraft) Catalina | 1 T. (.5 oz.) | 172 | 5.2 | | | |
| (Kraft) *Miracle* | 1 T. (.5 oz.) | 303 | 5.3 | | | |
| (Lawry's) | 1 T. (.5 oz.) | | 5.8 | | | |
| (Lawry's) San Francisco | 1 T. (.5 oz.) | | 5.4 | | | |
| (Marzetti) Blue, refrigerated | 1 T. (.5 oz.) | | 6.1 | | | 6 |
| (Marzetti) Country | 1 T. (.5 oz.) | | 6.3 | | | 5 |

(USDA): United States Department of Agriculture
*Prepared as Package Directs
[1]Principal sources of fat: soybean oil, cottonseed oil, corn oil & cheese.
[2]Principal sources of fat: butter, milk & egg.
[3]Principal source of fat: corn oil.
[4]Principal source of fat: cottonseed oil.
[5]Principal sources of fat: soybean oil, cottonseed oil & corn oil.
[6]Principal sources of fat: vegetable oil & egg yolk.

| Food and Description | Measure or Quantity | Sodium (mg.) | Fats in grams — Total | Satu- rated | Unsatu- rated | Choles- terol (mg.) |
|---|---|---|---|---|---|---|
| (Nalley's) | .5 oz. | | .5 | | | |
| (Wish-Bone) | 1 T. (.6 oz.) | 163 | 1.1 | Tr. | <1. | |
| (Wish-Bone) Deluxe | 1 T. (.6 oz.) | 83 | 5.5 | <1. | 5. | |
| (Wish-Bone) Garlic | 1 T. (.6 oz.) | 317 | 6.0 | <1. | 5. | |
| Fruit (Kraft) | 1 T. (.5 oz.) | 103 | 4.6 | | | |
| Garlic: | | | | | | |
| French (Hellmann's) *Old Home-stead*[1] | 1 T. (.6 oz.) | 240 | 6.1 | 1. | 5. | 5 |
| (Marzetti) creamy | 1 T. (.5 oz.) | | 7.2 | | | 4 |
| (Marzetti) creamy, refrigerated | 1 T. (.5 oz.) | | 9.0 | | | 9 |
| (Wish-Bone) creamy | 1 T. (.5 oz.) | 174 | 8.1 | 1. | 7. | |
| German Style (Marzetti) | 1 T. (.5 oz.) | | 5.0 | | | 0 |
| Green Goddess: | | | | | | |
| (Bernstein's) | 1 T. (.5 oz.) | 225 | 4.4 | <1. | 4. | |
| (Kraft) | 1 T. (.5 oz.) | 138 | 8.2 | | | |
| (Kraft) Imperial | 1 T. (.5 oz.) | 64 | 9.4 | | | |
| (Lawry's) | 1 T. (.5 oz.) | | 6.1 | | | |
| (Wish-Bone) | 1 T. (.5 oz.) | 150 | 7.0 | 1. | 6. | <1 |
| Green onion (Kraft) | 1 T. (.5 oz.) | 152 | 7.6 | | | |
| Hawaiian (Lawry's) | 1 T. (.6 oz.) | | 5.5 | | | |
| Herb & garlic (Kraft) | 1 T. (.5 oz.) | 147 | 9.7 | | | |
| Italian: | | | | | | |
| (USDA)[2] | 1 T. (.5 oz.) | 314 | 9.0 | 2. | 8. | |
| (Bernstein's) | 1 T. (.5 oz.) | 184 | 6.4 | 1. | 5. | |
| (Hellmann's) True[3] | 1 T. (.5 oz.) | 315 | 9.0 | 1. | 8. | 0 |
| (Kraft) | 1 T. (.5 oz.) | 222 | 9.7 | | | |
| (Lawry's) | 1 T. (.5 oz.) | | 8.1 | | | |
| (Lawry's) with cheese | 1 T. (.5 oz.) | | 4.5 | | | |
| (Marzetti) creamy | 1 T. (.5 oz.) | | 7.3 | | | 4 |
| (Marzetti) Sunny | 1 T. (.5 oz.) | | 8.8 | | | 0 |
| (Wish-Bone) | 1 T. (.5 oz.) | 362 | 8.1 | 1. | 7. | |
| (Wish-Bone) Rosé | 1 T. (.5 oz.) | 317 | 6.3 | <1. | 5. | 0 |
| Mayonnaise (See **MAYONNAISE**) | | | | | | |
| Mayonnaise-type salad dressing (USDA)[4] | 1 T. (.5 oz.) | 88 | 6.3 | 1. | 5. | 8 |
| Mayonnaise, imitation (Healthlife) | .5 oz. | 71 | 6.4 | <1. | 6. | 0 |
| *Miracle Whip* (Kraft) | 1 T. (.5 oz.) | 90 | 7.0 | | | |
| Oil & vinegar (Kraft) | 1 T. (.5 oz.) | 231 | 7.1 | | | |
| Onion, California (Wish-Bone) | 1 T. (.5 oz.) | 164 | 8.0 | 1. | 7. | |

(USDA): United States Department of Agriculture
*Prepared as Package Directs
[1]Principal sources of fat: vegetable oil & egg yolk.
[2]Principal sources of fat: soybean oil, cottonseed oil & corn oil.
[3]Principal source of fat: vegetable oil.
[4]Principal sources of fat: soybean oil, cottonseed oil, corn oil & egg.

| Food and Description | Measure or Quantity | Sodium (mg.) | Total | Satu-rated | Unsatu-rated | Choles-terol (mg.) |
|---|---|---|---|---|---|---|
| | | | —Fats in grams— | | | |
| Potato salad (Marzetti) | 1 T. (.5 oz.) | | 5.8 | | | 9 |
| Ranch Style (Marzetti) | 1 T. (.5 oz.) | | 5.3 | | | 0 |
| Red wine vinegar & oil (Lawry's) | 1 T. (.6 oz.) | | 4.6 | | | |
| Rich 'n' Tangy (Dutch Pantry) | 1 T. (.6 oz.) | 188 | 6.0 | <1. | 5. | 0 |
| Romano Caesar (Marzetti) | 1 T. (.5 oz.) | | 7.2 | | | <1 |
| Roquefort: | | | | | | |
| (USDA)[1] | 1 T. (.5 oz.) | 164 | 7.8 | 2. | 6. | |
| (Bernstein's) | 1 T. (.5 oz.) | 142 | 5.0 | <1. | 4. | |
| (Kraft) refrigerated | 1 T. (.5 oz.) | 172 | 5.7 | | | |
| (Kraft) refrigerated, Imperial | 1 T. (.5 oz.) | 145 | 7.1 | | | |
| (Marzetti) refrigerated | 1 T. (.5 oz.) | | 8.3 | | | 9 |
| Russian: | | | | | | |
| (USDA)[2] | 1 T. (.5 oz.) | 130 | 7.6 | 1. | 6. | |
| (Kraft) | 1 T. (.5 oz.) | 126 | 4.3 | | | |
| (Kraft) creamy | 1 T. (.5 oz.) | 56 | 6.7 | | | |
| (Marzetti) creamy | 1 T. (.5 oz.) | | 7.4 | | | 6 |
| (Wish-Bone) | 1 T. (.5 oz.) | 167 | 2.9 | Tr. | 2. | |
| (Saffola) | 1 T. (.5 oz.) | 88 | 4.8 | Tr. | 4. | 3 |
| Salad Bowl (Kraft) | 1 T. (.5 oz.) | 99 | 5.0 | | | |
| Salad 'n Sandwich (Kraft) | 1 T. (.5 oz.) | 92 | 4.7 | | | |
| Salad Secret (Kraft) | 1 T. (.5 oz.) | 245 | 5.3 | | | |
| Sherry (Lawry's) | 1 T. (.5 oz.) | | 5.3 | | | |
| Slaw (Marzetti) regular or refrigerated[3] | 1 T. (.5 oz.) | | 6.8 | | | 14 |
| Spin Blend (Best Foods) | 1 T. (.5 oz.) | 100 | 5.0 | <1. | 4. | 5 |
| Spin Blend (Hellmann's)[3] | 1 T. (.5 oz.) | 100 | 5.0 | <1. | 4. | 5 |
| Sweet & Saucy (Marzetti) | 1 T. (.5 oz.) | | 6.7 | | | 0 |
| Sweet 'n' Sour (Dutch Pantry) | 1 T. (.6 oz.) | 63 | 7.1 | 2. | 5. | 0 |
| Sweet & Sour (Kraft) | 1 T. (.5 oz.) | 64 | .2 | | | |
| Tahitian Isle (Wish-Bone) | 1 T. (.5 oz.) | 167 | 2.9 | Tr. | 2. | |
| Tang (Nalley's) | | | 4.5 | | | |
| Tart & Creamy (Bama) | 1 T. (.5 oz.) | 196 | 8.2 | | | |
| Thousand Island: | | | | | | |
| (USDA)[2] | 1 T. (.6 oz.) | 112 | 8.0 | 1. | 7. | |
| (Bernstein's) | 1 T. (.5 oz.) | 127 | 4.6 | <1. | 4. | |
| (Best Foods) | 1 T. (.5 oz.) | 180 | 5.4 | 1. | 4. | Tr. |
| (Kraft) | 1 T. (.5 oz.) | 99 | 7.1 | | | |
| (Kraft) Imperial | 1 T. (.5 oz.) | 60 | 7.9 | | | |
| (Kraft) pourable | 1 T. (.5 oz.) | 127 | 5.2 | | | |
| (Kraft) refrigerated | 1 T. (.5 oz.) | 78 | 7.3 | | | |

(USDA): United States Department of Agriculture
*Prepared as Package Directs
[1]Principal sources of fat: soybean oil, cottonseed oil, corn oil & cheese.
[2]Principal sources of fat: soybean oil, cottonseed oil, corn oil & egg.
[3]Principal sources of fat: vegetable oil & egg yolk.

| Food and Description | Measure or Quantity | Sodium (mg.) | Fats in grams — Total | Satu- rated | Unsatu- rated | Choles- terol (mg.) |
|---|---|---|---|---|---|---|
| (Lawry's) | 1 T. (.5 oz.) | | 6.4 | | | |
| (Marzetti) | 1 T. (.5 oz.) | | 6.7 | | | 5 |
| (Marzetti) refrigerated | 1 T. (.5 oz.) | | 6.9 | | | 6 |
| Tomato 'n' Spice (Dutch Pantry) | 1 T. (.6 oz.) | 200 | 6.1 | <1. | 5. | 0 |
| Vinaigrette (Bernstein's) | 1 T. (.5 oz.) | 180 | 4.2 | <1. | 4. | |
| (Wish-Bone) | 1 T. (.5 oz.) | 138 | 6.7 | 1. | 6. | 5 |

## SALAD DRESSING, DIETETIC
## or LOW CALORIE:

Bleu or blue cheese:

| Food and Description | Measure or Quantity | Sodium (mg.) | Total | Satu- rated | Unsatu- rated | Choles- terol (mg.) |
|---|---|---|---|---|---|---|
| Low fat, 6% fat (USDA)[1] | 1 T. (.6 oz.) | 177 | .9 | Tr. | <1. | |
| Low fat, 1% fat (USDA) | 1 T. (.5 oz.) | 170 | .2 | | | |
| (Frenchette) chunky | 1 T. (.5 oz.) | 286 | 1.4 | | | 4 |
| (Kraft) | 1 T. (.5 oz.) | 286 | .9 | | | |
| (Marzetti) | 1 T. (.5 oz.) | | 1.5 | | | 4 |
| (Slim-ette) | 1 T. (.5 oz.) | | 1.0 | | | |
| Caesar (Frenchette) | 1 T. (.5 oz.) | | 2.7 | | | 4 |
| Catalina (Kraft) | 1 T. (.5 oz.) | 110 | .5 | | | |
| Cheese (Tillie Lewis) | 1 T. (.5 oz.) | | 1.1 | | | |
| Chef Style (Kraft) | 1 T. (.5 oz.) | 107 | .6 | | | |
| Chef's (Slim-ette) | 1 T. (.5 oz.) | | 1.5 | | | |
| Chef's (Tillie Lewis) | 1 T. (.5 oz.) | | Tr. | | | |
| Coleslaw (Kraft) | 1 T. (.5 oz.) | 165 | 1.6 | | | |
| *Diet Mayo 7* (Bennett's) | 1 T. (.5 oz.) | 164 | 1.5 | | | |
| French: | | | | | | |
| Low fat, 6% fat (USDA)[2] | 1 T. (.6 oz.) | 126 | .7 | Tr. | <1. | |
| Low fat, 1% fat, with artificial sweetener (USDA) | 1 T. (.5 oz.) | 118 | <.1 | | | |
| Medium fat, with artificial sweetener (USDA)[2] | 1 T. (.5 oz.) | 118 | 2.5 | Tr. | 2. | |
| (Bennett's) | 1 T. (.5 oz.) | 148 | 1.0 | | | 0 |
| (Frenchette) | 1 T. (.5 oz.) | 138 | <.1 | | | 0 |
| (Kraft) | 1 T. (.5 oz.) | 267 | 1.5 | | | |
| (Marzetti) | 1 T. (.5 oz.) | | Tr. | | | 0 |
| (Tillie Lewis) | 1 T. (.5 oz.) | | Tr. | | | |
| Gourmet (Frenchette) | 1 T. (.5 oz.) | 202 | 1.3 | | | 0 |
| Green Goddess (Frenchette) | 1 T. (.5 oz.) | 254 | 1.5 | | | 6 |
| Green Goddess (Slim-ette) | 1 T. (.5 oz.) | | 1.0 | | | |
| Italian: | | | | | | |
| (USDA)[2] | 1 T. (.5 oz.) | 118 | .7 | Tr. | <1 | |
| (Bennett's) | 1 T. (.5 oz.) | 288 | .4 | | | 0 |

(USDA): United States Department of Agriculture
*Prepared as Package Directs
[1]Principal source of fat: cheese.
[2]Principal sources of fat: soybean oil, cottonseed oil & corn oil.

| Food and Description | Measure or Quantity | Sodium (mg.) | —Fats in grams— | | | Choles- terol (mg.) |
|---|---|---|---|---|---|---|
| | | | Total | Satu- rated | Unsatu- rated | |
| (Bernstein's) | 1 T. (.4 oz.) | 209 | <.1 | Tr. | Tr. | |
| (Bernstein's) with cheese | 1 T. (.4 oz.) | 209 | .2 | Tr. | Tr. | |
| *Italianette* (Frenchette) | 1 T. (.5 oz.) | 300 | .2 | | | 0 |
| (Kraft) | 1 T. (.5 oz.) | 173 | .8 | | | |
| (Marzetti) | 1 T. (.5 oz.) | | .2 | | | 0 |
| (Slim-ette) | 1 T. (.5 oz.) | | .6 | | | |
| (Tillie Lewis) | 1 T. (.5 oz.) | | Tr. | | | |
| (Wish-Bone) | 1 T. (.5 oz.) | 193 | 1.5 | Tr. | 1. | |
| Mayonnaise, imitation: | | | | | | |
| (USDA)[1] | 1 T. (.6 oz.) | 19 | 2.0 | Tr. | 2. | |
| *May-Lo-Naise* (Tillie Lewis) | 1 T. (.5 oz.) | | .9 | | | 2 |
| *Mayonette Gold* (Frenchette) | 1 T. (.5 oz.) | 203 | 2.8 | | | 10 |
| Remoulade (Tillie Lewis) | 1 T. (.5 oz.) | | .9 | | | |
| Russian (Wish-Bone) | 1 T. (.6 oz.) | 162 | .6 | Tr. | Tr. | |
| Slaw (Frenchette) | 1 T. (.5 oz.) | | 1.8 | | | 13 |
| Slaw (Marzetti) | 1 T. (.5 oz.) | | 1.8 | | | 13 |
| Supreme (McCormick) | 1 oz. | | 6.0 | | | |
| Thousand Island: | | | | | | |
| (USDA)[1] | 1 T. (.5 oz.) | 105 | 2.1 | Tr. | 2. | |
| (Frenchette) | 1 T. (.5 oz.) | 158 | 1.1 | | | |
| (Kraft) | 1 T. (.5 oz.) | 133 | 2.1 | | | |
| (Marzetti) | 1 T. (.5 oz.) | | 1.0 | | | 7 |
| (Wish-Bone) | 1 T. (.5 oz.) | 173 | 1.6 | Tr. | 1. | 5 |
| Vinaigrette (Bernstein's) | 1 T. (.4 oz.) | 132 | <.1 | Tr. | Tr. | |
| Whipped (Tillie Lewis) | 1 T. (.5 oz.) | | .9 | | | 2 |

## SALAD DRESSING MIX, regular

| Food and Description | Measure or Quantity | Sodium (mg.) | —Fats in grams— | | | Choles- terol (mg.) |
|---|---|---|---|---|---|---|
| & low calorie: | | | | | | |
| Bacon (Lawry's) | 1 pkg. (.8 oz.) | | 1.0 | | | |
| Bleu or blue cheese: | | | | | | |
| *(Good Seasons) | 1 T. (.5 oz.) | 170 | 9.3 | | | Tr. |
| *(Good Seasons) thick, creamy | 1 T. (.5 oz.) | 106 | 9.2 | | | 7 |
| (Lawry's) | 1 pkg. (.7 oz.) | | 5.0 | | | |
| Caesar garlic cheese (Lawry's) | 1 pkg. (.8 oz.) | | 2.4 | | | |
| *Cheese garlic (Good Seasons) | 1 T. (.5 oz.) | 166 | 9.2 | | | Tr. |
| *French, old fashion (Good Seasons) | 1 T. (.5 oz.) | 270 | 9.2 | | | 0 |
| *French (Good Seasons) thick, creamy | 1 T. (.5 oz.) | 203 | 9.1 | | | 5 |
| French, old fashion (Lawry's) | 1 pkg. (.8 oz.) | | <.1 | | | |
| *French, Riviera (Good Seasons) | 1 T. (.6 oz.) | 285 | 9.2 | | | 0 |
| *Garlic (Good Seasons) | 1 T. (.5 oz.) | 166 | 9.2 | | | Tr. |

(USDA): United States Department of Agriculture
*Prepared as Package Directs
[1]Principal sources of fat: soybean oil, cottonseed oil, corn oil & egg.

| Food and Description | Measure or Quantity | Sodium (mg.) | Total | Fats in grams — Satu-rated | Unsatu-rated | Choles-terol (mg.) |
|---|---|---|---|---|---|---|
| Green Goddess (Lawry's) | 1 pkg. (.8 oz.) | | .9 | | | |
| Italian: | | | | | | |
| *(Good Seasons) | 1 T. (.5 oz.) | 166 | 9.2 | | | Tr. |
| *(Good Seasons) cheese | 1 T. (.5 oz.) | 170 | 9.3 | | | Tr. |
| *(Good Seasons) mild | 1 T. (.5 oz.) | 170 | 9.3 | | | Tr. |
| *(Good Seasons) thick, creamy | 1 T. (.5 oz.) | 183 | 9.2 | | | 6 |
| (Lawry's) | 1 pkg. (.6 oz.) | | <.1 | | | |
| (Lawry's) cheese | 1 pkg. (.8 oz.) | | 2.3 | | | |
| *Low calorie (Good Seasons) | 1 tsp. | 55 | Tr. | | | 0 |
| *Onion (Good Seasons) | 1 T. (.5 oz.) | 166 | 9.2 | | | Tr. |
| *Thousand Island (Good Seasons) thick, creamy | 1 T. (.6 oz.) | 98 | 7.7 | | | 5 |
| **SALAD HERBS** (Spice Islands) | 1 tsp. | <1 | | | | (0) |
| **SALAD SEASONING:** | | | | | | |
| (Durkee) | 1 tsp. (4 grams) | 1151 | .5 | | | |
| *Salad Mate* (Durkee) | 1 tsp. (4 grams) | 1296 | .6 | | | |
| With cheese (Durkee) | 1 tsp. (3 grams) | 786 | .7 | | | |
| *Salad Lift* (French's) | 1 tsp. (4 grams) | 640 | .1 | | | |
| **SALAMI:** | | | | | | |
| Dry (USDA) | 1 oz. | | 10.8 | | | |
| Cooked (USDA) | 1 oz. | | 7.3 | | | |
| Cotto, all meat (Oscar Mayer) | .8-oz. slice (10 per ½ lb.) | 217 | 4.4 | 2. | 3. | 9 |
| Cotto, pure beef (Oscar Mayer) | .8-oz. slice | 251 | 4.4 | | | |
| Dilusso Genoa (Hormel) | 1 oz. | 454 | 11.1 | | | |
| For beer (Oscar Mayer) | .8-oz. slice | 251 | 4.1 | | | |
| Hard (Hormel) dairy | 1 oz. | 425 | 10.3 | 3. | 5. | 18 |
| Hard, all meat (Oscar Mayer) | 1 slice (.4 oz.) | 177 | 3.6 | | | |
| Machiaeh Brand, pure beef, cooked (Oscar Mayer) | .8-oz. slice | 251 | 4.8 | | | |
| **SALISBURY STEAK:** | | | | | | |
| Frozen: | | | | | | |
| (Banquet) buffet | 2-lb. pkg. | | 103.1 | | | |
| (Banquet) cooking bag | 5-oz. bag | | 16.2 | | | |
| (Morton House) & mushroom gravy | 4¹/₆-oz. serving | 512 | 11.0 | 5. | 6. | 38 |
| (Swanson) *Hungry Man* | 17-oz. dinner | 1999 | 56.5 | | | |
| (Swanson) with potato | 6-oz. pkg. | 775 | 18.9 | | | |

(USDA): United States Department of Agriculture
*Prepared as Package Directs

| Food and Description | Measure or Quantity | Sodium (mg.) | —Fats in grams— | | | Choles- terol (mg.) |
|---|---|---|---|---|---|---|
| | | | Total | Satu- rated | Unsatu- rated | |
| Dinner (Banquet): | | | | | | |
| Meat compartment | 6.3 oz. | | 17.2 | | | |
| Potato compartment | 2.8 oz. | | .4 | | | |
| Peas & carrots compartment | 1.9 oz. | | .8 | | | |
| Complete dinner | 11-oz. dinner | | 18.4 | | | |
| Dinner (Morton) | 11-oz. dinner | 1000 | 22.5 | | | |
| Dinner (Morton) 3-course | 1-lb. 1-oz. dinner | 1570 | 27.3 | | | |
| Dinner (Swanson) 3-course | 16-oz. dinner | 1653 | 24.5 | | | |
| **SALMON:** | | | | | | |
| Atlantic (USDA): | | | | | | |
| Raw, whole | 1 lb. (weighed whole) | | 39.5 | | | |
| Raw, meat only | 4 oz. | | 15.2 | | | |
| Canned, solids & liq., including bones | 4 oz. | | 13.8 | | | |
| Chinook or King (USDA): | | | | | | |
| Raw, steak | 1 lb. (weighed with bones) | 180 | 62.3 | 19. | 43. | |
| Raw, meat only | 4 oz. | 51 | 17.7 | 6. | 12. | |
| Canned, solids & liq., including bones, no salt added | 4 oz. | 51 | 15.9 | 4. | 11. | |
| Chum, raw, meat only (USDA) | 4 oz. | 60 | | | | |
| Chum, canned, solids & liq., including bones, no salt added (USDA) | 4 oz. | 60 | 5.9 | | | |
| Coho, raw, meat only (USDA) | 4 oz. | 54 | | | | |
| Coho, raw, meat only, dipped in brine (USDA) | 4 oz. | 244 | | | | |
| Coho, canned, solids & liq., no salt added (USDA) | 4 oz. | 54 | 8.1 | | | |
| Coho, canned, solids & liq., salt added (USDA) | 4 oz. | 398 | 8.1 | | | |
| Pink or Humpback: | | | | | | |
| Raw, steak (USDA) | 1 lb. (weighed with bones) | 255 | 14.8 | 4. | 11. | |
| Raw, meat only (USDA) | 4 oz. | 73 | 4.2 | 1. | 3. | |
| Raw, meat only, dipped in in brine (USDA) | 4 oz. | 536 | 4.2 | 1. | 3. | |
| Canned, solids & liq.: | | | | | | |
| No salt added (USDA) | 4 oz. | 73 | 6.7 | 2. | 4. | |
| Salt added (USDA) | 4 oz. | 439 | 6.7 | 2. | 4. | |
| (Del Monte) | 7¾-oz. can | 1371 | 9.2 | | | |
| (Del Monte) | 1 cup (8 oz.) | 1414 | 9.5 | | | |

(USDA): United States Department of Agriculture
*Prepared as Package Directs

| Food and Description | Measure or Quantity | Sodium (mg.) | Fats in grams — Total | Satu- rated | Unsatu- rated | Choles- terol (mg.) |
|---|---|---|---|---|---|---|
| Sockeye or Red or Blueback: | | | | | | |
| Raw, meat only (USDA) | 4 oz. | 54 | | | | 40 |
| Raw, steak (USDA) | 1 lb. | 192 | | | | 141 |
| Canned, solids & liq.: | | | | | | |
| Including bones, no salt added (USDA) | 4 oz. | 54 | 10.5 | | | 40 |
| Including bones, salt added (USDA) | 4 oz. | 592 | 10.5 | | | 40 |
| (Del Monte) | 7¾-oz. can | 1217 | 16.7 | | | |
| (Del Monte) | 1 cup (8 oz.) | 1255 | 17.2 | | | |
| Unspecified kind of salmon, baked or broiled with vegetable shortening: | | | | | | |
| (USDA) | 4-oz. steak (approx. 4″ x 3″ x ½″, 4.2 oz.) | 139 | 8.9 | | | 53 |
| (USDA) | 6¾″ x 2½″ x 1″ (5.1 oz.) | 168 | 10.7 | | | 68 |
| **SALMON RICE LOAF,** home recipe (USDA) | 4 oz. | | 5.1 | | | |
| **SALMON, SMOKED:** | | | | | | |
| (USDA) | 4 oz. | | 10.5 | | | |
| Lox, drained (Vita) | 4-oz. jar | | 6.7 | | | |
| Nova, drained (Vita) | 4-oz. can | | 14.6 | | | |
| **SALSIFY** (USDA): | | | | | | |
| Raw, without tops, freshly harvested | 1 lb. (weighed untrimmed) | | 2.4 | | | 0 |
| Raw, without tops, after storage | 1 lb. (weighed untrimmed) | | 2.4 | | | 0 |
| Boiled, drained, freshly harvested | 4 oz. | | .7 | | | 0 |
| Boiled, drained, after storage | 4 oz. | | .7 | | | 0 |
| **SALT:** | | | | | | |
| Butter-flavored, imitation: | | | | | | |
| (Durkee) | 1 tsp. (5 grams) | 1362 | .3 | | | |
| (French's) | 1 tsp. (4 grams) | 1090 | .9 | | | |
| Garlic (French's) | 1 tsp. (6 grams) | 1850 | .1 | | | |
| Garlic, parslied (French's) | 1 tsp. (4 grams) | 1050 | .1 | | | |
| Hickory smoke (French's) | 1 tsp. (4 grams) | 1170 | Tr. | | | |
| Garlic (Lawry's) | 2.9-oz. pkg. | | .3 | | | |

(USDA): United States Department of Agriculture
*Prepared as Package Directs

| Food and Description | Measure or Quantity | Sodium (mg.) | —Fats in grams— | | | Choles- terol (mg.) |
|---|---|---|---|---|---|---|
| | | | Total | Satu- rated | Unsatu- rated | |
| Garlic (Lawry's) | 1 tsp. (4 grams) | | Tr. | | | |
| Lite Salt (Morton) | 1 tsp. (6 grams) | 1188 | 0. | | | |
| Onion (French's) | 1 tsp. (5 grams) | 1620 | .1 | | | |
| Onion (Lawry's) | 3-oz. pkg. | | 1.0 | | | |
| Onion (Lawry's) | 1 tsp. (3 grams) | | <.1 | | | |
| Seasoning (French's) | 1 tsp. (5 grams) | 1620 | .1 | | | |
| Seasoned (Lawry's) | 3-oz. pkg. | | .5 | | | |
| Seasoned (Lawry's) | 1 tsp. (5 grams) | | <.1 | | | |
| Substitute (Adolph's) | 1 tsp. (4 grams) | <1 | 0. | | | 0 |
| Substitute (Morton) | 1 tsp. (6 grams) | <1 | 0. | | | |
| Substitute, seasoned (Adolph's) | 1 tsp. (4 grams) | <1 | <.1 | Tr. | Tr. | 0 |
| Substitute, seasoned (Morton) | 1 tsp. (6 grams) | <1 | 0. | | | |
| Table (USDA) | 1 tsp. (6 grams) | 2325 | 0. | | | 0 |
| Table (Morton) | 1 tsp. (6 grams) | 2544 | 0. | | | (0) |

**SALT PORK, raw (USDA):**

| Food and Description | Measure or Quantity | Sodium (mg.) | —Fats in grams— | | | Choles- terol (mg.) |
|---|---|---|---|---|---|---|
| | | | Total | Satu- rated | Unsatu- rated | |
| With skin | 1 lb. (weighed with skin) | 5278 | 370.0 | 141. | 229. | |
| Without skin | 1 oz. | 344 | 24.1 | 9. | 15. | |

**SALT STICK (See BREAD STICK)**

**SAND DAB, raw (USDA):**

| Food and Description | Measure or Quantity | Sodium (mg.) | —Fats in grams— | | | Choles- terol (mg.) |
|---|---|---|---|---|---|---|
| | | | Total | Satu- rated | Unsatu- rated | |
| Whole | 1 lb. (weighed whole) | 117 | 1.2 | | | |
| Meat only | 4 oz. | 88 | .9 | | | |

**SANDWICH SPREAD:**

| Food and Description | Measure or Quantity | Sodium (mg.) | —Fats in grams— | | | Choles- terol (mg.) |
|---|---|---|---|---|---|---|
| | | | Total | Satu- rated | Unsatu- rated | |
| (USDA) | 1 cup (8.7 oz.) | 1540 | 89.1 | | | |
| (USDA) | 1 T. (.5 oz.) | 94 | 5.4 | | | |
| (USDA) low calorie | 1 T. (.5 oz.) | 94 | 1.4 | | | |
| (Bama) | 1 T. (.5 oz.) | 238 | 4.2 | | | |
| (Bennett's)[1] | 1 T. (.5 oz.) | 139 | 3.2 | | | 5 |
| (Best Foods) | 1 T. (.5 oz.) | 185 | 5.8 | <1. | 5. | 2 |
| (Hellmann's)[1] | 1 T. (.5 oz.) | 185 | 5.8 | <1. | 5. | 2 |
| (Kraft) | 1 oz. | 183 | 9.4 | | | |
| (Kraft) Salad Bowl | 1 oz. | 183 | 8.9 | | | |
| (Nalley's) | 1 oz. | | 7.9 | | | |
| (Oscar Mayer) | 1 oz. | 243 | 3.4 | | | |
| Chicken salad (Carnation)[2] | 1/3 can (1.5 oz.) | 164 | 7.0 | <1. | 6. | 12 |

(USDA): United States Department of Agriculture
*Prepared as Package Directs
[1]Principal source of fat: oil.
[2]Principal sources of fat: chicken & corn oil.

| Food and Description | Measure or Quantity | Sodium (mg.) | —Fats in grams— | | | Cholesterol (mg.) |
|---|---|---|---|---|---|---|
| | | | Total | Saturated | Unsaturated | |
| Corned beef (Carnation)[1] | ¹/₃ can (1.5 oz.) | 277 | 6.5 | 1. | 5. | 13 |
| Ham & cheese (Carnation)[2] | ¹/₃ can (1.5 oz.) | 280 | 4.7 | 2. | 3. | 7 |
| Ham salad (Carnation)[3] | ¹/₃ can (1.5 oz.) | 265 | 6.3 | 1. | 5. | 8 |
| Pimento (Kraft) | 1 oz. | 231 | 11.3 | | | |
| Tuna salad (Carnation)[4] | ¹/₃ can (1.5 oz.) | 141 | 5.3 | <1. | 5. | 14 |
| Turkey salad (Carnation)[5] | ¹/₃ can (1.5 oz.) | 156 | 6.0 | <1. | 5. | 13 |
| **SANGRIA MIX** (Party Tyme) | ½-oz. pkg. | <1 | 0. | | | (0) |
| **SAPODILLA,** fresh (USDA): | | | | | | |
| Whole | 1 lb. (weighed with skin & seeds) | 44 | 4.0 | | | 0 |
| Flesh only | 4 oz. | 14 | 1.2 | | | 0 |
| **SAPOTE or MARMALADE PLUM,** fresh (USDA): | | | | | | |
| Whole | 1 lb. (weighed with skin & seeds) | | 2.1 | | | 0 |
| Flesh only | 4 oz. | | .7 | | | 0 |
| **SARDINE:** | | | | | | |
| Atlantic, canned in oil (USDA): | | | | | | |
| Solids & liq. | 3¾-oz. can | 541 | 25.9 | | | 127 |
| Drained solids | 3¾-oz. can | 757 | 10.2 | | | 129 |
| Atlantic, canned in tomato sauce, solids & liq. (Del Monte) | 1½ large sardines | 321 | 6.8 | | | |
| Norwegian, canned: | | | | | | |
| (Snow) | 1 oz. | | 6.3 | | | |
| In mustard sauce (Underwood) | 3¾-oz. can | 837 | 14.2 | | | |
| In oil, drained (Underwood) | 3¾-oz. can | 182 | 16.0 | | | |
| In tomato sauce (Underwood) | 3¾-oz. can | 422 | 9.8 | | | |
| Pacific (USDA): | | | | | | |
| Raw | 4 oz. | | 9.8 | | | |
| Canned, in brine or mustard, solids & liq. | 4 oz. | 862 | 13.6 | | | |
| Canned in tomato sauce, solids & liq. | 4 oz. | 454 | 13.8 | | | |

(USDA): United States Department of Agriculture
*Prepared as Package Directs
[1]Principal sources of fat: beef & corn oil.
[2]Principal sources of fat: ham, milk & cottonseed oil.
[3]Principal sources of fat: ham & corn oil.
[4]Principal sources of fat: tuna & corn oil.
[5]Principal sources of fat: turkey & corn oil.

| Food and Description | Measure or Quantity | Sodium (mg.) | Total | —Fats in grams— Satu- rated | Unsatu- rated | Choles- terol (mg.) |
|---|---|---|---|---|---|---|
| **SARSAPARILLA SOFT DRINK,** | | | | | | |
| sweetened: | | | | | | |
| (Hoffman) | 6 fl. oz. | 3 | 0. | | | 0 |
| (Yukon Club) | 6 fl. oz. | 3 | 0. | | | 0 |
| | | | | | | |
| **SAUCE,** regular & dietetic: | | | | | | |
| *A1* | 1 T. (.6 oz.) | 278 | Tr. | | | |
| Barbecue: | | | | | | |
| (USDA) | ½ cup (4.4 oz.) | 1019 | 8.6 | 1. | 7. | |
| (USDA) | 1 T. (.6 oz.) | 130 | 1.1 | Tr. | <1. | |
| (Contadina) oven | 1 fl. oz. (1.2 oz.) | 105 | Tr. | | | 0 |
| (French's) | 1 T. | 190 | Tr. | | | |
| (French's) mild | 1 T. | 165 | Tr. | | | |
| (French's) smoky | 1 T. | 210 | Tr. | | | |
| (General Foods) hickory smoke, *Open Pit* | 1 T. (.6 oz.) | 258 | .2 | | | 0 |
| (General Foods) hot 'n spicy, *Open Pit* | 1 T. (.6 oz.) | 211 | .2 | | | 0 |
| (General Foods) original, *Open Pit* | 1 T. (.6 oz.) | 224 | .2 | | | 0 |
| (General Foods) original flavor, with onions, *Open Pit* | 1 T. (6. oz.) | 226 | .2 | | | 0 |
| (Heinz) with onions, regular | 1 T. | 196 | .1 | | | |
| (Heinz) with onions, hickory smoke | 1 T. | 197 | .1 | | | |
| (Kraft) | 1 oz. | 466 | .5 | | | |
| (Kraft) garlic | 1 oz. | 484 | .3 | | | |
| (Kraft) hickory smoke | 1 oz. | 466 | .5 | | | |
| (Kraft) hot | 1 oz. | 572 | .6 | | | |
| (Kraft) mustard-flavored | 1 oz. | 399 | .6 | | | |
| (Kraft) onion | 1 oz. | 371 | .7 | | | |
| Cheese (Kraft) *Deluxe Dinner* | 1 oz. | 510 | 5.8 | | | |
| Chili (See **CHILI SAUCE**) | | | | | | |
| Creole (Contadina)[1] | 1 fl. oz. (1.1 oz.) | 138 | .3 | Tr. | Tr. | 0 |
| *Escoffier Sauce Diable* | 1 T. (.6 oz.) | 49 | .2 | | | |
| *Escoffier Sauce Robert* | 1 T. (.6 oz.) | 62 | Tr. | | | |
| *Famous* (Durkee) | 1 T. (6½-oz. bottle, .5 oz.) | 435 | 6.4 | 2. | 5. | |
| *Famous* (Durkee) | 1 T. (10-oz. bottle, .5 oz.) | 435 | 6.1 | 1. | 5. | |
| 57 (Heinz) | 1 T. | 265 | .2 | | | |
| Hard (Crosse & Blackwell) | 1 T. (.5 oz.) | | 3.4 | | | |

(USDA): United States Department of Agriculture
*Prepared as Package Directs
[1]Principal sources of fat: soybean oil & olive oil.

| Food and Description | Measure or Quantity | Sodium (mg.) | Total | Satu- rated | Unsatu- rated | Choles- terol (mg.) |
|---|---|---|---|---|---|---|
| Horseradish (Marzetti) | 1 T. (.5 oz.) | | 5.4 | | | 8 |
| *H.P. Steak Sauce* (Lea & Perrins) | 1 T. (1 oz.) | 280 | Tr. | 0. | Tr. | 0 |
| Marinara (Buitoni) | 4 oz. | | 2.5 | | | |
| Marinara (Chef Boy-Ar-Dee) | ¼ of 15-oz. can | 912 | 2.0 | | | |
| Meat loaf (Contadina)[1] | 1 fl. oz. (1.1 oz.) | 237 | Tr. | Tr. | Tr. | Tr. |
| Mushroom (Contadina)[2] | 1 fl. oz. (1.1 oz.) | 138 | 1.2 | 1. | 0. | 0 |
| Mushroom steak, *Dawn Fresh* | 5¾-oz. can | 823 | 0. | | | |
| Newburg, canned (Snow) | 4 oz. | | 9.1 | | | |
| Savory (Heinz) | 1T. | 162 | .1 | | | |
| Seafood (Bernstein's) | 1 T. (.5 oz.) | 172 | Tr. | | | |
| Seafood cocktail (Crosse & Blackwell) | 1 T. (.6 oz.) | 204 | 0. | | | |
| Seafood cocktail (Del Monte) | 1 T. (.6 oz.) | 261 | <.1 | | | |
| Sloppy Joe (Contadina) | 1 fl. oz. (1.1 oz.) | 212 | Tr. | | | |
| Sloppy Joe, chili (Contadina) | 1 fl. oz. (1.1 oz.) | 188 | Tr. | | | |
| Sloppy Joe, pizza (Contadina)[1] | 1 fl. oz. (1.1 oz.) | 204 | .2 | Tr. | Tr. | <1 |
| Soy (USDA) | 1 oz. | 2077 | .4 | | | |
| Spaghetti (See **SPAGHETTI SAUCE**) | | | | | | |
| Steak (Crosse & Blackwell) | 1 T. (.7 oz.) | 276 | | | | |
| Steak (Marzetti) | 1 T. (.5 oz.) | | .2 | | | 0 |
| Stroganoff (Contadina) | 1 fl. oz. (1.1 oz.) | 148 | .7 | | | |
| Sweet 'n sour (Contadina)[3] | 1 fl. oz. (1.2 oz.) | 88 | .6 | Tr. | <1. | 0 |
| Sweet & sour (Kraft) | 1 oz. | 128 | .5 | | | |
| Swiss steak (Contadina) | 1 fl. oz. (1.1 oz.) | 133 | .1 | | | 0 |
| Tartar: | | | | | | |
| (USDA) regular | 1 T. (.5 oz.) | 99 | 8.1 | | | 7 |
| (USDA) low calorie | 1 T. (.5 oz.) | 99 | 3.1 | | | |
| (Bama) | 1 T. (.5 oz.) | 162 | 9.6 | | | |
| (Bennett's) | 1 T. (.5 oz.) | 103 | 8.5 | | | 12 |
| (Best Foods)[4] | 1 T. (.5 oz.) | 182 | 8.0 | 1. | 7. | 4 |
| (Hellmann's)[4] | 1 T. (.5 oz.) | 182 | 8.0 | 1. | 7. | 4 |
| (Kraft) | 1 oz. | 401 | 15.6 | | | |
| (Marzetti) | 1 T. (.5 oz.) | | 7.3 | | | 6 |
| (Mrs. Paul's) | 4.2-oz. pkg. | | 70.2 | | | |
| Tomato (See **TOMATO SAUCE**) | | | | | | |
| White, home recipe (USDA): | | | | | | |
| Thin[5] | 1 cup (8.8 oz.) | 878 | 21.8 | 12. | 9. | 36 |
| Medium[5] | 1 cup (9 oz.) | 966 | 31.9 | 18. | 14. | 36 |
| Thick[5] | 1 cup (8.7 oz.) | 986 | 38.5 | 22. | 16. | 30 |

(USDA): United States Department of Agriculture
*Prepared as Package Directs
[1]Principal source of fat: milk.
[2]Principal source of fat: modified coconut oil.
[3]Principal source of fat: soybean oil.
[4]Principal source of fat: oils.
[5]Principal sources of fat: butter & milk.

| Food and Description | Measure or Quantity | Sodium (mg.) | —Fats in grams— Total | Satu-rated | Unsatu-rated | Choles-terol (mg.) |
|---|---|---|---|---|---|---|
| Worcestershire: | | | | | | |
| (Crosse & Blackwell) | 1 T. | 265 | 0. | | | |
| (French's) | 1 T. | 150 | Tr. | | | |
| (Heinz) | 1 T. | 234 | Tr. | | | |
| (Lea & Perrins) | 1 T. (.6 oz.) | 175 | Tr. | 0. | Tr. | 0 |
| **SAUCE MIX:** | | | | | | |
| *A la King (Durkee) | 1 cup (1½-oz. pkg.) | 1799 | 17.5 | | | |
| *Barbecue (Kraft) | 1 oz. | 550 | .2 | | | |
| *Bordelaise (Betty Crocker) | ¼ cup | 280 | 2.0 | | | |
| Cheese: | | | | | | |
| *(Betty Crocker) | ¼ cup | 678 | 9.2 | | | |
| *(Durkee) | 1 cup (1.1-oz. pkg.) | 1978 | 20.7 | | | |
| (French's) | 1¼-oz. pkg. | 1150 | 9.3 | | | |
| *(French's) | ¼ cup | 313 | 4.6 | | | |
| *Cheddar (Kraft) | 1 oz. | 107 | 3.9 | | | |
| (McCormick) | 1¼-oz. pkg. | 685 | 12.6 | | | |
| *McCormick) | 2-oz. serving | 200 | 5.0 | | | |
| Hollandaise: | | | | | | |
| *(Betty Crocker) | ¼ cup | 308 | 7.2 | | | |
| *(Durkee) | ⅔ cup (1¼-oz. pkg.) | 63 | 18.0 | | | |
| (French's) | 1⅛-oz. pkg. | 1000 | 16.3 | | | |
| *(French's) | 1 T. | 83 | 1.4 | | | |
| *(Kraft) | 1 oz. | 49 | 4.8 | | | |
| *(McCormick) | 2-oz. serving | 140 | 6.2 | | | |
| Miracle (Mrs. Paul's) | ½-oz. pkg. | | <.1 | | | |
| *Mushroom (Betty Crocker) | ¼ cup | 236 | 1.7 | | | |
| *Newburg (Betty Crocker) | ¼ cup | 399 | 3.8 | | | |
| Sloppy Joe (See **SLOPPY JOE MIX**) | | | | | | |
| Sour Cream: | | | | | | |
| *(Durkee) | ⅔ cup (1.1-oz. pkg.) | 954 | 16.0 | | | |
| (French's) | 1¼-oz. pkg. | 300 | 15.0 | | | |
| *(French's) | 1 T. | 34 | 1.8 | | | |
| *(Kraft) | 1 oz. | 397 | 4.3 | | | |
| *(McCormick) | 2-oz. serving | 131 | .5 | | | |
| Spaghetti (See **SPAGHETTI SAUCE MIX**) | | | | | | |
| Stroganoff (French's) | 1¾-oz. pkg. | 1300 | 9.2 | | | |
| *Stroganoff (French's) | ⅓ cup | 387 | 5.5 | | | |
| *Sweet-sour (Durkee) | 1 cup (2-oz. pkg.) | 1053 | 5.7 | | | |
| Tartar (Lawry's) | .6-oz. pkg. | | 1.4 | | | |
| *Teri-yaki (Durkee) | ⅔ cup (1¼-oz. pkg.) | 3484 | .1 | | | |

(USDA): United States Department of Agriculture
*Prepared as Package Directs

| Food and Description | Measure or Quantity | Sodium (mg.) | Total | Fats in grams Satu-rated | Unsatu-rated | Choles-terol (mg.) |
|---|---|---|---|---|---|---|
| **White:** | | | | | | |
| *(Durkee) | 1 cup (1-oz. pkg.) | 799 | 19.7 | | | |
| *(Kraft) | 1 oz. | 94 | 3.3 | | | |
| *Supreme (McCormick) | 2-oz. serving | 268 | 1.5 | | | |
| **SAUERKRAUT, canned:** | | | | | | |
| Solids & liq. (USDA) 1.9% salt | 1 cup (8.3 oz.) | 1755 | .5 | | | 0 |
| Drained solids (USDA) | 1 cup (5 oz.) | | .4 | | | 0 |
| Solids & liq. (Del Monte) | 1 cup (8 oz.) | 1655 | .4 | | | 0 |
| Solids & liq. (Stokely-Van Camp) | 1 cup (7.8 oz.) | | .4 | | | |
| **SAUERKRAUT JUICE, canned** | | | | | | |
| (USDA) 2% salt | ½ cup (4.3 oz.) | 952 | Tr. | | | 0 |
| **SAUGER, raw (USDA):** | | | | | | |
| Whole | 1 lb. (weighed whole) | | 13.2 | | | |
| Meat only | 4 oz. | | .9 | | | |
| **SAUSAGE (See also individual kinds):** | | | | | | |
| Breakfast (Hormel) | 8-oz. can | | 80.6 | | | |
| Breakfast, smoked, all meat (Oscar Mayer) | 1 link (7 to 5-oz. pkg.) | 172 | 6.0 | | | |
| Brown & serve: | | | | | | |
| Before browning (USDA) | 1 oz. | | 10.2 | | | |
| After browning (USDA) | 1 oz. | | 10.7 | | | |
| (Hormel) | 1 piece (.8 oz.) | 209 | 7.1 | 2. | 4. | 12 |
| After browning (Swift) | 1 link (.8 oz.) | 193 | | | | 7.9 |
| New England Brand, all meat (Oscar Mayer) | .8-oz. slice | 260 | 2.1 | | | |
| In sauce, canned (Prince) | 3.7-oz. can | | 14.2 | | | |
| **SAUTERNES:** | | | | | | |
| (Barton & Guestier) French white Bordeaux, 13% alcohol | 3 fl. oz. | 3 | 0. | | | (0) |
| (Gold Seal) dry, 12% alcohol | 3 fl. oz. | 3 | 0. | | | (0) |
| (Gold Seal) semi-soft, 12% alcohol | 3 fl. oz. (3.2 oz.) | 3 | 0. | | | (0) |
| (Great Western) Aurora, 12.5% alcohol | 3 fl. oz. | 34 | 0. | | | 0 |
| **SAVORY (Spice Islands)** | 1 tsp. | <1 | | | | (0) |

(USDA): United States Department of Agriculture
*Prepared as Package Directs

| Food and Description | Measure or Quantity | Sodium (mg.) | —Fats in grams— Total | Satu- rated | Unsatu- rated | Choles- terol (mg.) |
|---|---|---|---|---|---|---|
| **SCALLION** (See **ONION, GREEN**) | | | | | | |
| **SCALLOP:** | | | | | | |
| Raw, muscle only[1] (USDA) | 4 oz. | 289 | .2 | | | 40 |
| Steamed (USDA) | 4 oz. | 301 | 1.6 | | | 60 |
| Frozen: | | | | | | |
| Breaded, fried, reheated (USDA) | 4 oz. | | 9.5 | | | |
| Breaded, fried (Mrs. Paul's) | 7-oz. pkg. | | 14.0 | | | |
| Crisps (Gorton) | ½ of 7-oz. pkg. | 175 | 7.0 | | | |
| **SCHAV SOUP** (Manischewitz) | 8 oz. (by wt.) | | .2 | | | |
| ***SCOTCH BROTH,** canned (Campbell) | 1 cup | 1009 | 2.7 | 1. | 1. | |
| *SCOTCH-COMFORT* | 1 fl. oz. | Tr. | 0. | | | (0) |
| **SCOTCH WHISKY** (See **DISTILLED LIQUOR**) | | | | | | |
| **SCRAPPLE:** | | | | | | |
| (USDA) | 4 oz. | | 15.4 | | | |
| (Oscar Mayer) | 4 oz. | | 14.7 | | | |
| **SCREWDRIVER:** | | | | | | |
| Canned (National Distillers) | | | | | | |
| *Duet*, 12½% alcohol | 8-fl.-oz. can | Tr. | 0. | | | 0 |
| Dry mix (Bar-Tender's) | 1 serving (⅝ oz.) | 57 | .2 | | | (0) |
| **SCUP** (See **PORGY**) | | | | | | |
| **SEABASS, WHITE,** raw, meat only (USDA) | 4 oz. | | .6 | | | |
| **SEAFOOD CHOWDER,** New England (Snow) | 8 oz. | | 5.6 | | | |
| **SEAFOOD PLATTER,** breaded, fried, with potato puffs, frozen (Mrs. Paul's) | 9-oz. pkg. | | 21.4 | | | |
| **SEAFOOD SEASONING** (French's) | 1 tsp. (5 grams) | 1410 | Tr. | | | (0) |

(USDA): United States Department of Agriculture
*Prepared as Package Directs
[1]Frozen scallops, possibly brined.

| Food and Description | Measure or Quantity | Sodium (mg.) | —Fats in grams— | | | Choles- terol (mg.) |
|---|---|---|---|---|---|---|
| | | | Total | Satu- rated | Unsatu- rated | |
| **SENEGALESE SOUP** (Crosse & Blackwell) | ½ can (6½oz.) | | 2.0 | | | |
| **SESAME SEED:** | | | | | | |
| Dry, whole (USDA) | 1 oz. | 17 | 13.9 | 2. | 12. | 0 |
| Dry, hulled (USDA) | 1 oz. | | 15.1 | 2. | 13. | 0 |
| Hulled (Spice Islands) | 1 tsp. | 2 | | | | (0) |
| Liquid, Tahini (A. Sahadi) | 1 T. (8 grams) | | 5.1 | | | |
| *SEVEN-UP,* soft drink: | | | | | | |
| Regular | 6 fl. oz. | 16+ | 0. | | | 0 |
| Low calorie | 6 fl. oz. (6.3 oz.) | 19+ | 0. | | | 0 |
| **SHAD** (USDA): | | | | | | |
| Raw, whole | 1 lb. (weighed whole) | 118 | 21.8 | | | |
| Raw, meat only | 4 oz. | 61 | 11.3 | | | |
| Cooked, home recipe: | | | | | | |
| Baked with butter or margarine & bacon slices | 4 oz. | 90 | 12.8 | | | |
| Creole, made with tomatoes, onion, green pepper, butter & flour | 4 oz. | 83 | 9.9 | | | |
| Canned, solids & liq. | 4 oz. | | 10.0 | | | |
| **SHAD, GIZZARD,** raw (USDA): | | | | | | |
| Whole | 1 lb. (weighed whole) | | 21.0 | | | |
| Meat only | 4 oz. | | 15.9 | | | |
| *SHAKE 'N BAKE,* seasoned mixes: | | | | | | |
| Chicken-coating, regular | 2⅜-oz. pkg. | 2557 | 10.2 | | | 0 |
| Chicken-coating, Italian | 2⅜-oz. pkg. | 2557 | 10.2 | | | 3 |
| Fish-coating | 2-oz. pkg. | 2486 | 7.8 | | | 0 |
| Hamburger-coating | 2-oz. pkg. | 4889 | .8 | | | 0 |
| Pork-coating | 2⅜-oz. pkg. | 2863 | 4.3 | | | 0 |
| **SHALLOT,** raw (USDA): | | | | | | |
| With skin | 1 oz. | 3 | <.1 | | | 0 |
| With skin removed | 1 oz. | 3 | <.1 | | | 0 |

**SHEEFISH** (See **INCONNU**)

(USDA): United States Department of Agriculture
*Prepared as Package Directs

| Food and Description | Measure or Quantity | Sodium (mg.) | —Fats in grams—<br>Total | Satu-rated | Unsatu-rated | Choles-terol (mg.) |
|---|---|---|---|---|---|---|
| **SHEEPSHEAD,** Atlantic, raw (USDA): | | | | | | |
| Whole | 1 lb. (weighed whole) | 142 | 3.9 | | | |
| Meat only | 4 oz. | 115 | 3.2 | | | |
| **SHERBET** (See also individual brands): | | | | | | |
| Orange (USDA) | 1 cup (6.8 oz.) | 19 | 2.3 | | | |
| Orange (USDA) | ¼ pint (3.4 oz.) | 10 | 1.2 | | | |
| Any flavor (Borden) | ¼ pint (3 oz.) | | 1.3 | | | |
| Orange (Sealtest) | ¼ pint (3.1 oz.) | 29 | 1.0 | | | |
| **SHERRY:** | | | | | | |
| (Great Western) Solera, 18% alcohol | 3 fl. oz. | 34 | 0. | | | 0 |
| Cocktail (Gold Seal) 19% alcohol | 3 fl. oz. (3.1 oz.) | 3 | 0. | | | (0) |
| Cooking (Great Western) 18% alcohol | 3 fl. oz. | 31 | 0. | | | 0 |
| Cream (Gold Seal) 19% alcohol | 3 fl. oz. (3.3 oz.) | 3 | 0. | | | (0) |
| Cream (Great Western) 18% alcohol | 3 fl. oz. | 32 | 0. | | | 0 |
| Dry (Great Western) Solera, 18% alcohol | 3 fl. oz. | 34 | 0. | | | 0 |
| **SHORTENING** (See **FATS**) | | | | | | |
| **SHREDDED OATS,** cereal (USDA)[1] | 1 oz. | 173 | .6 | Tr. | <1. | 0 |
| **SHREDDED WHEAT,** cereal: | | | | | | |
| (USDA) plain, without salt | 1 cup (1.2 oz.) | 1 | .7 | Tr. | <1. | 0 |
| (USDA) with malt, salt & sugar | 1 cup (2.1 oz.) | 418 | 1.7 | Tr. | 2. | 0 |
| (Kellogg's) cinnamon or sugar-frosted, *Mini-Wheats* | 4 biscuits (1 oz.) | 4 | .3 | | | (0) |
| (Nabisco) | 1 biscuit (.9 oz.) | <1 | .5 | | | (0) |
| (Nabisco) *Spoon Size* | ⅔ cup (1 oz.) | <1 | .5 | | | (0) |
| (Nabisco) *Spoon Size* | 1 piece (1 gram) | Tr. | <.1 | | | (0) |
| (Quaker) | 2 biscuits (1⅓ oz.) | 2 | .7 | | | (0) |
| **SHRIMP:** | | | | | | |
| Raw (USDA): | | | | | | |
| Whole | 1 lb. (weighed in shell) | 438 | 2.5 | | | 470 |

(USDA): United States Department of Agriculture
*Prepared as Package Directs
[1]Includes protein & other added nutrients.

| Food and Description | Measure or Quantity | Sodium (mg.) | —Fats in grams— | | | Cholesterol (mg.) |
| --- | --- | --- | --- | --- | --- | --- |
| | | | Total | Saturated | Unsaturated | |
| Meat only | 4 oz. | 159 | .9 | | | 170 |
| Canned, dry pack or drained (USDA) | 1 cup (22 large or 76 small, 4.5 oz.) | | 1.4 | | | 192 |
| Cooked, french-fried[1] (USDA) | 4 oz. | 211 | 12.2 | | | |
| Frozen: | | | | | | |
| Raw: | | | | | | |
| Breaded, not more than 50% breading (USDA) | 4 oz. | | .8 | | | |
| Breaded (Gorton) | ¼ of 1-lb. pkg. | 80 | .8 | | | |
| Cooked (Sau-Sea) | 4 oz. | | .5 | | | |
| Cooked (Weight Watchers) | ½ pkg. (4 oz.) | | 1.0 | | | |
| Fried (Mrs. Paul's) | 4 oz. | | 13.1 | | | |
| Scampi (Gorton) | ½ of 7½-oz. pkg. | 415 | 23.0 | | | |
| **SHRIMP CAKE:** | | | | | | |
| Frozen, fried, breaded (Mrs. Paul's) | 1 cake (3 oz.) | | 1.9 | | | |
| Frozen, thins (Mrs. Paul's) | 10-oz. pkg. | | 29.5 | | | |
| **SHRIMP COCKTAIL:** | | | | | | |
| (Sau-Sea) | 4-oz. jar | | .6 | | | |
| (Sea Snack) | 4-oz. jar | 3 | 1.7 | | | |
| **SHRIMP DINNER,** frozen: | | | | | | |
| (Morton) | 7¾-oz. dinner | 480 | 16.4 | | | |
| (Swanson) | 8-oz. dinner | 1035 | 13.1 | | | |
| **SHRIMP PASTE,** canned (USDA) | 1 oz. | | 2.7 | | | |
| **SHRIMP PUFF,** frozen (Durkee) | 1 piece (.5 oz.) | | 4.3 | | | |
| **SHRIMP SOUP,** Cream of: | | | | | | |
| *Canned (Campbell) | 1 cup (8 oz.) | 988 | 10.4 | | | |
| Canned (Crosse & Blackwell) | ½ can (6½ oz.) | | 5.3 | | | |
| Frozen: | | | | | | |
| Condensed (USDA) | 8 oz. (by wt.) | 1950 | 22.5 | | | |
| *Prepared with equal volume water (USDA) | 1 cup (8.5 oz.) | 1032 | 12.0 | | | |
| *Prepared with equal volume milk (USDA) | 1 cup (8.6 oz.) | 1117 | 16.4 | | | |
| *SIMBA,* soft drink | 6 fl. oz. | 12 | Tr. | | | 0 |

(USDA): United States Department of Agriculture
*Prepared as Package Directs
[1]Dipped in egg, bread crumbs & flour or in batter.

| Food and Description | Measure or Quantity | Sodium (mg.) | —Fats in grams— | | | Choles-terol (mg.) |
|---|---|---|---|---|---|---|
| | | | Total | Satu-rated | Unsatu-rated | |
| **SKATE,** raw, meat only (USDA) | 4 oz. | | .8 | | | |
| | | | | | | |
| *SLENDER* (Carnation): | | | | | | |
| Dry: | | | | | | |
| Chocolate[1] | 1 pkg. (1 oz.) | 170 | .5 | Tr. | Tr. | Tr. |
| Chocolate malt[2] | 1 pkg. (1 oz.) | 150 | .6 | Tr. | Tr. | 1 |
| Chocolate marshmallow[1] | 1 pkg. (1 oz.) | 170 | .7 | Tr. | Tr. | Tr. |
| Coffee[3] | 1 pkg. (1 oz.) | 170 | .2 | Tr. | Tr. | Tr. |
| Dutch chocolate[1] | 1 pkg. (1 oz.) | 170 | .9 | <1. | Tr. | Tr. |
| Milk chocolate[1] | 1 pkg. (1 oz.) | 160 | .5 | Tr. | Tr. | Tr. |
| Strawberry, wild[3] | 1 pkg. (1 oz.) | 170 | .2 | Tr. | Tr. | Tr. |
| Vanilla, French | 1 pkg. (1 oz.) | 150 | .2 | Tr. | Tr. | Tr. |
| Liquid: | | | | | | |
| Butterscotch | 10-fl.-oz. can | 420 | 5.0 | <1. | Tr. | <1 |
| Chocolate[4] | 10-fl.-oz. can | 370 | 5.0 | <1. | Tr. | Tr. |
| Chocolate fudge[4] | 10-fl.-oz. can | 440 | 5.0 | <1. | Tr. | Tr. |
| Chocolate malt[5] | 10-fl.-oz. can | 430 | 5.0 | 1. | 4. | <1 |
| Chocolate marshmallow[4] | 10-fl.-oz. can | 345 | 5.0 | 1. | 4. | Tr. |
| Coffee | 10-fl.-oz. can | 310 | 5.0 | 1. | 4. | <1 |
| Eggnog[6] | 10-fl.-oz. can | 390 | 5.0 | 1. | 4. | <1 |
| Milk chocolate[4] | 10-fl.-oz. can | 400 | 5.0 | 1. | 4. | Tr. |
| Vanilla[6] | 10-fl.-oz. can | 350 | 5.0 | 1. | 4. | <1 |
| | | | | | | |
| *SLIM JIM:* | | | | | | |
| Sausage | 1 piece (½ oz.) | 252 | 7.1 | | | |
| Polish sausage, all beef | 1 piece (1¾ oz.) | 461 | 9.1 | | | |
| | | | | | | |
| **SLOPPY JOE:** | | | | | | |
| Frozen (Banquet) cooking bag | 5-oz. bag | | 16.4 | | | |
| Mix, including seasoning mix: | | | | | | |
| (Durkee) | 1½-oz. pkg. | 3512 | .2 | | | |
| *With tomato paste & meat | | | | | | |
| (Durkee) | 3 cups (1½-oz. pkg.) | 3866 | 97.0 | | | |
| (French's) | 1½-oz. pkg. | 3300 | .3 | | | |
| *(Kraft) | 1 oz. | 101 | 2.8 | | | |
| (Lawry's) | 1½-oz. pkg. | | 1.5 | | | |
| *(Wyler's) | ¾ cup | | .5 | | | |

(USDA): United States Department of Agriculture
*Prepared as Package Directs
[1]Principal sources of fat: milk, cocoa & lecithin.
[2]Principal sources of fat: wort solids, milk, cocoa & lecithin.
[3]Principal sources of fat: milk & lecithin.
[4]Principal sources of fat: milk, cocoa & corn oil.
[5]Principal sources of fat: wort solids, milk, cocoa & corn oil.
[6]Principal sources of fat: milk & corn oil.

| Food and Description | Measure or Quantity | Sodium (mg.) | —Fats in grams— | | | Cholesterol (mg.) |
|---|---|---|---|---|---|---|
| | | | Total | Saturated | Unsaturated | |
| **SMELT,** Atlantic, jack & bay (USDA): | | | | | | |
| Raw, whole | 1 lb. (weighed whole) | | | | | |
| Raw, meat only | 4 oz. | | 2.4 | | | |
| Canned, solids & liq. | 4 oz. | | 15.3 | | | |
| **SMOKIE SAUSAGE:** | | | | | | |
| (Hormel) | 1 piece (.8 oz.) | 261 | 6.6 | 2. | 4. | 14 |
| (Oscar Mayer): | | | | | | |
| 8 links per ¾ lb. | 1 link (1.5 oz.) | 360 | 11.6 | 4. | 7. | 18 |
| 7 links per 5 oz. | 1 link (.7 oz.) | 168 | 5.4 | 2. | 3. | 8 |
| Cheese | 1.5-oz. link | 369 | 11.6 | | | |
| Little Smokies, all meat | 1 link (16 per 5 oz.) | 76 | 2.7 | | | |
| Smoky Snax | 1 link (4 oz.) | 1106 | 29.5 | | | |
| (Wilson) | 1 oz. | 293 | 7.3 | | | 17 |
| *SMOKY SNAX SPREAD* (Oscar Mayer) | 1 oz. | 287 | 9.4 | | | |
| **SNACK** (See **CRACKER, POPCORN, POTATO CHIPS,** etc.) | | | | | | |
| **SNAIL,** raw: | | | | | | |
| (USDA) | 4 oz. | | 1.6 | | | |
| Giant African (USDA) | 4 oz. | | 1.6 | | | |
| **SNAPPER** (See **RED SNAPPER**) | | | | | | |
| *SNO BALL* (Hostess) 2 to pkg. | 1 cake (1.5 oz.) | 117 | 3.5 | | | |
| **SODA or SOFT DRINK** (See individual kinds listed by flavor or brand name) | | | | | | |
| *SOFT SWIRL* (Jell-O): | | | | | | |
| *All flavors except chocolate | ½ cup (3.8 oz.) | 301 | 5.8 | | | 9 |
| *Chocolate | ½ cup (4 oz.) | 302 | 8.0 | | | 9 |
| **SOLE:** | | | | | | |
| Raw, whole (USDA) | 1 lb. (weighed whole) | 117 | 1.2 | | | |
| Raw, meat only (USDA) | 4 oz. | 88 | .9 | | | |

(USDA): United States Department of Agriculture
*Prepared as Package Directs

| Food and Description | Measure or Quantity | Sodium (mg.) | —Fats in grams— | | | Choles-terol (mg.) |
|---|---|---|---|---|---|---|
| | | | Total | Satu-rated | Unsatu-rated | |
| **Frozen:** | | | | | | |
| (Gorton) | ⅓ of 1-lb. pkg. | 117 | 1.2 | | | |
| Dinner (Weight Watchers) | 18-oz. dinner | | 3.6 | | | |
| & cauliflower, luncheon (Weight Watchers) | 9½-oz. luncheon | | 5.4 | | | |
| In lemon butter (Gorton) | ⅓ of 9-oz. pkg. | 173 | 11.0 | | | |
| **SORGHUM** (USDA): | | | | | | |
| Grain | 1 oz. | | .9 | Tr. | <1. | 0 |
| **SORREL** (See **DOCK**) | | | | | | |
| **SOUP** (See individual listing by kind) | | | | | | |
| **SOUP BASE:** | | | | | | |
| Beef (Wyler's) no salt added | 1 tsp. (6 grams) | 12 | 1.4 | | | |
| Chicken (Wyler's) no salt added | 1 tsp. (6 grams) | 4 | 1.4 | | | |
| **SOURSOP,** raw (USDA): | | | | | | |
| Whole | 1 lb. (weighed with skin & seeds) | 43 | .9 | | | 0 |
| Flesh only | 4 oz. | 16 | .3 | | | 0 |
| **SOUSE** (USDA)[1] | 1 oz. | | 3.8 | 1. | 2. | |
| ***SOUTHERN COMFORT*** | 1 fl. oz. | Tr. | 0. | | | (0) |
| **SOYBEAN** (USDA): | | | | | | |
| Young seeds: | | | | | | |
| Raw | 1 lb. (weighed in pods) | | 12.3 | 2. | 10. | 0 |
| Cooked without salt, drained | 4 oz. | | 5.8 | 1. | 5. | 0 |
| Canned, solids & liq. | 4 oz. | 268 | 3.6 | 1. | 2. | 0 |
| Canned, drained solids | 4 oz. | 268 | 5.7 | 1. | 5. | 0 |
| Mature seeds, dry: | | | | | | |
| Raw | 1 lb. | 23 | 80.3 | 12. | 68. | 0 |
| Raw | 1 cup (7.4 oz.) | 10 | 37.2 | 6. | 31. | 0 |
| Cooked without salt | 4 oz. | 2 | 6.5 | 1. | 5. | 0 |
| Roasted: | | | | | | |
| Unsalted, *Soy Town* | 1 oz. | 6 | 10.5 | 1. | 9. | 0 |
| Sea-salted, *Soy Town* | 1 oz. | 249 | 10.5 | 1. | 9. | 0 |

(USDA): United States Department of Agriculture
*Prepared as Package Directs
[1]Principal source of fat: pork.

| Food and Description | Measure or Quantity | Sodium (mg.) | — Fats in grams — | | | Choles- terol (mg.) |
|---|---|---|---|---|---|---|
| | | | Total | Satu- rated | Unsatu- rated | |
| **SOYBEAN CURD or TOFU** | | | | | | |
| (USDA) | 4.2-oz. cake (2¾" x 2½" x 1") | 8 | 5.0 | 1. | 4. | 0 |
| **SOYBEAN FLOUR** (See **FLOUR**) | | | | | | |
| **SOYBEAN GRITS,** high fat | | | | | | |
| (USDA) | 1 cup (4.9 oz.) | 1 | 16.7 | 3. | 14. | 0 |
| **SOYBEAN MILK** (USDA): | | | | | | |
| Fluid | 4 oz. | | 1.7 | | | 0 |
| Powder | 1 oz. | | 5.8 | <1. | 5. | 0 |
| Sweetened: | | | | | | |
| Liquid concentrate[1] | 4 oz. (by wt.) | 49 | 8. | 1. | 7. | 0 |
| Dry powder[2] | 1 oz. | <1 | 6.6 | 3. | 4. | 0 |
| **SOYBEAN PROTEIN** (USDA) | 1 oz. | 60 | <.1 | | | 0 |
| **SOYBEAN PROTEINATE** (USDA) | 1 oz. | 340 | <.1 | | | 0 |
| **SOYBEAN SPROUT** (See **BEAN SPROUT**) | | | | | | |
| **SOYNUT,** unsalted, *Soy Ahoy* | 1 oz. | 6 | 10.2 | 1. | 9. | 0 |
| **SOY SAUCE** (See **SAUCE**) | | | | | | |
| **SOY SPREAD,** *Soy Town* | 1 oz. | 113 | 14.2 | | | 0 |
| **SPAGHETTI** (USDA): | | | | | | |
| Dry | 1 oz. | <1 | .3 | | | 0 |
| Dry, broken | 1 cup (2.5 oz.) | 1 | .9 | | | 0 |
| Cooked: | | | | | | |
| 8-10 minutee' "al dente" | 1 cup (5.1 oz.) | 1 | .7 | | | 0 |
| 8-10 minutes, "al dente" | 4 oz. | 1 | .6 | | | 0 |
| 14-20 minutes, tender | 1 cup (4.9 oz.) | 1 | .6 | | | 0 |
| 14-20 minutes, tender | 4 oz. | 1 | .5 | | | 0 |
| **SPAGHETTI DINNER:** | | | | | | |
| *With meat balls (Chef Boy-Ar-Dee) | 8¾-oz. pkg. | 1451 | 5.7 | | | |

(USDA): United States Department of Agriculture
*Prepared as Package Directs
[1]Principal source of fat: soybean.
[2]Principal sources of fat: soybean, coconut oil & olive oil.

| Food and Description | Measure or Quantity | Sodium (mg.) | Total | —Fats in grams— Satu- rated | Unsatu- rated | Choles- terol (mg.) |
|---|---|---|---|---|---|---|
| *With meat sauce (Chef Boy-Ar-Dee) | 7-oz. pkg. | 1818 | 4.6 | | | |
| *With meat sauce (Kraft) *Deluxe* | 4 oz. | 423 | 3.4 | | | |
| *With mushroom sauce (Chef Boy-Ar-Dee) | 7-oz. pkg. | 1819 | 3.2 | | | |
| Frozen, with meat balls: | | | | | | |
| (Banquet): | | | | | | |
| Spaghetti compartment | 7.1 oz. | | 12.6 | | | |
| Apple compartment | 2.5 oz. | | .2 | | | |
| Peas compartment | 1.9 oz. | | 1.2 | | | |
| Complete dinner | 11.5-oz. dinner | | 14.0 | | | |
| (Morton) | 11-oz. dinner | 1329 | 10.7 | | | |
| (Swanson) | 12-oz. dinner | 1138 | 9.8 | | | |
| **SPAGHETTI & FRANK-FURTERS in TOMATO SAUCE, canned:** | | | | | | |
| *SpaghettiO's* (Franco-American) | 1 cup | 816 | 12.7 | | | |
| (Heinz) | 8½-oz. can | 1475 | 16.9 | | | |
| **SPAGHETTI & GROUND BEEF in TOMATO SAUCE, canned:** | | | | | | |
| (Buitoni) | 8 oz. | | 14.9 | | | |
| (Chef Boy-Ar-Dee) | ½ of 15-oz. can | 1202 | 6.2 | | | |
| (Franco-American) | 1 cup | 1150 | 13.9 | | | |
| (Nalley's) | 8 oz. | | 7.8 | | | |
| **SPAGHETTI & MEATBALLS in TOMATO SAUCE:** | | | | | | |
| Home recipe (USDA)[1] | 1 cup (8.7 oz.) | 1009 | 11.7 | 5. | 7. | 75 |
| Canned: | | | | | | |
| (USDA)[1] | 1 cup (8.8 oz.) | 1220 | 10.2 | 5. | 5. | 39 |
| (Buitoni) | 8 oz. | | 13.1 | | | |
| (Chef Boy-Ar-Dee) | 1/5 of 40-oz. can | 1061 | 8.2 | | | |
| (Franco-American) | 1 cup | 1107 | 13.6 | | | |
| *SpaghettiO's* (Franco-American) | 1 cup | 1411 | 8.9 | | | |
| (Hormel) | 15-oz. can | | 16.6 | | | |
| (Van Camp) | 1 cup (7.8 oz.) | | 9.0 | | | |
| Frozen (Buitoni) | 8 oz. | | 9.1 | | | |
| **SPAGHETTI with MEAT SAUCE:** | | | | | | |
| Canned (Heinz) | 8½-oz. can | 1246 | 6.8 | | | |

(USDA): United States Department of Agriculture
*Prepared as Package Directs
[1]Principal sources of fat: olive oil, pork, beef, cheese, egg, bread crumbs & milk.

| Food and Description | Measure or Quantity | Sodium (mg.) | Fats in grams — Total | Satu- rated | Unsatu- rated | Choles- terol (mg.) |
|---|---|---|---|---|---|---|
| **Frozen:** | | | | | | |
| (Banquet) cooking bag | 8-oz. bag | | 15.1 | | | |
| (Banquet) buffet | 2-lb. pkg. | | 73.4 | | | |
| (Banquet) entrée | 8-oz. pkg. | | 14.4 | | | |
| (Kraft) | 12½-oz. pkg. | 1143 | 11.7 | | | |
| (Morton) | 8-oz. casserole | 937 | 13.1 | | | |
| (Morton) | 20-oz. casserole | 2342 | 32.8 | | | |
| **SPAGHETTI MIX:** | | | | | | |
| *American style (Kraft) | 4 oz. | 318 | 1.9 | | | |
| *Italian style (Kraft) | 4 oz. | 338 | 2.2 | | | |
| **SPAGHETTI SAUCE:** | | | | | | |
| Clam, red (Buitoni) | 4 oz. | | 7.3 | | | |
| Clam, white (Buitoni) | 4 oz. | | 9.6 | | | |
| Italian (Contadina)[1] | 4 fl. oz. (4.4 oz.) | 492 | 2.8 | Tr. | 2. | 0 |
| Italian, frozen (Celeste) | ½ cup | 740 | 2.4 | | | |
| Meat: | | | | | | |
| (Buitoni) | 4 oz. | | 8.4 | | | |
| (Chef Boy-Ar-Dee) | ¼ of 15-oz. can | 953 | 4.3 | | | |
| (Heinz) | ½ cup | 754 | 3.8 | | | |
| (Prince) | ½ cup (4.9 oz.) | 1030 | 5.0 | | | |
| Meatball (Chef Boy-Ar-Dee) | ⅓ of 15-oz. can | 940 | 9.2 | | | |
| With ground meat (Chef Boy-Ar-Dee) | ¹/₇ of 29-oz. jar | 1088 | 8.0 | | | |
| Meatless or plain: | | | | | | |
| (Buitoni) | 4 oz. | | 2.7 | | | |
| (Chef Boy-Ar-Dee) | ¼ of 16-oz. jar | 829 | 1.9 | | | |
| (Heinz) | ½ cup | 770 | 2.7 | | | |
| (Prince) | ½ cup (4.6 oz.) | 970 | 3.6 | | | |
| Mushroom: | | | | | | |
| (Buitoni) | 4 oz. | | 2.7 | | | |
| (Chef Boy-Ar-Dee) | ¼ of 15-oz. can | 974 | 1.8 | | | |
| (Heinz) | ½ cup | 794 | 3.0 | | | |
| Mushroom with meat (Heinz) | ½ cup | 822 | 3.9 | | | |
| **SPAGHETTI SAUCE MIX:** | | | | | | |
| *(Kraft) | 4 oz. | 572 | 2.4 | | | |
| (McCormick) | 1½-oz. pkg. | | | | | |
| *(McCormick) | 4-oz. serving | 878 | 3.0 | | | |
| Italian (French's) | 1½-oz. pkg. | 3600 | .4 | | | |
| *Italian (French's) | ⅝ cup | 918 | 5.8 | | | |

(USDA): United States Department of Agriculture
*Prepared as Package Directs
[1]Principal source of fat: olive oil.

| Food and Description | Measure or Quantity | Sodium (mg.) | —Fats in grams— | | | Choles-terol (mg.) |
| --- | --- | --- | --- | --- | --- | --- |
| | | | Total | Satu-rated | Unsatu-rated | |
| *Prepared without oil (Spatini) | ½ cup (4.2 oz.) | 402 | .2 | | | 0 |
| *Prepared with oil (Spatini) | ½ cup (4.2 oz.) | 380 | 2.8 | | | 0 |
| With meatballs (Lawry's) | 3½-oz. pkg. | | 2.2 | | | |
| With mushrooms (French's) | 1⅜-oz. pkg. | 3940 | 3.3 | | | |
| *With mushrooms (French's) | ⅝ cup | 1003 | 3.8 | | | |
| With mushrooms (Lawry's) | 1½-oz. pkg. | | 3.3 | | | |
| *With mushrooms & tomato paste (Durkee) | 2⅔ cups (1.2-oz. pkg.) | 3106 | .8 | | | |
| *Without meat (Durkee) | 2½ cups (1½-oz. pkg.) | 3937 | 1.0 | | | |
| *(Wyler's) | ¾ cup | | .5 | | | |
| **SPAGHETTI WITH TOMATO SAUCE:** | | | | | | |
| Twists (Buitoni) | 8 oz. | | 1.7 | | | |
| (Van Camp) | 1 cup (7.8 oz.) | | 1.4 | | | |
| With cheese: | | | | | | |
| Home recipe (USDA)[1] | 1 cup (8.8 oz.) | 955 | 8.8 | 2. | 6. | |
| Canned: | | | | | | |
| (USDA) | 1 cup (8.8 oz.) | 955 | 1.5 | | | |
| (Chef Boy-Ar-Dee) | ⅕ of 40-oz. can | 1283 | 1.4 | | | |
| (Franco-American) | 1 cup | 925 | 1.6 | | | |
| SpaghettiO's (Franco-American) | 1 cup | 1064 | 2.3 | | | |
| Italian Style (Franco-American) | 1 cup | 982 | 2.0 | | | |
| (Heinz) | 8½-oz. can | 1330 | 3.5 | | | |
| *SPAM* (Hormel), canned: | | | | | | |
| Regular | 3 oz. | 1020 | 22.5 | 6. | 12. | 45 |
| Spread | 1 oz. | 360 | 6.7 | 2. | 4. | 8 |
| & cheese | 3 oz. | 1020 | 22.3 | | | |
| **SPANISH MACKEREL,** raw (USDA): | | | | | | |
| Whole | 1 lb. (weighed whole) | 188 | 28.8 | | | |
| Meat only | 4 oz. | 77 | 11.8 | | | |
| **SPANISH-STYLE VEGE-TABLES,** frozen (Birds Eye) | ⅓ of 10-oz. pkg. | 339 | 6.6 | | | 0 |
| **SPEARMINT,** dry (Spice Islands) | 1 tsp. | 2 | | | | (0) |
| *SPECIAL K,* cereal (Kellogg's) | 1¼ cups (1 oz.) | 168 | .1 | | | |

(USDA): United States Department of Agriculture
*Prepared as Package Directs
[1]Principal sources of fat: olive oil & cheese.

| Food and Description | Measure or Quantity | Sodium (mg.) | —Fats in grams— | | | Choles-terol j)mg.) |
|---|---|---|---|---|---|---|
| | | | Total | Satu-rated | Unsatu-rated | |
| **SPICE CAKE MIX:** | | | | | | |
| *(Duncan Hines) | ¹/₁₂ of cake (2.7 oz.) | 384 | 6.1 | | | 50 |
| *Apple with raisins, layer (Betty Crocker) | ¹/₁₂ ofcake | 272 | 5.5 | | | |
| *Layer (Betty Crocker) | ¹/₁₂ of cake | 261 | 5.6 | | | |
| Honey: | | | | | | |
| (USDA)[1] | 1 oz. | 106 | 4.0 | 1. | 3. | |
| *Prepared with eggs, water, caramel icing (USDA)[2] | 2 oz. | 139 | 6.1 | 2. | 4. | |
| **SPICE PARISIENNE** (Spice Islands) | 1 tsp. | <1 | | | | (0) |
| **SPINACH:** | | | | | | |
| Raw (USDA): | | | | | | |
| Untrimmed | 1 lb. (weighed with large stems & roots) | 232 | 1.0 | | | 0 |
| Trimmed or packaged | 1 lb. | 322 | 1.4 | | | 0 |
| Trimmed, whole leaves | 1 cup (1.2 oz.) | 23 | <.1 | | | 0 |
| Trimmed, chopped | 1 cup (1.8 oz.) | 37 | .2 | | | 0 |
| Boiled without salt, whole leaves, drained (USDA) | 1 cup (5.5 oz.) | 78 | .5 | | | 0 |
| Canned, regular pack: | | | | | | |
| Solids & liq. (USDA) | ½ cup (4.1 oz.) | 274 | .5 | | | 0 |
| Drained solids (USDA) | ½ cup (4 oz.) | 264 | .7 | | | 0 |
| Drained liq. (USDA) | 4 oz. | 268 | 0. | | | 0 |
| Drained solids (Del Monte) | ½ cup (4 oz.) | 389 | .6 | | | 0 |
| Solids & liq. (Stokely-Van Camp) | ½ cup (3.9 oz.) | | .5 | | | (0) |
| Canned, dietetic pack, low-sodium: | | | | | | |
| Solids & liq. (USDA) | 4 oz. | 39 | .5 | | | 0 |
| Drained solids (USDA) | 4 oz. | 36 | .6 | | | 0 |
| Drained liq. (USDA) | 4 oz. | 36 | 0. | | | 0 |
| Solids & liq. (Blue Boy) | 4 oz. | 39 | .4 | | | (0) |
| Frozen: | | | | | | |
| Chopped: | | | | | | |
| Not thawed (USDA) | 4 oz. | 65 | .3 | | | 0 |
| Boiled, drained (USDA) | 4 oz. | 59 | .3 | | | 0 |
| (Birds Eye) | ⅓ of 10. oz. pkg. | 86 | .3 | | | 0 |
| Deviled, with cheddar cheese, casserole (Green Giant) | ⅓ of 10-oz. pkg. | 387 | 3.3 | | | |
| In cream sauce (Green Giant) | ⅓ of 10-oz. pkg. | 359 | 2.8 | | | |
| Leaf: | | | | | | |
| Not thawed (USDA) | 4 oz. | 60 | .3 | | | 0 |

(USDA): United States Department of Agriculture
*Prepared as Package Directs
[1]Principal source of fat: vegetable shortening.
[2]Principal sources of fat: vegetable shortening & egg.

| Food and Description | Measure or Quantity | Sodium (mg.) | Fats in grams — Total | Satu- rated | Unsatu- rated | Choles- terol (mg.) |
|---|---|---|---|---|---|---|
| Boiled, drained (USDA) | 4 oz. | 56 | .3 | | | 0 |
| (Birds Eye) | ⅓ of 10-oz. pkg. | 82 | .3 | | | 0 |
| Creamed (Birds Eye) | ⅓ of 10-oz. pkg. | 277 | 3.8 | | | Tr. |
| In butter sauce (Green Giant) | ⅓ of 10-oz. pkg. | 340 | 2.6 | | | |

**SPINACH, NEW ZEALAND** (See
**NEW ZEALAND SPINACH**)

**SPINACH SOUFFLE,** frozen

| | | | | | | |
|---|---|---|---|---|---|---|
| (Stouffer's) | 12-oz. pkg. | 2206 | 32.0 | | | |

**SPINY LOBSTER** (See
**CRAYFISH**)

**SPLEEN,** raw (USDA):

| | | | | | | |
|---|---|---|---|---|---|---|
| Beef & calf | 4 oz. | | 3.4 | | | |
| Hog | 4 oz. | | 4.3 | | | |
| Lamb | 4 oz. | | 4.4 | | | |

**SPONGE CAKE,** home recipe
(USDA)[1]

| | | | | | | |
|---|---|---|---|---|---|---|
| | ¹/₁₂ of 10" cake (2.3 oz.) | 110 | 3.8 | 1. | 2. | 162 |

**SPOT,** fillets (USDA):

| | | | | | | |
|---|---|---|---|---|---|---|
| Raw[2] | 1 lb. | 277 | 72.1 | | | |
| Baked, salt added | 4 oz. | 354 | 24.8 | | | |

| | | | | | | |
|---|---|---|---|---|---|---|
| *SPRITE,* soft drink | 6 fl. oz. | 21 | 0. | | | 0 |

**SQUAB,** pigeon, raw (USDA):

| | | | | | | |
|---|---|---|---|---|---|---|
| Dressed | 1 lb. (weighed with feet, inedible viscera & bones) | | 45.1 | | | |
| Meat & skin | 4 oz. | | 27.0 | | | |
| Meat only | 4 oz. | | 8.5 | | | |
| Light meat only, without skin | 4 oz. | | 4.8 | | | |
| Giblets | 1 oz. | | 2.0 | | | |

**SQUASH SEEDS,** dry (USDA):

| | | | | | | |
|---|---|---|---|---|---|---|
| In hull | 4 oz. | | 39.2 | 7. | 32 | 0 |
| Hulled | 1 oz. | | 13.2 | 2. | 11. | 0 |

(USDA): United States Department of Agriculture
*Prepared as Package Directs
[1]Principal source of fat: egg.
[2]Based on samples caught in October. Fat content may vary greatly in samples caught at other seasons of year.

| Food and Description | Measure or Quantity | Sodium (mg.) | —Fats in grams— | | | Choles-terol (mg.) |
|---|---|---|---|---|---|---|
| | | | Total | Satu-rated | Unsatu-rated | |

## SQUASH, SUMMER:
Fresh (USDA):
Crookneck & Straightneck, yellow:

| | | | | | | |
|---|---|---|---|---|---|---|
| Whole | 1 lb. (weighed untrimmed) | 4 | .9 | | | 0 |
| Boiled, drained, diced | ½ cup (3.6 oz.) | 1 | .2 | | | 0 |
| Boiled, drained, slices | ½ cup (3.1 oz.) | <1 | .2 | | | 0 |
| Scallop, white & pale green: | | | | | | |
| Whole | 1 lb. (weighed untrimmed) | 4 | .4 | | | 0 |
| Boiled, drained, mashed | ½ cup (4.2 oz.) | 1 | .1 | | | 0 |
| Zucchini & Cocozelle, green: | | | | | | |
| Whole | 1 lb. (weighed untrimmed) | 4 | .4 | | | 0 |
| Boiled, drained slices | ½ cup (2.7 oz.) | <1 | 2.1 | | | 0 |
| Canned, zucchini in tomato sauce (Del Monte) | ½ cup (4.1 oz.) | 416 | .1 | | | |
| Frozen: | | | | | | |
| Not thawed (USDA) | 4 oz. | 3 | .1 | | | 0 |
| Boiled, drained (USDA) | 4 oz. | 3 | .1 | | | 0 |
| Fried, breaded, zucchini (Mrs. Paul's) | 9-oz. pkg. | | 30.1 | | | |
| Parmesan, zucchini (Mrs. Paul's) | 12-oz. pkg. | | 13.5 | | | |
| Summer squash, slices (Birds Eye) | ½ cup (3.3 oz.) | 3 | .1 | | | 0 |
| Zucchini (Birds Eye) | ⅓ of 10.-oz. pkg. | 1 | .1 | | | 0 |

## SQUASH, WINTER:
Fresh (USDA):
Acorn:

| | | | | | | |
|---|---|---|---|---|---|---|
| Whole | 1 lb. (weighed with skin & seeds) | 3 | .3 | | | 0 |
| Baked, flesh only, mashed | ½ cup (3.6 oz.) | 1 | .1 | | | 0 |
| Boiled, mashed | ½ cup (4.1 oz.) | 1 | .1 | | | 0 |
| Butternut: | | | | | | |
| Whole | 1 lb. (weighed with skin & seeds) | 3 | .3 | | | 0 |
| Baked, flesh only | 4 oz. | 1 | .1 | | | 0 |
| Boiled, flesh only | 4 oz. | 1 | .1 | | | 0 |
| Hubbard: | | | | | | |
| Whole | 1 lb. (weighed with skin & seeds) | 3 | .9 | | | 0 |

(USDA): United States Department of Agriculture
*Prepared as Package Directs

| Food and Description | Measure or Quantity | Sodium (mg.) | Total | Satu-rated | Unsatu-rated | Choles-terol (mg.) |
|---|---|---|---|---|---|---|
| Baked, flesh only | 4 oz. | 1 | .5 | | | 0 |
| Baked, flesh only, mashed | ½ cup (3.6 oz.) | 1 | .4 | | | 0 |
| Boiled, flesh only, diced | ½ cup (4.2 oz.) | 1 | .4 | | | 0 |
| Boiled, flesh only, mashed | ½ cup (4.3 oz.) | 1 | .3 | | | 0 |
| Frozen: | | | | | | |
| Not thawed (USDA) | 4 oz. | 1 | .3 | | | 0 |
| Heated (USDA) | ½ cup (4.2 oz.) | 1 | .4 | | | 0 |
| (Birds Eye) | ⅓ of 12-oz. pkg. | 1 | .3 | | | 0 |
| **SQUID,** raw, meat only (USDA) | 4 oz. | | 10.2 | | | |
| **STARCH** (See **CORNSTARCH**) | | | | | | |
| *START,* instant breakfast drink | ½ cup (4.7 oz.) | 45 | .1 | | | 0 |
| *STOCKPOT SOUP,* canned (Campbell) | 1 cup | 925 | 3.9 | <.1 | 3. | |
| **STOMACH, PORK,** scalded (USDA) | 4 oz. | | 10.2 | | | |
| **STRAINED FOOD** (See **BABY FOOD**) | | | | | | |
| **STRAWBERRY:** | | | | | | |
| Fresh, whole (USDA) | 1 lb. (weighed with caps & stems) | 4 | 2.2 | | | 0 |
| Fresh, whole, capped (USDA) | 1 cup (5.1 oz.) | 1 | .7 | | | 0 |
| Canned, unsweetened or low calorie: | | | | | | |
| Water pack, solids & liq. (USDA) | 4 oz. | 1 | .1 | | | 0 |
| Solids & liq. (Blue Boy) | 4 oz. | 1 | .7 | | | (0) |
| Low calorie, solids & liq. (S and W) *Nutradiet* | 4 oz. | 1 | <.1 | | | (0) |
| Frozen: | | | | | | |
| Sweetened, whole, not thawed: | | | | | | |
| (USDA) | 16-oz. can | 5 | .9 | | | 0 |
| (USDA) | ½ cup (4.5 oz.) | 1 | .3 | | | 0 |
| Sweetened, sliced, not thawed (USDA) | 10-oz. pkg. | 3 | .6 | | | 0 |
| Sweetened, sliced, not thawed (USDA) | ½ cup (4.5 oz.) | 1 | .3 | | | 0 |

(USDA): United States Department of Agriculture
*Prepared as Package Directs

| Food and Description | Measure or Quantity | Sodium (mg.) | —Fats in grams— | | | Cholesterol (mg.) |
|---|---|---|---|---|---|---|
| | | | Total | Saturated | Unsaturated | |
| Whole (Birds Eye) | ¼ of 1-lb. pkg. | 1 | .2 | | | 0 |
| Halves (Birds Eye) | ½ cup (5.3 oz.) | 2 | .6 | | | 0 |
| Quick-thaw (Birds Eye) | ½ cup (5 oz.) | 6 | .3 | | | 0 |
| **\*STRAWBERRY CAKE MIX** (Duncan Hines) | ¹/₁₂ of cake | 240 | 6.1 | | | 50 |
| **STRAWBERRY DRINK MIX** *Quik* | 2 heaping tsps. (.6 oz.) | 5 | 0. | | | |
| **STRAWBERRY ICE CREAM** (Sealtest) | ¼ pt. (2.3 oz.) | 38 | 5.3 | | | |
| **STRAWBERRY PIE:** | | | | | | |
| Home recipe, made with lard (USDA)[1] | ¹/₆ of 9" pie (5.6 oz.) | 307 | 12.5 | 5. | 8. | |
| Home recipe, made with vegetable shortening (USDA)[2] | ¹/₆ of 9" pie (5.6 oz.) | 307 | 12.5 | 3. | 9. | |
| Creme (Tastykake) | 4-oz. pie | | 15.3 | | | |
| Frozen: | | | | | | |
| (Morton) | ¹/₆ of 20-oz. pie | 232 | 10.9 | | | |
| Cream (Banquet) | 2½-oz. serving | | 7.8 | | | |
| Cream (Morton) | ¼ of 14.4-oz. pie | 186 | 13.9 | | | |
| Cream (Mrs. Smith's) | ¹/₆ of 8" pie (2.3 oz.) | 95 | 11.8 | | | |
| **STRAWBERRY PIE FILLING:** | | | | | | |
| (Comstock) | ½ cup (5.4 oz.) | 77 | .2 | | | |
| (Lucky Leaf) | 8 oz. | 150 | .6 | | | |
| **STRAWBERRY PRESERVE or JAM:** | | | | | | |
| Sweetened (Bama) | 1 T. (.7 oz.) | 2 | <.1 | | | (0) |
| Dietetic or low calorie: | | | | | | |
| (Diet Delight) | 1 T. (.6 oz.) | <1 | Tr. | | | (0) |
| (Kraft) | 1 oz. | 36 | <.1 | | | (0) |
| (S and W) *Nutradiet* | 1 T. (.5 oz.) | | <.1 | | | (0) |
| (Slenderella) | 1 T. (.7 oz.) | 20 | Tr. | | | (0) |

(USDA): United States Department of Agriculture
\*Prepared as Package Directs
[1]Principal sources of fat: lard & butter.
[2]Principal sources of fat: vegetable shortening & butter.

| Food and Description | Measure or Quantity | Sodium (mg.) | —Fats in grams— | | | Choles- terol (mg.) |
|---|---|---|---|---|---|---|
| | | | Total | Satu- rated | Unsatu- rated | |
| (Smucker's) | 1 T. (.7 oz.) | Tr. | <.1 | | | (0) |
| (Tillie Lewis) | 1 T. (.5 oz.) | 3 | Tr. | | | 0 |
| **STRAWBERRY RENNET MIX:** | | | | | | |
| Powder: | | | | | | |
| Dry (Junket) | 1 oz. | 11 | <.1 | | | |
| *(Junket) | 4 oz. | 56 | 3.9 | | | |
| Tablet: | | | | | | |
| Dry (Junket) | 1 tablet (<1 gram) | 197 | Tr. | | | |
| *& sugar (Junket) | 4 oz. | 98 | 3.9 | | | |
| **STRAWBERRY-RHUBARB PIE:** | | | | | | |
| (Tastykake) | 4-oz. pie | | 14.6 | | | |
| Frozen: | | | | | | |
| (Morton) | ⅛ of 46-oz. pie | 382 | 16.5 | | | |
| (Mrs. Smith's) | ⅙ of 8″ pie (4.2 oz.) | 395 | 14.2 | | | |
| (Mrs. Smith's) old fashion | ⅙ of 9″ pie (5.8 oz.) | 470 | 22.7 | | | |
| (Mrs. Smith's) | ⅛ of 10″ pie (5.6 oz.) | 509 | 18.4 | | | |
| **STRAWBERRY-RHUBARB PIE FILLING,** canned (Lucky Leaf) | 8 oz. | 192 | .4 | | | |
| **STRAWBERRY SOFT DRINK:** | | | | | | |
| Sweetened: | | | | | | |
| (Canada Dry) | 6 fl. oz. | 14+ | 0. | | | 0 |
| (Clicquot Club) | 6 fl. oz. | 11 | 0. | | | 0 |
| (Cott) | 6 fl. oz. | 11 | 0. | | | 0 |
| (Fanta) | 6 fl. oz. | 7 | 0. | | | 0 |
| (Hoffman) | 6 fl. oz. | 14 | 0. | | | 0 |
| (Mission) | 6 fl. oz. | 11 | 0. | | | 0 |
| (Shasta) | 6 fl. oz. | 36 | 0. | | | 0 |
| (Yukon Club) | 6 fl. oz. | 14 | 0. | | | 0 |
| Low calorie: | | | | | | |
| (Canada Dry) bottle or can | 6 fl. oz. | 14+ | 0. | | | 0 |
| (Clicquot Club) | 6 fl. oz. | 45 | 0. | | | 0 |
| (Cott) | 6 fl. oz. | 45 | 0. | | | 0 |
| (Hoffman) | 6 fl. oz. | 56 | 0. | | | 0 |
| (Mission) | 6 fl. oz. | 45 | 0. | | | 0 |
| (Shasta) | 6 fl. oz. | 47 | 0. | | | 0 |
| **STRAWBERRY SYRUP,** low calorie | | | | | | |
| (No-Cal) | 1 tsp. | <1 | 0. | | | (0) |

(USDA): United States Department of Agriculture
*Prepared as Package Directs

| Food and Description | Measure or Quantity | Sodium (mg.) | —Fats in grams— | | | Cholesterol (mg.) |
|---|---|---|---|---|---|---|
| | | | Total | Satu-rated | Unsatu-rated | |
| **STRAWBERRY TURNOVER,** | | | | | | |
| frozen (Pepperidge Farm) | 1 turnover (3.3 oz.) | 251 | 19.9 | | | |
| | | | | | | |
| **STRUDEL,** frozen (Pepperidge Farm): | | | | | | |
| Apple | $\frac{1}{6}$ of strudel (2.5 oz.) | 146 | 10.2 | | | |
| Blueberry | $\frac{1}{6}$ of strudel (2.5 oz.) | 156 | 9.8 | | | |
| Cherry | $\frac{1}{6}$ of strudel (2.5 oz.) | 160 | 9.8 | | | |
| Pineapple-cheese | $\frac{1}{6}$ of strudel (2.3 oz.) | 208 | 12.1 | | | |
| | | | | | | |
| **STURGEON** (USDA): | | | | | | |
| Raw, section | 1 lb. (weighed with skin & bones) | | 7.3 | | | |
| Raw, meat only | 4 oz. | | 2.2 | | | |
| Smoked | 4 oz. | | 2.0 | | | |
| Steamed | 4 oz. | 122 | 6.5 | | | |
| | | | | | | |
| **SUCCOTASH,** frozen: | | | | | | |
| Not thawed (USDA) | 4 oz. | 51 | .5 | | | 0 |
| Boiled, drained (USDA) | ½ cup (3.4 oz.) | 36 | .4 | | | 0 |
| (Birds Eye) | ½ cup (3.3 oz.) | 39 | .5 | | | 0 |
| | | | | | | |
| **SUCKER, CARP,** raw (USDA): | | | | | | |
| Whole | 1 lb. (weighed whole) | | 5.7 | | | |
| Meat only | 4 oz. | | 3.6 | | | |
| | | | | | | |
| **SUCKER,** including **WHITE and MULLET,** raw (USDA): | | | | | | |
| Whole | 1 lb. (weighed whole) | 109 | 3.5 | | | |
| Meat only | 4 oz. | 64 | 2.0 | | | |
| | | | | | | |
| **SUET,** raw (USDA) | 1 oz. | | 26.6 | | | |
| | | | | | | |
| **SUGAR,** beet or cane (There is no difference in values among brands): | | | | | | |
| Brown: | | | | | | |
| (USDA) | 1 lb. | 136 | 0. | | | 0 |
| Brownulated (USDA) | 1 cup (5.4 oz.) | 46 | 0. | | | 0 |
| Firm-packed (USDA) | 1 cup (7.5 oz.) | 64 | 0. | | | 0 |
| Firm-packed (USDA) | 1 T. (.5 oz.) | 4 | 0. | | | 0 |

(USDA): United States Department of Agriculture
*Prepared as Package Directs

| Food and Description | Measure or Quantity | Sodium (mg.) | — Fats in grams — | | | Choles- terol (mg.) |
|---|---|---|---|---|---|---|
| | | | Total | Satu- rated | Unsatu- rated | |
| Confectioners': | | | | | | |
| (USDA) | 1 lb. | 5 | 0. | | | 0 |
| Unsifted (USDA) | 1 cup (4.3 oz.) | 1 | 0. | | | 0 |
| Unsifted (USDA) | 1 T. (8 grams) | <1 | 0. | | | 0 |
| Sifted (USDA) | 1 cup (3.4 oz.) | <1 | 0. | | | 0 |
| Sifted (USDA) | 1 T. (6 grams) | <1 | 0. | | | 0 |
| Stirred (USDA) | 1 cup (4.2 oz.) | 1 | 0. | | | 0 |
| Stirred (USDA) | 1 T. (8 grams) | <1 | 0. | | | 0 |
| Granulated: | | | | | | |
| (USDA) | 1 lb. | 5 | 0. | | | 0 |
| (USDA) | 1 cup (6.9 oz.) | 2 | 0. | | | 0 |
| (USDA) | 1 T. (.4 oz.) | <1 | 0. | | | 0 |
| (USDA) | 1 lump (1⅛" x ¾" x ⅜", 6 grams) | <1 | 0. | | | 0 |
| Maple (USDA) | 1 lb. | 64 | 0. | | | 0 |
| Maple (USDA) | 1¾" x 1¼" x ½" piece (1.2 oz.) | 4 | 0. | | | 0 |
| **SUGAR APPLE,** raw (USDA): | | | | | | |
| Whole | 1 lb. (weighed with skin & seeds) | 22 | .6 | | | 0 |
| Flesh only | 4 oz. | 12 | .3 | | | 0 |
| *SUGAR CHEX,* cereal, dry | ⅞ cup (1 oz.) | 220 | 2.2 | | | (0) |
| *SUGAR FROSTED FLAKES,* cereal (Kellogg's) | ¾ cup (1 oz.) | 170 | 0. | | | (0) |
| *SUGAR JETS,* cereal (General Mills) | 1 cup (1 oz.) | 218 | 1.1 | | | (0) |
| *SUGAR POPS,* cereal (Kellogg's) | 1 cup (1 oz.) | 68 | .1 | | | (0) |
| *SUGAR SMACKS,* cereal (Kellogg's) | 1 cup (1 oz.) | 22 | .5 | | | (0) |
| *SUGAR SPARKLED TWINKLES,* cereal (General Mills) | 1 cup (1 oz.) | 230 | .8 | | | (0) |
| **SUGAR SUBSTITUTE:** | | | | | | |
| (Adolph's) | 1 tsp. (4 grams) | Tr. | 0. | | | 0 |
| *Superose* (Whitlock) | 1 packet (1 gram) | 4 | 0. | | | (0) |

(USDA): United States Department of Agriculture
*Prepared as Package Directs

| Food and Description | Measure or Quantity | Sodium (mg.) | — Fats in grams — | | | Choles-terol (mg.) |
|---|---|---|---|---|---|---|
| | | | Total | Satu-rated | Unsatu-rated | |
| **SUKI-YAKI MIX:** | | | | | | |
| (Durkee) | 1.7-oz. pkg. | 6271 | .9 | | | |
| *With meat & vegetables (Durkee) | 6 cups (1.7-oz. pkg.) | 7226 | 122.7 | | | |
| **SUNFLOWER SEED** (USDA): | | | | | | |
| In hulls | 4 oz. (weighed in hull) | 18 | 29.0 | 4. | 25. | 0 |
| Hulled | 1 oz. | 9 | 13.4 | 2. | 12. | 0 |
| **SUNFLOWER SEED FLOUR** (See **FLOUR**) | | | | | | |
| *SUPER ORANGE CRISP WHEAT PUFFS,* cereal | 1 cup (1 oz.) | 146 | .3 | | | 0 |
| *SUPER SUGAR CRISP WHEAT PUFFS,* cereal (Post) | ⅞ cup (1 oz.) | 40 | .2 | | | 0 |
| **SURINAM CHERRY** (See **PITANGA**) | | | | | | |
| *SUZY Q* (Hostess) 2 to pkg. | 1 cake (2¼ oz.) | 137 | 9.2 | | | |
| **SWAMP CABBAGE** (USDA): | | | | | | |
| Raw, whole | 1 lb. (weighed untrimmed) | | 1.1 | | | 0 |
| Boiled, trimmed, drained | 4 oz. | | .2 | | | 0 |
| **SWEETBREADS** (USDA): | | | | | | |
| Beef, raw | 1 lb. | 435 | 72.6 | | | 1134 |
| Beef, braised | 4 oz. | 132 | 26.3 | | | 528 |
| Calf, raw | 1 lb. | | 9.1 | | | |
| Calf, braised | 4 oz. | | 3.6 | | | |
| Hog (See **PANCREAS**) | | | | | | |
| Lamb, raw | 1 lb. | | 17.2 | | | |
| Lamb, braised | 4 oz. | | 6.9 | | | |
| **SWEET POTATO:** | | | | | | |
| Raw (USDA): | | | | | | |
| All kinds, unpared | 1 lb. (weighed whole) | 37 | 1.5 | | | 0 |
| All kinds, pared | 4 oz. | 11 | .5 | | | 0 |
| Firm-fleshed, Jersey types, pared | 4 oz. | 11 | .8 | | | 0 |

(USDA): United States Department of Agriculture
*Prepared as Package Directs

| Food and Description | Measure or Quantity | Sodium (mg.) | Fats in grams — Total | Satu-rated | Unsatu-rated | Choles-terol (mg.) |
|---|---|---|---|---|---|---|
| Soft-fleshed, Puerto Rico variety, pared | 4 oz. | 11 | .3 | | | 0 |
| Baked, peeled after baking (USDA) | 3.9-oz. sweet potato (5″ x 2″) | 13 | .6 | | | 0 |
| Boiled, peeled after boiling (USDA) | 5-oz. sweet potato (5″ x 2″) | 15 | .6 | | | 0 |
| Candied, home recipe (USDA)[1] | 6.2-oz. sweet potato (3½″ x 2¼″) | 74 | 5.8 | 4. | 2. | 0 |
| Canned, regular pack: | | | | | | |
| In syrup, solids & liq. (USDA) | 4 oz. | 54 | .2 | | | 0 |
| Vacuum or solid pack (USDA) | ½ cup (3.8 oz.) | 52 | .2 | | | 0 |
| Heavy syrup, solids & liq. (Del Monte) | ½ cup (4.2 oz.) | 52 | Tr. | | | |
| Vacuum pack (Taylor's) | ½ cup | | .1 | | | (0) |
| Canned, dietetic pack, without added sugar & salt (USDA) | 4 oz. | 14 | .1 | | | 0 |
| Dehydrated flakes, dry (USDA) | ½ cup (2 oz.) | 105 | .3 | | | 0 |
| *Dehydrated flakes, prepared with water (USDA) | ½ cup (4.4 oz.) | 57 | .1 | | | 0 |
| Frozen: | | | | | | |
| Candied (Mrs. Paul's) | ⅓ of 12-oz. pkg. | | .2 | | | |
| Sweets & Apples, candied (Mrs. Paul's) | ⅓ of 12-oz. pkg. | | .1 | | | |
| Candied yams (Birds Eye) | ⅓ of 12-oz. pkg. | 10 | .3 | | | 0 |
| With brown sugar, pineapple glaze (Birds Eye) | ½ cup (3.3 oz.) | 36 | 2.5 | | | 0 |

**SWEET POTATO PIE:**

| Food and Description | Measure or Quantity | Sodium (mg.) | Fats in grams — Total | Satu-rated | Unsatu-rated | Choles-terol (mg.) |
|---|---|---|---|---|---|---|
| Home recipe, made with lard (USDA)[2] | ¹/₆ of 9″ pie (5.4 oz.) | 331 | 17.2 | 6. | 11. | |
| Home recipe, made with vegetable shortening (USDA)[3] | ¹/₆ of 9″ (5.4 oz.) | 331 | 17.2 | 5. | 13. | |
| (Tastykake) | 4-oz. pie | | 15.0 | | | |

**SWEETSOP** (See **SUGAR APPLE**)

| Food and Description | Measure or Quantity | Sodium (mg.) | Fats in grams — Total | Satu-rated | Unsatu-rated | Choles-terol (mg.) |
|---|---|---|---|---|---|---|
| *SWISS BURGER, mix, dinner (Jeno's) Add n' Heat | 30-oz. pkg. | | 78.2 | | | |

(USDA): United States Department of Agriculture
*Prepared as Package Directs
[1]Principal source of fat: butter.
[2]Principal sources of fat: lard & butter.
[3]Principal sources of fat: vegetable shortening & butter.

| Food and Description | Measure or Quantity | Sodium (mg.) | Total | Satu-rated | Unsatu-rated | Choles-terol (mg.) |
|---|---|---|---|---|---|---|
| | | | | *—Fats in grams—* | | |
| **SWISS STEAK,** frozen: | | | | | | |
| (Stouffer's) | 10-oz. pkg. | | 33.0 | | | |
| Dinner (Swanson) | 10-oz. dinner | 682 | 15.6 | 5. | 10. | |
| **SWORDFISH** (USDA): | | | | | | |
| Raw, meat only | 1 lb. | | 18.1 | | | |
| Broiled, with butter or margarine | 3″ x 3″ x ½″ steak (4.4 oz.) | | 7.5 | | | |
| Canned, solids & liq. | 4 oz. | | 3.4 | | | |
| **SYRUP** (See also individual listings by kind, such as **PANCAKE & WAFFLE SYRUP** or by brand name, such as *LOG CABIN*): | | | | | | |
| All fruit flavors (Smucker's) | 1 T. (.7 oz.) | Tr. | 0. | | | (0) |

# T

| Food and Description | Measure or Quantity | Sodium (mg.) | Total | Satu-rated | Unsatu-rated | Choles-terol (mg.) |
|---|---|---|---|---|---|---|
| *TABASCO* (McIlhenny) | ¼ tsp. (1 gram) | 6 | Tr. | | | (0) |
| **TACO SEASONING MIX:** | | | | | | |
| (French's) | 1¾-oz. pkg. | 3800 | 1.2 | | | |
| (Lawry's) | 1¼-oz. pkg. | | 2.1 | | | |
| *TAHITIAN TREAT,* soft drink (Canada Dry) bottle or can | 6 fl. oz. | 15+ | 0. | | | (0) |
| **TAMALE:** | | | | | | |
| Canned: | | | | | | |
| (Armour Star) | 15½-oz. can | | 31.6 | | | |
| (Hormel) beef | 1 tamale (2.1 oz.) | 357 | 6.0 | 2. | 3. | 5 |
| (Wilson) | 15½-oz. can | 2949 | 29.9 | 16. | 14. | 75 |
| Frozen: | | | | | | |
| (Banquet) cooking bag | 2 tamales with sauce (3 oz. each) | | 15.7 | | | |
| (Banquet) buffet | 2-lb. pkg. | | 83.6 | | | |
| **TAMARIND,** fresh (USDA): | | | | | | |
| Whole | 1 lb. (weighed with pods & seeds) | 111 | 1.3 | | | 0 |
| Flesh only | 4 oz. | 58 | .7 | | | 0 |

(USDA): United States Department of Agriculture
*Prepared as Package Directs

| Food and Description | Measure or Quantity | Sodium (mg.) | —Fats in grams— | | | Choles- terol (mg.) |
|---|---|---|---|---|---|---|
| | | | Total | Satu- rated | Unsatu- rated | |
| ***TANDY TAKE*** (Tastykake): | | | | | | |
| Chocolate | .7-oz. cake | | 6.2 | | | |
| Choc-o-mint | .6-oz. cake | | 5.2 | | | |
| Dandy Kake | .6-oz. cake | | 5.2 | | | |
| Karamel | .7-oz. cake | | 4.9 | | | |
| Orange | .6-oz. cake | | 4.8 | | | |
| Peanut butter | .7-oz. cake | | 6.5 | | | |
| ***\*TANG,*** instant breakfast drink: | | | | | | |
| Grape | ½ cup (4.7 oz.) | 8 | Tr. | | | 0 |
| Grapefruit | ½ cup (4.7 oz.) | 40 | Tr. | | | 0 |
| Orange | ½ cup (4.7 oz.) | 54 | .1 | | | 0 |
| **TANGELO,** fresh (USDA): | | | | | | |
| Juice from whole fruit | 1 lb. (weighed with peel, membrane & seeds) | | .3 | | | 0 |
| Juice | ½ cup (4.4 oz.) | | .1 | | | 0 |
| **TANGERINE or MANDARIN ORANGE,** fresh: | | | | | | |
| Whole (USDA) | 1 lb. (weighed with peel, membrane & seeds) | 7 | .7 | | | 0 |
| Whole (USDA) | 4.1-oz. tangerine (2⅜" dia.) | 2 | .2 | | | 0 |
| Peeled (Sunkist) | 1 large tangerine (4.1 oz.) | 2 | Tr. | | | 0 |
| Sections, without membranes (USDA) | 1 cup (6.8 oz.) | 4 | .4 | | | 0 |
| **TANGERINE JUICE:** | | | | | | |
| Fresh (USDA) | ½ cup (4.4 oz.) | 1 | .2 | | | 0 |
| Canned, unsweetened (USDA) | ½ cup (4.4 oz.) | 1 | .2 | | | 0 |
| Canned, sweetened (USDA) | ½ cup (4.4 oz.) | 1 | .2 | | | 0 |
| Frozen concentrate, unsweetened: | | | | | | |
| Undiluted (USDA) | 6-oz. can | 4 | 1.5 | | | 0 |
| \*Prepared with 3 parts water by volume (USDA) | ½ cup (4.4 oz.) | 1 | .2 | | | 0 |
| Frozen concentrate, sweetened: | | | | | | |
| \*(Minute Maid) | ½ cup (4.2 oz.) | 1 | <.1 | | | 0 |
| \*(Snow Crop) | ½ cup (4.2 oz.) | 1 | <.1 | | | 0 |

(USDA): United States Department of Agriculture
\*Prepared as Package Directs

| Food and Description | Measure or Quantity | Sodium (mg.) | —Fats in grams— | | | Choles-terol (mg.) |
|---|---|---|---|---|---|---|
| | | | Total | Satu-rated | Unsatu-rated | |
| **TAPIOCA,** dry, quick cooking, granulated: | | | | | | |
| (USDA) | 1 cup (5.4 oz.) | 5 | .3 | | | 0 |
| (USDA) | 1 T. (10 grams) | <1 | <.1 | | | 0 |
| (Minute Tapioca) | 1 T. | 2 | Tr. | | | |
| **TAPIOCA PUDDING:** | | | | | | |
| Apple, home recipe (USDA) | ½ cup (4.4 oz.) | 64 | .1 | | | |
| Cream, home recipe (USDA) | ½ cup (2.9 oz.) | 128 | 4.2 | 2. | 3. | 80 |
| Chilled (Sealtest) | 4 oz. | 229 | 3.5 | | | |
| Canned (Hunt's) | 5-oz. can | 210 | 5.8 | 1. | 5. | |
| Mix: | | | | | | |
| *All flavors (Jell-O) | ½ cup (5.1 oz.) | 166 | 4.6 | | | 13 |
| *Chocolate (Royal) | ½ cup (5.1 oz.) | 120 | 5.5 | | | 14 |
| *Fluffy (Minute Tapioca) | ½ cup (4.4 oz.) | 76 | 5.9 | | | 82 |
| *Vanilla (Royal) | ½ cup (5.1 oz.) | 120 | 4.6 | | | 14 |
| **TARO,** raw (USDA): | | | | | | |
| Tubers, whole | 1 lb. (weighed with skin) | 27 | .8 | | | 0 |
| Tubers, skin removed | 4 oz. | 8 | .2 | | | 0 |
| Leaves & stems | 1 lb. | | 3.6 | | | 0 |
| **TARRAGON** (Spice Islands) | 1 tsp. | <1 | | | | (0) |
| **TASTE AMERICA,** frozen (Green Giant): | | | | | | |
| Florida style | ⅓ of 10-oz. pkg. | 335 | 2.8 | | | |
| New Orleans style | ⅓ of 10-oz. pkg. | 572 | 3.6 | | | |
| Northwest style | ⅓ of 10-oz. pkg. | 454 | 3.3 | | | |
| Pennsylvania Dutch style | ⅓ of 10-oz. pkg. | 340 | 2.8 | | | |
| San Francisco Style | ⅓ of 10-oz. pkg. | 501 | .9 | | | |
| **TAUTOG or BLACKFISH,** raw: | | | | | | |
| Whole (USDA) | 1 lb. (weighed whole) | | 1.8 | | | |
| Meat only (USDA) | 4 oz. | | 1.2 | | | |
| **TEA:** | | | | | | |
| Bag (Lipton) | 1 bag | 0 | 0. | | | (0) |
| Bag (Tender Leaf) | 1 bag | Tr. | Tr. | | | 0 |
| Canned (Lipton) | 12 fl. oz. | 12 | | | | (0) |

(USDA): United States Department of Agriculture
*Prepared as Package Directs

| Food and Description | Measure or Quantity | Sodium (mg.) | —Fats in grams— | | | Cholesterol (mg.) |
|---|---|---|---|---|---|---|
| | | | Total | Saturated | Unsaturated | |
| Instant: | | | | | | |
|   Dry powder, slightly sweetened (USDA) | 1 tsp. (<1 gram) | | Tr. | | | 0 |
|   *Beverage, slightly sweetened (USDA) | 1 cup (8.4 oz.) | | Tr. | | | 0 |
|   *(Lipton) | 1 cup | 0 | 0. | | | (0) |
|   *Nestea* | 1 tsp. (<1 gram) | 7 | 0. | | | (0) |
|   (Tender Leaf) | 1 rounded tsp. | Tr. | Tr. | | | 0 |
| *TEAM,* cereal | 1⅓ cups (1 oz.) | 214 | .4 | | | (0) |
| **TEA MIX,** iced: | | | | | | |
|   *All flavors (Salada) | 1 cup (.5 oz. dry) | 6 | <.1 | | | (0) |
|   *(Tender Leaf) | 1 cup | 80 | | | | 0 |
|   Lemon-flavored: | | | | | | |
|     *Low calorie (Lipton) | 1 cup | 0 | <.1 | | | (0) |
|     *Low calorie (Tender Leaf) | 1 cup | 50 | Tr. | | | 0 |
| *TEMPTYS* (Tastykake): | | | | | | |
|   Butter creme | ⅔-oz. cake | | 4.4 | | | |
|   Chocolate | ⅔-oz. cake | | 2.5 | | | |
|   Lemon | ⅔-oz. cake | | 2.6 | | | |
| **TENDERGREEN (See MUSTARD SPINACH)** | | | | | | |
| **TEQUILA** (See **DISTILLED LIQUOR**) | | | | | | |
| **TERRAPIN, DIAMOND BACK,** raw (USDA): | | | | | | |
|   In shell | 1 lb. (weighed in shell) | | 3.3 | | | |
|   Meat only | 4 oz. | | 4.0 | | | |
| **TEXTURED VEGETABLE PROTEIN:** | | | | | | |
|   Breakfast links, *Morningstar Farms* | 1 link (.8 oz.) | 227 | 3.6 | <1. | 2. | 0 |
|   Breakfast patties, *Morningstar Farms* | 1 pattie (1.3 oz.) | 378 | 6.0 | 2. | 5. | 0 |
|   Breakfast slices, *Morningstar Farms* | 1 slice (1 oz.) | 468 | 3.1 | 1. | 2. | 0 |
|   *Burger Builders* (Betty Crocker) | ¼ cup | | 1.0 | | | |
|   *Pathmark Plus:* | | | | | | |
|     Dry | ⅓ oz. | | 0. | | | |
|     *Prepared | 4 oz. | | 7.9 | | | |

(USDA): United States Department of Agriculture
*Prepared as Package Directs

| Food and Description | Measure or Quantity | Sodium (mg.) | —Fats in grams— | | | Cholesterol (mg.) |
|---|---|---|---|---|---|---|
| | | | Total | Saturated | Unsaturated | |
| **THICK & FROSTY** (General Foods) | 1 cup (8.3 oz.) | 144 | 14.0 | | | 13 |
| **THURINGER,** sausage: | | | | | | |
| (USDA) | 1 oz. | | 6.9 | | | |
| (Hormel) Old Smokehouse | 1 oz. | 292 | 8.9 | | | |
| Summer sausage, all meat (Oscar Mayer) | .8-oz. slice | 287 | 6.4 | | | |
| Summer sausage, pure beef (Oscar Mayer) | .8-oz. slice | 278 | 5.8 | | | (0) |
| **THYME** (Spice Islands) | 1 tsp. | <1 | | | | (0) |
| **TIKI,** soft drink (Shasta): | | | | | | |
| Sweetened | 6 fl. oz. | 22 | 0. | | | (0) |
| Low calorie | 6 fl. oz. | 37 | 0. | | | (0) |
| **TILEFISH** (USDA): | | | | | | |
| Raw, whole | 1 lb. (weighed whole) | | 1.2 | | | |
| Baked, meat only | 4 oz. | | 4.2 | | | |
| **TOASTER CAKE:** | | | | | | |
| *Corn Treats* (Arnold) | 1.1-oz. piece | | 3.7 | | | |
| *Toastee* (Howard Johnson's): | | | | | | |
| Blueberry | 1 piece (1¼ oz.) | | 5.0 | | | |
| Cinnamon raisin | 1 piece (1.1 oz.) | | 4.0 | | | |
| Corn | 1 piece (1¼ oz.) | | 3.4 | | | |
| Orange | 1 piece (1 oz.) | | 4.8 | | | |
| Pound | 1 piece (1 oz.) | | 4.5 | | | |
| *Toastette* (Nabisco): | | | | | | |
| Apple | 1 piece (1⅔ oz.) | 159 | 5.4 | | | |
| Blueberry | 1 piece (1⅔ oz.) | 148 | 4.9 | | | |
| Brown sugar, cinnamon | 1 piece (1⅔ oz.) | 161 | 5.9 | | | |
| Cherry | 1 piece (1⅔ oz.) | 162 | 4.9 | | | |
| Orange marmalade | 1 piece (1⅔ oz.) | 175 | 5.0 | | | |
| Peach | 1 piece (1⅔ oz.) | 175 | 4.8 | | | |
| Strawberry | 1 piece (1⅔ oz.) | 145 | 5.1 | | | |
| *Toast-r-Cake* (Thomas): | | | | | | |
| Bran | 1 piece (1.2 oz.) | 335 | 3.1 | | | |
| Corn | 1 piece (1.2 oz.) | 345 | 3.9 | | | |
| Orange | 1 piece (1.2 oz.) | 335 | 3.8 | | | |

(USDA): United States Department of Agriculture
*Prepared as Package Directs

| Food and Description | Measure or Quantity | Sodium (mg.) | —Fats in grams— | | | Choles-terol (mg.) |
|---|---|---|---|---|---|---|
| | | | Total | Satu-rated | Unsatu-rated | |
| ***TOASTERINO,*** frozen (Buitoni): | | | | | | |
| Cheese, grilled | 4 oz. | | 9.3 | | | |
| Pizzaburger | 4 oz. | | 12.4 | | | |
| Sloppy Joe | 4 oz. | | 11.7 | | | |
| **TODDLER FOOD** (See **BABY FOOD**) | | | | | | |
| **TOFFEE KRUNCH BAR** | | | | | | |
| (Sealtest) | 3 fl. oz. (1.7 oz.) | 29 | 10.4 | | | |
| **TOFU** (See **SOYBEAN CURD**) | | | | | | |
| **TOMATO:** | | | | | | |
| Fresh, green, whole, untrimmed (USDA) | 1 lb. (weighed with core & stem end) | 12 | .8 | | | 0 |
| Fresh, green, trimmed, unpeeled (USDA) | 4 oz. | 3 | .2 | | | 0 |
| Fresh, ripe (USDA): | | | | | | |
| Whole, eaten with skin | 1 lb. | 14 | .9 | | | 0 |
| Whole, peeled | 1 lb. (weighed with skin, stem ends & hard core) | 12 | .8 | | | 0 |
| Whole, peeled | 1 med. (2″ x 2½″, 5.3 oz.) | 4 | .3 | | | 0 |
| Whole, peeled | 1 small (1¾″ x 2¼″, 3.9 oz.) | 3 | .2 | | | 0 |
| Sliced, peeled | ½ cup (3.2 oz.) | 3 | .2 | | | 0 |
| Cooked without salt | ½ cup (4.3 oz.) | 5 | .2 | | | 0 |
| Canned, regular pack: | | | | | | |
| Whole, solids & liq. (USDA) | ½ cup (4.2 oz.) | 155 | .2 | | | 0 |
| (Contadina) | ½ cup (4 oz.) | 225 | Tr. | | | |
| Solids & liq. (Del Monte) | ½ cup (4.2 oz.) | 159 | 1.0 | | | 0 |
| Diced, in puree (Contadina) | ½ cup (4 oz.) | 232 | Tr. | | | (0) |
| Sliced (Contadina) | ½ cup (4 oz.) | 352 | Tr. | | | (0) |
| Stewed (Contadina) | ½ cup (4 oz.) | 216 | Tr. | | | (0) |
| Stewed (Del Monte) | ½ cup (4.2 oz.) | 342 | .2 | | | 0 |
| Wedges, solids & liq. (Del Monte) | ½ cup (4.1 oz.) | 336 | .2 | | | 0 |
| Whole, peeled (Hunt's) | ½ cup (4.2 oz.) | 368 | .2 | | | (0) |
| Whole, solids & liq. (Stokely-Van Camp) | ½ cup (4.1 oz.) | | .2 | | | (0) |

(USDA): United States Department of Agriculture
*Prepared as Package Directs

| Food and Description | Measure or Quantity | Sodium (mg.) | —Fats in grams— | | | Cholesterol (mg.) |
|---|---|---|---|---|---|---|
| | | | Total | Saturated | Unsaturated | |
| Canned, dietetic pack, low sodium: | | | | | | |
| Solids & liq. (USDA) | 4 oz. | 3 | .2 | | | 0 |
| Solids & liq. (Blue Boy) | 4 oz. | 5 | .1 | | | (0) |
| Solids & liq. (Tillie Lewis) | ½ cup (4.3 oz.) | 15 | .2 | | | 0 |
| Whole, peeled (Diet Delight) | ½ cup (4.3 oz.) | 9 | .1 | | | (0) |
| Whole, unseasoned (S and W) | | | | | | |
| *Nutradiet* | 4 oz. | 10 | .1 | | | (0) |
| **TOMATO JUICE:** | | | | | | |
| Canned, regular pack: | | | | | | |
| (USDA) | 6 fl. oz. (6.4 oz.) | 364 | .2 | | | 0 |
| (USDA) | ½ cup (4.3 oz.) | 244 | .1 | | | 0 |
| (Campbell) | 6 fl. oz. | 618 | .2 | | | (0) |
| (Del Monte) | ½ cup (4.3 oz.) | 197 | .1 | | | 0 |
| (Heinz) | 5½-fl.-oz. can | 537 | .3 | | | (0) |
| (Hunt's) | 5½-fl.-oz. can | 566 | .2 | | | (0) |
| (Stokely-Van Camp) | ½ cup (4.3 oz.) | | .1 | | | (0) |
| Canned, dietetic pack, low sodium: | | | | | | |
| (USDA) | 4 oz. (by wt.) | 3 | .1 | | | 0 |
| (Blue Boy) | 4 oz. (by wt.) | 1 | <.1 | | | (0) |
| (Diet Delight) | ½ cup (3.9 oz.) | 8 | <.1 | | | (0) |
| Unseasoned (S and W) *Nutradiet* | 4 oz. (by wt.) | 7 | .1 | | | (0) |
| Concentrate, canned (USDA) | 4 oz. (by wt.) | 896 | .5 | | | 0 |
| *Concentrate, canned, diluted with 3 parts water by volume | | | | | | |
| (USDA) | 4 oz. (by wt.) | 237 | .1 | | | 0 |
| Dehydrated (USDA) | 1 oz. | 1115 | .6 | | | 0 |
| *Dehydrated (USDA) | ½ cup (4.3 oz.) | 312 | .1 | | | 0 |
| **TOMATO JUICE COCKTAIL:** | | | | | | |
| (USDA) | 4 oz. (by wt.) | 227 | .1 | | | 0 |
| *Snap-E-Tom* | 6 fl. oz. | 1066 | .2 | | | |
| **TOMATO PASTE, canned:** | | | | | | |
| (USDA) regular, no salt added | 6-oz. can | 65 | .7 | | | 0 |
| (USDA) regular, no salt added | ½ cup (4.6 oz.) | 49 | .5 | | | 0 |
| (USDA) regular, no salt added | 1 T. (.6 oz.) | 61 | .6 | | | 0 |
| (USDA) salt added | 6-oz. can | 1343 | .7 | | | 0 |
| (USDA) salt added | ½ cup (4.6 oz.) | 1019 | .5 | | | 0 |
| (USDA) salt added | 1 T. (.6 oz.) | 126 | .6 | | | 0 |
| (Contadina) | 1 T. (.5 oz.) | 5 | Tr. | | | (0) |
| (Del Monte) | 1 T. (.6 oz.) | 9 | <.1 | | | 0 |
| (Hunt's) | ½ cup (4.6 oz.) | 497 | .5 | | | (0) |

(USDA): United States Department of Agriculture
*Prepared as Package Directs

| Food and Description | Measure or Quantity | Sodium (mg.) | —Fats in grams— Total | Satu- rated | Unsatu- rated | Choles- terol (mg.) |
|---|---|---|---|---|---|---|
| (Hunt's) | 1 T. (.6 oz.) | 62 | <.1 | | | (0) |
| (Stokely-Van Camp) | ½ cup (4.6 oz.) | | .5 | | | (0) |
| **TOMATO PUREE:** | | | | | | |
| Canned, regular pack: | | | | | | |
| (USDA) | 1 cup (8.8 oz.) | 998 | .5 | | | 0 |
| (Contadina) | 1 cup | 24 | .7 | | | (0) |
| (Hunt's) | 1 cup (8.8 oz.) | 497 | .5 | | | (0) |
| Canned, dietetic pack (USDA) | 8 oz. | 14 | .5 | | | 0 |
| **TOMATO SALAD,** jellied | | | | | | |
| (Contadina) | ½ cup | 592 | Tr. | | | (0) |
| **TOMATO SAUCE,** canned: | | | | | | |
| (Contadina) | 1 cup | 1296 | Tr. | | | (0) |
| (Del Monte) plain | 1 cup (8.8 oz.) | 1252 | .3 | | | (0) |
| (Del Monte) with mushrooms | 1 cup (8.8 oz.) | 1262 | .3 | | | |
| (Del Monte) with onions | 1 cup (8.8 oz.) | 1218 | 1.3 | | | |
| (Del Monte) with tomato tidbits | 1 cup (8.8 oz.) | 1212 | .2 | | | |
| (Hunt's) plain | 1 cup (8.7 oz.) | 1662 | .4 | | | (0) |
| (Hunt's) herb[1] | 1 cup (8.8 oz.) | 942 | 8.5 | 2. | 7. | |
| (Hunt's) special | 1 cup (8.7 oz.) | 825 | .5 | | | |
| (Hunt's) with bits | 1 cup (8.7 oz.) | 1647 | .4 | | | |
| (Hunt's) with cheese[2] | 1 cup (8.8 oz.) | 1672 | 1.7 | | | |
| (Hunt's) with mushrooms | 1 cup (8.8 oz.) | 1669 | 4.2 | | | |
| (Hunt's) with onions | 1 cup (8.8 oz.) | 1704 | .5 | | | |
| **TOMATO SOUP:** | | | | | | |
| Canned, regular pack: | | | | | | |
| Condensed (USDA) | 8 oz. (by wt.) | 1796 | 4.8 | | | |
| *Prepared with equal volume water (USDA) | 1 cup (8.6 oz.) | 970 | 2.4 | | | |
| *Prepared with equal volume milk (USDA)[3] | 1 cup (8.8 oz.) | 1055 | 7.0 | 2. | 4. | |
| *(Campbell) | 1 cup | 801 | 1.8 | Tr. | 2. | 3 |
| *(Heinz) California | 1 cup (8.5 oz.) | 868 | .7 | | | |
| (Heinz) *Great American* | 1 cup (8¾ oz.) | 1585 | 5.7 | | | |
| *(Manischewitz) | 1 cup | | 1.7 | | | |
| *Beef (Campbell) *Noodle-O's* | 1 cup | 727 | 3.3 | | | |
| *Bisque (Campbell) | 1 cup | 988 | 2.4 | 1. | 1. | |

(USDA): United States Department of Agriculture
*Prepared as Package Directs
[1]Principal source of fat: cottonseed oil.
[2]Principal source of fat: cheese.
[3]Principal source of fat: milk.

| Food and Description | Measure or Quantity | Sodium (mg.) | —Fats in grams— | | | Cholesterol (mg.) |
|---|---|---|---|---|---|---|
| | | | Total | Saturated | Unsaturated | |
| *Rice, old fashioned (Campbell) | 1 cup | 752 | 2.8 | <1. | 2. | |
| *Rice (Manischewitz) | 1 cup | | 2.3 | | | |
| With vegetables (Heinz) *Great American* | 1 cup (8¾ oz.) | 1007 | 5.2 | | | |
| Canned, dietetic pack: | | | | | | |
| Low sodium (Campbell) | 7¼-oz. can | 30 | 2.3 | | | |
| *With rice (Claybourne) | 8 oz. | 34 | 1.0 | | | |
| *With rice (Slim-ette) | 8 oz. (by wt.) | 28 | .1 | | | |
| (Tillie Lewis) | 1 cup (8 oz.) | 35 | 1.4 | | | |
| **TOMATO SOUP MIX:** | | | | | | |
| (Lipton) *Cup-a-Soup* | 1 pkg. (.8 oz.) | 670 | .5 | Tr. | Tr. | 1 |
| Vegetable: | | | | | | |
| With noodles (USDA)[1] | 1 oz. | 1740 | 2.3 | <1. | 2. | |
| *With noodles (USDA)[1] | 1 cup (8 oz.) | 974 | 1.4 | | | |
| *With noodles (Lipton) | 1 cup (8 oz.) | 1304 | 1.6 | Tr. | 1. | 10 |
| **TOMCOD, ATLANTIC,** raw (USDA): | | | | | | |
| Whole | 1 lb. (weighed whole) | | .7 | | | |
| Meat only | 4 oz. | | .5 | | | |
| **TOM COLLINS MIX** (Party Tyme) | ½-oz. pkg. | 66 | 0. | | | (0) |
| **TOM COLLINS or COLLINS MIXER SOFT DRINK:** | | | | | | |
| (Canada Dry) bottle or can | 6 fl. oz. | 13† | 0. | | | 0 |
| (Dr. Brown's) | 6 fl. oz. | 9 | 0. | | | 0 |
| (Hoffman) | 6 fl. oz. | 9 | 0. | | | 0 |
| (Kirsch) | 6 fl. oz. | <1 | 0. | | | 0 |
| (Shasta) | 6 fl. oz. | 22 | 0. | | | 0 |
| (Yukon Club) | 6 fl. oz. | 9 | 0. | | | 0 |
| **TONGUE** (USDA): | | | | | | |
| Beef, medium fat, raw, untrimmed | 1 lb. | | 52.0 | | | |
| Beef, medium fat, braised | 4 oz. | 69 | 18.9 | | | |
| Beef, smoked | 4 oz. | | 32.7 | | | |
| Calf, raw, untrimmed | 1 lb. | | 18.5 | | | |
| Calf, braised | 4 oz. | | 6.8 | | | |
| Hog, raw, untrimmed | 1 lb. | | 53.8 | | | |
| Hog, braised | 4 oz. | | 19.7 | | | |

(USDA): United States Department of Agriculture
*Prepared as Package Directs
[1]Principal sources of fat: vegetable shortening & egg.

| Food and Description | Measure or Quantity | Sodium (mg.) | —Fats in grams— | | | Choles- terol (mg.) |
|---|---|---|---|---|---|---|
| | | | Total | Satu- rated | Unsatu- rated | |
| Lamb, raw, untrimmed | 1 lb. | | 50.7 | | | |
| Lamb, braised | 4 oz. | | 20.6 | | | |
| Sheep, raw, untrimmed | 1 lb. | | 72.2 | | | |
| Sheep, braised | 4 oz. | | 28.7 | | | |
| **TONGUE, CANNED:** | | | | | | |
| Pickled (USDA) | 1 oz. | | 5.8 | | | |
| Potted or deviled (USDA) | 1 oz. | | 6.5 | | | |
| (Hormel) | 1 oz. (12-oz. can) | | 5.0 | | | |
| **TOPPING** (See also **CHOCOLATE SYRUP**): | | | | | | |
| Sweetened: | | | | | | |
| Butterscotch (Kraft) | 1 oz. | 80 | 1.2 | | | (0) |
| Butterscotch (Smucker's) | 1 T. (.7 oz.) | 35 | .2 | 0. | Tr. | |
| Caramel: | | | | | | |
| (Smucker's) | 1 T. (.7 oz.) | 55 | <.1 | Tr. | Tr. | |
| Chocolate (Kraft) | 1 oz. | 55 | .6 | | | |
| Vanilla (Kraft) | 1 oz. | 65 | <.1 | | | |
| Cherry (Smucker's) | 1 T. (.6 oz.) | Tr. | 0. | | | |
| Chocolate or chocolate flavored: | | | | | | |
| (Kraft) | 1 oz. | 25 | .4 | | | |
| Fudge (Hershey's) | 1 oz. | 111 | 3.8 | | | |
| Fudge (Kraft) | 1 oz. | 96 | 3.6 | | | |
| Fudge (Smucker's) | 1 T. (.7 oz.) | 18 | .6 | Tr. | Tr. | |
| Fudge, mint (Smucker's) | 1 T. (.6 oz.) | 18 | .6 | Tr. | Tr. | |
| Milk (Smucker's) | 1 T. (.7 oz.) | 23 | 1.4 | <1. | <1. | |
| Marshmallow creme (Kraft) | 1 oz. | 17 | 0. | | | |
| Pecan (Kraft) | 1 oz. | 4 | 7.8 | | | |
| Pecan in syrup (Smucker's) | 1 T. (.7 oz.) | Tr. | 5.1 | Tr. | 4. | |
| Pineapple (Kraft) | 1 oz. | <1 | <.1 | | | |
| Pineapple (Smucker's) | 1 T. (.6 oz.) | Tr. | 0. | | | |
| *Spoonmallow* (Kraft) | 1 oz. | 16 | 0. | | | |
| Strawberry (Kraft) | 1 oz. | <1 | <.1 | | | |
| Strawberry (Smucker's) | 1 T. (.6 oz.) | Tr. | 0. | | | |
| Walnut (Kraft) | 1 oz. | <1 | 6.3 | | | |
| Walnut in syrup (Smucker's) | 1 T. (.6 oz.) | Tr. | 4.3 | Tr. | 4. | |
| Dietetic, chocolate (Diet Delight) | 1 T. (.6 oz.) | 13 | Tr. | | | |
| **TOPPING, WHIPPED:** | | | | | | |
| (USDA) pressurized | 1 cup (2.5 oz.) | | 17.0 | 15. | 2. | |
| (USDA) pressurized | 1 T. (4 grams) | | 1. | <1. | Tr. | |
| (Birds Eye) *Cool Whip* | 1 T. (4 grams) | 1 | 1.2 | | | 0 |

(USDA): United States Department of Agriculture
*Prepared as Package Directs

| Food and Description | Measure or Quantity | Sodium (mg.) | — Fats in grams — | | | Choles- terol (mg.) |
|---|---|---|---|---|---|---|
| | | | Total | Satu- rated | Unsatu- rated | |
| (Kraft) | 1 oz. | 19 | 7.0 | | | |
| (Lucky Whip) | 1 T. (4 grams) | 3 | 1.2 | Tr. | 1. | 0 |
| (Sealtest) *Big Top* | 1.5 fl. oz. (.5 oz.) | 1 | 1.4 | | | |
| (Sealtest) *Zip Whipt*, real cream | 1.5 fl. oz. (.4 oz.) | 3 | 2.0 | | | |
| **TOPPING, WHIPPED, MIX:** | | | | | | |
| *(D-Zerta) | 1 T. | 6 | .6 | | | Tr. |
| *(Dream Whip) | 1 T. (.2 oz.) | 4 | .8 | | | Tr. |
| *(Lucky Whip) | 1 T. (4 grams) | 3 | .6 | Tr. | <1. | 0 |
| **TORTILLA** (USDA) | .7-oz. tortilla (5″) | | .6 | | | |
| *TOTAL,* cereal (General Mills) | 1¼ cups (1 oz.) | 48 | .5 | | | (0) |
| **TOWEL GOURD,** raw (USDA): | | | | | | |
| Unpared | 1 lb. (weighed with skin) | | .8 | | | 0 |
| Pared | 4 oz. | | .2 | | | 0 |
| *TREET* (Armour) | 1 oz. | | 7.4 | | | |
| **TRIPE,** beef (USDA): | | | | | | |
| Commercial | 4 oz. | 82 | 2.3 | | | |
| Pickled | 4 oz. | 52 | 1.5 | | | |
| **TROPICAL PUNCH SOFT DRINK** (Yukon Club) | 6 fl. oz. | 14 | 0. | | | 0 |
| **TROUT:** | | | | | | |
| Brook, fresh, whole (USDA) | 1 lb. (weighed whole) | | 4.7 | | | |
| Brook, fresh, meat only (USDA) | 4 oz. | | 2.4 | | | |
| Lake (See **LAKE TROUT**) | | | | | | |
| Rainbow (USDA): | | | | | | |
| Fresh, meat with skin | 4 oz. | | 12.9 | 3. | 10. | 62 |
| Canned | 4 oz. | | 15.2 | 5. | 11. | |
| Frozen (1000 Springs): | | | | | | |
| Boned | 5-oz. trout | 29 | 4.2 | | | |
| Dressed | 5-oz. trout | 35 | 5.1 | | | |
| Boned & breaded | 5-oz. trout | | | | | |
| **TUNA:** | | | | | | |
| Raw, bluefin, meat only (USDA) | 4 oz. | | 4.6 | 1. | 4. | |

(USDA): United States Department of Agriculture
*Prepared as Package Directs

| Food and Description | Measure or Quantity | Sodium (mg.) | Total | Fats in grams — Satu- rated | Unsatu- rated | Choles- terol (mg.) |
|---|---|---|---|---|---|---|
| Raw, yellowfin, meat only (USDA) | 4 oz. | 42 | 3.4 | 1. | 2. | |
| Raw, yellowfin, meat only, brined (USDA) | 4 oz. | 498 | 3.4 | 1. | 2. | |
| Canned in oil: | | | | | | |
| Solids & liq.: | | | | | | |
| (USDA)[1] | 6½-oz. can | 1472 | 37.7 | 9. | 29. | 100 |
| (Breast O' Chicken) | 6½-oz. can | | 36.8 | | | |
| Chunk, light (Chicken of the Sea) | 6-oz. can | 1196 | 25.6 | 3. | 22. | 74 |
| Chunk, light (Del Monte) | 6½-oz. can | 1150 | 32.8 | | | |
| Chunk, light (Del Monte) | 1 cup (4.7 oz.) | 831 | 23.7 | | | |
| White albacore (Del Monte) | 6½-oz. can | 1019 | 37.7 | | | |
| White albacore (Del Monte) | 1 cup (4.7 oz.) | 528 | 27.3 | | | |
| Drained solids: | | | | | | |
| (USDA)[2] | 6½-oz. can | | 12.9 | 5. | 8. | 102 |
| Albacore (Del Monte) | 1 cup (5.6 oz.) | 858 | 13.1 | | | |
| Chunk, light (Chicken of the Sea) | 6½-oz. can | 1072 | 12.5 | 2. | 11. | 36 |
| Canned in water: | | | | | | |
| Solids & liq., no salt added: | | | | | | |
| (USDA) | 6½-oz. can | 75 | 1.5 | | | 116 |
| Solids & liq., salt added: | | | | | | |
| (USDA) | 6½-oz. can | 1610 | 1.5 | | | 116 |
| (Breast O' Chicken) | 6½-oz. can | | 1.8 | | | |
| Drained, solid, light (Chicken of the Sea) | 6½-oz. can | 1105 | 3.4 | | | |
| Drained, solid, white (Chicken of the Sea) | 6½-oz. can | 1105 | 1.7 | | | |
| Canned, dietetic, drained, chunk, white (Chicken of the Sea) | 6½-oz. can | 74 | 2.6 | | | |
| **TUNA CAKE,** frozen, thins (Mrs. Paul's) | 10-oz. pkg. | | 43.3 | | | |
| **TUNA PIE,** frozen: | | | | | | |
| (Banquet) | 8-oz. pie | | 27.0 | | | |
| (Morton) | 8-oz. pie | 715 | 19.8 | | | |
| **TUNA SALAD,** home recipe[3,4] | | | | | | |
| (USDA) | 4 oz. | | 11.9 | 3. | 9. | |

(USDA): United States Department of Agriculture
*Prepared as Package Directs
[1]Principal sources of fat: cottonseed oil & tuna.
[2]Principal sources of fat: tuna & cottonseed oil.
[3]Prepared with tuna, celery, mayonnaise, pickle, onion & egg.
[4]Principal sources of fat: cottonseed oil, soybean oil, corn oil, tuna & egg.

| Food and Description | Measure or Quantity | Sodium (mg.) | —Fats in grams— | | | Choles-terol (mg.) |
|---|---|---|---|---|---|---|
| | | | Total | Satu-rated | Unsatu-rated | |
| **TUNA SOUP,** Creole, canned | | | | | | |
| (Crosse & Blackwell) | 6½ oz. (½ can) | | 1.3 | | | |
| **TURBOT, GREENLAND:** | | | | | | |
| Raw, whole (USDA) | 1 lb. (weighed whole) | | 19.8 | | | |
| Raw, meat only (USDA) | 4 oz. | 64 | 9.5 | 2. | 8. | |
| Frozen (Weight Watchers) | 18-oz. dinner | | 25.1 | | | |
| Frozen, with apple (Weight Watchers) | 9½-oz. luncheon | | 16.4 | | | |
| **TURKEY:** | | | | | | |
| Raw, ready-to-cook (USDA) | 1 lb. (weighed with bones) | | 48.7 | 14.0 | 35. | 272 |
| Raw, meat & skin only (USDA) | 4 oz. | | | | | 84 |
| Raw, dark meat (USDA) | 4 oz. | 92 | 4.9 | | | 85 |
| Raw, light meat (USDA) | 4 oz. | 58 | 1.4 | | | 68 |
| Raw, skin only (USDA) | 4 oz. | | 44.5 | | | 125 |
| Roasted (USDA): | | | | | | |
| Flesh, skin & giblets | From 13½-lb. raw, ready-to-cook turkey | | 603.5 | | | 3864 |
| Flesh & skin | From 13½-lb. raw, ready-to-cook turkey | | 338.9 | 106. | 233. | 3283 |
| Flesh & skin | 4 oz. | | 10.9 | 3. | 7. | 105 |
| Meat only: | | | | | | |
| Chopped | 1 cup (5 oz.) | 183 | 8.6 | 3. | 6. | |
| Dark | 4 oz. | 112 | 9.4 | 2. | 7. | 115 |
| Dark | 1 slice (2½" x 1⅝" x ¼", .7 oz.) | 21 | 1.8 | Tr. | 1. | 21 |
| Diced | 1 cup (4.8 oz.) | 176 | 8.2 | 3. | 6. | |
| Light | 4 oz. | 93 | 4.4 | 1. | 3. | 87 |
| Light | 1 slice (4" x 2" x ¼", 3 oz.) | 35 | 1.7 | Tr. | 1. | 32 |
| Skin only | 1 oz. | | 11.9 | 3. | 9. | 36 |
| Giblets, simmered (USDA) | 2 oz. | | 8.7 | | | |
| Smoked, cooked, pressed (Oscar Mayer) | .8-oz. slice | 266 | .4 | | | |
| Canned, boned: | | | | | | |
| (USDA) | 4 oz. | | 14.2 | 5. | 10. | |
| Solids & liq. (Lynden Farms) | 5-oz. jar | 527 | 10.5 | 4. | 6. | |
| (Swanson) with broth | 5-oz. can | 650 | 9.0 | | | |
| Canned, roast (Wilson) *Tender Made* | 4 oz. | 480 | 2.4 | <1. | 2. | 76 |

(USDA): United States Department of Agriculture
*Prepared as Package Directs

| Food and Description | Measure or Quantity | Sodium (mg.) | —Fats in grams— | | | Choles- terol (mg.) |
|---|---|---|---|---|---|---|
| | | | Total | Satu- rated | Unsatu- rated | |
| **TURKEY DINNER:** | | | | | | |
| Canned, noodle (Lynden Farms) | 15-oz. can | 254 | 25.2 | 9. | 16. | |
| Frozen: | | | | | | |
| Sliced turkey, mashed potato, peas (USDA)[1] | 12 oz. | 1360 | 10.2 | 3. | 7 | |
| (Banquet): | | | | | | |
| Meat compartment | 6.8 oz. | | 5.2 | | | |
| Peas compartment | 1.9 oz. | | 1.0 | | | |
| Potato compartment | 1.8 oz. | | .6 | | | |
| Complete dinner | 11.5-oz. dinner | | 6.8 | | | |
| (Morton) | 12-oz. dinner | 1397 | 20.2 | | | |
| (Morton) 3-course | 1-lb. 1-oz. dinner | 1575 | 24.1 | | | |
| (Swanson) | 11½-oz. dinner | 1058 | 12.5 | 4. | 9. | |
| (Swanson) 3-course | 16-oz. dinner | 1747 | 17.0 | | | |
| With gravy, dressing & potato (Swanson) | 8¾-oz. pkg. | 955 | 10.5 | | | |
| (Weight Watchers) | 18-oz. dinner | | 9.9 | | | |
| **TURKEY FRICASSEE,** canned (Lynden Farms) | 14.5-oz. can | 1669 | 13.0 | 5. | 8. | |
| **TURKEY GIZZARD** (USDA): | | | | | | |
| Raw | 4 oz. | 66 | 8.3 | | | 164 |
| Simmered | 4 oz. | 58 | 9.8 | | | 260 |
| **TURKEY PIE:** | | | | | | |
| Home recipe, baked (USDA)[2] | ⅓ of 9″ pie (8.2 oz.) | 633 | 31.3 | 9. | 22. | 72 |
| Frozen: | | | | | | |
| Commercial, unheated (USDA)[2] | 8 oz. | 837 | 23.6 | 7. | 17. | 20 |
| (Banquet) | 8-oz. pie | | 20.1 | | | |
| (Banquet) | 2-lb. 4-oz. pie | | 57.3 | | | |
| (Morton) | 8-oz. pie | 1080 | 21.9 | | | |
| (Swanson) | 8-oz. pie | 960 | 22.9 | | | |
| (Swanson) deep-dish | 1-lb. pie | 1963 | 40.9 | | | |
| **TURKEY, POTTED** (USDA) | 1 oz. | | 5.4 | | | |
| **TURKEY SOUP,** canned: | | | | | | |
| (Campbell) *Chunky* | 1 cup | 848 | 4.0 | | | |
| Broth (Lynden Farms) | 1 cup (8 oz.) | 953 | 0. | | | |

(USDA): United States Department of Agriculture
*Prepared as Package Directs
[1]Principal sources of fat: turkey & butter.
[2]Principal sources of fat: vegetable shortening, cream, turkey & butter.

| Food and Description | Measure or Quantity | Sodium (mg.) | Fats in grams | | | Cholesterol (mg.) |
| --- | --- | --- | --- | --- | --- | --- |
| | | | Total | Saturated | Unsaturated | |
| Noodle: | | | | | | |
| Condensed (USDA) | 8 oz. (by wt.) | 1887 | 5.4 | | | |
| *Prepared with equal volume water (USDA) | 1 cup (8.8 oz.) | 1040 | 3.0 | | | |
| *(Campbell) | 1 cup | 814 | 3.0 | <1. | 2. | |
| *(Heinz) | 1 cup (8½ oz.) | 1072 | 3.1 | | | |
| (Heinz) *Great American* | 1 cup (8¾ oz.) | 1205 | 2.7 | | | |
| Low sodium (Campbell) | 7½-oz. can | 40 | 3.2 | | | |
| Rice, with mushrooms (Heinz) *Great American* | 1 cup (8½ oz.) | 1293 | 3.0 | | | |
| *Vegetable (Campbell) | 1 cup | 854 | 3.2 | <1. | 2. | |
| Vegetable (Heinz) *Great American* | 1 cup (8½ oz.) | 1032 | 2.8 | | | |
| **\*TURKEY SOUP MIX,** noodle (Lipton) | 1 cup (8 oz.) | 933 | 2.1 | <1. | 2. | 12 |
| **TURKEY TETRAZZINI,** frozen (Stouffer's) | 12-oz. pkg. | 1345 | 32.4 | | | |
| **TURMERIC** (Spice Islands) | 1 tsp. | 1 | | | | (0) |
| **TURNIP** (USDA): | | | | | | |
| Fresh, without tops | 1 lb. (weighed with skins) | 191 | .8 | | | 0 |
| Fresh, pared, diced | ½ cup (2.4 oz.) | 33 | .1 | | | 0 |
| Fresh, pared, slices | ½ cup (2.3 oz.) | 31 | .1 | | | 0 |
| Boiled without salt, drained, diced | ½ cup (2.8 oz.) | 27 | .2 | | | 0 |
| Boiled without salt, drained, mashed | ½ cup (4 oz.) | 39 | .2 | | | 0 |
| **TURNIP GREENS,** leaves & stems: | | | | | | |
| Fresh (USDA) | 1 lb. (weighed untrimmed) | | 1.1 | | | 0 |
| Boiled, in small amount water, short time, drained (USDA) | ½ cup (2.5 oz.) | | .1 | | | 0 |
| Boiled, in large amount water, long time, drained (USDA) | ½ cup (2.5 oz.) | | .1 | | | 0 |
| Canned, solids & liq.: | | | | | | |
| (USDA) | ½ cup (4.1 oz.) | 274 | .4 | | | 0 |
| (Stokely-Van Camp) | ½ cup (3.9 oz.) | | .4 | | | (0) |
| Frozen: | | | | | | |
| Not thawed (USDA) | 4 oz. | 26 | .3 | | | 0 |

(USDA): United States Department of Agriculture
*Prepared as Package Directs

| Food and Description | Measure or Quantity | Sodium (mg.) | Total | Satu- rated | Unsatu- rated | Choles- terol (mg.) |
|---|---|---|---|---|---|---|
| | | | —Fats in grams— | | | |
| Boiled, drained (USDA) | ½ cup (2.9 oz.) | 14 | .2 | | | 0 |
| Chopped (Birds Eye) | ½ cup (3.3 oz.) | 22 | .3 | | | 0 |
| **TURNOVER** (See individual kinds) | | | | | | |
| **TURTLE, GREEN** (USDA): | | | | | | |
| Raw, in shell | 1 lb. (weighed in shell) | | .5 | | | |
| Raw, meat only | 4 oz. | | .6 | | | |
| Canned | 4 oz. | | .8 | | | |
| **TV DINNER** (See individual listing such as **BEEF DINNER, CHICKEN DINNER, CHINESE DINNER, ENCHILADA DINNER,** etc.) | | | | | | |
| *TWINKIE* (Hostess): | | | | | | |
| 2 to pkg. | 1 cake (1.5 oz.) | 241 | 4.3 | | | |
| 12 to pkg. | 1 cake (1.3 oz.) | 214 | 3.8 | | | |

# U

| | | | | | | |
|---|---|---|---|---|---|---|
| *UPPER-10*, soft drink | 6 fl. oz. (6.5 oz.) | 10+ | 0. | | | 0 |

# V

| | | | | | | |
|---|---|---|---|---|---|---|
| **VANILLA,** bean (Spice Islands) | 2″ piece | <1 | | | | (0) |
| **VANILLA CAKE,** frozen (Pepperidge Farm) | ¹/₆ of cake (3.1 oz.) | 258 | 14.6 | | | |
| **VANILLA ICE CREAM** (See also individual brand names): | | | | | | |
| (Borden) 10.5% fat | ¼ pt. (2.3 oz.) | 29 | 7.0 | | | |
| *Lady Borden* 14% fat | ¼ pt. (2.5 oz.) | 26 | 10.0 | | | |
| (Sealtest) *Party Slice* | ¼ pt. (2.3 oz.) | 48 | 6.7 | | | |
| (Sealtest) 10.2% fat | ¼ pt. (2.3 oz.) | 48 | 6.7 | | | |
| (Sealtest) 12.1% fat | ¼ pt. (2.3 oz.) | 51 | 7.8 | | | |
| French (Prestige) | ¼ pt. (2.6 oz.) | 42 | 12.0 | | | |
| Fudge royale (Sealtest) | ¼ pt. (2.3 oz.) | 51 | 5.6 | | | |

(USDA): United States Department of Agriculture
*Prepared as Package Directs

| Food and Description | Measure or Quantity | Sodium (mg.) | —Fats in grams— | | | Choles- terol (mg.) |
| | | | Total | Satu- rated | Unsatu- rated | |
|---|---|---|---|---|---|---|
| **VANILLA ICE MILK** | | | | | | |
| (Borden) *Lite-line* | ¼ pt. | | 1.9 | | | |
| | | | | | | |
| **VANILLA PIE FILLING MIX** | | | | | | |
| (See **VANILLA PUDDING MIX**) | | | | | | |
| | | | | | | |
| **VANILLA PUDDING:** | | | | | | |
| Blancmange, home recipe, with starch base (USDA)[1] | ½ cup (4.5 oz.) | 83 | 5.0 | 3. | 2. | 18 |
| Canned (Betty Crocker) | ½ cup | 190 | 4.9 | | | |
| Canned (Del Monte) | 5-oz. can | 321 | 5.1 | | | |
| Canned (Hunt's)[2] | 5-oz. can | 186 | 12.4 | 2. | 10. | |
| Canned (Thank You) | ½ cup (4.5 oz.) | | 4.7 | | | |
| Chilled (Breakstone) | 5-oz. container | 170 | 13.3 | | | 0 |
| Chilled (Sealtest) | 4 oz. | 147 | 3.3 | | | |
| | | | | | | |
| **VANILLA PUDDING or PIE FILLING MIX:** | | | | | | |
| Sweetened: | | | | | | |
| *Regular, plain or French (Jell-O) | ½ cup (5.2 oz.) | 224 | 4.6 | | | 13 |
| *Instant, plain or French (Jell-O) | ½ cup (5.3 oz.) | 406 | 4.7 | | | 13 |
| *Regular (Royal) | ½ cup (5.1 oz.) | 230 | 4.8 | | | 14 |
| *Instant (Royal) | ¼ cup (5.1 oz.) | 310 | 4.6 | | | 14 |
| *Low calorie (D-Zerta) | ½ cup (4.6 oz.) | 142 | 4.5 | | | |
| | | | | | | |
| **VANILLA RENNET MIX:** | | | | | | |
| Powder: | | | | | | |
| Dry (Junket) | 1 oz. | 11 | .1 | | | |
| *(Junket) | 4 oz. | 56 | 3.9 | | | |
| Tablet: | | | | | | |
| Dry (Junket) | 1 tablet (<1 gram) | 197 | Tr. | | | |
| *& sugar (Junket) | 4 oz. | 98 | 3.9 | | | |
| | | | | | | |
| **VEAL,** medium fat (USDA): | | | | | | |
| Chuck, raw | 1 lb. (weighed with bone) | 327 | 36.0 | 17. | 19. | 258 |
| Chuck, braised, lean & fat | 4 oz. | 91 | 14.5 | 7. | 8. | 115 |
| Flank, raw | 1 lb. (weighed with bone) | 404 | 121.0 | 60. | 61. | 319 |

(USDA): United States Department of Agriculture
*Prepared as Package Directs
[1]Principal source of fat: milk.
[2]Principal source of fat: soybean oil.

| Food and Description | Measure or Quantity | Sodium (mg.) | Total | Saturated | Unsaturated | Cholesterol (mg.) |
|---|---|---|---|---|---|---|
| Flank, stewed, lean & fat | 4 oz. | 91 | 36.6 | 18. | 18. | 115 |
| Foreshank, raw | 1 lb. (weighed with bone) | 212 | 19.0 | 10. | 9. | 168 |
| Foreshank, stewed, lean & fat | 4 oz. | 91 | 11.8 | 6. | 6. | 115 |
| Loin, raw | 1 lb. (weighed with bone) | 338 | 41.0 | 20. | 21. | 267 |
| Loin, broiled, medium done, chop, lean & fat | 4 oz. | 91 | 15.2 | 8. | 7. | 115 |
| Plate, raw | 1 lb. (weighed with bone) | 322 | 61.0 | 30. | 31. | 254 |
| Plate, stewed, lean & fat | 4 oz. | 91 | 24.0 | 12. | 12. | 115 |
| Rib, raw, lean & fat | 1 lb. (weighed with bone) | 314 | 49.0 | 23. | 26. | 248 |
| Rib, roasted, medium done, lean & fat | 4 oz. | 91 | 19.2 | 9. | 10. | 115 |
| Round & rump, raw | 1 lb. (weighed with bone) | 314 | 31.0 | 16. | 15. | 248 |
| Round & rump, broiled, steak or cutlet, lean & fat | 4 oz. (weighed without bone) | 91 | 12.6 | 7. | 6. | 115 |

**VEAL DINNER,** frozen:

| | | | | | | |
|---|---|---|---|---|---|---|
| Parmigiana (Kraft) | 11-oz. dinner | 1962 | 30.3 | | | |
| Parmigiana (Swanson) | 12¼-oz. dinner | 1335 | 23.0 | | | |
| Parmigiana (Weight Watchers) | 9½-oz. luncheon | | 16.1 | | | |
| Breaded veal with spaghetti in tomato sauce (Swanson) | 8¼-oz. pkg. | 974 | 11.5 | | | |

**VEGETABLE BOUILLON CUBE:**

| | | | | | | |
|---|---|---|---|---|---|---|
| (Herb-Ox) | 1 cube (4 grams) | 900 | .1 | | | |
| (Steero) | 1 cube (4 grams) | | .1 | | | |
| (Wyler's) | 1 cube (4 grams) | | .3 | | | |

**VEGETABLE FAT** (See **FAT**)

**VEGETABLE JUICE COCKTAIL,**
canned:

| | | | | | | |
|---|---|---|---|---|---|---|
| (USDA) | 4 oz. (by wt.) | 227 | .1 | | | 0 |
| Unseasoned (S and W) *Nutradiet* | 4 oz. (by wt.) | 16 | .1 | | | (0) |
| V-8 (Campbell) | ¾ cup | 618 | .2 | | | (0) |

(USDA): United States Department of Agriculture
*Prepared as Package Directs

| Food and Description | Measure or Quantity | Sodium (mg.) | — Fats in grams — | | | Choles- terol (mg.) |
|---|---|---|---|---|---|---|
| | | | Total | Satu- rated | Unsatu- rated | |

**VEGETABLES, MIXED:**
Canned, regular pack:

| Food and Description | Measure or Quantity | Sodium (mg.) | Total | Satu-rated | Unsatu-rated | Choles-terol (mg.) |
|---|---|---|---|---|---|---|
| (Veg-All) | ½ cup (4 oz.) | | .1 | | | 0 |
| Solids & liq. (Del Monte) | ½ cup (4 oz.) | 518 | .5 | | | (0) |
| Drained solids (Del Monte) | ½ cup (2.8 oz.) | 354 | .4 | | | (0) |
| Drained liq. (Del Monte) | 4 oz. | 536 | .3 | | | (0) |
| Solids & liq. (Stokely-Van Camp) | ½ cup (3.8 oz.) | | .4 | | | (0) |
| Canned, Chinese, | | | | | | |
| Chop Suey (Hung's) | 4 oz. | | .3 | | | |
| Frozen: | | | | | | |
| Not thawed (USDA) | 4 oz. | 67 | .3 | | | 0 |
| Boiled, drained (USDA) | ½ cup (3.2 oz.) | 48 | .3 | | | 0 |
| (Birds Eye) | ½ cup (3.3 oz.) | 46 | .3 | | | 0 |
| In butter sauce (Green Giant) | ⅓ of 10-oz. pkg. | 354 | 1.9 | | | |
| Chinese (Birds Eye) | ⅓ of 10-oz. pkg. | 443 | 4.1 | | | 0 |
| Jubilee (Birds Eye) | ⅓ of 10-oz. pkg. | 321 | 6.5 | | | Tr. |
| With onion sauce (Birds Eye) | ½ cup (2.7 oz.) | 393 | 6.5 | | | Tr. |

**VEGETABLE OYSTER (See SALSIFY)**

**VEGETABLE SOUP:**
Canned, regular pack:

| Food and Description | Measure or Quantity | Sodium (mg.) | Total | Satu-rated | Unsatu-rated | Choles-terol (mg.) |
|---|---|---|---|---|---|---|
| *(Campbell) | 1 cup | 776 | 1.6 | Tr. | 1. | 3 |
| (Campbell) *Chunky* | 1 cup | 904 | 3.0 | | | |
| *(Campbell) old fashioned | 1 cup | 811 | 2.4 | <1. | 2. | |
| Beef, condensed (USDA) | 8 oz. (by wt.) | 1937 | 4.1 | | | |
| *Beef, prepared with equal volume water (USDA) | 1 cup (8.6 oz.) | 1046 | 2.2 | | | |
| *Beef (Campbell) | 1 cup | 858 | 2.6 | <1. | 2. | 6 |
| *Beef (Heinz) | 1 cup (8½ oz.) | 1005 | 1.5 | | | |
| Beef (Heinz) *Great American* | 1 cup (8¾ oz.) | 1157 | 3.4 | | | |
| With beef broth, condensed (USDA) | 8 oz. (by wt.) | 1565 | 3.2 | | | |
| *With beef broth, prepared with equal volume water (USDA) | 1 cup (8.8 oz.) | 862 | 1.8 | | | |
| With beef broth (Heinz) *Great American* | 1 cup (8¾ oz.) | 1116 | 3.7 | | | |
| *With beef stock (Heinz) | 1 cup (8½ oz.) | 1049 | 2.1 | | | |
| With ground beef (Heinz) *Great American* | 1 cup (8¾ oz.) | 1161 | 5.3 | | | |

(USDA): United States Department of Agriculture
*Prepared as Package Directs

| Food and Description | Measure or Quantity | Sodium (mg.) | —Fats in grams— Total | Satu- rated | Unsatu- rated | Choles- terol (mg.) |
|---|---|---|---|---|---|---|
| *& *Noodle-O's* (Campbell) | 1 cup | 975 | 2.5 | | | |
| Vegetarian: | | | | | | |
| Condensed (USDA) | 8 oz. (by wt.) | 1551 | 3.9 | | | |
| *Prepared with equal volume water (USDA) | 1 cup (8.6 oz.) | 838 | 2.0 | | | |
| *(Campbell) | 1 cup | 585 | 1.7 | Tr. | 2. | 7 |
| *(Heinz) | 1 cup (8¾ oz.) | 1250 | 2.0 | | | |
| (Heinz) *Great American* | 1 cup (8½ oz.) | 1326 | 3.5 | | | |
| *(Manischewitz) | 1 cup | | 1.8 | | | |
| Canned, dietetic pack: | | | | | | |
| Low sodium (Campbell) | 7½-oz. can | 40 | 1.8 | | | |
| Beef, low sodium (Campbell) | 7½-oz. can | 40 | 2.7 | | | |
| *(Claybourne) | 8 oz. | 45 | .7 | | | |
| *(Slim-ette) | 8 oz. (by wt.) | 16 | .2 | | | |
| (Tillie Lewis) | 1 cup (8 oz.) | 60 | 1.1 | | | |
| Frozen: | | | | | | |
| With beef, condensed (USDA) | 8 oz. (by wt.) | 1796 | 5.2 | | | |
| *With beef, prepared with equal volume water (USDA) | 8 oz. (by wt.) | 898 | 2.7 | | | |
| **VEGETABLE SOUP MIX:** | | | | | | |
| *(Wyler's) | 1 cup | | 1.1 | | | |
| *Beef (Lipton) | 1 cup | 1217 | 1.5 | Tr. | 1. | |
| *Chicken (Wyler's) | 1 cup | | .8 | | | |
| *& noodle (Lipton) Country | 1 cup | 1169 | 1.1 | Tr. | <1. | 13 |
| Spring (Lipton) *Cup-a-Soup* | ½-oz. pkg. | 1065 | .8 | Tr. | <1. | 4 |
| **VEGETABLE STEW,** canned | | | | | | |
| (Hormel) *Dinty Moore* | 8 oz. | 1021 | 8.4 | 4. | 4. | 11 |
| **"VEGETARIAN FOODS":** | | | | | | |
| Canned or dry: | | | | | | |
| Beans, rich brown (Loma Linda) | ½ cup (3.7 oz.) | 700 | 1.4 | | | 0 |
| Bean, soy: | | | | | | |
| Boston style (Loma Linda) | ½ cup (3.7 oz.) | 779 | 4.3 | | | 0 |
| Green, drained (Loma Linda) | ½ cup (3.7 oz.) | 333 | 4.7 | | | 0 |
| Tomato sauce (Loma Linda) | ½ cup (3.7 oz.) | 454 | 3.4 | | | 0 |
| Big franks, drained (Loma Linda) | 1 frank (1.6 oz.) | 229 | 5.6 | | | 0 |
| Breading meal (Loma Linda) | 1 cup (3.7 oz.) | 2625 | 5.4 | | | 0 |
| Breading meal (Worthington) | ¼ cup (1.1 oz.) | 936 | .5 | | | |
| Burger aid (Worthington) | 1 oz. | | .2 | | | |
| Cheze-O-Soy (Worthington) | ½" slice (2.5 oz.) | | 7.1 | | | |
| Chili (Worthington) | ¼ can (5 oz.) | | 6.0 | | | |

(USDA): United States Department of Agriculture
*Prepared as Package Directs

| Food and Description | Measure or Quantity | Sodium (mg.) | Total | Satu-rated | Unsatu-rated | Choles-terol (mg.) |
|---|---|---|---|---|---|---|
| | | | — Fats in grams — | | | |
| Chili with beans (Loma Linda) | ½ cup (4.7 oz.) | 498 | 3.3 | | | 0 |
| Choplet (Worthington) | 1 choplet (2.2 oz.) | 350 | 1.2 | | | |
| Choplet burger (Worthington) | ⅓ cup (3.2 oz.) | | 1.9 | | | |
| Cutlet (Worthington) | 1 cutlet (2.2 oz.) | | 1.2 | | | |
| Dinner bits, drained (Loma Linda) | 1 bit (.5 oz.) | 96 | 1.2 | | | 0 |
| Dinner cuts, drained (Loma Linda) | 1 cut (1.6 oz.) | 252 | .8 | | | 0 |
| Dinner cuts, no salt added, drained (Loma Linda) | 1 cup (1.6 oz.) | 5 | .8 | | | 0 |
| Fry stick (Worthington) | 1 piece (2.3 oz.) | | 3.4 | | | |
| Garbanzo (Loma Linda) | ½ cup (4.1 oz.) | 534 | 1.3 | | | 0 |
| GranBurger (Worthington) | 1 oz. | 798 | .3 | | | |
| Granola (Loma Linda) | ½ cup (2 oz.) | 107 | 8.5 | | | |
| Gravy Quik, brown (Loma Linda) | ¹/₆ of pkg. (6 grams) | 194 | .4 | | | 0 |
| J-7901 or J-7901A (Worthington) | 1 oz. | | .3 | | | |
| Jell Quik, dry (Loma Linda) | 1 oz. | 291 | .8 | | | 0 |
| Kaffir Tea (Worthington) | 1 bag (1 gram) | | Tr. | | | |
| Lentils, drained (Loma Linda) | ¾ cup (3.5 oz.) | 472 | .7 | | | 0 |
| Linketts, drained (Loma Linda) | 1 link (1.3 oz.) | 231 | 5.0 | | | 0 |
| Little links, drained (Loma Linda) | 1 link (.8 oz.) | 120 | 2.8 | | | 0 |
| Madison burger (Worthington) | ⅓ cup (2 oz.) | | 2.3 | | | |
| Meat-like loaf (Loma Linda): | | | | | | |
| Beef, drained | ¼" slice (2 oz.) | 400 | 7.1 | | | 0 |
| Chicken | ¼" slice (2 oz.) | 403 | 6.9 | | | 0 |
| Luncheon | ¼" slice (2 oz.) | 591 | 7.3 | | | 0 |
| Turkey | ¼" slice (2 oz.) | 554 | 7.5 | | | 0 |
| Meat loaf mix (Worthington) | 2 oz. | 921 | 8.0 | | | |
| Multigen powder (Loma Linda) | ½ cup (2.1 oz.) | | 2.1 | | | 0 |
| Non-meatballs (Worthington) | 1 piece (.6 oz.) | | 1.9 | | | |
| Non-meat with tomato (Worthington) | 2⅓-oz. | | 11.6 | | | |
| Numete (Worthington) | ½" slice (2.3 oz.) | | 11.0 | | | |
| Nuteena (Loma Linda) | ½" slice (2.5 oz.) | 331 | 11.8 | | | 0 |
| Oven-cooked wheat (Loma Linda) | ½ cup (2.6 oz.) | 7 | 2.5 | | | 0 |
| Peanuts & soya (USDA) | 4 oz. | | 19.2 | | | |
| Prime vegetable burger (Worthington) | ½" slice (2.1 oz.) | 444 | 0. | | | |
| Proteena (Loma Linda) | ½" slice (2.6 oz.) | 385 | 7.5 | | | 0 |
| Protose (Worthington) | ½" slice (2.7 oz.) | | 8.5 | | | |
| Rediburger (Loma Linda) | ½" slice (2.5 oz.) | 259 | 9.3 | | | 0 |

(USDA): United States Department of Agriculture
*Prepared as Package Directs

| Food and Description | Measure or Quantity | Sodium (mg.) | Fats in grams — Total | Satu- rated | Unsatu- rated | Choles- terol (mg.) |
|---|---|---|---|---|---|---|
| Redi-loaf mix, beef (Loma Linda) | ⅓ cup (1.2 oz.) | 770 | 8.0 | | | 0 |
| Redi-loaf mix, chicken (Loma Linda) | ⅓ cup (1.2 oz.) | 490 | 7.5 | | | 0 |
| Ruskets, biscuits (Loma Linda) | 1 biscuit (.6 oz.) | 47 | .5 | | | 0 |
| Ruskets, flakes (Loma Linda) | 1 cup (1 oz.) | 73 | .8 | | | 0 |
| Sandwich spread (Loma Linda) | 1 T. (.6 oz.) | 97 | 1.4 | | | 0 |
| Sandwich spread (Worthington) | 3 T. (1.2 oz.) | | 5.1 | | | |
| Saucette (Worthington) | 1 link (.6 oz.) | | 2.6 | | | |
| Savita (Worthington) | 1 tsp. (.4 oz.) | 465 | 0. | | | |
| Savorex (Loma Linda) | 1 oz. | | <.1 | | | 0 |
| Seasoning, chicken (Loma Linda) | 1 T. (3 grams) | 84 | .2 | | | 0 |
| Soyagen: | | | | | | |
| A.P. & malt powder (Loma Linda) | ¼ cup (1.4 oz.) | 204 | 9.0 | | | 0 |
| Carob, powder (Loma Linda) | ¼ cup (1.4 oz.) | 212 | 8.6 | | | 0 |
| Liquid (Loma Linda) | 1 cup (8.6 oz.) | 303 | 8.5 | | | 0 |
| Soyalac, concentrate, liquid (Loma Linda) | 1 fl. oz. (1.1 oz.) | 16 | 2.5 | | | 0 |
| Soyalac, infant powder (Loma Linda) | 1 oz. | 78 | 7.4 | | | 0 |
| Soyalac, ready-to-use (Loma Linda) | 1 oz. | 9 | 1.1 | | | 0 |
| Soyameat (Worthington): | | | | | | |
| Sliced beef | 1 slice (1 oz.) | 140 | 3.3 | | | |
| Diced beef | 1 oz. | 174 | 1.4 | | | |
| Diced chicken | 1 oz. | | 1.7 | | | <1 |
| Fried chicken | 1 piece (1.2 oz.) | 230 | 4.9 | | | 0 |
| Sliced chicken | 1 slice (1.1 oz.) | | 2.2 | | | <1 |
| Salisbury steak | 1 slice (2.5 oz.) | 5530 | 9.0 | | | |
| Soyamel, any kind (Worthington) | 1 oz. | | 5.9 | | | 0 |
| Soy flour (Loma Linda) | ¼ cup (.9 oz.) | 3 | 5.8 | | | 0 |
| Stew pac, drained (Loma Linda) | ½ cup (3 oz.) | 481 | 7.7 | | | 0 |
| Stripple Zips (Worthington) | 1 oz. | 943 | 6.8 | | | |
| Tamales (Worthington) | 1 oz. | | <.1 | | | |
| Tastee cuts (Loma Linda) | 1 cut (1.5 oz.) | 222 | .7 | | | 0 |
| Tenderbit (Loma Linda) | 1 piece (.9 oz.) | 126 | 1.2 | | | 0 |
| Vegeburger (Loma Linda) | ½ cup (3.9 oz.) | 385 | 2.7 | | | 0 |
| Vegeburger, no salt added (Loma Linda) | ½ cup (3.9 oz.) | 17 | 2.7 | | | 0 |
| Vegechee (Loma Linda) | ½" slice (2.5 oz.) | 397 | 6.8 | | | 0 |
| Vegelona (Loma Linda) | ½" slice (3.3 oz.) | 439 | 6.5 | | | 0 |

(USDA): United States Department of Agriculture
*Prepared as Package Directs

| Food and Description | Measure or Quantity | Sodium (mg.) | — Fats in grams — Total | Satu- rated | Unsatu- rated | Choles- terol (mg.) |
|---|---|---|---|---|---|---|
| Vegetarian burger (Worthington) | ⅓ cup (2.5 oz.) | | 4.4 | | | |
| Vegetable skallop (Worthington) | 1 piece (.7 oz.) | | .3 | | | 0 |
| Vegetable steaks (Worthington) | 1 piece (.7 oz.) | | .3 | | | |
| Veja-links (Worthington) | 1 link (1.2 oz.) | 225 | 5.6 | | | <1 |
| Wham, sliced or loaf (Worthington) | 1 slice (1 oz.) | | 2.5 | | | 1 |
| Wheat germ, natural or toasted (Loma Linda) | 1 T. (.4 oz.) | 21 | 1.2 | | | 0 |
| Wheat protein (USDA) | 4 oz. | | .9 | | | |
| Wheat protein, nuts or peanuts (USDA) | 4 oz. | | 8.1 | | | |
| Wheat protein, vegetable oil (USDA) | 4 oz. | | 12.1 | | | |
| Wheat & soy protein (USDA) | 4 oz. | | 1.4 | | | |
| Wheat & soy protein, soy or other vegetable oil (USDA) | 4 oz. | | 6.4 | | | |
| *Worthington 209* | 1 slice (.5 oz.) | 96 | 1.1 | | | 0 |
| Yum (Worthington) | 1 serving (1.5 oz.) | | 4.0 | | | |
| Frozen (Worthington): | | | | | | |
| Beef pie | 1 pie (7.9 oz.) | | 28.4 | | | |
| Beef style, loaf or sliced | 1 slice (1 oz.) | 156 | 2.7 | | | |
| Chicken pie | 1 pie (7.9 oz.) | | 26.9 | | | |
| Chicken style, diced, roll or sliced | 1 oz. or 1 slice | 294 | 5.0 | | | |
| Chic-Ketts | 1 oz. | | 2.5 | | | |
| Chili | ¼ can (5 oz.) | | 5.9 | | | |
| Corned beef, loaf or sliced | 1 slice (.5 oz.) | 179 | 2.3 | | | 0 |
| Croquettes | 1 croquette (1 oz.) | | 3.2 | | | |
| FriPats | 1 pat (2.6 oz.) | 607 | 10.6 | | | 0 |
| Holiday roast | 1 slice (2 oz.) | | 9.1 | | | 0 |
| Non-meatballs | 1 piece (.6 oz.) | | 3.3 | | | |
| Prosage | ⅜" slice (1.2 oz.) | 354 | 4.8 | | | <1 |
| Salisbury steak | 1 slice (2 oz.) | | 5.3 | | | |
| Smoked beef, roll or sliced | 1 slice (7 grams) | | .7 | | | |
| Stripples | 1 slice (7 grams) | 95 | 1.0 | | | |
| Turkey, smoked, loaf or sliced | 1 slice (.7 oz.) | 214 | 3.0 | | | 0 |
| Wham, diced, sliced or loaf | 1 slice (1 oz.) | | 2.7 | | | 1 |
| **VENISON,** raw, lean meat only (USDA) | 4 oz. | | 4.5 | 3. | 1. | |

(USDA): United States Department of Agriculture
*Prepared as Package Directs

| Food and Description | Measure or Quantity | Sodium (mg.) | —Fats in grams— | | | Choles- terol (mg.) |
|---|---|---|---|---|---|---|
| | | | Total | Satu- rated | Unsatu- rated | |
| **VERMOUTH,** dry or sweet (Great Western) 16% alcohol | 3 fl. oz. | 20 | | | | |
| **VERNORS,** soft drink: | | | | | | |
| Regular | 6 fl. oz. (6.2 oz.) | 1 | 0. | | | 0 |
| Low calorie | 6 fl. oz. (6.2 oz.) | 3 | 0. | | | 0 |
| **VICHYSSOISE SOUP** (Crosse & Blackwell) | ½ can (6½ oz.) | | 5.2 | | | |
| **VIENNA SAUSAGE,** canned: | | | | | | |
| (USDA) | 1 oz. | | 5.6 | | | |
| (USDA) | 1 sausage (from 5-oz. can, .6 oz.) | | 3.2 | | | |
| (Armour Star) | 5-oz. can | | 36.1 | | | |
| (Armour Star) | 1 sausage (.6 oz.) | | 4.1 | | | |
| (Hormel) | 1 sausage (.6 oz.) | 127 | 3.7 | | | |
| (Van Camp) | 1 oz. | | 5.6 | | | |
| (Wilson) | 1 oz. | 228 | 7.9 | | | 13 |
| **VINEGAR:** | | | | | | |
| Cider: | | | | | | |
| (USDA) | ½ cup (4.2 oz.) | 1 | 0. | | | 0 |
| (USDA) | 1 T. (.5 oz.) | <1 | 0. | | | 0 |
| Distilled: | | | | | | |
| (USDA) | ½ cup (4.2 oz.) | 1 | | | | 0 |
| (USDA) | 1 T. (.5 oz.) | <1 | | | | 0 |
| Red or white wine (Regina) | 1 T. (.5 oz.) | <1 | Tr. | | | (0) |
| Red wine: | | | | | | |
| Plain (Spice Islands) | 2 T. | 6 | | | | (0) |
| Eschalot (Spice Islands) | 2 T. | 10 | | | | (0) |
| Garlic (Spice Islands) | 2 T. | 9 | | | | (0) |
| Tarragon (Spice Islands) | 2 T. | 11 | | | | (0) |
| Rose (Spice Islands) | 2 T. | 10 | | | | (0) |
| White wine: | | | | | | |
| Plain (Spice Islands) | 2 T. | 11 | | | | (0) |
| Basil (Spice Islands) | 2 T. | 10 | | | | (0) |
| Tarragon (Spice Islands) | 2 T. | 10 | | | | (0) |
| **VINESPINACH or BASELLA,** raw (USDA) | 4 oz. | | .3 | | | 0 |
| **VIN ROSE** (See **ROSE WINE**) | | | | | | |
| **VIRGIN SOUR MIX** (Party Tyme) | ½-oz. pkg. | 61 | 0. | | | (0) |

(USDA): United States Department of Agriculture
*Prepared as Package Directs

343

| Food and Description | Measure or Quantity | Sodium (mg.) | Total | Satu- rated | Unsatu- rated | Choles- terol (mg.) |
|---|---|---|---|---|---|---|
| | | | | **—Fats in grams—** | | |

**VODKA,** unflavored (See
**DISTILLED LIQUOR)**

**VODKA SOFT DRINK,**
  sweetened (Shasta) | 6 fl. oz. | 22 | 0. | | | 0

# W

**WAFER** (See **COOKIE** or
**CRACKER)**

**WAFFLE:**
  Home recipe (USDA)[1] | 2.6-oz. waffle (7" dia.) | 356 | 7.4 | 2. | 5. |

  Frozen:
    (USDA)[2] | 1.6-oz. waffle (8 in 13-oz. pkg.) | 296 | 2.9 | <.1 | 2. |
    (USDA)[2] | .8-oz. waffle (6 in 5-oz. pkg.) | 155 | 1.5 | Tr. | 1. |
    Buttermilk (Aunt Jemima) | 1 section (¾ oz.) | 170 | 2.3 | | |
    Original (Aunt Jemima) | 1 section (¾ oz.) | 160 | 2.4 | | |

**WAFFLE MIX** (USDA) (See also
**PANCAKE & WAFFLE MIX):**
  Dry, complete mix[2] | 1 oz. | 291 | 5.4 | 1. | 4. |
  *Prepared with water[2] | 2.6-oz. waffle (½" x 4½" x 5½", 7" dia.) | 420 | 10.5 | 2. | 8. |
  Dry, incomplete mix | 1 oz. | 406 | .5 | | |
  *Prepared with egg & milk[3] | 2.6-oz. waffle (7" dia.) | 514 | 8.0 | 3. | 5. | 45
  *Prepared with egg & milk[3] | 7.1-oz. waffle (9" x 9" x ⅝", 1⅛ cup batter) | 1372 | 21.2 | 8. | 13 | 120

**WAFFLE SYRUP** (See **SYRUP)**

**WALNUT:**
  Black:
    In shell, whole (USDA) | 1 lb. (weighed in shell) | 3 | 59.2 | 4. | 55. | 0

(USDA): United States Department of Agriculture
*Prepared as Package Directs
[1]Principal sources of fat: vegetable shortening, egg & milk.
[2]Principal sources of fat: vegetable shortening & egg.
[3]Principal sources of fat: vegetable shortening, egg & milk.

| Food and Description | Measure or Quantity | Sodium (mg.) | —Fats in grams— | | | Choles-terol (mg.) |
|---|---|---|---|---|---|---|
| | | | Total | Satu-rated | Unsatu-rated | |
| Shelled, whole (USDA) | 4 oz. | 3 | 67.2 | 5. | 63. | 0 |
| Chopped (USDA) | ½ cup (2.1 oz.) | 2 | 35.6 | 2. | 33. | 0 |
| Kernels (Hammons) | 4 oz. | | 63.8 | | | 0 |
| English or Persian: | | | | | | |
| In shell, whole (USDA) | 1 lb. (weighed in shell) | 4 | 130.6 | 9. | 122. | 0 |
| Shelled, whole (USDA) | 4 oz. | 2 | 72.6 | 4.5 | 68. | 0 |
| Chopped (USDA) | ½ cup (2.1 oz.) | 1 | 38.4 | 2. | 36. | 0 |
| Chopped (USDA) | 1 T. (8 grams) | <1 | 4.8 | Tr. | 4. | 0 |
| Halves (USDA) | ½ cup (1.8 oz.) | 1 | 32.0 | 2. | 30. | 0 |
| (Diamond) | 3-oz. bag (¾ cup) | 2 | 54.7 | 5. | 50. | (0) |
| (Diamond) | 15 halves (.5 oz.) | <1 | 9.7 | <1. | 9. | (0) |
| **\*WALNUT CAKE MIX, BLACK,** | | | | | | |
| (Betty Crocker) | ¹/₁₂ of cake | 271 | 5.6 | | | |
| **WATER** (See page 353) | | | | | | |
| **WATER CHESTNUT, CHINESE,** | | | | | | |
| raw (USDA): | | | | | | |
| Whole | 1 lb. (weighed unpeeled) | 70 | .7 | | | 0 |
| Peeled | 4 oz. | 23 | .2 | | | 0 |
| **WATERCRESS,** raw (USDA): | | | | | | |
| Untrimmed | ½ lb. (weighed untrimmed) | 108 | .6 | | | 0 |
| Trimmed | ½ cup (.6 oz.) | 8 | <.1 | | | 0 |
| **WATERMELON,** fresh (USDA): | | | | | | |
| Whole | 1 lb. (weighed with rind) | 2 | .4 | | | 0 |
| Wedge | 2-lb. wedge (4″ x 8″, measured with rind) | 4 | .9 | | | 0 |
| Slice | ½ slice (12.2 oz., ¾″ x 10″) | 2 | .3 | | | 0 |
| Diced | 1 cup (5.6 oz.) | 2 | 3 | | | 0 |
| **WATERMELON RIND** (Crosse & Blackwell) | 1 T. (.6 oz.) | 210 | 0. | | | (0) |

(USDA): United States Department of Agriculture
*Prepared as Package Directs

| Food and Description | Measure or Quantity | Sodium (mg.) | — Fats in grams — | | | Choles- terol (mg.) |
|---|---|---|---|---|---|---|
| | | | Total | Satu- rated | Unsatu- rated | |
| **WATERMELON SOFT DRINK,** sweetened: | | | | | | |
| (Hoffman) | 6 fl. oz. | 14 | 0. | | | 0 |
| (Nedick's) | 6 fl. oz. | 14 | 0. | | | 0 |
| **WAX GOURD,** raw (USDA): | | | | | | |
| Whole | 1 lb. (weighed with skin & cavity contents) | 19 | .6 | | | 0 |
| Flesh only | 4 oz. | 7 | .2 | | | 0 |
| **WEAKFISH** (USDA): | | | | | | |
| Raw, whole | 1 lb. (weighed whole) | 163 | 12.2 | | | |
| Broiled, meat only, salt added | 4 oz. | 635 | 12.9 | | | |
| **WELSH RAREBIT:** | | | | | | |
| Home recipe (USDA)[1] | 1 cup (8.2 oz.) | 770 | 31.6 | 16. | 15. | 72 |
| Canned (Snow) | 4 oz. | | 11.4 | | | |
| **WEST INDIAN CHERRY** (See **ACEROLA**) | | | | | | |
| **WHALE MEAT,** raw (USDA) | 4 oz. | 88 | 8.5 | 1. | 7. | |
| *WHEAT CHEX,* cereal (Ralston) | ⅔ cup (1 oz.) | 217 | .3 | | | (0) |
| *\*WHEATENA,* cereal | ½ cup (.9 oz. dry) | | .5 | | | (0) |
| **WHEAT FLAKES,** cereal, crushed (USDA) | 1 cup (2.5 oz.) | 722 | 1.1 | | | 0 |
| **WHEAT GERM,** crude, commercial, milled (USDA) | 1 oz. | <1 | 3.1 | <1. | 3. | 0 |
| **WHEAT GERM, CEREAL:** | | | | | | |
| (USDA) | ¼ cup (1 oz.) | <1 | 3.2 | <1. | 3. | 0 |
| (Kretschmer) | ¼ cup (1 oz.) | 1 | 3.1 | | | (0) |
| With sugar & honey (Kretschmer) | ¼ cup (1 oz.) | | 2.3 | | | (0) |
| *WHEATIES,* cereal (General Mills) | 1¼ cups (1 oz.) | 393 | .5 | | | (0) |
| *WHEAT OATA,* cereal, dry | ¼ cup (1 oz.) | 1 | 1.4 | | | (0) |

(USDA): United States Department of Agriculture
*Prepared as Package Directs
[1]Principal sources of fat: cheese, butter & milk.

| Food and Description | Measure or Quantity | Sodium (mg.) | — Fats in grams — | | | Choles- terol (mg.) |
|---|---|---|---|---|---|---|
| | | | Total | Satu- rated | Unsatu- rated | |
| **WHEAT, PUFFED,** cereal: | | | | | | |
| Added nutrients, without salt (USDA) | 1 cup (.4 oz.) | <1 | .2 | | | 0 |
| Frosted with sugar and honey (USDA) | 1 cup (.4 oz.) | 19 | .3 | | | 0 |
| (Checker) | ½ oz. | 3 | .3 | | | (0) |
| (Quaker) | 1⅓ cups (½ oz.) | <1 | .2 | | | (0) |
| (Sunland) | ½ oz. | 3 | .3 | | | (0) |
| (Whiffs) | ½ oz. | 3 | .3 | | | (0) |
| **WHEAT, ROLLED** (USDA): | | | | | | |
| Uncooked | 1 cup (3.1 oz.) | 2 | 1.7 | | | 0 |
| Cooked, salt added | 1 cup (7.7 oz.) | 640 | .9 | | | 0 |
| **WHEAT, SHREDDED,** cereal (See **SHREDDED WHEAT**) | | | | | | |
| **WHEY,** fluid (USDA) | 1 cup (8.6 oz.) | | .7 | | | |
| ***WHIP 'N CHILL*** (Jell-O): | | | | | | |
| All flavors except chocolate | ½ cup (3 oz.) | 60 | 5.3 | | | 3 |
| Chocolate | ½ cup (3 oz.) | 48 | 5.5 | | | 3 |
| **WHISKEY or WHISKY** (See **DISTILLED LIQUOR**) | | | | | | |
| **WHISKEY SOUR MIX** (Party Tyme) | ½-oz. pkg. | 87 | 0. | | | (0) |
| **WHISKEY SOUR SOFT DRINK,** sweetened (Shasta) | 6 fl. oz. | 22 | 0. | | | (0) |
| **WHITEFISH, LAKE** (USDA): | | | | | | |
| Raw, whole | 1 lb. (weighed whole) | 111 | 17.5 | | | |
| Raw, meat only | 4 oz. | 59 | 9.3 | | | |
| Baked, stuffed, home recipe[1] | 4 oz. | 221 | 15.9 | | | |
| Smoked | 4 oz. | | 8.3 | | | |
| **WHITEFISH & PIKE** (See **GEFILTE FISH**) | | | | | | |
| **WIENER** (See **FRANKFURTER**) | | | | | | |

(USDA): United States Department of Agriculture
*Prepared as Package Directs
[1]Prepared with bacon, butter, onion, celery & bread crumbs.

| Food and Description | Measure or Quantity | Sodium (mg.) | —Fats in grams— | | | Cholesterol (mg.) |
|---|---|---|---|---|---|---|
| | | | Total | Saturated | Unsaturated | |
| **WILD BERRY,** fruit drink (Hi-C) | 6 fl. oz. (6.3 oz.) | Tr. | Tr. | | | 0 |
| **WILD RICE,** raw (USDA) | ½ cup (2.9 oz.) | 6 | .6 | | | 0 |
| **WINE** (Most wines are listed by kind, brand, vineyard, region or grape name): | | | | | | |
| Cooking, Sauterne or Burgundy (Regina) | ½ cup (3.9 oz.) | 657 | 0. | | | (0) |
| Cooking, Sherry (Regina) | ½ cup (3.9 oz.) | 657 | 0. | | | (0) |
| Dessert (USDA) 18.8% alcohol | 3 fl. oz. (3.1 oz.) | 4 | 0. | | | 0 |
| Table (USDA) 12.2% alcohol | 3 fl. oz. (3.1 oz.) | 4 | 0. | | | 0 |
| **WINK,** soft drink (Canada Dry) bottle or can | 6 fl. oz. | 15+ | 0. | | | (0) |
| **WORCESTERSHIRE SAUCE** (See **SAUCE,** Worcestershire) | | | | | | |
| **WRECKFISH,** raw, meat only (USDA) | 4 oz. | | 4.4 | | | |

# Y

| Food and Description | Measure or Quantity | Sodium (mg.) | —Fats in grams— | | | Cholesterol (mg.) |
|---|---|---|---|---|---|---|
| | | | Total | Saturated | Unsaturated | |
| **YAM** (USDA): | | | | | | |
| Raw, whole | 1 lb. (weighed with skin) | | .8 | | | 0 |
| Raw, flesh only | 4 oz. | | .2 | | | 0 |
| Canned & frozen (See **SWEET POTATO**) | | | | | | |
| **YAM BEAN,** raw (USDA): | | | | | | |
| Unpared tuber | 1 lb. (weighed unpared) | | .8 | | | 0 |
| Pared tuber | 4 oz. | | .2 | | | 0 |
| **YEAST:** | | | | | | |
| Baker's: | | | | | | |
| Compressed (USDA) | 1 oz. | 5 | .1 | | | 0 |
| Compressed (Fleischmann's) | ³/₅-oz. cake | 3 | .1 | | | |
| Dry (USDA) | 1 oz. | 15 | .5 | | | 0 |
| Dry (USDA) | 1 pkg. (7 grams) | 4 | 1 | | | 0 |
| Dry (Fleischmann's) | ¼ oz. (pkg. or jar) | 5 | .1 | | | 0 |

(USDA): United States Department of Agriculture
*Prepared as Package Directs

| Food and Description | Measure or Quantity | Sodium (mg.) | —Fats in grams— | | | Cholesterol (mg.) |
|---|---|---|---|---|---|---|
| | | | Total | Saturated | Unsaturated | |
| Brewer's dry, debittered (USDA) | 1 oz. | 34 | .3 | | | 0 |
| Brewer's dry, debittered (USDA) | 1 T. (8 grams) | 10 | <.1 | | | 0 |
| **YELLOWTAIL,** raw, meat only | | | | | | |
| (USDA) | 4 oz. | | 6.1 | | | |
| **YOGURT:** | | | | | | |
| Made from whole milk (USDA) | ½ cup (4.3 oz.) | 57 | 4.1 | 2. | 2. | |
| Made from partially skimmed milk, plain or vanilla: | | | | | | |
| (USDA) | ½ cup (4.3 oz.) | 62 | 2.1 | 1. | <1. | 10 |
| (USDA) | 8-oz. container | 116 | 3.9 | 2. | 2. | 18 |
| Made from partially skimmed milk, fruit-flavored (USDA) | 8-oz. container | | 2.7 | | | 15 |
| Plain: | | | | | | |
| (Borden) Swiss style | 5-oz. container | 101 | 1.4 | | | |
| (Borden) Swiss style | 8-oz. container | 161 | 2.3 | | | |
| (Breakstone) | 8-oz. container | 168 | 3.9 | | | 10 |
| (Breakstone) | 1 T. (.5 oz.) | 10 | .2 | | | <1 |
| (Dannon) | 8-oz. container | 170 | 3.6 | 2. | 1. | 11 |
| Apple, Dutch (Dannon) | 8-oz. container | 125 | 2.5 | 2. | 1. | 8 |
| Apricot: | | | | | | |
| (Breakstone) | 8-oz. container | 128 | 2.9 | | | 8 |
| (Breakstone) *Swiss Parfait* | 8-oz. container | 128 | 3.6 | | | 10 |
| (Dannon) | 8-oz. container | 125 | 2.5 | 2. | 1. | 8 |
| Black cherry (Breakstone) *Swiss Parfait* | 8-oz. container | 136 | 3.6 | | | 10 |
| Blueberry: | | | | | | |
| (Breakstone) | 8-oz. container | 136 | 2.9 | | | 8 |
| (Breakstone) *Swiss Parfait* | 8-oz. container | 136 | 3.6 | | | 10 |
| (Dannon) | 8-oz. container | 125 | 2.5 | 2. | 1. | 8 |
| (Sealtest) *Light n' Lively* | 8-oz. container | 114 | 1.8 | | | |
| (SugarLo) | 8-oz. container | 141 | 2.3 | 1. | 1. | 7 |
| Boysenberry (Dannon) | 8-oz. container | 125 | 2.5 | 2. | 1. | 8 |
| Cherry: | | | | | | |
| (Dannon) | 8-oz. container | 125 | 2.5 | 2. | 1. | 8 |
| Dark (SugarLo) | 8-oz. container | 141 | 2.3 | 1. | 1. | 7 |
| Cinnamon apple (Breakstone) | 8-oz. container | 128 | 2.9 | | | 8 |
| Coffee (Dannon) | 8-oz. container | 152 | 3.2 | 2. | 1. | 11 |
| *Danny* (Dannon) | 2½-oz. pop | 51 | 5.0 | 3. | 2. | |
| Honey (Breakstone) *Swiss Parfait* | 8-oz. container | 128 | 3.6 | | | 10 |
| Lemon: | | | | | | |
| (Breakstone) *Swiss Parfait* | 8-oz. container | 128 | 3.6 | | | 10 |
| (Sealtest) *Light n' Lively* | 8-oz. container | 127 | 1.9 | | | |

(USDA): United States Department of Agriculture
*Prepared as Package Directs

349

| Food and Description | Measure or Quantity | Sodium (mg.) | —Fats in grams— | | | Choles-terol (mg.) |
|---|---|---|---|---|---|---|
| | | | Total | Satu-rated | Unsatu-rated | |
| Lime (Breakstone) *Swiss Parfait* | 8-oz. container | 128 | 3.9 | | | 10 |
| Mandarin orange: | | | | | | |
| (Borden) Swiss style | 5-oz. container | 76 | 1.0 | | | |
| (Borden) Swiss style | 8-oz. container | 121 | 1.6 | | | |
| (Breakstone) *Swiss Parfait* | 8-oz. container | 128 | 3.6 | | | 10 |
| Peach: | | | | | | |
| (Borden) Swiss style | 5-oz. container | 74 | 1.0 | | | |
| (Borden) Swiss style | 8-oz. container | 119 | 1.6 | | | |
| (Breakstone) *Swiss Parfait* | 8-oz. container | 128 | 3.4 | | | 8 |
| Melba (Breakstone) *Swiss Parfait* | 8-oz. container | 128 | 3.4 | | | 8 |
| (Sealtest) *Light n' Lively* | 8-oz. container | 116 | 1.8 | | | |
| (SugarLo) | 8-oz. container | 141 | 2.3 | 1. | 1. | 7 |
| Pineapple: | | | | | | |
| (Breakstone) | 8-oz. container | 128 | 2.9 | | | 8 |
| (Sealtest) *Light n' Lively* | 8-oz. container | 120 | 1.8 | | | |
| (SugarLo) | 8-oz. container | 141 | 2.3 | 1. | 1. | 7 |
| Pineapple-orange (Dannon) | 8-oz. container | 125 | 2.5 | 2. | 1. | 8 |
| Prune whip (Breakstone) | 8-oz. container | 128 | 2.9 | | | 8 |
| Prune whip (Dannon) | 8-oz. container | 125 | 2.5 | 2. | 1. | 8 |
| Raspberry: | | | | | | |
| (Borden) Swiss style | 5-oz. container | 82 | 1.1 | | | |
| (Borden) Swiss style | 8-oz. container | 132 | 1.8 | | | |
| (Breakstone) | 8-oz. container | 136 | 2.9 | | | 8 |
| Red (Breakstone) *Swiss Parfait* | 8-oz. container | 144 | 3.9 | | | 10 |
| (Dannon) | 8-oz. container | 125 | 2.5 | 2. | 1. | 8 |
| Red (Sealtest) *Light n' Lively* | 8-oz. container | 125 | 1.9 | | | |
| (SugarLo) | 8-oz. container | 143 | 2.3 | 1. | 1. | 7 |
| Strawberry: | | | | | | |
| (Borden) Swiss style | 5-oz. container | 81 | 1.1 | | | |
| (Borden) Swiss style | 8-oz. container | 129 | 1.8 | | | |
| (Breakstone) | 8-oz. container | 128 | 2.9 | | | 8 |
| (Breakstone) *Swiss Parfait* | 8-oz. container | 128 | 3.6 | | | 9 |
| (Dannon) | 8-oz. container | 125 | 2.5 | 2. | 1. | 8 |
| (Sealtest) *Light n' Lively* | 8-oz. container | 127 | 1.9 | | | |
| (SugarLo) | 8-oz. container | 141 | 2.3 | 1. | 1. | 7 |
| Vanilla: | | | | | | |
| (Borden) Swiss style | 5-oz. container | 87 | 1.3 | | | |
| (Borden) Swiss style | 8-oz. container | 139 | 2.0 | | | |
| (Breakstone) | 8-oz. container | 208 | 3.4 | | | 10 |
| (Dannon) | 8-oz. container | 152 | 3.2 | 2. | 1. | 11 |

**YOUNGBERRY,** fresh (See
**BLACKBERRY,** fresh)

(USDA): United States Department of Agriculture
*Prepared as Package Directs

| Food and Description | Measure or Quantity | Sodium (mg.) | —Fats in grams— | | | Choles- terol (mg.) |
|---|---|---|---|---|---|---|
| | | | Total | Satu- rated | Unsatu- rated | |

# Z

**ZELLERSCHWARZE KATZ,** wine
(Julius Kayser) 9% alcohol    3 fl. oz.    2    0.    (0)

*ZING,* cereal beverage, 0.4%alcohol    12 fl. oz. (12 oz.)    41    0

**ZITI,** baked, with sauce, frozen
(Buitoni)    4 oz.    1.6

**ZUCCHINI** (See **SQUASH, SUMMER**)

**ZWIEBACK:**
(USDA)[1]    1 oz.    71    2.5    <1.    2.
(Nabisco)    1 piece (7 grams)    6    .7

(USDA): United States Department of Agriculture
*Prepared as Package Directs
[1]Principal sources of fat: vegetable shortening & egg.

# BIBLIOGRAPHY

Dawson, Elsie H., Gilpin, Gladys L., and Fulton, Lois H., *Average weight of a measured cup of various foods.* U.S.D.A. ARS 61-6, February 1969, 19 pp.

Durfor, C. N., and Becker, E., *Geological Survey Water Supply Paper* 1812, Washington, U. S. Government Printing Office, 1964, pp. 1–364.

Feeley, R. M., Criner, P. E., and Watt, B. K., "Cholesterol Content of Food," *Journal of the American Dietetic Association,* 61, August 2, 1972, pp. 134–149.

Merrill, A. L. and Watt, B. K., *Energy value of foods — basis and derivation.* U.S.D.A. Handb. 74, 105 pp., 1955.

Pecot, Rebecca K., Jaeger, Carol M., and Watt, Bernice K., *Proximate composition of beef from carcass to cooked meat: Method of derivation and tables of values.* U.S.D.A. Home Economics Research Report 31, 32 pp. 1965.

Pecot, Rebecca K. and Watt, Bernice K., *Food yields: Summarized by different stages of preparation.* U.S.D.A. Handb. 102, 93 pp., 1956.

U.S.D.A. *Nutritive value of foods.* Home and Garden Bul. 72, 36 pp., 1964, and revised edition, 1970, 41 pp.

U.S.D.A. Unpubl. Data 1969.

Watt, Bernice K., Merrill, Annabel L., *et al., Composition of foods: Raw, processed, prepared.* U.S.D.A. Agriculture Handb. 8, 190 pp., 1963.

# APPENDIX

## WATER SUPPLIES

This chart covers the largest cities in the United States and their principal sources of water supplies. The two types of resources are ground water (wells and infiltration galleries) and surface water (streams, lakes and reservoirs). Most cities use but one source; a second group always uses more than one source; a third group uses different sources only part of the year. Therefore, the column headed "% of water supply" includes both primary and auxiliary sources wherever used.

## SODIUM CONTENT OF LOCAL WATER SUPPLIES

| State, city & plant, reservoir or lake | % of water supply | Finished water or raw water | Sodium (mg.) 1 cup |
|---|---|---|---|
| **ALABAMA:** | | | |
| Birmingham: | | | |
| Inland Lake | 10% | R | .5 |
| Putnam Station filter plant | 10% | F | .4 |
| Cahaba River | 90% | R | 2.4 |
| Shades Mountain filter plant | 90% | F | 2.3 |
| Mobile: | | | |
| Big Creek | 100% | R | .5 |
| Treatment plant | 100% | F | .6 |
| Montgomery: | | | |
| Court Street plant, 18 wells | 39% | R | 12.1 |
| Court Street treatment plant | 39% | F | 13.0 |
| Day Street plant, 31 wells | 61% | R | 12.1 |
| Day Street treatment plant | 61% | F | 12.6 |
| **ARIZONA:** | | | |
| Phoenix: | | | |
| Verde River | 12% | R | 31.0 |
| Verde River filter plant | 12% | F | 31.0 |
| Squaw Peak filter plant | 30% | F | 32.7 |
| Verde well field | 17% | F | 9.7 |
| Scottsdale well 36 | 15% | F | 22.8 |
| Tucson: | | | |
| Composite of southside wells | 33% | F | 15.9 |

| State, city & plant, reservoir or lake | % of water supply | Finished water or raw water | Sodium (mg.) 1 cup |
|---|---|---|---|
| Composite of northside wells | 33% | F | 8.1 |
| Composite of Upper Santa Cruz wells | 33% | F | 7.8 |
| **CALIFORNIA:** | | | |
| Fresno: | | | |
| Composite or wells | 100% | R | 4.0 |
| Long Beach: | | | |
| Long Beach well water | | R | 16.8 |
| Long Beach treatment plant | 60% | F | 17.5 |
| La Verne treatment plant | 40% | F | 46.9 |
| Los Angeles: | | | |
| Colorado River | 20% | R | 21.8 |
| San Fernando Reservoir | 60% | F | 7.6 |
| Weymouth treatment plant | 20% | F | 35.8 |
| Oakland: | | | |
| Orinda filter plant | 99% | F | .6 |
| San Pablo filter plant | | F | .2 |
| Upper San Leandro filter plant | | F | 1.6 |
| Chabot filter plant | | F | 5.5 |
| Sacramento: | | | |
| Sacramento River | 85% | R | 2.4 |
| Filter plant | 85% | F | 2.8 |
| San Diego: | | | |
| Lake Hodges Reservoir | 10% | R | 23.5 |
| Alvarado treatment plant | 47% | F | 23.5 |
| Torrey Pines treatment plant | 10% | F | 25.4 |
| Lower Otay Reservoir | 4% | R | 21.3 |
| San Francisco: | | | |
| Calaveres Reservoir | 18% | F | 2.8 |
| Crystal Springs Reservoir | 8% | F | .8 |
| San Andreas Reservoir | 2% | F | 1.2 |
| Hetch Hetchy Reservoir | 72% | R | .3 |
| Hetch Hetchy treatment plant | 72% | F | .7 |
| San Jose: | | | |
| Wells | 80% | F | 6.9 |
| **COLORADO:** | | | |
| Denver: | | | |
| Frazer River & Williams Fork | 47% | R | .5 |
| Moffat filter plant | 46% | F | .6 |
| South Platte River & Bear Creek | 38% | R | 5.7 |
| Marston Lake, northside filter plant | 31% | F | 5.7 |
| South Platte River | 15% | R | 8.1 |
| Kassler filter plant | 15% | F | 7.3 |
| Marston Lake, southside filter plant | 8% | F | 6.4 |
| **CONNECTICUT:** | | | |
| Bridgeport: | | | |
| Easton Reservoir | 21% | R | .9 |
| Easton treatment plant | 21% | F | .9 |

| State, city & plant, reservoir or lake | % of water supply | Finished water or raw water | Sodium (mg.) 1 cup |
|---|---|---|---|
| Hemlocks Reservoir | 51% | R | .9 |
| Hemlocks treatment plant | 51% | F | .9 |
| Trap Falls Reservoir | 26% | R | .9 |
| Trap Falls treatment plant | 26% | F | 1.0 |
| Hartford: | | | |
| West Hartford filter plant | 97% | F | .7 |
| New Haven: | | | |
| Whitney filter plant | 13% | F | 1.4 |
| Lake Gaillard | 41% | F | .7 |
| Lake Saltonstall | 12% | F | 1.5 |
| Woodbridge system | 12% | F | .9 |
| Lake Wintergreen | 9% | F | .6 |
| Lake Bethany | 4% | F | .8 |
| Beaver Brook Lake | 4% | F | 2.6 |
| Maltby Lakes | 2% | F | 1.3 |
| **WASHINGTON, D.C.:** | | | |
| Potomac River | 100% | R | 1.8 |
| Dalecarlia filter plant | 45% | F | 1.9 |
| McMillan filter plant | 55% | F | 2.4 |
| **FLORIDA:** | | | |
| Jacksonville: | | | |
| Well | 100% | R | 3.3 |
| Chlorination plant | 100% | F | 3.3 |
| Miami: | | | |
| Hialeah well fields | 40% | R | 5.2 |
| Hialeah treatment plant | 40% | F | 5.5 |
| Orr well field | 60% | R | 2.8 |
| Orr treatment plant | 60% | F | 3.1 |
| St. Petersburg: | | | |
| Cosme well field | 100% | R | 1.4 |
| Treatment plant | 100% | F | 1.4 |
| Tampa: | | | |
| Hillsborough River | 97% | R | 1.9 |
| Tampa waterworks | 97% | F | 1.9 |
| **GEORGIA:** | | | |
| Atlanta: | | | |
| Chattahoochee River | 100% | R | .5 |
| Hemphill filter plant | 100% | F | .5 |
| Savannah: | | | |
| Abercorn Creek | 100% | R | .8 |
| Cherokee Hill plant | 100% | F | 1.0 |
| Well 2 | 100% | R | 2.1 |
| **HAWAII:** | | | |
| Honolulu: | | | |
| Kaimuki pumping station | 13% | R | 15.2 |
| Beretania pumping station | 23% | R | 8.3 |
| Kalihi underground station | 21% | R | 8.1 |

| State, city & plant, reservoir or lake | % of water supply | Finished water or raw water | Sodium (mg.) 1 cup |
|---|---|---|---|
| **ILLINOIS:** | | | |
| Chicago: | | | |
|   Lake Michigan | 100% | R | .9 |
|   Chicago Avenue station | 46% | F | .9 |
|   Lake View station | 20% | F | .9 |
|   South District filtration plant | 34% | F | 1.0 |
| Rockford: | | | |
|   Unit well 15 | 92% | F | .8 |
|   Composite of 6 group wells | 8% | F | 1.8 |
| **INDIANA:** | | | |
| Evansville: | | | |
|   Filtration plant | 100% | F | 3.1 |
| Fort Wayne: | | | |
|   St. Joseph River (impounded) | 100% | R | 2.3 |
|   Three Rivers filtration plant | 100% | F | 3.6 |
| Gary: | | | |
|   Gary-Hobart filter plant | 100% | F | 1.1 |
| Indianapolis: | | | |
|   Fall Creek purification plant | 45% | F | 1.9 |
|   White River purification plant | 55% | F | 3.3 |
| South Bend: | | | |
|   Coquillard Station well 3 | 18% | F | 1.8 |
|   Pinhook Station well 3 | 18% | F | 1.3 |
|   North Station wells 5 & 7 | 18% | F | 2.0 |
|   Oliver Station well 4 | 20% | F | 2.8 |
| **IOWA:** | | | |
| Des Moines: | | | |
|   Infiltration gallery | 75% | R | 3.1 |
|   Des Moines waterworks | 77% | F | 7.8 |
| **KANSAS:** | | | |
| Kansas City: | | | |
|   Missouri River | 100% | R | 6.2 |
|   Quindaro treatment plant | 100% | F | 5.9 |
| Topeka: | | | |
|   Kansas River | 100% | R | 1.7 |
|   Treatment plant | 100% | F | 26.3 |
|   Well 2 | 1% | R | 15.6 |
|   Well 3 | 1% | R | 16.6 |
| Wichita: | | | |
|   Wells in Equus Beds | 100% | R | 14.2 |
|   Treatment plant | 100% | F | 14.5 |
|   Well 4 near Bentley | | R | 35.1 |
| **KENTUCKY:** | | | |
| Louisville: | | | |
|   Ohio River | 100% | R | 3.8 |
|   Filtration plant | 100% | F | 6.2 |

| State, city & plant, reservoir or lake | % of water supply | Finished water or raw water | Sodium (mg.) 1 cup |
|---|---|---|---|
| **LOUISIANA:** | | | |
| Baton Rouge: | | | |
| Lula Street plant, 7 wells | 26% | F | 17.1 |
| Lafayette Street plant, 3 wells | 10% | F | 23.0 |
| Government Street plant, 5 wells | 37% | F | 18.5 |
| Bankston Street plant, 5 wells | 27% | F | 15.9 |
| New Orleans: | | | |
| Mississippi River | 100% | R | 4.0 |
| Algiers purification plant | 3% | F | 4.3 |
| Carrollton purification plant | 97% | F | 4.3 |
| Shreveport: | | | |
| Cross Lake | 100% | R | 5.7 |
| Cross Lake treatment plant | 74% | F | 5.7 |
| McNeill Street treatment plant | 26% | F | 5.7 |
| **MARYLAND:** | | | |
| Baltimore: | | | |
| Loch Raven Reservoir | 55% | R | .9 |
| Montebello filtration plant | 55% | F | .7 |
| Liberty Reservoir | 45% | R | .9 |
| Ashburton filtration plant | 45% | F | .9 |
| **MASSACHUSETTS:** | | | |
| Boston: | | | |
| Quabbin Reservoir | 100% | R | .4 |
| Norumbega Reservoir | 100% | F | .6 |
| Springfield: | | | |
| Little River (Cobble Mountain Reservoir) | 91% | F | .7 |
| Ludlow Reservoir | 9% | F | .7 |
| Worcester: | | | |
| Holden Reservoir | 35% | F | .5 |
| Lynde Brook & Holden Reservoir | 65% | F | .8 |
| **MICHIGAN:** | | | |
| Detroit: | | | |
| Detroit River | 100% | R | 1.0 |
| Water Works Park Station | 100% | F | .9 |
| Flint: | | | |
| Flint River (impounded) | 100% | R | 3.6 |
| Filtration plant | 100% | F | 6.6 |
| Grand Rapids: | | | |
| Lake Michigan | 100% | R | 1.0 |
| Filtration plant | 100% | F | 1.2 |
| **MINNESOTA:** | | | |
| Minneapolis: | | | |
| Mississippi River | 100% | R | 1.7 |
| Fridley filtration plant | 51% | F | 1.6 |
| Columbia Heights filtration plant | 49% | F | 1.5 |
| St. Paul: | | | |
| Mississippi River | 90% | R | 1.6 |

| State, city & plant, reservoir or lake | % of water supply | Finished water or raw water | Sodium (mg.) 1 cup |
|---|---|---|---|
| McCarron purification plant | 90% | F | 1.4 |
| **MISSISSIPPI:** | | | |
| Jackson: | | | |
| Treatment plant | 100% | F | .8 |
| **MISSOURI:** | | | |
| Kansas City: | | | |
| Missouri River | 100% | R | 8.3 |
| Treatment plant | 100% | F | 9.0 |
| St. Louis: | | | |
| Missouri River | 34% | R | 4.0 |
| Howard Bend purification plant | 34% | F | 5.2 |
| Mississippi River | 66% | R | 4.0 |
| Chain of Rocks purification plant | 66% | F | 5.2 |
| **NEBRASKA:** | | | |
| Lincoln: | | | |
| Composite of Ashland wells, 6, 9, 54-1, -4, -7, -9, -11 | 96% | R | 5.9 |
| Lincoln wells | 4% | R | 5.9 |
| Ashland purification plant | 100% | F | 5.9 |
| Omaha: | | | |
| Missouri River | 100% | R | 15.4 |
| Minne Lusa treatment plant | 100% | F | 15.4 |
| **NEW JERSEY:** | | | |
| Jersey City: | | | |
| Boonton Reservoir | 100% | F | 1.1 |
| Newark: | | | |
| Wanaque River | 45% | R | .9 |
| Wanaque Reservoir | | F | .8 |
| Cedar Grove treatment plant | 55% | F | 1.0 |
| Paterson: | | | |
| Passaic River | 47% | R | .5 |
| Little Falls treatment plant | 47% | F | 1.1 |
| Wanaque River | 53% | R | .9 |
| Wanaque Reservoir | | F | .8 |
| **NEW MEXICO:** | | | |
| Albuquerque: | | | |
| West Mesa Station, 40 wells | 4% | F | 25.4 |
| Santa Barbara Station | 34% | F | 12.3 |
| Eubank Station, 44 wells | 50% | F | 7.8 |
| Thomas Station, 8 wells | 6% | F | 11.1 |
| **NEW YORK:** | | | |
| Albany: | | | |
| Alcove Reservoir | 92% | R | .4 |
| Feura Bush filter plant | 92% | F | .4 |
| Buffalo: | | | |
| Lake Erie | 100% | R | 2.3 |

| State, city & plant, reservoir or lake | % of water supply | Finished water or raw water | Sodium (mg.) 1 cup |
|---|---|---|---|
| Filtration plant | 100% | F | 2.2 |
| New York City: | | | |
| Catskill & Delaware supplies | 79% | F | .4 |
| Croton supply | 18% | F | 1.0 |
| Jamaica wells (8, 8A, 17A & 31) | 3% | F | 4.0 |
| Rochester: | | | |
| Lake Ontario | 21% | R | |
| Lake Ontario filter plant | 21% | F | 2.4 |
| Hemlock Lake | 79% | R | 1.2 |
| Upland supply | 79% | F | 1.1 |
| Candice Lake | | R | .7 |
| Syracuse: | | | |
| Skaneateles Lake | 100% | R | 3.8 |
| Treatment plant | 100% | F | 4.0 |
| Yonkers: | | | |
| Saw Mill Reservoir | 18% | F | 4.7 |
| Grassy Sprain Reservoir | 17% | F | 4.5 |
| Catskill Aqueduct | 65% | F | .4 |

**NORTH CAROLINA:**

| State, city & plant, reservoir or lake | % of water supply | Finished water or raw water | Sodium (mg.) 1 cup |
|---|---|---|---|
| Charlotte: | | | |
| Catawba River | 100% | R | .9 |
| Hoskins treatment plant | 100% | F | 1.0 |
| Greensboro: | | | |
| Lake Brandt | 100% | R | .7 |
| Filter plant | 100% | F | .6 |

**OHIO:**

| State, city & plant, reservoir or lake | % of water supply | Finished water or raw water | Sodium (mg.) 1 cup |
|---|---|---|---|
| Akron: | | | |
| Treatment plant | 100% | F | 1.5 |
| Cincinnati: | | | |
| Ohio River | 100% | R | |
| Treatment plant | 100% | F | 4.3 |
| Cleveland: | | | |
| Nottingham filtration plant | 100% | F | 2.6 |
| Columbus: | | | |
| Big Walnut Creek | | R | |
| Morse Road treatment plant | 55% | F | 13.7 |
| Scioto River | | R | |
| Dublin Road treatment plant | 45% | F | 8.1 |
| Dayton: | | | |
| Well water | 100% | R | 2.6 |
| Ottawa Street treatment plant | 100% | F | 4.0 |
| Toledo: | | | |
| Lake Erie | 100% | R | 2.8 |
| Collins Park treatment plant | 100% | F | 2.8 |
| Youngstown: | | | |
| Meander Creek treatment plant | 100% | F | 6.2 |

| State, city & plant, reservoir or lake | % of water supply | Finished water or raw water | Sodium (mg.) 1 cup |
|---|---|---|---|
| **OKLAHOMA:** | | | |
| Oklahoma City: | | | |
|   Lake Hefner | 100% | R | 21.3 |
|   Lake Hefner treatment plant | 100% | F | 19.9 |
| Tulsa: | | | |
|   Sapvinaw Creek | | R | |
|   Treatment plant | 100% | F | 1.0 |
| **OREGON:** | | | |
| Portland: | | | |
|   Bull Run Headworks | 100% | F | .3 |
| **PENNSYLVANIA:** | | | |
| Erie: | | | |
|   Lake Erie | 100% | F | 1.9 |
|   Chestnut Street filtration plant | 100% | F | 2.8 |
| Philadelphia: | | | |
|   Delaware River | | R | |
|   Torresdale filter plant | 50% | F | 1.1 |
|   Schuykill River | | R | |
|   Belmont filter plant | 50% | F | 1.7 |
| Pittsburgh: | | | |
|   Allegheny River | | F | |
|   Aspinwall filter plant | 60% | F | 1.6 |
|   Aldrich filter plant | 40% | F | 4.0 |
| **RHODE ISLAND:** | | | |
| Providence: | | | |
|   Scituate Reservoir | 92% | R | .7 |
|   Filter plant | 92% | F | .8 |
| **TENNESSEE:** | | | |
| Chattanooga: | | | |
|   Tennessee River | 100% | R | 1.9 |
|   Treatment plant | 100% | F | 2.0 |
| Memphis: | | | |
|   Allen well field | 28% | R | 1.8 |
|   Allen filtration plant | 28% | F | 1.8 |
|   Sheadan well field | 28% | R | 2.8 |
|   Sheadan filtration plant | 28% | F | 2.8 |
|   McCord well field | 16% | R | 1.5 |
|   McCord filtration plant | 16% | F | 1.5 |
|   Parkway well field | 28% | R | 4.0 |
|   Parkway filtration plant | 28% | F | 4.0 |
| Nashville: | | | |
|   Cumberland River | 100% | R | .7 |
|   Treatment plant | 100% | F | .8 |
| **TEXAS:** | | | |
| Amarillo: | | | |
|   Composite of wells southwest of city | 55% | F | 5.9 |
|   Palo Duro well field | | R | 4.5 |
|   McDonald well 2 | | R | 4.0 |

| State, city & plant, reservoir or lake | % of water supply | Finished water or raw water | Sodium (mg.) 1 cup |
|---|---|---|---|
| Bush well 4 | | R | 6.9 |
| Westex well 3 | | R | 6.4 |
| Well 6, section 49 | | R | 8.3 |
| Composite of 25 wells in Carson County | 45% | F | 5.0 |
| Austin: | | | |
| Colorado River | 100% | R | 8.1 |
| Filter plant 1 | 53% | F | 7.8 |
| Filter plant 2 | 47% | F | 7.8 |
| Tap at 807 Brazos Street | 100% | F | 7.8 |
| Corpus Christi: | | | |
| Nueces River | 100% | R | 14.7 |
| Cunningham treatment plant | 100% | F | 14.7 |
| Dallas: | | | |
| Garza-Little Elm Reservoir | 67% | R | 9.2 |
| Elm Fork treatment plant | 67% | F | 9.7 |
| Grapevine & Garza-Little Elm Reservoir | 26% | R | 8.1 |
| Bachman plant | 26% | F | 9.7 |
| Lake Lavon | 7% | F | 3.6 |
| El Paso: | | | |
| Rio Grande | 14% | R | 39.1 |
| Rio Grande treatment plant | 14% | F | 43.6 |
| Wells at Mesa Station | 16% | F | 22.0 |
| Canutillo Station, 6 wells | 25% | F | 20.9 |
| Airport Station, 3 wells | 13% | F | 28.2 |
| Nevins Stationn 7 wells | 14% | F | 20.1 |
| Well V-70 in lower valley | 15% | F | 40.8 |
| Fort Worth: | | | |
| Lake Worth | 99% | R | 4.7 |
| North Holly treatment plant | 99% | F | 4.7 |
| Lake Benbrook | | R | 3.6 |
| Houston: | | | |
| Heights well field | 14% | F | 26.3 |
| East End well field | 5% | F | 41.9 |
| South Park well field | 3% | F | 38.2 |
| South End well field | 6% | F | 23.7 |
| Meyerland well | 1% | F | 20.6 |
| Northeast well field | 9% | F | 25.1 |
| Southwest well field | 18% | F | 20.4 |
| Central well field | 3% | F | 33.9 |
| San Jacinto River | 24% | R | 2.6 |
| San Jacinto purification plant | 24% | F | 2.6 |
| Lubbock: | | | |
| City well 62 at Northwest well field | 7% | R | 30.6 |
| Composite of wells in South part Lubbock | 4% | F | 26.3 |
| Northeast well field | 13% | F | 25.1 |
| Composite of wells in Sand Hills well field | 65% | F | 6.4 |

| State, city & plant, reservoir or lake | % of water supply | Finished water or raw water | Sodium (mg.) 1 cup |
|---|---|---|---|
| Well 102 in Shallowater well field | 10% | R | 24.2 |
| San Antonio: | | | |
| Market Street Station, 4 wells | | F | 1.9 |
| Wells of Bexar Metropolitan | | | |
| Water District | | R | 2.1 |
| Artesia Station, 5 wells | | F | 1.8 |
| Mission Station, 5 wells | | F | 2.4 |
| Basin Station, 4 wells | | F | 1.7 |
| 34th Street Station, 3 wells | | F | 1.6 |
| **UTAH:** | | | |
| Salt Lake City: | | | |
| Deer Creek Reservoir | 24% | R | 1.0 |
| Little Cottonwood treatment plant | 11% | F | 2.8 |
| Big Cottonwood Creek | 33% | R | 1.0 |
| Big Cottonwood treatment plant | 30% | F | 1.3 |
| Mountain Dell treatment plant | 14% | F | 5.2 |
| City Creek treatment plant | 9% | F | 1.0 |
| Artesian wells, 3rd East Station | 4% | F | 6.6 |
| **VIRGINIA:** | | | |
| Norfolk: | | | |
| Lake Wright | 62% | R | 3.3 |
| Moores Bridges treatment plant | 62% | F | 2.6 |
| Lake Prince | 38% | R | 1.1 |
| 37th Street treatment plant | 38% | F | 1.4 |
| Lake Burnt Mills | | R | 1.0 |
| Richmond: | | | |
| James River | 100% | R | .7 |
| Douglasdale Road filtration plant | 100% | F | .9 |
| **WASHINGTON:** | | | |
| Seattle: | | | |
| Cedar River | 100% | R | .5 |
| Lake Youngs purification plant | 100% | F | .4 |
| Spokane: | | | |
| Parkway well 5 | 32% | F | .7 |
| Electric well 2 | 45% | F | .7 |
| Tacoma: | | | |
| Treatment plant | 94% | F | .6 |
| Treatment plant | | F | .5 |
| **WISCONSIN:** | | | |
| Madison: | | | |
| Main Station wells | 25% | F | .9 |
| Unit well 6 | 25% | F | .7 |
| Unit well 11 | 25% | F | .7 |
| Unit well 12 | 25% | F | .5 |
| Milwaukee: | | | |
| Lake Michigan | 100% | R | 1.0 |
| Linnwood Avenue purification plant | 100% | F | 1.0 |

# Visual Meat Portions and Their
## Sodium, Fat, and Cholesterol Content
*(Source: USDA)*

**This Thick**

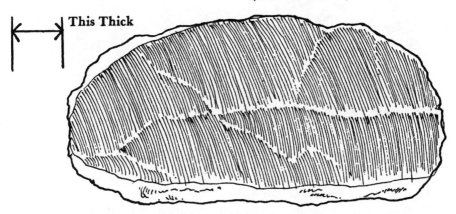

One piece of *round steak* (lean only) of this size (3 oz., cooked medium) has approximately 5 gr. total fat, of which 2 gr. are saturated and 3 gr. are unsaturated; 77 mg. of cholesterol; and 51 mg. of sodium (See also p. 37).

**This Thick**

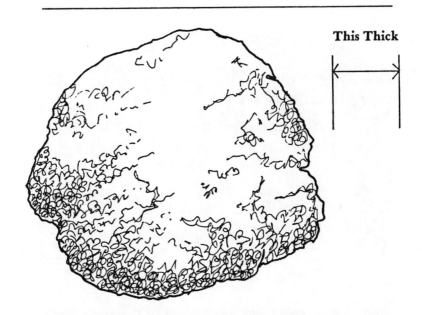

One *hamburger* (lean only) of this size (3 oz., cooked medium) has approximately 10 gr. total fat, of which 5 gr. are saturated and 5 gr. are unsaturated; 77 mg. of cholesterol; and 41 mg. of sodium (See also p. 36).

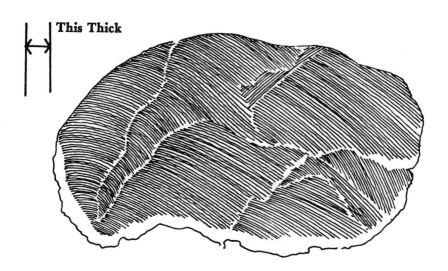

Two slices of *roast beef round* (lean only) of this size (3 oz., cooked medium) have approximately 5 gr. total fat, of which 2 gr. are saturated and 3 gr. are unsaturated; 77 mg. of cholesterol; and 51 mg. of sodium (See also p. 37).

---

**This Thick**

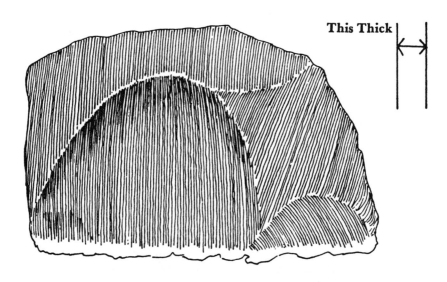

Two slices of *cured ham* (lean only) of this size (3 oz., cooked) have approximately 8 gr. total fat, of which 3 gr. are saturated and 5 gr. are unsaturated; 75 mg. of cholesterol; and 790 mg. of sodium (See also p. 259).

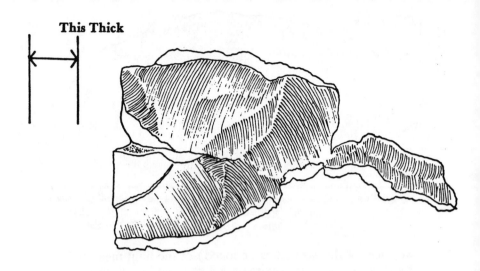

**This Thick**

Two *lamb chops* (lean only) of this size (3 oz., cooked medium) have approximately 7 gr. total fat, of which 4 gr. are saturated and 3 gr. are unsaturated; 85 mg. of cholesterol; and 60 mg. of sodium (See also p. 190).

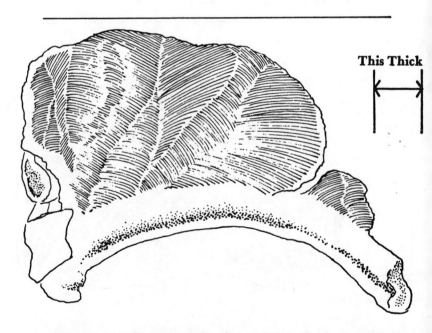

**This Thick**

Two *pork chops* (lean only) of this size (3 oz., cooked) have approximately 13 gr. total fat, of which 5 gr. are saturated and 8 gr. are unsaturated; 75 mg. of cholesterol; and 55 mg. of sodium (See also p. 259).

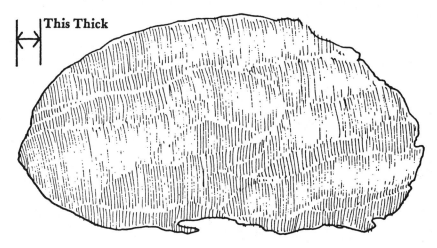

**This Thick**

Two slices of this size (3 oz., cooked) of the light meat of a *roast turkey* have approximately 3 gr. total fat, of which 1 gr. is saturated and 2 gr. are unsaturated; 55 mg. of cholesterol; and 70 mg. of sodium. Two slices of this size (3 oz., cooked) of the dark meat of a *roast turkey* have approximately 7 gr. total fat, of which 2 gr. are saturated and 5 gr. are unsaturated; 73 mg. of cholesterol; and 84 mg. of sodium (See also p. 332).

---

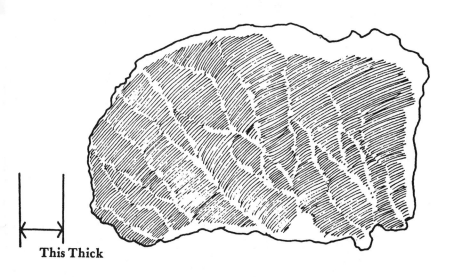

**This Thick**

One *veal cultlet* (trimmed) of this size (3 oz., cooked medium) has approximately 10 gr. total fat, of which 5 gr. are saturated and 5 gr. are unsaturated; 84 mg. of cholesterol; and 68 mg. of sodium (See also p. 337).